1/12

PREHISTORIC HUNTER-GATHERERS OF THE HIGH PLAINS AND ROCKIES

Third Edition

PREHISTORIC HUNTER-GATHERERS
OF THE HIGH PLAINS AND ROCKIES

Third Edition

Marcel Kornfeld, George C. Frison, and
Mary Lou Larson

WITH CONTRIBUTIONS BY:

Bruce A. Bradley, George W. Gill, Julie E. Francis, and
James C. Miller

Walnut Creek, California

LEFT COAST PRESS, INC.
1630 North Main Street, #400
Walnut Creek, CA 94596
http://www.LCoastPress.com

New edition of Prehistoric Hunters of the High Plains by George C. Frison, published in 1991 by Academic Press under ISBN 978-0-12-268561-3

ISBN 978-1-59874-467-5 hardcover

Library of Congress Cataloging-in-Publication Data:

Kornfeld, Marcel.
Prehistoric Hunter-Gatherers of the High Plains and Rockies / Marcel Kornfeld, George
C. Frison, Mary Lou Larson; with contributions by Bruce A. Bradley ... [et al.]. — 3rd ed.
    p. cm.
Rev. ed. of: Prehistoric hunters of the High Plains / George C . Frison. 2nd ed. 1991
Includes bibliographical references and index.
ISBN 978-1-59874-467-5 (hardcover : alk. paper)
1. Indians of North America—Hunting—Great Plains. 2. Indians of North America—
Great Plains—Antiquities. 3. Great Plains—Antiquities. I. Frison, George C. II. Larson,
Mary Lou, 1954- III. Bradley, Bruce A., 1948- IV. Frison, George C. Prehistory of the Plains
and Rockies. V. Title.
E78.G73F74 2009
978—dc22 2009037368

Printed in the United States of America

11 12 13 5 4 3 2

CONTENTS

LIST OF ILLUSTRATIONS

Figures

Tables

Plates

PREFACE

A Ph.D. dissertation entitled *A Preliminary Historical Outline for the Northwestern Plains* by William Mulloy was accepted by the Department of Anthropology at the University of Chicago in 1953 and later published by the University of Wyoming in 1958. Although supported by a limited database, it was a remarkable document reflecting a profound knowledge of anthropological and archaeological principles and is still widely used and quoted. The 1st edition of *Prehistoric Hunters of the High Plains* in 1978 was strongly influenced by Mulloy's earlier work that strictly and artificially delineated the Plains from the Rocky Mountains and appeared to perceive a separation between prehistoric cultural groups living in these areas. Part of this thinking reflected a dearth of upland and higher-altitude investigations at that time.

Subsequent to this, new data began to suggest this separation was not well enough supported. By the time the 2nd edition of *Prehistoric Hunters of the High Plains* appeared in 1991, there was ever-increasing evidence of interaction between plains and mountain prehistoric cultural groups, as well as better anthropological understanding of hunter-gatherer settlement strategies. With the appearance of the 3rd edition, the database has now expanded, and is discussed in this book, to a condition that we believe demands the inclusion of the Rocky Mountains in the title.

Another revision with the 3rd edition is a change in emphasis. The first edition of this volume emphasized cultural chronology. Nearly 30 years after William Mulloy presented his *A Preliminary Historical Outline for the Northwestern Plains,* and after a great deal of research in the intervening time, it was necessary to reformulate the chronological scheme for the region. A significant amount of the research in these years focused on communal bison procurement and processing sites, hence these sites played a large role in the 1st edition. The 2nd edition continued refining the cultural chronology as new data inevitably raised temporal questions. That volume, however, focused on adaptive strategies of past High Plains and Rocky Mountain peoples, although bison procurement and processing was still emphasized. To be sure, data from these types of sites provided some of the most secure information for making inferences about the past. This 3rd edition continues to refine the thorny chronological issues that remain unresolved and continues to focus on adaptive strategies. However, in the nearly 20 intervening years since the 2nd edition, the archaeological database has doubled, tripled, or more. In addition to bison bone beds, we now have significantly more information on a wide array of botanical and zoological remains and their procurement, processing, and consumption to inform archaeological interpretations. Moreover, raw data and inferences detailing a great deal more about the richness and complexity of aboriginal life in the Plains and Rockies have come to light. In this volume, we begin the process of integrating these data into a more complete picture of prehistoric lifeways and sociocultural systems of the Northwestern Plains and Rocky Mountains.

Plains and Rocky Mountain archaeology continues to grow by leaps and bounds. Much of the material reported in this book has its origin in cultural resource management (CRM) and salvage projects of the past two decades. The number of archaeologists in the public sector has increased, federal agencies—namely, the United States Forest Service, Bureau of Land Management, Bureau of Reclamation, and United States Fish and Wildlife Service—now have numerous trained professionals in nearly all field offices and often several students for seasonal employment. University involvement in CRM and salvage projects has generally declined, at least as a percentage of total, and academic institutional involvement has waxed and waned. For example, the University of Colorado at Boulder (CU) and Colorado State University (CSU) have not been at the forefront of CRM for several decades, while the University of Denver has steadily increased its contract programs. However, archaeologists at both CU and CSU have continued to do research, train students, and work with the public. While CU remains focused on the Southwest and Mesoamerica, it maintains a secondary Plains and Rockies emphasis. To the north, Montana State University (MSU) has successfully integrated pure research and publicly funded research into its archaeological program, as has the University of Wyoming (UW), but MSU faculty have recently diversified beyond the original Plains and Rocky Mountain focus. The University of Montana contributed to Plains archaeology from the 1950s through the 1970s, but has shifted focus to other regions in the 1980s and 1990s. It may be coming back on track with new faculty hired over the last several years.

Museums in the region have turned their backs on archaeology. The Museum of the Rockies at MSU showed great promise of becoming a serious contributor to Rocky Mountains prehistory a few decades ago, but their efforts unfortunately faltered as their emphasis shifted to paleontology. The same is true with the Denver Museum of Natural History (now Denver Museum of Science and Technology); although not focused on paleontology, Plains archaeology remains a relatively unappreciated component of their overall program, a situation that may be changing for the better.

Universities, however, continue to provide young professionals to fill the jobs in government agencies and the private sector. Nearly 40 years have passed since UW awarded its first Master's degree in anthropology, and it has recently instituted a Ph.D. program. The MSU anthropology department has recently grown to the point where it now offers a BA in anthropology. All these events have fostered and contributed to a growing archaeological database that holds a great deal of information about prehistory, but is becoming more difficult to synthesize. Most state historic preservation offices in the region have online computerized data availability, which alleviates some problems, but creates others. Without these databases, however, this book could not have been completed.

In no sense is this project complete, nor can it ever be. We continue to learn more about prehistory daily, and the data are multiplying exponentially. All we can do is periodically assess the state of our knowledge and understanding of the region's prehistory. In that sense, we hope this volume is one small step in that direction.

ACKNOWLEDGMENTS

The revision and expansion of any work is the result of efforts of many individuals and institutions. We wish to thank Mitch Allen of Left Coast Press, Inc., for seeing the publication of this edition through to completion. Research support during the past 45 years from a number of institutions, foundations, and organizations is gratefully acknowledged. These include the University of Wyoming (UW), the National Science Foundation, the National Endowment for the Humanities, the Wenner-Gren Foundation, the National Geographic Society, the L.S.B. Leakey Foundation, the Smithsonian Institution, the Wyoming Department of State Parks and Cultural Resources, the Office of the Wyoming State Archaeologist, the Wyoming State Historic Preservation Office, the Wyoming Game and Fish Commission, the Wyoming Council for the Arts, the Wyoming Council for the Humanities, the Zimbabwe Department of Wildlife, the Wyoming Archaeological Society, the Wyoming Archaeological Foundation, the U.S. Forest Service, the Bureau of Land Management (BLM) of Wyoming, BLM of Colorado, BLM of Montana, the U.S. Fish and Wildlife Service, UW College of Arts and Sciences, UW International Programs, UW Research Office, Wyoming Geographic Information Science Center, UW NASA Space Grant Consortium, Colorado State Historic Preservation Office, the National Park Service, the Bureau of Reclamation, the Carter Mining Company, the Kerr-McGee Mining Company, University of Arizona, and the Dubois Historical Center. We are also indebted to many individuals for research support. These include at least: Jean and Ray Auel, Joseph and Ruth Cramer, Mark Mullins, Betsy Mecom, Forrest Fenn, Mike McGonigal, Phillip Krmpotich, Mike Kammerer, Bill Tyrrell, Bonita Wyse, Susan Bupp, and Ed Bailey. The Friends and the Board of the Friends of the Frison Institute have been relentless in providing, as well as searching for research support for our endeavors. Especially noted should be Susan Bupp, Terry Wilson, Gail and the late Ray Gossett, P. Jaye Rippley, Jim Chase, the late Rhoda O. Lewis, and Ed and Shirley Cheramy.

The individuals who have directly or indirectly contributed to this volume would comprise a list far too long and one that would inevitably be incomplete. It would include persons from many walks of life, but who all had or have a common interest in prehistoric human life on the Plains and Rocky Mountains. It would include many who lack this interest but respect the efforts and wishes of others. Most of the specialists are acknowledged by reference to their published works.

However, there are others whom we wish to mention. From 1973 to 1995, Connie Robinson, a widely known and recognized artist from Sheridan, Wyoming, produced outstanding pen and ink drawings of flaked stone artifacts for the Department of Anthropology at the University of Wyoming. Many of these are reproduced in this volume. Pencil drawings by Marcia Bakry and pen and ink drawings by Sarah Moore are also included. Other line drawings of artifacts and maps were done by Abbe Current, Isobel Nichols, Patty Walker-Buchannan, Marion Huseas, David J. Rapson, and Charles A. Reher. Much of the photography is the work of Robert Swaim, Victor Krantz, Danny Walker, Charles A. Reher, and Curtis Martin. Others who have provided single illustrations are acknowledged directly on the figures.

Numerous individuals deserve special mention and include "Bison Pete" Gardner, Arthur Busskohl, George Crouse, Henry Jensen, Fred Finley, Gerald Clark, Dave Fraley, James Davis, Irving Friedman, Margaret Powers, Irene Morgan, Mr. and Mrs. Earl Davis, Lucille and Jim Adams, Burt Williams, Linda Ward-Williams, Bill Meckem, Keith Stillson, Mr. and Mrs. Wayne Darnell, Josephine Spencer, Amos Welty, Kay Bowles, Rex Corsi, Mr. and Mrs. Martin Maland, Milford and Imogene Hanson, George Wood, Maurice Bush, Donald Colby, Terrill Gibbons, John Potter, Bonnie Johnson, Marshall Dominick, Earl Holding, Joan Bugas, Jesse and Kathy Schultz, Mr. and Mrs. Dale Valentine, Dr. and Mrs. Orvill Bunnell, Dr. J. David Love, Dr. Luna Leopold, Mr. and Mrs. Bill Barlow, Mr. and Mrs. Paul Allen, Mr. and Mrs. Robert Larson, Tony Smith, Ralph and Ruth Phillips, Mary Helen Hendry, Joe Bozovich, Jack Krmpotich, Robert Sheaman, Berneil McCord, Glenn Sweem, Mike Toft, Mike Dollard, Tom Young, Bob Godsoe, Mary Hopkins, Steve Sutter, Paul Burnett, Terry Lietzman, Leslie Wildesen, Mike Fosha, Dan Eakin, Paul Sanders, Mark Miller, Kevin Black, Meg Van Ness, Maria Zedeño, Carolyn Sherve-Bybee, Mike Bies, Frank Rupp, Dewey and Janice Baars, Alan and Terry Korell, Alice Tratebas, Lynn Harrell, Mike Metcalf, Carl Conner, Sally Crum, Barbara Davenport, Curtis Martin, Rich Adams, John Brogan, Don Davis, Les Davis, Todd Surovell, Dennis DeSart, Dudley Gardner, Jim Wilson, Stan and Mary Flitner, Leroy Gonsoir, Cheryl Harrison, Ross Hilman, Aline LaForge, Tom Larson, Kevin O'Hanlon, Brian O'Neil, Bret Overturf, Les Peterson, Mike Peterson, Charles Reher, Nicole Waguespack, Tom Roll, Russ Tanner, Dave Vlcek, Alan Wimer, Judy Wolfe, Terry Craigie, George Zeimens, John and Evelyn Albanese, Harry Earl, Ed Peterson, the Frederick family, Helen Lookingbill, Bob Edgar, Ada Bouril, Debbie Chastain, Jana Pastor, Russ Tanner, Doris Vore, and the late Woody Vore. Our sincere apologies to the many others who deserve to be on this list. This book, however, would not have come to completion if it wasn't for the last final push by Joe Gingerich, Brigid Grund, Sara Ewing, Price Heiner, Jeremy Meerkreebs, and Christy Montgomery. Lee Steadman, copyeditor, and Allison Harkin, indexer, put the final authoritative touches on the volume. The heroic efforts of Kathy Fowler and Willa Mullen in dealing with the bureaucratic aspects of our projects are duly acknowledged.

A special kind of acknowledgment is directed to our students of the past nearly half century. Many of them are now in the forefront of American archaeology. They continually force us to keep abreast of the latest developments in the profession and have taught us a great deal more than we were able to teach them.

1

THE NORTHWESTERN PLAINS AND THE CENTRAL ROCKY MOUNTAINS
An Ecological Area for Prehistoric Hunters and Gatherers

INTRODUCTION

The Great Plains of North America constitute a large share of the continent, extending north and south from well into Canada to the border of Mexico and from the base of the Rocky Mountains on the west to the Eastern Woodlands (Wedel 1961:20–45). The Rocky Mountains likewise extend from northern Canada to Mexico and from their eastern boundary with the Great Plains to their more diffuse western boundary with the Northwest Plateau, Great Basin, and other physiographic regions. Actual boundaries between the Plains and Rocky Mountains are somewhat flexible, depending on the reactions to the area by the particular observer. There are some places where one can almost point to a line separating the Rocky Mountains and the Plains. Elsewhere on the western border of the Plains, mountain ranges extend deep into the Plains and often form intermontane basins, obscuring the line of demarcation. This is especially true in the case of the Central Rocky Mountain region. The eastern boundaries of the Plains are even less distinct, since there is none of the contrast formed by mountain slope and flat plain. Rainfall generally increases gradually to the east across the Plains, accompanied by lushness of the flora; the same is true with increasing elevation in the mountains. There is no sharp line of demarcation separating short-grass plains from tall-grass plains and the latter from Eastern Woodlands. Both short- and long-term changes in annual precipitation cause these boundaries to shift from time to time (Wedel 1961:20–45).

The seasoned Plains traveler can always detect the subtle difference that identifies the Plains. Prehistorically, the area was at the periphery of eastern cultural developments such as Hopewellian and Mississippian, but both influenced the peoples of the Northwestern Plains. Rainfall, frost-free days, and the available technology apparently held back the development of agriculture, limiting Plains horticultural efforts mostly to the floodplains of the rivers on the eastern margins. The Plains villagers living there may have been on the threshold of greater cultural developments when their efforts were disrupted by European incursion.

Various landforms, including stream valleys, uplifts, erosional remnants, and other less important features resulting from geologic processes, form integral parts of Plains and Rocky Mountain environments. These landforms provide relief to an otherwise monotonous and rather drab scene, and are reminiscent of oases in the desert. They often appear rather abruptly among seemingly endless rolling hills with little change in flora or fauna. The sudden appearance of a stream flowing from the higher elevations, or a spring in an arroyo with the surrounding green grass, trees, and shrubs, changes the entire aspect of the country. Without these niches or microenvironments, the region would not be the same and would certainly be less bearable for humans.

Such niches were every bit as important to the prehistoric inhabitants as to the present ones, animals as well as humans. The buffalo were grazers, but they had to go to water regularly, and they liked to stand in water and roll in dirt wallows. They sought shade on hot summer days, and they sought the protection of cut banks and brush thickets during winter and spring blizzards. Many animals, such as deer and mountain sheep, were not true open plains dwellers and favored areas of topographic relief, such as buttes, arroyos, river breaks, and dissected mountain slopes. Pronghorn do well with the forbs available on the sagebrush steppe of the intermountain basins to the west. These animals were important to the prehistoric economy. Human survival required a planned and careful utilization of the entire ecosystem; the instinctive behavior of the animals brought about culturally conditioned responses on the part of the humans.

The day-to-day life of the Plains and Rockies was generally harsher than life in adjacent geographic areas. Summer sun and winter storms were (and are today) brutal, reaching intensities from which there is little protection in the natural environment. Although there are differences in mean annual temperatures from north to south, a blizzard on the open areas of the Southern Plains can cause every bit as much discomfort as one on the Canadian border. However, both the human and animal populations were able to adapt to these harsh climatic conditions.

Though the Great Plains and Rocky Mountains of North America are marked by certain elements that distinguish them from adjacent areas, there is great internal diversity (e.g., Wood 1998). Depending on the person's home ground, a great many descriptions of the Plains are possible. Early on William Mulloy (1958) realized and described the great diversity of Northwestern Plains physiography. The short-grass plains are different from the tall-grass areas; the glaciated areas east of the Missouri River contrast sharply with areas to the west; small intermontane basins in the rain shadows of mountain ranges differ from the more open and expansive river basins. As a result, there is no single prehistoric ecological or cultural model that will suffice for the entire area.

This volume attempts to document only the prehistoric cultures of what is commonly called the Northwestern Plains (Mulloy 1958; Wedel 1961) along with the adjoining Rocky Mountains. For the purposes of this volume, the terms "Northwestern Plains" and "Rocky Mountains" refer to the archaeological culture area that encompasses the physiographic regions of the High Plains, Northwestern Plains, Central Rocky Mountains, portions of the Northern and Southern Rocky Mountains, the Black Hills uplift, and the Wyoming Basin. The area includes all of Wyoming in addition to southern Montana, eastern Idaho, southwest North Dakota, western South Dakota and Nebraska, and the area along the northern border of Colorado (Figure 1.1). In this volume, we also discuss pertinent data from the surrounding region. Although the boundaries are somewhat vague, the core of this region covers an area of more than 200,000 square miles that demonstrates considerable ecological diversity over short distances but shows strong suggestions of cultural homogeneity during prehistoric times. The area is extensive enough to detect many subtle changes in patterns of prehistoric exploitation, yet small enough to handle in terms of a research area.

The Northwestern Plains and surrounding regions demonstrate a wide variety of landforms. Mountain ranges and lesser uplifts project abruptly from the floor of the Plains. Many intermontane basins are at elevations above 7000 feet (2134 m);

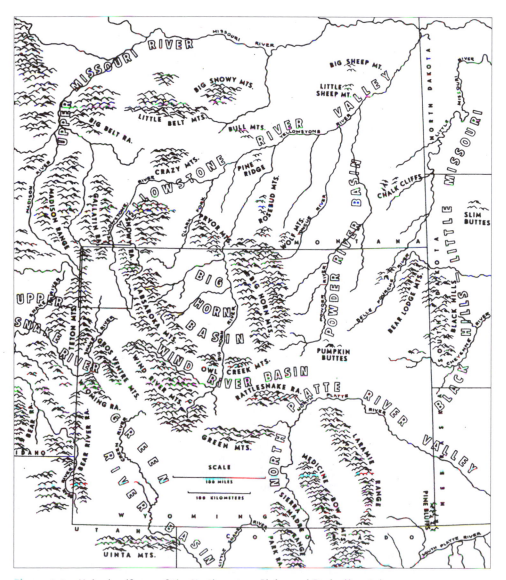

Figure 1.1 Major landforms of the Northwestern Plains and Rocky Mountains.

others are at less than 4000 feet (1219 m). Some areas of the open High Plains are subject to almost constant wind, whereas other areas are better protected. Floral changes are rapid in response to changes in elevation, precipitation, soils, and topography. Straddling both sides of the Continental Divide, the mountains adjacent to the Northwestern Plains are the source of many large rivers, which were avenues of human group movements from many directions. It is a unique area that requires careful analysis to understand its potentialities and failings in providing a subsistence base for past human populations. But no amount of analysis can entirely replace a long-term familiarity with the area during all seasons. Prehistoric hunters and gatherers had to deal with the adverse times of year as well as with the favorable ones.

Different areas within the Northwestern Plains and Rocky Mountains demonstrate ecological changes over short distances. The southern part of the region is dominated by an area of intermountain basins to the west of the Great Plains. The Wyoming Basin, sandwiched between the Central and Southern Rocky Mountains, is only interrupted from a nonmountainous passage between the Great Plains and the Great Basin by the Wasatch Range in Utah. While some consider the Wyoming Basin to be part of the Rocky Mountain System because of its location between the Central and Southern Rocky Mountains others consider it an extension of the Great Plains, with its comparatively lower altitude and unique character. Within the Wyoming Basin, there are several distinctive sub-basins.

The Laramie Basin in southeastern Wyoming is over 7000 feet (2134 m) above sea level and is composed mainly of rolling hills, with some areas of "breaks," or rough, deeply dissected landscapes. Transitional between the Plains on the east and intermountain basins to the west, it has a good grass cover, with some patches of sagebrush and greasewood in places. Playa lakes are common, although deeper lakes may hold water continuously or nearly so. The wind keeps large areas bare, allowing animals winter access to feed but forming deep snow drifts in arroyos and depressions.

Moving further west in south-central Wyoming, we find that elevations are lower and grass cover is not as good as in the Laramie Basin, with more sagebrush in evidence. This area is marked by some extremely rough country caused mainly by the deeply trenched North Platte River and its numerous permanent and intermittently flowing tributaries. The Hanna, Great Divide, Green River, and Washakie Basins and the Red Desert area further west in the Wyoming Basin lack good grass cover, but to some extent this may reflect overuse by livestock since the latter part of the nineteenth century. Here sagebrush, greasewood, and salt-tolerant desert shrubs form a vegetative mosaic throughout the lower elevations, with juniper, mountain mahogany, pine, and sagebrush in surrounding foothills.

One of the more unique aspects of the western Wyoming Basin is a large complex of active and stable sand dunes that span much of the area from southwest to northeast (Ahlbrandt 1974; Knight 1994:120). These dunes add to the ecological diversity present in the area today and formed an integral part of the environment in which the prehistoric inhabitants of southwestern Wyoming lived. The dune fields provide an environment that produces greater plant biomass than the surrounding sagebrush steppes (Knight 1994:122). Moisture falling on large sand dune areas often percolates through the sand to an impervious level and then comes to the surface in interdunal ponds. Some of these are large and provide water and green feed to animals who seek out these areas. Dune areas existed in varying sizes and distributions throughout at least the past 12,000 years in southwestern Wyoming and are found associated with buried artifact-bearing deposits.

To the south of the Green River Basin, the Green River flows into rough canyon country on the northern periphery of the Southwest and joins the Colorado River in western Colorado. The east–west trending Uinta Mountains, mostly in Utah, bring an end to the High Plains–like country of the southern Bridger Basin, located in extreme southwest Wyoming. A series of north–south trending ranges and divides on the Wyoming–Utah border, including the Bear River Divide, the Salt River Range, and the Wyoming Range, form the western border of the Green River and Wyoming Basins. West of this, the rivers flow into the Great Salt Lake. To the north of the Uinta Mountains, the character of the country changes gradually from plains to mountains in northwest Wyoming with the Wind River Mountains, the Gros Ventre Range, the Absaroka Mountains, and the Teton Range. Jackson Hole is nestled between the Teton and Gros Ventre ranges and is part of the upper Snake River drainage, which begins on the southern edge of the Yellowstone Plateau and flows south, west, and then northwest into the Columbia River. Yet, for all its mountain character, there are open, sagebrush-covered flats bordering the Snake River in Jackson Hole.

The Snake River Plain and adjoining areas in southeastern Idaho present an ecological and archaeological situation that bears a close relationship to the Northwestern Plains. The Yellowstone River, beginning at Yellowstone Lake, a large body of water at an elevation of 7200 feet (2195 m) on the northern part of the glaciated Yellowstone Plateau, drains north into Montana and then turns east and flows diagonally across Montana and meets the Missouri River at the Montana–North Dakota border. The headwaters of the Madison and Gallatin rivers also begin on the Yellowstone Plateau and flow north into Montana and then directly north to Three Forks and the beginning of the Missouri River. West of the Yellowstone Plateau in southeast Montana lies the Jefferson River, the third major stream that forms the Missouri River. The Sun and Milk rivers join the Missouri from the north, having their source in the Northern Rocky Mountains.

The Plains-like country continues to South Pass at 7550 feet (2301 m) elevation, straddling the Continental Divide in southwestern Wyoming at the southern end of the Wind River Mountains. It then merges with other Plains-like areas along the Sweetwater River, which flows into the North Platte River, and the Wind River, which farther on becomes the Bighorn River and eventually flows into the Yellowstone River in Montana. To the east of an imaginary line connecting the southern end of the Bighorn Mountains and the northern end of the Laramie Range is a true Plains environment of open rolling country along the North Platte River, the upper drainages of the Cheyenne, Belle Fourche, and Powder rivers, and extending southward along the North Platte River into the North Park area of Colorado. The first two flow east to the Missouri River and the third flows north to the Yellowstone River.

A unique enclave of the Northwestern Plains is the Bighorn Basin, lying between the Bighorn, Absaroka, and Owl Creek mountains in north-central Wyoming and the Pryor Mountains in southern Montana. The western and southern parts of the Bighorn Basin are reasonably good grasslands, but the eastern part at the base of the western slopes of the Bighorn Mountains is extremely dry and closer to a Great Basin rather than Plains environment. The Bighorn Basin, however, grades into a true Plains environment north in the area of the Clark's Fork of the Yellowstone River and northeast through the gap between the Pryor and Bighorn mountains and from there through the vast stretch of country along the Yellowstone River.

The character of the Northwestern Plains changes markedly to the east of the Bighorn Mountains along the drainages of the Little Bighorn, Tongue, Powder, and Little Missouri rivers in southern Montana and northern Wyoming. There is more moisture here and the grass improves. Besides open plains, the area is marked by buttes, escarpments, and shallow but rough canyons covered with sagebrush, ponderosa pine, and juniper. Mesas are a common feature and the entire area in general was good bison range. In southern Montana there are several small but important landform features including the Wolf and Rosebud Mountains.

The Yellowstone River and its wide valley comprise a special part of the Northwestern Plains. The stream valley has several broad terraces, and tributaries provide rough country; bluffs and escarpments are seen on both sides of the valley and deep, narrow canyons drain a large land area on both sides of the river. The Yellowstone River and its major tributaries provide a natural entrance from the east into the heart of the Northwestern Plains and Rocky Mountains, as does the North Platte River farther to the south. The drainages of the Yellowstone River east of the Bighorn Mountains include some of the best grass country and, in the past, some of the best buffalo country known for the entire Plains. Elevations here are lower and winter climates are less harsh than those of some of the higher intermontane basins.

The Black Hills area of Wyoming and South Dakota provides another somewhat special environment. Rising out of the Plains, the area attracts more rainfall than its surroundings. The flora is unique, and heavy stands of a hybrid species of oak and ponderosa pine predominate. Scattered throughout are open parks with excellent grass, although the higher elevations are deeply dissected and covered with heavy brush and timber. A number of small streams make the Black Hills a true oasis-like environment.

Between the Black Hills and the Laramie Range is an area of open plains with occasional minor uplifts such as the Rochelle Hills, the Pumpkin Buttes, and the Pine Ridge escarpment extending eastward from the northern part of the Laramie Range. The Hartville uplift begins just east of the North Platte River in eastern Wyoming and extends northward to the vicinity of Lusk, Wyoming. Just south of the North Platte River is another landmark known as Goshen Hole, a circular depression 100 or more feet (30 m) deep and nearly 62 miles (100 km) in diameter eroded out of the High Plains. This is another excellent grass area with good protection from the constant wind. Surrounding Goshen Hole is butte-like country, with open plains, long, steep scarps, and brushy canyons, extending well into western Nebraska before the more flat, typical Great Plains area begins. In the extreme southeast corner of Wyoming and extending a short distance into Colorado, the open plains are interrupted by an erosional remnant known as the Pine Bluffs, with a vegetation cover of sparse to thick stands of ponderosa pine. Similar erosional features occur farther to the south at Colorado's Palmer Divide and still farther to the south at the Mesa de Mayo. Many lesser features such as geological faults and deeply eroded sandstone formations add variety to the topography of the Northwestern Plains.

Major mountain ranges, such as the Bighorn, Absaroka, Wind River, and Bear Tooth ranges, have steep and deeply dissected slopes. At higher elevations above

7500 feet (2285 m), there are many relatively flat, open areas supporting excellent grass along with tall sagebrush and occasional stands of timber. At even higher elevations where thick stands of timber begin, numerous open, grassy parks provide feed during the warmer months. Above the timberline there are thick stands of grass and, though much of the country is extremely rough, bleached bison skulls were common a few years ago at elevations above 13,000 feet (3962 m). Evidence of prehistoric occupation is also found at these higher altitudes.

From the above, it is obvious that it is difficult to describe a true Northwestern Plains and Rocky Mountain environment. Nevertheless there is distinctiveness. In most of the Northwestern Plains one can climb to the top of a rise and on a clear day see some form of uplift or mountain range in the distance, which is in sharp contrast to the view from the open plains farther east. The wind blows almost incessantly, usually from the west. Violent changes in weather are always to be expected. Long, cold winters and short summers lead to a short growing season, and when rainfall is scarce, grass is short. Early warm spring days give a false promise of continuing good weather, but spring blizzards can be more deadly to animal life than those of winter because this is the critical birthing period. Indian summers seldom linger very long and are usually cut short by snow and cold weather.

It is not an area that even under present technology can support large human populations. Domestic livestock operations rely on irrigation, high-protein supplements, and domesticated crops adapted to high altitudes and short growing seasons in order to raise enough feed to survive the long, hard winters. There is little to recommend the Northwestern Plains as a place to live, but its uniqueness did foster some distinctive cultural patterns in prehistoric times.

The climate of the Northwest Plains is highly variable, as several major continental and maritime air masses meet over the Central Rocky Mountains and Western Plains. The movement of some or all of these air masses in any direction can have dramatic effects on weather from day to day and ultimately on the environment if patterns change over the decades or longer. Within the broader Rocky Mountain chain, the Northern Rockies receive cool, moist air masses from the Pacific Northwest, while the Southern Rocky Mountains are dominated by storm flows from the maritime tropical Pacific. During the summer, monsoonal flow from the Gulf of Mexico and the Pacific bring thunderstorms and severe weather to the Southern and Central Rockies. Warm, dry westerlies from the Pacific bring heat to the area at various times of the year.

In winter, Canadian cold fronts bringing cold, dry air from the Arctic plunge the Rockies and Plains into a deep freeze. Pacific storm fronts from the west coast can combine with moisture from the Gulf of Mexico to cause heavy snows in upslope conditions on the eastern front of the Southern Rocky Mountains and out into the Plains (Kittel et al. 2002). Significantly, the Central Rocky Mountains and Northwestern Plains receive a combination of all of these storm types that can vary greatly from one year to the next. The north–south, east–west movement of the jet stream determines the position of northern or southern air masses on the Northwestern Plains. The seemingly almost constant winds in some areas of the region are produced by the mix of highly mobile air masses and mountain uplifts.

Orographic precipitation and rain shadows affect the amount of precipitation, and elevation influences temperature; both of these can vary greatly over smaller areas compared to the flat-lying areas to the west and east (Kittel et al. 2002).

Precipitation within the Central Rocky Mountains varies from a high of 59 in./ year (150 cm) in high elevations in northwest Wyoming to 2.4 in./year (six cm) in south-central Wyoming and in the Bighorn Basin. Elevation and topographic relief affect temperature, as the highest temperatures in summer and winter occur in the low-elevation, eastern side of the state and the basins to the west, whereas the lowest temperatures in winter and summer are found in the mountains. Modern frost-free days vary from 65 to over 203 days per year (Western Regional Data Center 2008). The effects of elevation, slope, and aspect add to microenvironmental variation within the mountains. The timing, amount, and type (rain vs. snow) of seasonal precipitation combined with temperature affects the types and distribution of plants and, as a result, animal species.

It is tempting to place the events of the past entirely within the limits of present ecological conditions. However, the archaeologist must remember that the landforms and vegetative cover of the land have changed in various ways through time as a result of climatic changes. Short-term as well as long-term changes have significantly altered the landscape. There are deep, perpendicular-sided arroyos now where gently sloping, sodded swales were present a half-century ago. The dust bowl years of the 1930s changed the looks of the Plains as well as their livestock carrying capacity for several years both during and after the event. We can only hypothesize what the Plains looked like before the Europeans came, both before and after Upper Republican sites in western Nebraska were covered with a thick mantle of loess (Wedel 1961:101) or during the late Pleistocene when Clovis hunters were present and hunting the last remnants of mammoth populations. In the Late Archaic period some arroyos were in the process of aggrading and presented a meandering pattern with shallow banks; now they are marked by deep, perpendicular banks and a much less meandering pattern. Trapping bison on landforms present then (Albanese 1971; Frison 1971a) and now would be different matters and would require entirely different procurement strategies.

Another example of landform change over time is provided by an arroyo in the Bighorn Basin of northern Wyoming where mammoths were killed during Clovis times. The geology of the area indicates that the arroyo was steep sided at that time and at least 30 feet (9 m) wide, with banks nearly the same height (Albanese 1986). Today the same area is drained by a shallow, meandering arroyo with gently sloping banks (Figure 4.2). The presence of mammoths approximately 11,000 years ago in an area that today supports only small sagebrush, greasewood, and occasional bunch grass also indicates significant floral changes. Although the major features of the macroenvironment such as the mountain ranges, intermontane basins, and stream valleys remained relatively unchanged through late Pleistocene and Holocene times, the microenvironmental changes have been many and significant during the same period, and all have affected prehistoric human subsistence strategies in the area.

Paleoenvironments

The following section paints a broad picture of the natural environment of prehistoric hunters and gatherers on the Northwestern Plains and Rocky Mountains. This reconstruction synthesizes data collected from many sources of paleoenvironmental information (Table 1.1). Because some of the studies reported

Table 1.1   Studies used in the summary of paleoenvironmental data from the Plains and Rocky Mountains. CO=Colorado, MI=Michigan, MT=Montana, TX=Texas, UT=Utah, WY=Wyoming.

Pollen/Phytoliths

Fall et al. 1995	Wind River Mountains, WY
Fredlund and Tieszen 1997	Canada to TX
Lynch 1998	Wind River Mountains, WY
Munroe 2003	Uinta Mountains, UT
Whitlock and Bartlein 1993	Yellowstone Plateau, WY
Whitlock et al. 1995	Yellowstone Plateau, WY
Whitlock et al. 2002	Yellowstone, Pacific Northwest
Whitlock et al. 2003	Yellowstone, Pacific Northwest

Plant Macrofossils

Jackson et al. 2002	Wind River Canyon, WY
Lyford et al. 2002	Bighorn Basin, MT
Lyford et al. 2003	WY, MT, UT

Dendrochronology

Gray et al. 2003	Central & Southern Rockies
Gray, Fastie, Jackson, and Betancourt 2004	Bighorn Basin, WY & MT
Gray, Jackson, and Betancourt 2004	Uinta Basin, UT

Geostratigraphy/Geoarchaeology

Forman et al. 2001	Plains & Wyoming dunes
Mayer 2002	Krmpotich site, WY
Mayer 2003	Killpecker Dunes, WY
Mayer and Mahan 2004	Killpecker Dunes, WY

Isotopic Studies

Rux et al. 2000	Northeast Wyoming
Sjostrom et al. 2004	Northern & Southern Rockies

Insects/Beetles

Elias 1996	MT & CO

Ice Cores Plus Modeling and Overviews of Paleoenvironmental Indicators

Alley and Ágústsdóttir 2005	North Atlantic, global
Bradley 2000	Global
Ganopolski et al. 1998	Global

Multiple Data Sets

Booth et al. 2005	Midcontinent, WY to MI
Forman et al. 1995	Geochronology, geostratigraphy, pollen, modeling, NE Colorado
Mayewski et al. 2004	Rapid climatic change, Global
Miao et al. 2007	Geochronology, geostratigraphy, soil, organic carbon, SE Nebraska
Whitlock et al. 2003	Lake sediment cores, dendrochronology, NW United States, MT, WY

in this section calibrate their dates into calendar years before present (BP) while we provide our dates throughout this volume in uncalibrated radiocarbon years before present, Table 1.2 provides a simplified comparison of calibrated calendar years, both in BP and BC/AD formats, and uncalibrated radiocarbon years BP.

It now appears that hunters and gatherers living at the very end of the Pleistocene and start of the Holocene lived with drastic changes in weather patterns that produced equally dramatic changes in the availability of plants and animals as the earth lurched into the current interglacial from the last ice age. Scientists are now viewing many changes in Pleistocene and Holocene climates as reactions to massive, swift shocks from orbital, solar, atmospheric, oceanic, and physical forces that overlay changes associated with the gradual warming of the earth at the end of the ice age.

As warming at the end of the Pleistocene (about 11,500–10,000 BP) brought about the final melting of the Cordilleran and Laurentide ice sheets, climatic

Table 1.2 Comparison of calibrated calendar years BP and BC/AD to uncalibrated radiocarbon years BP. Calibrated date range is given for one sigma of 50 years. Calib Rev. 5.0.1 (Stuiver and Reimer 1993) used for calibration. Dates in text are uncalibrated radiocarbon years BP unless otherwise noted.

Radiocarbon years before present	Calibrated calendar year date range BC /AD	Calibrated calendar year date range BP
12,000	11,967–11,841 BC	13,916–13,790 BP
11,500	11,440–11,340 BC	13,389–13,289 BP
11,000	11,011–10,928 BC	12,960–12,877 BP
10,500	10,679–10,443 BC	12,628–12,392 BP
10,000	9656–9387 BC	11,695–11,336 BP
9500	9117–8729 BC	11,066–10,678 BP
9000	8286–8024 BC	10,235–9973 BP
8500	7583–7534 BC	9532–9483 BP
8000	7048–6828 BC	8997–8777 BP
7500	6433–6354 BC	8382–8215 BP
7000	5980–5838 BC	7929–7787 BP
6500	5515–5464 BC	7829–7464 BP
6000	4950–4805 BC	6899–6754 BP
5500	4444–4296 BC	6393–6218 BP
5000	3793–3757 BC	5875–5656 BP
4500	3338–3103 BC	5287–5052 BP
4000	2573–2471 BC	4522–4420 BP
3500	1885–1757 BC	3834–3706 BP
3000	1370–1131 BC	3319–3080 BP
2500	770–541 BC	2719–2490 BP
2000	AD 48–60	1997–1890 BP
1500	AD 470–635	1480–1315 BP
1000	AD 987–1150	963–800 BP
500	AD 1334–1448	616–502–BP

conditions and associations of plants and animals were unlike any seen after this time (Graham and Lundelius 1994; Whitlock et al. 2002). While many plants and animals had already become extinct, it is the co-occurrence of ancient megafauna and the remains of human activities that provide the first evidence we have of human existence on the Northwestern Plains. Clovis, the first clear, unequivocal evidence for human occupation of the Northwest Plains, appears at sites with mammoth, bison, and small numbers of horse and camel around 11,200 BP.

Bison were the only megafauna left when the abruptly colder and wetter conditions known as the Younger Dryas began about 10,900 BP. There is some evidence that this change may have happened within as little as 100 years. A black stratum known as the "black mat" formed in low-elevation, cold, wet meadows at many locations throughout the west (Haynes 2008), although not all places evidence this paleosol. Several sites on the Northwestern Plains contain this black stratum, including Carter-Kerr McGee, Hell Gap, Agate Basin, Sheaman, Fetterman Mammoth, Lindenmeier, Frazier, Jim Pitts, Seawright, and Lange/Ferguson. While no single factor caused the extinction of all megafauna and other organisms as well, the shift to Younger Dryas conditions may have been the one event in a series of events, both catastrophic and gradual, that brought about major changes in the resources available to hunter-gatherers.

By 10,600 BP continuing existence of glacial conditions to the north brought cool, wet conditions to eastern Wyoming and the east slope of the Colorado Rockies, while comparatively dry and warm conditions existed to the west in Idaho and northwestern Wyoming (e.g., Beiswenger 1991; Fall et al. 1995; Whitlock et al. 2002). Shifts in the earth's axis and tilt increased the amount of summer sun, raising summer temperatures but having less effect on winter cold. Summer precipitation and temperature continued to increase until sometime after 9600 BP, producing grassland environments ideal for grazing bison in eastern Wyoming (Fredlund 2009). The intensity of storms in the Central and Southern Rocky Mountains increased (Elias 1996; Reider 2009).

The time between 9500 and 6000 BP is marked by continued warming, although temperatures were still cooler than today. Between 7900 and 7200 BP, spectacular shifts in global climate resulted from the final melting of the Pleistocene glaciers to the north and a massive influx of freshwater into the north Atlantic from Canadian lakes. As the ice disappeared, major disruptions in wind and weather patterns as well as ocean temperatures are postulated. Conditions appear to have shifted to cold and wet for a brief period on the High Plains (Rux et al. 2000), but the continuing influence of increased summer insolation brought about warmer and potentially much drier conditions to the entire Northwestern Plains. In low-elevation areas of central and southwestern Wyoming, dune fields expanded and vegetation better adapted to warmer, drier conditions colonized new areas. The makeup of high-altitude vegetation also fluctuated from the late Pleistocene into the early Holocene. Between 9600 and 8500 BP high-elevation vegetation varied from tundra above tree line and/or spruce-fir forests to a coniferous forest that combined different percentages of whitebark pine, spruce, and fir.

All evidence suggests that summer temperatures increased on the Northwest Plains between 8000 and 6000 BP. Precipitation seems to have increased in at least some parts of the region at this time. The input of summer moisture from subtropical air masses from the Gulf of California and the Gulf of Mexico likely strengthened, pulling moisture in summer. Pollen records, in particular, pick up this trend in the foothills and higher elevations of mountains east of the Continental Divide and in the Uinta Mountains on the edges of the Wyoming Basin. Evidence at the Hawken site on the western edge of the Black Hills confirms this finding as well. At the same time, summer drought in the Pacific Northwest brought drier conditions to the Yellowstone Plateau and areas northwest of the Wind River Mountains (Whitlock et al. 2002). The line dividing summertime monsoon from drought no doubt varied, but was surely part of the reality of mid-Holocene life for foragers living on the Northwest Plains and Rocky Mountains.

Cooler, moister conditions returned to northwestern Wyoming sometime between 6000 and 5000 BP. In their model of paleoclimate of the Hell Gap site, Bryson and Bryson (2009) suggest wetter summers and drier winters, as well as cooler summers in relation to annual average temperature, beginning at this time. More severe summer storms, causing cutting and filling, appeared for the first time at Hell Gap in mid to late Holocene strata. In southwest Wyoming and the Uinta Mountains, cool moist conditions appear to have returned around the same time (e.g., Miller 1992; Munroe 2003), and site stratigraphic studies in south-central Wyoming and north-central Colorado indicate similar conditions at this time (Metcalf et al. 2006).

One indicator of warmer and drier conditions is the macrofossils of Utah juniper (*Juniperus osteosperma)* deposited in fossil wood rat (*Neotoma* sp.) middens in the foothills of the Pryor and Bighorn Mountains (Jackson et al. 2002; Lyford et al. 2002). Initial movement of *J. osteosperma* occurred as early as 8410 calendar years BP in one site in the Pryor Mountains; at another on Mahogany Butte in the southern Bighorns, migration of this shrub continued until about 4700 calendar years BP. Expansion of this juniper appears to have stopped in the Bighorn region until about 2700 calendar years BP, when the shrub begins to expand its range once again. The absence of *J. osteosperma* in middens between about 4700 and 2700 calendar years BP is taken as evidence of wetter conditions in the areas within the wood rat habitat. Wetter conditions are documented between 4600 and 2100 calendar years BP in the Uinta mountains in southwestern Wyoming. Evidence for paleosol development between 4600 and 3400 BP occurs along the Little Snake, Yampa, and White River drainages of southern Wyoming and northern Colorado (Metcalf et al. 2006). Finally, deposition begins in the dune fields of southwest Wyoming between calendar years 5300 and 2800 BP. Between calendar years 2800 and 1000 BP conditions dried and warmed in the Bighorn foothills, and the Killpecker dunes experienced renewed erosion between calendar years 2000 and 1500 BP (e.g., Lyford et al. 2003; Mayer and Mahan 2004).

Dendrochonological studies reaching back 800 years ago are providing evidence of the complexity of climatic variation that we cannot yet see in earlier indicators. Since approximately AD 1200 climatic conditions have fluctuated much like we see today (e.g., Gray et al. 2003). However, the longer time span provides a perspective on the nature of Northwestern Plains environments and climate not evident in historic records. Drought has been with us throughout the 800 years, as have wetter periods; temperatures have varied from warmer than today to colder.

It was within the past millennium that bison reached their zenith on the Plains, until they were hunted out in the eighteen hundreds. This was also the time of the Little Ice Age and the Medieval Warm Period. The relationship between climate and faunal availability deserves much more in-depth research, given the quantity of paleoclimatic data we currently have available to us. If we had the resolution on climate for the last 13,000 years that we have for the last 800, we would no doubt see as much variation stretching back through time as is apparent in our recent paleoclimatological data.

When one views the climate of the past 13,000 calendar years, several overall conclusions may be drawn. First of all, one cannot understand the variability in climate as if it were a single system from winter to summer or from high to low elevations. Difference between the seasons in both temperature and rainfall has produced many variations of the climate and therefore the environment of the Northwestern Plains and Rocky Mountains. In the early Holocene, winter temperature ranges were not synchronous with summer temperature ranges, as each season responded from different inputs. Variable moisture regimes from northwest and south-southwest of the Northwest Plains and Rocky Mountains have led to different conditions through time and space. In some cases, the weather patterns observed at high elevations differ significantly from nearby lower elevations, meaning that both xeric and mesic conditions coexisted at various times in the past within close proximity of each other. Finally, while the lag time between climate change and vegetation change is relatively short and of little consequence, it will be interesting to investigate the evidence for the effects of climate change on the large mammals that occupied the Northwest Plains during the Holocene. A few studies have begun to observe lags between faunal abundance in stratified archaeological sites and indicators of climate change (e.g., Bryan 2006), but further research is clearly needed.

As a result, there is actually no stereotype environment for the area, either past or present, because of the differences in elevation and the wide variety of landforms, flora, and fauna. Nor can we consider the foothills and mountains without considering the plains, or vice versa; neither one by itself is sufficient as a basis for intelligent discussion of past human exploitation of the area. The prehistoric occupants did not make these kinds of distinctions and neither can we. Mountain ranges, minor uplifts, intermontane basins, major rivers, high-altitude plateaus, and many other landforms intrude into the Northwestern Plains, and all form a part of the natural environment that was utilized by the prehistoric inhabitants.

The Subsistence Base

The main source of subsistence on the prehistoric Plains and adjacent mountains was a variety of grasses, forbs, and shrubs that supported grazing and browsing mammalian fauna, which, along with a number of seeds, roots, tubers, berries, greens, and fruit, provided economic resources for a small number of human groups sometimes rather precariously perched at the top of the food chain. The short, sparse grasses and low shrubs are deceiving. To strangers unfamiliar with the area, they appear to be incapable of supporting much in the way of large animal life, but they are actually rich in available protein. The native grazing and browsing animals are well adapted to their intake. These animals can survive and maintain excellent body condition here as well as in areas where there are less harsh climates and large quantities of lower protein grasses.

The present-day livestock operator has more descriptive terms for grass than the polar Inuit has terms for snow, and each type of grass results directly from soil and weather conditions. Moisture and temperature determine grass conditions, although perhaps the former is more critical. Wet, cold springs usually produce better grass than hot, dry springs. Heavy spring snow or rain followed by warm days produces the large quantities of nutritious grasses that rapidly bring the animals out of the long, downhill physiological trends of winter. No artificial feeding program yet devised can replace green grass as a means of reviving metabolic processes of grazing and browsing animals.

Although spring storms help the grass, they can be devastating for the animals, especially with blizzard conditions that include deep snow, high winds, and low temperatures. Early spring is bison birthing time, a particularly critical period even though bison are surprisingly tough. A calf born in a snow bank has a good chance of surviving if temperatures do not drop too low for prolonged periods. Once on its feet, dried off, and suckling, its chances are good even though temperatures may drop to 0°F and below, a possibility even as late in the year as April. Deer and pronghorn give birth during May and June, but blizzards do occur and can be of sufficient intensity to cause the death of many young animals.

Ideal grass conditions result from a warm, moist spring followed by enough summer moisture to bring the grass to slow, even maturity. Hot, dry periods, even after an ideal spring, force early maturity and poor seed development. Dry, brittle grass breaks off easily from movements of animal herds and is consequently lost. Because the critical element is moisture, and precipitation differs over short distances in the Plains, grass production is seldom uniform over large areas during any given year. Also, an area good one year may not be good the next. Hail storms can denude large areas of grass, causing the grazing animals to shift locations from year to year or even during a single season.

A combination of dry years, short grass, and hard winters have many negative effects on grazing animals. The number of offspring can be directly correlated to the condition of the animals, which is dependent on food supply. Bison calf crops especially suffer if animals are unable to achieve a certain level of conditioning. The teeth of grazing and browsing animals are also adversely affected by poor grass. Grazers and browsers are able to survive only as long as their teeth last. When grass is abundant, the animal can fill its belly without grubbing the grass close to the ground and so does not take in as much particulate matter, which accelerates the wear on incisor and molar teeth. Poor grass years also force animals to ingest greater quantities of coarser feed. As the animals approach old age, the incisor teeth no longer present a straight, uninterrupted occlusal edge.

To view the Plains in terms of animal survival, we must understand both the nature of the vegetation and how it is utilized by the animals. The Plains are characterized by different kinds of soils and topographic relief. Heavy clays or "gumbo" soils support bunchgrass; buffalo grass favors the areas of well-drained light soils and sandy soils; low-lying, saline areas provide conditions favorable for the salt bushes. River bottoms and arroyos with intermittent watercourses are favorable for a wide variety of tall, coarse grasses, trees, and shrubs.

The year-round patterns of plant utilization are in general the same for all grazers and browsers, although some minor variations may be unique to an individual species. The grasses begin to grow in the early spring and the animals, desperate for green feed, have sometimes been known to run themselves to death in order to find it, especially if they happen to be weak from a hard winter. This is the time when a good many animals die, strangely enough after they have managed to survive the long, difficult winter. After the grasses grow enough to provide sufficient feed, the animals begin to lose their winter coats of hair. In a short time they have regained their strength and begin to replace the fat lost during the winter. Females drift off to prepare for the birthing period and the males usually congregate in separate groups, displaying little or none of the belligerent behavior of the rutting season that follows. Extremely old males unable to compete with the young and stronger ones may remain solitary.

Spring rains usually provide enough moisture to give the Plains a false appearance of lush abundance for a few short weeks, and this is a good time for the animals. Feed and water are everywhere and conditions are ideal. The young are growing fast from the soft grass and good supplies of mother's milk. The days are warm and nights are cool; insects are not yet abundant in large quantities. One hardly recognizes the sleek, healthy animals that were listless and sickly appearing only a few weeks earlier. Even the very old, with teeth nearly gone, that barely made it through the winter can ingest sufficient grass and regain good body condition well into the fall.

It is not long, however, before the pleasantly warm days of spring turn into the hot days of summer. Spring ponds and watercourses begin to dry up and disappear; plants are suddenly forced into maturity while there is enough ground moisture to produce viable seeds. Animal utilization patterns of the Plains flora change. Longer and longer treks to water are necessary as the available feed around ponds and springs is consumed and the number of water sources decreases. The animals change to a pattern of early morning and late evening grazing to avoid the midday heat and the clouds of insects. Buffalo seek mud and dirt wallows and shady places. Another favorite spot is a clump of trees in a high place, where the breezes can circulate freely while the animals are in shade. In areas close to mountains many larger species move to the higher elevations for the summer.

As the grasses and other plants mature, the character of the Plains changes gradually from green to brown. A blindfolded person can sense the difference as the inevitable afternoon winds carry the smell of curing vegetation. This critical change in the nature of the vegetation brings about subtle changes in the animals. Their protein intake is comparatively higher because the seeds are now mature and the stems and leaves of the plants contain less moisture. This is the period when the animals begin to accumulate the layers of fat so crucial for winter survival. At the end of summer and early fall, with hot days and cool nights, the animals are in prime condition. Long strips of fat are found along the top of the back from the tail to the shoulders, in thick layers on the brisket and ribs, and in the form of long strings and blobs of loose or "gut" fat in the intestinal cavity. The hump of the buffalo is a choice cut of meat with alternating layers of fat and flesh. The true meat hunter knows that this is the period when the animals are in the best of condition and will loudly and justifiably proclaim the excellence of "grass fat" meat obtained at this time over the artificial products of forced feeding in a modern feedlot.

The rutting season begins in midsummer and lasts through fall. Buffalo have a gestation period of about 280 days and usually begin the rut in late July. Pronghorn have a gestation period of about 252 days and begin the rut about a month later than the buffalo. Deer and mountain sheep, with much shorter gestation periods, rut later in the fall. Rutting periods completely change animal behavior patterns. Docile and retiring males that once avoided the nursery herds become belligerent and aware of the females. The rut is short, however, and when it is over the males revert to their former behavior patterns but, in the meantime, have expended much of their fat reserves.

On the Plains and especially in the mountains, the salubrious days of late summer usually terminate abruptly. One day may be warm and sunny, and the next can bring cold winds, snow, and even blizzard conditions. These first storms never last but are signs of winter not to be ignored. Changes in animal behavior can be detected. Summer coats are lost and gradually replaced with the heavier ones of winter. Animals are more active during the day because the weather is cooler and insect hordes have decreased. Antlers and horns have been brought to top condition; the results of this are evident from numerous shrubs and small trees with the bark and branches rubbed and twisted into various shapes. A male deer or elk will attack a small tree or several shrubs in a thicket and literally strip all the bark and leaves while removing the velvet and polishing the tines of its antlers. Bison will go into a thicket of long, slender willows and encircle a number of trees with a horn. With a circular motion of their heads, they form bundles of branches several feet long resembling giant pieces of twisted cordage.

As fall progresses into winter, snow becomes deeper and the weather colder. Animal activity is more evident, largely because their habitat is reduced and also because there is less vegetation in which to hide. As long as the higher concentrations of grass along the bottoms of streams and arroyos are available, the grazers will take advantage of it. As the arroyos fill with snow and the snow becomes too crusted, the animals move to the bare, windswept ridges and southern exposures where feed is available. In the dead of winter feed generally becomes even scarcer. The animals use up their fat reserves and exploit the less desirable food sources. If the winter is really severe, bison will eat willows, cottonwood, and branches of other trees as large in diameter as a man's thumb. They also will eat yucca leaves (which are little more than heavy twine with a small amount of barely nourishing filler) and tall, coarse grasses such as Canadian wild rye (*Elymus canadensis*), which grows to heights of over 6 feet (2 m) and is usually ignored entirely because of its low feed value. Life spans of these animals are shortened because of the intense wear on teeth needed to masticate the coarse grasses and branches. Bison use their large heads to push away the snow while other grazers paw the snow with a front foot to expose feed.

Extended periods of below-zero weather are particularly difficult for the animals. This is the time when the old, the sick, and the crippled begin to die and/or fall victim to predators. Occasionally the conditions are so severe that even some healthy animals die before the arrival of spring. Winter culls the old and the weak, and it is the bad winter following a summer of sparse vegetation that is disastrous to the grazing and browsing animals. When the situation is such that another summer of poor grass follows a bad winter, the animals' condition, particularly in the case of bison, never improves sufficiently for proper breeding to take place and the next year's calf crop is consequently below normal. All animals going into a normal winter in poor condition can be in serious trouble before green grass appears the following spring.

THE HUMAN GROUP

Prehistoric life on the Northwestern Plains and in the Rocky Mountains was not gentle for prehistoric hunters and gatherers. Human skeletal material is not plentiful, but what there is strongly indicates that long life was not one of the concomitants of these hunting and gathering groups. Although some individuals may have lived to be quite old, a life span of 35 to 45 years was probably all the average person could expect. However, this means that for about 20 or 30 years a prehistoric individual lived within a family group that formed the basic social and economic unit of the band.

On the basis of analogy from ethnological studies, we can conclude that concepts of territoriality must have existed within prehistoric Plains groups. Hunters and gatherers favor patterns of economic exploitation in areas they are familiar with, since locating and procuring animal or plant resources in unfamiliar territory is a difficult and unpredictable task. Animals are predictable within limits, and familiarity with a territory means that the hunter has a chance to observe the way the animals behave in a given area. The hunting strategy that, from past experience, has the best chance of success can then be applied. The same is true with respect to the floral resources. It takes a long time to learn where the berry patches, seeds, greens, tubers, roots, and other resources are located and then provide constant monitoring to determine when they are available.

Many times during the year the prehistoric human group had to pack up all personal belongings and move. A dry year resulted in different patterns of distribution of plant and animal resources, and the human groups had to respond accordingly. Other factors such as infestations of insects, intensity of runoff water affecting stream crossing, and time of snow melt on mountain passes could also have caused changes in year-to-year resource procurement strategies. These would have been short-term events. Major climatic changes would have resulted in long-term events that changed the entire settlement pattern.

We may think of such movements as mobility strategies or the plan of movements across the landscape. Archaeologists define two polar extremes of such types: residential and logistical mobility (Binford 1980, 2001). In the former, an entire family group moves from one location to another, usually closer to a resource, and exploits the resources close to camp until it is no longer profitable. In the latter, a few people travel, usually longer distances from camp, and bring back food for the entire group. Some correlates of these strategies are that in residentially mobile groups virtually everyone procures resources for themselves, while in logistical groups a few procure for the rest. Such patterns of procurement, of course, create a variety of secondary social structures. For example, distribution of resources returned by logistical groups, sharing, obligations for future return, as well as others that form the fabric of prehistoric societies. Much of what we find in the archaeological record is the product of such social patterns. All groups use some combination of these two strategies and the Northwestern Plains and Rocky Mountains are no exception.

It seems very likely that a prehistoric family group of hunters and gatherers may have moved camp as many as 50 to 100 times during the year. They probably tended to revisit the same campsites or campsite areas from year to year. Water was always an important consideration on the Plains during part of the year, and many campsites were close to water. Sites on buttes and high spots were favored by some of these prehistoric groups. Ultimately, the prehistoric family of the Northwestern Plains and Rocky Mountains left a large number of campsites of different duration, intensity, and purpose, manifested by differing amounts of cultural evidence. Expressed another way, there are different degrees of archaeological visibility regarding these cultural manifestations.

Pursuing the same line of thought further, we can estimate that every prehistoric family or social group must have contributed several hundred campsites to the archaeological record. Multiply that number by the number of families or groups that could have occupied the area over the proven 11,000 radiocarbon years and slightly more of human occupation of the Plains and mountains and the result is a large number of potential archaeological sites. However, we know of only a tiny fragment of this total.

Postulating still further, it is immediately obvious that most sites on the Northwestern Plains and Rocky Mountains consist of very limited archaeological evidence. Suppose a family, or more than a single family, camped at a location for a single night. Very likely a pit would have been dug, a fire would have been built, and some food prepared. Some sort of shelter was probably used, depending upon the weather and the time of the year. And, depending on the nature of the activities performed, there may or may not have been some stone tools used or manufactured that might have left some evidence of the episode. If the site was rapidly covered over as the result of some geological process, it might some day come to light and be used as archaeological evidence. On the other hand, if it was not covered, the wind would disperse the charcoal, bones would disintegrate, and the edges of the fire pit would crumble. Over a long period of time only a few flakes and perhaps a broken tool would remain. And unless the tool was diagnostic of a time period, the chronology of the event would be lost. We might be able to say something about the function of the tool, but what else can such data tell us? Most sites on the Northwestern Plains and Rocky Mountains are of this nature (e.g., Ebert 1986; Kornfeld 2003), but with limited methodology to handle such data our knowledge of the prehistoric foragers is incomplete, and archaeologists base their interpretations on a small fraction of the total evidence. The large animal kill and less often the large campsite receive the bulk of our attention. Sites of low visibility that consist of, for example, a few flakes, a broken tool, and a few fire-fractured rocks can add greatly to our knowledge, but such studies are in their infancy.

There is sufficient evidence from both archaeology and ethnology to confirm the past use of plant food resources on the Plains and Rocky Mountains. How much such resources contributed to the total food supply is a matter of some debate, but it was undoubtedly significant. The contribution of plants foods to the human diet would have changed as forage and other conditions for animals fluctuated.

The availability of plant food for human groups changed throughout the year, as it did for the animals. Early spring in the plains and mountains is the time for tender shoots of plants and greens. Fruits and berries begin to appear in late spring and continue into early fall. Spring and early summer is the time also for certain roots and bulbs. Grass seeds usually mature in late summer but vary with available moisture. Some seeds are dispersed by wind, animals, or other natural agents shortly after maturity, and some are retained on the plants well into the winter, such as the seeds of the saltbush (*Atriplex* sp.). Some, such as the seeds of the limber pine (*Pinus flexilis*) and whitebark pine (*Pinus albicaulis*), are most easily gathered during short periods of time when the cones open in late summer. Fruits and berries appear and disappear rapidly, but since the same plants often grow at different elevations, they may be mature at one elevation and immature higher up.

Human plant food resources were limited during the winter months and consisted mostly of a few seeds, fruits, and berries that remained on plants, a condition that varied from year to year (see Bach 1997 for variation in yield of Indian rice grass throughout the year). For the prehistoric Plains hunter-gatherers, the best insurance for the winter was a calculated amount of food gathered for short-term storage during favorable periods for food procurement. However, gathering food surpluses was not always limited to summer. Based on data to be presented later, there is strong evidence for frozen meat caches as part of a Paleoindian subsistence strategy.

The present evidence strongly indicates that prehistoric economic strategies were seldom limited to any given life zone or food source. Narrow economic specializations were often the road to disaster, and broad spectrum hunting and gathering is proposed here as having best characterized most of prehistoric life on the Northwestern Plains and Rocky Mountains. The balance between the two strategies changed in response to climatic conditions which directly affected the animal populations.

ORGANIZATION OF THE DATA

This book is divided into 13 chapters that provide an outline of Northwestern Plains and Rocky Mountain prehistory as well as a discussion of the methods used to gain an understanding of the past. In Chapter 2 we begin with the basic temporal scheme of past cultures in the spatial setting described above. Time is an essential archaeological dimension, allowing for comparison across sites and regions. Chapter 2 is thus the backbone of the rest of the book. Chapter 3 covers the main inferential methods developed for understanding prehistory in this region. The archaeological record is dominated by bones of animals and chipped stone; the former the remains of prehistoric culinary activities and the latter of manufacturing and use of stone tools. Although a complete presentation of archaeological methods is beyond the goal of this chapter and indeed impossible in chapter length, a selected set of methods is critical to understanding the region's prehistory and enhances the understanding of the following chapters. In the next two chapters we discuss the main animal procurement strategies. First, developments and changes in mammoth and bison procurement throughout prehistory are the topics of Chapter 4. In Chapter 5, we consider a variety of other animals hunted, trapped, or otherwise procured and consumed. Both chapters cover some of the most important and most intensively excavated sites on the Northwestern Plains and the Rocky Mountains. These animal procurement and processing sites, however, leave out a huge portion of the archaeological record. Several chapters address aspects of the archaeological record not considered previously (Chapters 6–8, 10, and 11), and provide much needed breadth to the picture of prehistoric lifeways presented in Chapters 4 and 5. Significant aspects of regional archaeology are discussed in these chapters, including domestic structures, stone alignments, trails, rock images, caches, human interments, sucking tubes, atlatl weights, ceramics, various perishable items, and other features and artifacts. While some of these are quite rare and unusual, others, such as stone circles, are among the most ubiquitous archaeological manifestations in the region. Stone tools and the raw material for their manufacture comprise the bulk of the data for interpreting Northwestern Plains and Rocky Mountain prehistory. Regional geology, as it bears on the raw material sources, is discussed in Chapter 12, while Paleoindian chipped stone manufacturing technology is the subject of Chapter 9. We conclude the book with a discussion of prehistoric lifeways as we have come to understand them through the archaeological record.

2

THE ARCHAEOLOGICAL RECORD FOR THE NORTHWESTERN PLAINS AND ROCKY MOUNTAINS

INTRODUCTION

The temporal and spatial aspects of prehistoric human occupations are an important part of archaeological study. Stratified sites with individual components separated by sterile strata comprise the ideal units for analysis. However, only on rare occasions is the entire chronological sequence for a geographic area, whether large or small, contained in a single stratigraphic sequence. Cultural complexes are discrete units of study, usually established on the basis of diagnostic artifacts and relative stratigraphic relationships to other diagnostic artifacts, and placed in absolute time on the basis of radiocarbon dates. Depending on the nature of the evidence, it may then be possible to analyze and interpret further, and to formulate hypotheses and models defining the institutional and other systematic aspects of the various human groups involved.

The ability of the investigator to evaluate site integrity becomes an important aspect of archaeology. The inability to detect the mixing of components can introduce errors into the final interpretations. Archaeologists in recent years have realized that their science requires the expertise of a number of specialists in many disciplines. However, they have also realized that the information they need usually comes from studies on the fringes of other disciplines rather than in their mainstream. Consequently, a new generation of specialists has evolved with names such as "geoarchaeologist" and "zooarchaeologist," among others.

Most reliable data for interpreting cultural chronology are recovered from a subsurface geological context. Every site is unique, and its investigation requires a specially formulated research design. Unfortunately, there is no written source the archaeologist can fall back upon to tell him or her exactly how to investigate any given site. Consequently, no matter how well the research design or data-recovery plan is prepared ahead of time,

only in exceedingly rare cases will it survive the site investigation without modification. Methods of recovering and recording archaeological data are continually changing and usually improved by utilizing new techniques developed and
tested by well-trained, innovative investigators.

Chronology emerges as a major theme in both local and regional archaeological
studies. Time-space charts are an integral part of most final reports because they
provide a convenient way to organize and present data. They should be formulated in such a way as to provide a framework within which revisions can be
made as the analysis and interpretation of new data demand.

The present cultural chronology for the Northwestern Plains is based mainly
on stratigraphy and projectile point, tool, and ceramic typology and is buttressed
strongly by an ever-increasing number of radiocarbon dates. Obsidian hydration
dating, optical stimulated luminescence (OSL), thermoluminescence, and infrared
stimulated luminescence (IRSL) currently provide corroboration and promise to
be of great benefit as the methods are refined (e.g., Davis 1972, Mayer and Mahan
2004). Even though the chronological picture is continually becoming less clouded,
there are still many questions about what cultural groups are represented and
what their settlement and subsistence strategies were. Many projectile points are
not always the reliable chronological determiner they were once considered to be,
and as larger samples are collected from high-integrity components, the ranges
of variation of projectile points, types, and styles tend to overlap. Time relationships are becoming better known (Figure 2.1) but must remain flexible to allow
for the accumulation of more exact data. The first part of this chapter provides
the methods used to arrive at the establishment of the cultural chronology for the
Northwestern Plains and adjacent Rocky Mountains, while the second part is a
presentation of the cultural sequence as it is currently understood.

Establishing the Cultural Chronology

Prehistoric human occupations were rarely uniform over large areas, particularly where there were significant ecological changes over short distances.
This situation was and still is particularly true on the Northwestern Plains and
adjacent mountains. Consequently, changes in the cultural chronology may be
detected over relatively short distances. Cultural complexes are defined mainly
on the basis of artifact assemblages recovered in high-integrity site components.
Typology enters the picture and is used to determine the degree of similarity
or range of variation to be allowed between different artifact types. Projectile
points in combination with radiocarbon dates are usually the best temporal indicators in site components of preceramic age. Ceramics entered the archaeological
record of the Northwestern Plains late and in small amounts so that, in most
cases, projectile points and, to a lesser extent, certain tools are the prime temporal indicators.

Studies of tool and weaponry function through experimentation and the analysis of use and wear patterns have enhanced the value and meaning of typology.
In addition, studies of stone flaking technology as a cultural process have added
a new understanding to typology. We find, for example, that what have often
been described as discrete types and styles of chipped stone tools and weaponry
are actually a single type or style at different stages of manufacture or use. We

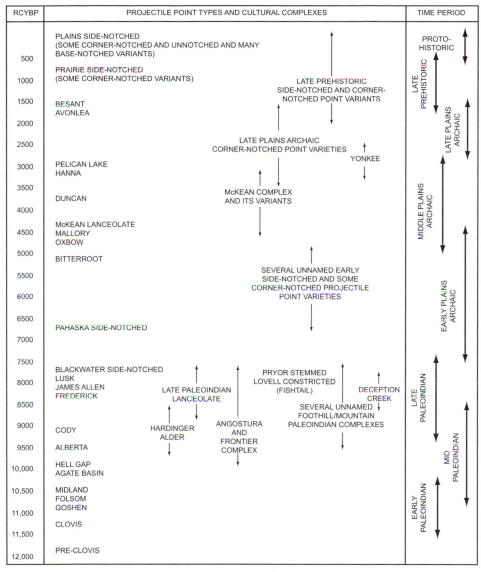

Figure 2.1   Northwestern Plains and Rocky Mountains chronology.

find also that some were used at different stages of their manufacture and did not always reach what some investigators have considered a final stage.

Usable pieces of broken projectile points were more often than not modified for reuse (Figure 2.2), and what emerged usually had little resemblance to the original, although function remained unchanged (e.g., Frison et al. 1976:41–46). But sometimes broken projectile points were reused in their altered condition or modified for use as tools. And most tools were designed so that as points or edges were dulled they could be rejuvenated through some kind of resharpening process. In the process, the object acquired different configurations, and the function associated with each must be recognized if its contribution to the ongoing cultural system is to be properly evaluated (e.g., Frison 1968b). Archaeologists in many instances have spent much time and effort attempting to assign specific functions to worn out and discarded tools and weaponry.

Here, experimental archaeology is proving to be of great value. Although we can never achieve exact past conditions, we can establish some limitations and possibilities. We have found, for example, that a projectile point must be properly designed to penetrate the rib cage of a bison or elephant. We have also found

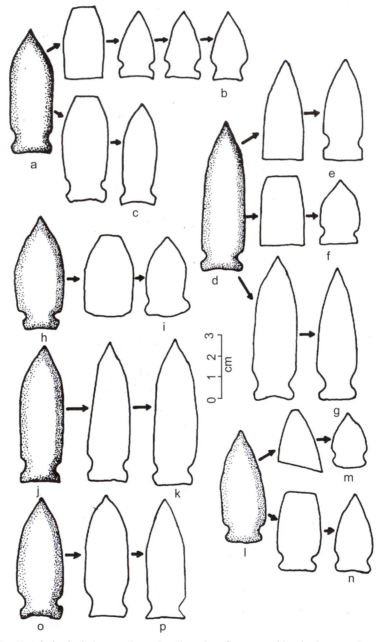

Figure 2.2 Morphological changes in projectile points from reworking broken specimens (Hawken site 48CK303); a, d, h, i, l, and o are complete and unbroken while b, c, e, f, g, i, k, m, n, and p demonstrate breakage and reworking.

that in the process many things that happen are predictable and can be interpreted from an examination of the utilized projectile point and remaining fragments. Breakage as the point impacts, for example, leaves a different kind of flake debitage in the deposits than those resulting from tool sharpening. We now know the limitations on the butchering process imposed by the use of stone and bone tools compared to an assemblage of metal tools and that certain materials such as quartzite maintain a functional cutting edge longer than a tool made of chert. From such experimental/functional studies, better descriptions of past lifeways are appearing. In this sense, typology is not a narrow study destined to be an end in itself. On the contrary, it is an ever-expanding means of inquiry into other aspects of culture.

The archaeologist and the geologic stratigrapher are heavily dependent on one another. The archaeologist is able to provide relative and often absolute dates for stratigraphic units. The development of the accelerator mass spectrometer radiocarbon dating process, although more costly, allows accurate dates on much smaller amounts of organic material. This is of particular value to the Paleoindian archaeologist in situations where amounts of charcoal are usually small and the datable fraction often shrinks during the initial treatment process. The geoarchaeologist is often able to reconstruct landforms that may have had considerable bearing on the cultural activities of the time represented. Human artifacts serve as index fossils where materials for radiocarbon dating are lacking. Soil scientists, palynologists, and paleontologists can utilize the same chronological data to establish climatic, plant, and animal successions. As a result, cultural chronologies and knowledge of past ecologies are expanded and continually become more reliable.

Topographic relief is high and annual precipitation is low on the Northwestern Plains and the adjacent foothills and mountains, providing optimum conditions for accelerated geologic activity. Consequently, much of the prehistoric record has eroded away and much of what remains is deeply buried. Once exposed, archaeological components are highly visible and vulnerable to loss through continued geologic activity and the activities of artifact collectors. Sites may be exposed briefly, and if their presence is not observed, they disappear and the information is irrevocably lost.

With the possible exception of the historic Plains Indian tribes, cultural groups on the Northwestern Plains and in the Rocky Mountains were band-level hunter-gatherers who never achieved more complex forms of sociopolitical organization found elsewhere. Neither could they support New World crop domestication and agriculture. As a result, the archaeological record lacks the evidence for increasing cultural complexity of the various stages of development found in other areas. Lacking entirely is the development of village life, ceramics (until very late and then mostly ceramic traditions from outside areas), craft specializations, and other things that preserve over long periods of time and provide the archaeologist with additional reliable temporal indicators.

Site visibility is a major problem for the Rocky Mountain and High Plains archaeologist. The faunal remains, site features, and weaponry assemblages from large animal kills are of high visibility but provide evidence of only a little segment of the total cultural system. Most cultural activities of a hunting and gathering group were of small magnitude and short duration. Consequently, cultural assemblages were small, and relatively little in the way of artifact material was left behind.

TOOL ASSEMBLAGES AND DEBITAGE AS CHRONOLOGICAL INDICATORS

As chronological indicators, tool assemblages are not as reliable as project-ile points. The sharp gravers and borers of the Clovis and Folsom complexes (Figure 2.3) are distinctive, but these sometimes continue on into later Paleoindian assemblages. The Cody knife (Figure 2.4a, b, f) was once regarded as a diagnostic of the Cody complex but one was recovered in an earlier Alberta complex bison kill (Agenbroad 1978a) and another in an Alberta-Cody context of about the same age (Frison and Todd 1987:269). In addition, there are a number of variations of the Cody knife, as was demonstrated at the Horner site (Bradley and Frison 1987:221). The Scottsbluff II projectile point (Figure 6.36) may actually be a knife, as suggested by the presence of one barb that is usually longer than the other. Hell Gap and Frederick knives have been described (Irwin-Williams et al. 1973; Irwin and Wormington 1970), but whether or not these are actual tool types or incidental cases of reworking a projectile point for a different use is still unproven. Consequently, their value as chronological indicators is open to question.

Some Paleoindian tools are quite distinctive but others, such as large butcher-ing tools found in communal bison kill sites, are not, since similar types were retained over long periods of time. From Folsom until the historic period, butcher-ing tools made from large percussion flakes were sharpened with a lateral retouch along one edge or, less frequently, both edges (Figure 2.5). It is easy to see why this is so, since it was the most functional stone tool for butchering large animals such as bison. Similar tools have been found at the Paleoindian Casper and Agate Basin sites as well as at the Piney Creek site (Frison 1967b), a presumed late Crow Indian buffalo jump.

Spurred end scrapers (Figure 2.6) are another possible Paleoindian diagnos-tic, but again they are not absolutely reliable. Of a large sample of end scrapers from the Folsom complex Hanson site and the Agate Basin component of the Agate Basin site, many lack a spur or spurs and are indistinguishable from those found in Late Prehistoric period sites. An occasional spurred scraper appears in

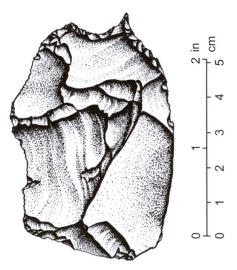

Figure 2.3   Folsom graver from the Hanson site.

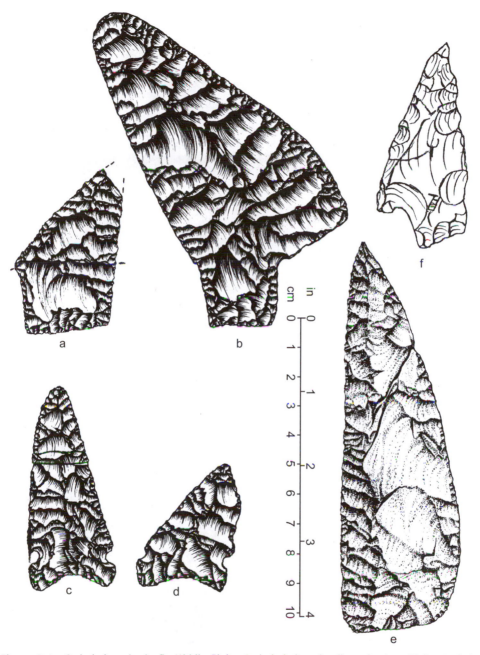

Figure 2.4 Cody knives (a, b, f), Middle Plains Archaic knives (c, d), and a Late Plains Archaic knife (e). (Figure 2.4f courtesy of Leon Lorentzen.)

post-Paleoindian site components but, in general, the true spurred end scraper is extremely rare in tool assemblages of the post-Paleoindian period.

Burins and evidence of what appears to be deliberate burination appear occasionally in certain Paleoindian assemblages but in no way comparable to the numbers found in Alaskan Arctic or Old World Upper Paleolithic assemblages.

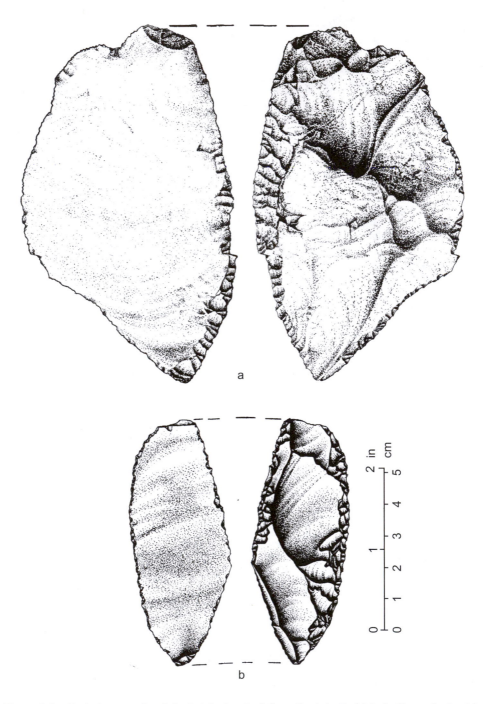

Figure 2.5 Typical percussion flake butchering tool from the Late Prehistoric Glenrock site (a), and a similar tool from the Casper Hell Gap site (b).

Burination performed on transverse breaks of proximal projectile points was common in Pryor Stemmed assemblages (Figure 2.7) as well as on other types of broken projectile points (Figure 2.8). Caution is needed also in identifying

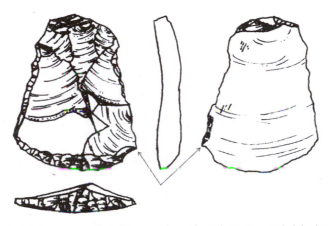

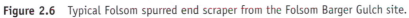

Figure 2.6   Typical Folsom spurred end scraper from the Folsom Barger Gulch site.

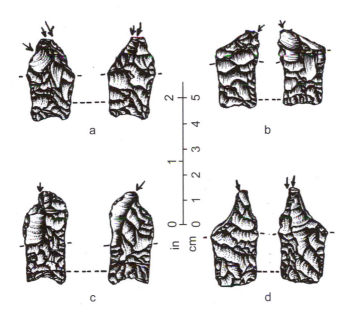

Figure 2.7   Broken Pryor Stemmed points reworked into burins from the Bighorn Mountains.

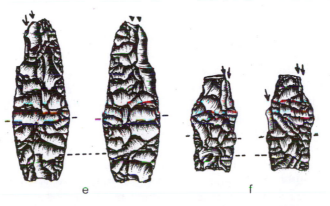

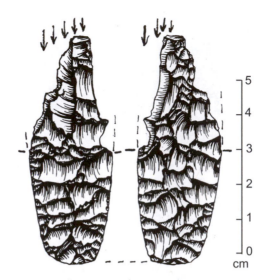

Figure 2.8   Classic Agate Basin point modified by burin spalls found in the Bighorn Mountains.

deliberate burination of broken projectile points versus impact damage. In experiments, broken projectile points recovered after spearing large animals occasionally demonstrate what could easily be identified in a different context as deliberate burination. Burins in Paleoindian contexts seldom demonstrate use wear on the edge formed by the burin spall in front of its striking platform; instead, wear is on edges adjacent to the striking platform and on the points formed by removal of the burin spall.

Cody complex projectile point fragments have been recovered that demonstrate unmistakable evidence of burination. Two obvious specimens are midsections of typical Cody projectile points with true burin spalls; in one specimen the spalls are on two opposite corners and on the other the spalls are on adjacent corners. These were recovered from a surface Cody complex site in the same general area as the Finley site. On the other hand, there were no recorded burins from the relatively large Cody complex assemblage at the Horner Site (Frison and Todd 1987). Consequently, the burination process is of limited value as a useful chronological indicator for the area.

Pieces esquilleés (wedges) were recovered in the Mill Iron site (Goshen complex) and Horner site (Cody complex) assemblages. At the latter site, they were made on both flakes and broken bifaces. Refitting of the use flakes on a specimen recovered at the Mill Iron site (Bradley and Frison 1996:62–64) leaves little doubt that they resulted from use as a wedge and not from a bipolar flaking process (Frison 1996). They may be a reliable Paleoindian diagnostic but their use may also have been limited to restricted contexts. There is some evidence also that certain Paleoindian tools may have carried over into the Early Plains Archaic, so that their presence there without the association of better diagnostics can be misleading (Frison 1983b).

One tool type of the Plains Archaic periods is a reliable diagnostic. It is a biface knife with a rounded base and sharp point. Initially it was a large symmetrical biface, but as it was used it was sharpened by means of a steep bevel on one side along one blade edge. As a result, one face remained nearly flat because all resharpening was done from one side. It also became progressively more asymmetrical through attrition as it was used and resharpened (Figure 2.4e). After a tool of this nature was sharpened beyond a certain point, it was no longer functional. There is evidence that this tool may have developed in Early Plains Archaic times at sites in the higher elevations (Frison 1983b).

A knife type known to occur occasionally in McKean components and possibly earlier was made in the shape of a large projectile point (Figure 2.4c). It was resharpened on both faces along one blade edge and gradually acquired an asymmetrical outline shape (Figure 2.4d). Resharpening finally reached a stage where the tool had to be discarded.

During the Late Plains Archaic, notches were sometimes added to this tool, usually on the corner opposite the working edge, forming what is usually referred to as a corner tang knife. It is arguable whether or not the notches were placed there so a handle could be added or merely to tie a thong around it for carrying purposes. To date, at least, this tool seems to be a reliable diagnostic of the Late Plains Archaic period. Two of these were found in a Late Plains Archaic component at the Garrett Allen site in southern Wyoming: one (Figure 2.9b) is unused while the other (Figure 2.9a) is nearly worn out, apparently from use and resharpening.

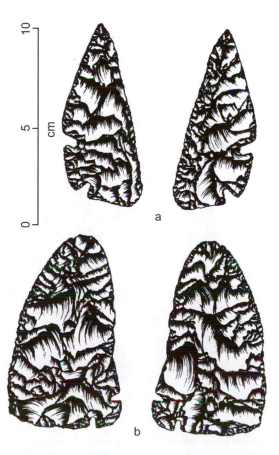

Figure 2.9   Well-worn (a) and unused (b) corner tang knife from Late Plains Archaic component in southwest Wyoming.

A possible diagnostic of late Shoshonean occupation is a tool that was made on a leaf-shaped biface. Both blade edges were resharpened bilaterally so that the tool remained symmetrical in outline form and the working end retained a lenticular transverse cross section. As in the case of the Late Plains Archaic knife, this tool type was often resharpened until the blade became so long and thin that it broke and the pieces were discarded (Figure 2.10). Apparently it was utilized as a knife, and it appears to be a fairly reliable horizon marker in late Shoshonean sites (Frison 1971b:269). It appears occasionally also in sites that demonstrate mixing of Crow and Shoshonean pottery.

Other chipped stone tool types of the post-Paleoindian period have little diagnostic value. As with Paleoindian assemblages, some tools are made from projectile points; these have essentially the same diagnostic value as the projectile points themselves, provided enough remains for reliable type identification and if it can be assumed that older projectile points were not picked up and reused as tools.

Figure 2.10 Late Prehistoric ("Shoshonean") biface knives continually resharpened from opposite blade edges; Bugas-Holding site (a), Shirley Basin Lodge site (b–d).

This occurs frequently in Archaic sites where broken Paleoindian projectile points were occasionally picked up and modified for tool use. In these cases, there is usually unmistakable evidence of use and wear.

Debitage as Diagnostic Indicator

The one unquestionable cultural specific in terms of debitage is the Folsom channel flake (Figure 2.11). Even then, unless the context is well established and striking platforms are preserved, certain impact flakes may be misidentified as Folsom channel flakes and vice versa. Clovis debitage may also be identified if a large

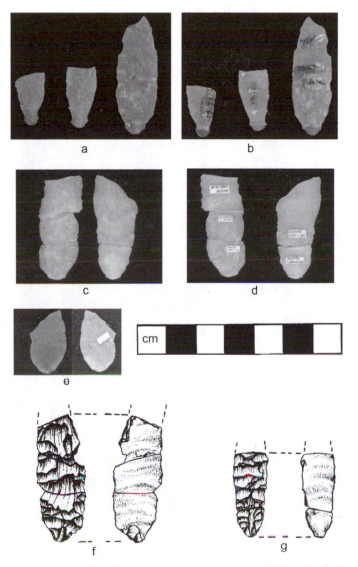

Figure 2.11   Folsom channel flake fragments from the Carter-Kerr/McGee site in Wyoming (a, b), the Barger Gulch site in Middle Park of Colorado (c–e), and the Hanson site in Wyoming (f, g).

debitage sample is present. Clovis biface production includes regular *outrepassé* flaking visible on both the bifaces and the resulting detritus, making both diagnostic of the period (Frison and Bradley 1999; Collins 2005). Even without a clear *outrepassé* flake, certain techniques of platform preparation may be identified in some cases, especially by well-trained lithic technologists. However, there is evidence of highly accomplished flint knappers at all times in the archaeological record, and it is dangerous for the investigator to attempt to read too much in terms of cultural affiliations from debitage samples alone. Another technological feature of the Clovis period is blade production. Although both blades and blade cores are diagnostic Clovis artifacts (Collins 1999), fluke blades are occasionally produced in all periods and intentional blade cores are sporadically manufactured throughout prehistory. Thus, while a true blade may indicate a Clovis occupation, it does so with certainty only if there are other indicators.

Other Useful Diagnostics

The serrated metatarsal scraper (Figure 2.12a) and grooved maul (Figure 2.13) are widespread diagnostic items of the Late Prehistoric period. The former was

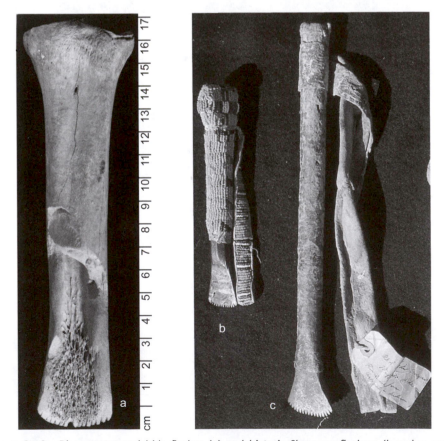

Figure 2.12   Bison metatarsal hide flesher (a) and historic Cheyenne fleshers (b and c, not to scale). The beaded flesher (b) was manufactured on a gun barrel. (Figures 2.12b and c courtesy of Ed and Shirley Cheramy.)

Figure 2.13   Typical grooved maul of the Late Prehistoric period.

usually made from a bison metatarsal, but occasionally the metatarsal of an elk was used. Grooved mauls were usually made of river cobbles. Grooves may be continuous, or discontinuous as shown in Figure 2.13. Sustained periods of use were necessary in order to produce the amount of wear found on many specimens. According to ethnographic evidence, they were used in food preparation activities such as pounding dried meat for the manufacture of pemmican. Mauls were hafted with either split stick or twisted rawhide handles, as demonstrated by examples found in protected places such as dry caves and as documented in the ethnographic record. Some of these are quite large and, again from ethnographic accounts, small trees were bent over and heavy cords were attached from the tree tips to the groove in the maul to provide a spring action to lift the maul while in use. There are apparently reliable claims that they were also used as horse hobbles.

Known Paleoindian fire hearths were almost always on the surface or in shallow depressions; the stone-filled fire pit with all of its variations appears to be an Archaic and Late Prehistoric period diagnostic. Evidence of small living structures are found in some Paleoindian sites such as Hell Gap, Agate Basin, and the Hanson Folsom site but the semisubterranean pithouse and true stone circle that are the archaeological remains of living structures belong to the post-Paleoindian period.

Ceramics

Pottery also appeared on the Northwestern Plains and Rocky Mountains at the end of the Late Plains Archaic and continued through the Late Prehistoric period.

Several pottery traditions are represented. The Intermountain pottery tradition (Mulloy 1958:196–200) is usually regarded as having cultural affiliations with Shoshonean groups. The oldest Intermountain pottery dates to about 750 years BP at the Myers-Hindman site in southwest Montana (Lahren 1976). Other dated occurrences are from Mummy Cave (Husted and Edgar 2002), Eden-Farson (Frison 1971b), and Eagle Creek (Arthur 1966) and are much later. At the Bugas-Holding site the date is AD 1500. Mandan tradition pottery occurs in the northeast quarter of Wyoming, a large share of southeastern Montana, and northwestern South Dakota. It is believed this pottery (Figure 2.14) was left by Crow Indians (see Frison 1976b). A bison jump and camp/processing area at the base of the eastern slopes of the Bighorn Mountains in northern Wyoming known as the Big Goose Creek site (Frison, Wilson, and Walker 1978) produced two radiocarbon dates between AD 1400 and 1500 with ceramics that could represent the Mandan tradition, based on comparison with those from the Hagen site in eastern Montana (Mulloy 1942). The erosional remnant known as the Pine Bluffs in extreme southeast Wyoming is peripheral to the Late Prehistoric horticultural groups that lived on the plains of western Nebraska and Kansas, and the area has yielded sites with Woodland (1560–1060 BP), Upper Republican (930–710 BP), and Dismal River (420–380 BP) ceramics. A nearly complete Woodland vessel was recovered at the Greyrocks site near the confluence of the Laramie and North Platte rivers in southeast Wyoming in good cultural context with a date of about 1750 BP (Figure 2.15). Farther up the North Platte River, the Butler-Rissler site produced Besant projectile points and the partial remains of a large Woodland vessel (Miller and Waitkus 1989). Pottery found in the camp/processing area of the Wardell bison corral site of proposed Avonlea affiliations is puzzling. Pueblo pottery, both corrugated and painted sherds, has been found along the southern border of Wyoming west of the North

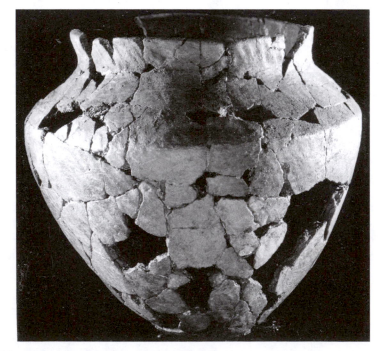

Figure 2.14 Crow-style vessel from northern Wyoming.

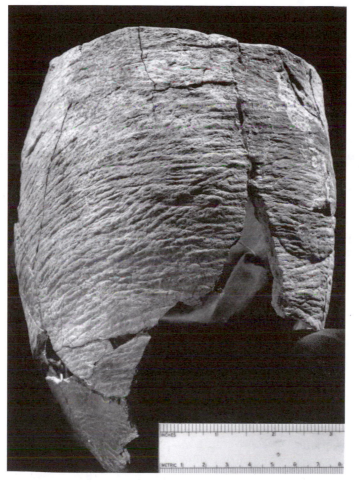

Figure 2.15   Woodland-style vessel from the Greyrocks site in southeast Wyoming.

Platte River and represents items brought into the area. These sherds have not yet been found in datable contexts or in association with diagnostic materials. Small amounts of Fremont (Promontory?) pottery have been found in southwestern Wyoming in the Green River drainage but only as surface finds. Middle Missouri ceramics in small amounts appear in the northeast part of the area. Other small finds of ceramics in the Black Hills and the buttes area of South Dakota have also been identified as Extended Coalescent (Johnson et al. 1990).

CHRONOLOGICAL ORDERING

The first serious attempt to synthesize the archaeological data and establish a cultural chronology for the Northwestern Plains was by William T. Mulloy (1958). Mulloy analyzed the material obtained from a deep, stratified cave site known as Pictograph Cave (24YL1), located a short distance south of the Yellowstone River near Billings, Montana. The site had been excavated earlier under the direction of Oscar T. Lewis, Field Supervisor of the Montana Archaeological Survey. In addition, Mulloy synthesized the data from the relatively few single and multiple component sites known at that time to establish a chronology that is still useful and one that he continually modified as new data appeared (Reeves 1983b). His work reflects the value of long, uninterrupted stratigraphic cultural sequences or "key sites" for establishing valid cultural chronologies. The situation has changed slightly with radiocarbon dating (Libby 1952) and some single-component sites can be included in this category; however, no amount of refinement in radio-carbon chronology can substitute for stratigraphic integrity.

Mulloy's scheme was simple. He proposed an Early Prehistoric period from 13,000 to 6000 years ago; a cultural hiatus from 6000 to 3500 years ago; an Early Middle period from 3500 to 2000 years ago; a Late Middle period from 2000 to 1500 years ago: and a Late Prehistoric period from 1500 years ago to historic times at about AD 1800. The accumulation of new data required continual modification of Mulloy's scheme (Frison 1978, 1991) (Figure 2.16). Aside from the chronological refinements necessitated by the accumulation of radiocarbon dates, new cultural complexes were identified. In particular, the term "Archaic" is firmly entrenched in American archaeology, although not all Plains archaeologists accept the term for use in the Plains area. On the other hand, the area described here as the Northwestern Plains and Rocky Mountains is such that the concept of an Archaic stage (Willey and Phillips 1958:107) is appropriate. The area is not "plains" in the same sense as the northern parts of the region, such as the plains of Alberta and northern Montana, are considered plains. Bison were present in the mountains and plains throughout the late Pleistocene and Holocene, but their distribution and density varied. There were a few local spots rich enough in plant and animal resources to have supported a true hunting economy comparable to the Northern Plains but many more spots were relatively marginal and required close attention to gathered resources. As a result, the prehistoric economic adaptations of the Northwestern Plains and Rocky Mountains fit into an Archaic way of life perhaps more so than that of plains hunters who are traditionally regarded as more oriented economi-cally toward procurement of large game animals, particularly bison.

Mulloy's Early Prehistoric period was also slowly divided up into a series of what came to be known as Paleoindian complexes (Frison 1978; Irwin-Williams et al. 1973; Wormington 1957). The "classic" Plains Paleoindian complexes were largely defined on the basis of open Plains and Plains-like intermountain basin bison bone bed sites that are, according to Wormington, those sites associated with "extinct" Pleistocene bison. Ironically, the linchpin of the chronological ordering was not a bison bone bed, but rather a campsite, Hell Gap. This simple scheme was, however, short lived. Excavations at Mummy Cave and Bighorn Canyon shelters, followed by Medicine Lodge Creek, soon showed temporally overlap-ping and spatially separated complexes that one of us (Frison) termed Foothill/ Mountain complexes (Frison 1976a; Husted 1969; Husted and Edgar 2002). Many of both the classic Plains and the Foothill/Mountain complexes have now been well established and additional ones have been defined.

Although we continue the separation of the cultural complexes of the Northwestern Plains and the Rocky Mountains, the geographical distribution is becoming blurry. For the Paleoindian period there are some tentative demonstra-tions of differences between the areas (e.g., Pitblado 2003), but we do not fully understand the interrelationships of groups in the two regions. However, we introduce Early, Middle, and Late terminology for the Paleoindian complexes. To begin, "Early" is commonly used for the fluted point complexes in the literature

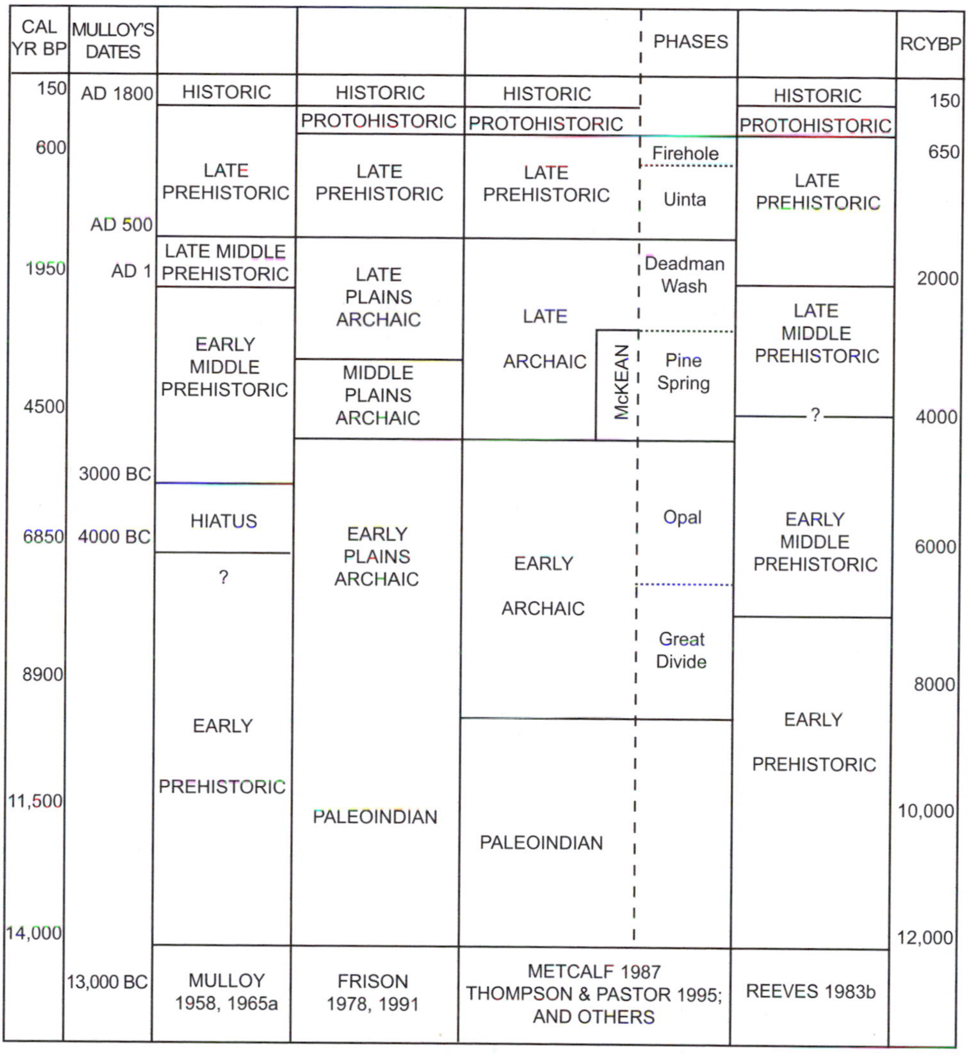

CAL YR BP	MULLOY'S DATES				PHASES		RCYBP
150	AD 1800	HISTORIC	HISTORIC	HISTORIC		HISTORIC	150
		PROTOHISTORIC	PROTOHISTORIC	PROTOHISTORIC		PROTOHISTORIC	
600		LATE PREHISTORIC	LATE PREHISTORIC	LATE PREHISTORIC	Firehole	LATE PREHISTORIC	650
	AD 500				Uinta		
1950	AD 1	LATE MIDDLE PREHISTORIC	LATE PLAINS ARCHAIC	LATE ARCHAIC	Deadman Wash	LATE MIDDLE PREHISTORIC	2000
		EARLY MIDDLE PREHISTORIC	MIDDLE PLAINS ARCHAIC		McKEAN — Pine Spring		
4500						——?——	4000
	3000 BC						
6850	4000 BC	HIATUS	EARLY PLAINS ARCHAIC	EARLY ARCHAIC	Opal	EARLY MIDDLE PREHISTORIC	6000
		?					
8900		EARLY			Great Divide	EARLY	8000
		PREHISTORIC	PALEOINDIAN	PALEOINDIAN		PREHISTORIC	
11,500							10,000
14,000							12,000
	13,000 BC	MULLOY 1958, 1965a	FRISON 1978, 1991	METCALF 1987 THOMPSON & PASTOR 1995; AND OTHERS		REEVES 1983b	

Figure 2.16 Comparison of Northwestern Plains, southwestern Wyoming, and Northern Plains regional chronologies.

and we do nothing but codify this use. We include Goshen in here because of its stratigraphic position and at least some radiocarbon dates. We should mention, however, that a point type named Boxelder recovered by Wesley Bliss (1950), but not in a datable context, bears a remarkable similarity to the Goshen point. Also included is the Midland complex as this is seen as a Folsom variant. The time period between approximately 10,300 and 9000 BP is given a Middle Paleoindian period designation. This includes the Agate Basin, Hell Gap, and Cody complexes. Following 9000 BP are the Late Paleoindian complexes of Frederick, James Allen, Lusk, Angostura, and some other variants commonly thought to occur on the Plains. The Foothill/Mountain complexes of Alder, Hardinger, Lovell Constricted, Pryor Stemmed, and a variety of other projectile point types have been found in a series of stratified sites throughout the Central and Southern (e.g., Pitblado 2003) Rocky Mountains. The sample of sites with Plains or Rocky Mountain Middle and Late Paleoindian projectile points is small and the exact stratigraphic relationship and geographic distribution of them is uncertain. Further work is necessary to understand the chronological ordering of these projectile points within the Middle and Late Paleoindian periods.

The Early, Middle, and Late Paleoindian categories are not a perfect subdivision; there certainly appears to be some overlapping radiocarbon dating (e.g., Grund 2009), but to the best of our knowledge these form a stratigraphic sequence of Paleoindian complexes, and the subdivision makes an otherwise unwieldy array of terms and complexes a little more manageable. There may also be a prehistoric reality to this new scheme. The Early Paleoindians can be seen as the first colonizers, at least some of which have a continent-wide distribution, that then "settle in" to the various Plains regions; the Middle Paleoindians operate in the still unstable earliest Holocene environments; and the Late Paleoindians begin to look more and more like the following Archaic groups. Rigid horizontal time boundaries are not always valid. Foothill/Mountain groups were living an Archaic way of life during Late Paleoindian times as were many other cultural groups in intermontane basins and open plains up to historic times.

For the sake of convenience of reference, Mulloy's "gap without evidence," previously referred to as Altithermal period cultural groups, are subsequently referred to in this volume as Early Plains Archaic; Mulloy's (1958) Early Middle Prehistoric period is referred to as the Middle Plains Archaic; Mulloy's Late Middle Prehistoric period is the Late Plains Archaic; and Mulloy's Late Prehistoric period is retained in its original form. This scheme has functioned quite well over the past several decades although some new data acquired since then have been incorporated (Figure 2.16).

The Chronology of the Wyoming Basin

The currently accepted prehistoric chronology for southwestern Wyoming subdivides the time between 11,500 and 150 BP into four periods, with phases in all but the Paleoindian and Protohistoric periods. Metcalf (1987; Figure 2.16) used radiocarbon date frequencies to build the chronology in reaction to the existence of archaeological materials that did not conform completely with chronologies used for surrounding areas. Investigators working in the Wyoming Basin argue the threefold Early/Middle/Late Plains Archaic time divisions fail to capture the chronology of the area. Instead the time between 8500 and 2000 BP is divided into the Early and Late Archaic with two phases each. The Late Prehistoric is also subdivided into two phases. Although some working in the Wyoming Basin argue that the absence of bison hunters of the McKean complex in the Wyoming Basin obviates the Middle Archaic, others recognize the presence of McKean complex projectile points in mid-Holocene sites in the area. The chronology developed for southwest Wyoming has been refined since Metcalf's pioneering effort, given the vast increase in the number of radiocarbon-dated components from archaeological studies associated with extensive oil, natural gas, and mining activities starting in the 1990s. Significant alterations to Metcalf's original chronology include renaming the Early Archaic Green River phase as the Opal phase and moving the start of the Archaic period back to 8500 BP from 7500 BP.

Another argument for the use of a different chronology in southwest Wyoming is the presence of Great Basin projectile point types occurring in Wyoming Basin archaeological sites. Their presence should not be a surprise as this area of Wyoming shows affinities with both the Great Basin and the Northern Colorado River Basin (Metcalf et al. 2006; Reed and Metcalf 1999).

Radiocarbon Dates

Beginning in the 1950s (Libby 1952), radiocarbon dates have provided a backbone for cultural chronologies throughout the world and have established absolute (in earth years) ages of cultural complexes. Since its inception, the methodology has been improved through calibration formulas and new technologies such as Accelerator Mass Spectrometry (AMS) dating (Renfrew 1973; Stuiver et al. 1998). The former have allowed for a better correlation between earth years and radiocarbon assays, while the latter has allowed for dating very small samples, often a necessity in Northwestern Plains and Rocky Mountain sites. As important have been improvements in dating various materials, mainly bone, such that now quite accurate assays can be achieved (Stafford et al. 1991). This is significant as bone is often a direct consequence of human occupation while charcoal is frequently a natural occurrence in the sediment. Improvements in bone dating have allowed the placement of many more sites in chronological context than would otherwise be possible.

Many specific radiocarbon dates used in establishing the Northwestern Plains and Rocky Mountain cultural sequence are mentioned in the second part of this chapter under the heading of the complexes to which they belong. The cultural chronology is also summarized on the basis of index fossils and radiocarbon dates in Figure 2.1. Independent of cultural complexes and chronology, radiocarbon assays have been used to make a variety of arguments about human occupation, demographics, abandonment, and use of landscapes throughout the world. Although such arguments are fraught with difficulties, some of which are discussed below, the Northwestern Plains and Central Rocky Mountain radiocarbon dates are worth considering because of their sheer numbers.

For the purpose of this illustration, we will confine ourselves to the radiocarbon assays from the state of Wyoming, but similar samples exist in the surrounding areas (Freeman 2006). The Wyoming radiocarbon database contains 3277 processed samples (Wyoming State Historic Preservation Office 2006), with new ones arriving daily. However, in terms of the overall distribution, the additional dating seems to be redundant (Figure 2.17a, b). Even though there are now twice as many dates in Wyoming, the new sample (n=3277) produces a virtually identical distribution to the old sample (n≈1600) published in the 2nd edition of this book. There is no reason to think that additional assays will change the outcome, and in this sense they are redundant. This is not to say that additional dates are not required and indispensable for an accurate dating of specific cultural complexes and subregional chronologies.

What might the Wyoming radiocarbon dates tell us? Arranging the dates in 200 year intervals, we observe a general increase in frequency from 15,000 to 1300 BP, and then rapid decrease over the next 400 years. More specifically, there is a gradual increase in dates from the first occupation of Wyoming through the Paleoindian and into the Early Plains Archaic periods. This is followed by a

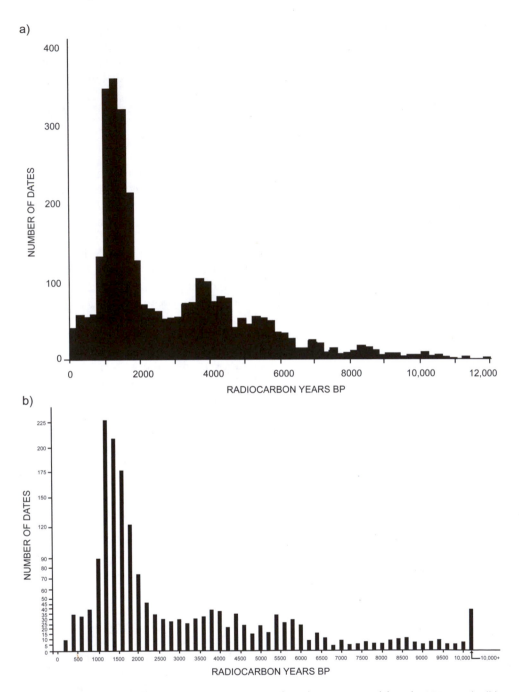

Figure 2.17 Age distribution of Wyoming radiocarbon dates: current (a) and 1991 sample (b), both in uncorrected radiocarbon years before present.

quicker rate of increase through the Middle Plains Archaic period and into the Late Plains Archaic, at which point the curve rises sharply into the Late Prehistoric period. The Late Prehistoric period peak in radiocarbon dates is followed by a rapid decrease in the frequency of dates nearly to the Early Plains Archaic level.

In analysis of radiocarbon dates in other areas of the world, population dynamics (Rick 1987), the timing of first occupations or colonizations of an area (Kuzmin and Keates 2005), and greater destruction of earlier sites have all been inferred to explain fluctuations in radiocarbon date frequencies. However, all such explanations must be carefully evaluated. For example, if the frequency of sites (as represented by radiocarbon dates) from different time periods is a function of the greater destruction of older sites, we should see a linear or curvilinear increase in the number of dates through time, punctuated by some erosional episodes. This may be the case until 1300 yrs BP, and site destruction could be a contributing factor to the distribution of dated sites (e.g., Albanese 1978). However, destruction does not seem to explain the distribution altogether; in particular it does not explain the rapid Late Prehistoric drop-off after 1300 yrs BP. It is tempting to see the curve as representing population increase through prehistory and then a dramatic decrease in the Protohistoric period caused by population decline resulting from Euroamerican contact through war and disease (Dippie 1982; Dobyns 1983; cf. Fawcett and Swedlund 1984). In fact, this is what Kornfeld (2003:82) suggested; however, in that case his data were based on the number of sites and the median date for each cultural complex (Figure 2.18) and was too coarse grained to detect a correct timing for the beginning of the drop-off. It is clear now that the drop-off occurs much too early to have been caused by European colonization, unless the Norse sailors had a much greater and deeper effect on the North American continent than we realize (McGovern 1994). Although, we think, population decline is the likely explanation for the Protohistoric decrease of the last 500–200 years, the decrease in the numbers of radiocarbon dates beginning at 1300 yrs BP must have a different cause. As archaeologists invariably focus more effort at dating hearths, we can suggest that following 1300 BP the use of hearths changed or decreased. Hearths serve three main functions in hunter-gatherer societies: as lighting, warming, or cooking facilities. Lighting fires tend to be surface features, using highly flammable materials such as grass and likely have little or no long-lasting archaeological visibility (e.g., Dunlap et al. 1966). Warming hearths are likely also surface features, designed to dissipate the heat to the nearby occupants (Yellen 1977:143), and while they have some archaeological visibility, it is not as much as cooking hearths. Cooking hearths are of numerous types and sizes, depending on the amount and type of food and type of processing (Black et al. 1997). Roasting

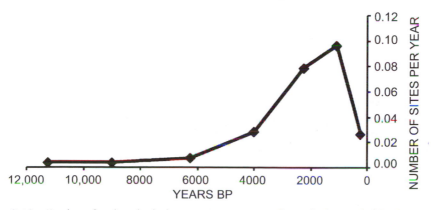

Figure 2.18 Number of archaeological components per year for each time period in the western Black Hills.

hearths, roasting pits, pit ovens, and stone boiling facilities are among the many variations. All or most leave ample archaeological remains, are easily visible, easily sampled, and produce much of the charcoal that has been dated in the Plains and Rocky Mountains. It is therefore reasonable to suggest that the number of these facilities drastically decreased after 1300 BP. The question is why? As we shall see later in this volume, plant processing appears to have intensified through prehistory, a fact that would cause an increase in the use of cooking hearths as well as radiocarbon dates, and perhaps a new subsistence system replaced the increasing plant use. The Late Prehistoric period bison hunting might have overwhelmed the subsistence system at this time, thus causing a drop in the use of cooking hearths and in the number of radiocarbon dates we see today.

Radiocarbon dates are useful, but must be used cautiously. There are currently too many uncontrolled variables to make absolute statements about the implications of the radiocarbon date curve. Our present suggestion is that the causes are multivariate, with at least a changing population density, differential erosion and destruction of sites, changing settlement and cooking strategies, and perhaps other variables included. Testing these propositions will have to wait until information is collected that can be used to control some of the variables while evaluating the effects of others. To be sure, there are apparent peaks in this curve, notable at 10,100, 8400, 6900, 5300, and 3500 BP, but whether these have any implications beyond being an archaeological artifact is as yet unexplored.

STRATIFIED ARCHAEOLOGICAL SITES

Archaeological sites on the Northwestern Plains vary from something as insignificant as a small surface scatter of flakes distributed over a small area to deep, stratified, multicomponent sites covering large areas. Site integrity varies from in situ components separated by sterile levels to mixed components that have resulted from various forms of geological, rodent, and insect activity. Each site, regardless of size and/or complexity, has the potential to add an increment or increments of knowledge to the prehistoric record. However, archaeological sites are not equal in their potential to produce meaningful information for all possibly relevant questions. Some sites can yield important data for developing chronologies, others provide evidence of subsistence strategies, some have implications for social strategies, others for religious or ritual practices, and all provide some data for settlement system dynamics.

The "key" sites are usually the result of geological accidents that have resulted in sites that have escaped to varying extents the geologic processes of weathering and stream scouring and transport, so that in situ archaeological components were preserved in stratigraphic sequences that can extend over long periods of time. The Hell Gap Paleoindian site in southeast Wyoming is one such open site with a long record of deposition that left stratified, in situ components of nearly all of the known Paleoindian cultural complexes presently known for that area. Geologists are not yet able to satisfactorily explain why the alluvial and colluvial deposits in the Hell Gap Valley were preserved and those in nearby valleys were not.

None of these key sites contains the complete archaeological record for the region in general or the immediate area in which the site is located. Some cover broad slices of time with continuous or nearly continuous depositional records, while others have hiatuses of unknown duration, and some are located well beyond the boundaries of the study area. Locations of 29 major sites are presented (Figure 2.19); when all the stratigraphic data from these sites are compiled, they provide a chronological key to the prehistoric record (Figure 2.1).

With the exception of Clovis, the above sites have produced diagnostics of all the known cultural complexes on the Northwestern Plains and the adjacent mountain ranges, so that a reasonably accurate relative cultural chronology has been developed. The absolute chronology has been developed using radiocarbon dates from all of these sites except Pictograph Cave and Kobold. Clovis sites to date are in single-component situations.

Pre-Clovis Possibilities and/or Ancestral Clovis

The origins of Clovis and/or the presence of cultural groups in North America in pre-Clovis times with no ancestral position to Clovis remains as one of the more vexing problems in North American archaeology; opinions on the subject number about the same as the number of archaeologists working on the problem. There are no known stratigraphic sequences on the Northwestern Plains and Rocky Mountains that provide a continuous record from pre-Clovis to Clovis, nor are we aware of any archaeological assemblage in the two areas that was recovered in a context that can unequivocally claim pre-Clovis status. There have been some claims of possible pre-Clovis occupations, but none that have withstood the test of critical analysis required in the understanding of site formation processes. However, the evidence for their presence may yet be found on the Northwestern Plains and in the Rocky Mountains.

The Late Pleistocene–Early Holocene faunal record for the area is known from several cave sites including Little Boxelder Cave in central Wyoming (Anderson 1968); Bell Cave (Zeimens and Walker 1974) and Horned Owl Cave (Guilday et al. 1967) from southern Wyoming; and Natural Trap Cave from northern Wyoming (Chomko and Gilbert 1987), but no paleontological site assemblage has yet yielded evidence of human remains or artifacts dating to pre-Clovis times.

An especially interesting line of research has been carried on by Steve Holen. At several sites in Nebraska and elsewhere on the Plains, Holen (1995, 2008) has attempted to use spatial analysis to argue for human action as a cause in the distribution of mammoth bone elements. In the analysis, Holen carefully evaluated the possible geologic and zoological processes as factors in such distributions and has concluded that human action is the most parsimonious explanation. Similar arguments are being proposed elsewhere in North America, where mastodon bones recovered essentially without a lithic assemblage are being evaluated for human modification (Joyce 2008). Johnson (2008) has carefully evaluated marks on mastodon bones and proposes that the location of some marks as well as their statistical distribution across bone elements bespeaks of intentional human disarticulation and butchering practices.

These arguments for an essentially osseous, perhaps pre-Lithic stage in North American prehistory have been proposed before and crop up periodically. Perhaps what is driving them is the relatively widespread belief in the antiquity of Monte Verde in southern Chile and its position as pre-dating the Clovis period

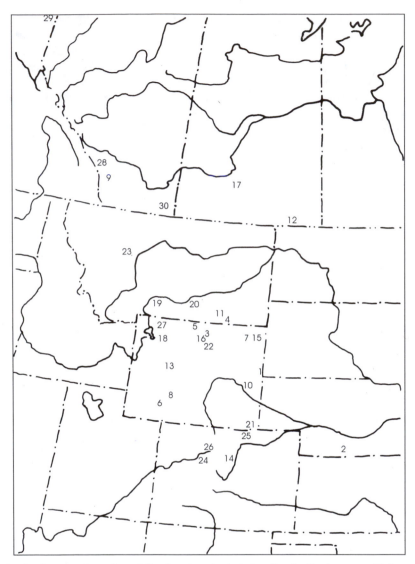

Figure 2.19   Twenty-nine selected "key" archaeological sites for the Northwestern Plains: 1. Agate Basin 48NO201 (Frison and Stanford 1982); 2. Allen (Holder and Wike 1949); 3. Beehive 48BH346 (Frison 1988a); 4. Benson's Butte 24BH1726 (Fredlund 1979); 5. Bighorn Canyon caves, Sorenson 24CB202, Mangus 24CB221, Bottleneck 48BH206 (Husted 1969); 6. Bozner 48SW5809 (Anonymous 1985); 7. Carter/Kerr-McGee 48CA12 (Frison 1984); 8. Deadman Wash 48SW1455 (Armitage et al. 1982); 9. Head-Smashed-In (Reeves 1978); 10. Hell Gap 48GO305, Patten Creek 48PL68 (Irwin-Williams et al. 1973); 11. Kobold 24BH406 (Frison 1970b); 12. Long Creek (Wettlaufer and Mayer-Oakes 1960); 13. Lookingbill 48FR308 (Frison 1983b); 14. Magic Mountain (Irwin-Williams and Irwin 1966); 15. McKean 48CK7 (Mulloy 1954b); 16. Medicine Lodge Creek 48BH499 (Frison and Walker 2007); 17. Mortlach (Wettlaufer 1955); 18. Mummy Cave 48PA201 (Wedel et al. 1968); 19. Meyers-Hindman 24PA504 (Lahren 1976); 20. Pictograph Cave 24YL1 (Mulloy 1958); 21. Pine Bluffs Project sites (Charles Reher, personal communication 1990); 22. Southsider Cave 48BH363 (Huter 2003); 23. Sun River 24CA74 (Greiser et al. 1985); 24. Vail Pass Camp 5ST85 (Gooding 1981); 25. Wilbur-Thomas 5WL45 (Breternitz 1971); 26. Middle Park Paleoindian localities (Barger Gulch Locality B, Upper Twin Mountain; Kornfeld and Frison 2000); 27. Bugas-Holding (Rapson 1990); 28. Vermillion Lakes (Fedje et al. 1995); 29. Charlie Lake (Fladmark 1996); 30. Stampede (Gryba 1975).

(Dillehay 1997) as well as the arguments for other early sites in North and South America (e.g., Cactus Hill, Meadowcroft, and Topper). All this continues to spark lively debates about dates, geologic contexts, human versus nonhuman production of patterns, and other issues about each of the proposed pre-Clovis cases (Smallwood 2008). For now, none of these sites are in the area of our immediate study; however, Kanorado and La Sena (Holen 1995, 2008) are close.

THE EARLY PALEOINDIAN PERIOD

What is known about prehistory comes mainly from data recovered in a limited number of archaeological sites. Major Paleoindian site locations are presented in Figure 2.20, although most of the key sites (Figure 2.19) have Paleoindian components as well. The earliest known archaeological sites on the Northwestern Plains and in the Rocky Mountains with unequivocal evidence of human occupation are of Clovis age.

The Clovis Complex

Clovis is widespread on the Northwestern Plains and in the Rocky Mountains, based on the surface distribution of Clovis projectile points, which have been recovered in most of the area from the lowest elevations to timberline. In many ways, the Rocky Mountains broadly defined can be said to teem with Clovis finds. One of us (Kornfeld 1999) has mapped all Clovis occurrences from Alberta and British Columbia to New Mexico, along a corridor extending approximately 75 km east and west of the Rocky Mountains. This corridor contains arguably some of the better-known Clovis localities, including Colby and Dent mammoth procurement sites, Anzick, Fenn, and Crook County caches, Mockingbird Gap camp, and perhaps 100 or more miscellaneous surface finds (see also Prasciunas et al. 2008). The interesting aspect of the distribution of these localities is that they are not only in the Plains or basins surrounding the Rocky Mountains, but a significant number occur in the mountains themselves. Clearly these earliest Americans were already familiar with the still partially glaciated Rocky Mountains, and one wonders if the glaciated landscape was not more of a home they were familiar with than the areas to the east or west. All this gets us to further wonder about the routes of peopling of the Americas and if this distribution has any relevance to that question.

On the other hand, sites with unequivocal evidence of mammoth–human association are rare in the region. The Colby site in northern Wyoming (Frison and Todd 1986) suggests planned, predictable mammoth hunting, while others such as the Lange-Ferguson site in western South Dakota (Hannus 1990) and the Union Pacific mammoth site in central Wyoming (McGrew 1961) may represent a more opportunistic kind of hunting. Although the Dent site in northern Colorado produced several mammoths and three Clovis points, the actual nature of the human–mammoth relationship is not at all clear. There are several other sites with mammoth remains and dates in the range of Clovis but the lithics or other evidence to confirm the human presence is not present or else remain in serious doubt.

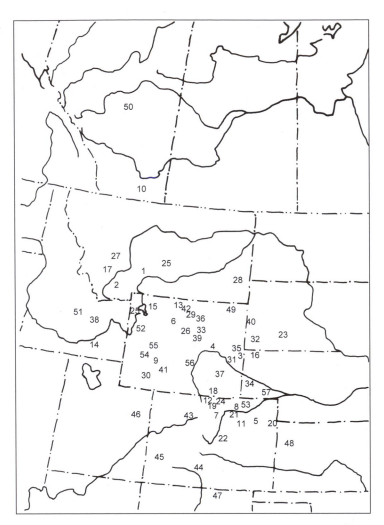

Figure 2.20   Paleoindian sites: 1. Anzick 24PA407 (Lahren and Bonnichsen 1974); 2. Barton Gulch 24MA171 (Davis et al. 1988); 3. Betty Greene 48NO203 (Greene 1967); 4. Casper 48NA304 (Frison 1974); 5. Claypool 5WN18 (Dick and Mountain 1960); 6. Colby 48WA322 (Frison and Todd 1986); 7. Dent 5WL268 (Figgins 1933); 8. Drake (Stanford and Jodry 1988); 9. Finley 48SW5 (Moss et al. 1951); 10. Fletcher (Forbis 1968); 11. Frazier 5WL268 (Wormington 1988); 12. Gordon Creek 5LR99 (Breternitz et al. 1971); 13. Hanson 48BH329 (Frison and Bradley 1980); 14. Haskett (Butler 1965); 15. Horner 48PA29 (Frison and Todd 1987); 16. Hudson-Meng 25SX115 (Agenbroad 1978b); 17. Indian Creek 24BW626 (Davis 1984); 18. James Allen 48AB4 (Mulloy 1959); 19. Johnson 5LR26 (Galloway and Agogino 1961); 20. Jones-Miller 5YM8 (Stanford 1978); 21. Jurgens 5WL53 (Wheat 1979); 22. Lamb Springs 5AH125 (Wedel 1963); 23. Lange-Ferguson 39SH33 (Hannus 1990); 24. Lindenmeier 5LR13 (Wilmsen and Roberts 1978); 25. Osprey Beach (Johnson et al. 2004); 26. Little Canyon Creek Cave 48WA323, Bush Shelter 48WA324 (K. Miller 1988; Shaw 1980); 27. MacHaffie (Forbis and Sperry 1952); 28. Mill Iron 24CT30 (Frison 1988b); 29. Paint Rock V 48BH349 (Frison 1976a); 30. Pine Spring 48SW101 (Sharrock 1966); 31. Powars II 48PL330 (Stafford 1990); 32. Ray Long 39FA65 (Hughes 1949); 33. Schiffer Cave 48JO319 (Frison 1973a); 34. Scottsbluff Bison Quarry (Barbour and Schultz 1932); 35. Agate Basin localities (48NA201; Sheaman 48NA211) (Frison and Stanford 1982); 36. Sister's Hill 48JO314 (Agogino and Galloway 1965); 37. China Wall (Brian Waitkus, personal communication 2008); 38. Wasden (Butler 1968); 39. 48JO303 (Frison and Grey 1980); 40. Jim Pitts (Sellet et al. 2009); 41. Krmpotich and Krmpotich Waterhole No. 3 (this

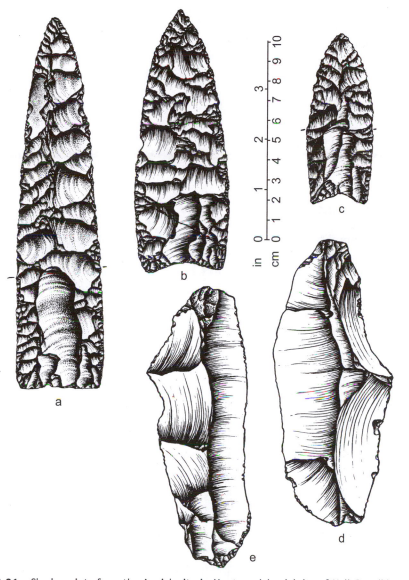

Figure 2.21   Clovis points from the Anzick site in Montana (a), vicinity of Hell Gap (b), and the Casper site (c), and Clovis blades from the Sheaman site in the Agate Basin locality (d, e).

volume); 42. Two Moon Shelter (Finley et al. 2005); 43. Middle Park Paleoindian sites (Upper and Lower Twin Mountain, Jerry Craig, Phillips-Williams Fork, Hay Gulch, Barger Gulch Localities A–G; Kornfeld and Frison 2000); 44. Linger, Zapata, and Cattle Guard (Jodry 1999a); 45. Mountainair (Steiger 2006); 46. Montgomery (Davis 1985); 47. Folsom (Figgins 1927); 48. Laird and Norton (Hofman and Blackmar 1997; Hofman et al. 1995); 49. Crook County Fenn Cache (Tankersley 2002); 50. Sibbald (Gryba 1983); 51. Simon (Butler 1963); 52. Game Creek 48TE1573 (Dan Eakin, personal communication 2008); 53. Nelson (Kornfeld et al. 2007); 54. Blue Point (Johnson and Pastor 2003); 55. Deep Hearth (Rood 1993); 56. Seminoe Beach (Miller 1986); and 57. Clary Ranch (Myers et al. 1981). In Figure 2.19, sites 1, 2, 5–8, 10, 13, 16, 18–22, 24, 26, 28, and 29 contain Paleoindian components.

The Sheaman site in the Moss Agate Arroyo in eastern Wyoming was first thought to contain only a Clovis component (Frison and Stanford 1982), although it is now known to have, in addition, an Agate Basin component. The site produced a large quantity of debitage, which was used by Bradley (1982) to attempt a study of Clovis biface technology. More recent data indicate that his observations were substantially correct. Clovis blades were also recovered at the Sheaman site (Figure 2.21d, e), as well as a carved antler object (Frison and Craig 1982) with a single, cross-hachured bevel on one end (Figure 2.22a). The other end was broken but apparently came to a sharp point. It closely resembles bone and ivory objects found in other Clovis contexts. Pronghorn and bison comprised the remainder of the faunal assemblage.

The Goshen Complex

The Goshen complex, named for Goshen County, Wyoming, was first recognized at the Hell Gap site in southeast Wyoming. It was below a Folsom component (Figure 2.23) and was first thought to be a variant of Clovis. It was named on

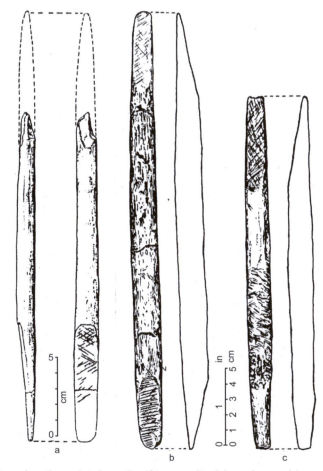

Figure 2.22 Carved antler point from the Sheaman site (a), and carved bone points from the Anzick site (b, c).

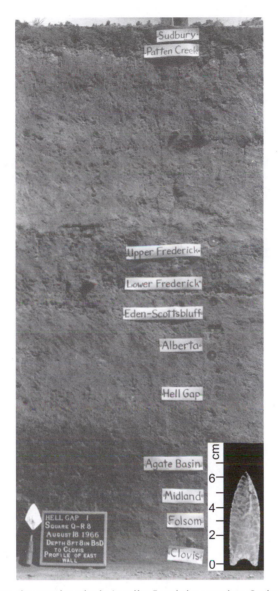

Figure 2.23   Hell Gap site stratigraphy in Locality I and the complete Goshen point from the site (inset).

the basis of a single complete projectile point (see Figure 2.23, inset) which has disappeared from the collections, although photographs, drawings, and replicas remain for study (Larson et al. 2009). The concept of Goshen as a cultural complex was seriously questioned until recently, but its validity was better substantiated with the discovery and investigation of the Mill Iron site (Figure 2.24) in southeast Montana (Frison 1988b). This site consists of a bison bone bed presumably related to a nearby campsite area. There are two series of AMS radiocarbon dates on both site areas: one averages over 11,000 BP and the other averages just under 11,000 BP. If the older dates are correct, the site would be contemporaneous with Clovis and if the younger ones are correct, it would be among the older Folsom sites.

Figure 2.24 View of the Mill Iron site in southeast Montana.

Goshen projectile points are technologically and morphologically neither Clovis nor Folsom, but do retain some characteristics of both. They demonstrate a pressure-flaking technology and a final edge retouch reminiscent of Folsom but are basally thinned and not fluted (Figure 2.25). A biface from the bison bone bed is strongly reminiscent of Clovis manufacture technology as are several blade tools.

As in the case of the Hell Gap site, the lowest level of the Carter/Kerr-McGee Paleoindian site in the Powder River Basin of Wyoming (Frison 1984) was first thought to be Clovis but is now thought to be Goshen. The one complete project-ile point (Figure 2.25e) from the bottom cultural component was made of a local material named clinker, which is a metamorphosed shale formed by heat and pressure as the result of burning coal beds in the later Tertiary (see Chapter 12). What were first thought to be flutes are now believed to be basal thinning flake scars. Also, as was the case at Hell Gap, the cultural level underlies a well-defined and radiocarbon-dated Folsom level which, along with the questions at that time as to the validity of Goshen, lent further support to a Clovis interpretation.

Many Goshen projectile points bear a strong resemblance to the Plainview type as it is known from the Southern Plains and which is considered to be later than Folsom. It is now apparent that Goshen points have been found regularly on the Northwestern Plains and Rocky Mountains but were identified as Plainview and given a post-Folsom date. The Mill Iron site has eliminated much of the uncer-tainty about the existence of Goshen but its relationship to Clovis and Folsom and its actual age still need to be better resolved, as indicated by both the Jim Pitts and Upper Twin Mountain sites. At the Jim Pitts site, Goshen underlies Folsom, confirming the Hell Gap cultural stratigraphy (Sellet et al. 2009). However, the radiocarbon dates of around 10,200 BP are late and do not fit well with the pre-Folsom stratigraphic position. The Upper Twin Mountain bone date of around 10,400 BP is slightly better, but it is still fully within the Folsom age range, while

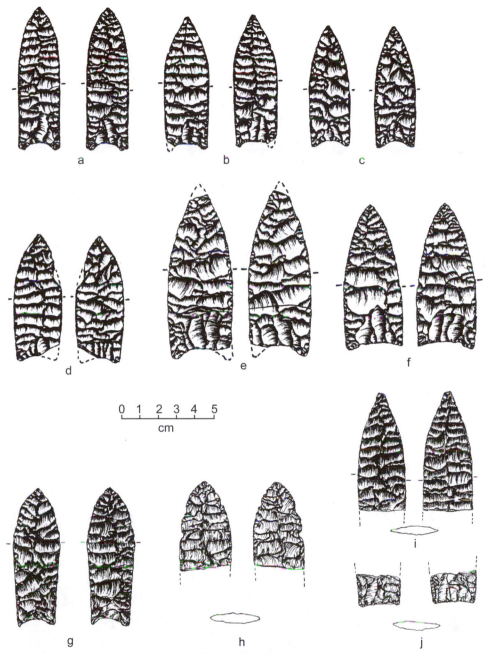

Figure 2.25 Goshen points from the Mill Iron campsite area in Montana (a–d), Carter/Kerr-McGee site (e), Kaufmann Cave (f) in northern Wyoming, and Upper Twin Mountain (g–j) in the Middle Park of Colorado. (Figure 2.25 g–j by Kelley J. Hankins.)

another date, also on bone, of around 10,200 BP is close to the Jim Pitts assay. At present our best evidence is the stratigraphic position of Goshen below Folsom at three sites—Hell Gap, Carter/Kerr-McGee, and Jim Pitts—while the absolute dating needs much further refinement.

The Folsom and Midland Complexes

Folsom follows the Clovis period, and the two complexes likely overlap as they both do with Goshen. However, a lack of mammoth remains in Folsom sites, but their presence in Clovis sites, suggests that these animals may have disappeared by Folsom times. As is the case with Clovis, Folsom projectile points are widespread on the Northwestern Plains and in the Rockies and have been found up to the timberline.

The number of radiocarbon-dated Folsom sites or sites with Folsom components is increasing. Today these include at least the Lindenmeier site in extreme northern Colorado (Roberts 1935, 1936); the Brewster site in the Moss Agate Arroyo in eastern Wyoming (Agogino 1972); the Folsom component in Area 2 of the Agate Basin site (Frison and Stanford 1982); several Folsom components at the Hell Gap site in southeast Wyoming (Irwin-Williams et al. 1973); the Hanson site (Figures 2.26–2.28) in extreme northern Wyoming (Frison and Bradley 1980); the Folsom component at the Carter/Kerr-McGee site (Frison 1984); the McHaffie site in Montana (Forbis and Sperry 1952); and the Indian Creek site in Montana (Davis 1984; Davis and Greiser 1992). Radiocarbon dates indicate that Folsom may have had a relatively long residence in the Rocky Mountains and adjacent Plains from about 10,900 to 10,200 BP.

At the Hell Gap site (Irwin-Williams et al. 1973), the investigators felt there was a Midland level with dates estimated between 10,700 and 10,400 BP. Midland presence is generally based on projectile points closely resembling Folsom except for a lack of fluting (but see Bradley 2009). Folsom site assemblages, including Lindenmeier, Hanson (Figures 2.27 and 2.28), and Agate Basin, contain both fluted and unfluted specimens so that what is labeled as Midland could be the unfluted part of Folsom assemblages. Whether or not Midland is a valid cultural complex

Figure 2.26 View of the Hanson site in northern Wyoming showing site areas 1 and 2.

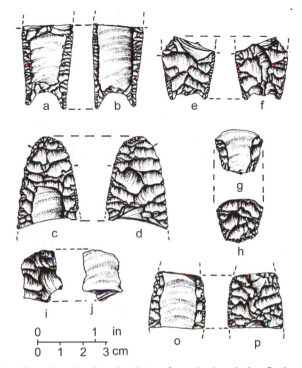

Figure 2.27 Projectile points (a, e) and point preforms broken during fluting (c, g, i, p) from the Hanson site.

here and in areas outside the Central Rocky Mountains and Northwestern Plains is an open question begging for more data.

Folsom flint knapping was exquisite, with the highest quality pressure flaking recognized worldwide. The purpose of fluting remains unexplained and is argued by some to have been more of an art form rather than functional. Both Folsom stone and bone tool assemblages exhibit a high degree of fine workmanship. This is indicated by small pieces of delicately incised bone at the Agate Basin and Lindenmeier sites, presumably for decorative purposes. Eyed bone needles that compare favorably with present-day metal examples (Figure 2.29) suggest fine work, possibly in clothing manufacture (see Frison and Craig 1982). This excellence of workmanship probably carried through into wood and other perishables as well. What appear to be bone and antler projectile points were also recovered in the Folsom component at the Agate Basin site (Frison and Zeimens 1980). However, their specific function is unknown; we do not know if they were generalized hunting tools or designed for procurement of a specific class of animals.

Two artifacts interpreted to have been punches designed for removal of Folsom flutes were recovered in the Agate Basin site Folsom level (Frison and Bradley 1981). The two items, one made from the brow tine (Figure 2.30) of an elk antler (Figure 2.31) and the other a bison metatarsal (Figure 2.32), were recovered in a scatter of channel flakes, broken projectile point preforms, and debitage. They support the argument that the fluting process may have been accomplished in more than one way but depended upon simple principles of proper application of pressure, selection of the proper raw material, and careful preparation of the preform and the channel flake platform.

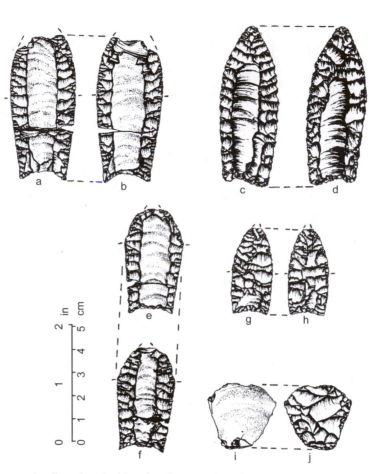

Figure 2.28   Projectile points (a–h) and end scraper (i, j) from the Hanson site.

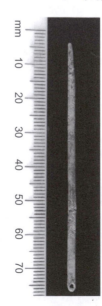

Figure 2.29   Bone needle from the Folsom component at the Agate Basin site.

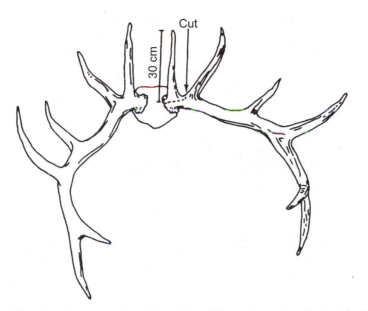

30 cm

Cut

Figure 2.30   Elk antlers demonstrating the location of the cut to remove the tool in Figure 2.31.

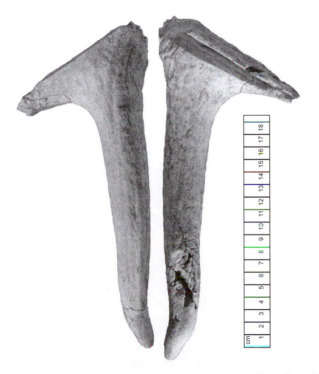

cm 1 2 3 4 5 6 7 8 9 10 11 12 13 14 15 16 17 18

Figure 2.31   Postulated Folsom fluting punch made from the brow tine of an elk antler from the Folsom component at the Agate Basin site.

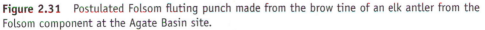

Whether or not the fluting of Folsom points served a functional, ritual, or other purpose can be and will continue to be argued. However, it is apparent that, along with a well-developed level of expertise, successful fluting required

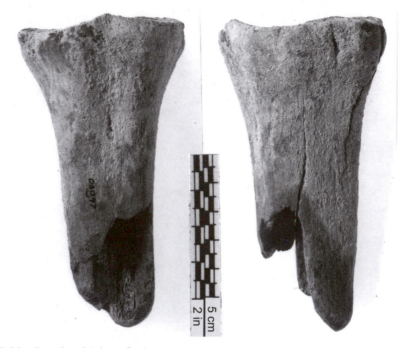

Figure 2.32   Postulated Folsom fluting punch made from a bison metatarsal from the Folsom component at the Agate Basin site.

careful selection for the best of raw materials. That it was a wasteful process can be argued also, judging from the number of preforms broken at different stages during the fluting process. Some have estimated that 50% of the Folsom preforms were broken in manufacturing stages, mostly fluting (Winfrey 1990).

Elk antler tools in the Folsom level at the Agate Basin site indicate the presence of *Elaphus canadensis*, although other skeletal remains of the species were not found. Nor do other skeletal elements found at the Hanson or Lindenmeier sites suggest their procurement or use as part of the food supply. A Folsom component at Agate Basin produced a *Canis* sp. maxilla, argued as evidence of a domesticated dog during Folsom times (Walker 1982:291–294).

THE MIDDLE PALEOINDIAN PERIOD

The Agate Basin Cultural Complex

The Agate Basin complex at the Hell Gap site was proposed to fall between 10,500 and 10,000 BP, according to the investigators (Irwin-Williams et al. 1973) and was the best-represented component of all Paleoindian complexes at the site. A recent date of 10,260 ± 95 BP (AA-16108, Haynes 2009) confirms their hunch. Dates on the Agate Basin level at the Agate Basin site fall within this time period. A date on the Agate Basin level at the Brewster site (Agate Basin site locality) of about 9300 years BP is probably too young while another of nearly 10,000 BP may be nearly correct. A mixed but undated Agate Basin–Hell Gap level is present at the Carter/Kerr-McGee site near Gillette, Wyoming. It overlies the Folsom level and is separated from it and an overlying mixed Alberta and Cody component by sterile levels.

The Agate Basin projectile point is long and narrow with a thick, lenticular cross section (Figure 2.33). In terms of killing bison or other large animals, it was without doubt an excellent design. Contrary to general opinion, it is relatively easy to haft to either a notched or a socketed foreshaft, and its design allows easy penetration of vital parts of the animal. Breakage could produce proximal, medial, and distal segments that were easily reworked and reused. Agate Basin points are technologically equal to Folsom points in terms of manufacturing technology but still are very different morphologically from Folsom points, although the archaeological record indicates that both were effective. This difference raises the question of relationships between the two cultural complexes. Agate Basin components are

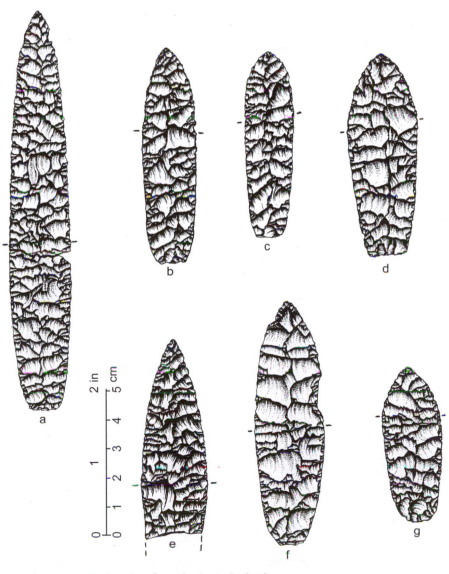

Figure 2.33 Agate Basin points from the Agate Basin site.

always above Folsom components in stratified sites, but radiocarbon dates suggest the possibility of an overlap between the two. It is difficult to detect significant differences between tool assemblages of the two complexes.

The Hell Gap Cultural Complex

A number of Hell Gap radiocarbon dates are available. None are from Hell Gap components at the Hell Gap site, but the investigators (Irwin-Williams et al. 1973) claim a radiocarbon date of about 10,300 BP from below the Hell Gap level and postulate dates of between 10,000 and 9500 years BP for its duration. Sister's Hill (Agogino and Galloway 1965), a Hell Gap site in north central Wyoming, yielded two radiocarbon dates of about 9600 years BP; one is from channel fill overlying the occupational levels and the other is from a composite sample taken from three occupational levels. Two dates were obtained from the Casper site (Frison 1974): one is from charcoal and the other is from bone and both are close to 10,000 years BP, which seems to be a reliable date for the Hell Gap complex. The Casper site along with the Jones-Miller site in eastern Colorado (Stanford 1978) have produced a large sample of Hell Gap projectile points and have provided detailed information on the range of variation of the type, which apparently resulted largely from reworking of broken specimens and utilization of points at different production stages (Figure 2.34). The Jones-Miller site is the largest bison kill known of the Hell Gap complex: radiocarbon dates demonstrate an unexpected spread but one at about 10,000 years BP is probably not far from correct.

The Hell Gap projectile point apparently developed directly out of the Agate Basin point. The Hell Gap projectile point shoulder is beginning to develop on some of the Agate Basin specimens (Figure 2.33e). It is difficult in terms of performance in killing large mammals to understand the change from the long, narrow Agate Basin type to the wide, shouldered type seen in Hell Gap. However, both were apparently successful in killing bison.

Other Middle Paleoindian Complexes

The deepest levels at the Helen Lookingbill site have no in situ diagnostics but are associated with a $10,405 \pm 95$ BP radiocarbon date. The material from the lowest levels are located in pink clay and clearly separated from the later Late Paleoindian deposits. One projectile point recovered during excavations in the 1970s reportedly came from the pink clay, and several projectile points found out of context (Figure 2.44p–s) may be either Haskett found further west along the Snake River (Butler 1965) or Hell Gap from the Plains to the east (Figure 2.47i). As only four one by one meter units have been excavated into this early deposit, the age, nature, and extent of this level is subject to question.

The Cody Cultural Complex

The Alberta projectile point introduced a different idea into Paleoindian weaponry. The hafting part is a large, parallel-sided stem with a definite shoulder

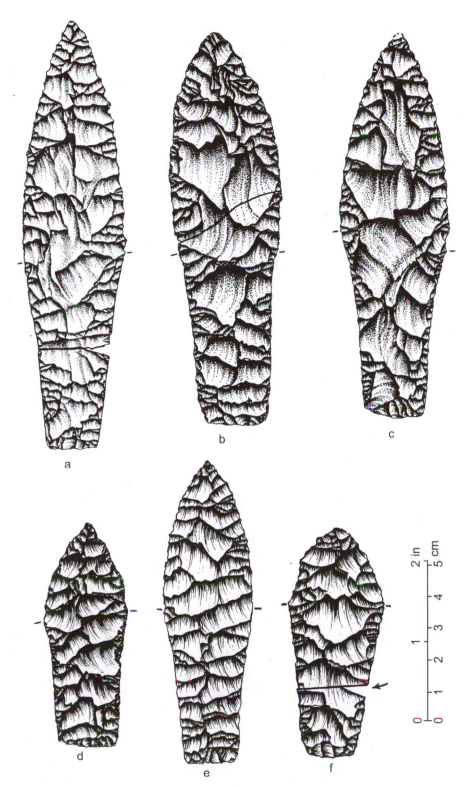

Figure 2.34 Hell Gap points from the Casper site.

(Figure 2.35a–c) that required some technological changes from Agate Basin–Hell Gap points to haft properly. Upon impact, pressure is delivered to the base and shoulders. A nocked foreshaft with sinew bindings properly applied to prevent the point from being driven backward and splitting the shaft upon impact was necessary. The shoulders of the point probably took on significance since they had to absorb most of the shock of heavy impact, which is substantial indeed in the case of penetrating the rib cage of a bison. The technological solution to these hafting problems was not difficult using only pitch and sinew. Alberta points are relatively large and quite heavy; the hafting part or stem is also quite large, but not out of proportion to the rest of the projectile point.

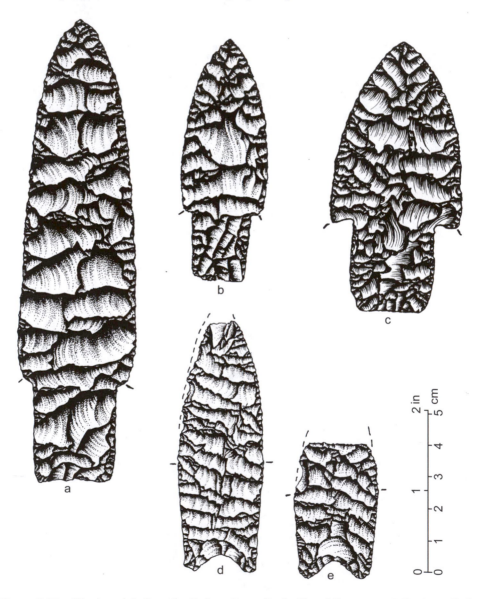

Figure 2.35 Alberta points from the Hudson-Meng site (a, b) and the arroyo at the Agate Basin site (c), and James Allen points from the James Allen site (d, e).

An Alberta component present at the Hell Gap site was radiocarbon dated only recently between 10,560 ± 80 BP (AA-20545) and 9410 ± 95 BP (AA-28774; Haynes 2009), but is probably closer to the later date. A duration from 9500 to 9000 BP was, however, already suggested some time ago for the Alberta complex (Irwin-Williams et al. 1973). The Alberta projectile point introduced the idea of a large stem and abrupt shoulders in the hafting of Paleoindian projectile points. The Hudson-Meng Alberta bison bone bed in northwest Nebraska (Agenbroad 1978b) yielded radiocarbon dates from 9800 to 9000 years BP along with several project-ile points (Figure 2.35a, b). There was a mixed Alberta and Cody component at the Carter/Kerr-McGee site in the Powder River Basin in north-central Wyoming (Frison 1984:301). Surface finds of Alberta projectile points occur regularly. A specimen found in the arroyo at the Agate Basin site (Figure 2.35c) suggests that there may be an Alberta component or components somewhere in that locality.

The Princeton-Smithsonian excavations at the Horner site in northwest Wyoming during the late 1940s and early 1950s were concentrated in an area that contained a bone bed or bone beds near the present surface. They obtained a large assemblage of weaponry and tools that formed the basis for establishing the Cody cultural complex. Further excavations at the Horner site in 1977 and 1978 by the University of Wyoming revealed a bison bone bed under more than a meter of deposits and a projectile point assemblage similar to part of the assemblage recovered over a quarter of a century earlier (Frison and Todd 1987).

Two radiocarbon dates from the 1977–1978 bison bone bed were close to 10,000 years BP, which seemed too old for the Cody complex. An analysis of the projectile points (Bradley and Frison 1987:199–231) confirmed that there were rather subtle differences technologically between them and the ones known to be of the Cody complex. Although the radiocarbon dates would suggest an Alberta age, the tech-nology and morphology of the projectile points were different enough not to clas-sify them as Alberta. A compromise was made and they were tentatively named Alberta-Cody (Figures 2.36f and 2.37d, e). The differences were obvious enough that the Alberta-Cody points in the Princeton-Smithsonian assemblage were easily separated out, leaving only the Eden and Scottsbluff points of the Cody complex. Further analysis revealed also that the Alberta-Cody assemblage could be further divided into Alberta-Cody I and Alberta-Cody II on the basis of technological differences in manufacture. To date, this is the only known in situ occurrence of Alberta-Cody, which may be a regional variant of Alberta, a separate complex ancestral to the Cody complex, or something else as yet unknown or unidentified.

The Horner site became the type site of the Cody complex (Frison and Todd 1987) because of the occurrence of the Eden and Scottsbluff projectile points together along with the various styles of the Cody knife. A large assemblage that included Eden (Figure 2.36g) and Scottsbluff (Figure 2.36h) projectile points along with Cody knives was recovered in the Princeton-Smithsonian excavations. Radiocarbon dates on the Cody complex are two hundred or so years on both sides of 9000 years BP. The Cody level at Locality I of the Hell Gap site was radio-carbon dated to 9120 ± 490 BP (AA-27675, Haynes 2009), while a bulk sediment organic residue date on the Eden floor at Locality V of Hell Gap is 8665 ± 70 BP (AA35655, Haynes 2009). Two radiocarbon dates from the Finley site are both close to 9000 BP, although both are bone dates which have not proven to be reliable in all cases. The Finley site produced both Eden (Figure 2.36a–c) and Scottsbluff (Figure 2.36d) projectile points. Two earlier radiocarbon dates on burned bone

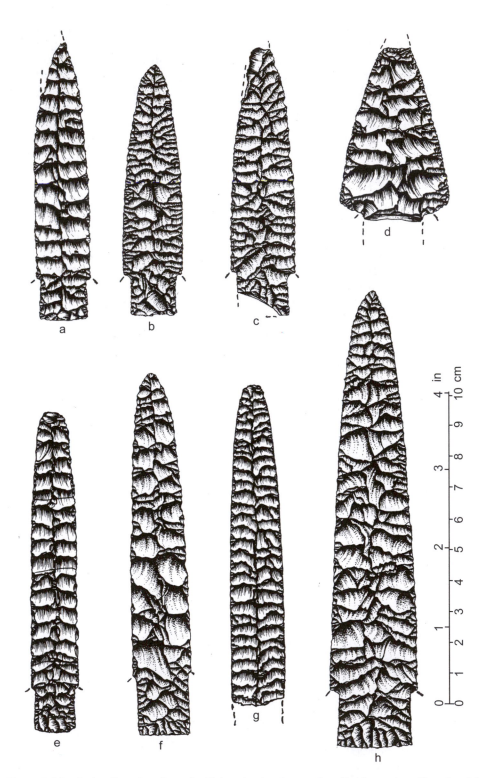

Figure 2.36 Projectile points from the Finley site (a–d), a surface find in western Wyoming (e), and from the Horner site (f–h).

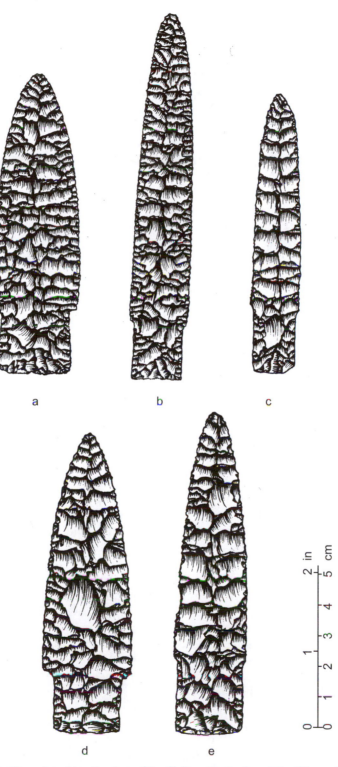

Figure 2.37 Projectile points from the Carter/Kerr-McGee site (a–c) and the Alberta-Cody component at the Horner site (d, e).

from the Princeton-Smithsonian excavations at the Horner site were about 8800 years BP, as was a Cody component at the Medicine Lodge Creek site. A date of 9260 ± 20 BP (UCIAMS-26939) was assessed on bone from the Nelson site, while 9310 ± 50 BP (Beta 10946) and 8490 ± 50 BP (Beta 109466) are charcoal dates bracketing the Cody level of the Jerry Craig site in the high country of Colorado (Kornfeld and Frison 2000), adding several dates in confirmation of Cody chronology. Both Stanford (1999) and Holliday and colleagues (1999) place Cody within this range of dates.

Cody, once thought to be one of the classic Plains Paleoindian projectile point styles, turns out to be far more complex. Its recent discovery at the Osprey Beach site in Yellowstone National Park as well as other localities indicates its more widespread occurrence (Johnson et al. 2004). Several years earlier a Cody component was investigated at Mammoth Meadow in southwestern Montana (Bonnichsen et al. 1992). Most interesting are the recent studies of substantial surface collections in the far western Great Basin, where some of the stemmed projectile points appear to be of Cody affiliation (Amick 2007). These new data open the way for new perspectives on the Cody complex and its distribution, undoubtedly an area rife with possibilities for future research.

THE LATE PALEOINDIAN PERIOD

The Frederick and/or James Allen Cultural Complex

A duration from about 8400 to 8000 BP was postulated for the Frederick complex at the Hell Gap site (Irwin-Williams et al. 1973), and several residual organic and humate dates suggest that deposition of stratigraphic unit F, containing the Frederick complex, ended by 8000 BP (Haynes 2009). However, the Frederick component predates the cessation of deposition by some time and dates at the contact of stratigraphic units E and F at the Hell Gap Site of 8690 ± 380 BP (A-501) and 8890 ± 110 BP (A-753A) may more closely approximate the age of Frederick. There is an abrupt change from the stemmed projectile points with transverse pressure flaking of the Cody complex to the lanceolate style with parallel-oblique flaking that followed (Figure 2.38). Except for slight differences in outline form, these projectile points bear a close similarity to those known as James Allen points (Figure 2.35d, e) from the James Allen site, a small bison kill site in the Laramie Basin in southern Wyoming (Mulloy 1959) with a radiocarbon date (on bone) of about 7900 years BP. This date, however, must now be rejected along with the many early bone dates that yielded inaccurate, usually late, assays. A new assay, based on the fractionation protocols developed by Stafford and colleagues (1991), has yielded a date of 8405 ± 25 BP (Knudson and Kornfeld 2007). This is in the range of the original assessment of the Frederick complex at Hell Gap and not unreasonably late for the current Hell Gap chronostratigraphy (Haynes 2009).

Although a bit farther afield, a bison bone bed in Kansas, the Norton site, contains similar projectile points to those discussed here (Hofman et al. 1995). The Norton site date of 9080 BP may mark the beginning of Frederick/James Allen complexes, although the Norton points have significantly deeper basal indentation than Frederick and are more similar to James Allen (Jack Hofman, personal communication 2002). The date is also not out of line with the recent Hell Gap

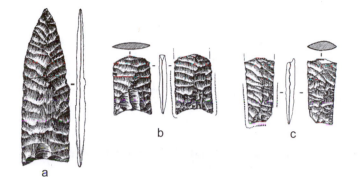

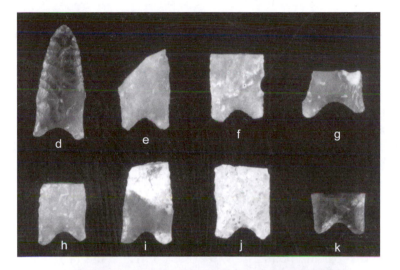

Figure 2.38 Frederick projectile points from Hell Gap site (a–c), James Allen points from the Phillips-Williams Fork site (d–k), and Lusk points from the Betty Green site (l–o).

assessment of this complex. Parallel-oblique, lanceolate projectile points of the same complex occur at the Phillips-Williams Fork site in the Colorado mountains, but in an as yet undated context (Figure 2.38d–k; Wiesend and Frison 1998), as well as numerous other plains and mountain settings at least from Texas to South Dakota (LaBelle 2005; Pitblado 2003). Another site with similar projectile points is Clary Ranch, a bison bone bed in Nebraska. Originally reported as Meserve (Myers et al. 1981), the site has recently been reevaluated as Frederick or James Allen (Hill 2005). However, Dalton complex is sometimes mentioned in the context of discussion of some of these localities, and Kay (2003) has recently reported on a revision of the Dalton dates from Rodgers Shelter that puts them more in line with the revised Frederick and James Allen dates.

Two other sites in Kansas also provide significant dates for estimating the spatial and temporal distribution of this Late Paleoindian complex—Laird and Winger. The Laird date of 8495 ± 40 BP and the Winger date of around 9000 BP (Blackmar 2002; Mandel and Hofman 2002), along with the Norton site, demonstrate both spatial and temporal continuity of the James Allen/Frederick components in the Northern Plains and Rockies with those in the Central Plains, and LaBelle has shown that this continuity extends to the Southern Plains. These Late Paleoindian complexes demonstrate a great deal of chronologic and stylistic variation. The meaning of this variation is yet unclear; however, as the data accumulate, questions of spatial and temporal contemporaneiety will resolve and the more interesting issues of cultural variation will become approachable.

The Lusk Cultural Complex

Lusk as a cultural complex was proposed on the basis of a small assemblage of tools and projectile points from the Betty Greene site near the Wyoming–Nebraska–South Dakota tristate border and from out-of-context artifacts from the Hell Gap site about 64 km to the south (Greene 1967). The best description of the few Lusk projectile points known to have come from either the Hell Gap or Betty Greene sites is that they exhibit parallel-oblique flaking similar to the Frederick points but they tend to be considerably narrower and thicker, and thus have a smaller width-to-thickness ratio (Figure 2.38l–o). They are usually made on flakes or blades with a triangular cross section, so that the projectile points tend to be plano-convex in cross section. Bases tend to be more concave than Frederick points and blade edges vary from convex to those with pronounced lateral restrictions. However, tools including scrapers and gravers demonstrate a definite Paleoindian influence. On the basis of projectile point characteristics, Pitblado (2003) would include them in the Foothill/Mountain complex, along with Angostura, Alder, and others.

There was never an adequate geological study of the Betty Greene site area. It is now known that there is more than a single cultural component present. A date of about 7900 years BP was obtained (Greene 1968) but from what level in the site the charcoal was collected is not clear. Many of the artifacts used to describe the Lusk projectile point type were recovered by the landowner as surface finds in an area of secondary deposits that produces other Paleoindian projectile point types as well as Lusk.

THE FOOTHILL/MOUNTAIN PALEOINDIAN COMPLEXES

About 10,000 BP there were apparently two concurrent and separate Paleoindian occupations with different and mutually exclusive subsistence strategies, since several radiocarbon dates of around 10,000 years BP have been recovered in caves and rockshelters in the foothills-mountain areas. The Foothill/Mountain complexes favored more hunting and gathering subsistence in foothill and mountain slope areas and were more Archaic in terms of subsistence strategies. Cody followed a part-time bison hunting way of life on the Plains as well as a forager subsistence in the foothills. Two deep, stratified rockshelters—Mummy Cave (Husted and Edgar 2002; Wedel et al. 1968) and Medicine Lodge Creek (Frison 1976a; Frison and Walker 2007; Frison and Wilson 1975); the open Lookingbill site (Frison 1983b; Kornfeld, Larson, Rapson, and Frison 2001); and several smaller rockshelters in Bighorn Canyon in Wyoming and Montana (Husted 1969) and in the southern Bighorn Mountains (Frison 1973a) have helped to define somewhat the Foothill/Mountain complex. Still another manifestation of the Foothill/ Mountain groups is the Alder complex in southwest Montana at the Barton Gulch site, which falls in about the same age bracket as Cody and possibly slightly older (Davis et al. 1988). The stratified Hell Gap, Carter/Kerr-McGee, and Agate Basin sites (Frison 1984; Frison and Stanford 1982; Irwin-Williams et al. 1973) and a number of single-component sites have aided in establishing the chronology of the Plains big game hunting groups. The Cody complex may have been present in a somewhat transitional period since its evidence occurs in foothill sites.

There are now sufficient data to support the concept of a dichotomy in subsistence strategies between plains and foothill-mountains ecosystems that varied in intensity throughout prehistoric times. This is based on the results of investigations from a number of stratified sites with long records of human habitation. Explanations are still in the formative stages, largely because of a paucity of comparative data from the foothill-mountain areas, but a distinct separation in lifeways between the two ecosystems appears to be the only conclusion at this time.

Mummy Cave (Figure 2.39), with several meters of stratified deposits extending from Late Prehistoric times to about 9000 years BP, is located along the North Fork of the Shoshone River in northwest Wyoming well into the Absaroka Mountains (Husted and Edgar 2002; Wedel et al. 1968). Mountain sheep remains dominated the faunal remains in all levels. There is no evidence there of the Cody complex as was found at the Horner bison bone bed site, which is located only 50 km to the east in the interior Bighorn Basin. All of the late Paleoindian occupation levels in Mummy Cave suggest cultural groups with different subsistence strategies than those living on the open plains and interior intermontane basins. Husted (1969) suggested the existence of a subsistence dichotomy based on the evidence from Mummy Cave and from cave sites along the Bighorn River on both sides of the Montana–Wyoming boundary. The same evidence for a subsistence dichotomy is found at the Medicine Lodge Creek site (Figure 2.40), located on the ecotone between plains and mountains in the eastern Bighorn Basin. The site has stratified Paleoindian levels dating from 10,000 to 8000 years BP. As mentioned earlier, both Clovis (Figure 2.41) and Folsom evidence is found in the higher elevations. Their presence there may have been to acquire raw stone flaking materials found only in geologic formations exposed there. Evidence of the fluted projectile points

Figure 2.39   Mummy Cave in northwest Wyoming. (Photo by Jack Richard.)

Figure 2.40   The Medicine Lodge Creek site in northern Wyoming.

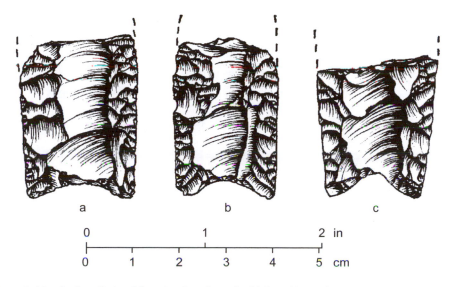

a   b   c

0   1   2 in
|——————————|——————————|

0   1   2   3   4   5 cm

Figure 2.41 Surface finds of fluted points from the Bighorn Mountains.

are found regularly in mountain meadows in the immediate vicinity of several of these geologic features. However, their frequency is rather sparse.

The earliest human occupation of a mountain-foothill comes from Two Moon shelter near Shell, Wyoming (Finley et al. 2005), where a Folsom level is under investigation. The next earliest occupation to occur in caves and rockshelters is at just over 10,000 BP in sites including Medicine Lodge Creek (Frison and Walker 2007), Little Canyon Creek Cave, Bush Shelter (K. Miller 1988) and Two Moon Shelter, all in the foothills on the western slope of the Bighorn Mountains. All of these mountain-foothill sites produce small numbers of diagnostics (projectile points) compared to the large numbers found in animal kill sites of the Plains Paleoindian, so that typologies at this time are tenuous and based on small samples. At Medicine Lodge Creek there are a number of projectile points between the Cody complex and 10,000 BP that are markedly different than those during the same time period at Hell Gap, Carter/Kerr-McGee, and Agate Basin sites (Figure 2.42j, o–r). The same is true from Cody times until the end of the Paleoindian period at about 8000 years BP (Figure 2.42b–h, k, l). The one exception was found in a Cody component dated to 9000 BP (Figure 2.42n). Several complexes in the time range of 9500 to 8000 BP have been proposed, some of which are well enough established to warrant discussion.

The Alder and Hardinger Complexes

Current research in southwest Montana has revealed stratified evidence of Paleoindian occupation that does not appear to be directly related to the classic Plains Paleoindian and could be something more akin to the Foothill/Mountain Paleoindian. The Barton Gulch site 24MA171 is stratified with one component producing a distinctive lanceolate projectile point with a deep basal notch (Figure 2.43d–f) and radiocarbon dates around 8800 years BP. The investigator has termed these Metzal points and has defined the Hardinger complex on this basis.

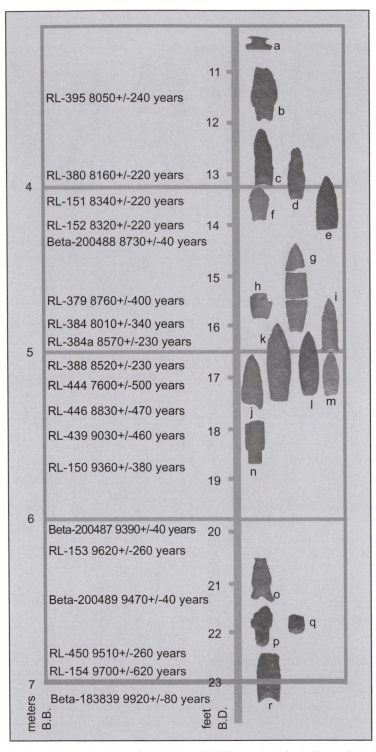

Figure 2.42   Early Plains Archaic point (a), Foothill/Mountain Paleoindian points (b–m, o–q), a Cody point (n), and a concave-base possible Goshen point (r) from the Medicine Lodge Creek site, arranged by depth with associated radiocarbon ages indicated.

A deeper component produces very different lanceolate projectile points with definite parallel-oblique flaking and radiocarbon dates of 9400 years BP. Ruby Valley points (Figure 2.43a–c) are designated as a diagnostic of the Alder complex

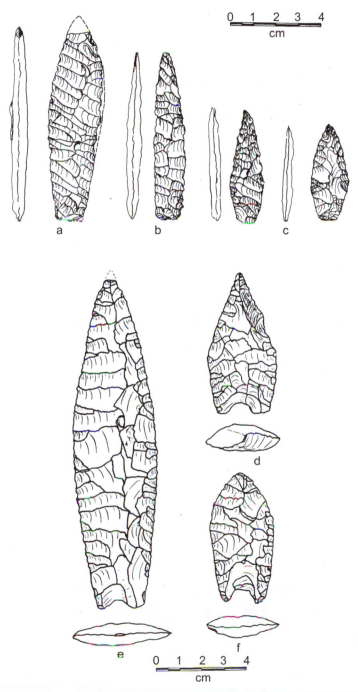

Figure 2.43 Ruby Valley points from the Alder complex (a–c) and Metzal points from the Hardinger complex (d–f) of the Barton Gulch site in southwest Montana. (Courtesy of Leslie B. Davis.)

(Davis et al. 1988). This pushes the age of the parallel-oblique flaking back into pre-Cody or at least earliest Cody times and demonstrates parallel transverse flaking well into post-Cody times.

The Alder complex has been corroborated by data from the Helen Lookingbill site in Wyoming (Kornfeld, Larson, Rapson, and Frison 2001). The site has two terminal Paleoindian components with Early Plains Archaic immediately above them. The lower of these Paleoindian components has yielded a series of lanceolate, usually parallel-oblique flaked points with slightly insloping lateral basal edges and convex to straight bases (Figure 2.44g–o). The dates on these specimens are 8800 ± 60 BP and 8980 ± 80 BP. Although later than the Barton Gulch dates by 500 years, some projectile points could easily be lost between the two assemblages (Figure 2.45). It is certainly possible that Barton Gulch and Lookingbill occupations represent the Alder complex. Similar Late Paleoindian materials can be found at other Foothill/Mountain localities, in particular Southsider Cave, Medicine Lodge Creek site, Bass-Anderson Cave, and Schiffer Cave. Furthermore, Pitblado (2003) recognizes these types of specimens throughout the Southern Rocky Mountains.

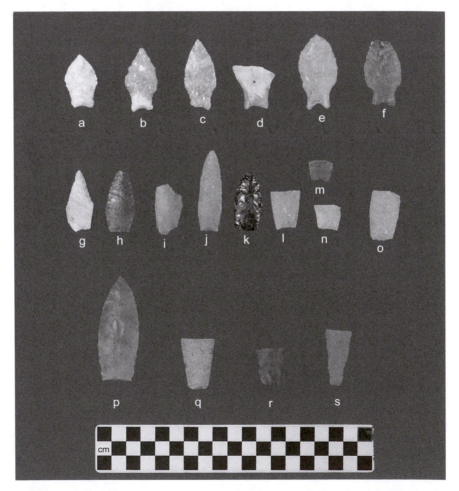

Figure 2.44 Lookingbill site Paleoindian projectile points: Lovell Constricted (a–f), Alder complex (g–o), and Haskett (p–s).

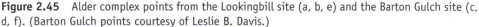

Figure 2.45   Alder complex points from the Lookingbill site (a, b, e) and the Barton Gulch site (c, d, f). (Barton Gulch points courtesy of Leslie B. Davis.)

Parallel-oblique flaked projectile points were also recovered at the Ray Long site (Hughes 1949) in western South Dakota and were given the name of Angostura. Angostura, Frederick, James Allen, Lusk, and others may also be local or regional variants of the terminal Paleoindian manifestation for the Northwestern Plains that crosscut plains and foothill-mountain areas.

The Lovell Constricted Complex

Two of the Bighorn Canyon cave sites and the Medicine Lodge Creek site produced several lanceolate points below Pryor Stemmed levels characterized by crude parallel-oblique flaking, slightly restricted blade edges, and concave bases (Figure 2.42e, f). Husted (1969) gave these the type name of Lovell Constricted after the nearby town of Lovell, Wyoming. A Lovell Constricted projectile point was recovered in the Medicine Lodge Creek site and another at the lowest cultural level at Mummy Cave (Husted and Edgar 2002), and they are occasionally recovered on the surface, particularly on the western slopes of the Bighorn Mountains.

The Lookingbill site contains a large sample of Fishtail points in stratified and dated contexts between the Alder complex and the Early Archaic components of the site (Figure 2.44a–f). Although the vertical stratigraphic separation of the

Alder and Fishtail assemblage as a whole is difficult to discern, the two styles of projectile points are stratigraphically distinct, with the Fishtail overlying the Alder. The Fishtail or Lovell Constricted component produced radiocarbon dates of 8525 ± 100 BP. With the extant information from Mummy Cave and Medicine Lodge Creek, the Lovell Constricted complex is beginning to find its place in the Late Paleoindian chronology.

The Pryor Stemmed Complex

The Bighorn and Pryor Mountains in Montana and Wyoming, respectively, have produced a distinctive horizon marker in the form of a projectile point that was given the type name of Pryor Stemmed (Husted 1969) based on specimens of this type in radiocarbon-dated cave and rockshelter deposits near Pryor Mountain in southern Montana and northern Wyoming. There are a number of radiocarbon dates for other sites in the Bighorn Mountains along with surface finds that have produced this type of projectile point. Consequently, Pryor Stemmed was proposed as a cultural complex (Frison and Grey 1980). Radiocarbon dates indicate that Pryor Stemmed was present from about 8300 to 7800 BP.

Small bits of evidence recovered in the last decade suggest that Pryor Stemmed or something very similar may have had a much wider distribution in the area than just the Bighorn Mountains. Surface finds from along the North Platte River in central Wyoming and from the Laramie Range, along with several specimens from stratified cave sites in the Hartville uplift not far from the Hell Gap site but in a foothill-mountain ecosystem, suggest variants of the Pryor Stemmed projectile point.

Pryor Stemmed points are unique in that they were continually reworked on alternate blade edges (Figure 2.46) to produce a steep beveling. The archetype was apparently lenticular in transverse cross section and usually but not always characterized by parallel-oblique pressure flaking. They may be lanceolate in outline form or have an expanding, parallel-sided, or slightly contracting stem, usually with a basal concavity. Beveling of the blade edges was a continually repeated process so that, in some cases, the blade edges became narrower than the stem. When this occurred, however, projections at the shoulder suggest the point was still on a haft. The beveling was often carefully applied to give serrated blade edges. Reworking was common also on broken specimens and in many cases a deliberate burination was applied to blade edges and/or faces using transverse breaks as striking platforms. The latter specimens were apparently reused as tools (Figure 2.7).

Deception Creek

Deception Creek projectile points were described as early as the 1970s (Collins 1970; Rood 1993). They were recognized as being distinct and suspected of being Paleoindian. However, no dates were available on them at the time and they had not been found in stratigraphic or dated context. The Deep Hearth site changed this situation. The Deep Hearth site is a multicomponent locality near Cumberland Gap in southwestern Wyoming. The deeply buried Component 2 was dated with a series of radiocarbon assays from features in the range of 8610 ± 90 to

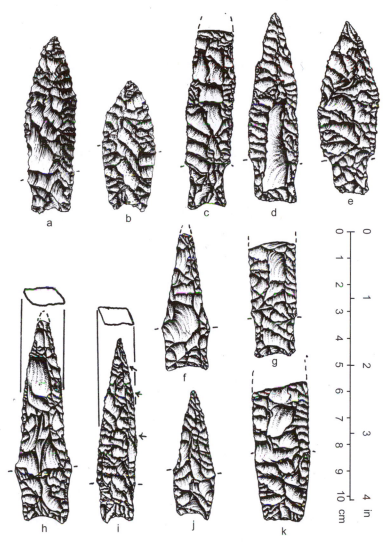

Figure 2.46 Pryor Stemmed points from the Bighorn Mountains.

8220 ± 130 BP (Rood 1993). Associated with these features were small lanceolate, projectile points with distinct lateral ears, flat bases, and lenticular, but sometimes diamond-shaped, cross sections.

At present these projectile points are relatively rare, but they occur at least from southwestern Wyoming to adjacent areas of northwestern Colorado and on to the North and Middle Parks of the Central Rocky Mountains (Kornfeld 1998; Lischka et al. 1983). The same type of points are part of a surface collection from the Krmpotich Waterhole No. 1 site (48SW13617) on the western edge of the Killpecker Dune field. The site is situated around a small interdunal pond, but artifacts may be eroding from a slip face that tapers off to a bedrock bench that forms one side of the pond. Buried intact portions of the site may be present in the dune. Although multiple complexes are represented by the diagnostic assemblage, five of them are Deception Creek type. This site has not been excavated, but in situ material may be present and if so the site forms a significant archaeological locality that could yield data on this, currently poorly defined, Late Paleoindian Foothill/Mountain complex.

Other Foothill/Mountain Paleoindian Manifestations

Southsider Cave on the western slopes of the Bighorn Mountains produced parallel-oblique flaked projectile points (Figure 2.47a, b) and a similar rockshelter nearby, Paint Rock V (Figure 2.48), produced what may be a variant of Pryor

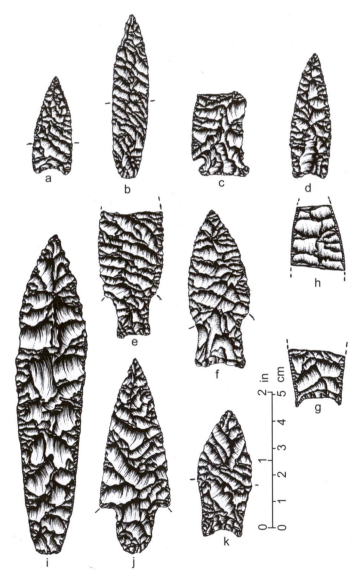

Figure 2.47 Projectile point sequence from Foothill/Mountain Paleoindian (a, b) to Early Plains Archaic (c) to Middle Plains Archaic (d) from Southsider Cave in the Bighorn Mountains. Foothill/ Mountain Paleoindian points from Paint Rock V (e, f), surface finds of possible unfluted Folsom or Midland points (g, h), Haskett point from the Haskett site in Idaho (i), surface finds of a rounded-stem point (j), and a Lovell Constricted point (k).

Stemmed (Figure 2.47e, f). Surface finds in the immediate area of these two sites include possible unfluted Folsom or Midland points (Figure 2.47g, h), Lovell Constricted points (Figure 2.47k), and one point with a rounded stem (Figure 2.47j).

Evidence of the local nature of Foothill/Mountain groups has been found at Bass-Anderson Cave in the interior Hartville uplift (Eisenbarth and Earl 1989). A radiocarbon date of 8900 BP came from a level that produced large, lanceolate points

Figure 2.48 The Paint Rock V site in the Bighorn Mountains.

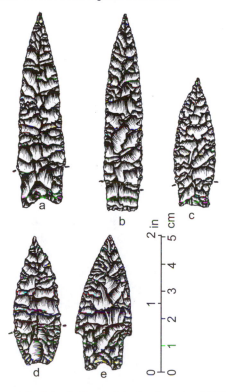

Figure 2.49 Foothill/Mountain Paleoindian points (a–d) and a Middle Plains Archaic point (e) from the Bass-Anderson Cave site in the Hartville uplift in southeast Wyoming.

(Figure 2.49b, c). An overlying and presumably younger level yielded what appear to be Pryor Stemmed (Figure 2.49a), as well as Alder (Figure 2.49d) projectile points. Evidence of later Foothill/Mountain occupation at Bass-Anderson is based on the straight stemmed, shouldered projectile point (Figure 2.49e) reminiscent of one known from the Yarmony House site in the northern Colorado mountains (Metcalf and Black 1991).

Another stratified site of value to late Paleoindian studies is the Myers-Hindman site in the Upper Yellowstone River Valley near Livingston, Montana (Lahren 1976). A thick, sterile level separates the two deepest cultural units; the oldest contains several projectile points reminiscent in style and technology to those from the Bighorn Canyon and Medicine Lodge Creek sites. Included are rounded-base and concave-base styles with both parallel-oblique and/or parallel-transverse flaking (Lahren 1976).

The deepest cultural level at the Medicine Lodge Creek site produced a projectile point with a concave base, parallel-transverse flaking, and blade edges parallel for a distance from the base before they begin to converge toward the point (Figure 2.42r). Two similar projectile point bases were found in the bottom cultural level of Bush Shelter in the foothills of the southern Bighorn Basin. Radiocarbon dates on both are at about 10,000 years BP. They are strongly reminiscent of the Goshen type and, in addition, a typical Goshen point (Figure 2.25f) was found in the lowest level of Kaufmann Cave in northern Wyoming in association with a broken mammoth scapula (Grey 1962a). These specimens bring up the possibility of a relationship between Goshen and the early Foothill/Mountain groups, although there is not enough information at this point to do more than offer the suggestion and await the acquisition of new data.

Cultural levels at Medicine Lodge Creek with radiocarbon dates between about 10,000 and 9000 BP produced split-based points (Figure 2.42o); points with lateral restrictions; points with rounded stems (Figure 2.42p, q); and lanceolate points (Figure 2.42j) all with ground blade edges toward the base. None is well enough known as yet to warrant assignment of type names, although all are found occasionally on the surface. The same is true of projectile points at Medicine Lodge Creek stratigraphically above Cody complex materials (Figure 2.42b, g, h, k, l), except for the Pryor Stemmed and Lovell Constricted types.

Another caution must be mentioned in assuming that the parallel-oblique flaking and a lanceolate shape is characteristic of the post-Cody Paleoindian alone. Certain sites of Late Prehistoric and Early Historic age in the Snake River Valley in Idaho have produced a tool type known as the "Wahmuza lanceolate point" from the site of the same name (Holmer 1986) that has the appearance of a late Paleoindian projectile point with parallel-oblique flaking (Wood 1987). Out of context these could be considered as late Paleoindian in age (Figure 2.50, from Wood 1987). Since most known specimens of Wahmuza lanceolate points are made of obsidian, hydration rinds can be checked on surface finds.

THE EARLY PLAINS ARCHAIC PERIOD

The change from the lanceolate and stemmed projectile points of the Late Paleoindian to the side-notched types of the Early Plains Archaic was abrupt and is easily detected in the archaeological record. It also represented the finalization of an Archaic lifeway that probably began in late Paleoindian times. At one time

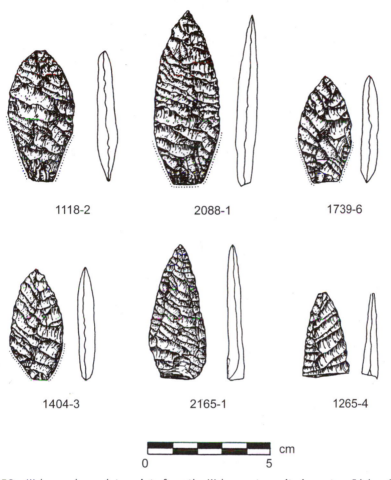

1118-2   2088-1   1739-6

1404-3   2165-1   1265-4

cm

0   5

Figure 2.50 Wahmuza lanceolate points from the Wahmuza type site in eastern Idaho. (Courtesy of James Wood.)

it was thought that the Altithermal or Early Plains Archaic period might have coincided with a cultural hiatus over the entire Northwestern Plains (see Mulloy 1958). In the light of more recent evidence, it is becoming obvious that there are still many unanswered questions about the geographic spread, duration, and nature of the climatic conditions of the period and how this affected human and animal populations. Selected site locations are given in Figure 2.51.

On the Northwestern Plains and Rocky Mountains, several radiocarbon dates of the Early Plains Archaic place its beginnings between 8000 and 7500 BP. These dates are from caves, rockshelters, and open sites. The best radiocarbon-dated chronological record of Early Plains Archaic occupations for this area is found in Mummy Cave (Figure 2.39), which is located along the Shoshone River a few miles east of Yellowstone National Park in Park County, Wyoming (Hughes 2003; Husted and Edgar 2002; Wedel et al. 1968). Sites such as Mummy Cave were in locations of continuous deposition controlled by conditions within the cave so that the stratigraphic record there was independent of conditions outside. In southwestern Wyoming and northwestern Colorado some characteristics of the Early Archaic begin at 8500 BP.

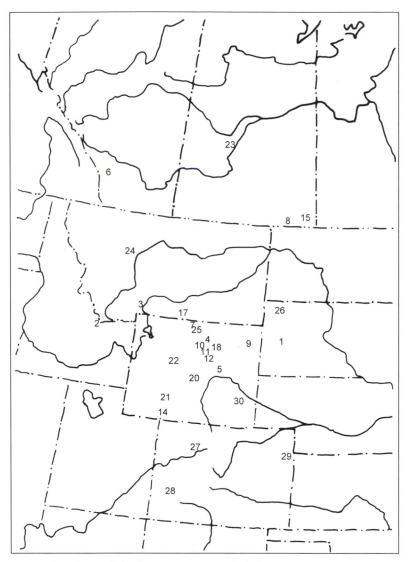

Figure 2.51 Early Plains Archaic sites: 1. Beaver Creek Shelter (Martin et al. 1988); 2. Birch Creek (Swanson et al. 1964); 3. Carbella 24PA302 (Arthur 1966); 4. Carter Cave 48WA365 (unpublished); 5. Dunlap-McMurry Burial 48NA675 (Zeimens et al. 1976); 6. Gap (Reeves and Dormaar 1972); 7. Granite Creek Rockshelter 48BH330 (Frison and Wilson 1975); 8. Gray Burial (Millar et al. 1972); 9. Hawken I and III 48CK303 (Frison et al. 1976); 10. Laddie Creek 48BH345 (Larson 1990); 11. Leigh Cave 48WA304 (Frison and Huseas 1968); 12. Little Canyon Creek Cave 48WA323 and Bush Shelter 48WA324 (K. Miller 1988; Shaw 1980); 13. Medicine House 48CR2353 (McGuire et al. 1984); 14. Maxon Ranch 48SW2590 (Harrell and McKern 1986); 15. Oxbow Dam (Nero and McCorquodale 1958); 16. Patten Creek 48PL68 (Keller 1971); 17. Pretty Creek 24CB4 (Loendorf et al. 1981); 18. Rice Cave 48WA363 (unpublished); 19. Shoreline 48CR122 (Walker and Zeimens 1976); 20. Split Rock Ranch 48FR1484 (Eakin 1987); 21. Sweetwater Creek 48SW5175 (Newberry and Harrison 1986); 22. Wedding of the Waters Cave 48HO301 (Frison 1962); 23. Gowen (Walker 1992); 24. Sun River (Greiser et al. 1985); 25. BA Cave (Finley et al. 2005); 26. Licking Bison (Fosha 2001); 27. Yarmony House (Metcalf and Black 1991); 28. Tenderfoot (Steiger 2002); 29. Hutton-Pinkham (Larson et al. 1992); 30. China Wall (Brian Waitkus, personal communication 2008). In Figure 2.19, sites 4–6, 8–10, 13–16, 18, 19, 21–24, 29, and 31 contain Early Plains Archaic components.

At this time, the Early Plains Archaic projectile points are referred to as "early side-notched" (Figure 2.52a, b, d–f), although Husted has isolated and named two specific types, the Pahaska Side-Notched and Blackwater Side-Notched types (Husted and Edgar 2002:102), both local place names along the North Fork of the Shoshone River in the vicinity of Mummy Cave. Side-notched projectile points are not the only styles diagnostic of the Early Plains Archaic period. Large corner-notched points, some with and some without base notches, were found in culture layer 16 at Mummy Cave (Husted and Edgar 2002) and in the Early Plains Archaic levels at the Laddie Creek site with dates of around 7600 to 7000 BP (Figure 2.52b–d). The same style of point appeared also in stream gravels lying between the terminal Paleoindian and Middle Plains Archaic levels at the Medicine Lodge Creek site. Toward the end of the Early Plains Archaic, an even wider range of projectile point styles appears. For example, at culture layer 24 of Mummy Cave (Husted and Edgar 2002), which was dated at about 5400 BP, a number of projectile points were found that out of context could easily fit into the Late Plains Archaic. The same holds true for the Laddie Creek site, Rice Cave (Figure 2.52f), Southsider Cave (Figure 2.52g), and the Sorenson site in Bighorn Canyon (Husted 1969). Similar undated materials were found at the lowest level of the Kobold buffalo jump site (Frison 1970b), but these were below the bison-jumping levels and apparently represent a small camp-site. From this, it is obvious that it is not always possible to look at an Early Plains Archaic projectile point recovered out of context and assign it to the proper time period.

Unlike the preceding Late Paleoindian period, few people have assigned names to these different projectile point styles, partially perhaps because we do not completely understand the stratigraphic relationship of the different styles. A useful statistical distinction between these and several other side-notched styles was developed by Ernie Walker (1992). He showed that several styles can be differentiated on the basis of quantitative data with robust statistical analyses. Although quantitative analysis is not always useful, particularly when styles are differentiated by discrete traits such as flaking patterns, assemblages with similar discrete traits can sometimes be shown to differ and such differences may have cultural meanings. Regardless of the style, the youngest Early Plains Archaic radiocarbon date from Mummy Cave is about 5250 BP.

At Medicine Lodge Creek, a small area containing stratified deposits with Early Plains Archaic (and Late Paleoindian) projectile points is present. Unfortunately, the remainder of the Early Plains Archaic material at the site was recovered from disturbed contexts (Frison and Walker 2007). However, all the Early Plains Archaic projectile point types that appeared at Mummy Cave were also found at Medicine Lodge Creek (Figure 2.53). A corner-notched variety (Figure 2.53t, u) appeared at Medicine Lodge Creek from a level that is undated but stratigraphically should be terminal Early Plains Archaic. Further excavations at Medicine Lodge could reveal intact deposits dating to this time period.

The Laddie Creek site is an open site at an elevation of about 6800 feet (2072 m) in the foothills on the western slope of the Bighorn Mountains. The unusual condition of springs in the area resulted in the slow aggradation of deposits throughout the Early Plains Archaic period (Larson 1992). Radiocarbon dates from the upper two of four levels from this period were 5700 ± 160 BP and 6650 ± 480 BP. The projectile points from the Early Plains Archaic levels show a wide range of variation in form, much like Mummy Cave and Medicine Lodge Creek.

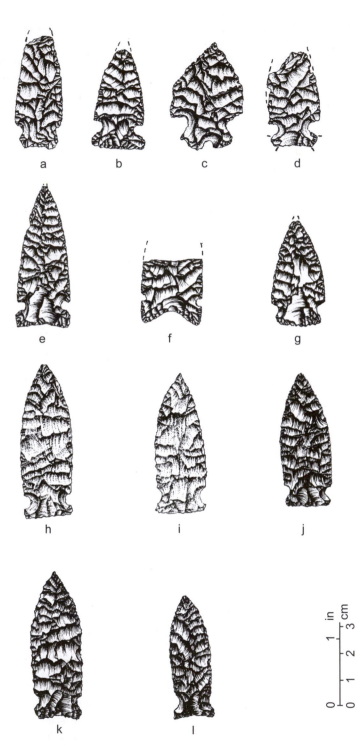

Figure 2.52   Early Plains Archaic points from Wedding of the Waters Cave (a), Laddie Creek site (b–d), Lookingbill site (e), Rice Cave (f), and Southsider Cave (g), all in the foothills on the eastern side of the Bighorn Basin in northern Wyoming, and points from the Hawken bison kill in northeastern Wyoming (h–l).

Figure 2.53 Early Plains Archaic projectile points from the Medicine Lodge Creek site, Area 1.

The Lookingbill site (Frison 1983b; Kornfeld, Larson, Rapson, and Frison 2001) in the southern Absaroka Mountains at an elevation of 8600 feet (2621 m) contains well-stratified levels of late Paleoindian and Early Plains Archaic age as the result of interfingering of colluvial material between cultural levels deposited on low-gradient spring-fed stream deposits. A series of radiocarbon dates from Early Archaic deposits range from 6460 ± 90 BP to 7140 ± 160 BP. Projectile points from the site are virtually all of the classic side-notched variety with ground, straight to slightly concave bases. Several of the points show evidence of resharpening while still in the haft, as the basal width of one of the most completely resharpened points (Figure 2.54k) is the same as a point that has not been resharpened (Figure 2.54j). However, not all Lookingbill Early Archaic points are side notched. A series of convex-based points present a very different basal morphology (Figure 2.54h, i).

Figure 2.54 Projectile point sequence from the Lookingbill site (a–l) and Oxbow projectile points from the Sun River site in west-central Montana (m, n): Early Plains Archaic (h–l), Middle Plains Archaic (f, g, m, n), Late Plains Archaic (d, e), and Late Prehistoric (a–c). (Oxbow points courtesy of Sally T. Greiser and T. Weber Greiser.)

These types are reminiscent of the styles described as the Mount Albion complex on the basis of Hungry Whistler and other sites and originating between 5800 and 5600 BP (Benedict and Olson 1978).

Most rockshelters in the foothill-mountain areas that demonstrate any prehistoric evidence of human habitation contain Early Plains Archaic components. One of the best series of dates, with a range from 7650 ± 200 BP to 5420 ± 160 BP for the period, was recovered from Southsider Cave in the western foothills of the Bighorn Mountains. The site is a deep cave with little or no opportunity for introduction of outside materials, and the cultural levels were separated by levels of sterile roof fall. A reinvestigation of Wedding of the Waters Cave (Frison 1962) at the south end of the Bighorn Basin produced an Early Plains Archaic component with side-notched projectile points (Figure 2.52a).

In the foothills at the north end of the Laramie Range at the lowest level in Maneater Cave and dated at just over 6000 years ago are several slab-lined pits probably used for storage in a pithouse. Associated with these pits are distinctive projectile points (Zeimens and Alkire 2005:134–143) that have also been recovered in mixed contexts and on the surface in that area.

A bison kill containing an extinct variant of bison (*Bison bison occidentalis*) in the Wyoming part of the Black Hills produced the largest known sample of Early Plains Archaic projectile points from a single site component (Figure 2.52h–l). This site, the Hawken site, has two radiocarbon dates of about 6400 years BP. The site was an arroyo trap, but no camp, butchering, or meat processing areas were found (Frison et al. 1976). Another site (Hawken III) was discovered in the same general area. It contained a large sample of butchered bison and had the same general characteristics found at Hawken; the site yielded a radiocarbon date of about 6000 years BP. Recent analysis of carbon isotopes from the Hawken site indicates that while temperatures were warmer, precipitation was greater (Rux et al. 2000) at the time of the occupation.

Side-notched projectile points known as Bitterroot have been known and described from further west in Idaho for some time and apparently represent a mid-Holocene occurrence there (Swanson et al. 1964). A Bitterroot component was recorded at the Myers-Hindman site near Livingston, Montana, in the upper Yellowstone River valley area (Lahren 1976). Relationships further to the east are not yet resolved, but materials from Logan Creek in eastern Nebraska (Kivett 1962) seem to have close relationships both temporally and typologically.

The Oxbow complex with side-notched projectile points is well known on the Northern Plains, especially in northern Montana, Alberta, and Saskatchewan. It appears at about the same time as the later Early Plains Archaic and lasts well into the Middle Plains Archaic period farther south. Sites in southern Saskatchewan have been dated to around 5200 BP at the Oxbow Dam (Nero and McCorquodale 1958) and somewhat later at the Long Creek site (Wettlaufer and Mayer-Oakes 1960). The Sun River site in west-central Montana has a stratified series of Oxbow complex occupation levels dating from about 5700 to 3500 years BP (Greiser et al. 1985; see also Bryant 2007 and Green 2005).

The typical Oxbow projectile point is side-notched with a pronounced basal indentation. Good examples were obtained from the Sun River site (Figure 2.54m, n). Northern Wyoming sites have produced projectile points that fit well in the Oxbow complex and include Mummy Cave at about 5000 BP and the nearby Dead Indian Creek site at about 4500 BP (Frison and Walker 1984). Undated Oxbow materials were found in a stratified cave site in the northern Bighorn Mountains known as Rice Cave. This mixing of Oxbow materials with those of the Middle Plains Archaic in the northern Wyoming area remains unexplained. The Sun River dates suggest a long temporal overlap of Oxbow and Middle Plains Archaic complexes. However, Morlan's (1994) careful reanalysis of dates from the Herder site, as well as all radiocarbon dates in Saskatchewan, favors pre-5000 BP as the correct time range of the Oxbow Complex.

Reeves (1978) has named the Mummy Cave phase to accommodate the earliest known components at Head-Smashed-In Buffalo Jump in Alberta, based apparently on projectile point similarities. The Head-Smashed-In Buffalo Jump, a World Heritage site, is an especially important site for the Northern Plains and has produced a long sequence of radiocarbon dates that document continuous bison jumping beginning in Early Archaic times (Brink 2008).

Although initially thought to represent a cultural hiatus, the extant database reveals much diversity within the time ascribed to the Early Plains Archaic. As more data are found it is likely that we will gain much insight into the occupation of the mountains and plains at this time. Future research will undoubtedly address this variability and answer many of the questions we have today.

THE MIDDLE PLAINS ARCHAIC OR MCKEAN PERIOD

Ever since the investigation of McKean and several nearby Black Hills sites in the early 1950s (Mulloy 1954b; Wheeler 1996) and the definition of the McKean complex, the terms McKean and Early Middle period have been synonymous. After the restructuring of Northwestern Plains chronology and the introduction of the Archaic concept, the term Middle Plains Archaic period replaced Early Middle period, but McKean continued to refer to this time frame (Frison 1978). With the appearance of the Middle Plains Archaic there are more sites than in the preceding period (Figure 2.55) and apparently an increased emphasis on plant foods. Grinding stones (manos and grinding slabs) that appeared in terminal Paleoindian and increased during Early Plains times now become even more common (Figure 2.56).

The term McKean has been the subject of much controversy, largely because of the wide variance in projectile point types found in the various site assemblages regarded as part of the McKean complex. The McKean site in northeast Wyoming produced a large assemblage of projectile points of different styles, which Mulloy (1954b) interpreted as representing a range of variation in a single point type. Another investigator who worked in the same area (Wheeler 1996) and excavated in a number of sites of the McKean complex named separate projectile point types rather than regarding the points as variations of a single type. However, Wheeler excavated in sites that produced only one of the several point styles recognized at the McKean site. Several models have been proposed to resolve this problem: 1) some investigators have suggested that the different variants in a single site might represent different bands coming together for special occasions, 2) both functional differences and differences in raw materials have been suggested as causes for the variants, and 3) variability in the projectile points might be due to different occupations of the same site that represent slight temporal differences, which we are as yet unable to detect in the stratigraphic record. Recent reinvestigations at the McKean site, as well as data from other sites, appear to be supporting the third model.

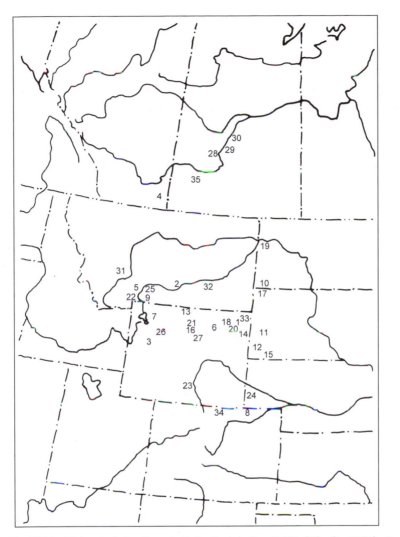

Figure 2.55 Middle Plains Archaic sites: 1. Belle Rockshelter 48CK4 (Wheeler 1996); 2. Billings Bison Trap (Mulloy 1958); 3. Birdshead Cave 48FR54 (Bliss 1950); 4. Cactus Flower (Brumley 1975); 5. Carbella 24PA302 (Arthur 1966); 6. Cordero Mine 48CA75 (Reher et al. 1985); 7. Dead Indian 48PA551 (Frison and Walker 1984); 8. Dipper Gap 5GL101 (Metcalf 1973); 9. Eagle Creek 24PA301 (Arthur 1966); 10. Fisher 32BO207, Red Fox 32BO213 (Syms 1969); 11. Gant 39ME9 (Gant and Hurt 1965); 12. George Hey 39FA302 (Tratebas and Vagstad 1979); 13. Granite Creek Rockshelter 48BH330 (Frison and Wilson 1975); 14. Hawken II 48CK303 (unpublished); 15. Kolterman 39FA68 (Wheeler 1985); 16. Leigh Cave 48WA304 (Frison and Huseas 1968); 17. Lightning Spring 39HN204 (Keyser and Davis 1984); 18. McKean 48CK7 (Mulloy 1954b); 19. Mondrian Tree (Keyser and Davis 1985); 20. Mule Creek 48CK204 (Wheeler 1996); 21. Paint Rock V 48BH349 (Frison and Wilson 1975); 22. Rigler Bluffs 24PA401 (Arthur 1966); 23. Scoggin 48CR304 (Lobdell 1973); 24. Signal Butte (Strong 1935); 25. Sphinx 24PA508 (Lahren 1971); 26. Wedding of the Waters Cave 48HO301 (Frison 1962); 27. 48JO303 (Grey 2004; Haynes et al. 1966); 28. Sjovold (Dyck and Morlan 1995); 29. Graham (Walker 1984); 30. Redtail, Thundercloud, Cutarm, and Meewasin (Ramsay 1993; Webster 1999, 2004); 31. Quinn Creek (Rennie and Hughes 1998); 32. Dodge (Davis 1976); 33. Red Canyon Rockshelter (Tratebas 1998); 34. Phoebe Rockshetler, Packrat Rockshelter, Spring Gulch, and Kinney Spring (Morris et al. 1985); 35. Gray site (Millar et al. 1972). In Figure 2.19 all sites except Agate Basin, Allen, Carter/Kerr-McGee, and Bugas-Holding have at least one component of Middle Plains Archaic age.

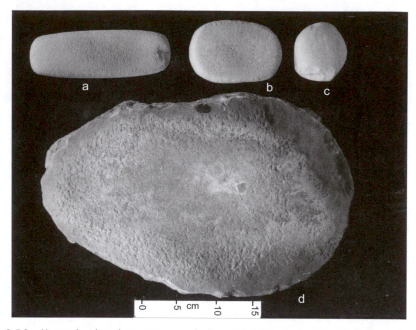

Figure 2.56   Manos (a–c) and a metate or grinding slab (d) typical of the Plains Archaic periods.

The projectile points in question include the true McKean lanceolate type with indented base and convex blade edges that are slightly narrower at the base than toward the middle (Figures 2.47d and 2.57a). A stemmed form with sloping shoulders and a straight stem has been called Duncan (Figure 2.57b), and a form with distinct shoulders and a slightly expanding stem (Figure 2.57c) has been named Hanna by Wheeler (1954a). Wheeler (1985) named other point types, including Kolterman, Harney, Landers, Lewis, Thompson, and Hilton and observed at least six other unnamed styles for the Middle Plains Archaic period. Even the lanceolate form may vary considerably. One persistent form (in terms of numbers) is a

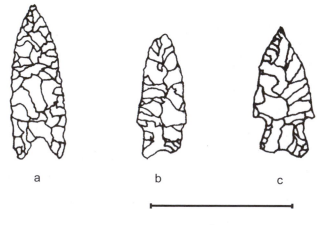

5 cm

Figure 2.57   McKean (a), Duncan (b), and Hanna (c) projectile points from the McKean type site.

relatively large heart-shaped variety that could be a tool type and not a projectile point. Unlike certain Late Paleoindian projectile points that are often similar in outline form to the lanceolate and stemmed Middle Archaic points, the heart-shaped points rarely evidence grinding of stems or blade edges and, in addition, demonstrate a less careful manufacture technology.

Another variant point style found in McKean sites is wide, very thin, with deep side notches placed well forward, and with either straight, slightly concave, or deeply indented bases. Sometimes the addition of a deep, narrow basal notch is seen (Figure 2.58c–f). These points were found at the Signal Butte site in western Nebraska, where they were given the type name of Mallory (Forbis et al. 1965). This type along with true McKean lanceolates (Figure 2.58a, b) occurred in a temporally restricted bison trap site situation in central Wyoming, leaving no doubt of their co-occurrence (Lobdell 1973).

McKean and Other Sites

The McKean site is located in northeast Wyoming and was one of several sites investigated ahead of construction of the Keyhole Dam on the Belle Fourche River. The early investigations at the McKean site were done by Mulloy (1954b) while several other sites nearby were investigated by Wheeler (1996). These include Belle Rockshelter and Mule Creek Rockshelter along the Belle Fourche River in Wyoming and the Kolterman site at the Angostura Reservoir along the Cheyenne River in western South Dakota. All of these sites are located at the western and southern edge of the Black Hills.

From 1983 to 1986, a reinvestigation of the McKean site and the other sites in the Keyhole Reservoir area was supported by the Bureau of Reclamation. A long series of dry years lowered the level of Keyhole Reservoir which, along with rapidly fluctuating reservoir levels, was beginning to destroy parts of the sites. The most significant results clarified the site stratigraphy. Instead of two cultural levels as defined by Mulloy (1954b), the geologic and geomorphic studies showed that these geomorphic units represent two soil horizons (Albanese 1985; Reider 1985) and that in different parts of the site there can be up to nine separate soils. However, these nine soils are frequently superimposed, and there is no necessary consistency from one area of the site to another as to where the breaks in the superposition occur. There are two implications of this interpretation. One, Mulloy's levels and consequently assemblages represent multiple occupations of the site over long time spans, thus the co-occurrence of chronologically or culturally distinct artifacts is not surprising (that is, McKean Lanceolate, Duncan, and Hanna points). To define the complex solely on the basis of the McKean site data is problematic. Two, because the breaks in the superimposed soils are not consistent throughout the site, an artifact recovered from the "upper" soil in one part of the site may not be temporally related to a specimen recovered in the "upper" soil in another part of the site. In other words, the "upper" and "lower" levels defined by Mulloy do not have consistent dates in all areas of the site. The 1980s investigation also discovered a Middle Archaic pithouse, similar to those of the Early Plains Archaic, in a trench profile. These data along with a regional synthesis of the Middle Plains Archaic (see Kornfeld and Todd 1985) and a more recent synthesis of the Northern Plains data (Ramsay 1993) provide a better understanding of the time period and indicate directions for future research.

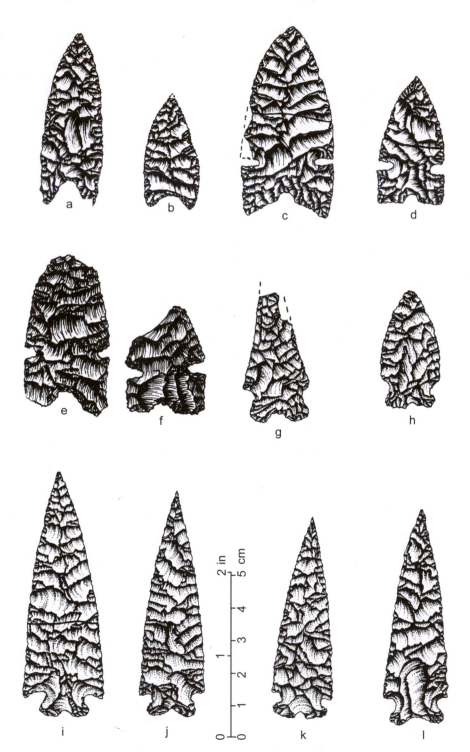

Figure 2.58 McKean (a, b) and Mallory points (c–f) from the Scoggin site in Wyoming. Yonkee points from the Kobold site (i) in southern Montana, the Powder River site (g, h, j, k), and the Mavrakis-Bentzen-Roberts site (l), the latter two sites in northeast Wyoming.

Mulloy was unable to obtain a radiocarbon date on the McKean component at the site, but the 1983 excavations yielded a date of about 4600 years BP on charcoal from a continuation of one of Mulloy's old trenches that dates the lower portions of the McKean component (Kornfeld et al. 1995). Wheeler had obtained radiocarbon dates earlier of about 4200 and 3600 years BP on McKean components at the Kolterman site. The earliest known dates for the McKean complex are those from the Bighorn Mountain area. Husted (1969) reported a date of 4900 years BP on a McKean component from the Sorenson site in southern Montana along the Bighorn River. A date of about 4700 years BP was obtained from Granite Creek Rockshelter (Figure 2.59) in Shell Canyon (Frison and Wilson 1975) not far from the Sorenson site but in the higher elevations of the Bighorn Mountains. The charcoal used in dating at Granite Creek was recovered from a context in good association with lanceolate McKean projectile points and at least two other of Wheeler's types.

The Dead Indian Creek site located in the Sunlight Basin of northern Wyoming, a small mountain basin adjacent to the west side of the Bighorn Basin (Frison and Walker 1984), yielded three radiocarbon dates of 4400, 4200, and 3800 BP. It was a winter camp, based on the age of deer mandibles (Simpson 1984), reflecting extensive use of mule deer and lesser use of mountain sheep. All the known McKean projectile point variants were present (Figure 2.60). A pithouse was also partially uncovered during excavations (Figure 2.61).

Mummy Cave, located along the North Fork of the Shoshone River in the Absaroka Mountains in northwest Wyoming, yielded a radiocarbon date of about 4400 BP on McKean artifacts (Wedel et al. 1968). Two localities at the Medicine Lodge Creek site contained stratified units with McKean and other as yet poorly

Figure 2.59   Granite Creek Rockshelter in the northern Bighorn Mountains.

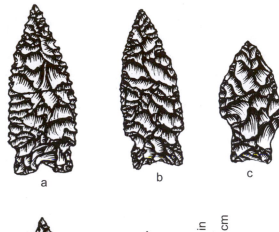
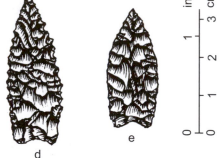

Figure 2.60   Projectile points from the Dead Indian Creek site in the Absaroka Mountains in northwest Wyoming.

Figure 2.61   Profile through a pithouse at the Dead Indian Creek site.

known Middle Plains Archaic diagnostics (Figure 2.62). Stream cobbles one meter thick mark the Middle Plains Archaic levels. A Middle Archaic date of just over 4000 BP was obtained from an in situ cultural level just above the cobbles in direct

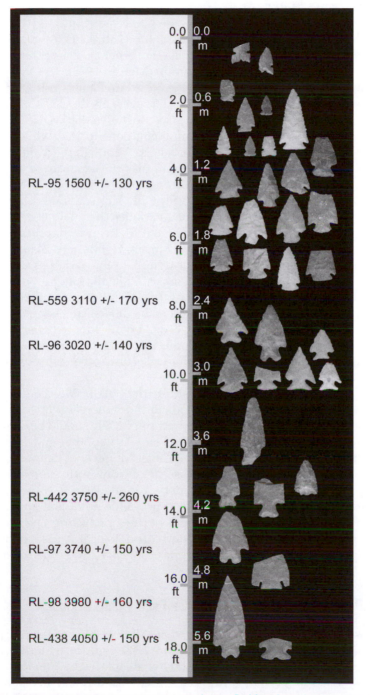

Figure 2.62   Middle Plains Archaic (bottom) through Late Prehistoric projectile points (top) from the Medicine Lodge Creek site, arranged by depth with associated radiocarbon ages indicated.

association with Duncan-type projectile points, and McKean lanceolate projectile points were found in the cobbles immediately below.

A number of sites with McKean and other Middle Plains Archaic components excavated in Wyoming, Nebraska, and Montana date to between 4400 and 3100 BP. Sites with Middle Archaic deposits include Paint Rock V, Leigh Cave, 48JO303, Southsider Cave in Wyoming, the Gant site (Gant and Hurt 1965) in western South Dakota, the Myers-Hindman site (Lahren 1976) in southwestern Montana, Signal Butte in western Nebraska (Forbis et al. 1965; Strong 1935), and the Dipper Gap site in northeastern Colorado (Metcalf 1973).

A recent synthesis of McKean sites in the Northern Plains finds a similar range of dates for the complex (Ramsay 1993). However, on the basis of Redtail and other sites in southern Canada Ramsay also concludes that McKean Lanceolate points predominate in earlier levels in multicomponent sites, while the Duncan and Hanna varieties predominate in later levels. Although the 1980s excavations at the McKean site provided inadequate samples to demonstrate a robust statistical distribution of projectile points through the sediment, the same pattern was suggested in the final site monograph, with McKean Lanceolates predominating early and followed by the stemmed varieties (Kornfeld et al. 1995). Thus, the data continue to support the notion of the McKean technocomplex, that is, the co-occurrence of McKean Lanceolate, Duncan, Hanna, and Mallory projectile points, but with a caveat that the former dominate the earlier assemblages and perhaps occur earlier in the McKean sequence, while the latter gradually replace them toward the end of the McKean period. While these recent studies answer some of the questions of co-occurrence and make others irrelevant, the functional question remains unresolved. In other words, the question whether the replacement of McKean Lanceolate projectile points by the Duncan and Hanna varieties is due to functional differences in the point styles or to other causes remains to be answered.

McKean projectile point variants constitute the bulk of Middle Plains Archaic diagnostics, but there are others. In the Medicine Lodge Creek sequence are corner-notched specimens (Figure 2.53t, u) that stratigraphically should be on the borderline between Early and Middle Plains Archaic. At the other end of the Middle Plains Archaic, directly under Pelican Lake levels of the Late Plains Archaic were projectile points that are vaguely reminiscent of Yonkee (to be discussed later) with large corner notches, sharp shoulders, rounded basal corners, and base indentations (Figure 2.62, 14–16 ft. level). A projectile point that appeared in the Middle Plains Archaic levels demonstrates notches projecting upward from the base (Figure 2.62, 16 ft. level). Its cultural and chronological status is poorly known at present, although similar specimens appear occasionally as surface finds.

THE LATE PLAINS ARCHAIC OR LATE MIDDLE PREHISTORIC PERIOD

The increase in sites of the Late Plains Archaic allows only a small representative sample of site locations to be presented (Figure 2.63). Cultural materials, especially the projectile points of the McKean complex, were replaced by later manifestations around 3000 years BP on the Northwestern Plains and Rocky Mountains. There are two of these; one is a widespread cultural horizon over both the Northwestern and Northern Plains known as Pelican Lake and identified by changes in projectile

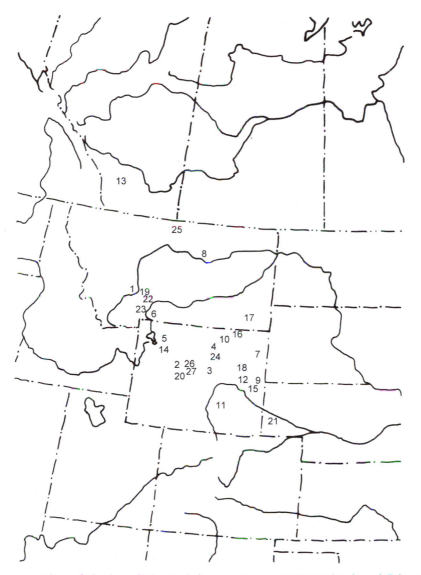

Figure 2.63 Sites of the Late Plains Archaic: 1. Antonson 24GA660 (Davis and Zeier 1978); 2. Birdshead Cave 48FR54 (Bliss 1950); 3. Cedar Gap 48NA83 (unpublished); 4. Daugherty Cave 48WA302 (Frison 1968a); 5. Dead Indian II 48PA551 (Frison and Walker 1984); 6. Eagle Creek 24PA301 (Arthur 1966); 7. Fulton 48WE302 (Niven 1997); 8. Keaster 24PH401 (Davis and Stallcop 1965); 9. Lance Creek 48NO204 (Haynes 1968); 10. Mavrakis-Bentzen-Roberts 48SH311 (Bentzen 1962b); 11. Muddy Creek 48CR324 (Reher 1978); 12. North Platte River 48PL23, 48PL24 (Mulloy 1965a); 13. Old Women's Jump (Forbis 1962); 14. Pagoda Creek 48PA853 (Eakin 1989); 15. Patten Creek 48PL68 (Keller 1971); 16. Powder River 48SH312 (Frison 1968c); 17. Powers-Yonkee 24PR5 (Bentzen 1962a); 18. Ruby 48CA302 (Frison 1971a); 19. Schmitt 48BW559 (Davis 1982); 20. Shoshone Basin 48FR5, 48FR33, 48FR34 (Mulloy 1954a); 21. Signal Butte (Strong 1935); 22. Small Emigrant Jump 24PA309 (Arthur 1962); 23. Sphinx 24PA508 (Lahren 1971); 24. Spring Creek Cave 48WA1 (Frison 1965); 25. Wahkpa Chu'gn 24HL101 (Davis and Stallcop 1966); 26. Wedding of the Waters Cave 48HO301 (Frison 1962); 27. Wind River Canyon Burial 48HO10 (Frison and Van Norman 1985). In Figure 2.19 only the Carter/Kerr-McGee, Allen, and Bugas-Holding sites have no Late Plains Archaic age components.

point types. Pelican Lake points are the oldest of several styles characterized by wide, open corner notches that form sharp points or barbs as they intersect blade edges and bases. Both blade edges and bases may be slightly convex, straight, or very slightly concave. The other is known as Yonkee and has a less widespread occurrence; it is best known from the Powder River Basin area of Montana and Wyoming.

The name Pelican Lake comes from the designation given the lower levels of the Mortlach site in south-central Saskatchewan (Wettlaufer 1955). Similar material was described from a component in the Long Creek site in extreme southeastern Saskatchewan (Wettlaufer and Mayer-Oakes 1960). Head-Smashed-In Buffalo Jump (Reeves 1978) produced a number of radiocarbon-dated Pelican Lake levels. Two Pelican Lake levels were dated at about 3100 and 3000 BP, respectively, at Medicine Lodge Creek and both levels contained projectile points (Figure 2.62, 8 ft. and 10 ft. level). Many variations of relatively large corner-notched dart points other than those found at Pelican Lake persist on the Northwestern Plains and Rocky Mountains until around AD 500, as is demonstrated in the sequence at the Medicine Lodge Creek site (Figure 2.62, 8 ft. and 10 ft. level).

The Laddie Creek site contains an undated level stratigraphically above the Early Plains Archaic levels that has a series of Pelican Lake projectile points associated with stone tools, faunal remains, and a buried stone circle. Further analysis of these materials will provide much more in-depth information about the Late Plains Archaic occupations of the foothills of the Bighorn Mountains.

In the late 1950s, a Pelican Lake cremation burial (Frison and Van Norman 1985) was excavated in the Wind River Canyon at the south end of the Bighorn Basin in Wyoming. A radiocarbon date on the burial was over 3500 years BP, which seems too early. However, the charcoal came from a juniper log at least 15 cm in diameter. The log could have been well over 100 years old when the tree died, and could easily have been dead longer than that before it was burned, so that the date, while not in error, is not actually dating the Pelican Lake burial.

A number of communal bison kills in the Powder River Basin in Montana and Wyoming were at one time thought to have begun early in the Middle Plains Archaic period and lasted until well into the Late Plains Archaic period. Both the kill sites and the associated projectile points are known as Yonkee from the site and the landowner located in southeast Montana close to the Powder River. First investigated in 1961 by the Sheridan Chapter of the Wyoming Archaeological Society, a charcoal sample reported as coming from the site produced a radiocarbon date of over 4400 years BP (Bentzen 1962a). In 1962, the same group investigated a bison kill site in northeast Wyoming on a tributary of Powder River (the Mavrakis-Bentzen-Roberts site) that produced projectile points identical to those from the Yonkee site, and a radiocarbon date of 2600 years BP was obtained (Bentzen 1962b). These dates were accepted at that time as representing the probable time span for Yonkee bison kill sites.

Later excavations at another Yonkee bison kill site, the Powder River site, produced charcoal with a radiocarbon date of 2900 years BP (Frison 1968c), and a reinvestigation of the Mavrakis-Bentzen-Roberts site in 1971 produced a radiocarbon date between 2500 and 2400 years BP, suggesting that the earlier date from that site was probably correct. These new data began to cast some doubt on the radiocarbon date of 4400 years BP from the Yonkee site. The problem was solved by careful geoarchaeological reinvestigation that showed the 4400 year old date was not associated with the Yonkee complex bison bone bed (Roll et al. 1992). The re-reinvestigation also produced a series of radiocarbon dates on both bone and charcoal that range from about 3100 to nearly 2300 years BP (Roll et al. 1992).

Radiocarbon dates of just over 2700 years BP from Site 48CA1391, a Yonkee site along the Belle Fourche River in Wyoming, further strengthens the Late Plains Archaic placement. Instead of bison, the faunal assemblage of the site was dominated by pronghorn, although there was no evidence to suggest a large communal kill. Instead, the site assemblage suggested a more hunting and gathering orientation. It may also be a seasonal representation of groups that were communal bison hunters at another time of the year (McKibbin et al. 1988).

The communal bison kills associated with Yonkee apparently represent different variations of arroyo traps. At the Mavrakis-Bentzen-Roberts site, posts and post holes suggest an addition to a natural landform. Bison jumping was also practiced by Yonkee groups, according to data from the Kobold Buffalo Jump in southeast Montana (Frison 1970b). A large number of Yonkee projectile points (see, for example, Figure 2.58i) were recovered at that site in the lowest bison bone bed at the foot of a perpendicular bluff that had been used for at least 3000 years during Late Plains Archaic and Late Prehistoric times to jump bison. No radiocarbon dates were obtained from the Yonkee component.

Recent excavations at the Kaplan-Hoover site in Fort Collins, Colorado, produced a bison bone bed with a diverse projectile point assemblage. While some specimens resemble the Yonkee variety (Todd et al. 2001), others appear more similar to Pelican Lake. The average date of 2724 ± 35 BP fits comfortably in the Yonkee age range. Although the site has experienced some fluvial transport of the bone that may have affected spatial patterns of site use, the investigators argue that only the top layers of bone have been affected by these geological processes. On the basis of the location of the bone bed in an arroyo and intense taphonomic analysis, the investigators argue that Kaplan-Hoover is an arroyo trap. As with similar arroyo traps discussed later in this volume, it is hard to imagine such a locality not affected by fluvial processes.

Later in time, shortly after AD 1, a distinctive projectile point appears on the Northwestern Plains that is diagnostic of what Wettlaufer (1955) named the Besant culture; the name is derived from the Mortlach site in south-central Saskatchewan. Besant on the Northwestern Plains represents an extremely sophisticated bison hunting manifestation. Radiocarbon dates of just before 1700 and just after 1800 years BP are known from bison corrals, built of logs and posts set in deep post holes, at the Ruby site (Frison 1971a) and Muddy Creek sites (Hughes 1981:30–36). Evidence of extensive religious activity is present at the former site. Large numbers of side-notched, dart-type projectile points from each site (Figure 2.64), plus a few corner-notched points, are apparently diagnostic of Besant on the Northwestern Plains. Woodland ceramics are also found occasionally in Besant sites in the area (Miller and Waitkus 1989).

A number of radiocarbon-dated cave and rockshelter sites suggest a relatively intense occupation in the Bighorn Mountain and Basin areas from about AD 200 to AD 500. Spring Creek Cave (Figure 2.65) on the western slopes of the Bighorn Mountains (Frison 1965) provided a large collection of perishable material of the Late Plains Archaic period. This included coiled basketry fragments, extensive debris from woodworking, bark cordage, sinew, hide, feathers, shell, and many other items, along with corner-notched projectile points. Atlatl fragments

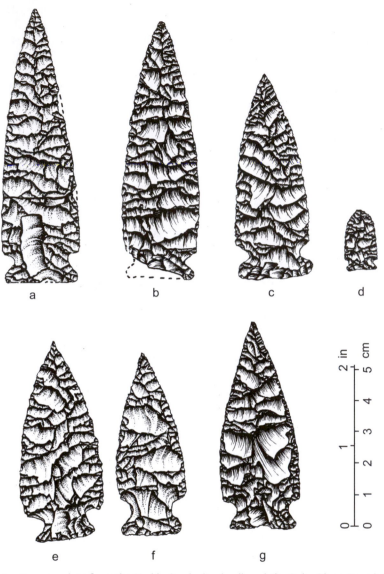

Figure 2.64   Besant points from the Muddy Creek site (a–d) and the Ruby Bison Pound (e–g).

(Figure 2.66e, f) and a nearly complete atlatl (Figure 2.66g) were recovered, along with atlatl weights, main shaft fragments (Figure 2.66d), and a number of broken and complete wooden foreshafts. One corner-notched projectile point was mounted with sinew and pitch on a foreshaft (Figure 2.66a) and a number of broken specimens (Figure 2.66b) and partially mounted specimens were recovered (Frison 1965).

Another large assemblage of nearly identical perishable material was recovered from Daugherty Cave located in the same general vicinity as Spring Creek Cave (Frison 1968a), but this site was not radiocarbon dated. Similar dated material was recovered, however, from Wedding of the Waters Cave (Frison 1962) and the cultural materials included several sharpened wooden foreshafts (Figure 2.66c).

Figure 2.65 Spring Creek Cave in the Bighorn Mountains.

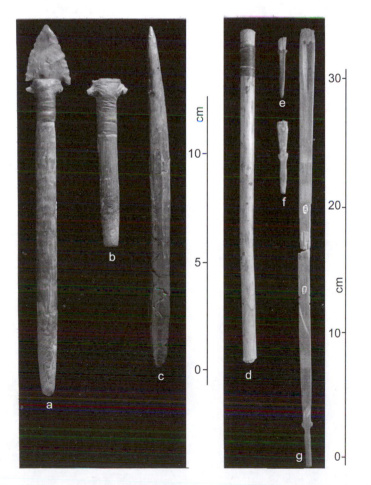

Figure 2.66 Hafted points (a, b), main shaft fragment (d), and atlatl fragments (e–g) from Spring Creek Cave. Sharpened wooden point from Wedding of the Waters Cave (c).

Occupation V at Bottleneck Cave in Bighorn Canyon in Wyoming (Husted 1969) apparently dates corner-notched projectile points. Analysis of coiled basketry (Figure 2.67) found in several of the rock shelters demonstrates a close similarity to Great Basin basketry of the same age. At least two fragments from different caves are identical to Fremont style parching trays. The number of basketry specimens from different rockshelter sites is considered to be a significant economic indicator of a hunting and gathering subsistence strategy more reminiscent of the Great Basin than of the Plains (Frison, Adovasio, and Carlisle 1986).

Other perishable items found in these dry rockshelters are now believed to be digging sticks. Tubers such as sego lily and wild onion and root crops such as biscuit root and bitterroot abound in the area, and a simple digging stick will rapidly produce enough for a meal during the right season. The wear patterns on wooden (Figure 2.68b–d) and antler specimens (Figure 2.68a) can be reproduced experimentally by digging sego lily bulbs. The point is driven into the ground alongside the stem of the plant with a light hammer stone; pulling back quickly on the top of the stake using the ground surface as a fulcrum brings the roots or tubers to the surface.

The surge of archaeological activity in the last two decades resulting from energy-extraction projects on federal land has substantially increased the number of radiocarbon dates, but mainly from areas directly affected. The present trend in radiocarbon dates for Wyoming indicates a significant increase toward the end of the Late Plains Archaic (Figure 2.17), but these data cannot be accepted as accurately reflecting the number of prehistoric occupations present since energy resources are not equally distributed. However, they do suggest quite strongly that something ecologically significant was happening toward the end of the period.

The human occupations of the Late Plains Archaic period demonstrate noticeable differences in subsistence strategies both diachronically and synchronically over short distances. Mulloy (1954a:59) interpreted the evidence from the Shoshone

Figure 2.67   Coiled basket from a rockshelter in the Bighorn Mountains.

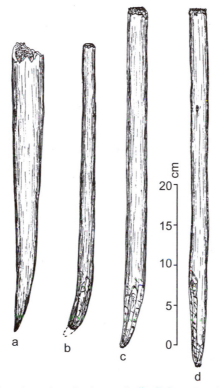

Figure 2.68 Elk antler (a) and wooden digging tools (b–d) from Daugherty Cave.

Basin as suggesting "small groups of miserable, probably chronically starving nomads with a way of life more similar to that of such Great Basin peoples as the Gosiute than to anything else in the region." However, a short distance away from the Shoshone Basin sites in any direction, the ecological situation changes dramatically for the better in terms of human subsistence. It is more likely that groups stopped temporarily at the Shoshone Basin sites in their yearly round of subsistence activities. While Pelican Lake, Yonkee, and Besant appear to have strong northern affiliations, other Late Plains Archaic materials appear to have strong roots in the Great Basin. We are only now beginning to have sufficient data and the interpretive potential to resolve these kinds of problems.

THE LATE PREHISTORIC PERIOD

As already mentioned, a significant part of the Northwestern Plains and Rocky Mountains has been affected by the accelerated energy extraction activities that began in the early 1970s. Much of the area is federal land and the subsurface minerals of much of the private land are federally owned. Federal cultural resource management developed rapidly, requiring massive archaeological surveys and subsequent mitigation of areas affected by extraction of energy resources. With the concomitant increase in funding, radiocarbon dates demonstrated a dramatic increase. These dates cannot be claimed as representing a true sample of all prehistoric occupations because the location of energy resources is determined by geologic factors that did not necessarily coincide with the settlement and subsistence patterns of aboriginal populations. Neither does this number of radiocarbon dates make allowance for the loss through natural conditions of erosion to deposits of earlier cultural components, so that the older the cultural complex, the less chance there is of finding datable evidence.

Acknowledging these discrepancies, it is nevertheless evident that beginning toward the end of the Late Plains Archaic the number of radiocarbon dates begins to increase rapidly, reaching a peak in the Late Prehistoric period at about 1200 to 1000 years BP and then falling off rapidly (see Figure 2.17). It would appear that something was happening ecologically in the region at this time. The intermontane basins demonstrate increased populations: movements to the area by Avonlea groups with their large bison kills suggest a several-hundred-year period of unusually good conditions for both humans and animals. Given the increase in the number of sites with Late Prehistoric period components, only a small sample of sites, restricted to the most relevant locations, is shown in Figure 2.69.

The Late Prehistoric period is rather arbitrarily assigned a beginning date of around AD 500. It is recognized in the archaeological record by a change in projectile point types and sizes that most investigators think is the result of the introduction of the bow and arrow. Projectile points early in the period are both side notched and corner notched, and later on base notching is added to the side notches. Apparently some of the corner-notched dart points were simply reduced in size for use with the bow.

The earliest of the late side-notched projectile points seem to have appeared first on the Northern Plains and apparently overlapped with Besant. These groups were given the name of Avonlea from a site in Saskatchewan (Kehoe and McCorquodale 1961). They are characterized by true side notches placed close to the base, although in assemblages on the Northwestern Plains and Rocky Mountains there is considerable variation in the placement of the notches (Figure 2.70). The cultural relationships between Avonlea in the north and similar projectile point assemblages in the region are unclear. A bison kill apparently related to Avonlea is located on the Green River in western Wyoming (Frison 1973b). Other Avonlea-related sites are widely scattered but distinctive. They are predicatively located on and around buttes (Figure 2.71), locations that suggest either defensive activity or a desire to be able to see great distances or both. Their sites produce large, slab-lined food preparation pits (Figure 2.72). Some of the sites produce ceramics thought to have possible relationships to Woodland.

A major edited publication explores the various Plains-wide aspects of Avonlea (see Davis 1988). The "pine breaks" area of southeast Montana and northeast Wyoming was proposed as a distinctive ecological area (Fredlund 1981). Three of the larger sites known in the area—Benson's Butte in southeast Montana (Fredlund 1979), Beehive Butte (Frison 1988a) (Figure 2.71), and Shiprock (unpublished) in northern Wyoming—were used to typify the kind of occupation manifest in this ecosystem by the Avonlea-like groups. Shiprock is just to the east of the Medicine Lodge Creek site (Figure 2.40). The first two of these sites are of importance because they are stratified with earlier components underlying the Avonlea occupations. Several burned juniper logs remained from a structure in the Avonlea component at the Beehive. A small rockshelter in the northern Bighorn Mountains yielded a large number of broken arrow shafts and projectile points, some retaining partial sinew bindings but none hafted (Greer 1978); and in nearby Bighorn Canyon, a rockshelter, the Mangus site, produced Avonlea points and a coiled basketry mat or tray along with several other perishable items (Husted 1969:35–40).

Two human burials from the Powder River Basin in Wyoming produced large numbers of projectile points that are unmistakably of Avonlea type (Galloway 1962, 1968). Avonlea weaponry along with a number of ground and flaked stone tools, bone tools, bone and shell decorative items, fire pit features, and site locations on and around buttes make Avonlea sites stand out from those of any other time period or cultural group. Radiocarbon dates from Avonlea sites produce the peak observed in radiocarbon dates during the Late Prehistoric period in Wyoming.

Sites that produce the small corner-notched projectile points have a wide distribution throughout the Northwestern Plains and Rocky Mountains. Long, narrow projectile points with sharp barbs, serrated edges, and deep corner notches were recovered in Mummy Cave with dates between AD 700 and AD 800, and they were very likely associated with the Shoshonean occupation of the mountainous areas of the region. By AD 1100, the side-notched varieties had replaced the earlier type.

Small corner-notched projectile points (Figure 2.70) are found widespread in sites throughout the area with dates that coincide with Avonlea. However, they can easily be separated out from the Avonlea sites because they lack the abundance of debitage, weaponry, tools, decorative items, and faunal materials and suggest a much more Archaic hunting and gathering subsistence with numerous grinding stones and food preparation pits. On the other hand, bison kill sites in the Laramie Basin in southern Wyoming and in northern Colorado have produced large numbers of the small, corner-notched projectile points (Bupp 1981). Many archaeologists working in southwestern Wyoming note the existence of "Rose Spring" projectile points, after the site in the Owens Valley in California (Lanning 1963). While the use of this type implies some sort of direct cultural relationship, the presence of the projectile points in the Wyoming Basin, in particular, emphasizes the connections between this area and the Great Basin.

Several hundred years of bison jumping between about AD 1500 and AD 1800 are recorded at the Vore site (Reher and Frison 1980) in the Wyoming Black Hills area. As many as 22 components were found, each containing side-notched varieties of projectile points. The differences in appearance and quality of workmanship of projectile points cannot be attributed entirely to changes through time as much as to the use of different raw materials.

The side-notched and base-notched (tri-notched) projectile point (Figure 2.62, 0–2 ft. level) was apparently the favorite by Protohistoric times. They appear almost as a pan-Northwestern Plains and Rocky Mountain phenomenon and were used by a number of known tribes such as the Crow and Shoshone. Whether the base notch has functional value has been argued; certainly it does have some value if the nock in a foreshaft is constructed so that a central ridge is left to engage with the base notch. This, combined with a light sinew binding, aids in preventing movement of the point on impact.

Tri-notched projectile points have been recovered at numerous Northwestern Plains and Rocky Mountain localities, including the Bugas-Holding site in the Sunlight Basin of northwestern Wyoming. The site, located in the former floodplain of Sunlight Creek, is exquisitely preserved by gentle over-bank deposits from annual flood events. In addition to the tri-notched points, the investigations at Bugas-Holding recovered a rich assemblage of bone and stone tools, ornaments,

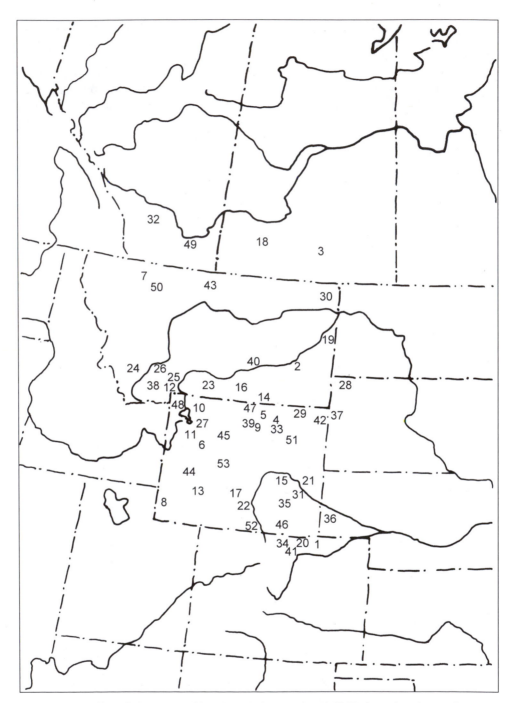

Figure 2.69 Sites of the Late Prehistoric Period: 1. Agate Bluff (Irwin and Irwin 1957); 2. Ash Coulee 24PE118 (Mulloy 1953); 3. Avonlea (Kehoe and McCorquodale 1961); 4. Big Goose 48SH313 (Frison et al. 1978); 5. Bighorn Medicine Wheel 48 BH302 (Grey 1963a); 6. Birdshead Cave 48FR54 (Bliss 1950); 7. Boarding School Bison Drive 24GL302 (Kehoe 1967); 8. Bridger Antelope Trap 48UT1 (Frison 1987); 9. Daugherty Cave 48WA302 (Frison 1968a); 10. Dead Indian III 48PA551 and Bugas-Holding (Frison and Walker 1984; Rapson 1990); 11. Dubois Animal Traps 48FR307, 48FR309 (Frison et al. 1990); 12. Eagle Creek 24PA301 (Arthur 1966); 13. Eden-Farson 48SW304 (Frison

Figure 2.70 Avonlea points from the Beehive Butte site (a–g, j) and from the Shiprock site (h–i).

1971b); 14. Foss-Thomas (Fry 1971); 15. Glenrock Buffalo Jump 48CO304 (Frison 1970a); 16. Grapevine Buffalo Jumps (Medicine Crow 1962); 17. Green Mountain Conical Lodge (unpublished); 18. Gull Lake (Kehoe 1973); 19. Hagen 24DW2 (Mulloy 1942); 20. Happy Hollow 5WL101 (Steege 1967); 21. Irvine 48CO302 (Duguid 1968); 22. John Gale 48CR303 (Brox and Miller 1974); 23. Keogh Buffalo Jump 24ST401 (Conner 1962a); 24. LaMarche Animal Trap 24BE1011 (Keyser 1974); 25. Large Emigrant Jump 24PA308 (Arthur 1962); 26. Logan Buffalo Jump (Malouf 1962); 27. Logan Mountain Lodges 48PA57 (Frison 1991); 28. Ludlow Cave (Over 1936); 29. Missouri Buttes Antelope Trap 48CK49 (unpublished); 30. Nollmeyer 24RL1225 (Johnson et al. 1990); 31. North Platte 48PL29 (Mulloy and Steege 1967); 32. Old Women's Jump (Forbis 1962); 33. Piney Creek 48JO311, 48JO312 (Frison 1967b); 34. Robert's Buffalo Jump 5LR100 (Witkind 1971); 35. Shirley Basin 48AB301 (Zeimens 1975); 36. Signal Butte (Strong 1935); 37. Smiley-Evans 39BU2 (Alex 1989); 38. Sphinx 24PA508 (Lahren 1971); 39. Ten Sleep Creek 48WA305 (Frison 1967a); 40. Thirty Mile Mesa (Mulloy 1965b); 41. T-W Diamond 5LR200 (Flayharty and Morris 1974); 42. Vore 48CK302 (Reher and Frison 1980); 43. Wahkpa Chu'gn 24HL101 (Davis and Stallcop 1966); 44. Wardell 48SU301 (Frison 1973b); 45. Wedding of the Waters Cave 48HO301 (Frison 1962); 46. Willow Springs Buffalo Jump 48AB30 (Bupp 1981); 47. Wortham Shelter 48BH730 (Greer 1978); 48. The Yellowstone National Park Tipis 48YE2 (Shippee 1971); 49. Cluny Village (Forbis 1977); 50. Bootlegger (Roll and Deaver 1980); 51. Harrier Nest site 48CA1366 (Winham et al. 2000); 52. 5JA7 (Colorado SHPO, unpublished); 53. Sand Draw Village (Walker 2004a). All the sites in Figure 2.19 except Agate Basin, Carter/Kerr-McGee, Allen, and Southsider Cave have some form of Late Prehistoric component.

Figure 2.71   Location of the Beehive Butte site in the foothills of the Bighorn Mountains.

Figure 2.72   Large, slab-lined fire pit at the Beehive Butte site.

pottery, and several types of hearths, surrounded by a bone bed containing pre-dominantly bighorn sheep and bison (Rapson 1990). The tri-notched projectile points (Figure 2.73), Shoshone knives (Figure 2.10a), Intermountain pottery, and

Figure 2.73   Late Prehistoric period tri-notched points from the Bugas-Holding site.

radiocarbon dates from the hearths of just under AD 1500, all point to occupation by a Sheepeater Shoshone group. A large artifact assemblage in context with stone circles composed of flat stones built up to as much as .5 m high in the Shirley Basin area in central Wyoming is believed to represent a Shoshonean occupation (Zeimens 1975).

THE PROTOHISTORIC PERIOD

To get from prehistoric to historic groups is a task fraught with difficulties. Sociocultural processes, migrations, ethnogenesis, mate exchanges, and a myriad of other processes mould both prehistoric and historic peoples. Pottery shapes, manufacturing techniques, decoration, and other characteristics are independent phenomena (as they are for other objects), and each can be affected independently from others. To read ethnicity into the archaeological record may or may not be possible, but the methodology, warranting arguments, and assumptions have not been adequately developed to this point. Nevertheless, some who study the Plains have tried this approach (Schlesier 1994 and articles within). But as Duke and Wilson (1994:70) warn, "We also suggest that archaeologists should be wary of assuming that ethnographically defined culture-area boundaries have any analytical relevance to the prehistoric archaeological record."

There is no doubt that it was the introduction of the horse that ultimately brought about the most significant cultural changes to the Indian occupations of the Northwestern Plains and Rocky Mountains. The precise date of this occurrence is not well documented in the archaeological record. However, from other sources we learn that the Shoshoneans were getting horses in significant numbers during the first quarter of the eighteenth century and the Crow obtained horses shortly afterward (see Ewers 1955:3–19; Haines 1938:430; Secoy 1953:33–38). On the other hand, Shoshonean groups commonly referred to as the Sheepeaters did not acquire the horse, probably because the mountains in which they lived would not support horses and travel on foot was often easier.

Along with the appearance of horses in Protohistoric times were small amounts of European goods. These were usually decorative in nature; they were highly prized and often appear as burial items. Shell beads from the west coast and several early European glass trade beads were found along with small tri-notched projectile points in the uppermost level at the Medicine Lodge Creek site. Horse bones and a few fragments of iron appeared along with small side-notched and also tri-notched projectile points in a Protohistoric site along the North Platte River in central Wyoming (McKee 1988) with probable Shoshonean cultural affiliations.

Farther up the North Platte River is what appears to be a Protohistoric Shoshonean campsite located along the shore of Seminoe Reservoir, an artificial body of water formed by a dam on the river. The site to date has produced sherds of unidentified ceramics, probably Intermountain tradition, steatite fragments that may be from a carved vessel, brass fragments that appear to have been hammered with stone tools, a broken blue European trade bead, and small side-notched and tri-notched projectile points. The site is submerged most of the time and is available for observation only on rare occasions when lake levels are extremely low.

One of us (Frison) recalls a multiple burial, found in the early 1930s in a crevice in the rocks on the western slopes of the Bighorn Mountains, that contained among other things a sinew-backed wooden bow and a bundle of hafted arrows, some with European metal trade points, some with hand-hammered iron projectile points (probably Indian made), and the remainder with small side-notched and tri-notched projectile points of obsidian and chert. Both European metal trade points and hand-hammered iron points were rather common surface finds a few decades ago, but most have now rusted away (Figure 2.74). A hand-hammered brass projectile point and a badly rusted iron awl were recovered at the grass-roots level of the Big Goose Creek site, directly above the radiocarbon-dated Crow campsite mentioned earlier (Frison, Wilson, and Walker 1978:13). There were, however, no tribally diagnostic materials in association with the metal products.

Metal lance points are occasionally found. These were usually larger pieces of metal pounded out with stone tools and smoothed by abrasion on pieces of hard sandstone. An unusually fine example was found sticking in a large pine tree on Torrey Creek in the Wind River Mountains near Dubois, Wyoming. This particular specimen is hammered and smoothed except for the notched base, which demonstrates laborious hammering, probably with stone tools, judging from the marks left on the metal where it was not later ground smooth (Figure 2.75).

The first metal knives acquired by the historic Native Americans in the area were treated in similar manner; they beveled the working edge of the blade on one edge only and instead of maintaining a continuous keen edge, they deliberately placed nicks at close intervals. These were common finds at the turn of the century (Figure 2.74g).

There are, however, many more Protohistoric sites in the region at which no historic or European items are found, which nevertheless date to the period (Sutton 2004). The Native Americans of the eighteenth and nineteenth centuries did not all have equal access to trade goods, valued the trade goods and discarded

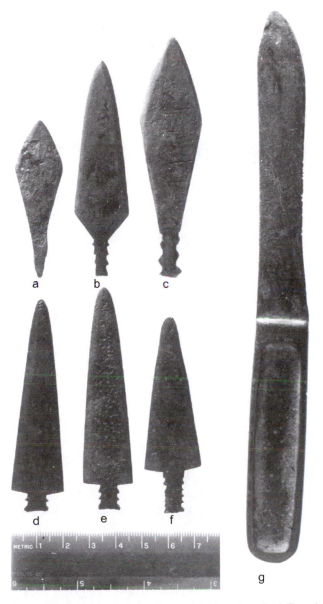

Figure 2.74 Hand-hammered metal points (a, c), metal trade points (b, d–f), and an early historic metal knife (g) from the Bighorn Mountains.

them reluctantly, or for other reasons did not deposit trade goods at every location they occupied. Hence many sites have radiocarbon or other chronometric assays of Protohistoric period, but are not necessarily identifiable on the basis of the artifact assemblage. For example, skeletal remains of a horse in southwestern Wyoming were found with no associated artifacts, but with metal tool butchery marks (Eckles et al. 1994). The date on this site placed the horse in the late 1600s, clearly of Protohistoric age and a very early occurrence of the horse in this area. Likewise a number of wooden structures around Wyoming's mountains have been dendrochronologically dated to the Protohistoric, although no European

Figure 2.75   Metal lance point from the Absaroka Mountains in northwest Wyoming.

items were located at them and indeed few or no artifacts were present (Frison et al. 1990). The point is that searching out all the sites of Protohistoric age and including them in the analysis of cultural processes provides for a more holistic picture of this period.

3

METHODOLOGY FOR THE HIGH PLAINS AND ROCKY MOUNTAINS
Animal Behavior, Experimentation, and High-Tech Approaches

INTRODUCTION

There are many approaches to archaeology that range from the pragmatic to the highly theoretical; all have their place and all contribute to the final product, which is to learn something of prehistoric lifeways. In a century and a half, since the inception of archaeology as a scientific discipline and a few centuries before in its nascent state (Trigger 2006; Willey and Sabloff 1993), the field of archaeology has assimilated into its repertoire a remarkable number of methods to carry on research (Renfrew and Bahn 2008). Many of these were developed by archaeologists, while others were borrowed from other sciences. As in any field, methods are developed to solve problems. Perhaps a unique feature of archaeology is the uniqueness of our database. Although patterns can be defined, no two artifacts are ever exactly alike, no two sites are ever exactly alike, no two regions are ever exactly alike, and no two cultures are ever exactly alike. Consequently, no matter how elaborate a methodology we posses as a discipline, questions inevitably arise in the research process and in field studies that require new and innovative approaches and methods.

During our careers, we have made it a point to be creative in the development of methods specifically geared for application to the archaeological record of the Northwestern Plains and the Rocky Mountains, as well as for interpreting specific sites we were investigating. This approach led us to rely on animal behavior studies (e.g., Frison 2004), personal experience with animals and plants, and experimentation with prehistoric tools, as well as other approaches leading to interpretation of the archaeological record (Larson and Kornfeld 1997; Shanks et al. 1999; Shanks, Kornfeld, and Ream 2005).

In this chapter we first review animal behavior, focusing on the two main prehistoric large game species, mammoth and bison, and the implication of their behavior on pedestrian hunting strategies. We argue that the detailed study of animal behavior can be used to understand the actions of prehistoric hunters. This is followed by zoological and paleontological approaches, taxonomy, and taphonomy as significant methods used and developed by archaeologists in search of answers to questions about animal procurement strategies. These approaches are considered in the next to the last section of this chapter. Experimentation with prehistoric tool kits with the intent of demonstrating functionality and potential use strategies follow. It is clear from these experiments that effective prehistoric tools existed for killing and processing large animals, but the experiments also provide inferential fodder for interpreting tool attributes (for example, impact damage on projectile points, edge damage on cutting implements, and so on). Finally, the last section considers the new, not completely proven, but potentially informative methods that archaeologists are beginning to apply to data. Specifically, blood residue, protein, DNA, and isotope analyses constitute a series of molecular and geochemical techniques now being applied cautiously that shows promise in expanding our knowledge of the past. Although we have developed or adapted some of these methods specifically for our Northwest Plains and Rocky Mountain problems, they are now in widespread use by our colleagues throughout the world.

MODERN ANIMALS AS BEHAVIOR ANALOGS

Elephant as Hunting Models for Clovis

The mammoth and mastodon are long extinct and we can only postulate on their behavior and/or attempt to use modern elephants as a model. The physiology of modern elephants is similar to that of mammoths and mastodons, whose frozen carcasses have been recovered from permafrost contexts. Mammoths recovered from permafrost have heavy coats of hair and fur but, by actual measurement, hide thickness is similar to that of modern African elephants. Whether or not mammoths in the warmer regions had heavy coats of fur and hair is an open question with little possibility of solution. These and other factors leave the impression that mammoths and mastodons were not too different from African and Asian elephants in their day-to-day behavior.

Few things have captured the interest and imagination of prehistorians more than mammoth hunting. Dioramas in museums and artists' depictions in textbooks worldwide follow a central theme: shouting hunters, usually with packs of barking dogs, are pursuing a mammoth that becomes immobilized in a bog or, in some cases, is forced over a precipice. Dead and/or crippled hunters who have been trampled are being removed from the scene while spears and rocks are hurled at the animal. In some cases, only the head of the animal is protruding out of the bog. Besides being contrary to the rules of intelligent hunting, no consideration is given to the next-to-impossible tasks of skinning, butchering, and retrieval of the meat from an animal in this kind of situation. A more realistic approach to mammoth hunting is badly needed if reliable interpretations of Clovis mammoth kill sites and Old World mammoth kill sites are to be realized.

With regard to bogging elephants, African elephants are attracted to wet areas, swamps, and bogs and spend much of their time in these kinds of areas. Elephants die in bogs only when they are sick, wounded, or starving (Gary Haynes, personal communication 1984). Although elephants are large, their feet are also large and constructed so that their weight exerts less pressure per unit of surface area than a human's does. When an elephant extracts its foot from mud, the morphology of its foot causes the toes to come together, preventing the suction that tends to hold the feet of other animals in boggy areas (Eltringham 1982). Another consideration is that animals that commonly frequent bogs on their own can be difficult or impossible to drive or otherwise entice into a bog if they decide not to do so.

The critical question in modeling a mammoth procurement strategy lies, to a large extent, in the behavioral characteristics of the species. Present-day elephants live under a matriarchal social system in which the eldest female and her offspring form a family exclusive of mature males. Families may contain 10 or less individuals or over 50 (Figure 3.1). As the family becomes too large, they tend to break up into smaller families. Large family aggregations tend to occur when feed conditions are good. However, as feed and water conditions worsen, submatriarchs tend to split off from the larger families with their offspring, allowing better utilization of diminishing resources.

Matriarch elephants are responsible for the welfare and protection of the family, a responsibility not taken lightly. Any threat to any member of the family immediately brings the matriarch to meet the source of the danger. From experience, direct confrontation of a matriarch (Figure 3.2) is a sobering experience; if the threat is a human hunter lacking the means to immediately bring down the matriarch, a fast retreat is the wise strategy. A matriarch elephant protecting her family is a formidable foe.

This matriarchal system has disadvantages for the elephants that are hunted by humans aware of its weaknesses. Wildlife managers in places such as Hwange National Park in Zimbabwe, where overpopulation is a serious problem, learn

Figure 3.1   African elephant family with matriarch and submatriarch standing guard.

Figure 3.2   Matriarch African elephant beginning the final charge.

quickly that indiscriminate killing of elephants is impractical as well as very dangerous to the hunters. Their present culling strategy is to remove entire families. The family is confronted and when, after a couple of false charges, the matriarch makes her final charge, she is downed by a large-caliber bullet placed in the brain cavity. The remainder of the family then crowds on the matriarch seeking protection. At this point, since their attention is focused on the dead matriarch, they are oblivious to the hunters and all are quickly and easily killed. Should any members of the family escape, they are pursued and killed because they will not be accepted by any other family, and they eventually become traumatized to the extent that they become dangerous to park visitors. On rare occasions, a submatriarch takes her offspring and hastily departs the scene instead of crowding on the matriarch for protection. In this situation also, the hunters are committed to pursuing and killing all members of the family.

This poses the question as to whether or not this has any relevance to Clovis mammoth hunting. We think the answer is yes if mammoths lived under the same matriarchal principles as present-day elephants. It is difficult to determine unequivocally whether or not the mammoths from sites such as Lehner Ranch (Haury et al. 1959) or Colby (Frison and Todd 1986) represent more than a single procurement event (e.g., Hoppe 2004). However, more recent data from a site in Texas does provide strong evidence for a mammoth family structure analogous to that of modern African elephants. The site is a catastrophic kill, but the investigators do not believe that it is archaeological. Its composition is a mature female, probably the matriarch, estimated to have been between 34 and just over 40 years of age. She and fourteen other individuals, the youngest of which was two years of age, comprised a typical family group. One was a mature male, indicating that one of the females was probably in her estrous period (Fox et al. 1992).

Experiments on African elephants have shown that Clovis weaponry (Figure 3.3), used with either thrusting spear or atlatl and dart, has the potential to inflict lethal wounds on elephants (Figure 3.4) of all ages and sexes (Frison 1989, 1991, 2004). However, the same weaponry does not have the potential to drop a charging matriarch or other elephant of any size in its tracks. Hunters on the elephant culls use a 500-grain, high-velocity, jacketed bullet to penetrate into

Figure 3.3   Experimental Clovis point used with atlatl and dart.

Figure 3.4   Penetration of the rib cage of a mature female African elephant with a point similar to that in Figure 3.3.

the brain cavity. However, a Clovis point used with either a thrusting spear or a throwing stick cannot be given the velocity needed to penetrate the hide and bone in order to reach the brain cavity (Figure 3.5).

Elephant hunting requires a clear understanding of the animal's behavior and the skills designed to capture large family groups or animals that have wandered away from the herd. The hunter who is self-disciplined enough to wait for the right opportunity and experienced enough in the use of weaponry should be able to place a stone projectile point in the desired part of the elephant's anatomy.

The optimum spot to place the projectile point is the rib cage, preferably the lung cavity. This requires a good degree of skill in the use of the atlatl and dart. The diaphragm separating the lung and stomach cavity is well forward, and hitting the animal too far forward requires penetration through added layers of flesh. Penetration still further forward brings on the danger of hitting the scapula, with little chance of further penetration into the rib cage. A Clovis point into the stomach cavity will eventually be lethal but takes much longer to do so than one placed into the lung cavity. The heart, located well toward the bottom of the rib cage where the ribs tend to become wider and flattened, is not a good target. The force of a Clovis point impacting at right angles on the flat surface of a rib may break the foreshaft and shatter the point (Figure 3.6). Farther up, the rib is more rounded, and a projectile point usually slides around it and on into the rib cage. Even if it breaks, it may still penetrate and produce a lethal wound.

Unless the projectile point hits a major blood vessel, a neck wound is not the best choice. Neck shots are more effective with the added velocity and shocking

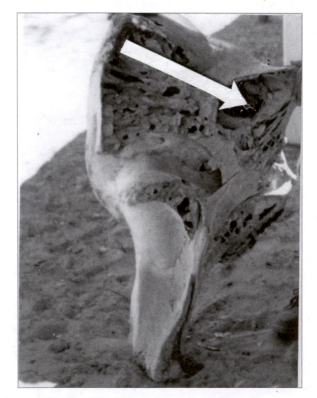

Figure 3.5   Elephant skull split to show the location of the brain case.

Figure 3.6 Shattered Clovis point and foreshaft (b), and the tip of the point in the elephant rib (a).

power produced with firearms and large-caliber bullets. Flesh wounds can be serious and cause an animal to lie down. However, in all cases with a wounded animal, the hunter must exercise patience and caution and not pursue the wounded animal too closely. A seriously wounded animal that is frightened enough to get back on its feet may travel for long distances and can sustain a surprising amount of further wounding before it collapses.

This is, without doubt, a more realistic strategy of mammoth hunting than is usually presented. Whether purposely or by accident, the Clovis projectile point is a well-designed bit of weaponry and a model of efficiency in terms of inflicting lethal wounds on large animals. Sharp points and blade edges allow deep penetration, the lenticular cross section strengthens it structurally, the fluted base allows easy attachment to a nocked foreshaft, and the grinding on the proximal blade edges prevents cutting of the sinew bindings under the added stress of heavy impact. Clovis hunters were undoubtedly knowledgeable enough in mammoth hunting to have been able to procure the animals on their own terms, although windfalls probably occurred at times, such as an animal incapacitated through mishap or natural causes.

Observations of Bison Today

The present-day bison is enjoying a new popularity (Figure 3.7). Breeding stock bring high prices and buffalo breeders are quick to defend their choice of bison over cattle. They claim a number of traits that make the bison in some ways equal to or superior to domestic cattle. There is little danger that the bison will replace domestic cattle, but as a result of their popularity, enough of them are around for us to make some meaningful observations on bison behavior and use this information toward a better understanding of prehistoric methods of bison procurement.

Anyone who works buffalo in the same corral, chute, and squeeze gate facilities that are used in handling domestic cattle has no doubt whatsoever that the buffalo is still a far-from-domesticated animal. They may appear docile, but in response to what seems the least provocation they can become extremely wild. They appear slow, awkward, and oblivious to what is happening around them. It is often at this point that they change character entirely and react so quickly that one often wonders whether one is seeing the same animals.

Figure 3.7   Modern bison cow and calf in Yellowstone National Park.

This does not mean that their reactions are always intelligent in terms of survival. However, their speed and agility can rapidly get them away from a given point and unless whoever or whatever is pursuing them has great mobility, there is small chance that they will be overtaken. It is easy to see why, even after the acquisition of horses, the Plains Indian tribes had strong sanctions against buffalo hunting before the communal hunt began. Even with horses, a herd of bison can be difficult to move in a given direction at the whim of the drivers.

In handling bison today, there are two general procedures that can be followed. One is to build a set of fences and structures strong enough to hold the animals and to use motorized vehicles with metal wings to herd them. The animals in this situation are handled by brute force, and they have no choice but to go into corrals, through chutes, and so on. In this kind of situation, the mortality rate is often high and crippled animals are common. The animals are strong and quick, and when frightened they often go completely berserk. If an animal happens to fall down, or gets a foot or head caught or wedged in part of the chute or corral structure, the force of the other animals can only cause serious injury or death.

The other, more intelligent and humane way to handle buffalo is to be aware of their behavior patterns and adjust your reactions to theirs. Buffalo will not ordinarily crowd a corral fence when inside it unless they want to rub on it. Otherwise they only crowd the fence if forced into it by other animals. The idea that a buffalo will try to push a fence over is erroneous. However, if a bison can get its head through a hole in the fence, it will try to force its way through it. A small group of animals (10 to 20) can be handled in a corral with relative ease, whereas a larger group (50 or more) can be difficult to handle.

It is common to move both cattle and bison back and forth through various sets of corrals during branding, working, inoculating, pregnancy testing, and the like. It is simple to move cattle into a corral, follow them closely, and then close the gate. Not so with bison. Often the group of bison will circle a person several times with unbelievable speed and agility. They may go through the gate into one corral from another, then turn around and come back through the open gate back into the original corral, circle it, and go back into the other corral again. If the person is quick, he or she may get the gate closed before the bison decide to come back out again. Once the gate is completely closed they will not force it, but if the person is slow in getting the gate closed and they spy an opening, they will crowd it and force their way through.

Bison are not always predictable in their reactions to various stimuli. Some days they may be docile and appear much like domestic cattle, whereas the next day they may be extremely wild and depart at full speed, running for a mile or more before looking back. Some days it is not worth the effort to try to work bison unless they are inside corrals where they can be forced. Cows with young calves are erratic in their behavior, and the cows are protective of the calves. It is not at all unusual for a young calf or a group of young calves to stampede in whatever direction they happen to be pointed at the time, and they do not always stick together. The cows take off and follow them and it can take a long time to get them back together.

Animals in rut are even more difficult to handle than the ones with young calves. At this time the mature bulls seek out the cows after ignoring them for the remainder of the year. The peak of the rut lasts for about two weeks and the entire season drags on for about a month. A cow in heat is the focus of attention of the mature males. A dominant male will try to separate the cow from the herd and at the same time fight off other males. With this kind of activity going on all through the herd there is little possibility of success in driving, corralling, or otherwise working with the herd.

Armed with this kind of information on bison behavior, we can look at prehistoric bison procurement sites as the result of band-level hunting groups familiar enough with the animals to take advantage of their natural behavior patterns. It was through the hunters' knowledge of the limits and possibilities offered by bison behavior that communal bison hunting became an institutionalized economic process during the entire Holocene period on the Great Plains.

Frank H. Mayer died in Fairplay, Colorado, at the age of 104 years. He was probably the last of the buffalo hunters (runners) who witnessed the end of the bison on the Great Plains in the late nineteenth century. He made his living for several years as a hide hunter. He recorded his experiences, including a number of references to bison behavior that demonstrate an intimate knowledge of the animals, pertaining to his exploitation of bison for a specific purpose—that of killing the animals in such a way as to maximize the monetary returns. Embedded in his narrative are numerous observations that any investigator concerned with prehistoric bison procurement should carefully pursue (Mayer and Roth 1958).

Pronghorn or Antelope

The American antelope or pronghorn (*Antilocapra americana*) is a distinctive animal in an evolutionary sense and in its behavior patterns. It is the only artiodactyl in North America that actually sheds its horns (Figure 3.8). The horn sheaths loosen and fall and are usually consumed by rodents or chewed by carnivores and scavengers, so they are not as common a find as might be expected. A unique physiological characteristic of the pronghorn is its lack of dewclaws, or external accessory digits, on its feet, allowing the hunter to immediately identify tracks as either pronghorn or deer if the ground is soft enough for the feet to sink in a short distance.

Pronghorns favor open, flat or rolling, treeless country. They will range into high elevations, even to timberline and above if there is access through fairly open country. They are more visible during the daylight hours than deer, who like to hide in brush or rough country during the day. Pronghorns have unusually good eyesight and like to stand or lie down on a rise where at least one or more of the group can see for long distances. Their cursorial ability is unmatched in North American mammals; it is not unusual to clock them at up to 95 km per hour for short distances.

During late fall, winter, and early spring, pronghorn herds numbering into the hundreds are common. Females have their young in late May and early June and are solitary during this period, but they start to run in small nursery herds as soon as the fawns are a few weeks old. Males may run in bunches of up to 20 or more during the summer. Tests of dominance among the males begin before the rut, which starts in earnest in early September. The gestation period is about 252 days.

Pronghorns exhibit a strange stubbornness at times. A single buck or a small herd of animals in level country will race alongside a vehicle. In some circumstances, the animals will exert every possible effort to cross in front of the

Figure 3.8   Modern pronghorn in the Laramie Basin. Buck (bottom), female and young (top).

vehicle and can be coaxed up to speeds of around 95 km/h in the process. If the vehicle goes too fast, however, they will veer away and run into the distance until they feel it is safe to stop. A horse-mounted hunter could potentially elicit similar behavior.

Another pronghorn characteristic that can be easily exploited by hunters is a great curiosity. Any unusual object that cannot be identified, such as a flag or other object placed on the open prairie or preferably on a rise where it can be seen for long distances, will cause the animals to come closer and closer until they can easily be killed. A sure method to obtain a pronghorn is to camp out in antelope country and put up a small tipi or tent or lay a blanket on top of sagebrush where it can be seen for long distances. Provided, of course, that there are animals in the area, the next morning a number of them are likely to be moving in to see what the object is and will usually approach to within easy shooting distance if the hunter has the patience to remain quiet. This pronghorn hunting strategy is mentioned for the Assiniboin (Denig 1930:535).

When frightened they may run away from the danger at top speed. However, once out of sight of whatever they were running from, they seemingly forget all about what it was that frightened them. Consequently, a hunter needs only to be patient and resume the stalk once the animals have stopped.

Fences have been a problem to pronghorn survival. They will not ordinarily jump fences, although some are now learning to do so. They have learned also in many areas to crawl under or through a hole in a fence. However, we have more than once seen a single strand of barbed wire stretched across sagebrush at about a meter off the ground contain a sizeable herd of pronghorn because the animals refused either to jump over it or crawl under it. In fact, when cornered, they would double back and run within a few feet of their pursuer rather than go over or under the barbed wire. All things considered, pronghorn are easy to hunt. They are creatures of habit and appear regularly at waterholes. Hunters can either stalk the animals or sit tight in a good location and let the animals come to them. Either method is effective. Pronghorn behavior invites communal hunting; immediately after the rut in September they form large herds until well into spring. They can be restrained within a brush enclosure that a deer or mountain sheep would pay little if any attention to. Their body size is relatively small (about 25 kg for a female and up to 35 kg for a male, both field dressed) so that single animal hunting is not too productive in terms of energy expenditure.

Bighorn Sheep

The mountain sheep (*Ovis canadensis*), usually portrayed as an almost exclusively mountain animal, was found in historic times in all areas of rough topography, such as minor uplifts, eroded canyons, river breaks, and isolated buttes at considerable distances from the major mountain ranges (Figure 3.9). As an example, one of us (Frison) observed two large ram skulls that were recovered in alluvial deposits along Powder River in southern Montana, a considerable distance from present mountain sheep populations. Taxonomically these specimens were probably *O. c. auduboni*, or the Audubon bighorn, which was reportedly found throughout northeast Wyoming, southeast Montana, and western South Dakota, especially the Black Hills and its extensions to the north before becoming extinct in historic times due to hunting pressure. Mountain sheep remains from prehistoric contexts follow about the same distribution.

As in the case of the pronghorn, mountain sheep very nearly became extinct in historic times, but small resident herds survived in the more inaccessible mountain areas of northwest Wyoming and adjacent areas of Montana, Idaho, and Colorado and formed the nucleus for a number of presently viable herds. Reports by Stuart (1935:188,191), Russell (1921), Fremont (1887:133,147), and many others attest to the presence of large numbers of the animals during the nineteenth century. Disease, and especially scab, was the agent that brought about the near demise of the mountain sheep. There is no agreement as to the source of the scab; some attribute it to domestic sheep but there are biological differences that prevent transmittal back and forth between the domestic sheep scab mite and the wild sheep scab mite. In addition, the scab epidemic that proved disastrous to

Figure 3.9 Modern bighorn sheep on slope.

mountain sheep occurred before the major incursions of domestic sheep into the area. This raises the possibility that similar epidemics may have caused fluctuations in mountain sheep populations more than once during prehistoric times.

Mountain sheep today have been forced into the higher altitudes usually in or close to rough country. With hunting pressure, the sheep (the older rams especially) become wild and extremely wary. Although usually pictured as inhabiting the high, rough, treeless area above the timberline, they are not entirely adverse to thick timber. Nursery herds are separate from the rams except during the rut. Probably the most successful way for the individual hunter to obtain mountain sheep is to spend enough time observing them to learn where the animals are located and something of their daily habits without alerting them to one's presence. In this way they can be successfully stalked. Going after mountain sheep without being aware of their exact location gives the animal all the advantages of seeing and hearing the hunter from superior vantage points. They have a habit of finding a protected location and dozing at times during the afternoon, at which time they are extremely vulnerable to a careful hunter who is aware of their hiding spot.

Mountain sheep behavior differs significantly from that of other medium-sized mammals that inhabit the plains and mountains of North America. These unique behavior patterns must be known and understood in order to be able to reconstruct any prehistoric procurement strategy. Observations made by Honess and Frost (1942) remain unchallenged in both the extent and depth of their experience with mountain sheep. The late Ned Frost was widely acknowledged as the foremost authority on mountain sheep hunting. In addition, he was a careful and articulate observer who passed much of his immense wealth of knowledge on to others.

A study of the large Whiskey Mountain mountain sheep herd in northwest Wyoming (Thorne et al. 1979) is another source of firsthand behavioral information. Observations on seasonal migrations, use of day and night bedgrounds, feeding habits, daytime movements, daytime resting, and reactions to predators, among many other things, affected any procurement strategy. Mountain sheep can negotiate rough terrain, going up and down with remarkable speed; this along with their excellent eyesight is their main protection from predators. Ewes with young lambs favor open areas just above timberline where they can better observe movements of predators such as mountain lions. They like to graze in open areas close to rough terrain into which they immediately retreat when pursued by coyotes. Bighorns are better equipped to go longer without water than animals such as deer and elk. Even in summer, bighorns have been observed spending three days on a dry mountainside without making a trip to water. They are seemingly oblivious to weather extremes compared to most species.

Mountain sheep seem to display many behavioral characteristics of their Old World relatives, the domestic sheep. For all of their apparent ruggedness, in addition to their inability to cope with parasites and diseases they can be easily injured during handling. During trapping for transplant purposes using drop nets, care must be taken to prevent pulling of muscles, damaging of eyes, and breaking of bones. If any of these does occur, the affected animal is likely to give up the battle and lay down and die without a struggle. When entangled in a net, they usually struggle briefly and become quite docile, unlike deer or pronghorn who will struggle to the last moment (Figure 3.10).

Deer

Both mule deer and whitetail deer are present in the region today (Figure 3.11). Unlike antelope, mule deer favor rough, brushy country and are not usually in evidence during the day, especially in warm weather. Livestock fences present

Figure 3.10   Behavior of mountain sheep under a drop net.

Figure 3.11 Two mule deer bucks. (Courtesy of Danny N. Walker.)

little problem to normal, healthy animals. However, weak animals are prone to putting their hind legs between the top and second wires of fences as they attempt to jump over, with disastrous results. They will also go through or under fences if necessary. Mule deer could have been trapped or netted but convincing evidence is lacking. They are not regarded as difficult to hunt. They usually demonstrate a fatal attribute in their behavior pattern, which is to nearly always run a short distance when frightened and then stop to look back. Mule deer are a dependable source of food when they are present in an area and not over exploited.

Elk

It is difficult to understand why elk (*Cervus canadensis*) remains are rare in prehistoric sites given their modern preponderance. When elk occur in sites, they are represented by only a few specimens, although recent investigations of two elk bone beds are discussed in Chapter 6. Elk are particularly desirable meat animals and they are not difficult to hunt. No unambiguous evidence is known for artificial elk traps or communal procurement practices (cf. Benedict 1996). Elk are able to adapt to a wide variety of ecological conditions. Today viable elk herds are located from low elevations to timberline. They are at home in rough country, open plains, thick timber, or brushy areas. Although usually regarded as a plains animal in early historic times, they are able to negotiate deep snow as well as or better than any other North American game animal. They can travel long distances at a distinctive gait that appears to be slow but is not. They are gregarious animals and tend to congregate in large herds, but they fragment into smaller groups when they are the subject of heavy hunting pressure (Figure 3.12). They are also particularly vulnerable to the well-trained hunter. The animals are predictable in their habits and usually easy to locate. Once a bunch is located, it is relatively easy to maneuver into position to kill one.

Figure 3.12   Cow elk in Yellowstone National Park protecting calves from a wolf pack. (Courtesy of Petra Brkić)

Elk are easily confused. A mature female is usually the bunch leader; if she is killed the remainder of the herd will often mill in circles and the entire herd or a good share of it can be killed. On the other hand, a herd that is frightened can travel for several kilometers and temporarily locate in a different area until disturbed again.

Elk are characterized by a distinctive odor that can be detected for several hundred meters if the air currents are right. Under hunting pressure they tend to hide in thick timber during the day. A favorite hunting trick is to scout out timber patches carefully from the leeward side, locate the animals by smell, and then run at top speed into the herd, most of which are usually bedded down. This confuses the animals, who usually charge in all directions. Unable to locate the rest of the herd, each animal goes entirely berserk for a few moments, charging first one way and then another. During this time the hunter can usually kill one or more. Trying to sneak up on the herd in thick timber is not usually as successful. The animals usually detect the hunter first and simply charge off in a group, leaving the hunter with nothing but an occasional flash of an animal's rear, but nothing that he or she can react to fast enough to obtain a lethal shot.

Whether or not the prehistoric hunter resorted to these elk-hunting techniques is not known. They have been described here only to provide an insight into elk behavior and to demonstrate the advantage that can be taken of the elk's distinctive odor. This technique will not work with deer or mountain sheep because they have no such smell and react differently than elk to the same stimuli. Pronghorns do not frequent thick timber, so in their case this technique is automatically excluded. Neither would it work for moose (*Alces alces*). The hunter would not be wise to charge into a thicket where a moose was lying since that animal's reaction would more than likely be to charge the hunter; the moose can be taken by other techniques. However, moose are nonexistent in the archaeological record of the Northwestern Plains and Rocky Mountains. The Jurgens site in Colorado is the only site in the region where moose is reported to occur in the deposits (Wheat 1979).

STUDIES OF ANIMAL POPULATIONS IN ARCHAEOLOGICAL SITES AND THEIR USE IN BIOLOGICAL AND CULTURAL INTERPRETATIONS

In any discussion of prehistoric hunting strategies as part of food procurement activities in the Plains and immediately adjacent areas, bison has top billing. Bison studies are complex; we are dealing with an animal whose evolutionary history from the first evidence of its appearance in North America to its later pursuit by human hunters is still imperfectly known. However, recovery and analysis of large and temporally controlled samples of bison are beginning to result in a better understanding of the evolutionary history of the species.

Bison Taxonomy and Pleistocene/Holocene Evolution

Earlier observers and collectors of fossil bison remains were hampered by a lack of temporal control and a compulsion to proliferate in their naming of species. One of the most variable characteristics of bison, the horn core, was used as the basis for designating species. At the same time, these observers were unaware of the possible range of variation in single bison populations due to age differences and sexual dimorphism (Figures 3.13, 3.14, 3.15, 3.16).

The earliest species of bison native to North America was *Bison latifrons* (Figure 3.17). Believed to be evolutionary descendants of *B. latifrons*, *B. antiquus* and *B. occidentalis* have been found in Paleoindian and Early Plains Archaic archaeological sites. *B. bison bison* appears archaeologically at about 5000 BP in sites in the Plains and Rocky Mountains. Size diminution of bison has been a gradual process during the entire Holocene, and there is some indication of a slight acceleration of this trend through the mid-Holocene (Figures 3.18 and 3.19). Along with dwarfing there was some dental microevolution involving the enlargement (molarization) of premolars.

The two chronosubspecies *B. bison occidentalis* and *B. bison antiquus* differ in measurable ways. The former or northern one is characterized by a more posterior deflection of horn cores, greater orbital protrusion, and less cranial breadth than the latter or southern one (Wilson 1975:138). We cannot as yet establish a precise dividing line between the two or the actual nature of southward clinal shifts at given points in time. We do know, however, that phenotypes of both did occur together at the Casper site at 10,000 BP and that *B. occidentalis* was present in the Wyoming Black Hills at 6400 BP, as is clearly demonstrated by complete crania recovered at the Hawken site (Figure 3.15; Frison et al. 1976).

Recent studies of bison DNA show that in the post-Pleistocene period, that is, as the Laurentide and Cordilleran ice sheets melted, the southern bison moved up the ice-free corridor and populated the area up to Athabasca by 10,400 BP (Shapiro et al. 2004). At the same time, the northern haplotype

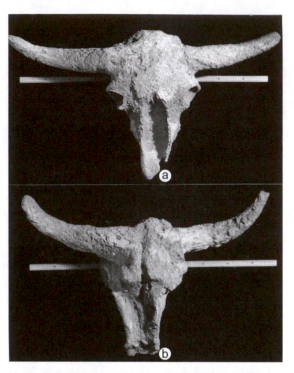

Figure 3.13   Male bison skulls from the Casper site. One (a) demonstrates characteristics of *B. bison antiquus*, and the other (b) has many characteristics of *B. bison occidentalis*.

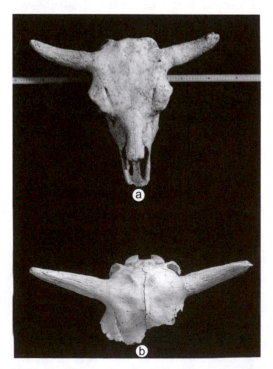

Figure 3.14   Female bison (*B. bison antiquus*) skulls from the Casper site (a) and *B. bison occidentalis* from the Hawken III site (b).

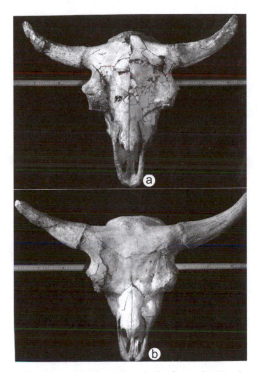

Figure 3.15 Male bison (*B. bison occidentalis*) skulls from the Hawken site. One (a) is badly deformed by crushing, and another (b) is the largest specimen from the site.

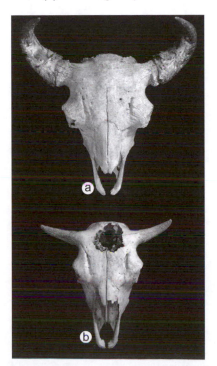

Figure 3.16 Male bison (*B. bison bison*) skull from an animal that died in 1887 (a), and a female bison (*B. bison bison*) skull from the Glenrock Bison Jump with frontal part opened (b).

Figure 3.17 Mr. and Mrs. Jerry Peery of Canadian, Texas, with *Bison latifrons* horns, Lipscomb County, northeast Texas. (From Wycoff and Dalquest 1997. Courtesy of Don Wycoff.)

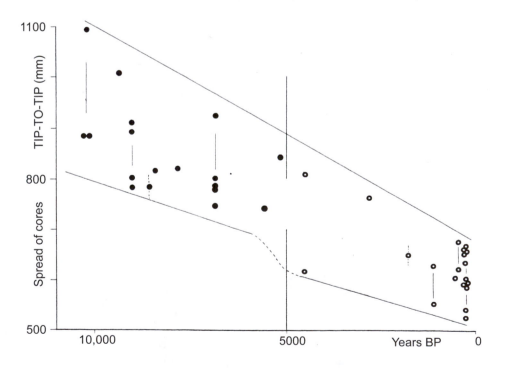

Figure 3.18 Changes in bison skulls through time. (From Wilson 1978.)

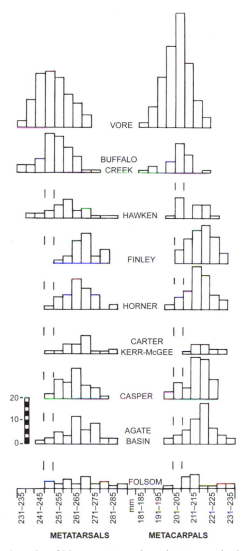

Figure 3.19 Changes in lengths of bison metatarsals and metacarpals through time. (From Frison 1984.)

reached south to the Peace River in British Columbia by 11,200 and 10,200 BP and the two varieties were in close association in this area at the time. The traditional hypothesis that the modern bison descended from Beringian bison that moved through the ice-free corridor after the last glacial maximum (McDonald 1981; Wilson 1996) has been put on ice with the DNA evidence. The DNA data are clear on the fact that the modern bison are the descendants of the bison populations that were south of the continental ice sheets prior to 12,000 BP.

> All modern bison belong to a clade distinct from Beringian bison. This clade has MRCA (most recent common ancestor) between 22 and 15 Ky BP, which is coincident with the separation of northern and southern populations by the western Canadian ice barrier. (Shapiro et al. 2004:1563, parentheses added)

These findings suggest the need to reevaluate the bison speciation described above with new techniques such as DNA.

The tip-to-tip spread of bison horn cores has decreased during the Holocene (the last 10,000 years) at a rate of about 32 mm/1000 years, with at least one fluctuation during the Altithermal (Wilson 1978), which supports the idea of a continual dwarfing trend (Figure 3.18). A study of metacarpals and metatarsals from a number of Holocene bison kill sites (Bedord 1974) indicates a continual decrease in size, and measurements of volumes of astragali (Zeimens and Zeimens 1974) give a similar result. We can now add the measurements on both these postcranial skeletal elements from a large sample of the original Folsom site bison in New Mexico; these are observably larger than those from the Casper site and other sites of about the same period. A sample of metatarsals and metacarpals was also recovered from Agate Basin and other Paleoindian sites. Comparing these to sites of the later periods, the dwarfing hypothesis is supported (Figure 3.19). The range of variation in size also points out the need for large samples of a bison population before meaningful assessments can be made. We do not at this time have an adequate comparative sample of postcranial elements of bison from dated Clovis period sites, but measurements on selected specimens from Murray Springs (Haynes and Huckell 2007) and a single specimen from the Union Pacific Mammoth site (McGrew 1961) suggest that the bison during Clovis times were larger than those of Folsom times.

The larger size of the extinct bison by itself may have been a determining factor in the selection of prehistoric procurement methods. A modern bison, especially a mature bull, is quite formidable, particularly when contained within a corral or other holding structure. Adding an average of several hundred more pounds per animal and another foot to each horn and projecting the horn more directly outward could hardly help but give any hunter cause for serious thought and judicious consideration before rushing into a direct confrontation with the animal, unless he or she had considerable experience and was equipped with well-proven weaponry.

With regard to actual bison procurement by humans, we may be on somewhat dangerous ground in assuming that the extinct variants of bison demonstrate identical or similar behavioral patterns to the modern form. Present-day bison congregate in large herds, but the extinct variants may not have done so. They may have been more solitary, less excitable, easier to approach, and more cursorial (Smiley 1979). On the other hand, the fact that large numbers were stampeded into deep, steep-walled arroyos (Wheat 1972), driven into parabolic sand dunes (Frison 1974), driven into arroyo traps (Frison et al. 1976; Frison and Stanford 1982), and driven into artificial corrals (Frison and Todd 1987) provides some basis for comparison. The modern bison can be put through all the paces that we know the extinct ones were put through, so they probably were not too dissimilar.

Age Determination and Mortality Profiles

In order for the archaeologist to derive meaningful interpretations from a sample of a population, accurate means of determining the age of each specimen represented are necessary. To date, tooth eruption and wear seem to offer the most reliable results, at least on the larger ungulates. The development of more precise age-determination techniques for bison came about from the analysis of tooth eruption and wear of known-age animals from present-day commercial and national park herds. Information on other animals (deer and pronghorn) were obtained from hunters and game management personnel.

Age determination using tooth eruption schedules accurate to a month or less is possible on young animals, especially those less than a year of age (Figure 3.20). Reasonably good results can be obtained on immature bison one year of age to maturity at about five years. Beyond this, age must be estimated according to tooth wear. As long as the sample being studied is from a single population that died at a single point in time, yearly increments of wear can be detected and age groups one year apart can usually be detected.

The principles involved in determining age are simple and straightforward because tooth eruption schedules are systematic and predictable. As long as

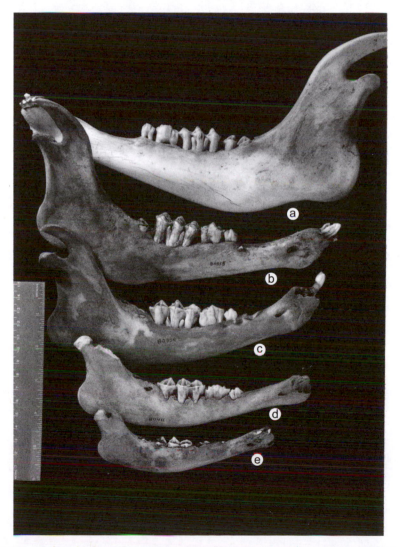

Figure 3.20   Modern bison calf mandibles from fetus (e) to newborn (d) to approximately 4 months old (a).

teeth are erupting, there is an interaction between eruption and wear that is age diagnostic. Earlier schemes for describing mammalian teeth (e.g., Crompton and Hiiemae 1969) were designed to give the evolutionary history of dental morphology, not to provide for accurate descriptions of tooth wear. Frison (Frison et al. 1976) proposed a descriptive model for bison tooth wear (Figure 3.21). Use of this descriptive, standardized method of determining bison tooth wear allows different investigators to compare results. The model has been applied to other artiodactyls, and similar wear diagrams can probably be constructed for the dentitions of other species. The first attempts at determining bison age were made using lower teeth, since these were better preserved and more frequently recovered in archaeological sites. However, the upper teeth have proven as reliable as lower teeth. Samples from the Hawken site were aged by two investigators independently, one using upper teeth and the other using lower teeth, and the results were nearly identical.

We know that rutting and birthing seasons are nearly constant from year to year for all the larger animals commonly hunted in North America. As a result, each year's crop of young will be spread over the birthing period. With bison for example, most calves are born within a period of four to six weeks. The calving begins slowly, builds up to a peak and ends like it began. An occasional calf is born out of normal calving period; such a calf usually has a poor chance of survival. The early calf faces cold spring weather and the summer calf may not achieve sufficient growth to survive a severe winter. As a result, those born outside the normal calving period may not seriously affect the structure of a given bison population. Even a surviving female calf born outside the normal calving period is as likely as any other to breed and have its offspring during the normal breeding and calving periods. However, a calf born late in the summer may not

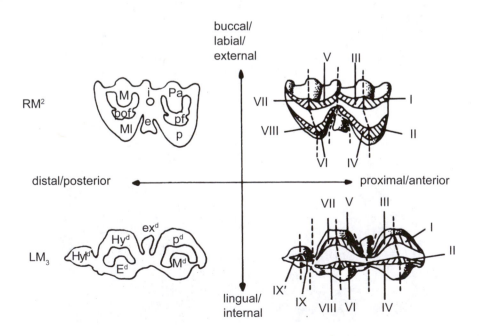

Figure 3.21 Occlusal surfaces of bison teeth. (From Frison et al. 1976.)

attain enough size and maturity to bear offspring until a year later than ones of the same calf crop born during the regular calving season. And sometimes the early calf that survives breeds a year early and dies because it is not developed enough to give birth to its calf.

Tooth eruption and wear criteria can be used to determine the ages of young animals and the season of communal events. Calves from the Olsen-Chubbuck site that were probably killed in late summer or early fall (Figure 3.22a, b) demonstrate lower first molars in a much earlier stage of eruption than those from the Casper site (Figure 3.22c–e) that were killed in late fall or early winter. Note also that although there is a noticeable size difference in the two Olsen-Chubbuck specimens (one is probably male and the other female), eruption stages are in close agreement.

The Vore site (Reher and Frison 1980) was a bison jump of the Late Prehistoric period with a number of components. Not all the jumping operations occurred at the same time of the year. Calves (Figure 3.23a–c) and yearlings (Figure 3.23d) in one level demonstrate tooth eruption indicative of a late fall operation, whereas calves and yearlings from another level were killed in late spring or early summer. Calves and yearlings from the Hawken site were killed about midwinter, according to mandibular tooth eruption and wear. Using the same criteria, we found that calves and yearlings from the Glenrock Buffalo Jump were killed in the fall.

The life span of grazing animals is variable and a function partly of the life of their teeth. For example, bison that are given supplemental feed during the winter can have their productive life span doubled simply because their teeth are not subjected to the intense wear resulting from chewing coarse grasses and shrubs during the winter months. Tall grass and open winters also extend bison life spans. Tooth attrition is greater among animals that graze in areas where dust and other abrasive materials adhere to grass and forbs in comparison to animals living in areas where the grasses are not so affected.

Catastrophic kill site populations offer the opportunity to calculate annual rates of tooth wear. These rates of wear vary from site to site and from time period to time period. The causes of this are not yet well understood. Obviously, if the first molar of a bison is shortened an average of 5 mm each year and there is 50 mm of tooth after it is fully erupted at the age of two years, the molar tooth will be gone after 12 years and the animal will require lush, available winter feed to survive another year. The potential for recovery of past ecological conditions from these kinds of data is high but remains to be fully explored.

The methodology used in zooarchaeological studies of bison kill site populations is readily applicable to the remains of animals other than bison. The pronghorn (*Antilocapra americana*) has shorter breeding/birthing seasons than bison, and close time-of-year determinations are possible (Nimmo 1971). Using these data, remains of over 200 antelope recovered at the Protohistoric Eden-Farson Shoshonean campsite were found to have been killed between late October and early December. This strongly suggests the animals were taken in some sort of a communal trap rather than through individual hunting (Frison 1971b). Studies of a large sample of mule deer (*Odocoileus hemionus*) remains from the Dead Indian Creek site of Middle Plains Archaic age described earlier indicate that the deer were killed throughout the winter months rather than at a single large kill. In this particular site situation it would be tempting to regard it as a single kill or several

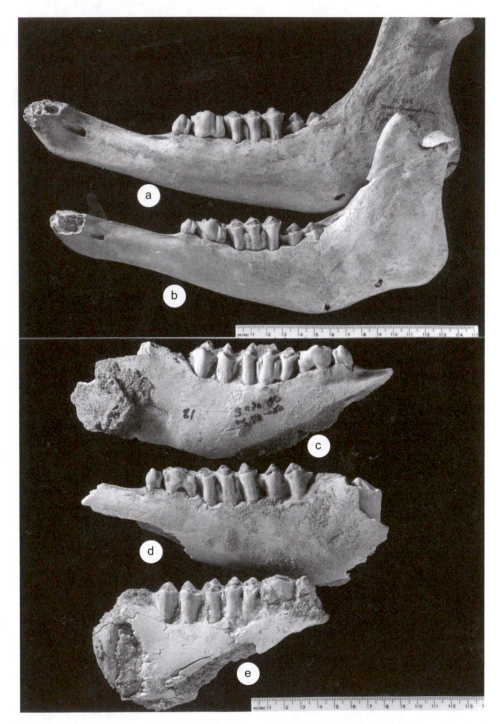

Figure 3.22   Bison calf mandibles from the Olsen-Chubbuck site (a, b) and the Casper site (c–e).

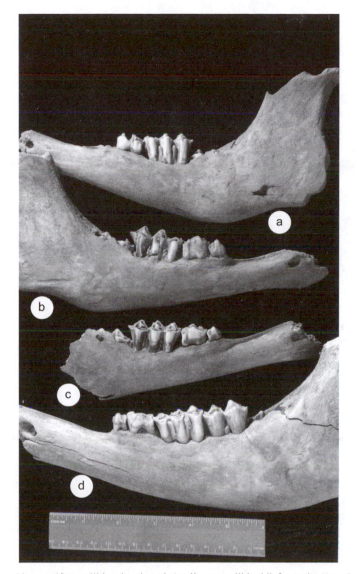

Figure 3.23   Bison calf mandibles (a–c) and yearling mandible (d) from the Vore Buffalo Jump.

closely spaced kills, were it not for the evidence from age determination (Simpson 1984).

A reevaluation of the seasonality of some bison kills has been possible using tooth eruption and wear as a time-of-year indicator. The Olsen-Chubbuck site (Wheat 1972) was apparently a late summer or early fall event rather than late spring as first claimed, since calves from the site are close to 0.4 years of age (Figure 3.22a, b). The Finley site (Moss et al. 1951) was apparently a late fall or early winter activity. Insufficient ageable material for a closer determination was recovered in the youngest age categories. Agate Basin bison procurement activities (Frison and Stanford 1982) took place throughout the winter on the basis of calf teeth recently recovered from both butchering and kill areas of an Agate Basin level at the site.

Large samples of the animal population in a kill site usually reveal individuals of all age groups within the population. With such data, we can derive life tables and survivorship curves, which tell us something of the viability of the population. In the Late Prehistoric period there is evidence that there were as many as 16 or 17 age groups for bison (Reher 1970, 1973:98–99), whereas at the Casper site we could find only about 12 age groups (Reher 1974:113–124). The same situation was confirmed for the *B. bison occidentalis* population at the Hawken site (Frison et al. 1976). There is evidence also of stress on the Casper bison population, as is demonstrated by tooth abnormalities. These include abnormal lower third molars (M/3) (Figure 3.24), congenital absence of a lower premolar tooth (Figure 3.25a, b),

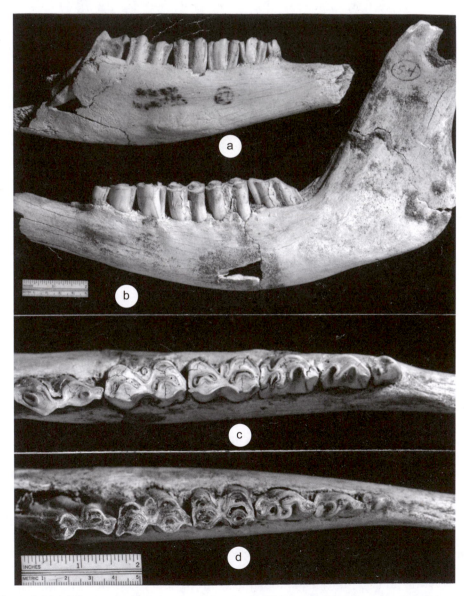

Figure 3.24   Side view (a, b) and occlusal view (c, d) of bison mandibles from the Casper site with pathological lower third molars. (From Wilson 1974a.)

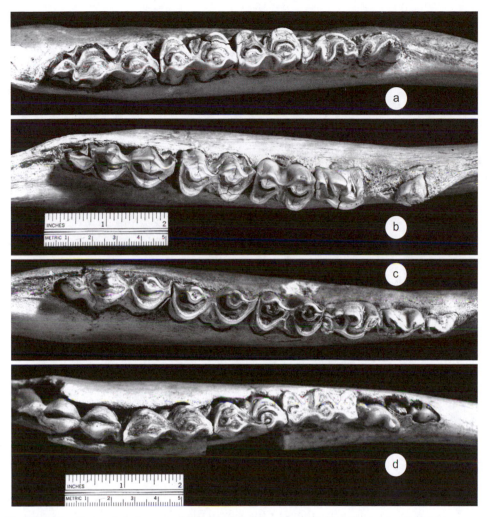

Figure 3.25   Congenital absence of P/2 (a), P/3 (b), and crooked tooth rows (c, d) in bison mandibles from the Casper site. (From Wilson 1974a.)

malformed lower teeth other than M/3, deflected tooth rows (Figure 3.25c, d), excessive amounts of cementum on molar exteriors (Figure 3.26a, b), lumpy jaw (Figure 3.26c), and others (Wilson 1974a). From these we may eventually understand why the larger, extinct bison were not able to survive. The solution of problems such as these may tell us more about the human populations as well. For example, the stress may have resulted from intense human predation or a combination of stressful circumstances.

Two other important concepts in the study of taphonomy and population dynamics are catastrophic and attritional mortality. Attritional mortality is the normal dying off of the population and can be detected by a look at the population structure (Deevey 1947:289). In a normal dying-off situation a large number of the very young die. The ones that pass a critical age are no longer subject to the earlier high probability of death and the remainder of the age groups gradually increase from a low value to a higher value and then decrease to zero as

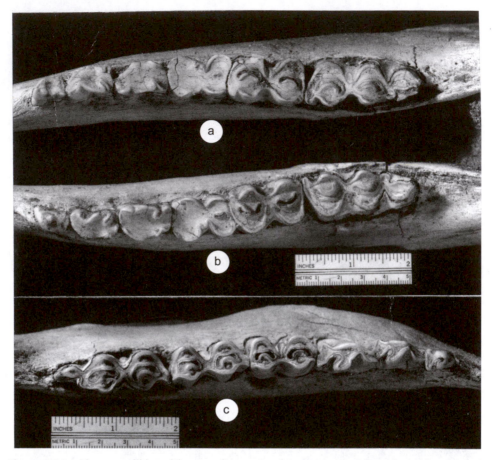

Figure 3.26 Bison mandibles with unusual amounts of cementum (a, b) and lumpy jaw (c) from the Casper site. (From Wilson 1974a.)

the maximum age of individuals in the population is reached. Results produce a population structure that contains mostly the very young and the middle aged (Figure 3.27a).

Catastrophic mortality is different and represents a sample of the total population at a given point in time. Large animal kills using traps or stampedes over bluffs are examples. A number of smaller kills in the same spot within a short period of time produce nearly identical results. The ideal population structure as seen in a catastrophic kill contains large numbers of young and grades into slightly smaller numbers of early mature animals and fewer old ones (Figure 3.27b).

The catastrophic kill and its analysis are of value in archaeological interpretation. These are the situations in which large populations were taken and, although human activities of butchering and processing resulted in considerable dismembering of the animals and removal of some parts, enough elements are usually left to form a base for analysis. Mandibles were one of the less desirable items on the bison carcass and were often discarded at the kill sites. Fortunately, not all mandibles were left at kill sites, and some were taken to camp and butchering areas. The presence of mandibles from the same population sample in both kill and camp and/or processing areas provides a means of checking one area against the other.

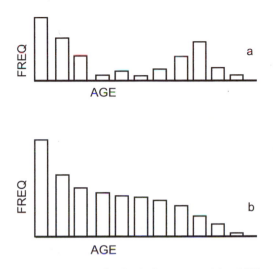

Figure 3.27 Generalized age structure of animals from an attritional kill sample (a) and a catastrophic kill sample (b). (From Frison and Todd 1987.)

The utility of this was demonstrated at the Big Goose Creek site (Frison et al. 1978), a Late Prehistoric period bison jump and campsite complex near Sheridan, Wyoming. The initial interpretation was that this was a bison jump with a butchering/processing area associated. Tooth eruption analysis of mandibles from the kill area left little doubt that the animals there were killed about the middle of fall. Analysis of the upper teeth from the camp area revealed that the animals there had been killed over a period of several months during the winter.

In the Big Goose Creek site winter camp area the seasonality of bison procurement was further supported by a study of fetal remains. Fetal bones appear at several growth stages, and from our rather limited sample of fetal bison material of known age, we feel the site specimens represent fetuses taken from animals killed from about November to February.

The Wardell Buffalo Trap (Frison 1973b) is another example of a bison kill that demonstrates the utility of determining the animals' ages in order to determine seasonality. The bison from the kill site (a corral or pound situation) were determined to be in age groups of about 0.4, 1.4, 2.4, and so on years (Reher 1973). A large butchering and/or processing area is immediately adjacent to the corral, and mandibles recovered from the processing area fall into the same time-of-year pattern as those from the kill. This provides strong evidence that the processing area is where the animals from the kill were taken. The site was a multicomponent one, indicating the strategy of fall procurement was repeated several times.

Studies of population dynamics can be extended to include small animal populations. Investigations in the deep, stratified Medicine Lodge Creek site in the Bighorn Basin of Wyoming revealed intensive use of rodents by Paleoindian hunting and gathering groups. Included in a cultural level dated at about 9500 BP was a bone midden containing a minimum number of 101 pocket gophers (*Thomomys talpoides*), 135 bushy-tailed wood rats (*Neotoma cinerea*), 134 montane voles (*Microtus montanus*), and 180 prairie voles (*Microtus ochrogaster*). Many other species were represented but in much smaller numbers. Only part of the midden was excavated.

All four species were present in quantities large enough for a population study to be done. Apparently the *Neotoma cinerea* (bushy-tailed wood rat) is characterized by a predictable yearly breeding season. A study of the wood rat dentitions from the site indicated three groups, those approximately two years of age, those approximately one year of age, and the year's newborns (Walker 2007). It is believed, based on tooth eruption and wear, that the wood rats were killed in late July or August, which provides a basis for suggesting a late summer occupation of this area of the site.

More reliable means of determining the age of animals from archaeological sites may appear in the future. Other indicators have been tried, such as bone ossification schedules, cementum annuli accumulation on roots of teeth, and chemical contents of bone (Spiess 1979). So far not enough is known about bone ossification rates to determine age as closely as with tooth eruption. Annual or seasonal rings on bison molar teeth have not been visible enough for meaningful age determinations, and the methods of analysis are destructive. Studies on incisor teeth have not been tried because few incisor teeth are preserved in most archaeological sites. General distinctions between young, juvenile, and mature animals may be made through the analysis of the chemical content of bone, but this is not yet precise enough for seasonality determinations.

Fetal material, if present, is of importance since it demonstrates systematic changes in size and development over short periods of time and often appears in both camp and kill sites. In fact, fetal material is proving to be of great value as an indicator of seasonality as better collections of known-age materials are becoming available (see Fenner and Walker 2008 for fetal pronghorn).

Sex Determination

The archaeologist requires sex determinations in animal populations for other reasons in addition to as an aid in determining the evolutionary history of the species. The population structure reveals the age and sex of the animals recovered in kill sites and the time of year the kill occurred. With this kind of information and knowledge of animal behavior, it is then possible to assess the procurement methods used because nursery herds behave differently than groups of mature males. Different procedures were used to butcher and process a mature male bison, a smaller female, or a still smaller calf. The nature of procurement, butchering, and processing methods indicates something of the size of the human group involved, and the time of year of the kill allows an investigator to formulate hypotheses about the seasonality of other economic activities. The amount of food products obtained differs also with the ranges of size and differences in sex. The amount and kind of food products obtained in a communal animal kill are important in the final analysis of site data. Reliable sex indicators other than skulls are therefore important.

Metacarpals, metatarsals, and astragali are bones that occur commonly in kill sites. Metapodials (both metacarpals and metatarsals) were occasionally broken for bone marrow, but as with the mandibles, they carried very little flesh and were not among the more desirable bones. Consequently, metatarsals, metacarpals, and astragali are usually present in numbers sufficient for analysis. These bones are important in supporting the animal's weight, and their relative size should reflect the size of the animal. Some positive results in determining bison sex have resulted from careful study of these bones (Bedord 1974). Volumes of astragali can easily be determined, and the idea is not new. Sellards (1955:138) and Lorrain (1968) used astragali volume measurements to demonstrate different size ranges between modern and extinct forms of bison in the Southern Plains.

Another means of sexing bison utilizes the height measurement of the mandible below M3 (Reher 1970, 1973, 1974). This is based on a principle that males have larger, more rugose mandibles than females. These measurements applied to bison populations yield bimodal distributions, but exact separation between males and females cannot be made. However, the method does appear to have a reasonably good validity. One major limitation is that in many sites the butchering process and/or bone deterioration has not left enough of the mandibles intact.

In summary, there are many things the archaeologist needs to know that can be extracted from studies of animal remains recovered in large kill sites. Studies of taphonomy and animal population dynamics can provide some of the evidence needed to reconstruct human cultural systems as well as the recent evolutionary histories of the various animal species. Bison kills have been the most productive in terms of data because many of the bison kill situations were communal efforts that resulted in the death of large segments of the population within a restricted time period, and the remains were preserved in datable, recoverable contexts. However, any animal kill will provide the necessary data if enough ageable specimens are present.

The archaeologist is especially concerned with the social implications of the communal animal kill. The distribution of food resources throughout most of the year required the humans to be dispersed in single or small multifamily groups in order to exploit the area most efficiently. The communal kills were probably the largest aggregations of people that commonly occurred at any time during the year among hunting and gathering bands. Band composition was determined by kinship and its extensions, and consolidating the kin group at intervals was an important mechanism for its continuing existence. It may have been that the social and other institutionalized benefits of communal animal kills were as important to these band-level societies as were the economic benefits.

THE USE OF TAPHONOMY IN ARCHAEOLOGICAL STUDIES

Nearly a century of investigating bison and other bone beds had demonstrated to previous generations of archaeologists that not all skeletal elements are present in these features (White 1952, 1953, 1954). The missing elements can be the result of past butchering practices, processing of animal products, natural consequences of death assemblages, or a combination of these and other factors. Paleontologists realized long ago that reconstructing animal behavior, past animal communities, paleoecology, and other topics of interest require the understanding of how animals pass from living, dynamic systems (a live animal herd) to a "static" pile of bones that are recovered by the investigators (Efremov 1940). To get from the pile of bones to animal behavior and paleoecology, paleontologists have developed the science (methodology) of taphonomy, the "study of death assemblages" (Efremov 1940). According to Voorhies (1969:21):

> Taphonomy is concerned with the factors intervening between a living fauna and the fossilization of a fraction of it. It deals mainly with the post-mortem history of animal remains (especially their decay, transportation, and burial) but also with the cause of death. Taphonomy overlaps paleoecology only insofar as the mode of life of an organism influences its choices of burial and preservation.

Voorhies (1969:2) distinguishes carefully between paleoecology and taphonomy but points out that information derived from the latter can be of importance for the reconstruction of the former.

Voorhies's initial study dealt with an early Pliocene vertebrate fauna. However, the principles involved and methodology used provide a usable and quantifiable means of analyzing faunal remains from archaeological sites. The results can then be used to determine a variety of characteristics of the animal populations, and these facts in turn provide information on what the humans who were exploiting the animals were doing. In this sense and toward these ends, a number of archaeologists, including ourselves, have utilized concepts of taphonomy and analyses of population structures with positive results. In their analysis of animal populations, archaeologists must allow for one variable that need not be considered in paleontological studies. This variable is the human element, which adds different dimensions in terms of its effects on the animals and their postmortem remains.

The last 30 years have seen an explosion of taphonomic studies in archaeology, intimately linked to the proliferation of middle-level theory, an archaeological concept not altogether divorced from taphonomy (Binford 1978a, 1981; Haynes 1980; Lyman 1994). By and large these studies have taken a cue from paleontology, as well as all that it offered in this regard, and carried the science of taphonomy to new heights. Even avocational archaeologists and collectors have incorporated taphonomy into their research agenda (Fenn 2004:104). Some of the archaeological studies are general and can be incorporated back into paleontology, but much of it is specific to archaeological problems, or rather to the human element in archaeological assemblages. In this sense, it is important to differentiate the marks of human hammerstone impact fractures from carnivore canines (Binford 1980; Capaldo and Blumenschine 1994), the effects of intentional burning on assemblages (Shipman et al. 1984), the differentiation of human and other marks from animal and soil processes (Shipman 1980), impact flakes from natural bone flakes (Ono 2001), and a myriad of other observations and their causes. These studies have developed incrementally to solve specific problems at specific sites, but the methodology developed for each case is widely applicable to archaeological problems throughout the world (e.g., Kreutzer 1992).

The continual developments in taphonomic study has greatly increased the potential for interpretation. Bone weathering studies (Behrensmeyer 1973) can yield information on past ecological conditions and site formation processes. For example, bison bone in the Goshen complex Mill Iron site in southeast Montana demonstrated extreme weathering stages on upper surfaces and nearly pristine bottom surfaces. The conclusion from this is that the bones were still in situ when recovered but were exposed for some time before burial (Kreutzer 1996). Observations on the dismemberment and final disposition of modern animal carcasses through various noncultural agents including weathering, geologic activity, water transport, carnivores, scavengers, and rodents, as well as cultural activities, aid in understanding and interpreting the faunal evidence in both paleontological and archaeological deposits. For example, experimental water transport studies using modern elephant bones and attempting to reestablish stream bed characteristics were used to buttress the argument that the mammoth bone piles at the Colby Mammoth Kill site in Wyoming were the result of cultural activity and not water transport (Frison and Todd 1986:61–68).

One of the most exhaustive analyses of a Paleoindian bison bone bed to date is the one completed on the Horner site (Todd 1987a). Todd not only utilized the most recently published archaeological and paleontological taphonomic methodology, but contributed to this methodology through field studies of recent animal deaths (the Nall Bos site), as well as detailed recording and observations of animal bone beds with known histories (Plumbago Canyon; Figures 3.28 and 3.29). These studies helped explain a variety of observations at bison bone beds, as well as contributed to the understanding of decomposition/disarticulation processes of size class 4 animals (Brain 1981).

Others have likewise made significant contributions to taphonomic studies. Lyman (1989) took the opportunity to collect data on elk killed by the Mount St. Helens eruption to show the immediate postmortem characteristics of skeletonization. At the same time, Hughes (1985) recorded a natural elk death assemblage in Wyoming to examine bone fractures occurring under known conditions. More recently, Lubinski (1997) reported on a pronghorn herd that died in Reiser Canyon in southwest Wyoming. The instant death of the herd provided Lubinski an analog for the age and sex composition of such an assemblage to compare with archaeological assemblages whose duration of death is uncertain. This type of natural death can, however, be further exploited. Recently Jack Fenner (2007) has used the Reiser Canyon assemblage to ask questions about the isotopic composition of the herd. Like Lubinski, Fenner was interested in whether prehistoric bone beds are the result of single (or a few closely spaced) mass kill events and thus represent communal hunting strategies, or accumulations of many single animal deaths and thus represent individual hunting. Through the determination of the oxygen and

Figure 3.28 Photo of Bos *taurus* bone bed at Plumbago Canyon locality, where a group of animals were killed in the 1930s.

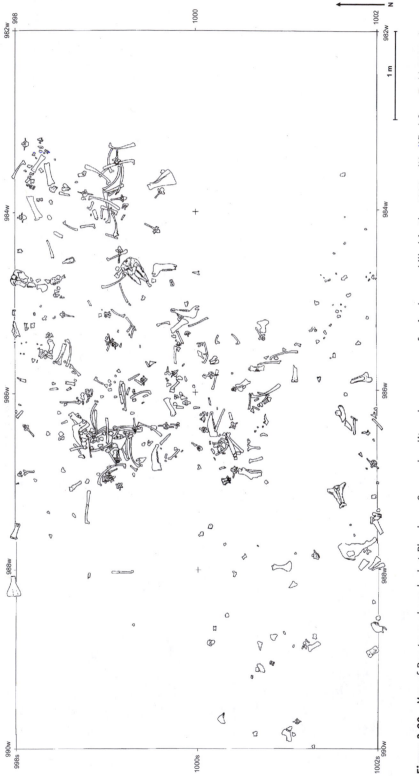

Figure 3.29 Map of *Bos taurus* bone bed at Plumbago Canyon locality, where a group of animals were killed in the 1930s. (Modified from Todd 1987a.)

strontium isotope signatures of a herd, Fenner has shown the history of prong-horn herd migration. He is building a method for the study of pronghorn of the Northwestern Plains and Rocky Mountains on the well-established precedents in other areas and animals (Hoppe 2004; Widga 2006). Such studies link taphonomy to interdisciplinary endeavors of great importance to prehistoric interpretation.

Significant recent advances in archaeological taphonomic studies have been achieved in the understanding of bone fragmentation processes in both the Americas and Europe (Enloe 1993; Outram 2001; Todd and Rapson 1988). Such studies not only lead to understanding how human action can alter assemblage or element frequency, but also allow for more nuanced understanding of bone processing behavior. Such research has led to the study of extremely fragmented assemblages that former generations of archaeologists thought uninterpretable (Bryan 2006).

Today taphonomy is firmly entrenched in archaeology. Not only is it concerned with faunal remains, but with it also comes the realization that all archaeological data are subject to taphonomic processes. For example, water transport, one of the foremost taphonomic processes Voorhies worried about, is as much relevant to chipped stone as it is to bone, as has been shown by Isaac (1967), Petraglia and Nash (1987), and Schick (1986), among others. It is not only missing skeletal elements that can be explained by taphonomy, but missing or displaced chipped stone of certain size categories can also be a function of taphonomy (Ammerman and Feldman 1978). Assemblages can therefore be easily misinterpreted unless they are carefully studied from a variety of perspectives and not blindly interpreted as the product of cultural processes alone.

On the Northwestern Plains and Rocky Mountains, investigations at Bugas-Holding (Rapson 1990), Lookingbill (Kornfeld, Larson, Rapson, and Frison 2001; Wasilik 2006); Mill Iron (Frison 1996), Barger Gulch (Surovell et al. 2005), Hell Gap (Larson et al. 2009), and other sites have been conducted with taphonomic processes at the forefront of the site investigations. These studies allow for confidence in statements about the spatial distributions of archaeological materials that previously relied on unstated and unevaluated assumptions (e.g., Dibble et al. 1997; McPherron et al. 2005).

EXPERIMENTS IN ARCHAEOLOGY

There are many activities that can be considered experimental archaeology. As anthropologists in general and archaeologists in particular, we are aware of the inadequacies of the archaeological record for purposes of interpretation. This is aptly demonstrated in an experiment in which a Cree Indian camp abandoned in the late 1960s was investigated shortly afterward according to established archaeological methods. After the investigation and interpretation, the woman who had lived in the camp was asked to look at the interpretations and comment on their validity. Very briefly, the results were the following:

1. Items were misidentified and assigned to the wrong functional categories.

2. False associations were made between items.

3. Activity areas were interpreted incorrectly.

4. The relationships between activity areas were misinterpreted (Bonnichsen 1972:286).

This should make any archaeologist think very carefully about his or her site interpretations. In Bonnichsen's case, the perishable items were still there, which raises the question of the validity of site interpretations when only the imperishable items are present.

Ethnographic analogy is in some ways another form of experimental archaeology. Its usefulness as well as its pitfalls for the archaeologist have been demonstrated many times (e.g., Binford 1967, 1978a, 1981). Another form of experimental archaeology is the actual testing of weaponry and tools in what we like to think are realistic reconstructions of past conditions. In reality, it is not possible to place the present-day weaponry and tool user with his or her replications of archaeological assemblages into an exact aboriginal context. However, this does not negate the possibilities of gaining insights into how the efficiency of weaponry and tool assemblages affected aboriginal lifeways. The main pitfall for the experimenter is not to forget the fact that any successful experiment represents a single possibility and not the only way in which the task could have been accomplished. On the other hand, because there are relatively unchanging limitations that can be tested, these can provide better parameters upon which to formulate interpretations than parameters derived from theory and conjecture alone.

In terms of experimentation, many of the characteristics of chipped stone raw materials used to manufacture tools and weaponry are unchanging, so that the technology of production is well established. Lithic technology was once considered almost a lost art; however, experimental work in the last few decades has demonstrated—through practice and learning the properties of different raw stone flaking materials—that tool production is a predictive process, and that any prehistoric flaked stone artifact can be duplicated. If we add to this the relatively small amount of perishable parts of weaponry that has been recovered, we can experiment with reliable reconstructions of prehistoric weaponry.

Weaponry Use

A prehistoric, communal bison kill is an example of a situation in which a number of hunters prepared for a specific activity that always had a fairly high potential of failure and also an element of danger. Knowledgeable hunters in this kind of situation do not ordinarily jeopardize their chances of success with inferior or poorly maintained weaponry. No matter how skillfully the animals were herded into the trap, if the weaponry was not properly designed and maintained to penetrate and kill the animals, the animals increased their probability of escaping and the hunters had a higher probability of going hungry and of being hurt physically in the process.

However, when we analyze the weaponry assemblage from a large communal bison kill, whether Paleoindian or Late Prehistoric, we discover a wide range of quality in the projectile points in terms of flaking technology and aesthetics. Apparently, not all of the excellence in flaking technology can be interpreted as purely functional. We would have to assume the less aesthetic projectile points were as lethal to a bison as the others. However, it appears that if a knapper acquired a superior piece of raw stone flaking material, the end product was sometimes something superior in terms of technology and aesthetics.

In order for a projectile point to be effective on large animals, it must penetrate more than the length of the point. The tip must be sharp enough to penetrate the hide and the blade edges must be sharp enough to widen the cut and allow the projectile and shaft to continue on into the carcass and reach a vital spot (Figure 3.30). If the shaft and binding are too bulky it is nearly impossible to drive this bulge through the hole formed by the projectile. The binding must be secure enough to prevent movement of the projectile in the haft, but it must not be so bulky as to hinder penetration. One noticeable attribute of projectile points from bison kills is the care taken to sharpen the point to obtain the best possible penetration of the hide (e.g., Figure 2.58i–l).

Whether or not Paleoindian projectile points were hafted to foreshafts that were in turn inserted into the end of a mainshaft (as can be demonstrated in Late Archaic times, e.g., Figure 2.66 a, b) or were hafted directly to a mainshaft is not known; perhaps both methods were used. The technological solutions for manufacturing

Figure 3.30   Distal end of a Yonkee point lodged in the centrum of a bison thoracic and undoubtedly a lethal shot.

an easily changeable, reliable bond between mainshaft and foreshaft are relatively simple although costly in terms of manufacture time. However, the advantages are many. It is relatively easy to carry several foreshafts and a single mainshaft; a person using a thrusting spear can spear a large animal such as a bison and pull off the mainshaft leaving the foreshaft in the animal. Another foreshaft can quickly and easily be inserted into the mainshaft, or the mainshaft can also be used for protection from other animals if the hunter is in the confines of a trap or corral. Maintenance is enhanced also since the foreshafts are carried separately and are not accidentally dulled or broken as easily. On the other hand, the mainshaft is also subject to breakage, particularly in the vicinity of its juncture with the foreshaft. A bundle of foreshafts without a mainshaft leaves the hunter in the same predicament as having a mainshaft and no foreshafts. From experience, the best solution is to use foreshafts but also carry along an extra mainshaft. After many experiments, the conclusions are that there are many ways in which the stone point can be attached to wood using simple materials. A strictly personal and individual tendency in these experiments was to underestimate the strength and flexibility of a wooden foreshaft and the binding elements to the extent that they were too bulky. What needs to be determined is the location of weak points where failure is most likely to occur and concentrate on improving weaponry design in these areas. The most common locations of failure are the projectile point itself distal to the bindings and the connection between the foreshaft and mainshaft.

A good demonstration of projectile point failure was a direct hit on a domestic cow rib using a thrusting spear. In this case, both the point and the haft of the projectile point broke. Almost identical results occurred in the case of using a thrusting spear with a foreshaft and Clovis point on an African elephant; the foreshaft broke ahead of the mainshaft connection, the projectile point broke transversely just ahead of the haft binding, and the point tip, besides crushing, penetrated almost to the cancellous part of the rib (Figure 3.6). No amount of strengthening of bindings or increase in foreshaft and mainshaft size would have aided the situation; it is simply not possible to drive a stone projectile through a bison or elephant rib with either thrusting spear or spear thrower and produce a lethal wound.

Projectile points hafted to darts used with atlatls on African elephants sustained surprising amounts of punishment without breakage (Frison 1989); one projectile point did break upon entry of the rib cage but the remainder of the point and the foreshaft continued on and resulted in a potentially lethal wound. One specimen manufactured of Edward's Plateau chert from Texas penetrated the rib cages of 12 elephants of both sexes from calves to mature animals with no damage except in one case, where about 2 mm of the distal end broke off. It required only a few seconds to restore it to usable condition.

Proper maintenance and continual practice are vital in order to maximize the potential from prehistoric weaponry. Even a slight bend in a mainshaft negatively affects the flight of the weapon and the direction of force to the base of the projectile. The conical base of the foreshaft must fit closely the matching hole in the distal end of the mainshaft. The spur of the throwing stick must engage properly with the cup in the proximal end of the mainshaft. During the experimental use of atlatl and dart on African elephants, a frustrating problem developed in which the mainshaft refused to follow a proper flight path; the cause was finally determined to be an atlatl spur that was too short to engage with the bottom of the cup on the mainshaft so that the force was delivered to the rim of the cup. No matter how well seasoned wooden equipment may be, certain weather changes and patterns can cause warping. Proper storage and continual monitoring of weaponry condition is necessary to keep it working efficiently.

In addition, weapons and tools are personal and individual items that require total familiarity to maximize results. Only by continual practice does the hunter arrive at the correct length and weight of the atlatl and mainshaft and the best projectile point size. Some wooden materials are superior to others. Willow (*Salix* sp.) for example, makes good shafts but chokecherry (*Prunus* sp.) is superior in strength and flexibility. The former functions quite well for small- and medium-sized animals, but for elephants, the latter is superior and will withstand better the force needed to penetrate their thick hide.

There are many pitfalls to avoid in using primitive weaponry. Patience is the first thing that must be ingrained into the prehistoric hunter, even throughout the most frustrating times. The atlatl and dart is a short-range weapon; it does no good to try long-range, desperation shots because the successful hunter knows that the chances of inflicting a lethal wound are very low. Sooner or later, the proper opportunity will present itself and a desperation shot usually only frightens the animals and decreases the probability of a good shot later.

Size and sex of the animal are determining factors in hunting success. It is relatively easy to place a projectile in the throat of a juvenile bison and the results are extremely effective. However, the neck of a mature bull with its thick hide and heavy coat of hair is a different proposition. In this case, the rib cage would probably be a better choice. The experienced hunter can usually call the results of his or her shot. For example, the immediate involuntary reaction of an animal after being hit with dart, spear, or bullet tells the hunter whether penetration is deep or shallow and whether it is a heart, lung, intestinal, or flesh shot. From that, the hunter knows whether or not the animal needs further attention. Confident of a lethal wound, the hunter can turn his or her attention to another animal in the herd; if the animal is only wounded, it is best to pursue the matter further and be sure of one animal rather than attempt to concentrate on another and lose both.

The thrusting spear and atlatl and dart are both effective though in different contexts. The former is more of a confrontation weapon while the latter is effective at longer distances. In open country, the first action of a bison upon seeing a human being is usually to run away, although they may also go through a short period of curiosity when they may first try to identify the nature of the intrusion. There are means to get close to wild bison, as demonstrated by McHugh (1972) in donning a buffalo hide and mingling with the Yellowstone National Park herd. On the other hand, the reaction of a bison when the hunter reveals his or her true identity is not always predictable. Should a bison decide to charge the hunter, it would be better to rely on the thrusting spear than the atlatl and dart. In a corral or trap, the animal may charge or try to escape; when it realizes escape is impossible, it usually does an about-face, possibly charges the hunter, tries to climb out of the trap, charges into other animals, or attempts some other form of irrational behavior. During this period, the animal is vulnerable to a calculating hunter armed with a thrusting spear. In addition, the spear shaft offers some protection to the hunter. Dispatching the younger animals presents little problem once the older ones are down, since the former will be looking to the latter for protection.

Most of us would hesitate to enter into a corral with a number of bison, reasonably and wisely so, particularly if there were mature animals present and especially a mature male or a female with a young calf. Actually, entering a corral that contains a single bison could be more dangerous than one containing a group. A single animal in this situation is often more unpredictable than the same animal in a group with other animals. A more prudent approach in this situation might be to throw a dart from atop the walls of the trap or from a platform on the top log of the corral.

Many hunters of today would probably argue that improved weaponry has been the greatest aid to the hunter. We would argue that an aid of equal importance to hunting has been optics. Field glasses greatly increase the hunter's chance of locating animals before they see the hunter. Once spotted, it is much easier for the hunter to map out a hunting strategy. This leads to considerations of familiarity with the hunting area. No hunter feels comfortable in unfamiliar territory; the topography must be known as well as how animals behave within it. Weather, time of day, time of year, herd composition, and terrain are only a few of the major factors that affect animal behavior. A good hunter can go into unfamiliar territory, make quick judgments, and have some success, but it is often the subtle things about a given hunting area that prove to be of greatest significance. The animals themselves know the area. They know where the best cover is. The hunter has to know what lies over the next rise in order to predict what the animals on this side of the rise are most apt to do when disturbed. In other words, absolute familiarity with a hunting area is of prime importance to success.

The strategy of the prehistoric hunting operation—except for the large communal procurement events—whose purpose was to alleviate hunger on a continuing basis, was to take animals regularly and disturb the remainder of the animals as little as possible. The more skillful the hunter and the more successful the technology, the less evidence there is of the hunter's activities in the actual hunting area. Hunting as it exists today bears little resemblance to the prehistoric situation. Many prehistoric species are still extant, but some have been forced into different behavior patterns because of changes in or loss of habitat, seasonal hunting patterns, and artificial limitations on age and sex of animals killed. Even so, a good deal can be learned by an experimental approach to prehistoric hunting.

Butchering and Processing Tools and Tool Use

Animal procurement does not stop with killing the prey. To be able to use the resources—largely meat, but also bone, sinew, horn, stomach content, and possibly other usable parts—the animal must be butchered, distributed, potentially processed for storage, or prepared for consumption. The following observations of such processes come directly from numerous ethnographic accounts.

The Plains Indian tribes reached their greatest cultural integration after the introduction of the horse and before the bison were eliminated in the later part of the nineteenth century, a period of less than 200 years. There are many accounts by explorers, fur trappers, mountain men, artists, and others that give some descriptions of Plains and Rocky Mountain Indian life. One account by a man known as Nick Wilson for whom the town of Wilson, Wyoming, (in Jackson Hole) was named tells the story of his time with historic Indian groups. Wilson came to the

Utah area in 1850, and in 1852 at the age of 12 he ran away from home to join the Wind River Shoshone tribe, which was at that time under the leadership of Chief Washakie.

His account of two years of life with the Wind River Shoshone (Wilson and Driggs 1919) is written in the simplest of language and may seem juvenile to most, but it reveals much of the everyday Native American lifeways. Above all, it clarifies the positions and expectations of male and female in this society. Studying Wilson's account leaves no doubt that the males were the hunters; they killed the animals, and if no females were nearby, they would field dress the animals to prevent spoilage. However, from that moment on the women took over, beginning with skinning the animal, and then butchering and processing the meat and fleshing and tanning the hides. At no place in Wilson's narrative is there mention of a woman killing an animal or a man processing the meat. Although quite accurate for the historic period, this description is a function of the impact of European economy on prehistoric social systems (Klein 1983), and not a reflection of the prehistoric division of labor.

Numerous other accounts describe similar gender-based divisions of labor for the historic period; however, some provide a role for a broader social base in hunting strategies. For example, it is clear that in many Northern Plains communal hunting situations the entire group participated in the drive (Verbicky-Todd 1984). Prehistoric gender division of labor is not well understood. The historic situation, as indicated above, is quite different, while hunting and gathering ethnographies rarely cover communal hunting events that are not a function of global economies, where labor systems have been altered as in the Plains case. It is almost certain that prehistorians will have to develop models for prehistoric communal hunting strategies independently of and free from historic biases.

Every animal used as food by humans requires some preparation to render it edible. Many things affect the degree and kind of preparation needed. Some are cultural, some are dictated by environmental conditions, and some reflect individual preferences. Ethnographic accounts of Plains bison hunters describe the immediate consumption of the warm, raw liver of a freshly killed bison as a delicacy. Its flavor was often enhanced by sprinkling the contents of the gall bladder over the liver. In our own culture, liver is regarded as a highly nutritious food, but only after it is properly aged and cooled. Modern butchers carefully remove the gall bladder without rupturing it in order not to spoil the liver by allowing the contents of the gall bladder to come in contact with it. Many people today categorically refuse to eat the liver of deer and elk (neither of which has a gall bladder), claiming the lack of a gall renders it inedible. There is no known record of prehistoric groups making this distinction.

There are many ways to butcher and process a large animal for human consumption. Some utilize more of the animal than others. Even today, some regard brains, eyes, tongue, spleen, heart, kidneys, etc., as desirable, while others feel the opposite. What has survived in the archaeological record indicates a difference in the intensity of utilization of animal products; much of this may have resulted from cultural factors and some from matters of convenience. A bison killed far from camp at the bottom of a canyon was not likely to have been as much utilized as one killed on level ground close to camp. Stripping only the meat from a carcass ignores the brains, the bone marrow, and the meat adhering to the bones. However, a good butcher can strip the meat from a carcass and leave very little in the way of edible products. Even so, boiling the bones after stripping the meat can provide a nourishing meal.

Killing an animal automatically obliges a hunter to perform further work to properly use the meat and other parts as food. Some limitations are imposed and leeway allowed by existing conditions, such as time of day, time of year, animal size, etc. Spoilage is of particular concern, especially on warm days. In the heat of the day, the contents of the stomach cavity should be removed within an hour or so to prevent the meat from beginning to sour. We know that flies were present prehistorically from thick layers of maggot cases preserved in bone deposits in some bison kills. On a warm fall day, fly eggs laid on meat in the early morning can hatch by sundown. Fly activity is governed largely by temperature and becomes of less concern as the weather grows colder.

One solution to the problem of flies on a hot day is to open the animal up and allow the animal heat to dissipate and the heat of the sun to form a glaze over the exposed flesh. This will prevent both souring and flyblowing of the meat until the cooler conditions of the evening. Another solution, and one undoubtedly used by prehistoric hunting groups, was to construct a simple rack or use the branches of a tree or shrub, cut the meat into strips, and hang it to dry. As soon as a hard film formed, a matter of a few minutes in the hot sun, the flies could no longer lay eggs, and if any had been laid, they would have been unable to hatch. The meat could have been black with flies, as many eyewitness accounts tell us, but their efforts at laying eggs in the meat would have been checked. The average American would be greatly disturbed at being asked to eat meat after seeing it covered with flies. The same American might also give up the great American institutions known as hamburger and hot dog if he or she were to visit certain slaughterhouses and meat processing plants and see the kinds of animal products that go into them.

There were many different kinds and different degrees of prehistoric butchering depending on the immediate situation, as mentioned briefly above. A communal kill presented one set of problems; a single hunter with an animal far from camp and the rest of the group had different problems. Since parts of this book deal with communal hunting, it might be well to reflect momentarily on the plight of the lone hunter. We shall use an example of a 1100 lb (500 kg) female bison killed on a warm, late summer or early fall evening. First, it had to be field dressed. The hide had to be slit from the base of the tail to the throat. In doing this, care was needed to avoid cutting into the intestines, since the quality of the meat is not enhanced if contaminated by the stomach contents.

If the animal was to be left on the ground overnight or for any length of time with the hide on, some provisions had to be made to ensure proper cooling or the animal would begin to sour, usually from the neck down the spinal column and eventually into the entire carcass. There is no mistaking sour meat; one whiff at close range is nauseating and no one is going to eat it.

In order to prevent souring in warm weather, the rib cage must be propped open and the front legs spread wide. As an added precaution, the shoulders of the animal should be elevated slightly off the ground. The neck should be opened and the tongue and windpipe removed. Many a fine animal sours because the hunter fails to open the throat completely and remove all the windpipe when field dressing the animal. Another added precaution against souring is to cut open the muscles between the front legs and rib cage to allow air to circulate. These precautions are not as critical in below-freezing weather, but even then, souring of large animals has resulted in the loss of much good meat. Another precaution is killing an animal in deep snow. Many hunters assume that the snow is cold enough to prevent souring of meat, but snow is also a good insulator and can hold the heat in the animal.

Sometimes part of an animal can be saved if the souring is detected in time and the bad part cut out. Small animals usually present no souring problems because of reduced bulk and more rapid cooling. Also it is a relatively simple matter to hang a smaller animal or simply elevate it over a bush, rock, or anything to get it up off the ground to allow faster cooling.

Once the animal is split open and the tongue and windpipe removed, the innards are ready for removal. Heart, liver, and spleen can be taken early or retrieved after the entire mass is removed. The diaphragm has to be cut, and the kidneys can either be left in the animal or removed. Some hunters like to bleed an animal as soon as possible while others do not. Sometimes this depends upon the nature of the wound that killed the animal. A spear in the rib cavity causes profuse internal bleeding while the same thrust into the stomach or spinal column does not. While the average American today believes that meat should not contain blood, the prehistoric hunter may not have been as likely to be upset by bloody meat and might have even considered it an asset rather than a liability.

After removal of the innards, the animal was ready to be propped open to cool. First a stick of proper length was used to spread the ribs. Lacking a stick, a situation not uncommon to the open plains, a lower leg could be cut off and used for this purpose. A stick, rock, or clump of brush could be used to elevate the shoulder slightly if the hunter felt this was necessary. Because of its hump, a mature bison is almost impossible for one person to roll over or keep on its back. Regardless of the species, the carcass needed to be blocked in the best position for proper cooling.

The hunter could not ignore carnivores or scavengers if the carcass had to be left for any length of time. The rapidity with which these animals can congregate at a freshly killed carcass always comes as a surprise. The hunter might not wish to challenge a grizzly's claim to a carcass, but others less formidable could be kept away. However, leaving the carcass for any length of time was taking a chance on other carnivores and scavengers causing varying amounts of damage. Coyotes are usually suspicious of a carcass the first night while human scent is strong but bear, the various cats, and others will gorge themselves whenever the opportunity presents itself. Eagles, magpies, ravens, and crows can consume a surprising amount of meat and ruin much more during the daylight hours. Brush piled over the carcass will deter the birds but not the animals. Many a hunter returns to the kill to discover varying degrees of loss and contamination from birds and animals.

Every kill and butchering situation is unique to some degree, so the prehistoric hunter continually added to basic skills and hunting knowledge. In addition, this uniqueness makes every archaeological kill site a challenge to the investigator. It also makes it difficult for the investigator to define an exact butchering process for any given site since there are so many variables affecting each kill and butchering situation. On the other hand, the basic butchering procedures and processes did not change greatly until the introduction of metal tools.

So much for philosophical reflections on the prehistoric person who completed a successful hunt and was then faced with the problems of caring for the meat so that it would not be wasted and its quality would not suffer. White (1952, 1953, 1954) initiated systematic studies of prehistoric butchering of large animals on the Plains. His approach was that prehistoric animal carcass handling and utilization could be interpreted from the skeletal units recovered in archaeological sites. Much the same approach is still being used, although modified somewhat by different investigators.

We know from the archaeological and ethnographic record that prehistoric hunting groups on the Plains and Rocky Mountains were able butchers and used a simple but functional set of tools. The communal kill placed demands on the butchers that individual hunting did not. Animals, whether pronghorn, bison, or elephant size, are easier to butcher when still warm from natural animal heat. As the animal cools, the hide adheres more to the carcass, the appendages stiffen, and the carcass becomes difficult to manipulate. It is possible (but not proven) that the initial butchering in a communal kill situation may also have been communal. A cooperating team of two or three can butcher a large animal much more efficiently and quickly than the same two or three operating separately.

Butchering animals the size of mature bison is hard work using a metal knife and axe. It is more difficult yet using a chipped stone tool (Figure 3.31), a stone chopper, and a hammerstone. Different motor habits are required when using a stone knife than when using a steel one. Grasping a stone knife and cutting a hide

Figure 3.31 Experimental butchering of a mature female bison using a large flake tool.

also brings into play an entirely different set of muscles than those used in performing the same action with a metal knife. However, when the proper muscles have been developed, a good deal of the supposed superiority of a metal knife over a stone knife is rapidly dissipated.

Frison (1978, 1991) has demonstrated that bone damage analogous to that found in bison bone beds can be produced by using certain bones as butchering tools (Figure 3.32). These same damage patterns, however, are frequently also

a

b

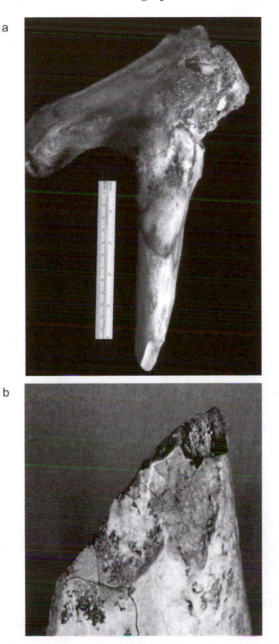

Figure 3.32   Experimental tibia with butchering damage (a) and a Dutton site tibia with damage similar to that produced experimentally (b).

produced by a variety of nonhuman agents, such as carnivores, rodents, and geologic processes, as has been demonstrated over the past 20 years by various taphonomic studies (Lyman 1994). The evidence is currently ambiguous, and we have no known methodology to differentiate expedient bone tools (if they exist, and they may well exist), from bone modified by nonhuman agents (Figure 3.33). Note that we are referring here only to expedient bone tools that might be used during the butchering process and not a variety of formed bone or horn implements such as needles, awls, beads, and other artifacts.

As mentioned earlier, the butchering tool regularly used in communal kill events was a large percussion flake requiring a minimum of preparation other than sharpening of the cutting edge and dulling of the part held in the hand (Figure 2.5).

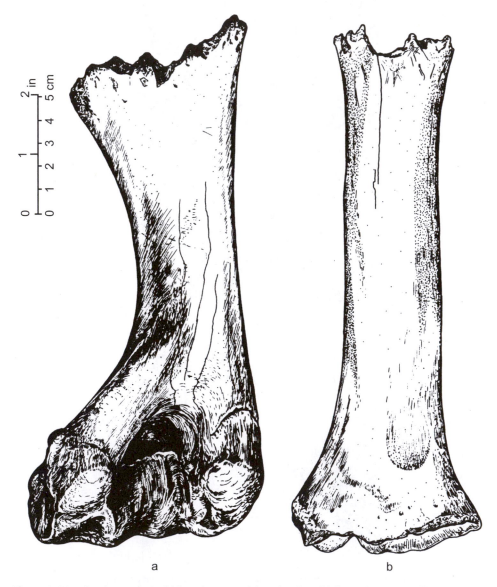

a   b

Figure 3.33   Carnivore-chewed bison humerus (a) and radius (b) from the Vore Buffalo Jump.

In fact, there is evidence in some sites of manufacture of these kinds of tools, presumably for gearing up for butchering animals in communal bison kills. These kinds of tools were efficient and easily resharpened. The user felt little remorse in discarding it when worn out or broken because little effort went into its manufacture and a new one was easily obtainable. Tools of this kind were usually sharpened unilaterally on the dorsal side of the flake; only occasionally were they sharpened bilaterally. These tools appear almost without exception in prehistoric bison butchering contexts on the Plains and Rocky Mountains from Clovis to historic times. They are functional for all cutting requirements in butchering a bison but are not equal to a metal knife. Many kill and butchering sites have produced only small numbers of these tools, but the use of a great many more can be indisputably demonstrated by the presence of flakes removed in the process of resharpening tools no longer present (e.g., Frison 1967b, 1968b, 1974). A similar tool of quartzite functioned quite well in cutting elephant hide (Figure 3.34).

Hammerstones and stone choppers also appear in prehistoric bison-butchering contexts. Breaking bones was common, and the amount and kind depended upon the butchering process employed in any given site. In some cases, joints were separated by cutting the ligaments; in other cases, the bone was crushed or broken on one or both sides of the joint. Hammerstones were usually unmodified river cobbles of the desired size and shape. Sometimes one end of a flat river cobble was flaked to provide a sharp edge or point. Muscle attachments were sometimes removed with a stone chopper, sometimes with a bone chopper, even in the same

Figure 3.34 Cut in the hide near the top of the back of a mature female African elephant using the quartzite biface reduction flake pictured alongside the cut. Hide thickness is 15 mm.

site. This may have been the result of differential availability of raw materials or the preferences of the individual butcher.

It should be emphasized again that during at least 11,000 years of prehistoric bison butchering on the Plains and Rocky Mountains, the basic process changed little (Figure 3.35). Some individuals or groups preferred one tool type or assemblage over another. Some groups favored a stripping and dissecting technique whereas others leaned toward stripping meat and breaking the bones. We are far from being able to analyze the butchering process at any given site and make meaningful statements about the time period or cultural affiliations involved. An exception might be something like the practice of opening the brain cavity from the front (Figure 3.16), which seems to be a diagnostic of the Late Prehistoric period on the Plains, and which may have been for ritual purposes rather than to merely gain access to the brain cavity. Certainly, this was the more difficult method for performing this operation.

Experimental Butchering with Stone Tools

We believe much about prehistoric butchering processes can be learned from the interpretation of various marks on bone, the composition of bone units remaining in kill and butchering sites, and experimentation in butchering animals, as well as from tool assemblages and ethnographic accounts. Experimental butchering has been a means of testing a number of ideas and hypotheses about butchering processes and techniques that arose as the result of observations made in prehistoric bison kill and butchering sites. It has also been the source of many new ideas on butchering and tool use. We strongly believe that if one wishes to become familiar

Figure 3.35   Butchered bison at the Vore Buffalo Jump.

with prehistoric butchering, there is no substitute for taking a prehistoric stone and bone butchering tool assemblage and applying it to freshly killed animals until such time that one is proficient at butchering. It may not be possible to recreate past conditions exactly or prove hypotheses beyond any doubt, but actually using the tools is a good way to understand the limitations imposed as well as the possibilities offered by a tool assemblage. One requirement in this kind of activity is to pursue the experimental work to an extent that some measure of expertise is acquired. This will certainly not come by butchering one or two animals; by about the tenth or twelfth animal, the butchering process using stone and possibly along with bone tools will begin to look professional.

Keeping these ideas on tool use in mind, we can refer once more to a typical 1100 lb (500 kg) female buffalo. One animal in particular was completely butchered following the procedures just described and using a tool assemblage as nearly as possible identical to that recovered from the Glenrock Buffalo Jump (Frison 1970a). This was an animal culled from a herd after losing her calf and the whole butchering process was performed under the watchful eye of an official meat inspector. After the animal was completely butchered, all of the meat was declared fit for human consumption, which should say something for being able to butcher a large animal with prehistoric tools and keep it as clean as if it were butchered with modern tools. The bones of the animal (except for the skull) were later cleaned and checked for evidence of tool use. Most but not all of the cutting, chopping, and hammerstone marks that had been recorded on bones from the Glenrock site were observed.

Weights for all of the separate butchered units were recorded and the total came to 358 lb (163 kg), somewhat short of the general rule that the average mature female bison should yield about 400 lb of fresh meat. On the other hand, the animal was on the open range well into the winter and was not in top condition, which is another factor that affects butchering and also the meat products. The common figure of 400 lb of meat from a female buffalo apparently refers to animals in prime condition in late summer and early fall. At this time there is fat in thick layers between the layers of meat and on the ribs, brisket, and into the hump. The back fat may be 2.5 cm or more thick, and gut fat is present also in large strings and blobs in the intestines. The animal in poor condition presents an entirely different picture. The fat is gone on ribs, brisket, and back. The hump shrinks to practically nothing, and the hide hangs tight to the animal and is difficult to remove. By actual weight, a buffalo cow in prime condition may have a hump of 20–30 lb and even more, made up of alternating layers of fat and flesh. A similar animal in poor condition, such as is encountered in early spring after a hard winter, may have a hump that weighs only 5–10 lb or less. A 15-year-old buffalo cow killed in very poor condition in early April yielded only 225 lb of flesh in contrast to the one in better condition killed in March that yielded 348 lb. The difference in weight makes a good deal of difference in the contours of the animals, which affects the ease of manipulation of the carcass during butchering.

Buffalo hide is tough but not as tough or as thick as the hide of the genus *Bos*. A sharp stone knife slices quite easily through bison hide but its keenness is soon lost. As the knife gets duller, more and more pressure is needed to force the tool against the hide, which in turn requires a tighter and tighter grip on the knife. Ultimately the only solution is to sharpen the tool. On the other hand, once the necessary cuts in the hide are made, the stone knife is about as useful as a metal one for actual skinning. In fact, the stone knife that is slightly dulled so that it will not slice into the hide but will still sever the tissues holding the hide to the animal is a superior skinning tool.

A working edge on a large percussion flake is surprisingly efficient as long as it is kept sharp and as free as possible of grease and body fluids. Animal grease increases the gripping pressure necessary to hold a tool properly during use. The greasy tool and the butcher's hand can both be wiped clean on the animal's hair or a handful of grass. Wrapping a handful of long bison hair on the part of the tool held in the hand helps also. The pain that results from tightly gripping a tool as a result of grease or liquids can become agonizing after a very short time. Fat can and does build up on a tool, but the effectiveness of this on limiting the function of the tool needs more study. Any limitation to the life of a tool used in bison butchering even though extra fat was rubbed on the tool several times was imperceptible.

This raises the question of tool hafting and why the prehistoric butcher did not simply use a tool with a substantial handle. The question is often posed also as to the use of projectile points as butchering tools. A properly hafted stone knife is easier to use than a hand-gripped one. On the other hand, flake and blade tools used in bison butchering were not amenable to hafting. Stone has little structural strength compared to steel, and a long handle cannot be attached to a stone knife unless a suitable means of attachment is provided. The handle must be well supported and properly attached to withstand the pressures encountered during intense butchering. This sort of haft can be provided, but consider also that the stone knife is rapidly dulled in some butchering operations so that the attrition rate through use and continued resharpening and breakage is extremely rapid. The butcher soon has a hafted tool that is no longer of any use, but in which there is a large investment of time, effort, and materials. It is better to use a large, hand-held flake or blade tool that is functional for intensive butchering and to discard it when it is broken or worn out.

The projectile point and its accompanying shaft and binding were designed to penetrate on impact with an animal. Most bison kill sites demonstrate that projectile points were reused whenever possible, but as projectile points and not as knives. We have yet to find convincing evidence that the same hafted projectile points used in killing animals were relied upon to any significant extent in heavy butchering. It is not difficult to understand the reasons. A projectile point, its wooden haft, and its sinew bindings were designed specifically for the purpose of killing animals. The pressures of thrust on impact are altogether different from the pressures resulting from heavy butchering. The shaft and the sinew bindings can be strengthened to the point where they will withstand this kind of abuse, but when they are so strengthened the haft and binding areas cover so much of the point that its penetrating qualities are hampered. Many kinds of activity areas yield evidence of the use of projectile points as tools, but these were not the ones chosen for heavy bison butchering in communal kills.

Another project in experimental butchering was an attempt to quantify what happens to the working edges of tools as the result of use and to explore various alternatives in the butchering processes. As with most tools that require continual maintenance, learning to prepare butchering tools for use is just as important as learning how to use them. We have found that it is difficult to analyze the working edges of tools in order to determine task-specific aspects of butchering. Butchering covers such a wide range of tool-use activity and makes so many different demands on a tool that its effects on working edges are next to impossible to separate in a task-specific sense. A tool no longer functional for one kind of butchering use may be perfectly functional for other uses. Certain butchering tasks result in a relatively high attrition of tool working edges whereas others do not. It is suggested from a large body of evidence that the high tool-attrition aspects of butchering were taken care of with special classes of easily made tools that were used up quickly and then discarded. A tool may have a short life in a high-attrition situation, but without modification it may then have a comparatively long life in another situation. For example, the tool that has been dulled quickly in cutting hide may then be used for some time in skinning or cutting flesh.

In one of the authors' (Frison's) experiments, none of the common cherts, quartzites, or obsidians would hold an edge for very long when used in cutting open the hide, especially if it was dirty as in the case of a bison just out of a mud or dirt wallow. However, in terms of working edge use, quartzite tool held an edge better than chert, while obsidian was the poorest in this respect of the three.

Some actual figures are available. An excellent flake tool skinning knife of high quality chert (Figure 3.36) with 15.1 cm (8.11 in) of cutting edge was used to cut 111.7 cm (44 in) of hide on a 15-year-old female buffalo. This included the inside of one hind leg from about the midpoint of the metatarsal and a short section of hide on the belly. By the time this amount of hide was cut, the tool was too dull; further cutting of the hide required so much effort that the tool had to be sharpened. It was also well beyond the point where a butcher would normally have stopped and resharpened the tool. This does not mean that the tool would no longer cut hide. It means that it would no longer cut hide in the context of slitting the hide of a dead animal for purposes of skinning. When the hide is removed from the animal and placed flesh side up on a solid base (such as over a log) so that it can be cut, the same tool can be used to cut strips of hide equal to many times the length of hide cut while it is still on the animal. In the process of making the necessary cuts for skinning, the butcher must depend more on the keenness of the tool edge since the hide does not rest on a solid base. In addition, the hide from the lower front foot of a buffalo (which is relatively thin compared to the hide on the back of the animal) was placed flesh side up over a log and an unmodified flake with a low-angle cutting edge (20–25°) was used to cut the hide into narrow strips. The tool cut 300 cm (118 in) of strips from the hide utilizing 32 mm (1.25 in) of tool edge. After this use the tool was dull but still (barely) functional.

Although the tool was nonfunctional at this point for purposes of cutting the hide while on the animal, it was just right for skinning and also cutting flesh from bones. It was, however, nonfunctional for cutting ligaments or large muscles at or near points of origin or insertion. In other words, in heavy butchering, a sharp tool will cut a small amount of hide, ligaments, and muscles near their origin and/or insertion and will subsequently cut a lot of meat before it needs to be resharpened. It should also be added that in cutting strips of hide, the cuts were made from the flesh side, which eliminated to some extent the effects of dirt on the hide. The same flake tool was used without any modification to disarticulate the front leg at the distal radius-ulna and radial-medial-ulnar carpal joint. The same tool was still in good enough condition to disarticulate the tibia-tibial-tarsal joint.

We can demonstrate what actually happens to the working edge of a tool between the time it is sharp and functional and the time it is dull and nonfunctional. The working edge of the tool in Figure 3.36 was photographed before and after

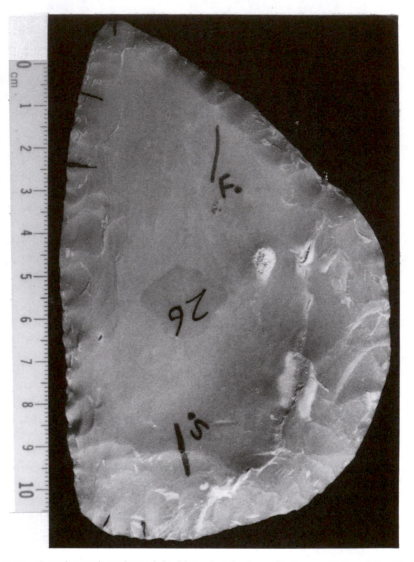

Figure 3.36 Experimental tool used in bison butchering. (Tool manufactured by Charles A. Reher.)

use. A part of the edge is sufficient to demonstrate the effects of cutting a typical bison hide on a mature female animal. The hair on the hide contains a normal complement of dirt, which affects the working edge of the tool. It can readily be seen that the sharp tool edge (Figures 3.37a and 3.38a) is characterized by a number of sharp projections. Some resharpening of the edge occurs as parts of the working edge are broken off during use leaving fresh sharp points. However, the projections soon lose their sharp points and edges, and once they are worn smooth (Figures 3.37b and 3.38b) the tool will no longer cut the hide. One part of the tool edge was deliberately not used and here the condition before use (Figure 3.39a) was identical to the condition after (Figure 3.39b) (see also Frison 1979).

Unmodified flake edges were also used experimentally in cutting the hide on the same animal. On the test tool, the working edge was relatively thin, forming a

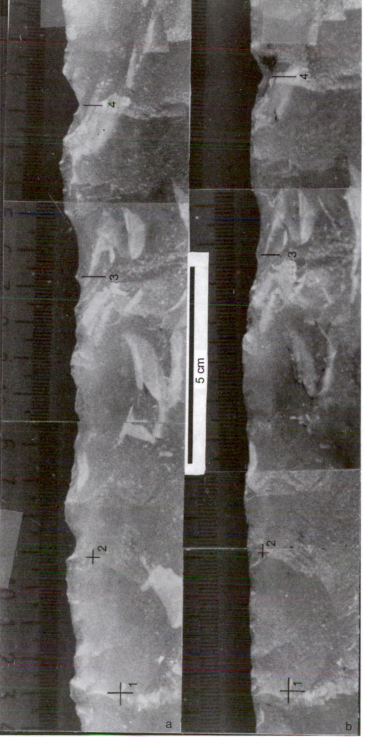

Figure 3.37 Enlarged section of the tool in Figure 3.36 showing a sharp edge (a) and the same section after it is too dull to cut bison hide (b).

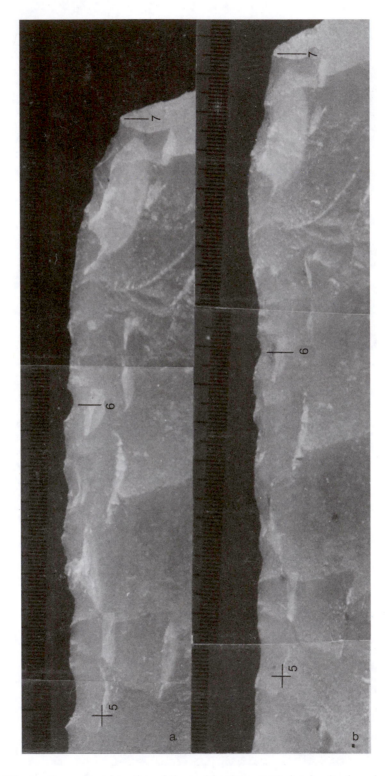

Figure 3.38   Another enlarged section of the tool in Figure 3.36 showing it when sharp (a) and after being dulled during cutting of a bison hide (b).

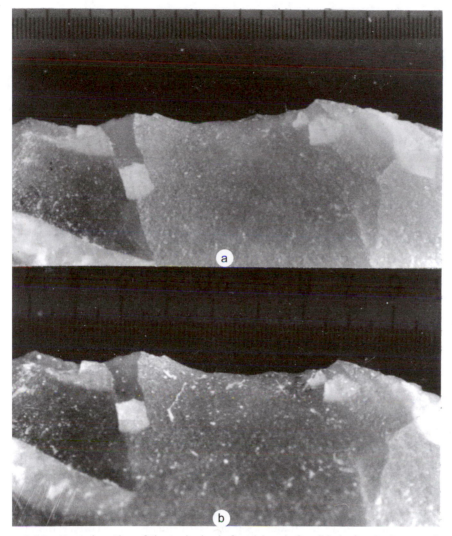

Figure 3.39   Unused portion of the tool edge before (a) and after (b) the butchering experiment, demonstrating no changes.

working edge angle of from 10 to 14°. Using an edge this thin to cut heavy bison hide resulted in rapid attrition of the working edge through breakage, which continued until the working edge became thick enough to withstand the heavy use encountered in cutting the hide. After this stage of use was reached, continued use dulled the projections on the working edge and the same resharpening was applied as in the case of the first tool.

The above should be regarded as a strictly pragmatic approach to chipped stone tool use in a narrowly focused, large animal butchering context. This is not the proper place to attempt an in-depth study of tool use wear and analysis, which is an extremely complex area of study. This type of analysis requires, among other things, special optical equipment and experimentation with tools made of many different types of raw stone flaking materials and their use in task-specific contexts (Hayden 1979). In somewhat different vein, a useful approach to late Paleoindian tool production and use systems has been developed by Knudson (1983). In this application, the term EU (employable unit) is used to describe "that implement segment or portion (continuous edge or projection) deemed appropriate for use in performing a specific task, e.g., cutting, scraping, perforating, drilling, chopping" (Knudson 1983:10). Employable unit is a useful concept and admittedly superior to the term "working edge" since all tool use is not confined to edges. The EU concept was used in the analysis of the Horner site tool assemblage (Frison and Todd 1987:233–274) and the Hell Gap site stone tool assemblages (Kornfeld 2009).

Limited butchering experiments with stone tools were extended to freshly killed elephants during culling operations in Zimbabwe in 1984 and 1985 (Frison 1989). Tools used in the experiment were large biface-production flakes that were similar to those recovered in the Sheaman Clovis site in the Agate Basin site locality in eastern Wyoming (Frison and Stanford 1982: Figure 2.92). A biface tool patterned after one from the same site (Frison and Stanford 1982: Figure 2.91a) was somehow lost and never recovered during a long chase after a small family of five elephants. This was unfortunate because one of the objectives of the 1985 project was to describe the efficiency of biface-production flake tools on fresh elephant carcasses. No suitable flaking material was available in that part of Zimbabwe with which to manufacture another tool.

The results were very much in line with those observed during the bison butchering experiments. Quartzite tools held an edge better than chert, which is thought to be due to the graininess of the former that causes the edge to wear unevenly and actually prolong cutting edge life. The main effort in butchering of elephants is cutting the thick hide (Figure 3.34). A tool made on a quartzite biface-production flake performed adequately but in no way comparable to a steel knife. The tool was used to cut a section of hide on a 6- to 7-year-old male elephant. The section was a rectangular piece between the front and hind quarters and from the centerline of the back to about three-fourths of the distance to the centerline of the belly. This required four sharpenings of the tool, but once the cuts in the hide were made the skinning was relatively easy.

The same quartzite tool (Figure 3.34) that was too dull to cut hide efficiently was used to strip a good share of the flesh from one hind quarter without resharpening. Disarticulation of the major long bones of the elephant carcass also is relatively easy, because the great weight of an elephant does not allow the amount of angular movement of the joints as in the case of smaller animals such as a horse or bison, and the resulting, deep-seated muscles are not present. Once the thick joint capsule is cut through, which was done with the same quartzite tool used in cutting hide and skinning, the joints literally fall apart. This can be done leaving no cut marks on the bone. The size of an elephant demands the cooperation of several butchers for any measure of efficiency. A young elephant in good condition produces a large quantity of tender meat of excellent flavor. If mammoth meat was comparable to that of the African elephant, it should have been sought eagerly by Clovis hunters.

We emphasize that the experimental butchering of bison and African elephants along with a number of other animal species including pronghorn, deer, elk, mountain sheep, domestic cattle, and domestic sheep has been instructive, and it has provided a background for a better understanding and appreciation of prehistoric butchering. On the other hand, it has by no means answered all our questions on the subject. Many more controlled experiments are needed that better replicate past conditions as closely as possible. Butchering processes as they are interpreted from site data need also to be more closely analyzed and described. Approaches along these lines were attempted by Brumley (1973) and Brose (1975). Even though mistaken observations and interpretations will continue to surface, continual site analysis, combined with experimentation and ethnoarchaeological observations such as that of Binford (1978a), appear to be the best approach to further our knowledge of prehistoric butchering.

New Methods at the Cutting Edge

To extract fine-grained data from current field investigations and extant collections as well as to confirm a myriad of occupations that form the basis of our interpretations of the archaeological record from the Northwest Plains and the Rocky Mountains, we and our students have been developing new methods or improving old ones. Below we discuss several specific recent contributions to archaeological methodology that are beginning to have an effect on how we do archaeology and interpret prehistory: minimum analytical nodule analysis, a set of geochemical and molecular techniques, and geophysical applications.

Minimum Analytical Nodule Analysis (MANA)

Several years ago when refitting studies were the rage in archaeological methodology (e.g., Cahen and Keeley 1980; Villa 1983), one of us (Larson) was in the process of refitting the chipped stone assemblage from the Laddie Creek site. Refitting was used to establish the discreteness of the archaeological layers, followed by the establishment of intrasite spatial relationships for the defined levels (e.g., Larson 1992, 1994; Larson and Ingbar 1992). Refitting, however, proved relatively unproductive with far fewer refits than expected. This led the investigator to a series of questions regarding refitting success rates and their implications for archaeological interpretation; but more immediately it led to asking questions about what could be learned from the nodules created in the refitting process.

The relationship of the archaeological record remaining on a site—that is, what one actually finds—with past human activities has always been ambiguous. Archaeologists gloat at pointing out that they dig other people's garbage, but how indicative is the garbage of human behavior? Binford (1978b) and others have shown us that what remains on a site and even the activities that go on at a site may have little to do with the real function that the site plays in the cultural system. Minimum Analytical Nodules (MAN) are argued to be one way to identify what chipped stone was brought to a site, what was done with it at the site, and what was carried away. This better defines the chipped stone technological organization at a site than other methods.

Minimum Analytical Nodules, the nodules arrived at in the process of refitting, are groups of chipped stone with intra–raw material similarity; that is, the pieces in a nodule share a specific constellation of features that differentiate these pieces from others of the same raw material type. Numerous archaeologists have recognized the characteristics of MANs and have utilized them to bolster their arguments about chipped stone technological organization. For example,

Frison (1974:98) defined such groups on the basis of "color, texture and stone type," then estimated the minimum number of tools represented by these resharpening flakes. He further examined the spatial distribution of the nodules and related this distribution to butchering activities. Kelly (1985:166) also grouped stone based on raw material "color, grain, inclusions, evidence of heat treatment, and patina." He divided nodules further based on production techniques (bipolar, biface, percussion flake, and biface flake). On the basis of inferences about hunter-gatherer mobility, he then predicted expected nodule constituents.

Minimum Analytical Nodule Analysis (MANA) lends itself to assemblages that contain materials that are highly variable in color, inclusions, and cortex. For example, with Madison Formation chert from the Bighorn Mountains, the nodules are highly variable in all of the attributes used in minimum nodule sorting, yet all of the material comes from the same geological formation. In our experience cherts are the easiest materials to subdivide, particularly those formed in highly variable environments. MANA begins with sorting all the recovered chipped stone, usually larger than 1 cm, into raw material categories and further subdividing each category into groups based on color, texture, inclusions, and other visual differences and similarities (Figure 3.40, Plate 1b). While we tend to limit our groups to materials from contiguous excavation areas in a site because of the overwhelming quantity of material, these limitations are not necessary and may, in fact, eliminate those rare, but well-documented long distance refits. Several sorts, in combination with mapping of the MAN constituents, are required before the final MANs are agreed upon. The mapping allows the analyst to evaluate if an identified MAN can be further subdivided on the basis of spatial clusters, or it constitutes a single cluster. Here spatial distribution, in combination with material characteristics, forms the criteria for analytically splitting or not splitting the nodule. Although the logic seems circular (nodule–space–(re)nodule), it is not

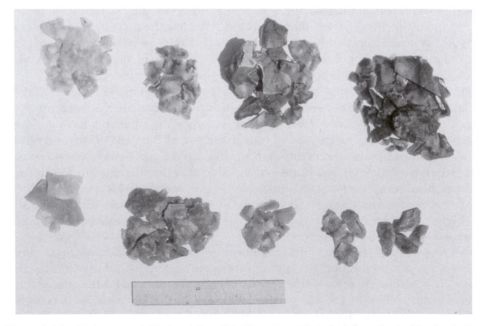

Figure 3.40   Minimum analytical nodules of Madison Formation chert from the Laddie Creek site.

necessarily detrimental to interpretation if one physical nodule becomes two ana-lytical nodules.

While refitting is possible after sorting chipped stone into MANs, the informa-tion available from MANA is not limited to whether or not pieces fit back together. In fact, some of the assemblages we have studied with this technique have not been overly impressive in the number of refits obtained, yet have yielded infor-mation on hunter-gatherer technological organization through analysis of MAN constituents. On a continuum, MANs measure some set of production events less than the entire raw material category, but more than individual items and usually refitted pieces (Figure 3.41). If an analyst unwittingly splits a block of raw mater-ial into several MANs, each nodule represents fewer discrete production events than the entire block, but probably more than an individual item. Even on sites in which the large majority of material is from a single local source, the identification and subdivision of raw materials into MANs has proven successful (for example, the Hell Gap site in southeastern Wyoming [Byrnes 2009; Knell 2009; Sellet 1999]). Hofman (1992) argued that refitting is useful for understanding depositional pro-cesses, horizontal distributions, and technological organization. In the absence of refitted pieces, or with few refitted pieces, MANA yields an understanding of those same processes. The method appears to be useful not only for what it was designed for, but also to answer other questions about human behavior and site formation processes.

Molecular and Geochemical Archaeology

A few years ago analysis of residues left on artifacts promised to provide another line of evidence for our interpretations, in particular for substances processed with

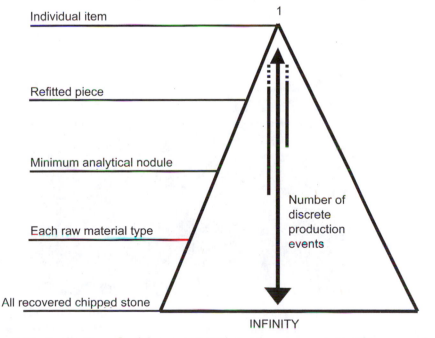

Figure 3.41 Implication of minimum analytical nodules compared to other raw material groupings.

various tools. This quickly developed in several directions, including the removal and identification of blood protein from stone tools and protein remaining on rocks in hearths, pottery, and other artifacts (Loy 1983; Quigg et al. 2001). As with any such new methods, controversy swirled and the method was almost buried alive. In the late 1980s we worked with one of our students who had developed an interest in this topic and had not only rescued the method, but explained and enhanced it. Shanks et al. (2001) showed that residue not only adheres to the surface of stone tools, but protein-sized pieces enter microcracks that develop during production of stone tools (Figure 3.42). This preserves the residue even from vehement washing, and it is only through sonification that this material is released and can be analyzed. By using experimental tools, Shanks, Kornfeld, and Ream (2005) also showed that blood residue survives for at least a dozen years after removal from the ground, something that had earlier been questioned. Their results also demonstrate that DNA can be recovered. Such analyses can also carry surprises, such as the presence at archaeological sites of animals other than those represented by bones. Thus at the protohistoric Bugas-Holding site where sheep and buffalo were processed and eaten in a winter Shoshone village, the tools also came into contact with mule deer and dog (Rapson 1990; Shanks, Hodges, Tilley, Kornfeld, Larson, and Ream 2005). The former possibly from a sheath covering a Shoshone knife and the latter either from using dogs as food during a harsh winter or from manufacture of ornaments, both activities with otherwise low

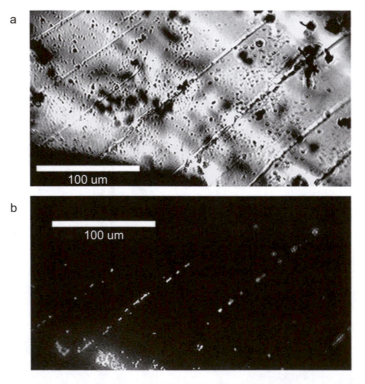

Figure 3.42 Microcracks in an experimental obsidian artifact photographed under visible light (a) and with xenon laser (b). Fluorescent latex beads, 1 μ in diameter, trapped in the microcracks are visible under the xenon laser light (b) and appear as light streaks (Shanks 2003:19). (Photo courtesy of Orin Shanks.)

archaeological visibility at this site but well known from ethnographic and archaeological literature.

Isotope analyses are being used for a variety of purposes in the sciences; in paleontology, zoology, and zooarchaeology the methodology has great promise. Fenner (2007) performed strontium, oxygen, and carbon isotope analysis of pronghorn teeth. Using samples from modern Wyoming hunt areas and archaeological specimens from a half-dozen pronghorn bone beds, he (Fenner 2007) has shown that some assemblages are single event death assemblages, while others show a pattern consistent with accumulation of single animal deaths stacked one on top of another. This line of research promises to provide additional information on communal pronghorn procurement and individual or small group single animal hunting strategies. It may buttress or alter our thinking of tried-and-true methods of tooth eruption as described earlier in this chapter and in the process will undoubtedly see those methods improved.

Another geochemical method of great significance is X-ray fluorescence (XRF) analysis of obsidian, which can be used to trace the direction of movement of this raw material from its source (e.g., Hughes 1989; Kunselman 1998). Unlike other sources of stone tool raw material, obsidian sources are readily identifiable through their chemical composition. This allows the matching up of the chemical signature of any archaeological specimen to its source, providing the source has been discovered and analyzed. Although obsidian is rare in Plains and Rocky Mountain assemblages, except very near the source locations, several interesting patterns are beginning to emerge (Baugh and Brosowske 2006). One is that obsidian is traveling quite widely and is being left at sites from sources that are not always the nearest to its discovery. Thus, for example, in southeast Wyoming as well as in eastern Colorado a significant amount of obsidian is from the Jemez Mountains of central New Mexico; in northeast Wyoming and nearby South Dakota Black Hills the obsidian is not only from the Yellowstone Plateau, but also from further away in Idaho and Utah (Kornfeld et al. 1995; Kunselman, personal communication 1995; Mollyneaux et al. 2001; Reher 2006). In at least one of these cases, the obsidian may be a part of the Hopewell Interaction Sphere, providing one of the rare instances of finding a route traveled by this raw material between the Yellowstone Plateau and the Ohio River (DeBoer 2004).

Geophysical Methods

Geophysical methods that had their origin in the mine sweeping technology of World War II were introduced to the Northwestern Plains and Rocky Mountains in the 1970s and 1980s (Fawcett and Larson 1984; Kornfeld 1985). Until recently their successful application was confined to historic sites with little use or productive results at prehistoric ones. However, improvements in methods, including data interpretations, have resulted in their successful use at prehistoric sites as well in recent years.

The three basic techniques employed by archaeologists are magnetometry, resistivity, and ground penetration radar (GPR) (Figure 3.43). In the most basic terms magnetometry measures the strength of the magnetic field, resistivity measures the ground's resistance to electrical current, while GPR measures radio pulses. One can imagine that this alone makes the methods more or less useful

Figure 3.43 Geophysical surveying in progress at Seminoe Fort. (Courtesy of Danny N. Walker.)

depending on the character of the sediment, depth of the detection desired, character of material one wishes to detect, and other constraints.

The use of geophysical techniques has been most prevalent at historic sites, and one of the most investigated ones has been Fort Laramie, a frontier trading post and military fort at the confluence of the Laramie and North Platte rivers (Larson 1978). Over a dozen years of investigation, much of the fort and its surroundings have been investigated using the three geophysical techniques with tremendous success. The results have included detecting the location of historically known features, including graves, and many surprises (Walker 2004b). Military records, no matter how accurate, do not include many on-the-spot decisions and adaptations encountered in field situations when constructing or remodeling a fort. Subsequent uses of the site are almost never completely recorded. Consequently, archaeology is the only means of arriving at the actual events that took place on the ground rather than what appears in the written record. Another successful use of geophysical surveying occurred at Seminoe's Fort. Here the survey showed the location of the main fort structures, a trail leading to the fort, a corral, trash areas, and other features (Figure 3.44, Plate 1a).

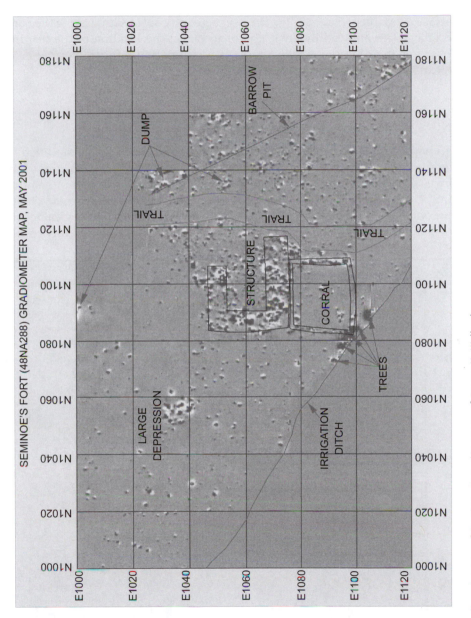

Figure 3.44 Gradiometer map of Seminoe Fort. (Courtesy of Danny N. Walker.)

Work at the Sand Draw Village site represents the potential use of geophysical techniques at a prehistoric site. A probable Shoshone pit house village dating to about 1200 years ago, the site today consists of 15 pithouses, most with internal storage or heating facilities distributed over approximately 1600 m² (Walker 2004a). After the discovery of the first few pithouses, the foremost characteristic of the research design was a massive geophysical survey that yielded numerous subsurface anomalies (Figure 3.45). The use of geophysical techniques at the Sand Draw Village site allowed the investigator to detect the location of the features and, based on their location, make informed decisions about future excavation of the features and their vicinity (Walker 2004a).

CONCLUSIONS

In this chapter we have presented a series of methods developed or modified by us, our students, or our colleagues specifically for the archaeological record of the Northwestern Plains and the adjacent Rocky Mountains. Critical to our understanding is the knowledge of animal behavior and how this behavior affects the data we obtain in the archaeological record. But, because the archaeological record is varied and in some sense every site is unique, the uniqueness frequently results

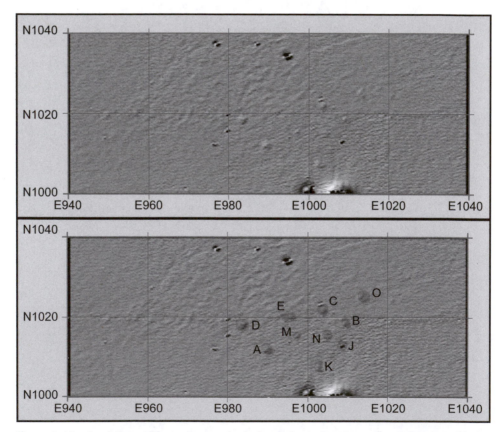

Figure 3.45 Sand Draw Village site geophysical survey results. Anomalies indicating pithouse locations (shadowed in lower map) are indicated by letters. (Courtesy of Danny N. Walker.)

in the necessity to adapt or develop new methodologies or interpretive techniques. The archaeological tool chest of observations, experiments, and field and analytical methodologies has only been supplemented by the specific methods discussed in this chapter. The remainder of this volume relies on all archaeological methods to tell the prehistory of the region, but is especially indebted to the established methods discussed in this chapter. The more cutting-edge methods discussed at the end of this chapter contribute to our interpretations, but their full potential lies in the future.

4

MAMMOTH AND BISON HUNTING

INTRODUCTION

No other place in North America or possibly even the world offers a better opportunity to study prehistoric large mammal hunting strategies than the Northwestern Plains and the adjoining Rocky Mountains. A wide variety of species were hunted there communally, as well as by small groups and single hunters. Animal kill sites can be documented there from Clovis to Protohistoric times, and the resulting bone beds are found in sites of high integrity; at most sites preservation is adequate, so that large samples are available for studies of butchering, processing, animal population, and seasonality studies. In many cases, enough of the old landforms are present to allow reconstructions of the topography at the time of the procurement events.

The short grass plains may appear to the outsider and the uninitiated to be devoid of the plant life necessary to sustain large herds of animals on a year-round basis, but this is not the case. The short grasses, along with a number of forbs and even some shrubs, contain high ratios of crude protein that build up the summer fat reserves necessary to carry the animals through the winter months. Even so, populations of large animals such as bison, elk, deer, pronghorn, and mountain sheep fluctuate in response to available food supplies. A series of dry summers and hard winters may drastically reduce animal numbers, but both the plants and animals rebound quickly from periods of adversity when conditions change for the better. Two good years with adequate feed will bring back deer, pronghorn, and mountain sheep populations that were in serious trouble. Bison populations require a year or so longer. During these periods of adversity in the past, prehistoric human populations had to either broaden their subsistence base to include less desirable species of both plants and animals or move to a more favorable area.

One of the problems that has plagued human populations on the Plains and Rocky Mountains throughout prehistory, and history as well, is the unpredictable nature of climate in both the short and long term. There is no way as yet to reliably predict yearly precipitation or the duration and intensity of winters. Consequently, prehistoric human groups had to prepare for the worst and hope for the best. An easy winter can be quite pleasant for a hunting society while a bad winter can be the exact opposite. The only recourse was to gather surpluses during the favorable months for use during periods of adverse weather. There were periods of time during the winters when hunting was not possible, there was nothing to gather, and stored food supported the group until conditions improved. Once the warm weather of spring arrived, the trauma of the past winter was shed in the optimism for better conditions to come.

There are many accounts of aboriginal hunting of large land mammals in the ethnographic records, but relatively few of these convey much of actual procurement strategies. Hunting is behavior learned and continually perfected over long periods of time. Few ethnologists and/or archaeologists have acquired the necessary experience to be familiar with prey animal behavior to an extent where they fully understand hunting processes. Many investigators apparently think that the same hunting strategy can be applied to just about any animal procurement situation while, in actual practice, every hunting event is affected by a host of factors both internal and external to the animal or animals pursued that can alter or diminish the possibilities of success. Unexpected occurrences, some as simple as a bird or rabbit flushing out of the brush, can cause a stampede and alter the movements of a herd of bison; only the experienced hunter can make the decision whether the best strategy then is to abandon the project or try to salvage it. The accomplished prehistoric hunter served a long apprenticeship with elders before absorbing enough knowledge and experience to almost instinctively know what strategy to apply in any given animal procurement situation.

Successful hunting requires the utmost in fine tuning of the senses as well as in physical ability. Once the human body begins to deteriorate through aging processes, the hunter then becomes the teacher and advisor and the younger hunter must take over to provision the group. It has been argued that gathering of plant products is more predictive and certain of success than hunting because the former cannot move. We believe this is open to question, since most animals stand little chance when pursued by an accomplished hunter. The large animals may appear as food a few hours or even days later than the plants and small animals but the ultimate fate of the large mammals is never in doubt when pursued by skilled human predators.

All animals, large and small, from wood rats to mammoths, demonstrate behavior patterns unique to their species. Successful procurement requires a familiarity with the behavior of the animals hunted under all conditions encountered. Internal controlling factors that affect animal procurement include species, sex, age, size, and condition. External conditions include time of year, time of day, weather, terrain, vegetative cover, insects, and other predators in the area. To begin to understand the body of knowledge a hunter must assimilate and command, simply permute all of these factors, both internal and external, and tabulate the results. The successful prehistoric plains hunter needed only to look outside the tipi at first light and integrate all of the above factors that would affect the coming hunt. The hunter left camp with the day's strategy well mapped out, along with alternatives in case the first choice failed to produce the desired results.

One lesson the hunter learns early is that hunting one species is generally mutually exclusive of hunting other species at the same time. Mule deer (*Odocoileus hemionus*), mountain sheep (*Ovis canadensis*), and pronghorn (*Antilocapra americana*) are about the same size and overlap to a certain extent in their use of habitats. However, each behaves differently enough that hunting one excludes hunting the other two, whether the procurement event is a single hunter, small group, or a communal operation. Fortunately, the above species are still around for observation in their native habitats. Bison herds are present but most are partially domesticated, although they rapidly revert to wild conditions when pressured.

Hunting has acquired a bad name, some of which is justified. The present-day hunter who heads for the hills on the first day of hunting season to pursue and kill an animal purely for sport has difficulty in justifying his or her actions. It is not usually good economic strategy to hunt, since it would be cheaper to buy meat at the local supermarket. It can be justified to some extent on the basis of wildlife management. Since most predators have been eliminated or are under tight control, animal populations need some sort of control to keep their numbers within the carrying capacity of the ecosystem, otherwise the environment suffers in the same way that is suffers from overgrazing by domestic animals. It can take long periods of time and effort to restore lands that have been denuded by too much animal pressure.

Although there are occasional hints in the archaeological record that prehistoric hunters placed some value on exceptionally fine trophies, the message from the record and the ethnographic literature is that human groups who rely on hunting for survival have a special regard for the animals they hunt. The concept prevails that animals make themselves available for the benefit of humans and in return, expect a certain measure of respect from the humans. This respect is manifest through proper ritual before and during the hunt and ritualistic treatment of dead animals. The animals make themselves unavailable to the humans if proper respect through ritual is ignored. In communal animal kills, certain features that appear unrelated to the actual drive lines, fences, barriers, and corrals needed for the containment of animals are probably for the use of the religious specialist (shaman) in order to perform the rituals accompanying these efforts. If there is one thing that separates present-day sport hunting from prehistoric hunting at a subsistence level, it is this respect for the animals and the resulting proscriptions placed on procurement.

Archaeologists can attempt to reconstruct prehistoric animal procurement strategies using archaeological and ethnological data, observations on animal behavior, replications of prehistoric weaponry, past hunting experience, and techniques for the pursuit of animals in their natural environments. These can reveal many past misconceptions and limitations for present and future interpretations, but they will not allow the archaeologist to assume that he or she can perform using the same thought processes as the prehistoric hunter. We continue to interpret prehistoric hunting based on pragmatic considerations, which are viewed with a certain amount of distrust by other investigators. With this caveat, our own thoughts on prehistoric hunting strategies are presented.

MAMMOTH HUNTING

In terms of procurement strategies, the interpretive value of mammoth sites with bona fide human association is limited (Figure 4.1). The Colby site in the Bighorn

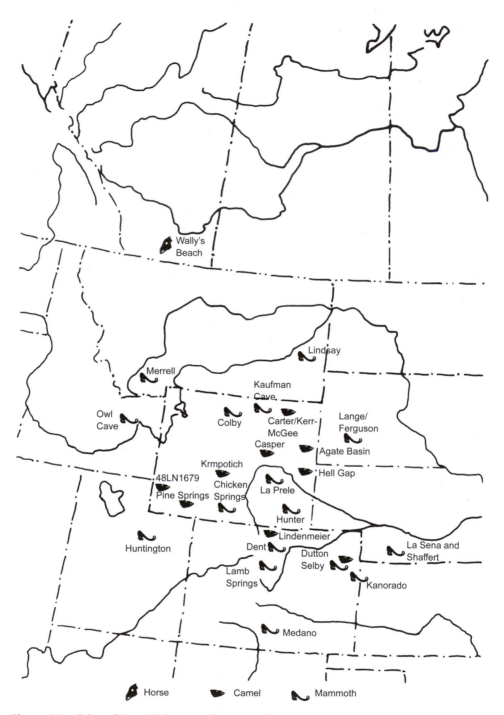

Figure 4.1 Selected Late Pleistocene faunal localities and procurement sites. Many localities include multiple species. All localities are referenced in Figures 2.19, 2.20, or in the text, except Wally's Beach (Kooyman et al. 2006), Merrell (Hill and Davis 2005), Huntington mammoth (Madsen et al. 1976), and Wasden (Miller 1978).

Basin in Wyoming (Frison and Todd 1986) is the only one in the area that provides enough data to speculate. We do not believe it was a single event. More likely it was a location that allowed single animals to be picked off only when the proper conditions were present. African elephant families are territorial, and they tend to cover a territory on a regular basis in search of forage. Mammoths probably did very much the same thing. In Late Pleistocene times, the Bighorn River valley was undoubtedly much better in terms of forage than it is today, although paleo-ecological studies have not produced the evidence to properly assess the differences. However, it is quite obvious that mammoths would not be able to survive on the greasewood, sagebrush, and sparse grasses present in the area today.

The short arroyo in which the Colby site is located drains into a larger arroyo known as Slick Creek, which is the only landform of its kind for several kilometers in any direction and which flows only during spring runoff and heavy rains. It formed a natural pathway for animals moving from the Bighorn River to grazing lands in the low hills away from the river floodplain. The floodplain and terraces of Slick Creek probably contained brush and trees which offered shade in summer and protection from winter winds and snow.

The arroyo containing the mammoth bones at the Colby site looked much different in Clovis times than at present. Instead of the dendritic drainage pattern now present (Figure 4.2), it was then a deep, steep-walled arroyo. In addition, it was and still is the first and only such arroyo to be found on the west side of the Bighorn River. A possible and probable hunting strategy was to carefully monitor a family of mammoths that had watered at the Bighorn River and follow them carefully until one member wandered far enough away from the group that it could be darted. Once wounded and away from the protection of the matriarch, it would drift naturally and/or would be maneuvered into the steep-walled arroyo from which it could not escape and where the final coup de grâce could be administered. This was probably repeated many times and would explain the number of animals present at the site.

Two mammoth bone piles at the site are believed to be the result of human activity. It is postulated also that they may be the remains of meat caches, based on a strong resemblance to meat caches in the Arctic. One (Figure 4.3) had been opened and the contents utilized but the other, containing the articulated left front quarter of a nearly mature animal (Figure 4.4), had not been opened. The configuration of mammoth bones in the arroyo apparently resulted from stream action. Besides mammoths, bones of other animals were recovered, including bison, pronghorn, camel, horse, possible ovibos, and jackrabbit (Frison 2004; Walker and Frison 1980). Projectile points recovered at the site (Figure 4.5) leave little doubt of human involvement.

It is difficult to evaluate other mammoth kills in the area in terms of mammoth procurement. The Lange-Ferguson site in the South Dakota badlands (Hannus 1990) is a Clovis site and appears to represent more of an opportunistic event than does Colby. On the other hand, it could also represent a situation in which animals drifted toward water when wounded. The Rawlins Mammoth (McGrew 1961) in southern Wyoming and the Lindsay Mammoth in eastern Montana (Davis 1971) are of the right age but there is a question of human association. If they are actual Clovis sites, they would represent killing of mature male mammoths. There are probably several dozen Late Pleistocene mammoth sites in Wyoming that contain between a few bones and what can be considered bone beds. Hunter and Jewett in

Figure 4.2 The Colby Mammoth Kill site: top, looking east, location of an earlier discovery of mammoth bone (1), site location (2), and the artificial reservoir (3); bottom, looking upstream at site location (2), modern arroyo and the artificial reservoir (3).

Figure 4.3 Mammoth bone pile 1 at the Colby site: projectile point in situ (1) and mandibles exposed at the surface (2).

Figure 4.4 Mammoth bone pile 2 at the Colby site.

Figure 4.5   Clovis points from the Colby site.

southeast Wyoming, Sheridan Cemetery in north-central Wyoming, and La Prele Creek near Douglas in central Wyoming are a few of the excavated mammoth localities (Frison and Kornfeld 2008). Although of the right age to have been used by early humans, none have demonstrated unequivocal evidence of human procurement. Given the Late Pleistocene extinction of mammoth, it is not surprising that many mammoth bone beds date to this age.

Clovis groups, as accomplished hunters, would have devised a strategy for killing mammoths. As discussed in Chapter 3, one strategy would have been to first kill a matriarch and then, as the remainder of the herd gathered around her, hunters could have killed several animals at a time. Since killing even a single mammoth resulted in an immediate surplus of meat, and band-level societies have no incentives to acquire more food than is needed, there would have been no incentive to expend extra effort in killing an entire family of mammoths at one time.

Any discussion of mammoth hunting inevitably brings forth the question of mammoth extinction. Since Martin's (1967) article, Pleistocene overkill versus extinctions by natural causes has been the subject of numerous articles and debates with no indication that the problem will be resolved, at least in the immediate future. Since the Colby site constitutes a significant part of the present database on Clovis mammoth hunting in North America, and one of us being the principal investigator of the site, we claim the privilege of making comments, being fully aware that they will probably serve only to fuel the controversy rather than resolve the problem.

The Colby site provides the best-known evidence to date in the area from which it is possible to propose an actual mammoth procurement strategy. This is because of the unequivocal association of Clovis materials in an identifiable landform—a deep, steep-walled arroyo, strongly suggesting some sort of natural trap. Juvenile animals were apparently the preferred target of long-term, systematic exploitation of a resident mammoth herd. Based on paleoecological analyses and climatic studies of the terminal Pleistocene and beginning Holocene, we can assume that a deterioration of animal carrying capacity, which was not favorable for the mammoth populations, was underway.

At the same time mammoths in the Colby site area were facing problems of diminishing forage, they were faced also with an intrusion of obviously successful human predators who were killing mostly young animals. For a species in which females produced young at the age of about 15 years, had a gestation period of under 2 years, and a mean calving interval of somewhere around 6 years (Laws et al. 1975), the combination of human predation and a deteriorating environment were operating against the survival of the species. Consequently, both human predation and climatic factors could have had strong implications for mammoth extinction on the Northwestern Plains and Rocky Mountains.

On the other hand, deterioration of the environment was toward present conditions, which were continually more favorable for horse habitat, as can be demonstrated today by ever-increasing herds of feral horses. The archaeological record has produced little if any reliable evidence that Clovis hunters were systematically hunting either the Pleistocene horse or camel (Frison, Wilson, and Walker 1978), and both species went extinct in the same area where mammoth were found. Interestingly, the bison and the pronghorn, which were the second and third most heavily hunted of all the species by human predators in post-Clovis times, managed to escape extinction. Although able to survive, bison underwent evolutionary stress beginning at the Pleistocene–Holocene transition, as seen in bone bed assemblages, and apparently evolved from *Bison antiquus* and *Bison occidentalis* into *Bison bison* by the mid-Holocene (Frison 2004:62–64). We are left with the conclusion that more data are needed before the Pleistocene extinction problem can be resolved.

BISON HUNTING

The various species of bison present on the Northwestern Plains and Rocky Mountains were the main target for prehistoric hunters. Except for some areas during the period between about 8000 and 5000 BP, bison hunting occurred continuously over a period of at least 12,000 calendar years and involved both extinct and modern species of these animals. Prehistoric bison hunters displayed great ingenuity in communal bison hunting, which included driving them into artificial corrals, up ramps into artificial corrals, over low bluffs and steep slopes into artificial corrals, into different kinds of arroyo traps, into parabolic sand dune traps, and the classic buffalo jump where the animals were stampeded over steep, high bluffs and were killed or crippled when they hit the ground. Small group and individual hunting probably resulted in more animals killed than the more spectacular communal kills, but the latter have attracted the most attention.

Different variations of traps utilizing the natural topography formed by dry arroyos probably accounted for most of the systematic communal bison hunting. This has created special problems for the archaeologist since dry arroyos are continually affected in many ways by fluvial transport. The Northwestern Plains and Rocky Mountain area is far enough to the north so that runoff ceases as soon as the temperature is low enough to prevent rain and/or snow melt. Only on rare occasions have temperatures from November through February been warm enough to cause appreciable runoff from snow melt. Since headcuts in dry arroyos often formed barriers that prevented further movement upstream by bison, and the slopes of the adjacent walls of the arroyos were usually high enough and steep enough to contain the animals, these landforms were ideal for trapping the animals (Figure 4.6).

Headcuts in dry arroyos continually migrate upstream except in special situations where the lip of the headcut is formed by bedrock, in which case the headcut may remain stationary for some time. We can document one site where this situation did occur and which was used as a bison trap (see Mann 1968). Depending upon the degree of carcass dismemberment, some parts of the carcasses from animal kills were left in the bottoms of the arroyos. Several things could subsequently occur depending upon whether the arroyo was experiencing a cycle of aggradation or degradation: heavy runoff could carry the animal remains downstream; the animal remains could collect mud and trash and form enough of a barrier to alter the course of the stream; or the animal remains could become buried and be exposed later as another headcut migrated upstream. However, the entire range of possibilities is too extensive to explore fully.

Arroyo kills investigated to date occurred in the fall or later, with little danger of flooding until the following spring. Unfortunately, little is known of butchering/processing areas associated with arroyo bison kills. If they were located close to the kills, there was a high probability of their destruction through continuing cycles of geologic activity. One exception is the Agate Basin site of Paleoindian age where one interpretation claims the animals were killed in the arroyo and then cut into units and piled on the arroyo floodplain. The hunting group then camped and spent the winter months at or near the piles of butchered units, which were

Figure 4.6   Headcut forming a natural animal trap in the Moss Agate Arroyo.

apparently preserved by freezing. Any of the butchered units that were not used when spring runoff began were simply allowed to spoil. This caused no problem for the hunting group because by this time, fresh meat was available.

Since the campsite at Agate Basin was located on the arroyo floodplain, run-off water could potentially cause many problems for the archaeologist. Material upstream could be picked up and deposited on the floodplain campsite, or the camp area could be scoured by flood waters and its material picked up and redeposited farther downstream. Apparently all of these conditions were present at the Agate Basin site. Had the hunting group camped on a terrace instead of the floodplains, the results would have been more components of higher integrity. However, investigations of arroyo bison kills must take into account these special conditions of site formation and destruction in order to recover data with any degree of reliability.

Bison hunting strategies have received their share of erroneous interpretation by those unfamiliar with the behavior of the species. Some artists' depictions show a group of bison frightened by hunters yelling and waving a hide or blanket, running toward a precipice, and jumping over the edge. Bison are commonly thought of as ungainly in their movements, which is not the case. They can move rapidly and change their direction as quickly as or more quickly than any animal of comparative size. A single animal or a small group of bison is almost impossible to drive over a precipice because they can easily perceive the danger and react immediately by swerving or reversing their direction. Stampeding a large herd of bison creates a different situation; in this case, the mass of animals is so great that the leaders cannot change direction and are pushed over the precipice, followed by many behind them.

Incapacitating bison by driving them into bogs has often been proposed as a bison procurement strategy, but would not have succeeded for many of the same reasons as those in the case of mammoths (see Chapter 3). Bison spend a good deal of time in wallows and swampy areas; they can be seen up to their bellies in mud fighting insects and grazing swamp grasses. They move in and out of bogs with ease, unless sick or incapacitated by wounds or old age. Consider for a moment trying to skin and butcher an animal the size of a bison that is submerged so deep in a bog that it could not readily extract itself. The better strategy would have been to first drive the animal out of the bog and then kill it on firm ground. Prehistoric bison hunters were capable of killing the animals under their own terms and not those of the animals.

BISON HUNTING DURING EARLY PALEOINDIAN TIMES

Although excellent evidence for a bison procurement during Clovis times comes from the Murray Springs site in Arizona (Haynes and Huckell 2007) and Jake's Bluff in Oklahoma (Bement 2003), we can document very little if anything about Clovis bison hunting on the Northwestern Plains and Rockies except that a small amount of bison bone was found in the Colby and Sheaman Clovis sites. However, we do have evidence shortly afterwards at the Goshen complex Mill Iron site in Montana and the Upper Twin Mountain site in Colorado of what appear to be communal bison kills. The actual kill location at Mill Iron was not preserved, nor do we know what method of procurement was utilized, because erosion of the surrounding area left only a small remnant of the site intact at the top of a small butte (Figure 2.24). The Mill Iron bone bed (Figure 4.7), with partial remains of at least 30 bison along with projectile points (Figure 4.8), is believed to be an artificially stacked pile of bones, but not the actual kill location. A population study of the mandibles and teeth reveals tight yearly age groups of animals either all killed at one time or more than one kill at the same time for more than one year (Todd et al. 1996). The former situation seems the most likely, and the bone bed probably represents the stacking of butchered bison that were killed nearby in a single event, probably late in the spring or in early summer.

The only other Goshen complex bison procurement site is Upper Twin Mountain in the Middle Park of Colorado's high country (Kornfeld et al. 1999). Although dated to only 10,470 ± 50 BP (CAMS-26782), its Goshen complex affiliation is clear. The date does, however, pose a problem to a clear definition of the Goshen complex, which has been firmly documented to underlie Folsom stratigraphically (e.g., Irwin-Williams et al. 1973). The Upper Twin Mountain bison bone bed is encased in a sheet flow alluvium that filled a late Pleistocene slump scar such as is common in the area. The scar itself speaks to the climatic conditions in the park at the end of the Pleistocene. The ameliorating Late Pleistocene climate was still cooler and wetter, the moisture causing widespread slumping. As the bottom of the scar began to collect sediment, a group of bison was apparently driven into it from the nearby drainage to the north and over an adjacent ridge (Figure 4.9).

The Upper Twin Mountain bone bed, while partially eroded and not completely excavated, still yielded thousands of faunal specimens from centimeter-sized fragments to 243 identifiable bison elements (Figure 4.10). Among these are 62 lower molars that provide excellent evidence of death in the early winter

Figure 4.7   The Mill Iron site bison bone bed.

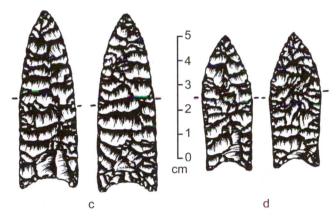

Figure 4.8   Goshen points from the Mill Iron site bison bone bed.

Figure 4.9   Upper Twin Mountain site (arrow). Filled slump scar is outlined with dashed line.

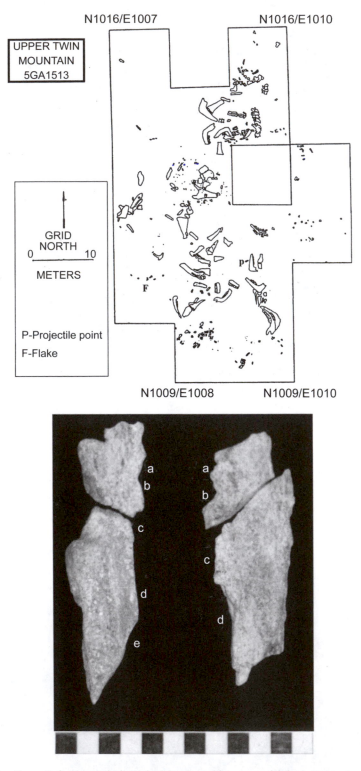

Figure 4.10 Upper Twin Mountain bone bed (top), and humerus with impact punctures (bottom). Five distinct blows are recorded by the impact scars a–e.

season (Todd et al. 1996). This evidence suggests, contrary to some models of high Rocky Mountain basin use, that human groups remained in the basins on a year-round basis, as snow accumulation on mountain passes might have precluded movement out of the basin. Currently, the open, low areas of the park serve as winter refuge for a variety of animals (Figure 4.11) and it probably did so during Goshen times, providing ready access to winter "storage-on-the-hoof" resource procurement. The dentiary bison elements also served to provide information about the size of the bison herd, which represents a minimum of 15 animals. The age structure of the Upper Twin Mountain site shows no yearlings, no animals in age groups 6 and 10 and one old animal in age group 11. Most animals were in age groups 2–5 and 7–9, that is prime and older-age adult animals. However, the small overall assemblage size makes the implications of this pattern suspect.

The faunal remains recovered show a high degree of weathering, desiccation, and deletion of elements from the assemblage. Of the thousands of centimeter-sized fragments, all or nearly all are heavily weathered pieces, the result of longitudinal bone cracking under exposed conditions. The complete specimens also show heavy chemical weathering of cortical bone, making all observations of cultural surface modification impossible. The only clear evidence of human action on the bone is a bison humerus cracked open for marrow. This is significant as it shows quite a high degree of processing relatively early in the Paleoindian period. Most Early Paleoindian faunal assemblages show minimal or no use of within-bone nutrients, relying largely on muscle mass and organs as the sought-after resource. Despite rather heavy natural destruction of the assemblage, the investigators were able to suggest that high-utility parts of the bison carcass may have been carried away from the site, presumably to a camp, where the bison would have been consumed (Kornfeld et al. 1999).

Two areas of the Agate Basin site provide evidence of Folsom bison procurement (Figure 4.12). Remains of 11 bison (eight adult and three subadults) were

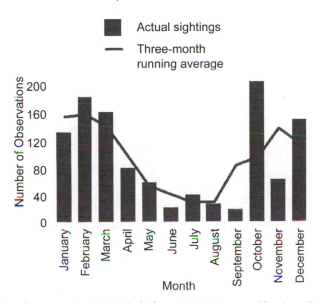

Figure 4.11 Deer frequency in Middle Park through the seasons. (Courtesy Todd Surovell; data from Carpenter et al. 1979.)

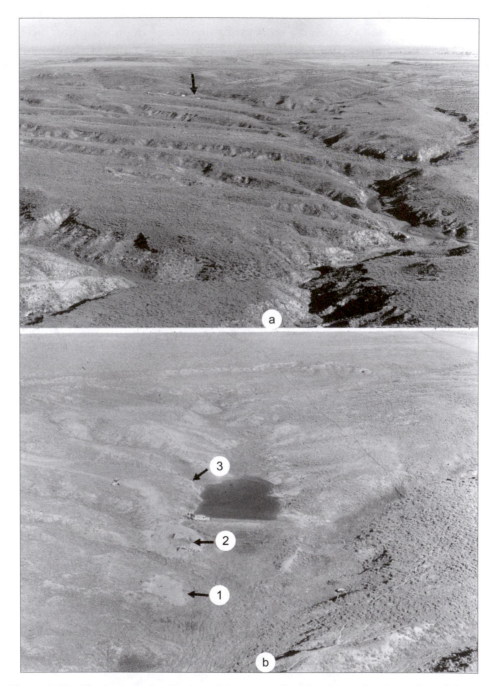

Figure 4.12 The Agate Basin site (arrow) in eastern Wyoming (a), and a closer view of the site (b). Roberts excavation in 1942 (1), main site area (2), and the Brewster site (3).

found in the Folsom component in Area 2 at the Agate Basin site (Figure 4.13; Hill 2008). Tooth eruption on the calf and the stage of development of the fetal bones suggest a late winter kill, although the sample is too small to be considered

Figure 4.13   Bison bone bed exposed in the Folsom level at the Agate Basin site.

reliable. Two other Folsom components with bison bones in Area 3 at the Agate Basin site probably represent small bison kills, but unknown amounts of these two components were removed by arroyo cutting so that the total number of animals involved is unknown (Frison and Stanford 1982:37–76), and no ageable mandibles or teeth were recovered to provide any indication of seasonality.

Undoubtedly there are more Folsom components intact in the deposits filling the old arroyo at the Agate Basin site. A recent investigation between Areas 2 and 3 discovered a bison bone bed that may be of Folsom age and will be investigated in the coming years. Some procurement strategy involving an arroyo trap was probably used for bison procurement, but whether it was something like an arroyo headcut, an artificial barrier, a corral, or some combination of all or part of these is open to question. However, there was something special about the old arroyo at the Agate Basin site since it was utilized for bison trapping for at least a thousand years during Folsom, Agate Basin, and Hell Gap times. Hill (2008) has produced an intensive study of the Folsom bone beds at the Agate Basin site.

Bison trapping probably occurred at the Lindenmeier Folsom site as well. Roberts (1936:13–17) described a "bison pit" with remains representing nine individuals. A photograph taken during the 1936 excavation at the Lindenmeier site shows a front leg unit (Roberts 1936:Plate 3-1) and it was mentioned that "several legs" were recovered. Partial remains of one animal consisted of "a forequarter, most of the ribs from one side, and the vertebral column still intact" (Roberts 1936:14). A damaged skull and parts of others were found. Roberts mentioned that this part of the site had similarities to the Folsom type site in New Mexico (Figgins 1927), which has strong indications of being a kill site.

According to tooth eruption schedules, ageable mandibles from the Folsom type site in northern New Mexico fall into four age groups a year apart (Todd et al. 1996:169–173). Although the sample is small, it suggests a fall kill, provided that the calving period for bison was the same time as it is at present on the Northwestern Plains. The number of bison killed at the Folsom site is at least 32, although given the collection practices of the 1920s and curation since that time, this is only the best estimate (Meltzer 2006). The authors suggest that the cow calf herd at the Folsom site died in a single catastrophic event.

The Carter/Kerr-McGee site, located at an arroyo headcut (Frison 1984), is thought to have been a large bison-procurement site throughout most of Paleoindian times (Figure 4.14). Because of headward erosion of the arroyo subsequent to the site activities, only a remnant of the site remained. Only a few bison bones were recovered in the Folsom level, but these nevertheless indicate the Folsom people's procurement of this animal in the site vicinity. The much larger Cody bone bed is discussed later in this chapter (Figure 4.15).

The Lipscomb Bison Quarry in the extreme northeast Texas Panhandle (Schultz 1943) appears to have been the scene of a large Folsom bison kill. Although far from the Rocky Mountains, the site provides an important dimension in Folsom bison procurement. According to the investigator, 14 skeletons (apparently complete or nearly so) were recovered in an area 12 feet by 20 feet, and nine more skulls were found nearby. This is not a total number since it was mentioned in the report that sporadic digging had occurred. In addition, a recent study of the bones from the site indicates a minimum number of 55 individuals based on astragali, which makes Lipscomb the largest Folsom bison bone bed (Todd et al. 1990). It may, however, be the result of multiple occupations. An assemblage of Folsom projectile points and tools leaves little doubt of its identity as a bison kill. The position of the 14 skeletons is puzzling to say the least: they "were headed in an easterly or southerly direction and overlapped one another considerably" (Schultz 1943:246). This description raises the question of how the animals were killed in order for them to be found in this position and whether or not they had been butchered. An ongoing reinvestigation of the site and the site area may answer some of these questions.

Figure 4.14   Location of the Carter/Kerr-McGee Paleoindian animal kill site.

Figure 4.15   Excavations at the Carter/Kerr-McGee site; Cody-level bone.

The San Luis Valley in southern Colorado, close to the Great Sand Dunes National Monument, was a major area of Folsom bison procurement activities. At the Linger site, first reported by Hurst (1943), five animals were mentioned associated with Folsom points and tools, but no systematic excavations were undertaken at that time, and subsequent looting and collecting resulted in the loss of much data. A reinvestigation of the site (Dawson and Stanford 1975) indicated that more of the site could still be intact. An intensive study of tool refitting and bison remains was performed on the Folsom assemblage from Stewart's Cattle Guard site, also in the San Luis Valley (Jodry 1999b; Jodry and Stanford 1992). These sites, along with the nearby Zapata site, provide evidence of bison procurement in this region (Jodry 1999a).

Folsom bison bone beds demonstrate that these hunters were able to take small numbers of the large Late Pleistocene/Early Holocene bison at one time and on a regular basis, although there is no strong evidence of large communal kills such as those that appear a short time later. This could have been a result of different animal behavior; the animals at that time may have been more solitary and may have lived in small family groups instead of larger herds (see Smiley 1979 for change in bison behavior). Regardless of the reason for smaller-sized procurement, Folsom people apparently involved ritual in their bison hunting activities. A bison skull from the Cooper site in Oklahoma was painted with a red zigzag pattern on the frontal bone, perhaps signifying a lightning bolt (Figure 4.16). It is hard to conceive of this type of design in the context of a bison kill as anything but ritual (Bement 1999).

Figure 4.16   Cooper site skull with ocher zigzag on a bison frontal bone in situ. Zigzag pattern digitally enhanced. (Courtesy Lee Bement.)

BISON TRAPPING AND PROCUREMENT DURING MIDDLE PALEOINDIAN TIMES

Agate Basin Complex

During Agate Basin times, the evidence for systematic, communal bison procurement is better demonstrated, although only five bison bone beds are known for the Agate Basin complex. These are from the Areas 1 and 2 of the Agate Basin site in Wyoming, one from the Frazier site in Colorado, one from Beacon Island along the Missouri River in North Dakota, and one from Locality II of the Hell Gap site in Wyoming.

The Agate Basin site is located in typical short-grass plains on an intermittent tributary of the Cheyenne River in extreme eastern Wyoming (Figure 4.12). The latter stream begins in eastern Wyoming and drains a large area of open, rolling plains but has no high-altitude headwaters. Consequently, stream flow fluctuates rapidly depending on spring snow melt and heavy rains.

The Cheyenne River flows around the southern end of the Black Hills, and arroyos and intermittent streams flowing into it form areas of typical "breaks" of relatively rough terrain. These kinds of areas have been and still are attractive to both wild and domestic grazing animals. North slopes provide good grass and shade while grass is lush in arroyo bottoms and stays green longer, creating an added attraction for large animals. The Agate Basin locality consists of a number of arroyos whose headcuts have encroached through time into a relatively flat Pleistocene surface (Figure 4.12a). The resulting landforms with good grass cover have been in the past and still are ideal bison habitat. Unless moisture conditions were unusually severe, water was available in ponds and seeps somewhere in the arroyo bottoms, and under extreme conditions when springs ceased to flow and there was no rain for runoff, animals such as bison could trek back and forth to the Cheyenne River for water.

There have been many events of cut and fill in the Agate Basin arroyo, which has been both good and bad for archaeology. Periods of fill have preserved archaeological components while periods of downcutting have had the opposite effect. As has been the case in other locations, notably at the Colby site, arroyos may aggrade and in a subsequent period of downcutting may not follow the same route as before, leaving parts of the old alluvium-filled arroyo intact. This was what preserved Paleoindian components at the Agate Basin site locality, since cultural components were preserved in the aggraded deposits.

While watering livestock sometimes in the 1930s, William Spencer, a general ranch hand who lived and worked in the area, happened to observe bones eroding out of the bank. The Agate Basin site is located across an arroyo from a spring that was one of the rare sources of potable water in the area. Digging among the bones with a stick produced several projectile point fragments, which were later shown to Robert Frison, an avid avocational archaeologist then living nearby in Newcastle, Wyoming. After confirming the earlier observations made by Spencer, he brought the site to the attention of Frank H. H. Roberts of the Smithsonian Institution. Test excavations were made in 1942 (Roberts 1943), but this was during the World War II years and further investigation had to be deferred to a later date.

Brief mention of Agate Basin was made by Roberts (1943), but at that time the projectile points were regarded as one of several variants of "Yuma." A decade later, Roberts (1951), after careful examination of 32 specimens recovered in 1942 and 38 specimens recovered by various local collectors, gave them the formal type name of Agate Basin, although their age and relationship to other Paleoindian projectile point types was not known. A large sample of bison bones was collected from the excavations in 1942, but these were tentatively identified as modern bison and by the time it was realized they might be extinct bison, they had been discarded. Based on pictures and descriptions of the site by Roberts, we are convinced that this part of the site—what we now call Area 1 (Figure 4.12b-1)—represented an actual bison kill location. Further excavations by Roberts were carried out at the site during the summer of 1961 that produced valuable data but little if any evidence for actual Paleoindian bison procurement (see Bass 1970). A recent visit to this area of the Agate Basin site (Area 1) resulted in the recovery of a significant quantity of faunal specimens discussed further below. Agogino (1972) had excavated in a Folsom component in the Agate Basin locality close to the area excavated by Roberts and gave this the name of the Brewster site (Area 3).

Subsequent geological investigations have demonstrated that the Brewster and Agate Basin sites are part of the same depositional units lying in the Agate Basin arroyo and that the former probably does not deserve separate site status.

Several years of surface survey and careful testing in the Agate Basin site and locality by Frison revealed that there were still in situ deposits remaining in other site areas (Areas 2 and 3). Because of the ease in finding Agate Basin projectile points there, the site was continually being looted, so that in 1975 the decision was made to initiate a long-term investigation. The main problems were determining the time of year the bison were killed, the type of topographic feature in which the animals were killed, the butchering and processing methods, something of the population structure and morphology of the bison in the site, and the presence or absence of other Paleoindian complexes besides Agate Basin.

During the reinvestigation of the Agate Basin site, it was divided into three areas. Area 1 is the location of Robert's first excavations; Area 2 is where Bass and Roberts worked in 1961; and Area 3 is the Brewster site area (Figure 4.12b). Very little of Area 1 was left intact, although a number of chipped stone artifacts were recovered in disturbed deposits that apparently resulted from digging by artifact hunters. Area 2, although it had been damaged by looting both before and after the 1961 investigation, still had a large part of the bison bone bed intact (Figure 4.17), and it was possible to integrate bone maps from that investigation into a final bone map of Area 2, lacking only the information from the looted sections. We do not believe that this represents a kill area, and although Area 1 probably was a kill, its true relationship to Area 2 cannot be determined. It is possible and even likely that the animals killed in Area 1 were partially butchered there and the butchered units moved to Area 2. On the other hand, an entirely different processing area may have been associated with the Area 1 kill.

Figure 4.17   The Agate Basin bison bone bed at the Agate Basin site.

A recent reinvestigation of Area 1, the Agate Basin type site (Meyer et al. 2005), resulted in recovery of thousands of faunal specimens from the backdirt of earlier investigations and looting activities. Although a small sample and of dubious context, since only one component is known for this area of the site and the bone is known to have been discarded, the sample can serve a useful function and is an indispensable addition to the few other Agate Basin complex bone beds. The recovered sample from Area 1 yielded 245 identifiable bison bone elements of which only one was a tooth, precluding determination of seasonality. Despite the difficulty of interpreting such a redeposited assemblage, the investigator was able to show that the assemblage consists of low-utility parts, a pattern consistent with use of this area of the site as a kill location. As this pattern may be the result of bone density mediated attrition or selective discard by the original investigators, we mention the results with caution.

According to tooth eruption schedules, the bison were killed during the winter (Frison and Stanford 1982:240–251), and we believe Area 2 to represent butchered bison units piled on the arroyo flood plain and frozen for temporary storage. There is a concentration of butchered units in one part of the area. Moving away from this part of Area 2, more disarticulated and heavily processed bones are encountered. The hunting group was camped nearby for the winter and withdrew frozen units from the pile as needed. Several intact butchered units were not needed and were allowed to spoil upon the arrival of warm weather. These kinds of short-term storage features have been quite appropriately labeled "insurance caches" (Binford 1978a:387).

A possible method of bison procurement at the Agate Basin site would have been to maneuver groups of possibly 10 to 20 animals into the arroyo bottom at an appropriate spot, which may have been several hundred meters or more from the trap. The actual spot would have depended upon the topography at the time. Once in the arroyo bottom, the animals would have been carefully maneuvered upstream until a headcut, artificial barrier, or corral, or a combination of these was reached. Hunters would have been stationed at critical spots, such as tributary arroyos or places where the banks were not steep enough to contain the animals. When the lead animal or animals reached the barrier and attempted to turn around, enough confusion would have been created so that the animals would have been vulnerable to experienced hunters. It is possible that a barrier of hides was dropped behind the animals once they were inside the enclosure. The animals had to be kept moving steadily up the bottom of the arroyo. This required close pursuit by the hunters, because if the animal or animals in the lead suspected danger ahead, they would turn and head in the opposite direction. The entire herd would then turn with the leaders and stampede back down the arroyo; they would have been impossible to stop and the entire venture would have had to be initiated from the beginning.

The actual method of killing is conjectural. Large numbers of projectile points found in the kill area bear evidence of heavy impact and breakage (Figures 4.18) and leave little doubt that they were used to kill the animals. Whether they were used in thrusting spears or with a throwing stick is not known. Most wild animals that realize they are trapped often have a tendency to go berserk for a time and charge blindly into the restraints, whether they are dirt walls or logs in a corral fence. An infuriated animal the size of a mature bison can cause an almost incredible amount of destruction in a very short time. It would probably have been a wise

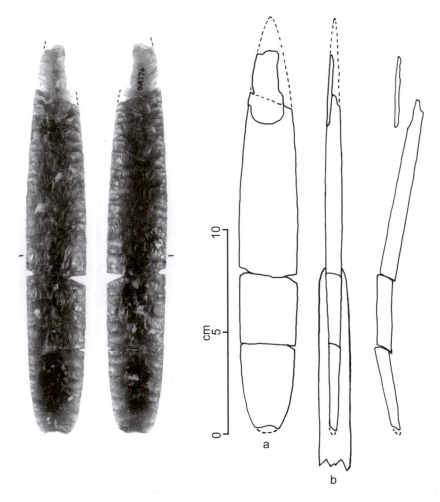

Figure 4.18 Refitted Agate Basin point from the bison bone bed (left and a), and postulated impact damage on the point shown by fragments and dotted lines (b).

move to spear or dart the animals from outside the trap, at least until the larger and more dangerous ones were no longer a serious threat. Once inside the trap, to dispatch the wounded animals, the thrusting spear would have been the ideal weapon in a close and direct confrontation situation. A cornered, wounded animal is likely to charge the hunter, making it extremely vulnerable, especially to a spear thrust. The hunter is left with the spear shaft which, from actual experience, affords a lot of protection from a charging bison. The real threat to the hunters in terms of charging animals would have been the older females and an occasional mature male. Once they were dispatched, the remainder would not have presented as much of a danger. The calves and even yearlings would probably have remained at the sides of their dead mothers.

An early interpretation of the Agate Basin site by Roberts was that it was a bog into which the animals were driven. Evidence for this was part of a bison skeleton with the rear legs intruded well into the deposits on the floor of the kill area, an observation made by Robert Frison when he worked with Roberts during the first site investigation in 1942. Judging from a verbal description given to one us (Frison), we are quite certain that the rear feet of this same animal were found in situ during the 1975 reinvestigations. The two feet were in an articulated position (Figure 4.19). The metatarsal was complete on one, but only the distal metatarsal remained on the other. However, it was a fresh break, indicating that the remainder of the bone had been removed during the first excavation at the site. The position of the phalanges indeed suggested that they had been forced into the soil deposits in the bottom of the arroyo. However, they were intruded at a low angle and, although the soil may have been wet at the time, the deposits do not appear to have been bog deposits. The position of the two rear legs suggests that the animal probably had its feet well into the muddy soil but it does not suggest that the animal was bogged down. Instead, it was probably an animal that had been wounded and was lying with its legs directly under its body.

In an intensive study of the Agate Basin site Area 2 bone bed, Hill (2008) argues that the bone bed is the actual location in which the animals were killed. The investigator's (Frison's) interpretation was that the animals were killed in the arroyo bottom, then cut into units and piled on the flood plain. We do not see any possibility of resolving the question whether or not the bone bed lay on the flood plain or arroyo bottom or if a definite answer would change the original interpretation of the actual procurement process.

The only other extensively excavated and reported Agate Basin complex bone bed is the Frazier site. Originally investigated by H. Marie Wormington from 1965 to 1970 (Borresen 2002; Wormington 1988), the collection lay largely unanalyzed until recently. Wormington recovered a chipped stone assemblage consisting of 1161 chipped stone artifacts and 19,815 bone specimens (Slessman 2004). The site is one of a series of well-known Paleoindian localities on the Kersey Terrace of the South Platte River (Dent, Jurgens, and Powars being the others). Several of these sites—as well as the terrace sequence, important for understanding these occupations, their ages, and site formation processes—have been intensively investigated

Figure 4.19 Bison rear feet in the area excavated by Frank H. H. Roberts in 1942 at the Agate Basin site.

(Haynes et al. 1998; Holliday 1988; Pitblado and Brunswig 2007). It appears that the Frazier site cultural material was quickly covered by sandy, windblown sediment (Malde 1988:88), indicating a rather dry climate.

A preliminary analysis of bison third molars suggests that the bison from the Frazier site died in the late winter or early spring (Todd et al. 1990). Although the bone at the site was relatively scattered and disarticulated, the investigator thinks that the site represents a bison kill rather than a processing location (Borresen 2002). Her interpretation is based on a thorough analysis that found that attrition by natural processes affected the bison bone assemblage. However, the assemblage composition still retained elements of human activity, including selective removal of high-utility packages and riders (bones that have no nutritional value, but are difficult to separate from those parts that are highly sought after [Emerson 1990]). Presumably, the high-utility parts were removed to a secondary processing location or a campsite. There are other aspects of the Frazier site bison bone assemblage that differ from other Paleoindian bison bone beds, in particular the apparent selective removal of metapodials. The investigator speculates that these were removed to be made into tools or for the extraction of marrow. Seasonal variation in the nutritional value of specific skeletal portions likely led to different decisions by the human users of the product from season to season. We still know very little about this aspect of seasonal variation in use of bison products, but studies of sites such as Frazier, Agate Basin, and Horner are beginning to give us glimpses into this aspect of Paleoindian behavior and decision making (Borresen 2002; Hill 2008; Todd 1987a). However, since the Agate Basin component at the same site is the only known component of the complex to offer enough evidence for interpretation of bison trapping, killing, butchering, processing, and utilization of the products, it is difficult to compare with the evidence from other Agate Basin sites or cultural complexes where more sites are known.

Bison Procurement during Hell Gap Times

Hell Gap bison procurement is at present better documented than the earlier cultural complexes because of investigations carried out on three large Hell Gap complex sites: the Casper site (Frison 1974), a Hell Gap component at the Agate Basin site in Wyoming, and the Jones-Miller (Stanford 1978) site in extreme eastern Colorado near the Colorado–Nebraska–Kansas meeting point. Although the latter site is somewhat south of the area with which this book is concerned, it does have a strong bearing on Hell Gap materials farther north and west. The Jones-Miller site contains the remains of several hundred animals thought to have been killed during a single winter, but probably not as a single event. There is not yet an exact interpretation of the use of any geomorphic feature that may have been a natural trap, although it is possible that some kind of artificial corral or other constraint was used. The investigator (Figure 4.20a; Stanford 1979b) suggested a possible procurement situation in which the animals were stampeded and sent floundering down a descending slope covered with packed snow into a simple structure where they were killed using both spears and spear throwers.

An unusual feature at the site is what the investigator believes to have been a "shaman's" pole; close to it were some paraphernalia that could have belonged to a shaman, including a possible antler flute and a miniature projectile point

Figure 4.20 Jones-Miller site bone bed (a), and posthole in the middle of the bone bed (b). (Figure 4.20b courtesy of Dennis Stanford.)

(Figure 4.20b; Stanford 1978). This interpretation seems reasonable, since there is ample archaeological evidence for shamanistic activity in Archaic bison kills (see, e.g., Frison 1971a) and ethnographic evidence for such activity during the Protohistoric period.

The Casper Hell Gap bison kill site investigations were published more than a quarter century ago (Frison 1974), but while in need of a full reanalysis, the site provides unequivocal evidence of the use of a parabolic sand dune in Paleoindian bison procurement. Today, the dune is part of the extensive Wind River Basin and Casper dune fields, a combination of active and stabilized dunes that stretch across much of central Wyoming (Kolm 1974).

Parabolic dunes are horseshoe or U-shaped, with open ends extending to the windward and the closed end or nose to the leeward. The area between the wings of the dune is the trough. The sides and the nose of the trough of the dune are generally steep toward the inside with the slopes at the angle of repose of the sand, or approximately 33°. Troughs of parabolic dunes vary in size from a few meters to half a kilometer in length, up to 100 m wide, and 10 to 15 m and even more deep. Often there is a perpendicular drop of 0.5 m or 1 m along the edges of the dune trough where the sand is held in place by deep root growth, making it difficult for an animal such as a bison to negotiate this last obstacle between it and freedom. Obviously dunes of this nature can form only in areas with extensive sand deposits (Figure 4.21).

The ecology of these dune fields is significant also. The wind often removes the sand in a trough between the wings of the parabola to a base level of clay and cobbles impervious to water so that interdunal ponds form, some of which are quite large and hold water year round. Grass is lush in the troughs of many dunes because of the availability of added moisture, and consequently these dune areas were favorite locations for bison. It is not uncommon to observe a parabolic dune with a pond of water and tall grass near the opening at the windward end. Further on toward the nose, the sand is active and forms a suitable trap. Even in late fall or early winter the ponds were not permanently frozen over if conditions then were similar to the present.

Humans would enjoy one definite advantage in killing the animals in this kind of trap. The split-hoofed bison would sink deep into the sand whereas humans would not. This kind of trap would impede the animals and not hold them immobile in the sand, but still they would be at a definite disadvantage. Surrounded by well-armed

Figure 4.21 Typical parabolic sand dune in the large dune field several kilometers north of the Casper site.

hunters around the rim of the dune, the animals would be forced to move uphill in the soft sand in their efforts to escape. Even in winter, sand dune activity often continues, unless the sand is wet enough to freeze solid. Snow and sand often move at the same time. Snow may drift first and the sand may then drift over the snow and preserve it well into summer (Steidtmann 1973). From these observations we can postulate that a sand dune trap at chosen times in winter could be every bit as effective in slowing the escape of bison as at other times of the year.

The Casper site is the prime example of the use of a parabolic sand dune for a bison trap. Bison were apparently driven into the dune from the west (windward) and killed in the deepest part of the trough just before it sloped upward toward the nose of the dune. It was probably not a single event although tooth eruption schedules indicate that it could be; an alternative possibility would be that it represents several events close together during the same year, or more than one annual event at the same time of the year. Again this is a problem that could be solved through a reanalysis of the faunal remains from the site.

Because of the nature of dune fields, animal traps in parabolic sand dunes are rarely preserved intact, especially in areas of high winds such as the Casper site area. Vegetation is a major factor controlling sand movement, so even short periods without rain usually bring about some sand movement. However, the particular characteristics of the parabolic dune located on a stream terrace above present-day Casper, Wyoming, preserved the remains of approximately 100 *B. antiquus* killed in late fall/early winter (Reher 1974) in the bottom of the trough of the dune. Sand quickly covered the partially butchered bison remains after their deposition. An interdunal pond formed on top of the sand covering the bones, and carbonates filtered down through the sand onto the bison remains. The bone had been covered by nine meters of sand and was only exposed by earth-moving equipment in the 1970s.

The skeletal remains at the Casper site were recovered in an unusually good state of preservation and with little if any postkill disturbance. Some carnivore damage could be observed, but even this was minimal compared to bone beds in many kill areas. However, many of the marks on bones that were earlier interpreted as the result of tool use were more likely the result of carnivore and scavenger activity. Many carcass parts remained in about the same position as when butchering was completed. Large articulated skeletal units, including both axial and appendicular skeletal parts, were recorded (Figure 4.22). A processing and/ or camp area for the Casper site was not located.

A high incidence of tooth pathologies, including loss of a premolar or a molar, loss of the third cusp on the third molar, both enlarged and reduced tooth size, and crooked tooth rows characterize the population of well-preserved cranial material (see Chapter 5, this volume). These suggest some kind of stress, which could have been the result of inbreeding, intense human predation, or geographic isolation of a bison herd in a worsening natural environment, or some combination of all three. This is one area of future study that deserves a strong effort.

Part of a Hell Gap bone bed was excavated at the Agate Basin site (Figure 4.23), although an unknown amount was removed by arroyo cutting. Animal ages based on tooth eruption from 11 immature individuals indicate a kill probably well into December. The tightness of the age groups suggests a single kill event. Presumably, the same kind of procurement activity was continued there from Agate Basin into Hell Gap times.

Figure 4.22   The bison bone bed at the Casper site.

Figure 4.23   Hell Gap bison bone bed at the Agate Basin site.

After investigating and analyzing the materials from both the Agate Basin and Casper sites, we see a close similarity between the tools and weaponry of both complexes. Hell Gap projectile points (Figure 2.34) appear to be Agate Basin points with a slight shoulder. In fact, at the Agate Basin site some of the Agate Basin points were beginning to acquire the shoulder that is the diagnostic of Hell Gap (Figure 2.33e). Each projectile point style has its apparent advantages and disadvantages. Whether a split foreshaft, a socket, or something else altogether was used for hafting we may never know, but both the Agate Basin and Hell Gap points are ideal for use in a socket, although a split or nocked foreshaft will function quite well also. From experiments on both domestic cattle and bison, both are satisfactory, but in the case of Agate Basin points, the socket with a sinew wrapping is superior in strength to a nocked foreshaft with a sinew wrapping. The thick lenticular cross section of the Agate Basin point gives it structural strength and enough weight to ensure penetration. Its tapering base and sinew wrapping absorb the shock of impact, and transverse breaks often leave sections that can be resharpened for future use. The expanding stem and shoulder of the Hell Gap point facilitates and improves the hafting. The Hell Gap point, if properly pointed, blade edges sharpened, and thrust into an animal, cuts a larger hole than the Agate Basin point and the wide blade slices very effectively into the internal organs during any subsequent movement of the animal. However, the Hell Gap point does not penetrate as deeply into an animal as the Agate Basin point.

Projectile points at both the Casper and Agate Basin sites demonstrate evidence of heavy use in the form of a number of impact scars and flakes. Breakage of projectile point stems is further evidence of heavy impact. Identical impact damage has been produced experimentally using both domestic cattle and bison as the targets. It should be noted, however, that ribs of domestic cattle are wider and the outside surfaces are flatter than bison ribs. Consequently, projectile points have a greater tendency on impact to slip off the rounded surface of the bison rib and continue on into the rib cage, instead of breaking as they usually do upon impact with the flat ribs of domestic cattle. Agate Basin and Hell Gap projectile points are efficient weaponry for killing bison, used properly with either thrusting spear or throwing stick. Each functions well in different kinds of encounters such as darting an animal from a distance or spearing one that is charging. Perhaps in actual practice some hunters were armed with throwing sticks and darts in the former situation, while in the latter situation some were using thrusting spears.

Cody Complex Bison Procurement

The Alberta complex Hudson-Meng site in western Nebraska is about the same age as the Casper site and produced the remains of around 600 animals. The investigator (Agenbroad 1978b) postulated that the site was a possible bison jump since he apparently felt that the terrain at the time of the bison kill was favorable for this kind of procurement strategy. Except for the early part of the excavation when the bone was removed, the bison bone was left in place after recording and the site backfilled. The reason for this was to develop the site for public viewing as an example of a Paleoindian bison kill site. The excavations also resulted in several observations relevant to bison procurement and use. First, tooth eruption schedules indicated bison mortality six months after birth (age + 0.5 years) or in the fall.

Second, there were some missing elements, in particular no complete crania, a paucity of third phalanges (hoofs), sacral elements, and caudal vertebrae relative to that expected for 600 animals. These patterns were attributed to specific butchering processes, a model of which was presented based partially on experimental butchering of a cow. The investigator calculated total available resource from this kill event in terms of meat weight, as well as the dried meat weight. These types of calculations were common at the time of the investigation (Wheat 1972). The investigator also linked the Alberta complex to the Cody complex on the basis of a Cody knife discovered at the site.

As a result of Agenbroad's original plan to make the site a public example of a Paleoindian bison kill, the United States Forest Service, the property owner, began in the 1990s to develop the site for research and visitors. In preparation for the project, the bone bed had to be re-exposed and testing in the vicinity of the proposed development had to be undertaken in order not to damage other parts of the site during construction (Figure 4.24). Twenty years after the initial investigation of Hudson-Meng, taphonomic studies had become central to any zooarchaeological analysis but especially to zooarchaeological analysis of bone middens, and the investigators that took on the Hudson-Meng project during the 1990s were at the cutting edge of this research (Todd 1987b). In particular, what was realized in the intervening years is that patterns in bone beds are created by a vast variety of processes prior, during, and after burial. The investigators' approach at Hudson-Meng, as it had been at other sites previously, was to investigate the archaeological record with the goal of understanding taphonomic processes and therefore identify those patterns that could be a function of zoological, geological, or other noncultural processes. As a part of these studies, animal remains and their patterning in the geological or paleontological record provided the source of information with which to interpret bone beds and human activity within them.

The most obvious pattern at Hudson-Meng, the lack of skulls and paucity of third phalanges, was thus investigated, and the new investigators concluded that both are consistent with what would be expected as a part of natural weathering and burial processes in a bone bed, without needing to resort to human intervention to explain these patterns (Todd and Rapson 1997). The other aspect of their work was to investigate the possibility of a bison jump as indicated by the initial investigator at the site. A backhoe trench placed in the area of the suggested bison jump showed that the early Holocene landform had not formed a steep drop-off, but had been a slope that would not have provided adequate topographic relief to either kill the bison or disable them so they could be killed by other means. The investigators then went on to analyze other aspects of the faunal assemblage, in particular skeletal element frequencies, and concluded that most are consistent with natural burial processes. They contend there is no reason to think that the Hudson-Meng site is anything but a paleontological locality.

Lest we think this issue is an esoteric debate between two opposing views, the United States Forest Service has developed a multimillion-dollar research and visitor facility at the Hudson-Meng site, and interpretation of the bone bed is a central part of that facility. It is quite clear that Alberta and other artifacts were recovered from the site, and the original investigator has on numerous occasions pointed to several of these artifacts, including one imbedded in a vertebra, to demonstrate that in fact the bison at Hudson-Meng were dispatched by prehistoric peoples of the Plains. The investigators of the 1990s, however, point out that

Figure 4.24   Bison bone bed at the Hudson-Meng site.

there are very few projectile points relative to the number of bison in the bone bed; in fact, Hudson-Meng is an outlier in this regard with the fewest number of points per bison of any Paleoindian site. Various test excavations in the 1990s, as well as more recently by a third set of investigators, have pointed out a number of overlying cultural layers, including a component at the very top of the Hudson-Meng bone bed that appears to be of Alberta age, as well as overlying Archaic components.

The present interpretation of Hudson-Meng is that it appears to be the result of a complex set of cultural and noncultural processes. Thirty years ago virtually all patterns in the archaeological record were interpreted as the result of human action, and models of human behavior were developed on this basis. Today we know that patterns can be created by a variety of processes, some caused or initiated by humans, some by other "actors." Which patterns at the Hudson-Meng site are caused by humans is still a matter of debate. Is Hudson-Meng a bison kill? Currently the evidence for this is not strong, but one projectile point imbedded in a vertebra is suggestive. Had the bison at Hudson-Meng been butchered or otherwise modified by humans? Currently only a little evidence for this exists in the form of a few cut marks on bone. All other statements about human involvement are ambiguous.

Within the same age bracket (around 10,000 years ago) as the Hell Gap Casper and the Alberta Hudson-Meng sites is a component at the Horner site, the type site of the Cody complex (Figure 4.25), because it yielded the Eden- and Scottsbluff-type projectile points and the Cody-type knife together at a single site. A bison bone bed separate from the one or ones excavated by Princeton and the Smithsonian in the late 1940s and early 1950s was discovered in 1977. It contained the skeletal remains of at least 68 bison killed in late fall or early winter. A few more animals may be present in a small part of the bone bed that is still intact. It was at first thought to be an Alberta component, but, although some of the projectile points demonstrated some resemblance to Alberta, they also demonstrated some resemblance to those of the Cody complex. A compromise was made, and it is now referred to as Alberta-Cody (Bradley and Frison 1987:201–231).

The bison bones lay in a shallow depression formed by a slow, meandering watercourse formed on top of a cobble terrace of the Shoshone River (Figure 4.26) and were covered by more than a meter of alluvium. At first, it appeared that the bones might have been dumped there from another location after butchering. However, after removal of individual bones and smaller articulated units, the remains of several nearly complete carcasses were revealed (Figure 4.27), strongly suggesting that this was indeed the location where the animals had actually been killed and butchered.

Geologic study indicates there was no landform present at the Horner site since the formation of the cobble terrace that could have served as a natural trap. The edges of the bison bone bed are distinct and end abruptly, but there is no evidence of postholes around its perimeter. In addition, the terrace cobbles are tightly packed, cemented to some extent by carbonate deposits, and are of a size that would have been difficult to dig even with metal tools. The presence of some sort of corral structure similar to a buck fence has been postulated. The timber

Figure 4.25   Aerial view of the Horner site, the type site of the Cody cultural complex in northwest Wyoming.

Figure 4.26   Bison bone bed at the Horner site during excavation.

necessary for such a structure would have been nearby and, although the depression in which the bones lay was less than half a meter in depth, in combination with a sturdy fence it would have helped contain the animals.

Since there is undisputed evidence for both Alberta-Cody and Cody complex bison kills at the Horner site (Frison and Todd 1987), it can be argued that the

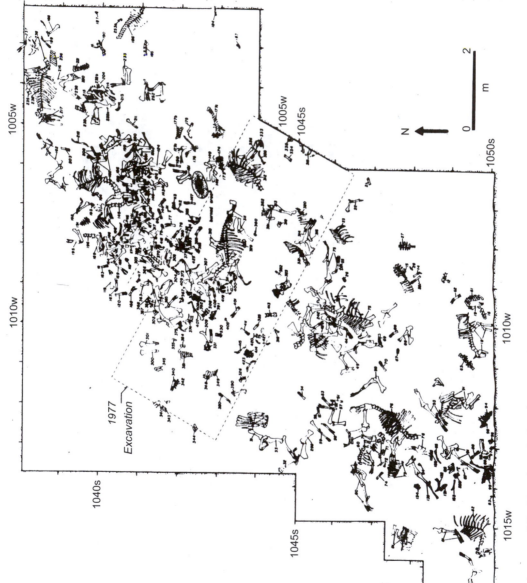

Figure 4.27 Plan view map of the bison bone bed at the Horner site.

Horner site area was the scene of systematic bison procurement for at least a thousand years of the Paleoindian period. Consequently, it can be argued further that the area must have been favorable bison habitat in a location also favorable for predictive kills. The cobble terrace at the Horner site by itself is difficult to envision as a prime spot for bison. However, the site is located near the confluence of the Shoshone River and a small stream known as Sage Creek. The latter forms a natural passage to and from highly productive grasslands located about 12 km to the east of the Horner site, which is a short distance for bison to travel. Regular and predictive movements from grass to trees and water are what probably made the Horner site area an ideal spot for bison procurement.

A study of the Horner site bison dentitions from the Alberta-Cody component demonstrated an annual rate of wear on molar teeth of 5.4 mm per year (Todd and Hofman 1987:508), which seems relatively high but still quite similar to annual attrition rates of other early Holocene bison from kill sites. At this rate of wear, the animal's life span was limited, since the total enamel height on the first molar was usually around 55 mm. This meant that at between 10 and 11 years of age the animal had no grinding area left on the first molar and the probability was low that it would again see green grass if the coming winter was long and the snow was deep.

The Olsen-Chubbuck site was one of the first modern, sophisticated investigations of a bison bone bed (Wheat 1972). The site dates within a range of other Eden and Scottsbluff sites as determined from a radiocarbon date on bone (Holliday et al. 1999). Located on the eastern Plains of Colorado, it is one of the few Paleoindian sites for which there is little doubt of the geomorphic feature involved in bison procurement. A herd of *B. occidentalis* were stampeded by some strategy into a deep, steeply-sided, narrow arroyo, killing about 190 animals of all ages and both sexes. It was regarded as an early spring kill event for some time, but later analyses of tooth eruption determined the kill occurred in late summer or early fall (Frison 1991:279–287).

The procurement situation at Olsen-Chubbuck appears to have been one of great success and a model of efficiency, at least in terms of killing animals. We might wonder why more sites of similar nature have not been found, since arroyos of the same or similar nature are a common geomorphic feature of the terrain in many areas of good bison habitat. It may be that there are many more undiscovered similar sites, since large quantities of bison bone in arroyo bottoms often do preserve quite well. Another possible explanation is that although these kinds of kills were effective in killing bison, they did not leave the dead animals in the optimum location for butchering and processing. A deep, narrow arroyo filled to the brim with dead bison cannot be regarded as a happy task to face in terms of salvaging the products of the kill for future consumption. Human groups wise in the ways of hunting might have generally preferred to utilize more favorable locations and have the dead animals where they could be butchered and processed more easily. Certainly a significant quantity of the Olsen-Chubbuck meat products were lost, judging from the number of animals in the bottom of the arroyo that were left intact and/or only partially butchered (Wheat 1972:28–38).

The Olsen-Chubbuck site deserves a special place in bison kill site studies. Up until that time, bison bones and faunal materials in general from archaeological sites received more or less cursory treatment in site analysis. The analysis of the Olsen-Chubbuck bone bed alerted archaeologists to the fact that the bones themselves contained a wealth of data on human activities that accompanied the animal procurement operation, as well as taphonomic and biological information on the animals themselves. As a result, zooarchaeology has become an integral part of archaeological studies.

Three Cody complex sites in Wyoming—the Horner site in the northern Bighorn Basin, the Finley site in the Green River Basin, and the Carter/Kerr-McGee site in the Powder River Basin—along with the Frasca, Jurgens, and Nelson sites in northeast Colorado and Jerry Craig in the Colorado mountains, were the scenes of bison procurement operations, perhaps at a large scale. All occurred apparently during the time when early Holocene bison numbers were diminishing due to unfavorable climatic conditions leading up to the Altithermal period about a millennium later.

The Finley site is located at the periphery of the Killpecker sand dune field, part of which is one of the larger of the presently active sand dune areas in North America. The site has undergone a good deal of investigation as well as looting since its discovery in 1939 by O. M. Finley (Hack 1943; Howard 1943; Howard et al. 1941; Moss et al. 1951). Like the Horner site, the Finley site has undergone a good deal of digging by people in search of Paleoindian projectile points. However, from 1971 to 1973 and still later in 1987, we have recovered additional faunal materials from the site that tell us quite a bit more about the associated bison and their procurement.

The Finley site (Moss et al. 1951) is located in an area of stabilized sand dunes about a quarter of a mile east of a spring near Eden, Wyoming. The spring apparently results from precipitation that falls on a large area of sand dunes overlying an impervious stratum. The spring runs strongest in the spring and tapers off in late summer, but does produce water year round. The water forms a bog area for several hundred meters beyond the spring source. The bog presents a danger to cattle in the spring of the year, especially to older animals that are relatively weak from the winter. However, cattle graze the bog in summer and it presents no problem to healthy cattle then, even though they may sink to their bellies in the mud.

The area excavated at the Finley site produced a number of bison bones but mostly foot bones such as distal metacarpals, metatarsals, phalanges, and very few long bones. Although a number of both Eden and Scottsbluff projectile points were recovered (Figure 2.36a–d), the evidence argues that this was some kind of specialized processing area rather than a kill area.

During the late 1960s, wind action began to uncover bison bone in a large sand dune about 200 meters north of the original Finley site excavations. Postulating that this might be an undisturbed kill area associated with the original site area, investigations were quickly initiated. However, it was soon evident that the bones were not in situ but had apparently been dug out and subsequently reburied. Sorting through the bones, one nearly complete *B. antiquus* skull was recovered (see Wilson 1974b:92) along with several broken Eden and Scottsbluff projectile points. One front leg and several single long bones were in situ in lightly cemented sand deposits, lending credence to the idea that this was indeed the kill area at Finley, but that persons unknown had discovered it subsequent to the original Finley site excavations and had excavated it looking for artifacts. Judging from the number of projectile points found in other communal Paleoindian bison kill sites, they were probably well rewarded for their efforts.

Even though not recovered in situ, the faunal collection is of considerable value. The minimum number of individuals represented is at least 59, based on left metacarpals (Haspel and Frison 1987). Based on tooth eruption, the animals were killed in late fall at about the same time as the ones at the Horner site (Todd and Hofman 1987). Unfortunately, no evidence exists to tell us the method employed to trap the animals.

The partial bone bed remaining at the Carter/Kerr-McGee site (Figure 4.15) was of Cody age, and both Eden and Scottsbluff projectile points (Figure 2.37a–c) were recovered in the bones. The minimum number of animals was 47 based on astragali, and seasonality based on tooth eruption followed closely that of the Horner and Finley sites (during late fall or early winter). Bone preservation was poor enough to make butchering analysis difficult, although a number of articulated units were identified. The bone bed is probably not the actual kill location, which was likely to have been in the bottom of the immediately adjacent arroyo; it resembles more closely the situation at the Agate Basin site where a large pile of butchered units were deliberately stacked and frozen and stripped of meat as needed.

An aerial view of the Carter/Kerr-McGee site (Figure 4.14) reveals the ideal situation for communal bison procurement using a headcut in an arroyo as a natural trap, although there is no evidence at present of the original geomorphic feature of Paleoindian age that formed such a trap. On the other hand, the general character of the site area has not changed from Paleoindian times. A lake bed to the north was present during that period and probably resulted from dropping of the land surface after burning of thick coal beds much earlier in time, probably during the late Pliocene or early Pleistocene. Arroyos then gradually formed that drained into the lake and were ideal for attracting animals up the bottoms to headcuts utilized as traps. The lake undoubtedly held water in Pleistocene times as it occasionally does at present. Feed would have been lush around its margins and up the arroyo bottoms.

The Frasca and Nelson sites in northeast Colorado have some similarities, and Frasca is further similar to the Olsen-Chubbuck site. The bison remains at Frasca were recovered in an old arroyo, although much of the site had eroded away. At least 56 animals were killed and processed possibly as late as January or February (Fulgham and Stanford 1982). A radiocarbon date of 8900 BP fits well with those from other Cody complex sites.

The Nelson site has received only cursory investigation of a chipped stone sample and approximately 200 bones recovered from the site surface (Kornfeld et al. 2007). However, these remains show that at least five bison were killed at the site in the middle of winter. The chipped stone assemblage is very small, similar to the Frasca site, but given that all the artifacts were recovered from the surface, excavation is expected to significantly increase the assemblage size of both bone and chipped stone (Figure 4.28a–c). At present the nature of the kill process at Nelson cannot be ascertained.

The Jurgens site is located on a South Platte River terrace about 14.5 km east of Greeley, Colorado. According to the investigator (Wheat 1979), three separate site areas represent a butchering station, a long-term campsite, and a short-term camp. A radiocarbon date of about 9100 BP places it in the time period of the Cody complex, although Wheat (1979:152) argues that Olsen-Chubbuck and Jurgens are part of a cultural development on the Central and Southern Plains that paralleled the Alberta-Cody complex development farther to the north.

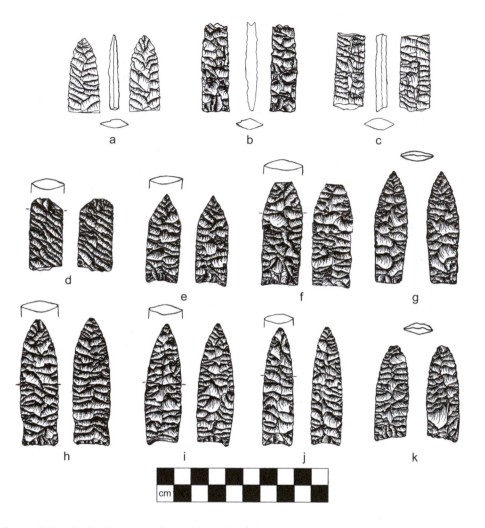

Figure 4.28   Projectile points from Nelson (a–c) and Jerry Craig (d–k) sites. (Figure 4.28a–f courtesy of Susan Davis.)

Area 3 at the Jurgens site was a bison bone bed containing partial remains of at least 35 animals, but it is believed to be a butchering station and not a kill area. Undoubtedly there was a kill area nearby, but no hint of its presence or means of procurement was found. Seasonality and age-group studies through tooth eruption schedules were not attempted but should be done since these kinds of studies can provide information on the nature of the procurement strategy involved.

A very unique Cody complex manifestation is the Jerry Craig site in the Middle Park of the Colorado Rocky Mountains. This is the only known bison procurement site of this age in a clear montane setting; a small and high mountain basin (Richings-Germain 2002). The site produced over 75 projectile points or fragments, most of them found eroding down a small rill over a period of more than 30 years. Excavations carried out at the site from 1993 to 1999 recovered a small faunal sample and chipped stone. The radiocarbon date from burned wood sample of

9310 ± 50 BP (Beta 109467) falls squarely in the Cody age. The projectile points, however, are quite variable, showing a range from typical Eden and Scottsbluff characteristics to points that look like those from Packard site in Oklahoma and Big Eddy in Iowa (Ray et al. 1998; Wycoff 1984). Of the 75 projectile points, 12 are complete and another five are nearly complete. Thus, essentially one quarter of the assemblage could have been rejuvenated, but were never recovered from the bone bed. Over 85% of the points were manufactured on local Troublesome Formation or Kremmling chert and a little over 10% were of other local materials. Only a small number of projectile points were manufactured on nonlocal materials. Two of the specimens retain their original form, while 10 complete points exhibit reworked tips or bases. Of the 75 projectile points, 44% of all specimens show reworking. Resharpened tips are present on 36% of the points, bases on 21%, both tips and bases on 18%, while 9% have been modified into another tool form. While the number of usable projectile points seems high, it is also clear that raw material conservation was of concern and tools were recycled to extend the use life of the raw material.

The excavation recovered 326 faunal specimens, including 191 identifiable to element, and enough dentiary material to establish that the season of death was late summer or fall (Hill et al. 1999). Furthermore, based on the tight tooth eruption and wear cluster showing the time of death, a single kill event is suggested. Mandibles, the most common element, show that the minimum number of animals that died at the site is seven. However, it should be emphasized that an unknown portion of this site has been destroyed by erosion and an unknown portion remains to be excavated. Based on the recovered assemblage, in particular the large number of projectile points exhibiting impact fractures, the Jerry Craig site appears to be a kill location.

BISON KILLS OF THE LATE PALEOINDIANS

The Late Paleoindian period database of bison procurement sites is still rather small, but it is growing. Furthermore, many of the sites were excavated long ago, when archaeologists were discarding the bone or not analyzing it consistently. Hence some recent field investigations, combined with reanalysis of curated fauna from previous excavations, are beginning to build a database for these sites. The James Allen site in the Laramie Basin of southern Wyoming, Clary Ranch in Nebraska, and the Laird site in western Kansas are three Late Paleoindian period sites that have some information on bison procurement, along with the Frederick component at the Hell Gap site.

James Allen was excavated in 1959 by William Mulloy of the University of Wyoming (Mulloy 1959). Mulloy recovered bison bone and 30 projectile points; today there are 41 projectile points in the assemblage, the result of continuous surface recovery over a 50-year period. Twenty other tools in the assemblage consist of drills, scrapers, and flake tools (Knudson and Kornfeld 2007). The bone from the site was not collected except for selected complete elements. These provided evidence that a minimum of 15 animals were present at the site, and Mulloy interpreted it as a single kill/butchery event. Dated at about 7900 years ago, it is among the latest known Paleoindian bison procurement sites, but unfortunately little can be said about the actual strategy of trapping and killing the animals. As was the case with the Agate Basin and Horner sites, the faunal materials from the site were discarded and seasonality or population studies are not possible.

Clary Ranch site in western Nebraska was excavated some time ago and recently reanalyzed in preparation for reinitiating field investigations (Hill 2008; Myers et al. 1981). Hill determined that the over 1500 faunal specimens recovered from the site represent 41 individual animals and that the kill occurred in the late summer or early fall. An exhaustive zooarchaeological analysis clearly shows that the site is a secondary butchering location. Animal parts were selected and brought to the site from a nearby kill and processed in a variety of ways including processing the bones for marrow, as evidenced by impact fractures and patterned opening up of the marrow cavities and stripping and drying of meat, a conjectural activity postulated to produce stores for overwintering.

Of similar cultural affiliation as Clary Ranch, the Laird site in Sherman County, Kansas, is identified as Dalton by the investigators (Hofman and Blackmar 1997). The site was identified by bone on the surface and was tested with only four 1 x 1 meter units and 14 auger holes. The excavation yielded 306 bison bones, 86 of them identifiable to element. The bones exhibit moderate amounts of root etching and some rodent gnawing, but are generally in good condition for zooarchaeological analysis, except for high degrees of dry bone breakage. Nevertheless there are a significant number (n=14) of green bone breaks, indicating the breakage of bone for marrow removal. Only two bison are represented in the sample of bone within the excavated portion of the site, with a mortality estimate of late winter or early spring based on two lower third molar teeth. The geologic context of the bison bone is a filled, narrow gully and the investigators suggest that it may represent a situation similar to the Olsen-Chubbuck arroyo kill in Colorado. The testing indicated that a portion of the site has eroded away, but at least another 15 m^2 of the sediment contains bone. Although we will never know the total extent of this bone bed, further investigation would yield additional relevant data for Late Paleoindian bison procurement.

Another site of similar age and in the area of Laird is the Norton site, again in Kansas. The site is in a gully that drains into Ladder Creek (Hofman et al. 1995). The gully has cut into Pleistocene sands and gravels containing mammoth, horse, turtle, and other Pleistocene fauna. The gully fill contains the bison bone bed, but the bone bed also extends to the gully margins in some portions of the site. Several dates on the overlying Holocene sediment and one assay on the bison bone that yielded a date of 9080 BP suggest an age for the site. If the associated diagnostic artifact is an Allen point this is a rather early date, but it may be Dalton, which would fit better with the radiocarbon date. The relationship of Allen, Dalton, Frederick, and Meserve, however, is rather unclear and deserves more attention (see Chapter 9).

The bone at the Norton site is predominantly bison, but pronghorn is present as well, as is the case in many other bison bone beds. Over 1600 specimens yielded a minimum of eight animals killed at the site. However, the orientation and inclination of specimens on the gully is highly variable, the weathered bone surfaces are frequently on the bottom, and the bone is fragmented. This suggests to the investigators that the bone has been redeposited from another location. The bone on the gully margins, on the other hand, contains several articulated units, and the weathering surfaces are on the top of the bone. This gully margin may be the origin of all the bone, before a redepositon event moved some of the bone to the bottom of the gully. Part of this site has been destroyed by recent quarrying activity and part has been removed by erosion. Nevertheless, a substantial amount of bone has been recovered and awaits further analysis.

Faunal remains recovered during the 1960s excavations in the Frederick level at the Hell Gap site are only incompletely analyzed because of problems with provenience, biased collection policies, and postexcavation treatment. However, the Locality I assemblage contains bison, deer, and pronghorn bone in larger proportions than earlier levels at the site (Rapson and Niven 2009). A pattern of the extraction of within-bone nutrients (e.g., marrow) characterizes the assemblage.

These sites, although of variable preservation and excavation effort, show that bison hunting was a significant part of Late Paleoindian economic activity. Bison processing appears more intensive than at most earlier Paleoindian bison bone beds, but an increase in the number of excavated sites and excavated areas of already investigated sites may change this perception. At present more earlier Paleoindian bone beds have been intensively investigated than later ones.

Bison Procurement during the Early Plains Archaic Period

The Black Hills of South Dakota and Wyoming form an uplift about 160 km long and about half that distance in width. The area is quite heavily timbered with ponderosa pine, quaking aspen, and a hybrid species of oak. This vegetation contrasts sharply with the flora of the Rocky Mountains farther west and with the surrounding sagebrush- and grass-covered plains. Within the Black Hills, however, there are numerous small stream valleys and other areas of open, grass-covered country that are quite different ecologically from the timber- and brush-covered parts. The Black Hills also enjoy slightly more yearly precipitation than the surrounding plains, and their grass cover is somewhat better. The Black Hills must have presented optimum conditions for the propagation of the bison herds in the past, and if our present data remain unchanged, this was true particularly during the mid-Holocene. The grass is lush and the area is well watered with several small but permanent streams flowing from the hills. Good winter protection is offered by brush- and timber-covered valleys along streams and dry arroyos, valleys that provided good browse even during deep snow periods.

Several years of archaeological survey, testing, and excavation have been done in an area of about 5 km² centered just south of Sundance, Wyoming. Triassic red sandstones form a scarp overlooking a basin-like area characterized by low, rolling hills and shallow, meandering arroyos with good grass cover. However, toward the base of the scarp, the slopes increase in gradient for a distance of a quarter of a kilometer or so, and soils derived from the erosion of the sandstones are quite deep and easily eroded. Arroyos here are narrow and deep with steep banks, and as they extend into areas of lower relief and their gradients decrease, they become wider with flat, grass-covered bottoms and low banks. For several thousand years they provided ideal avenues up which bison were driven as the sides of the arroyo became high enough and steep enough that the animals could not get out. Headcuts in the sandstone formation of some arroyos were sometimes up to several meters in height and formed animal traps analogous to those described earlier for the more open areas of the plains.

The Hawken site is located within the area described above and was discovered by artifact hunters who noticed bison bone and projectile points eroding out of a cut bank. The Hawken site is a classic example of the arroyo bison trap; at least 80 animals were driven up the bottom of the arroyo by hunters until a perpendicular headcut was reached (Figures 4.29 and 4.30). There were at least three disparate episodes of use at the Hawken site, but the time lapse between these periods is not known. Several centimeters of sediment separate each of the three levels. Radiocarbon dates from the site suggest an age of approximately 6600 BP. It is unknown whether the three levels at the site represent three kills in a single season or separate kills over a period of years.

A large sample of bison mandibles and maxillaries with intact tooth rows were used to determine the season of kill as late fall/early winter (Frison et al. 1976). Separate analyses of the lower teeth and the upper teeth correlated very closely and add a strong measure of credence to the methodology used (Frison et al. 1976). The presence of a large number of complete mature male skulls and measurements from metacarpals and metatarsals (Bedord 1974:234) suggests the hunters were taking mature male groups of animals as well as nursery herds. The Hawken site bison are larger than the modern form but smaller than those from the Casper site. They are believed to represent *B. occidentalis*, which is characterized by a more posterior deflection of horn core, greater orbital width, and less cranial breadth than that seen in *B. antiquus* skulls. The measurements on metatarsals and metacarpals (Bedord 1974) and on volumes of astragali (Zeimens and Zeimens 1974) provide further evidence of the intermediate size of the Hawken site bison around 6600 years ago. Analysis of the Hawken site bison remains strengthens the contention that there has been a steady decrease in size of the bison species during the Holocene.

Figure 4.29   Bison bone bed at the Hawken site in northeast Wyoming.

Figure 4.30   Postulated direction of bison movement into the Hawken site.

The measurable skulls at the Hawken site were all males, although metacarpal and metatarsal measurements (Bedord 1974:234) argue for only a slight preponderance of males in the total sample of mature animals (at least 61 animals) based on lower teeth. The total number of complete metatarsals and metacarpals with fused distal ends (attesting to animals four years of age and above) number 23 females and 27 males. This is the sample used in sex determinations but not the entire sample, since many were incomplete.

The Hawken site bison mandibles can be separated into yearly age groups. The population structure of the site, like that of the Casper site, suggests that most of the bison lived to an age of about 12 years, although an occasional animal might have lived longer. However, the tooth anomalies that were observed at the Casper site were not present at Hawken. Postcranial pathologies were infrequent also, and those noted could have resulted from normal mishaps and from male dominance displays.

A total of nearly 300 known projectile points has been recovered from the site and many more were collected by amateurs that have not been located. The ratio of projectile points to animals is high, which suggests a trapping situation. A significant amount of killing and crippling may have occurred among the animals themselves when crowded into the confines of a pound or trap, but most of the killing had to be done by the hunters.

The projectile points at the Hawken site are the earliest side-notched type known from the Northwestern Plains associated with a bison kill (Figure 2.52h–l). The use of notches to bind a projectile point to a wooden shaft was an innovation that appeared at the beginning of Early Plains Archaic times and spread rapidly over a wide area of the Plains and adjacent areas. However, side-notching had one disadvantage: it increased the number of points that break across their notch. One could consider the points from the Hawken site as nothing more than terminal Paleoindian types such as Frederick or Lusk with side notches added. On the other hand, the Hawken points are quite similar to projectile points known as Logan Creek in eastern Nebraska (Kivett 1962) and possibly also to those at the Simonsen site (Agogino and Frankforter 1960) and the Cherokee Sewer site (Anderson and Semken 1980), both bison kills in eastern Iowa. If the latter case is true, the early side-notched points on the Plains may have relationships elsewhere instead of being simply a local innovation derived from the terminal Paleoindians. Resolution of the problem is not expected until sites are found that will satisfactorily demonstrate the necessary cultural relationships.

Many Hawken site projectile points demonstrate the results of heavy impact. As in Paleoindian sites, all broken points that could be reworked into usable specimens were so treated. The seemingly wide variation in the Hawken site projectile point assemblage is largely the result of modification of broken specimens to restore functional utility (Figure 2.2). The Hawken site points are unquestionably designed to penetrate the hide of large animals such as bison. The notches and bases were ground smooth to withstand thrusting pressure without splitting the shaft or cutting a sinew binding. The tips were brought to a needle-sharp point to penetrate the hide. Evidence of this kind of penetration is demonstrated by the distal end of a projectile point embedded in the atlas of a bison calf. It was undoubtedly a lethal thrust that penetrated deep into the muscles of the neck (Figure 4.31) and into the bone.

In the spring of 1975, a concentration of bison bone was discovered eroding out of a different arroyo bank close to the Hawken site. Excavations revealed a pile of nine bison skulls along with several other postcranial elements. Tool marks on many of the latter along with two large, flake butchering tools indicate the animals had been butchered and the skulls deliberately stacked. The actual kill location may be nearby or it may have been removed by arroyo cutting. This site (Hawken III) is dated at just over 6000 years BP, which is several hundred years later than the original Hawken site.

Preliminary measurements of the Hawken III male crania indicate a close similarity to those from Hawken. Three partial female crania were recovered from the pile of nine from Hawken III. The female crania have long, slender horn cores that extend laterally and are quite distinct from those of modern female bison (see Chapter 3, this volume). The Hawken III operation probably took place very close to calving time; mandibles from two calves are almost exactly one year old and part of a fall-term fetus was present in the bone pile. This strongly suggests a kill between mid-March and early April. A closer determination might be possible with a larger sample of mandibles from juvenile animals.

A recent discovery of bison bone to the northeast of the Black Hills resulted in partial excavation of the only other known Early Plains Archaic bison kill in this part of the Northwestern Plains, the Licking Bison site (39HN570) in Harding County, South Dakota. Excavations were conducted here from 1995 to 2000 by Mike Fosha, after a collector showed him projectile points discovered in the area. The site is located on a terrace of Graves Creek, a relatively wide ephemeral tributary of the South Fork of the Grand River, below approximately 1.5 m of alluvial sediment of the first terrace of Graves Creek, thought to be of Holocene age (Fosha 2001). On the opposite side of the drainage were additional cultural and bison remains, but their relationship to the Licking Bison site remains unknown.

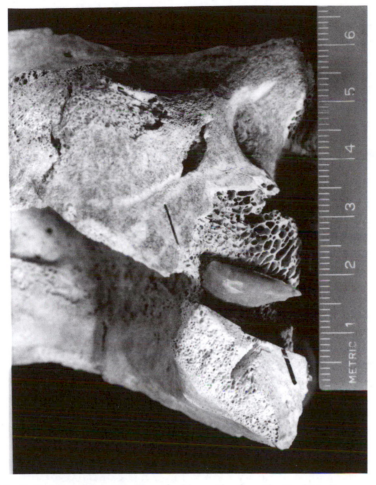

Figure 4.31 Projectile point penetration of a bison atlas from the Hawken site.

Excavation included a total of 26 units placed along the edge of the terrace where bison and artifacts were seen eroding out of the deposit. Although the zooarchaeological study has yet to be completed, field observations indicate that bone condition varies across the site, as does the distribution of skeletal elements. One part of the site contains complete or nearly complete carcasses, in another part of the site the carcasses are halved, in yet other parts of the site the remains are of articulated animal quarters, while in other areas smaller articulated sections or individual elements are present. In the latter area the excavations uncovered a small surface hearth with burned bison bone. A stream channel was observed in the area of the site where the fully articulated carcasses were located, and the investigator suggests that the channel may have played a role in bison trapping strategy.

The Licking Bison excavations yielded at least nine projectile points. The types of points are similar to those recovered at the Hawken site, although most have concave rather than straight bases. A radiocarbon assay on material from the site yielded a date of 5630 ± 40 BP (Beta-195191; Mike Fosha, personal communication 2009), an Early Plains Archaic date nearly identical to that from the Hawken site.

Local materials were used for the manufacture of most of the points, although some of the raw material originated in southeast Montana and the Minnelusa or Pahasapa formations of the northern Black Hills. At present neither the bison taxa nor the season of the kill are known. These and other questions about the site remain to be answered with the full analysis and reporting of the site material. Nevertheless, Licking Bison represents a critical addition to Early Plains Archaic procurement strategies, as it is only one of two bison kill sites of this time period in the Northwestern Plains and adjacent Rocky Mountains.

There is also evidence of bison jumping at Head-Smashed-In Buffalo Jump near Lethbridge, Alberta, by cultural groups that Reeves (1978) labels the Mummy Cave complex, which would be contemporaneous with the Early Plains Archaic. Radiocarbon dates are from about 7600 to 5000 years BP, and the diagnostics are side-notched dart points. Head-Smashed-In is a large, complex series of bison procurement locations that were utilized for thousands of years and intensified during the Late Plains Archaic period (Brink and Dawe 1989).

The Middle Plains Archaic Period Bison Kills

While there seems little doubt that the climate was not too favorable for the propagation of bison herds between approximately 7500 and 5000 BP, except in possible oasis areas such as the Black Hills of Wyoming and South Dakota, we can document a return to more favorable conditions about 5000 years BP. Climatological and paleoecological indicators point to a highly variable climatic regime between about 6500 and 5000 BP throughout many areas of the Northwestern Plains and Rocky Mountains and an intensification of summer storms (see Chapter 1). Bison appear once more in archaeological sites. The bison present by 5000 or so years BP are the modern species *Bison bison*.

The McKean cultural complex dominates the Middle Plains Archaic on the Northwestern Plains and Rocky Mountains, but it can claim little in the way of systematic, large-scale bison hunting. One exception is the Scoggin site located about 20 km west of the North Platte River in south-central Wyoming. In this case, bison were apparently driven over a steep talus slope about 7 m high formed as the result of a layer of cap rock covering a softer, claylike formation (Lobdell 1973). At the base of the slope, postholes connected by a low wall of stones rest on a terrace of a dry arroyo. An associated bone level is presently covered by as much as 75 cm of colluvium. Charred wood fragments were recovered from one posthole and long bones had been shoved into holes alongside the posts, presumably to straighten leaning posts. Stones, pieces of wood, and other items similarly placed are still used in livestock corrals to straighten a post that is leaning too far because of pressure from the animals inside.

Full details on the size and shape of the corral are lacking, since only a small part of the posthole pattern remained. We think the fence extended for several meters parallel to the base of the slope and then both ends were turned upslope, possibly to its top. The only means of escape from the enclosure was back up the slope, and, although the slope itself was not steep enough to hold the animals, the hunters would have had a definite advantage with the animals below them. One corner of the structure is still present, and extra postholes were placed in a way to provide added reinforcement at a critical part of the fence. Outside the enclosure was a feature similar to Late Prehistoric period stone-boiling pits containing large stones and a number of bison bones, including two male skulls well within the size range of modern bison and measurably smaller than the intermediate size Hawken site bison that were present in the Black Hills 2000 years earlier.

The site location was strategic in terms of normal bison herd movements. It is at the end of a natural access corridor that extends through a high hogback ridge several kilometers in length. Since the location was on a dry arroyo tributary of the North Platte River, animals would pass by the site area going to and from water. Both pine and juniper are present, as they most likely were in the past, so posts and logs for corral construction were available. In terms of bison procurement, the location and terrain were ideal and the restraining corral was ingeniously constructed. From the sample of mandibles and individual teeth that could be used for age determination, it was found that there were two separate periods of procurement, one in summer/early fall and one in late fall/early winter (Niven and Hill 1998), that could have taken place during the same or different years.

The bone bed produced lanceolate McKean projectile points (Figure 2.58a, b) and, in addition, tri-notched Mallory points (Figure 2.58c–f). However, the manufacturing technology of both the lanceolate and the tri-notched points at the Scoggin site is the same; the major difference between the two is the addition of the notches.

The bone deposit separates into two distinct levels toward the base of the slope. Few tools were recovered, although tool-sharpening flakes suggest the use of a number of tools no longer present. The site may be a forerunner of the great number of similar procurement operations known from the Late Prehistoric period. Its greatest advantage is that the short, steep slope combined with the low, perpendicular cap rock at the jump-off would have helped hold the animals in the corral. The corral structure was probably completely covered with something, perhaps hides, to prevent the bison from seeing through to the outside. Even a small hole could have precipitated an attempt on the part of the animals to force an exit unless the structure was solidly built.

The Cordero Mine site (48CA75) in the central Powder River Basin of northern Wyoming provides evidence for Middle Plains Archaic bison procurement with a radiocarbon date of 3520 ± 150 BP (RL-805) and a minimum of 12 bison (Niven and Hill 1998; Reher et al. 1985). The mortality of the bison was determined to be late fall/early winter. The bison assemblage was highly patterned, containing predominantly limb bones of adult cows. The skeletal elements exhibited intense processing in the form of cut marks and impact fractures. Buttressed by a total absence of complete long bones, the processing marks suggest an intense utilization of the carcass, including marrow and bone grease rendering. The latter is further supported by the features present on the site, indicating heating of rocks for the purpose of stone boiling. The Cordero Mine site is thus a specialized processing site, clearly located close to a kill location from which selected carcass parts could be brought for intensive resource extraction.

THE LATE PLAINS ARCHAIC PERIOD BISON KILLS

The Yonkee bison kill sites at around 3000 years ago ushered in a period of extensive and sophisticated bison trapping on the Northwestern Plains. According to the present state of our knowledge, the major sites are found in the drainages of the Tongue and Powder rivers in Montana and Wyoming. The wealth of projectile points and the high visibility of the bone beds in many Yonkee sites have led to their destruction by collectors. See Chapter 2 for a full discussion of the radiocarbon dating of the sites.

The first Yonkee bison kill to be investigated was the Yonkee site in southeast Montana. Located in an area of moderate relief, the actual kill site was in an arroyo, but erosion in the area and disturbance by artifact hunters had altered the original topography so that it was difficult to discern a procurement strategy. The possibility of a fence at the top of the old arroyo bank should not be ruled out. Both ponderosa pine and juniper are at present growing in the area and would have provided ample timber for fence posts and logs. A single bison skull collected near the site, but not in the bone bed, was first believed to be an "intermediate form between *B. bison* and *Bison antiquus*" (Bentzen 1962a:121), but subsequent analysis disproved this conjecture (Wilson 1975:216).

A small remnant of another Yonkee bison kill site is located on a short, dry tributary of the Powder River in northern Wyoming (Site 48SH312; Frison 1968c). The site is an arroyo trap and was formed by headward erosion in the Fort Union Formation. The banks of the arroyo at the time of the kill were believed to have been nearly vertical and 5–10 m high. The headcut that makes the trap was formed in more resistant strata in the Fort Union Formation (Mann 1968). The trap may have been as much as 30 m wide during the time it was used, but subsequent erosion left only a small part of the site intact above the present arroyo bottom (Figure 4.32). Large articulated parts of bison remained and, as at the Yonkee site, projectile points were commonly recovered in the rib cages of the animals.

Figure 4.32   Bison bone bed at the Powder River site, a Yonkee kill site along the Powder River in northern Wyoming.

The animals at the Powder River site had to be driven up the bottom of the arroyo for some distance from a location downstream where the walls were not as steep. It has been suggested that the animals might have been driven down the arroyo and forced over the headcut into the trap, but this would have been extremely difficult since the arroyo walls upstream from the headcut were low and gently sloping and would not have held the animals. In addition, bison do not react well to being driven down an arroyo of this nature.

Another Yonkee arroyo bison kill, the Mavrakis-Bentzen-Roberts site (48SH311), is located a few miles west of Site 48SH312 in terrain similar to that near the Yonkee site (Bentzen 1962b; Miller 1976). In this case, animals could have been driven either up or down a wide, flat-bottomed ravine and then turned into the mouth of a short, narrow, steep-walled arroyo that terminated in a perpendicular headcut. The main ravine has a running spring, which undoubtedly would have attracted the bison if it was present at the time the site was in use. Two separate excavations were made at the site, one by the Wyoming Archaeological Society and a later one by the University of Wyoming in 1971.

In the latter investigation, enough mandibles were recovered to determine that the main procurement event or events took place in late winter, probably not too far from calving time. There is evidence also that a small kill occurred much earlier, probably in late fall. The size and extent of the site suggests a number of kills rather than a single one. Two radiocarbon dates average about 2500 years BP. At three of the arroyo kills—Yonkee, Buffalo Creek (Miller 1976), and Powder River (Frison 1968b)—butchering consisted of the removal of muscles with little attention paid to the removal of articulated units. Although cutting-tool marks were present, bone breakage was largely absent. Similar treatment of the carcasses at site 48SH312 may suggest that this method of butchering was an established practice among the hunting groups associated with Yonkee communal bison kills.

Yonkee hunters were apparently familiar with bison jumping. On Rosebud Creek, a short tributary of the Yellowstone River to the west of the Tongue River in southern Montana, a stratified buffalo jump, the Kobold site (Frison 1970b), was discovered by archaeologists following drive lines to the edge of a perpendicular sandstone cliff. The cliff, about 8 m high (Figure 4.33a), is ideally situated for jumping bison. Large, well-watered gathering areas for bison are nearby and are considered to be one of the better short-grass areas of the Plains. The terrain allows only one approach to the jump-off, although it may have changed slightly through time due to erosion. The position of the bones at the bottom of the precipice indicates that the hunters were well able to take advantage of the topography. Drive lines consisting of continuous lines of small stone piles lead to the jump-off, but there is no way as yet to determine whether these date to the Yonkee use at the site. Our best guess at this time is that the drive lines are probably Late Prehistoric in age.

Bison carcass treatment in the Yonkee level at the Kobold site was similar to that in the Yonkee arroyo traps. The animals were separated into large articulated units but occasionally the completely stripped skeleton was left intact as described at Site 48SH311. A good deal more bone breakage occurred, but this is believed to be the result of the animals falling over the jump-off since it is different than breakage observed in marrow retrieval. Jump-off height was at least 1.5–2 m more at that time than at present. The time of year, based on a small number of calves, was about late October or early November. There were fewer projectile

Figure 4.33 The Kobold Buffalo Jump in southern Montana (a), and the Glenrock Buffalo Jump along the North Platte River in central Wyoming (b). (Figure 4.33b courtesy of Bart Rea.)

points per animal than in the arroyo traps, probably because a large number of animals were killed outright or badly maimed by the fall. Possibly after the first few animals piled up at the bottom of the jump-off, the later ones suffered varying degrees of crippling in the fall and had to be killed. This would account for the projectile points that were recovered.

The projectile points in the Yonkee component at the Kobold site demonstrate a wider variation of styles than in the Yonkee arroyo traps. Stemmed points reminiscent of Wheeler's (1954b) Duncan type are present, along with true side-notched points and points identical to those at the Yonkee, 48SH311, and 48SH312 sites (Figure 2.58g–l). This wider range of variation might be used to suggest some cultural relationship to the earlier McKean complex, although no McKean lanceolate points were found. No charcoal was recovered, so that radiocarbon dates are not available for the Kobold site, but a large part of the site is still intact for future research. Attempts at obsidian dating were made, but the specimens analyzed were made of a nonvolcanic glass which occurs in the burned-out coal beds in the Powder River Basin (see Frison et al. 1968; Miller, Chapter 12, this volume).

These Yonkee sites in the Powder River Basin discussed above demonstrate a similarity that suggests a strong cultural relationship and highly developed techniques of bison procurement. The evidence indicates a strong reliance on fall and winter communal bison procurement, but little is yet known of the Yonkee campsites or the economic activities that took place during the remainder of the year. A working hypothesis is that there was some kind of temporary storage of meat products for winter use. The method of butchering, in which muscles were stripped and bone marrow apparently disregarded, suggests procurement operations geared to the collection of surpluses and temporary storage, similar to those used during Paleoindian times. It is tempting to propose Yonkee as a cultural complex but more data on campsites and seasonality is needed.

Bison jumping continued at the Kobold site in Late Plains Archaic times, and cultural levels above Yonkee produced Pelican Lake and Besant projectile points. The bone levels for the Late Plains Archaic at Kobold showed severe deterioration, but large numbers of projectile points (Figure 4.34a, b) were recovered. Several

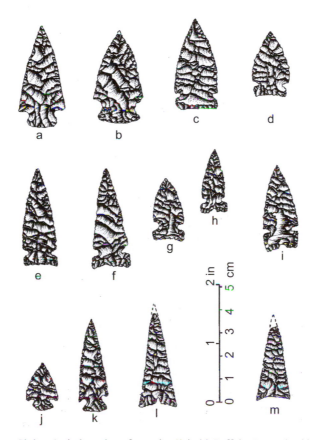

Figure 4.34 Late Plains Archaic points from the Kobold Buffalo Jump (a, b). Late Prehistoric period points from the Wardell Bison Trap (c–e) in western Wyoming, the Glenrock Buffalo Jump (f, g), the Piney Creek Buffalo Jump in northern Wyoming (h, i), the Willow Springs Buffalo Jump in the Laramie Basin in southern Wyoming (j, k), and the Vore Buffalo Jump in northeast Wyoming (l, m).

arroyo traps of Pelican Lake age are known, although few of the latter have been investigated. One along Powder River in southern Montana produced Yonkee points in the lowest bone bed and Pelican Lake points in an overlying bone bed, but unfortunately the site was completely destroyed by artifact hunters. Minimal investigation was done in the Fulton site, an arroyo trap in the central Powder River Basin in Wyoming with a radiocarbon date of about 2100 years BP. The Keaster site to the north (Davis and Stallcop 1965) is a Pelican Lake bison kill site, although it is more of a Northern Plains manifestation. Enumeration of other similar sites of the same general time period is possible but would be of little additional value to this discussion.

Around AD 100 or shortly afterward, Besant hunters from the north and/or northeast moved into the Northwestern Plains and initiated the most sophisticated bison procurement strategies known in the area during prehorse times. Three Besant bison kill sites in Wyoming are presently known: the Ruby Bison Pound in the southeastern Powder River Basin; the Muddy Creek site on a tributary of the North Platte River in south-central Wyoming; and the Cedar Gap site at the south end of the Bighorn Mountains in central Wyoming.

The Ruby site (Frison 1971a) was in operation at a time when the alluvial deposits of a dry tributary of the Powder River were aggrading and the tributary followed a broad meandering pattern. The aggradation process continued until the site was covered by up to 3 m of alluvial and colluvial deposits. Subsequently, the cycle changed to one of degradation, and most of the alluvial and colluvial deposits in the arroyo were removed except in some of the meander bends, one of which was the location of the Ruby site. The degradation pattern was also much less meandering than the earlier pattern of aggradation, so that many of the former meander bends were not affected. It has not been possible to perceive the advantages of the site location in terms of bison handling because of changes in the terrain. The degradation cycle cut into and destroyed part of the site, but also revealed its presence.

The Ruby bison pound (Figure 4.35) reflects a high level of knowledge, resourcefulness, and dedication in prehistoric bison procurement. If they were present today in their original form, the structures involved in the procurement operation would be adequate for corralling buffalo or cattle, and were probably equal or even superior to many present-day cattle corrals. Corrals for domestic cattle are usually constructed by planting posts in pairs separated by a distance equal to the diameter of the horizontal poles used in the aboveground part of the structure. The distance between pairs of posts is less than the length of the horizontal poles; therefore, the poles can be stacked alternately on top of one another so that the distance between the horizontal poles is also equal to the diameter of the poles used (see Figure 4.36). We would argue strongly that the Ruby site bison corral was built in precisely this manner (Figure 4.37). The horizontal poles were probably large enough and sturdy enough so that the bison could not force an exit even if they could see out between the poles. And properly motivated bison, both males and females, have been known to tear up corrals that appear quite strong and well built.

On the other hand, there is ample evidence that the Ruby site corral underwent varying degrees of destruction and rebuilding. It was built on a slope, which required the downslope side of the corral, where the greatest stress was exerted, to be the strongest. Few people have observed bison in corrals closely enough to realize their strength, especially when one is being gored by another one. This kind of situation undoubtedly happened many times during the Ruby site operations. By peeling thin layers off the downslope side of the corral, more than one building stage was revealed, and each one of these probably represents repair or rebuilding of parts of the structure.

Building the structure on a slope may at first seem like a poor decision, but actually it was not. We can assume that the prehistoric hunting group's only interest was to kill the animals. They were not interested in any of the operations that

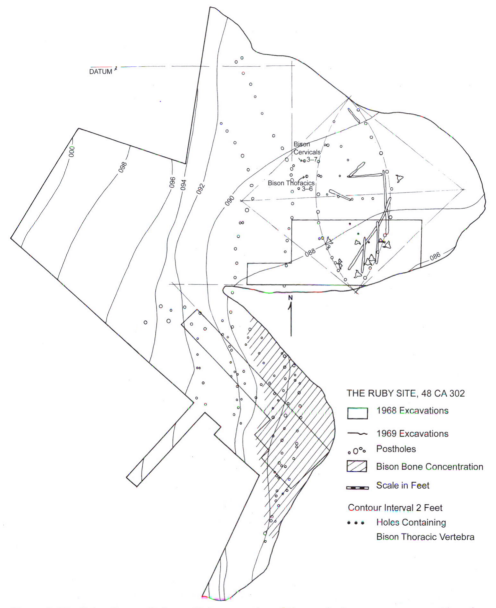

Figure 4.35 Ruby site postholes outlining a portion of the coral, shaman structure, and location of the bone bed.

Figure 4.36 Typical, present-day cattle corral.

Figure 4.37 The Ruby Bison Pound in the Powder River Basin of Wyoming: the shaman structure (1), the drive lane (2), and the corral (3). Arrow points to the remnants of a bison bone bed.

occur in a present-day corral, such as roping, cutting, branding, dehorning, and castrating. The Ruby site corral would not be functional for these types of operations performed on domestic cattle, but it would have been for the purpose of corralling bison for slaughter. An animal, whether bison or domestic cow, running uphill or along a steep slope is at a definite disadvantage in jumping or going through a fence. On the other hand, the downhill side of a corral built on a slope is the ideal spot for crowding animals for killing—provided it is strong enough. The upslope parts of the corral need not be as strong as the downslope parts, which would save effort in construction. The evidence at the Ruby site supports these ideas.

The actual construction and materials needed for a corral that would hold bison can be considered. Such a structure might be round and about 14 m in diameter, with poles 4 m long. Allowing for overlap, this would require paired postholes 3 m apart. Outside circumference would be about 40 m, so that 12 panels 3 m apart would require 26 posts and leave a 1.5 m gate. One hundred and twenty poles at least 15 cm in diameter on the small end and 18 cm on the large end, if stacked 10 high beginning 30 cm from the ground, would provide a structure just over 2 m high that would hold bison. Wings would have to be built out from the entrance. The several panels close to the entrance would have to be just as well constructed, but from there on out the wings need not be so strong nor the posts so close together. Wings need to extend for at least 100 m depending on the terrain and the number of persons heading the bison into the wings. Today the work would probably be done by a person using a chain saw and a mechanical posthole digger. The posts and poles would probably be purchased at the local lumberyard and one man could construct a bison-proof corral in a day or so. Wings out from the entrance to funnel the animals into the corral would probably require another day.

Without such sophisticated tools, two men using axes and crosscut saws would have spent 2 days cutting and hauling the poles and another day cutting and hauling the posts. At least two or three days would have been required to dig the postholes with an iron digging bar and shovel, set the posts, and lay up the poles. At least another day or two would have been needed to construct the wings. The dry arroyo has a good stand of juniper and cottonwood. Cottonwood groves and juniper thickets are always characterized by quantities of dead wood, much of which would be usable in the corral structure both for posts and poles. Remnants of posts left in several postholes at the site were juniper, much superior to cottonwood, which rots quickly and is structurally inferior.

We are quite certain that the postholes were dug with the aid of expedient bone tools such as bison ribs, broken long bones, and mandibles, some of which were found at the site and bore evidence strongly suggesting this kind of use. Wooden digging sticks could also have been used to dig into the relatively soft alluvial soil. We postulate that a hunting group consisting of 20 people mobilizing the efforts of the entire social group might have required a period of 10 days to two weeks to construct the Ruby site bison corral, final drive lane, and wings. This is a considerable investment in time and effort, although the structure was probably intended to be used for a long time.

The configuration of the final drive lane at the Ruby site indicates that the hunters were experienced and knowledgeable about bison behavior. Before the lane reaches the entrance to the corral, there is a deliberate bend, obscuring the corral entrance until the last possible moment (Figure 4.35). Those unfamiliar with the handling of bison and domestic cattle have attributed this to the fact that the builders were not able to build straight fences. In reality, however, this is a much superior design to a straight-line approach, as any livestock operator knows. Bison moving down a drive lane in which they are unable to see the end are much less apt to balk and turn around than they would be if the drive lane were straight. Also significant is the fact that projectile points begin to appear at the point inside the final drive lane where the corral entrance first becomes visible. This suggests actions analogous to the prodding of the animals today with a sharp stick or electric prod at the moment they can perceive the end of the drive lane and perhaps attempt to turn and reverse direction. The best insurance against bison turning is constant pursuit from the rear and a good prod from behind in exactly the right spot at the proper moment by persons stationed outside the drive lane.

In addition to the final drive lane, there were undoubtedly expanding wings to funnel animals into the trap. Natural features such as ridge tops and arroyo banks may have simplified construction, and one wing may not have been as long as the other. It is possible to crowd a bison herd against a fence and follow it toward a corral, so that the other wing need only be extended a short distance. Placing the corral structure on the arroyo floodplain may have been deliberate; it was several feet lower than the surrounding country so the operation was hidden from view until the animals were crowded well into the funnel formed by the expanding wings. At this point the close pursuit by the drivers worried the animals enough to distract them from their immediate surroundings.

The kinds of bison driving activities just described are not things that can be learned by reading books. The bison is a large animal that appears to move awkwardly and think slowly, but a few minutes in a corral with one will rapidly dispel this notion. Although large, they are anything but awkward. And although their reactions to the same stimuli used in handling domestic cattle are similar, they react much faster. Bison can be successfully handled in a corral such as the one at the Ruby site only by experienced personnel. They have to be pursued in exactly the right way and prodded at exactly the right moment from exactly the right position. Any other action will bring on an undesired reaction from the animal and the whole effort will be wasted.

The downslope side of the Ruby bison corral was filled to a depth of over 30 cm with badly decomposed bison bone (Figure 4.37), indicating that many animals had been killed there. Large dart points (Figure 2.64e–g) were recovered in the drive lane and bone bed. About 350 m up the arroyo and on the same side is a large processing area covering at least 900 m² that has been only minimally tested. It is covered by over 2 m of alluvial deposits, so proper investigation will require heavy equipment to remove overburden. Directly across the arroyo from the corral is another camp and/or processing area under more than a meter of alluvial deposits that could be larger yet. It is likely that more than one corral was present, since the processing area up the arroyo from the kill area seems to be an unusually and unnecessarily long distance from the corral.

Investigations to date in the processing area up the arroyo from the corral suggest a number of discrete but similar processing activity areas, further suggesting that although the kill effort was communal, once the distribution of the products of the kill was made, further processing was probably done at the family level. Based on eruption schedules from a small sample of teeth, the trapping occurred from early to late fall.

The corral and drive-line complex was not the only major building effort at the Ruby site. The procurement complex reflects a thorough knowledge of bison behavior but this was strongly buttressed by whatever additional help was available from supernatural sources. The sophistication of the corral and related structures was matched or superseded by a religious structure alongside the final drive line. The identification of the remains as a religious structure is based on a number of features associated with the structure and the architecture of the structure itself. A look at the site map (Figure 4.35) reveals a structure over 13 m in length and 5 m wide formed by two intersecting arcs of circles with radii of approximately 10.2 m. The structure was almost certainly outlined originally by setting two stakes 15.54 m apart and then marking off the two intersecting arcs. Postholes outlined the bipointed structure, the long axis of which was either deliberately or accidentally oriented very nearly true north or south.

The aboveground details of the structure are obscure, although the aggradation of the alluvial and colluvial deposits was fast enough to fill the structure for a depth of nearly half a meter before it collapsed, preserving many of its features. The structure was divided into two parts by five postholes across the widest part. The southern half of the structure was definitely roofed over, but the northern half may or may not have been roofed. The badly decomposed remains of a juniper log about 6 m long lies on top of a similar log nearly 5 m in length. The shortest is believed to have spanned the structure across the widest part and the longest one was a ridgepole that reached from the south end to the center. Two shorter juniper logs were on top of the longest and appear to have been rafters extending from the longest pole to the edge. Their positions would suggest the structure fell to the east with the ridgepole on top of the center cross log and the two rafters on top of the ridgepole. The rafters suggest some sort of a roof, but no evidence of this remains. The postholes outlining the structure were set perpendicularly, so we are assuming the sides were the same. The height is purely conjectural, but the remains of three other logs are present that may have been the aboveground parts of posts; if so, the sides of the structure would have been between 1.5 and 2.4 m high.

Other unusual features were associated with the structure. Three small holes in the southern half each contained a bison vertebra with the longest dorsal spine (the second or third thoracic vertebra) with distal ends in the ground and proximal ends aboveground. Three similar small holes in the north end of the enclosure contained nothing, unless perishable items were placed in them originally, which is highly probable. Two holes just outside the structure to the west contained, respectively, four thoracic vertebrae with dorsal spines downward and the entire series of articulated cervical vertebrae with the atlas at the bottom of the hole. Around the south end of the structure were eight male bison skulls with mandibles removed. Some disturbance was obvious, but most had been placed face up with noses pointed outward along the fence line of the structure. In addition, the area of the enclosure bore no evidence of having been a living structure. Lacking entirely were the fire hearths and activity areas associated with conventional living structures. Also, the structure and its associated features bear no resemblance to any known prehistoric living structures on the Plains.

Reliance on the supernatural was a common occurrence in communal kills. Mandelbaum (1940:190–191) mentions that the Cree pound or corral was built under a shaman's supervision and the latter was empowered to do so by a spirit helper. In addition, the tipi of the pound maker was placed by the entrance and it was here the shaman sang and smoked to invoke his spirit helpers. This sounds exactly like what was occurring at the Ruby site buffalo corral, only the shaman's structure there was much more than a simple tipi. Many other related examples of shaman activity associated with bison kills, as well as kills of other species, are known (Chittenden and Richardson 1905:1028–1029; Gilmore 1924:209; Grinnell 1961:12–14).

The other bison corral that is closely related culturally to the one at the Ruby site is in similar country but about 160 km to the southwest. Muddy Creek, a small, meandering, live stream at its beginnings, becomes an ephemeral one before flowing into the Little Medicine Bow River, which in turn flows into the North Platte River. The corral was situated about a quarter of a mile west of Muddy Creek but close to its headwaters. The site is at the base of a steep slope about 130 m high that forms a scarp extending several kilometers to the east. The flats along Muddy Creek provided excellent bison habitat in an area of several square kilometers of grazing and gathering areas.

An area of artificially placed boulders was found that created a pavement constructed at the edge of a flat area that forms part of the rim of the depression in which the corral lies. Postholes between the boulder pavement and the corral indicate a ramp was present; the animals were driven in the downstream direction onto the ramp, which dumped them into the corral and eliminated the need for an entrance gate. The corral lies in a depression so that the ramp itself was very nearly a continuation of the terrain leading to it (Figure 4.38).

As with the Ruby site, the Muddy Creek bison corral (Hughes 1981) was built on sloping ground. Details of the structure are not as clear as at the Ruby site, since most of the site deposits were only a few inches below the surface and were actually exposed in some places. The corral was apparently about 13 m in diameter and single postholes were used, possibly because of the large logs available. Two postholes excavated were of larger diameter than at the Ruby site, and bison long bones were used in the postholes, presumably to brace the posts in proper upright position. The Muddy Creek site is located close to stands of lodgepole and limber pine, which must have eased the problems of corral construction considerably.

The selection of the location for the Muddy Creek bison corral demonstrates a careful consideration of the natural features present. The terrain from a distance appears quite flat but considerable relief is actually present. The corral was placed in a depression, which hid the entire operation from view until the last possible moment. The boulder pavement was important; it would have been at this point that the stampeding animals would have realized that something was amiss and they were being driven into an unfamiliar situation. At the entrance to the ramp, the animals would have braced their feet and would have been able to stop and disrupt the drive if they could have dug their feet into the soft clay. The boulder pavement would have prevented this from happening. Fences would have been necessary to lead the animals into the ramp but no evidence of this in the form of postholes could be found; perhaps a buck fence was used.

We have no evidence of a religious structure at Muddy Creek but, if its location coincided with the one at the Ruby site, which seems a possible assumption, recent gullying would have removed any evidence of it. On the other hand, a large boulder pile with smaller piles nearby on the scarp above the site may have had some relationship to rituals performed in the trapping operations. Its location offered a clear view of all of the activities in the trap area.

Neither the Ruby nor the Muddy Creek site was designed to handle large numbers of animals at one time. A corral or pound of this nature was not strong enough to hold together even if only half filled with animals. A nursery herd of about 20 animals seems about right, although a few more animals would not have caused an undue strain on the structures.

Figure 4.38   The location of the Muddy Creek bison corral looking south (top) and north (bottom). Location of the corral (a), and the direction of bison herd movements (b).

Bison demonstrate distinctive behavior when inside a corral. The animals along the fence are not the ones that crowd a fence and break it down. In fact, the animals along the fence will push against the animals crowding them so that animals backed up one or two deep are not usually able to cause much strain on a fence. When too many animals are in a corral, the animals will be stacked up so deep that those along the fence are powerless and a strong barrier is necessary to withstand the pressure; corrals such as those described here were simply not that strong.

In the vicinity of the Muddy Creek trap there are numerous concentrations of stone circles believed to be the remains of the hunters' camps. Artifacts recovered in the tipi ring areas leave no doubt of their cultural affiliation as Besant, and their numbers and configuration has led one investigator of the site to refer to them as tipi ring villages (Reher 1983:201–204). They also strongly suggest use of the Muddy Creek bison-trapping complex over a long period of time.

The projectile points recovered at the Ruby (Figure 2.64e–g) and Muddy Creek (Figure 2.64a–d) sites stand out not only in quality of workmanship, but mostly in the choice of the best raw materials for their manufacture and in their shaping to best penetrate and produce lethal wounds to large animals. The hunters acquired the best quartzites and cherts available. One miniature projectile point recovered at the Muddy Creek site (Figure 2.64d) may possibly have been part of a shaman's equipment, analogous to the situation suggested for the Jones-Miller Hell Gap bison kill site (Stanford 1978).

The first analysis of the teeth and mandibles from the Ruby site was done before reliable techniques of aging were developed using tooth eruption and wear. The first estimate was that the calves at the Ruby site were four to six months of age (Frison 1971a:87). A reevaluation of the Ruby site bison materials based on a larger sample collected recently indicates that the age of the calves was actually about five to eight months, indicating a period of use throughout the entire fall. The Muddy Creek site provided a poor sample of preserved teeth because of the closeness of the site deposits to the surface, but those found suggest about the same range of calf ages and seasonal activity, with a possible extension of use to early winter. Both site samples were too small to allow meaningful population structure assessments.

Another Besant bison kill, meat processing, and camping location, the Cedar Gap site, has recently been identified and appears to be of similar extent and size as the other two. It is located at the southern end of the Bighorn Mountains in central Wyoming, increasing considerably the known geographic extent of Besant occupation. The site is in a strategic location with regard to bison herds moving back and forth from grasslands to water. Initial testing revealed large clusters of tipi rings and bison processing areas but, unfortunately, the corral appears to have been destroyed by a combination of road construction and flash floods. There is a definite association of Besant and Woodland ceramics at the Cedar Gap site.

THE LATE PREHISTORIC PERIOD BISON KILLS

We believe that the best indication of the beginning of the Late Prehistoric period on the Northwestern Plains and Rocky Mountains is the change from the atlatl and dart to the bow and arrow. Communal bison procurement reached its peak, at least in terms of numbers of animals killed, during the Late Prehistoric period, although all the known procurement strategies were present before this. Whether or not the bow and arrow resulted in more efficient killing of bison in corrals or in close-range situations is open to question. The bow and arrow seems to have been accepted quite rapidly, but it does not follow that its use directly resulted in the increased emphasis on communal procurement. There was, however, an increased emphasis during the Late Prehistoric period on the bison jump or slight variations of this, at least on the Northern and Northwestern Plains. Dart points and bow and arrow points can usually be distinguished by size. The dart—consisting of the long, heavy mainshaft and projectile point used with a foreshaft—does not travel as fast as the shorter, lighter shaft and projectile point used with a bow.

Perhaps the sudden popularity of the bow and arrow was due to a combination of many attributes. The smaller projectile points gave the arrow greater velocity, longer range, and better accuracy. Smaller points are easier to manufacture from more easily obtainable quarry materials. Arrow shafts are also easier to manufacture than dart shafts. The atlatl dart has to be relatively long and straight to allow accuracy and penetration, and it is difficult to carry very many of them. This is believed to be at least one reason for using a separate foreshaft, since a large bundle of these could be easily carried. When a projectile was lodged in an animal, it separated from the mainshaft, which was then retrieved to be used again with another foreshaft. A bundle of arrow shafts, each one complete, seems a much better solution.

In order for the atlatl to be used effectively, the hunter's entire body has to be brought into play to deliver the velocity needed for penetration of the hide of a bison. Underbrush constrains the action of throwing a dart more than the action required in drawing a bow. In addition, a bow can be drawn effectively from more positions (standing, kneeling, lying on the back and incorporating the use of feet) than possible with a dart and atlatl. Perhaps the greatest advantage of the bow is that it can be drawn slowly and deliberately, involving no violent movement on the part of the hunter, so that the bow was more versatile and easier to control than the atlatl. From experience, the atlatl and dart work best with animals that are either committed to a course of movement or watching someone or something besides the person actually throwing the dart. The movement on the part of the hunter in properly throwing the dart usually causes an immediate reaction on the part of the watching animal that is not always predictable. Another consideration is that the velocity of a dart is less than an arrow shaft, allowing a running animal to travel a greater distance between the time the projectile leaves the hunter's hand and the time it reaches the animal.

The earliest known evidence of a communal bison kill involving use of the bow and arrow on the Northwestern Plains and Rocky Mountains was found at a site in the Green River Basin near Big Piney, Wyoming. Known as the Wardell site (Frison 1973b), it was a bison corral close to the Green River (Figure 4.39). Intermittent use over a long period of time is suggested by nearly five feet of stratified bison bone levels (Figure 4.40) and radiocarbon dates that span about 500 years. A large butchering, processing, and camp area adjacent to the kill has been only partially investigated.

The corral, located at the base of a low, steep scarp at the confluence of two small arroyos, was well chosen. Steep slopes on three sides aided in the strengthening of the corral, part of which is outlined by both paired and single postholes. Parts of juniper posts remain in some of the holes. Groves of cottonwood are plentiful along the nearby Green River and juniper grows in the immediate site area. Erosion has removed all evidence of drive lanes and other structures that may have existed. Other than the fact that the kill area deposits at the Wardell site are

Figure 4.39 Location of the Wardell site in western Wyoming looking west away from the Green River.

Figure 4.40 Bison bone bed at the Wardell site.

characterized by large numbers of bow and arrow points (Figures 4.34c–e), the operation was similar to those at the Ruby and Muddy Creek sites.

Excavations involving less than an estimated quarter of the total kill area produced remains of nearly 150 animals killed in the early fall of several years. We have no way of knowing whether the corral was partly cleaned at various times or how much of the bone material was taken to the processing area, so the total count of animals killed would be a guess. Young animals, especially those in the first two age groups (calves and yearlings) are not properly represented in our sample (Reher 1973). This may be the result of butchering processes, although alternative hypotheses must be tested. Sixteen age groups (based on tooth eruption and wear) indicate a longer-lived bison population than for the Casper and Hawken sites, where only 12 age groups could be accounted for.

With the exception of obsidian, the raw materials used to manufacture Wardell site projectile points were of local origin. Neutron activation studies on obsidian sources and Wardell site specimens indicate that the obsidian sourced to Obsidian Cliff in Yellowstone National Park and to a location close to Teton Pass. Whether the obsidian came directly or indirectly from these sources or came from pebble obsidian found in many areas of the western Green River Basin has never been addressed.

Some of the limitations of arrow points are demonstrated quite well at the Wardell site. Two mature bison ribs demonstrate direct hits; in both cases the projectile point tips carried just into the interior cancellous bone and the remainder of the point broke. One of these points had been carried around in the rib for some time, judging from the buildup of pathological bone around it. The other specimen was a rib that bore no pathological buildup of bone around the projectile point and was probably from an animal killed at the same time the abortive rib shot was made. Neither of these wounds would have resulted in more than slight discomfort to the animal, demonstrating that an arrow point had to penetrate between the ribs in the same manner as a dart point or thrusting spear in order to be effective. In contrast, a rifle bullet of the common hunting calibers would have shattered the rib, penetrated the rib cavity, killed the animal, and then lodged against the hide on the opposite side.

About 65 m south of the Wardell bison corral is the edge of a processing/camping area that may cover as much as a hectare. Bison completely dominate the faunal assemblage here as expected, although small numbers of pronghorn, jackrabbit, cottontail, and sage grouse bones appear in the cultural deposits. The processing/camping area is characterized by several distinct features. These include stone-heating pits, stone-boiling pits, and cooking or roasting pits. The stone-heating pits are wide, shallow pits in which fires were built and into which stones were placed to be heated. The stone-boiling pits are about the same dimensions as the stone-heating pits but were first lined with possibly a green bison hide or emptied paunch and then filled with water, broken bones, and hot stones. The boiling water released the grease from the bone, and the grease was retrieved as it floated to the top of the water and solidified. Some meat may have been boiled also. Roasting or cooking pits are slightly different. At the Wardell site, these were usually in the shape of inverted cones up to 0.6 m in diameter and about 0.3 m deep, and were probably also lined with something before various butchered units and several hot stones were placed inside. The top of the pit was then covered with dirt and, in at least one case at the Wardell site, flat slabs of stone and sealed.One of the roasting pits at Wardell had never been opened. When excavated, the pit contained at least seven discrete butchered units from bison along with several large, fire-fractured stones. Several flat stone slabs and a layer of soil that covered the entire pit had never been removed. A more in-depth analysis of the methods used to butcher and process the meat at the kill and camp is long overdue.

THE CLASSIC LATE PREHISTORIC BISON JUMPS

Buffalo jump sites are characterized by a high bluff over which the animals were stampeded so that large numbers of them would be killed and crippled. There were many variations. Steep banks were used, as were perpendicular bluffs and especially ascending scarps of both cut and fill terraces along streams, as long as they were of sufficient height and gradient and the proper approach for the animals was present. The Late Prehistoric buffalo jump was usually characterized by long lines of cairns or stone piles, referred to as drive lines, leading to the jump-off. The stone piles were usually not large; some contained only four or five boulders, whereas others contained 20 or more. Even short grass can hide the drive lines during a normal grass year. Sometimes topographic features are combined as in the Vore Buffalo Jump (Figure 4.41; Reher and Frison 1980). The direction of any particular drive was determined largely by the initial location of the herd and possibly also wind direction.

There was a fundamental difference between the jump and the corral, and the necessary conditions for the operation of one in some ways excluded the operation

Figure 4.41   The opening in the karst that formed the Vore Buffalo Jump in northeast Wyoming.

of the other. The jump relied on a large number of animals. Small numbers of bison simply cannot be regularly and successfully stampeded over a jump-off. The secret of operating a jump is to have enough animals moving close together at a high rate of speed so that when the lead animals balk or try to turn sideways, the mass of moving animals behind prevents them from stopping or turning and carries them, along with many others, over the precipice. The leader or leaders of a small herd can detect a jump-off in time to stop, turn sideways, or do a 180° turn. Unless some force is there that is of sufficient magnitude to carry the animal over the jump-off, the animal in question will be able to avoid it.

Even with trained cow horses, no three knowledgeable cowhands could force a single bison or even four or five over a jump-off, at least with any regularity. In a herd of a dozen or so, the same three cowhands might be able to get an animal over, but only under special conditions—for example, if a large animal is frightened enough to charge through the rest of the herd and in the process gives a smaller animal or animals enough of a shove to push them over. The same three cowhands could collect a herd of 50 or so bison in the right position, stampede them toward a precipice, and occasionally get a few animals crowded over the edge. They would probably not be able to repeat the process with any regularity. On the other hand, 10 mounted, well-trained cowhands should be able to take 100 head of buffalo, maneuver them into proper position, and stand a better than even chance of stampeding a substantial number over the edge. There is one reservation even here, and that is that on some days even 10 cowhands on horses may not be able to maneuver the animals into the proper position, and if this is the case, the best alternative is to go back home and try again another day.

For trapping in a typical corral or arroyo trap the smaller herd is easier to handle. The animals have to be kept close together and they have to be maneuvered constantly to get them in exactly the right position. Individual animals will continually attempt to scale the banks of an arroyo as they are being driven up the bottom, and these animals must be turned back into the arroyo because if one is successful in getting away, the others will try to follow. In rougher country, which is usually encountered as the arroyo traps are approached from gathering areas, the lead of a herd tends to separate from the ones to the rear. This problem is not as difficult to rectify with a smaller herd, but it is a mistake to start out with a big herd thinking that small groups can be split off until the desired number of animals is reached. The only reliable method is to gather a herd of the proper size and keep it together for the entire operation. Such is the nature of the bison: the large herd could not be handled in a small corral or trap and the small herd could not be stampeded over a bluff.

Drive lines had an important function in the handling of bison. They were usually placed in such a manner as to impart the kinds of information to the drivers that would aid them in moving a bison herd. Moving a bison herd was more than merely running along behind them. The herd had to be prevented from stampeding at the wrong moment. It had to be manipulated in order to keep it on a predetermined path. Failure to do so usually resulted in the loss of the herd. Bison react positively and quickly to driving pressures. The secret to driving bison over a jump or into a trap without horses is to locate the proper feature and determine whether it is so situated that a bison herd can be brought to it. Then each hunter has to become totally familiar with the territory. The drive lines serve as reference points to help the hunters coordinate their movements with those of the buffalo. These movements have to be perfectly timed. Split-second responses to movements of the animals usually mean the difference between success and failure. Bison have been one of the most successful mammals in North America, and their near demise resulted largely from superior weaponry and horses introduced by Europeans.

The drive-line complex was normally composed of two parts. One is the part designed to bring a herd into the proper position for the final stampede that has just been described. The final drive lines usually consisted of two straight lines of stone piles that converge at the jump-off. Usually the bison herd was carefully maneuvered to a predetermined position back some distance from the jump-off and was then made to turn at almost a right angle. At this point an all-out effort was made to stampede the herd in a tightly packed formation toward the jump-off. The turn was important; the strategy was to keep the bison from seeing the jump-off until the very last minute. After the sharp turn the hunters changed tactics. Instead of carefully manipulating the animals, they did everything they could to make them panic. However, the stampede had to be controlled. The animals had to be kept together in tight formation, pushed at top speed, and headed in exactly the right direction. Even a slight deviation in the approach to many jump-offs would have sent the herd down a steep slope instead of over a perpendicular drop, wasting the entire effort. To make sure there was no deviation, hunters hid behind brush piles, hides, and other artificial means of concealment so they could appear at the stone piles at the proper moment and urge the stampeding animals even more. Very likely the drive lines marking the final stampede were actually stations for these hidden hunters.

The Glenrock Buffalo Jump (Frison 1970a) was a modest operation compared to many others, but it embodies all the principles of driving and jumping bison over a perpendicular precipice without horses. The location is along the North Platte River in east-central Wyoming, where a scarp several miles long forms several perpendicular drop-offs with adequate approaches. Behind the drop-offs there are streams, springs, and open, rolling country covered with grass. At least three and possibly four discrete bison jumps are known to be along the same scarp, but only one, the Glenrock site, has been investigated.

Drive lines extend for more than a kilometer and a half back from the jump-off at the site. More than one access route is present. One may have proven better than another, or the initial location of the herd may have determined which access route was used. Drive lines leading in another direction were the key to locating another jump at a different location along the same scarp. The effective part of the jump-off is only a few yards wide (Figure 4.33b), so tight control of the herd during the final stampede was essential, and final drive lines form a V that terminates precisely at this critical point.

The animals that went over suffered a 13 m vertical drop and then rolled a similar distance down a steep talus slope. Small arroyos toward the bottom of the slope were filled with bones (Figure 4.42). The paucity of projectile points in the bone deposits and a high incidence of fractured long bones not usually broken in ordinary butchering processes suggest the results of the fall were quite lethal. The direction of the final stampede was due north, but the herd movement leading up to the final drive was northwest, or into the prevailing wind. A campsite connected with the jump was never located and cultural affiliations are not known. Projectile points are side notched (Figure 4.34f, g) with occasional base notching. Most were made from quartzite probably taken from the Spanish Diggings about

Figure 4.42 Bison bone in the arroyos at the Glenrock Buffalo Jump.

60 miles east and slightly south of the site. The site represents a number of kill operations during the early fall of the year.

The Crow Indians were deeply involved in Late Prehistoric period buffalo jumping, and one main center at least of their activity was apparently in northern Wyoming and southern Montana east of the Bighorn Mountains on the drainages of the Little Bighorn, Tongue, and Powder rivers, in the best of bison habitat. Both the Big Goose Creek and Piney Creek sites illustrate the use of drive-line systems where animals were moved long distances over a relatively gentle slope before being forced onto steep slopes above significant jump-offs. At the Big Goose Creek site (Frison, Walker, Webb, and Zeimens 1978), the bison were moved for distances of up to 3 km. One nearly continuous part of a drive line, interrupted today by irrigation ditches and roads, is almost 1500 m long and consists of drive-line markers of 15 to 25 boulders spaced from 3.5 to 7.5 m apart. The animals were driven east or directly to the leeward of prevailing winds. Smell is important if one wishes to approach bison unseen, but in driving the animals are aware of the humans anyway, so wind direction is not as critical. The approximately 55° slope over which the animals were driven descends approximately 14 meters to the creek below.

A large camp and processing area was located upstream approximately 200 m. However, the mortality of the animals at the camp and at the kill do not match. One level at the kill site produced sufficient intact mandibles from immature animals to assign the time to death to late October to early November. Thirteen animals with intact tooth rows from the campsite indicated that the animals had been killed throughout the winter months, not in a single, mass kill. Fetal bone from 12 fetuses indicates their times of death as November through February, supporting the winter camp designation for the site. The processing area for the animals killed at the jump was probably alongside it and was removed by lateral movement of Big Goose Creek. Ceramics in the camp area are believed to be Crow, although no ceramics were found in the kill area. Prominent features of the camp area included stone-heating pits and stone-boiling pits.

The Piney Creek site (Frison 1967b) is located about 45 km south of the Big Goose Creek site. The kill, like that at the Big Goose Creek site, was made over a 13 m high, 48° slope onto the present floodplain of Piney Creek. Very likely there was some kind of enclosure at the bottom to hold the animals not killed or crippled in the trip over the jump-off, but no unequivocal evidence of such a structure was found (Figure 4.43a). The larger number of projectile points and fewer broken long bones that were not the result of butchering strongly suggest that this jump was not as effective in killing the animals as the one at Big Goose Creek. Projectile points were both side notched and tri-notched (Figure 4.34h, i). The one-time operation was carried out in early fall and processing area operations coincide in time of year with those at the kill.

About 50 m downstream from the kill area is a large processing area (Figure 4.43b). Large stone-heating pits are centrally located with regard to smaller stone-boiling pits. Large anvil stones are surrounded by heaps of broken bone, and hammerstones are present. Around the edges of stone-boiling pits are piles of crushed and broken bones that were presumably boiled for grease. Both belowground pits and aboveground stone rings were used as boiling pits. Cultural items, especially ceramics, found in both the campsite and the processing area are similar. The downstream campsite contains 20 stone circles or tipi rings (Figure 4.44) ranging in size from 3 to nearly 5 m in diameter. Each ring is believed to represent the remains of a conical lodge with stones piled around the bottom to hold it down. A single, exceptionally large ring of 6 m in diameter could have represented the lodge of the hunt leader. Central fires were detected in eight of the circles; deflation of soil in most of the remaining ones would have removed traces of fire. There seems little doubt that a campsite of several days or even weeks is represented. The Piney Creek processing area, unlike the campsite at Big Goose Creek, was not favorably located for a winter camp; it was damp and in heavy underbrush at the base of a high steep hill that today prevents sunlight from touching the area at any time during winter months.

One of the largest known buffalo procurement sites on the Northwestern Plains is the Vore site near Sundance, Wyoming (Reher and Frison 1980). Technically it can be considered a jump, although the geomorphic feature involved is unique. The animals were stampeded into a sinkhole 30 m in diameter at the top, with sides sloping steeply to the bottom about 15 m below, where the diameter is just over 26 m (Figure 4.41). Located toward the top of a gentle rise surrounded by open country of moderate relief, the sinkhole is difficult to see until one is close to its rim, and it is easy to understand why it was used as a bison jump. Stampeding herds of bison would not have realized that it was there until too late. Bison could have been and probably were stampeded into the sinkhole from all directions. Remnants of drive lines in the vicinity suggest that this was the case.

With one exception, all the bison driving at the Vore site was done in the fall of the year. One level with late spring mortality has large numbers of nursery herd (cows, calves, and yearlings) animals probably killed shortly after calving time. First used about AD 1500 or slightly later, with its last use around AD 1800, 22 discrete levels of bison bone reach to a depth of 5.5 m. These levels vary from a single bone in thickness to packed masses of bone a meter thick (Figure 4.45a).

Figure 4.43   The Piney Creek Buffalo Jump (a) and the processing area (b).

Figure 4.44 Tipi rings at the Piney Creek Buffalo Jump campsite.

Figure 4.45 Bison bones in profile (a) and in horizontal distribution (b) at the Vore site.

Horizontally, the levels extend completely across the sinkhole (Figure 4.45b). The deposits contain a wide variety of Late Prehistoric period side-notched and tri-notched projectile points along with stone and bone butchering tools. Near the top were both notched and unnotched varieties of projectile points (Figure 4.34l, m). Less than 10% of the site was excavated and from this it is estimated that the Vore Buffalo Jump could easily contain the remains of as many as 20,000 bison. Four feet of sterile deposits overlie the topmost bone level.

The lowest five components at the Vore site are contained in varved pond sediments, so that the sinkhole can be considered analogous to a rain gauge 35 m in diameter; in one profile 282 laminations represent 141 consecutive years of accumulation. The thickness of the laminations or varves is assumed to indicate past precipitation accurately. During a period of 141 years recorded in varves at the Vore site (beginning about AD 1540–1550), five buffalo kills occurred, averaging one about every 25 years, but only an average of four years after periods of high precipitation. One interpretation of this is that periods of high rainfall improved the grass, which improved breeding conditions and resulted in a better calf crop. After three years (the age of a bison generation), the female calves resulting from the initial spurt themselves had calves, and a minor population explosion resulted. This in turn triggered a communal bison kill (cf. Fawcett 1988 for an alternative interpretation).

Jumping Bison into Corrals

A common variation of the classic buffalo jump was the stampede over a low bluff or bank into a corral below. These were quite common and allowed the bison hunters to take advantage of many lesser topographic features for successful bison procurement. They were in locations where a perpendicular drop-off was not high enough to kill a lot of animals but would eliminate the need for a gate in the corral below. The idea was not new: it was essentially the same idea as the use of a ramp at the Muddy Creek Besant bison trap. However, the combination of jump and corral accounted for the death of many bison during the latter part of the Late Prehistoric period.

Many of these sites could be described in detail, but we shall discuss them only briefly since no new bison driving or hunting principles were employed. They seem to have supplanted the arroyo trap in some cases. Even though they required more effort to construct than the arroyo traps, the topographic features necessary for their placement are common and are located within easy access of some better bison habitat areas, at least in the region considered here. And although the arroyo trap was effective, the dead animals wound up in a spot where it was difficult to butcher them and remove the butchered parts, so that use of an arroyo trap was more restricted by adverse weather conditions and topographic features than a jump-off site.

The Foss-Thomas site (Fry 1971) is a typical jump and corral located along the Tongue River just inside Montana. A long, gentle slope extends from an inter-stream divide to an upper terrace of the Tongue River and is interrupted by a perpendicular sandstone scarp about 4 m high (Figure 4.46). At one spot, a dry wash spills over the wall of the scarp, and consequent headward erosion into the sandstone has produced a U-shaped notch in the wall and a shallow gully below. A stone fence, which presumably incorporated logs and brush, was built out from the base of the wall. The enclosure extends 7 m out from the wall at a right angle on the west side. From here it extends 13 m east to an isolated sandstone erosional remnant about 2 m high, 6 m across at the base, and 16 m from the base of the wall. The sandstone remnant formed an anchor for two sides of the enclosure, which was rectangular in shape and measured about 15 x 21 m. The 1 m deep and nearly 2 m wide gully was of some significance in the overall configuration of the holding structure, since it added to the height of the fence on one side.

Remnants of the final drive lines are present in back of the jump-off, but no part of a more extensive drive-line complex could be located. This could easily have been removed by road construction and mining activity in the area. The enclosure contained a thick level of bison bone and quantities of Late Prehistoric period side-notched projectile points, suggesting that the drop into the corral was not all that was needed to kill the animals. Based on the ages of calves present in the bone deposits, the operation occurred in fall. Whether this was a single- or multiple-event operation could not be determined. A radiocarbon date of nearly 500 years BP and its geographic location suggest that Foss-Thomas could have been an early Crow Indian bison procurement operation. However, no diagnostics were found to provide more positive cultural identification. No butchering/processing area was found. The site represents a successful, well-planned bison procurement operation and also one that required a good deal of communal cooperation for both the construction of the corral and the driving and killing of the bison.

Figure 4.46 Jump-off at the Foss-Thomas Buffalo Jump along the Tongue River in southern Montana. Person standing in center provides a scale.

The Willow Springs Bison Jump (Bupp 1981) is located on the southern edge of the Laramie Basin in southeast Wyoming. A perpendicular sandstone ledge about 2.5 m high was used as a jump-off into a corral, and a long, gentle rise just before the jump-off provided an ideal approach. Postholes and bases of several posts along with fragments of pitch pine logs outline a 15 m x 20 m corral that was nearly rectangular, but that had both corners away from the wall rounded and well braced. Extensive use of this corral is suggested, but in places the bone deposits (up to 60 cm in depth) were burned by an extremely hot fire or fires, and as a result the bones were difficult to collect intact. Only the bones from the last drive at the site were not burned. Burning is not uncommon in bison kills; whether it was accidental or deliberate is not known. The contents of the paunches of 100 bison, when dried, constitute a surprisingly large amount of highly combustible material. This, in addition to a heavy growth of annual weeds (supported by the added nutrients of dead animal products), would have provided a basis for an extremely hot fire.

The bone deposit contained literally thousands of small, corner-notched arrow points (Figure 4.34j, k), along with smaller numbers of the side-notched and side-notched/base-notched varieties, in the upper few inches. Once more this strongly suggests that the drop over the sandstone ledge did not kill the animals and served only as a gate to prevent their escape. Nothing is known of the cultural affiliations. A Late Plains Archaic use of the feature is suggested by several dart points at the bottom of the bone bed.

Late Prehistoric Period Arroyo Traps

In addition to the better known and more spectacular types of jumps and corrals, Late Prehistoric period use of the arroyo trap has been well documented. These Late Prehistoric kills were operated on principles only slightly different from those of the older Archaic and Paleoindian kills, except that they utilized locations with greater topographic relief and did not rely on headcuts or artificial barriers in the arroyos to contain the animals. Instead, they relied more on shallow arroyos and longer and steeper slopes. We know of at least four of these, three in northern Wyoming and one in southeast Montana, and there are undoubtedly many more. The actual kills are close to the heads of the arroyos where they are eroding into higher land surfaces and at the end of long, steep, uphill climbs for the animals reminiscent of the land forms at the Agate Basin site (Figure 4.6). Without doubt, the locations were and had to be carefully chosen in order to ensure regular success.

The 300-year-old Cache Hill site (Miller and Burgett 2000) is located in northern Wyoming. The Oshoto site is about 35 km northeast of Cache Hill, also in northern Wyoming, and the Marshall Lambert site is located about 190 km northeast near Ekalaka, Montana. The season of death for bison in the latter two sites is late fall or early winter, with multiple components demonstrated for the kills during a single year or closely spaced over several years. Analyses of these sites are still very preliminary and in need of further work.

The arroyo trap had at least one advantage over the jump: the hunters did not need a large herd of animals to stampede over a precipice to achieve the desired results. Five to as many as 30 or more bison could have been manipulated in this kind of procurement activity. The animals would have been collected in their normal grazing areas located some distance from the intended kill location. They were then started up the bottom of the arroyo, which would not have been difficult because there were no barriers to their progress and the animals naturally move well uphill. However, the head of the arroyo would have been as much as a kilometer or more away and the grade was continually increasing. The trailing hunters kept constant pressure on the animals. Since the bison were carrying large reserves of fat at the end of summer, they would have become tired and less aware of danger by the time they reached the kill location just short of the top of the ridge.

Just before they topped the rise at the beginning of the arroyo, hunters waiting behind the top of the ridge would have confronted the tired animals and would have been able to kill at least part of the herd. The effectiveness of this type of procurement was apparently quite high, judging from the bone beds found. Many more of these types of traps were undoubtedly present, but headward erosion has removed the evidence of most. These kinds of traps may have been used in earlier times also, but continual headcutting of the arroyos reduces their chances of preservation so that only the ones of the Late Prehistoric period are still visible. Combined with the various forms of jumps and corrals as described above, there were alternative strategies available for Late Prehistoric period bison procurement. If enough animals were present in an area, some form of communal operation could very likely have been devised.

OTHER EVIDENCE OF BISON PROCUREMENT

For various historic reasons, as well as their high archaeological visibility, bison and mammoth bone beds have become key sites in our understanding of Plains and Rocky Mountain prehistoric lifeways (Kornfeld 2003, 2007a). They have been intensively investigated, reinvestigated, analyzed, reanalyzed, and reinterpreted; much of this information has been synthesized in the previous sections of this chapter. Most if not all of these sites represent mass animal kills, likely employing communal hunting strategies. Individual animal hunting, however, was likely also an important subsistence pursuit, perhaps even more important than the apparently generational communal events (e.g., Fawcett 1988). Bison hunting and economic strategies have spurred numerous models that address the dynamic interactions between foraging resources, bison, and humans on the Plains, as well as change in such interaction over millennia (Bamforth 1988; Fisher and Roll 1999; Reeves 1990; Reher and Frison 1980; Roper 1997; Scheiber 2001).

Regardless of which model is correct, and they may all be correct for one or another epoch of prehistory, hunting of one or a few animals by individual or a small group of hunters, rather than communal events, was undoubtedly practiced and may have been the more significant subsistence pursuit in terms of its contribution to overall diets. Again, we do not necessarily know, but we have to account for this practice as well in prehistoric lifeways. Evidence for this type of bison procurement comes from thousands of sites in the region. Campsites, various plant procurement and processing sites, and single-animal kill sites often present us with small quantities of bison or other bone that indicate consumption and thereby animal procurement or hunting probably of single animals (Kornfeld and Larson 2008).

SOME THOUGHTS ON PREHISTORIC BISON PROCUREMENT

One of us proposed some time ago (Frison 1973b:3–7) that a critical number of bison is necessary in a given area before communal procurement is feasible or profitable. The rationale for this statement was that since the hunters lacked horses, the bison drive had a high probability of failure, and also that as a result of animal behavior patterns, bison driving was to some extent limited to certain times of the year. To speculate further, a bison herd that had been hazed part of the way through a drive and then allowed to escape was not likely to have been amenable to another try until at least the next day, provided of course it did not move several miles away where, without horses, the hunters might find the herd well out of range. Another herd then had to be available or the whole corral or jump complex would have been idle. As a result, unless there were large enough numbers of animals present, it would have been better to revert to a pattern of individual or small-group hunting.

Another idea was that the communal bison drive was an annual affair brought about by the need for meat to be dried for short-term storage and winter use. Obviously this was not the pattern for at least 140 years at the Vore site. The possibility of alternative sites must be considered, but if, as the Vore site evidence suggests, communal procurement was keyed into periods of high precipitation, the alternative-sites idea is not supported either. We must consider an alternative hypothesis. If the critical numbers of bison for jumping were not present, there may have been other procurement methods for which the critical numbers of bison needed were lower. These could have been some form of surround or small trap, but as yet we lack this evidence.

It now appears that we must take a new look at prehistoric bison procurement with the idea of testing some alternative hypotheses and proposing some new ones. If, for example, the Vore site was the only communal bison procurement site used by a single group of hunters and it was used on an average of once in 25 years, a person might see only two or three of these operations in a lifetime, an unlikely situation. There must have been alternative sites, alternative procurement methods, or alternative subsistence strategies within the territory claimed by the hunting group. Some of the decisions made were dependent upon local conditions affecting the bison populations.

Very likely, one could stand at the Roberts Buffalo Jump in northern Colorado (Witkind 1971) and look from one Late Prehistoric period bison jump to another all the way to the northern tip of the Plains in Canada. The exception to this would be certain areas such as the Bighorn Basin in northern Wyoming, not the best of bison habitats because of its aridity and consequent scarcity of grass. Bison were undoubtedly there but not in the numbers necessary for communal procurement except, of course, during the Paleoindian period. Many other excellent examples of buffalo jumps are known for the Northern Plains and should be mentioned (Figure 4.47). Among these are the Emigrant Bison Drives near the small town of Emigrant, Montana, located between Livingston and Gardiner (Arthur 1962; Brown 1932); the Madison (or Logan) Buffalo Jump, south of Logan, Montana, a small town between Manhattan and Three Forks (Malouf 1962); the Antonson site a short distance west of Bozeman, Montana (Davis and Zeier 1978); the Keogh Buffalo Jump, east of the foot of the Beartooth Mountains along the Stillwater River about 25 miles from Absarokee, Montana (Conner 1962a); the Grapevine

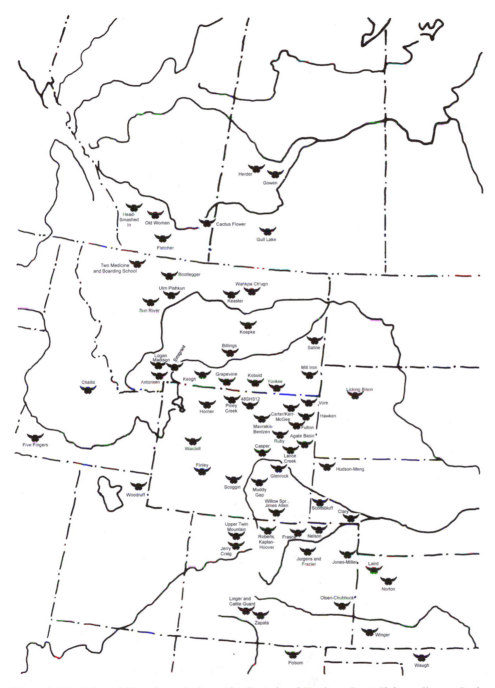

Figure 4.47 Selected bison bone beds on the Central and Northern Great Plains, adjacent Rocky Mountains, and vicinity. All localities are cited in Figures 2.19, 2.20, 2.51, 2.55, 2.63, 2.69, or in the text, except Chalis (Butler 1978), Five Fingers (Agenbroad 1978c), Koepke (Fisher and Roll 1999), and Saline (Fisher and Roll 1999).

Buffalo Jumps, located along Grapevine Creek in Bighorn County, Montana (Medicine Crow 1962); and 5JA7 just outside of North Park in Colorado (unpublished; Figure 4.48). The student of bison procurement must also be familiar with some of the more northerly sites including the Old Women's Buffalo Jump in Alberta (Forbis 1962); Head-Smashed-In Buffalo Jump in Alberta (Reeves 1978); the Boarding School Bison Drive site (Kehoe 1967) near Browning, Montana, as well as the Kutoyis and Two Medicine jumps in the same area (Lewis 1947; Zedeño 2008); the Gull Lake site in southwestern Saskatchewan (Kehoe 1973); the Wahkpa Chu'gn site in the Milk River Valley of north-central Montana (Davis and Stallcop 1966); and the Sun River (Greiser et al. 1985) and Ulm Pishkun sites in Montana (Davis 1978).

The numbers of bison killed in prehistoric times is impressive indeed. A good share of the evidence is no longer extant due to the earlier mining of bison bones for fertilizer. The quantities of bones involved is difficult to comprehend, but the extent of these operations has been well documented for the state of Montana (Davis 1978) and provides us with some idea of the amount of valuable archaeological data on prehistoric bison hunting that has been lost.

Prehistoric Hunters and Hunting Strategies on the North American Plains and in the Rockies

Zooarchaeological analyses of bone beds resulting from prehistoric human animal procurement activities require, in addition to archaeologists, a wide range

Figure 4.48   Jump-off at site 5JA7 (unpublished).

of specialists from a number of disciplines and, if properly integrated, can provide a wide range of cultural as well as biological and ecological information. Failure to pursue all these possible avenues of inquiry can result in erroneous and incomplete final interpretations, with repercussions that eventually return to haunt the original investigator. Zooarchaeology has progressed in positive ways since its fledgling beginnings a half century ago, but there still remain areas of concern.

Prehistoric hunters on the Western Plains and adjacent mountains of North America survived in close contact with the natural environment with the aid of simple but effective tools, weaponry, clothes, and shelter. Clovis hunters were taking mammoths, but not all Clovis sites contain mammoth, and their total contribution to the food supply remains in question. Following Clovis, however, bison, pronghorn, deer, and mountain sheep were the most important food animals, with the former probably of greatest importance on the Great Plains and, to a lesser extent, in the Rocky Mountains, while smaller mammals and birds comprised an additional food source. Elk present a nagging problem; we know they were present in Paleoindian and Early Archaic times, mostly from tools and decorative items made from antlers, but bone beds are absent until Late Archaic times. However, the sporadic presence of non-ornamental or non-tool elk bone at many sites may indicate their procurement for food throughout the Holocene. An occasional camel or horse bone is found in early Paleoindian sites, but their procurement and use as food is even more poorly understood than elk. Bear remains occasionally occur in kill sites and bear would have been attracted to this type of site but, as in the case of elk and camel, their importance as a food source is not known and may be minimal.

Any subsistence hunter familiar with wild animals, a hunting territory, and use of prehistoric weapons can easily feed a family under favorable external conditions. However, these conditions can rapidly deteriorate, requiring alternative strategies in the food quest. Too often ignored or deemphasized also is a large body of ethnographic evidence pointing to other influences, particularly in large animal procurement, where the demands of ritual and social behavior can profoundly affect procurement strategies.

Differential preservation between large and small, mature and immature animals and birds result in the loss of data and biased interpretations of archaeological site remains. In addition human, animal, and natural activities affected osteological materials in different but not always in satisfactorily identifiable ways. Consequently, bone modification has become a separate area of archaeological and faunal investigation, with specialists from several disciplines, resulting in multiple experimental ventures that have produced numerous interpretations along with some disagreements. Plant resources present a separate problem in prehistoric human economic studies because only in rare situations, such as dry caves, is there adequate preservation of the plant resources present and utilized. However, some tools and site features are believed to be reliable evidence of plant food utilization.

Forces that interrupted normal external conditions demanded adjustments to prevent catastrophic consequences to the human inhabitants. Extremely cold winters, droughts, floods, hail storms, insect infestations, and disease disrupted normal external conditions and required adjustments in both animal and plant procurement, but are often difficult if not impossible to detect in the archaeological record. For example, a severe hail storm can wipe out the year's crop of grasses and shrubs and kill many small mammals and birds and, in extreme cases, even some of the very young of larger mammals over large areas. This left little choice for the human group other than moving to an unaffected area. Grasses usually recover the following year but it may take longer for the shrubs and small animals and birds, adding further disruption to the normal human economic cycle. Undoubtedly, other past extreme weather conditions were equally disruptive to normal animal and plant procurement activities and difficult to identify in the archaeological record.

Bone beds from large animal kills provide the most visible evidence of past human animal procurement. They provide a wide range of information, including the ability of prehistoric hunters to choose locations that offered the necessary conditions to collect and detain the animals; identification of the landforms present at the time of the events; population structures of the animals involved; seasonality of the events; butchering and processing; weaponry utilized to dispatch the animals; and estimates of the amounts of food obtained. However, it is unlikely that these large, communal animal kills were the major, year-round source of food, which was instead most likely acquired by individual and small-group hunting and gathering throughout the year. An important part of the social system throughout the year, communal operations required the aggregation and cooperation of several groups of hunters rather than a single- or multi-family group that stayed together for most of the annual cycle.

Natural features such as headcuts in arroyos appear to have been the most commonly used landform to contain bison for procurement purposes, but some modifications were usually needed such as wooden barriers and drive lines. Arroyos are major features of the plains topography, but spring runoff and summer storms can rapidly change their configuration and alter a headcut favorable as an animal trap one day or year into one useless the next. In some cases, a pile of animal carcass remains may have been enough of a barrier to alter the course of a stream and leave the skeletal material intact. Changes in regimes from aggrading stream deposits to severe lateral movement and downcutting may, in the former situation, preserve or, in the latter case, totally eliminate the archaeological evidence. Consequently, we are aware of only a small but badly distorted portion of the animal kill sites originally present in arroyos.

We know of at least one parabolic sand dune that was used to impede bison but, as in the case of an arroyo headcut, the wind can rapidly alter the shape of a sand dune. Deep, loose sand can impede animal movements, especially split-hoofed animals such as bison. Corrals were often placed at favorable locations, including the base of a steep slope or perpendicular drop-off high enough to prevent the animals from reversing course. Even more sophisticated were wooden fences, corrals, and drive lines with high labor requirements for acquiring materials, construction, and maintenance. The classic bison jump was a situation where the distance from the drop-off to the base was enough to kill and cripple many animals.

Once the location was selected and the necessary modifications completed, a profound knowledge and understanding of animal behavior and cooperation of several hunters was needed to bring the animals to a specific location and into a feature where they could be detained and killed. Considering the complexity of these kinds of operations and possibility of failure, no one can argue for perfect past success records.

The communal kills may have been as important for many social functions that reinforced the structure and continued existence of the social group as it was for procurement of food resources. Killing large numbers of animals at one time and place indicates some level of authority to police the operation, and acquisition of more meat than can be consumed during normal day-to-day needs implies a need for some kind of storage. Time of year limits storage possibilities, but warm, dry conditions allow drying of meat while winter cold provides a means for frozen storage caches. Many of the present studies of prehistoric animal procurement tend to minimize the effects of adverse external conditions, animal behavior, and other factors that affected past procurement events. Prevailing attitudes among many investigators appear to be that the animals were "out there" and available about any time someone became hungry and needed to replenish their food supply. The contention here is that the realization of these goals was not always immediately achieved. The knowledgeable hunter is well aware that, for unknown reasons, animals may be in evidence one day and absent the next. The myriad of changes in the external environment must be allowed for to ensure survival. Carnivore and scavenger activity had to be contended with. Cold weather killing may have avoided hibernating bears but warm fall and early winter weather can delay the hibernation period and, if still moving about, a grizzly in particular can be extremely aggressive, and also endowed with a sense of smell that allow them to hone in on anything like a large animal kill from surprisingly long distances. Meat caches required adequate protection from a wide variety of threats. Historical accounts remind us that bad judgment and failure to allow for change has resulted in human suffering and death that could have been avoided with better knowledge and better preparation for the possible conditions and consequences of unexpected events.

This chapter has focused mainly on bison procurement. Although there were differing amounts of overlap in territories occupied by bison, pronghorn, mountain sheep, deer, and elk, behavioral differences required different procurement strategies for each species. Small mammals and birds demonstrate different behavior patterns and required different procurement strategies, but without preparation of elaborate features and the ritual activities present in large animal procurement. This indicates a vast reservoir of knowledge the hunter needed to learn to adequately insure the continued welfare of the family and the social group.

5

PREHISTORIC HUNTING OF OTHER GAME AND SMALL ANIMAL PROCUREMENT

INTRODUCTION

Ever since the earliest studies in Central Rocky Mountain and Northwestern Plains prehistory, archaeologists have known about a variety of animal remains in the archaeological record. Much effort, however, was geared toward excavations of bison procurement sites, and their remains fill our repositories. Along with vivid illustrations of nineteenth-century Plains Indian bison hunters on horseback (Figure 5.1), the sheer quantity of bison remains largely determine the present conceptions of the importance of buffalo in the Plains economy.

In this chapter we present evidence of the use of a variety of medium and small animals. The remains of such animals occur throughout North American prehistory, in a wide variety of sites and all time periods. This alone attests to their importance and persistence in Plains prehistoric economy. With this chapter we hope to demonstrate that the Native Americans of the Northwestern Plains and Rocky Mountains adapted their societies to a wide variety of daily, seasonal, and long-range variations and perturbations in the environment and consequently their resource base, and that such adaptability served them well in their lifeways, to a degree that some have called them "affluent foragers" (Kornfeld 2003).

A wealth of significant new data on the use of a variety of medium to small animals has come to light in the past several decades. These data are both the result of discoveries of new sites or components at these sites, as well as reanalyses and reinterpretations of extant collections. Sites such as Trappers Point yielded evidence of pronghorn procurement during the Early Archaic period, while the Early Archaic component at the Lookingbill site provided evidence of deer procurement, the Shoshonean Bugas-Holding site gave evidence of mountain sheep and bison use, and Blue Point in southwest Wyoming yielded data on the use of a variety of animal species (Johnson and Pastor 2003; Kornfeld et al. 2001; Miller and

Figure 5.1 Plains bison hunters on horseback. (From Catlin 1844. Photo courtesy of Toppan Rare Books Library, American Heritage Center, University of Wyoming. Anne M. Lane, archivist.)

Sanders 2000; Rapson 1990). Reanalyses of the Firehole Basin, Austin Wash, Allen, and other collections likewise yielded new evidence of procurement of a variety of medium to small animals (Hudson 2007; Lubinski 1997). These and other sites discussed in this chapter provide a significant new perspective on prehistoric Plains and Rocky Mountain economy, settlement, and subsistence. While these contributions to our understanding of the use of a wide range of animal species significantly expands our interpretations of prehistoric diet, the use of plants, discussed in the next chapter, will yet further broaden our understanding of the dietary habits of prehistoric peoples.

ANTELOPE OR PRONGHORN

Evidence for procurement methods and use of pronghorn comes from a variety of sources. First, pronghorn bone beds—large and dense concentrations of pronghorn skeletal material—like bison bone beds, are one significant source of information about the use of this resource. Second, pronghorn traps, or rather large architectural constructions whose features suggest their use for trapping pronghorn, provide us with evidence of procurement methods. And third, pronghorn bones found in small quantities at numerous sites in the region indicate the widespread use and importance of this animal.

Pronghorn remains have appeared in archaeological sites beginning with early Paleoindian times, but the only evidence we have for communal hunting is more recent. There is, however, no reason to believe that the practice does not have more time depth. A different procurement strategy was needed for pronghorn than for bison, and the fences and enclosures may simply have rotted away. The arroyo trap that works for bison trapping is worthless as a pronghorn trap. Pronghorn are amenable to both driving and trapping, but under an entirely different set of conditions than bison. Fortunately, there are eyewitness accounts of Shoshone trapping pronghorn in the Great Basin and Cheyenne and Sioux in the Plains (Egan 1917:238, 241; Grinnell 1923; Hyde 1974; Regan 1934:54; Wissler 1914). According to Steward (1938:33) pronghorn trapping was so successful in parts of the Great Basin that after one season, the population of animals was depleted to the extent that several years were required for regeneration of the herds to a point that another communal hunt was possible. Prehistoric human predation on pronghorns may have been successful enough to keep their numbers relatively small.

After the introduction of horses in historic times, pronghorns were easily hunted. According to one eyewitness account in the northern Great Basin, as many as 50 Shoshone on horseback were able to surround a herd of pronghorns and take turns running them in circles until they collapsed from fatigue and were easily killed (Wilson and Driggs 1919). In the Plains region, the Brule Sioux in the Sand Hills area of Nebraska are reported to have chosen

> a spot where there was a gap between the hills and, beyond the gap a small cliff or sudden drop to a considerable depth. The Indians built a tall hedge of timber and brush at the foot of the cliff, surrounding a large patch of ground. Part of the hunters concealed themselves behind this hedge; the others, mounted on fast horses, went off into the plain and drove a herd of antelope through the gap. The frightened animals poured through the gap, came to the cliff edge, and leaped over it, falling inside the pen formed by the tall hedge. The Sioux then shot them with arrows as they raced about inside the hedge. On lower Big White Clay Creek near Butte Cache, the Hinman party in 1874 saw one of these old traps, the hedge still there and the ground strewn thickly with antelope bones. (Hyde 1974:21)

Bone Beds

Currently, the earliest pronghorn bone bed and evidence of communal or mass pronghorn procurement is the Trappers Point site near Pinedale in northwest Wyoming. Stratum V, one of several early Archaic layers at the site, yielded the remains of at least 27 butchered pronghorn from over 57,000 bone specimens (Figure 5.2). The high fragmentation rate and a variety of bone breakage characteristics suggest heavy bone processing for marrow and grease. Fetal development, tooth eruption, and tooth wear indicate March to April as the procurement season (Miller and Sanders 2000:42). However, a reanalysis based on fetal growth pattern suggests an April to May procurement season (Fenner 2007:24).

Trappers Point is located at a bottleneck of a modern seasonal pronghorn migration corridor. A 270 km migration route between the summer range in Jackson Hole and winter range in the Rock Springs and Green River areas passes over Trappers Point (Figure 5.3). The pronghorn procurement was likely enhanced by this ecological fact. A question arises, however, whether Stratum V represents a single-event kill (a communal kill) or a series of smaller kill episodes (mass kills) during which several antelope were killed at a time. While a communal kill is a single event during which a large number of animals are dispatched

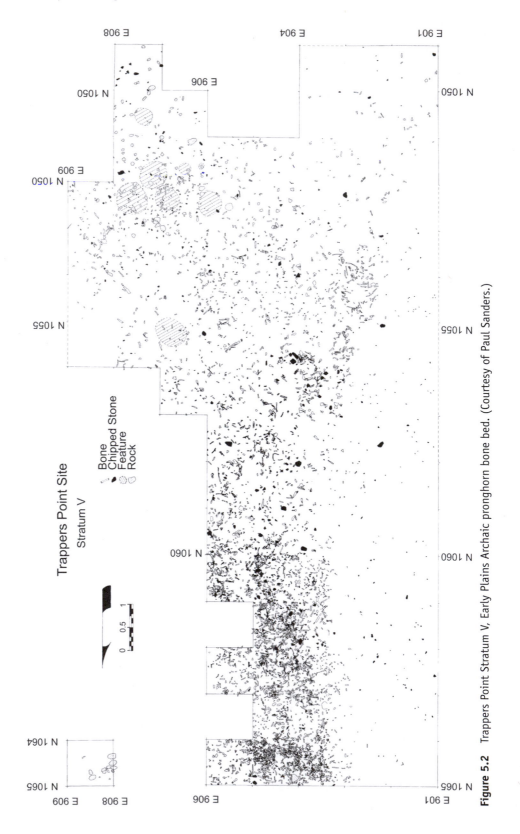

Figure 5.2 Trappers Point Stratum V, Early Plains Archaic pronghorn bone bed. (Courtesy of Paul Sanders.)

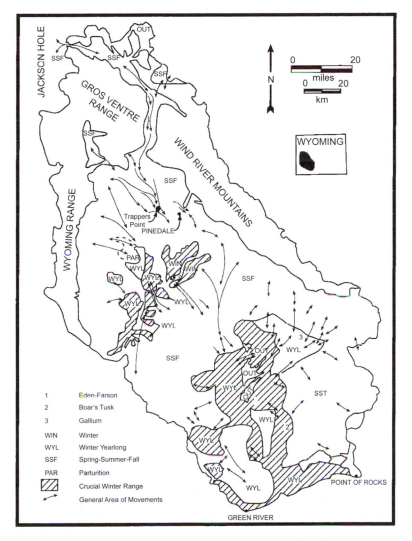

Figure 5.3   Pronghorn migration in western Wyoming. (Courtesy of Paul Sanders.)

at a "moment" in time (or at least a series of closely spaced procurement episodes) and that from a social perspective requires a cooperative social unit, a
mass kill requires no cooperation. In the latter case, a single hunter could kill one
pronghorn each day for a month, resulting in as many dead animals as a mass
kill but not a communal kill event. Thus, a communal kill is always a mass kill,
but a mass kill does not necessarily equal a communal kill. The animals procured
in a mass kill that involves no cooperative or group (communal) effort could be
stored or taken to a nearby village for consumption or processing for storage.

Another antelope bone bed discovered in the Upper Green River Basin near
Eden, Wyoming, the Eden-Farson site (Frison 1971b), consisted of a number of
lodges in a sheltered location in a patch of tall sagebrush in a much larger area of
open country covered with small sagebrush. Parts of at least 212 pronghorns were
found distributed among the lodges. All the pronghorn were killed between late
October or early November (Nimmo 1971). The existence of a trap was postulated

on the grounds that only a trap could have enabled a small group of hunters to take so many animals in such a short time.

Of the several possible ways the animals could have been trapped, one seems more feasible than the others. The site area is characterized by ridges of sand 6 m to 9 m across, 1 m to 1.5 m high, and several hundred meters long, presently stabilized by big sagebrush up to 2 m high. In more than one location the sand ridges form nearly complete outlines for suitable corrals, and the hunters could easily have constructed a brush fence by pulling and piling the sagebrush. We know from eyewitness accounts that sagebrush corrals a meter or slightly more in height are sufficient for holding pronghorns.

The Eden-Farson site is almost certainly of Shoshone origin. Flat-bottomed, flanged-based Intermountain ware ceramics were recovered, as well as a steatite elbow pipe of European style and broken in manufacture (Figure 5.4). A radio-carbon date of 230 years BP suggests an early Protohistoric occurrence, although no historic items were recovered and all the site activities were accomplished with stone and bone tools.

Pronghorn butchering and processing at the Eden-Farson site was a stylized process (Frison 1971b); bones demonstrate similar breakage patterns and skeletal remains strongly indicate intense utilization of all animal parts, although many skeletal elements are missing in the site deposits, leaving many details of carcass treatment in question. All bones were crushed and broken and probably cooked in pottery vessels to obtain bone grease.

The number of animals taken in such a short period suggests surpluses that were probably dried for later use. The lodges were preserved because they were located just over the leeward edge of a flat-topped, mesa-like landform; sand

Figure 5.4   Steatite pipe from the Eden-Farson site.

drifted over the edge so that in places the site was covered up to 40 cm deep in sand. A favorable location for meat drying would have been on top of the mesa, where bones and other perishable evidence would not have preserved.

The number of pronghorn killed at the site sounds impressive but the animals are not large. A male weighing as much as 40 kg field dressed with the head removed is one of better than average size; a fawn in the fall of the year weighs on the order of 14 kg. There were undoubtedly many more than the 212 animals recorded, but this number could have produced at least 2700 kg of flesh in addition to parts such as heart, liver, brains, and bone grease. If, in addition, we add at least one bison, several rodents, insects, and plant foods that were recorded at the site, then there was more food than the group (estimated at about 75) could have eaten before spoilage. We can thus make a strong argument that some of the meat was probably dried and saved for later use.

Other pronghorn sites comparable to Eden-Farson have not appeared, leaving it somewhat of an anomaly. The Boar's Tusk site in the same general area is a short-term campsite consisting of 11 features with fire hearths and small numbers of pronghorn bone (Fisher and Frison 2000).

Considering the relative scarcity of large quantities of prehistoric pronghorn remains in archaeological sites, we believe the Lost Terrace site (24CH68) on the Upper Missouri River to be important (Davis and Fisher 1988, 1990; Davis et al. 2000). This Avonlea site, dating to about 1200 BP (mean of 7 dates), represents one of the largest antelope bone beds in the region with a minimum number of 83 individuals. Along with pronghorn are 13 mammalian taxa, including bison, deer, rabbit, prairie dog, gopher, smaller animals, and bobcat, as well as three species of bird. Cut marks demonstrate that the bison, deer, rabbit, grouse, and crow were processed for food or other resource. Analysis of the pronghorn fetal specimens suggests December to March as the mortality period, but the dentition (a more developed methodology) indicates a January to February mortality, a more confined time span. A single or several communal events are suggested to have taken place to procure the pronghorn. The site also included a number of features interpreted as stone-boiling pits for extracting bone fat from the pronghorn bones. The tool kit consisted of 103 specimens of a variety of chipped, ground, and battered stone tools, as well as a number of bone tools. The pronghorn bone was heavily processed, with no complete elements in the assemblage. The lower limb bones are the most represented, followed by several upper limb portions and mandibles, while upper limbs and ribs are the least well represented in the assemblage. The investigators dismiss carnivore and other destructive processes as the cause of this assemblage composition and attribute it to extensive carcass processing during periods of winter food stress.

The significance of pronghorn for the Late Prehistoric inhabitants of the Northwestern Plains is also seen to the east of the Rocky Mountains, where several sites have pronghorn bone beds. One of these is an Initial Middle Missouri hunting camp in the southern Black Hills. Originally investigated by Richard Wheeler during the Missouri River Basin Surveys, site 39FA23 was reinvestigated in the 1980s (Lippincott 1996). The reinvestigation yielded over 10,000 faunal specimens (NISP), 501 of which were identified to taxa. Of these identifiable specimens, 426 were pronghorn yielding an MNI of 15, while 32 were bison with an MNI of 2. Four bird, one reptile, and one amphibian taxa round out the faunal assemblage with a few specimens each and none with an MNI of greater than one. A total of 36 pronghorn were procured at 39FA23, making it one of the larger pronghorn bone beds (Table 5.1). More significantly, however, the site demonstrates large-scale use of these animals throughout prehistory, even during the time that bison hunting is presumed to represent a dominant economic pursuit. Additionally, pronghorn hunting camps show the diversity of resource procurement by the more complex societies of the Plains Village dwellers further to the east.

Other Sites with Pronghorn Bone

The above can be described as "bone bed" sites, but just what does this term mean? And just how is a bone bed related to mass kills or to communal kills? The correspondences are rather loosely defined. Many sites on the Northwestern Plains and Rocky Mountains contain bone, but we would not call them bone beds. We all recognize that Olsen-Chubbuck is a bone bed and conversely we all recognize that Lindenmeier is not. Yet the former yielded quantities of stone tools and the latter yielded faunal remains. In general we would argue that bone beds are sites with large numbers of densely packed bone, sometimes even dominated by bone, and with little other material, but sometimes not; considerable quantity of chipped stone material, for example, can occur in bone beds. Bone beds represent mass kill and processing locations, although this must be demonstrated and not assumed just because there is a bone bed. Bone beds can be the result of long-term accumulations or they can be natural bone accumulations, as in numerous paleontological examples.

One way to address this issue is to use multiple analytical methods to investigate site formation processes; one such method is based on stable isotopes. A series of recent studies have found that stable isotope variation within a herd is less than variation between herds (Hoppe 2004; Widga 2006). Consequently, in a mass kill situation, where an entire herd or part of a herd is killed in a single event, there will be less variation in stable isotopes than if animals were killed one by one and they were from different herds. In his analysis of pronghorn bone beds from southwestern Wyoming, Fenner (2007) argues that some pronghorn bone beds are the result of a single mass kill event (Firehole Basin), others are accumulations of multiple kill events (Trappers Point and Austin Wash), while others are of uncertain formation processes (Eden-Farson).

Our interest here, however, is not just bone beds, but rather all sites yielding evidence of pronghorn procurement. In separate studies of archaeological sites in southwestern Wyoming, between 56% and 61% of the sites contain pronghorn bone—but no bone bed (Lubinski 2000; Smith and McNees 2000). These sites provide strong evidence for a widespread use of pronghorn across time and space.

The earliest presence of pronghorn in an archaeological site dates to the first demonstrable occupation of Wyoming, with the pronghorn presence at the Colby mammoth site. In post-Clovis times, pronghorn commonly occurred in Paleoindian bison bone beds, camps, and other localities. The Folsom bison bone bed at the Agate Basin Area 2 contains a minimum of four butchered and heavily processed pronghorn (Hill 2008:28), as evidenced by cut marks and breakage patterns that suggest hammerstone use to remove the marrow. The two occupations of the Horner bison kill also contain pronghorn, a minimum of one individual in each occupation (Walker 1987). Paleoindian campsites also commonly contain

Table 5.1 Pronghorn, deer, sheep, and elk bone beds in the Rocky Mountains and adjacent Plains. Dates are in radiocarbon years before present. Summary data for pronghorn from Lubinski (2000) and Smith and McNees (2000), and original data from Fisher and Frison (2000), Hughes (2003), Fedje et al. (1995), Davis et al. (1989), Eakin (1989), Lippincott (1996), Rapson (1990), and Miller and Sanders (2000).

Site	Radiocarbon years BP	NISP	MNI	TAXA	Season	Cultural affiliation	Species
Boar's Tusk	100	NA	6	2	Early Winter	Protohistoric, Shoshone	Pronghorn
Gailiun	150	NA	6	NA	Fall/Winter	Protohistoric, Shoshone	Pronghorn
Eden-Farson	230	NA	222	NA	Late Fall	Protohistoric, Shoshone	Pronghorn
Firehole Basin 11	628	433	31	NA	Fall/Winter	Late Prehistoric, Firehole Basin	Pronghorn
39FA23	710	426(10,000)*	36	14	No Estimate	Initial Middle Missouri	Pronghorn
48LN373	1170	18	6	NA	No Estimate	Late Prehistoric, Uinta	Pronghorn
Austin Wash	1187	1880	25	7	Winter		Pronghorn
Ceramic	1190	45	5	NA	Late Winter		Pronghorn
Lost Terrace	1200	1041	83	13	Winter	Avonlea	Pronghorn
Oyster Ridge	1375		5	NA	Summer		Pronghorn
48UT199	1460	67	12	NA	No Estimate		Pronghorn
Trappers Point	5587	1683(57,000)*	27	10	Late Winter	Early Plains Archaic	Pronghorn
Dead Indian	4180		50	NA	Winter	McKean	Deer
Lookingbill	6800	482	7	6	Midsummer/Early Fall	Early Plains Archaic	Deer
Barton Gulch	9410	NA	2	2		Alder	Deer
Vermillion Lakes	≈10,000	24	4	NA	NA	Late Paleoindian	Sheep
Vermillion Lakes	>10,000	136	12	NA	Fall and Spring	Early Paleoindian	Sheep
Bugas-Holding	450	780(45,000)*	14	NA	Late Fall/Early Winter	Shoshone	Sheep
Pagoda Creek	2850	1751	7	5	Early/Midwinter	Pelican Lake	Sheep
Mummy Cave	1230	834	47	12	Winter	Late Prehistoric (CL3)	Sheep
Mummy Cave	4090	1365	35	16	Winter	Middle Archaic (CL6/7)	Sheep
Mummy Cave	8136	73	6	2	Winter	Late Paleoindian (CL17)	Sheep
Mummy Cave	8307	72	6	2	Winter	Late Paleoindian (CL19)	Sheep
Joe Miller	1650	1442(7795)*	11	4	May/May-June	Late Plains Archaic	Elk
EhPv-126	NA	256(2171)*	5	NA	NA	Late Prehistoric	Elk

*Total number of specimens.

pronghorn remains, as seen at the Hell Gap and Allen sites. At the Hell Gap site, Goshen, Agate Basin, as well as Middle and Late Paleoindian occupations contain pronghorn, most commonly a minimum of one individual in each component (Rapson and Niven 2009). However, the heavily processed bone, some with cut and impact marks, is indistinguishable between pronghorn and deer, thus much more of the assemblage could be pronghorn. At the Allen site in central Nebraska, pronghorn is likewise a significant component of the assemblage. The three Middle to Late Paleoindian components (post-10,000 BP) contain between one and four pronghorn (Hudson 2007). Although bison dominates the lowest component, the remaining occupations have similar number of pronghorn and deer. Long-term continuity in procurement of small numbers of pronghorn is also seen in sites like Pictograph Cave near Billings, Montana (Mulloy 1958), where antelope remains occur from the Middle Plains Archaic period and continue through the Late Plains Archaic and Late Prehistoric periods.

Traps

The third line of evidence of communal pronghorn procurement—animal trapping—is well illustrated by the Laidlaw site in southern Alberta, near Medicine Hat, dated to over 3000 years BP (Brumley 1984). Hunters took advantage of the natural topography in driving the animals between two converging fences and into a small catch pen, part of which may have been a pit, although part may also have been above ground. Grinnell (1923:278–279) described how the Cheyenne built and used the pit:

> In a broad flat they began to build two straight, tight, brush fences, eight to ten feet high, as if for the opposite sides of a square pen. From the ends of these fences on one side two lines of brush heaps about five steps apart stretched away into the flat for 400 or 500 yards ... This made two wings, which ran out from the ends of the tight fences, to direct the antelope into the pit. Between the ends of the tight fences opposite the side from which the wings extended, the people dug a big hole.

After preparing the trap, young men were sent out to scout for the pronghorn and move the herds toward the wings of the trap and the pit. Grinnell (1923:281) further describes the hunt:

> As soon as the antelope had come to the opening between the fences, all the people who had been hidden in the trenches rose and rushed toward the opening and closed it by crowding into it. They ran toward the antelope, which now were frightened and were going so fast that they could not stop, and rushed on and fell into the pit. The men and women seized each a club, and jumping into the pit, knocked the antelope on their heads.

Remains of one aboriginal pronghorn trap, the Fort Bridger Antelope Trap (48UT1; Figure 5.5) are still visible in southwestern Wyoming close to the town of Fort Bridger. Playa lakes are a common feature here in flat areas and are favorite places for pronghorn to gather, especially after late summer and fall rains have rejuvenated dry summer grasses. The trap is strategically located between two

Figure 5.5   Location of the Bridger Antelope Trap in southwest Wyoming.

of these playa lakes in a faulted area characterized by alternating hogback ridges and narrow, flat valleys.

The entire trap complex covers an area of about 520 m x 213 m, or about 11 hectares. Dimensions of the oval-shaped corral are roughly 200 x 150 m. One end of the oval is open and a long, curving fence forms a drive line about 625 m in length (Figure 5.5), although there is an apparent 100 m interruption in the fence through tall sagebrush. The remaining fences were constructed of juniper. According to local residents the fence was originally several feet high. The missing part may have been constructed of sagebrush that has simply rotted away.

Unfortunately, the juniper part of the fence was an excellent source of firewood for early settlers in the area and much of it was removed for that purpose, leaving only enough for the outline of the trap to be traced. A few better-preserved sections of the fence suggest that it was around 1.3 m to nearly 2 m high and about 1 m wide at the base. There is an indication that part of the fence was abandoned and rebuilt at a slightly different location (Figure 5.6). However, this could have been deliberate, with one part of the fence used to get the animals into the trap and the other for circling the animals. Junipers are plentiful in the immediate site area, and enough dead trees would have normally been available for the construction of the trap. The procurement complex was entirely adequate to trap and contain pronghorn but it would have been worthless for trapping either bison or deer. The former would have simply gone through the juniper fence and the latter would have gone over it.

Operation of the trap was straightforward. Pronghorn would naturally congregate at the playa lake, especially after late summer and fall rains regenerated the vegetation. When a herd of sufficient size gathered, the hunters headed it downvalley, which is the natural way the animals would move if disturbed. When the animals came up against the curved wing, they followed it until they came into the oval enclosure. The animals were, of course, being urged on all the time by persons stationed in the proper locations.

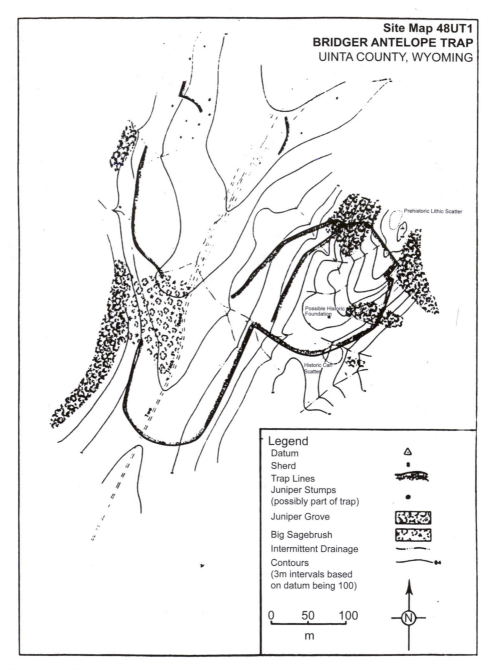

Figure 5.6 Map of the Bridger Antelope Trap, Uinta County, Wyoming. (Courtesy of Michael Metcalf.)

Once inside the oval, the animals were probably kept circling close to the fence until they were exhausted, an easy task since the animals would refuse to jump the fence, and the hunters could take turns chasing the animals from inside where they had the advantage of following a much shorter path than the animals. A definite anomaly in the north end of the fence was very likely a shaman's structure, but it was too badly deteriorated for us to determine its exact configuration. Animals could have been shot and killed as well as pursued until they fell from exhaustion.

The age of the trap is not known. Tree ring studies might have yielded some information had the trees not been removed for firewood. The country is arid and juniper lasts for some time so a date of 200–400 years ago is not unreasonable. A similar trap, known only from accounts by early settlers, located in the same general area was made of sagebrush and has completely disappeared, although at least one early settler claimed he had seen the trap in operation sometime well before the turn of the twentieth century. Details of the operation were not elaborated, but the fact that it was a functional pronghorn trap in historic times seems reliable.

Remains of another pronghorn trap complex are located in northeastern Wyoming on the headwaters of the Little Missouri River; one of the traps in this complex is reminiscent of the one described above by Hyde for the Brule Sioux (Figure 5.7). The Missouri Buttes Antelope Trap complex contains many sets of wings extending for several kilometers in all directions, with at least two traps of different configuration, suggesting multiple trapping strategies (Tratebas and Kornfeld 2004). One of the traps consists of a V-shaped set of wings terminating at a probable pit, while the other is oval shaped, reminiscent of the Great Basin facilities. The two traps are located on the opposite side of a gently sloping drainage with animal gathering areas that would have been outside of the drainage. The

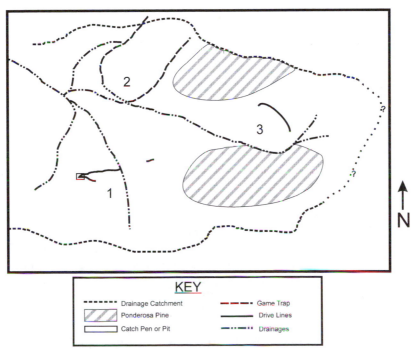

Figure 5.7 A portion of the Missouri Buttes Antelope Trap complex (also known as the Little Missouri Antelope Trap) on the Little Missouri River in the northwestern Black Hills. (Modified from Tratebas and Kornfeld 2004.)

animals would have been driven over a ridge from the south and in the other case from the north. The gathering areas in both cases consist of broad, gently undulating, sagebrush-grassland valleys surrounded by or interspersed with ponderosa pine savannahs. Antelope abound in these areas and deer are common as well. Sections of juniper fence similar to the fence described for the pronghorn trap near Fort Bridger still remain but the total outline is lacking, again because the fence was exploited by early homesteaders for firewood. Citing stories told by early settlers, residents of the area say it was an antelope trap. There seems no reason to doubt its original function. It is out of the area of Shoshonean influence and could possibly have been of Crow, Sioux, Cheyenne, or other Native American origin. Investigation of this trap is currently in process and each season additional drive lines are discovered, demonstrating the truly huge extent of the complex and attesting to its importance to prehistoric economies of the region (Great Plains Cooperative Ecosystem Studies Unit 2009).

MOUNTAIN SHEEP

The mountain areas of northwest Wyoming and immediately adjacent parts of Idaho and Montana contain a wealth of evidence of past mountain sheep procurement by individual and small-group hunting and larger communal strategies. Eleven traps are recorded in the high elevations around Dubois, Wyoming (Frison et al. 1990), and more are becoming known in the northern portions of the Shoshone National Forest near Cody. Some of the evidence for mountain sheep procurement is quite clear while much is not. Every high-altitude line of stones and cairn-like structures or fallen wood should not be interpreted as evidence of mountain sheep hunting and trapping. In terms of archaeology, it was fortunate that many Protohistoric and historic sheep procurement complexes were discovered and recognized as such before the perishable parts rotted away or were destroyed by wildfires. It is distressing to think of the number of such structures and the data lost in the 1988 and more recent fires in Yellowstone National Park and in the adjacent national forests (Eakin 2005).

Traps

Mountain sheep traps were constructed of dead juniper, lodgepole pine, and fir. Hunters took advantage of fallen trees as evidenced by the use of logs with intact roots, as well as deadfall from the surrounding area. Located at high, relatively inaccessible places, the effort put into collecting the wood and stones and building these traps suggests they were intended for repeated use over many years. Historic records of higher numbers of mountain sheep than are in existence today argue for use of these traps as part of a significant procurement method. Lines of stones in many cases are the only remnants of what at one time were wooden and stone sheep fences (Figure 5.8).

The construction employed in the catch pens of the traps appears identical to that used in dome-shaped, cribbed-log habitation structures scattered over the high country of the area and attributed to the Shoshone Sheepeater groups (Figure 6.47). In fact, a catch pen for a mountain sheep trap in the Absarokas close

Figure 5.8   Drive lines near timberline in the Absaroka Mountains in northwest Wyoming.

to the western boundary of Yellowstone National Park was once considered an elongate house structure because the fences had all rotted away. Even though the ramp on one end was clearly visible, it was not identified as a trap until the discovery of a nearly complete trap in another area revealed its true function. The traps were constructed out of whole logs up to 30 cm in diameter. Using logs with attached root systems added to their bulk and helped hold the structure together. Catch pens were, in some cases, anchored to rooted trees or braced with large logs. The configuration of the mountain sheep catch pen is truly ingenious, as they were wider at the bottom than the top, preventing the animals from escaping back out once they were moved into the pen from the ramp.

Animals coming down the converging fence line could see only a steep slope ahead of them, which was actually a ramp built of logs that was covered with dirt and rocks to mimic the terrain. Once at the top of the rise there was no choice but to jump into a cribbed-log catch pen where they were killed with clubs. Each trap complex was different due to the surrounding terrain, but they also demonstrated a remarkable similarity in response to mountain sheep behavior.

Drive lines vary from well-preserved wooden constructions to remnant stone and cairn lines. One example is the Boulder Ridge sheep trap, a complex of drive lines that begins at timberline (about 3048 m elevation) and extends to well above timberline on a high divide in the Absaroka Mountains in northwest Wyoming. The site is close to the center of an extensive area of high, bare ridges and deep stream valleys. Here, discontinuous lines of stone were strategically placed for nearly 1.6 km (Figure 5.8), so that animals were finally funneled into two converging lines of stones. Horseshoe-shaped stone piles were strategically placed on high points; with the addition of a small brush superstructure, each would have hidden a person inside. They may have been built for hunters to hide in before killing any animals that tried to slip away from the main group or they may have been for shamanistic purposes or perhaps both. The end of the converging lines of stones is on a flat at the top of a steep talus slope. It is possible that the talus slope served to slow and confuse the animals sufficiently so that they could be killed, but more likely there was some sort of wooden corral at the top of the slope of which no evidence remains.

There is unequivocal evidence for communal mountain sheep trapping in the late eighteenth century and the beginnings of the nineteenth century in the Absaroka and Wind River Mountain ranges of northwest Wyoming (Figure 5.9). Tree-ring dating of wooden components remaining in the best-preserved traps yields dates in the last two to three centuries, although we have evidence of mountain sheep taken en masse in archaeological sites dating to the Late Prehistoric period.

Two basic types of traps existed. One involved driving the animals directly into catch pens (a in Figure 5.10). In this trap, hunters drove the animals uphill between converging drive lines until the animals were within a short distance of the catch pen. At that point, the animals were turned downhill along drive lines that ended in a ramp at the entrance to the catch pen. In the second type, the animals were driven uphill into a holding pen and then downhill into a catch pen (b in Figure 5.10). Controlling the numbers of animals brought into the holding pen at any one time would allow hunters to slow the number of animals brought into the catch pen, potentially providing a better outcome in the number of animals killed.

The locations and designs of these trap complexes suggest strongly that they were designed mainly for taking nursery herds and, in many cases, the locations are predictable in relation to bedgrounds. Before and after the rutting season in November, ewes, lambs, and juveniles prefer a bare ridge or butte for a

Figure 5.9 Area in the southern Absaroka Mountains of Wyoming where a number of Late Prehistoric and Early Historic communal mountain sheep traps are found.

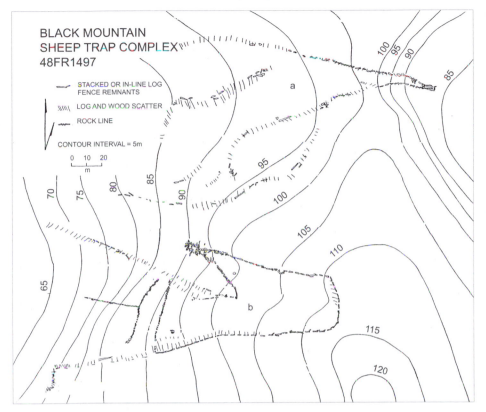

Figure 5.10   Map demonstrating two different types of mountain sheep traps.

bedground where they can see for long distances. If disturbed, they tend to first run downhill and then quickly turn upslope. Drive lines were placed so that the animals entered the open end of converging fences when they turned uphill and were then either driven directly into a catch pen, or into a holding corral where they could be driven later on into short converging lines leading to a catch pen (Figure 5.10).

In addition to this drive-line complex, there are several single manifestations of stone cairns, small wooden structures, and modified small rockshelters located in strategic spots throughout the high country that suggest hiding places for hunters lying in wait for mountain sheep. It was suspected that a processing and camping area associated with the Boulder Ridge trapping complex should be nearby. Recent fires in thick timber patches adjacent to the trapping features removed a thick layer of duff and exposed badly burned but still extensive identifiable evidence of the missing site activity areas.

Although most of the fences are badly deteriorated, the remaining ones demonstrate another facet of mountain sheep behavior; the ability of mountain sheep to scale high, perpendicular fences allows them to take a short run at a fence and use their feet and legs to propel them up and over the top (Figure 5.11a). Fences that lean inward toward the animals cause them to fall back into the corral when they try to jump over. The catch pens demonstrate well this same construction. At the Bull Elk Sheep Trap complex the catch pen was built to take advantage of a large rock that served as a ramp and also as one end of the catch pen (Figure 5.11b).

Figure 5.11   Mountain sheep's ability to scale a fence (a), and a catch pen at Bull Elk Pass in the Southern Absaroka Mountains (b). (Figure 5.11a courtesy of Jack Turnell.)

One of the timbers in the corral was placed in the forks of a then-living tree at about AD 1790. The fences leaning inward are easily visible, and the downhill slope would have obscured the catch pen hidden over a meter behind the rock. The mountain sheep would have had to jump on top of the rock and into the catch pen. Another trap demonstrates the convergence of drive lines into the catch pen on a steep downward slope (Figure 5.12). The animals were killed with clubs, since this was much more efficient than using arrows or spears. We have a record of one wooden club that was found at a sheep trap (Figure 5.13), and an elk antler with a sharpened bez tine found in the vicinity of several sheep traps was probably used to kill animals.

Variations exist in the construction of mountain sheep traps, but all are similar enough to be easily identifiable (Frison et al. 1990). One timberline trap consists of blinds either excavated out of deep deposits of slide rock or made using slide rock to build doughnut-shaped structures (Figure 5.14). Some larger branches used to

Figure 5.12   Looking down converging drive lines to the ramp leading into a catch pen of a mountain sheep trap.

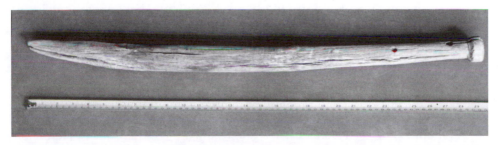

Figure 5.13   Wooden club presumably used to kill mountain sheep in a catch pen. One end is badly rotted where it was in contact with the ground.

Figure 5.14   Hunters' blind in slide rock above timberline.

cover the blinds are still present, although badly deteriorated critical areas where the animals might escape demonstrate evidence of fences with only stones remaining. The animals were driven through a natural gap, where there is evidence of an old corral that appears to have burned.

At each sheep trap is a feature that seems anomalous and functionally unrelated to the actual trapping operations. These are believed to be shamans' structures. These may be a small log and rock structure built into the fence or, as in the case of the timberline complex, a partially collapsed structure built of flat stones (Figure 5.15). There is ample evidence of shaman activity in communal bison hunting (Frison 1971a) and in communal antelope hunting by the Shoshone (Steward 1938), and there seems no reason not to generalize the same kind of activity to communal mountain sheep hunting. Besides the proposed shaman structures, large, mature ram skulls were placed in forks of trees in the vicinity of sheep traps. In many cases, the tree grew around parts of the skulls (Figure 5.16), while in other cases the tree was dead or the skull was not placed so that the tree could grow around it. We have documented twelve of these skulls, and in all but two, the brain case had been deliberately opened by smashing the foramen magnum. This strongly suggests ritual activity having to do with proper treatment of the animals' spirits.

Warren Angus Ferris described a ram skull partially embedded in a tree in southern Montana. He noted further that the local Flathead Indians left offerings when passing by (Ferris 1940). Weisel (1951) mentioned "medicine trees" and cited an account by a fur trader, Alexander Ross, who observed in 1824 what may have been the same skull seen later by Ferris and claimed the Indians always left offerings there. Weisel mentioned two other sections of trees with embedded mountain sheep skulls at a trading post in Missoula, Montana, and that one of these

Figure 5.15 Probable shaman's structure in the vicinity of a mountain sheep trap.

Figure 5.16 Ram head placed in the fork of a tree; the tree later grew around it.

was venerated by Indians. When the tree was cut (probably around 1920) there were "beads and trinkets at its base" (Weisel 1951:11). Although these accounts are some distance west of the Absaroka Mountains, the idea of ritualistic treatment of ram skulls was likely widespread wherever mountain sheep were extensively hunted.

Although these Protohistoric traps suggest mainly taking nursery herds, we do have evidence of a trapping situation in the Absaroka Mountains in which only rams were taken. The site was found by a hunter who mentioned that many years before he had observed a large ram skull in the fork of a dead tree. Investigation of the area revealed evidence of wooden fences placed to bring the animals into a natural trap formed by the perpendicular walls on both sides of a small stream. The dead tree in which the skull had been placed had recently fallen but the skull was still intact. A total of 25 badly deteriorated ram skulls remained at the site, but there were only a very few postcranial elements. A recent dating of the bone from this site yielded an age of 310 ± 40 BP (Beta 242606, Dan Eakin, personal communication 2008). Several mandibles may provide a key to seasonality, but the site needs further investigation since there are indications of buried deposits. This site probably represents more than a single kill event since it is difficult to envision either taking this number of rams at one time or building fences that were not intended for continued use.

It is not surprising to find a trap with evidence of rams only since the mature males often congregate in separate groups and display different behavior patterns than the females and juveniles. A trap that is properly located for nursery herds is not likely to be of use for rams. Very little skeletal material was recovered in the vicinity of the nursery herd traps and it is puzzling why the ram skulls were left in the trap area.

The LaMarche game trap, located in the Beaverhead National Forest in southwestern Montana, has a strong resemblance to those just described (Keyser 1974). This Montana complex apparently lacks the holding pen, but the corral or catch pen measures 2.1 x 7 m and is of cribbed-log construction, quite similar to the ones in Wyoming. The investigators thought the trap was probably one in which deer or mountain sheep were taken, but given its location and configuration, mountain sheep were the most likely prey. The site is at an elevation of about 2440 m and it is estimated to have been constructed somewhere between AD 1800 and 1850.

The Sheep Mountain Net

Small-group mountain sheep procurement in the Absaroka Mountains dates from at least late Paleoindian times as suggested by another line of evidence, a stored net. A folded net made of juniper bark fibers (*Juniperus* sp.) was recovered in a dry limestone alcove on Sheep Mountain at about 2440 m elevation in what is today a prime wintering area for mountain sheep (Frison et al. 1986). Sheep Mountain is situated in the V formed by the confluence of the North and South forks of the Shoshone River west of Cody, Wyoming. Wooden stakes incorporated into the net were radiocarbon dated at about 8800 years BP. The net was too fragile to be unfolded, but is estimated to be between 50 m and 65 m long and 1.5 m to 2 m high (Figure 5.17). The net was made of two-ply, S-twist juniper bark cordage of diameters ranging from 1.0 mm to 5.2 mm. Mesh gauge varies from about 0.71 cm to 3.01 cm. An estimated 2 km of two-strand cordage was employed in the manufacture of the net. It was reinforced, making it entirely adequate for the purpose of netting mountain sheep, which are the only large animals that frequent the area.

We propose that the Sheep Mountain net was stored for seasonal use on the resident mountain sheep herd. Two or more people probably held the net across a path where sheep commonly moved while others drove small numbers of animals into it. The net was designed to have the animals run into it and become entangled

Figure 5.17   Mountain sheep net from rockshelter near Cody, Wyoming.

long enough for the hunters to kill them with clubs. After taking a few animals, the hunters moved to other nearby areas with mountain sheep herds where nets were stored and the process was repeated. This was a viable and predictable animal procurement system that needed no stone projectile points and may help to explain in part the scarcity of these diagnostics at the higher elevations. The Sheep Mountain net was found not far from Mummy Cave, where fragments of a similar net date to the Late Archaic. Recorded also at Mummy Cave at about 8000 years BP were three stone slabs placed on end with an associated mountain sheep skull. This may have been some sort of shrine and, if so, the ritual treatment of mountain sheep skulls could have good time depth (Husted and Edgar 2002:39–40). Prehistoric sheep net hunting is supported by rock images depicting this activity (Figure 5.18; Sundstrom 1984). The Whoopup Canyon and other petroglyph sites on the southern and western slopes of the Black Hills were sheep country prehistorically, as were the Plains to the east, before such animals took refuge in the mountains after the onslaught of cattle, domestic sheep, and farming on the Plains. Hence net hunting likely had a wide geographical distribution in North America.

Mountain Sheep Bone and Bone Beds

Abundant evidence of sheep procurement comes from four sites: Vermillion Lakes outside of Calgary in Alberta, and Mummy Cave, Bugas-Holding, and Pagoda Creek, all in northwest Wyoming. Although the Vermillion Lakes site is outside of the primary regional coverage of this book, its relevance is the time depth of this economic activity. As with other medium and large mammals, many other sites attest to sheep procurement as well, but the evidence from such sites in minimal and difficult to interpret.

Figure 5.18   Net hunt scene from Whoopup Canyon, Wyoming. (Courtesy of Linea Sundstrom.)

The Vermillion Lakes site is located on the east side of the Canadian Rockies at the base of steep lower slopes where the mountains meet the terraces of the Bow River. The stratified Vermillion Lakes site spans the range from more than 10,000 years ago to the present, but of interest here are the Paleoindian components (Fedje et al. 1995). Components at the site are interpreted as representing short- to longer-term campsites, some with evidence of structures. Because of geomorphic context, these are divided into two groups for analytical purposes—an earlier group dating to the late fluted point period and a later group of Agate Basin/ Hell Gap age. The former group contains an MNI of four from 24 sheep specimens, while for the latter component the quantities are 12 and 136, respectively. Other taxa are present, but sheep are significantly more abundant than all other taxa combined. While individual occupations vary in skeletal element representation, as a composite sample all body parts are present, suggesting nearby procurement of the animals. Both fall and spring seasons are represented in the later cultural group, and animal processing tends to be heavy, including bone breakage to remove marrow. Certainly, one significant aspect of the Vermillion Lakes site is the evidence of economic reliance on sheep in the earliest Paleoindian components, associated with the late fluted point period. Not only does this add breadth to the overall economic activity of the earliest occupations of North America, but it suggests that such activity can dominate the economy.

Although it provides evidence of significant early prehistoric use of sheep, Vermillion Lakes cannot really be considered a bone bed. Neither can Mummy Cave; however, Mummy Cave does have a long occupation sequence with large quantities of sheep even during the Paleoindian period and some of the strata may be described as bone beds. Significant quantity of sheep bone was recovered in cultural layer 20, dated to 8430 BP, and continuing through the rest of the Paleoindian, Archaic, and Late Prehistoric cultural sequence at the site (Hughes 2003). Sheep dominate the Mummy Cave faunal assemblage with an NISP of 3769; deer are a distant second with an NISP of 113. The greatest sheep MNI (n=47) is in Late Prehistoric cultural layer 3, while the Middle Archaic layer 6/7 has an MNI of 35 (NISP=1365). The Paleoindian cultural layers 15–24 have MNI calculations between zero and six, showing significant use of this resource during this early period of prehistory. Especially notable is the large quantity of sheep bone in the Middle Archaic layer (cultural layer 6/7). Also notable are the over 30 other animal species present, including birds, as well as the total absence of bison. Sheep procurement at Mummy Cave occurred from winter to summer, although winter procurement is dominant and summer procurement is rare (Hughes 2003:105), with only two cultural layers showing summer as the season of occupation. Season of procurement changes through time, with the earliest Paleoindian cultural layers showing only winter procurement, later Paleoindian through Archaic layers showing winter and spring procurement, and only the most recent layers showing winter, spring, and summer sheep procurement.

Mummy Cave presents evidence for the most temporally consistent and intense use of bighorn sheep in the Rocky Mountain region. The Mummy Cave sheep bone was in excellent condition, preserved by the dry conditions of the Mummy Cave microenvironment (Hughes 2003). However, carnivore damage was extensive and probably responsible for the destruction of articular ends of bones. Butchering and processing of carcasses was nevertheless observable, and assemblage composition retains information about human procurement and processing methods. Hughes suggests that sheep carcasses were brought to the cave either whole or in portions for further processing. At the cave, the meat was stripped while long bones were opened for removal of the marrow. More intensive marrow processing appears in more recent cultural layers. Along with Bighorn Canyon caves (Husted 1969), it documents that early Holocene populations, at least in some regions, were highly dependent on midsize mammals rather than focused on bison, as is commonly suggested for the Plains east of the Rockies.

Two sites constitute mountain sheep bone beds. One of these, buried within terrace deposits of the Shoshone River, is the Pagoda Creek site. Two Pelican Lake layers (Figure 5.19) are encased in fine alluvial overbank silts of the Shoshone River that have left the cultural material relatively unaffected by horizontal movement

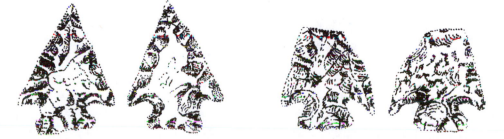

Figure 5.19   Pelican Lake projectile points from the Pagoda Creek site. (Courtesy of Dan Eakin.)

processes. The lower level, dating to 2850 and 2890 BP (Eakin 1989:62), is generally richer, but both layers contain hearths, fire-cracked rock, bone, and chipped stone, and sheep is the dominant species (Figure 5.20).

The nearly 23,000 faunal remains recovered from the site consist mostly of small bone fragments of less than 1 cm in any dimension. Of these, nearly 13,000 are from the lower layer, while the rest are from the upper layer or indeterminate context. In addition to sheep, small quantities of elk, deer (*Odocoileus hemionus*), grizzly bear, bobcat, and rabbit (*Lepus* sp.) are present. Based on 13 mandibles, at least seven sheep are present in the assemblage. The stage of tooth eruption indicates an early to midwinter death of the animals. The bone assemblage is characterized by high intentional fragmentation, representation of long bones mainly by shaft portion—a fact related to high fragmentation—and the absence of vertebrae. The bones, most of which exhibit well-preserved cortical surfaces, show numerous cut marks, especially on shaft fragments, indicative of muscle stripping, impact fractures, and burning. Along with hearths, fire-cracked rock, and stone tools, evidence indicating the dominance of tool-sharpening activities and minor amounts of other stone tool manufacturing, also seen from an antler flaker found in the deposits (Figure 5.21), has led the site investigator to suggest that Pagoda Creek is a processing and consumption locality. He surmises that carcasses were

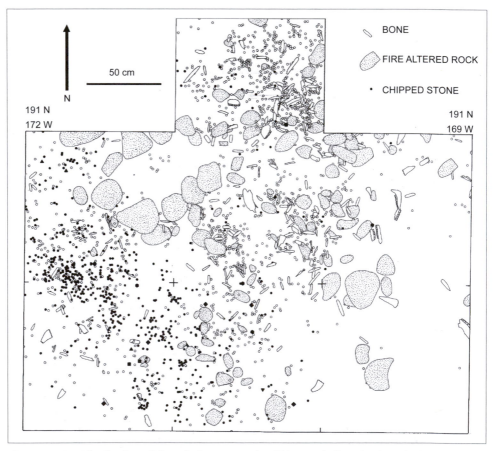

Figure 5.20 Distribution of faunal elements and cobbles encircling the Pagoda Creek hearths. (Courtesy of Dan Eakin.)

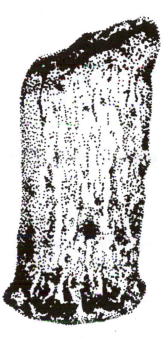

Figure 5.21   Antler flaker from the Pagoda Creek site. (Courtesy of Dan Eakin.)

brought to the site, butchered, and distributed to residential units, where the bone was prepared and processed for marrow and bone grease, resulting in the highly fragmentary bone assemblage (Eakin 1989).

The second major sheep bone bed consists largely of sheep and bison; however, other species are present in small quantities. The Bugas-Holding site is located about 30 km directly north of Pagoda Creek, but over a major mountain range raising 1800 m above the sites. Gentle overbank sedimentation from Sunlight Creek (Figure 5.22) buried the site shortly after occupation ended. Bugas-Holding is a Shoshone winter village dating between AD 1400 and AD 1600 that was occupied for 4–5 months (Rapson 1990). Excavations conducted in the 1980s yielded 51,000 pieces of point-plotted specimens, of which 5665 are chipped stone and the rest are bone (Rapson 1990). Based on a sample of screened material, at least 600,000 specimens were recovered from the excavated portion of the site. The mean size of the point-plotted chipped stone is 7.5 mm; however, including the screened material in our calculations would undoubtedly significantly decrease the mean artifact size.

Site size is estimated at about 5250 m² based on widely scattered test units across the terrace, but it may be significantly larger. An 84 m² excavation block also yielded eight hearths well delineated by rocks. Six of these are surface hearths or slightly basin shaped, while two are deep and filled with fire-cracked rock (Figure 5.23). At least one other feature was recognized and was interpreted as a trash midden. All of the hearths have downwind scatters of ash and upwind concentrations of small artifacts, suggesting they are outside features where people dropped small artifacts where they were sitting while the wind blew the smoke and ash away from them. Other artifacts recovered during the 1980s include 22 bone and 149 chipped stone tools, a few fragments of shell, and 129 pieces of pottery.

Figure 5.22 The Bugas-Holding site on the floodplain of Sunlight Creek. Approximate area of the site indicated by dashed line.

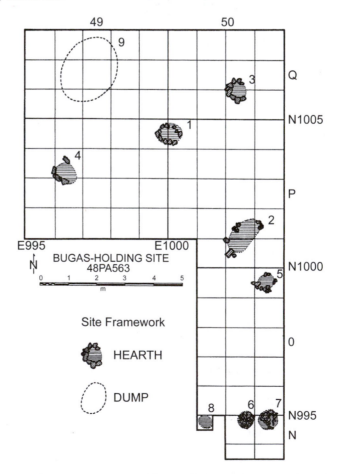

Figure 5.23 Bugas-Holding site features and fire-cracked rock. (Courtesy of David J. Rapson.)

The Bugas-Holding site was discovered during a house construction project, the house estimated to be no more than 275 m², which likely destroyed a portion of the site. A trench connecting the propane tank to the house cut across a thick cultural deposit recognized by one of the construction personnel, who recovered bone tools, pottery, 18 projectile points, 19 other stone tools, and reported organic matting from the trench. The assemblage suggests that the trench might have cut through a domestic structure. For practical reasons, the 1980s excavations could not expand on these findings, but was conducted slightly away from the occupied new house. Nevertheless similar cultural debris was discovered.

Around the eight hearths in the block excavation were dense concentrations of chipped stone—mostly debitage, but also stone tools. The chipped stone assemblage is dominated by debitage, but includes at least 14 tool types. The most common tools are 83 retouched and utilized flakes, followed by 22 broken and eight complete projectile points (Figure 2.73). The small, tri-notched points are typical of the Late Prehistoric Shoshone occupation of the Central Rocky Mountains. These projectile points are commonly a product of a complex manufacturing sequence that includes the production of preforms (small thin bifaces that are notched as the last step of the production process, thus becoming projectile points). Such preforms are generally triangular in shape and are referred to as Cottonwood Triangular types. Six preforms are found in the Bugas-Holding assemblage (Figure 5.24), suggesting that the group anticipated a longer stay at the site during which additional projectile tips may be needed. End scrapers are the next most common artifact category, showing that hide working was an important activity at the site. Four Late Prehistoric knives, referred to regionally as Shoshone knives but associated with a variety of Late Prehistoric groups in North America (Eccles 1997), form an important component of the chipped stone tool assemblage (Figure 5.25). The Shoshone knives occur in several stages of rejuvenation from relatively unrejuvenated, large

Figure 5.24 Cottonwood Triangular preforms from the Bugas-Holding site.

Figure 5.25   Bugas-Holding site Shoshone knives.

and thin bifaces, technologically the same as Folsom ultrathins with broad, diving flake scars (Jodry 1999b; Root et al. 1999), to heavily rejuvenated forms that constitute the typical type specimens. Other formal tools in the assemblage include a bipoint, large tri-notched projectile point or knife, three flake tools with long (about 5 mm) robust projections, three irregular bifaces, one denticulate, two cores, one bifacial pendant, two side scrapers, and the 83 informal flake tools (retouched or utilized flakes) mentioned above (Figures 5.26 and 5.27).

Molecular analysis of residue on the stone tools by Shanks et al. (1999; Shanks, Hodges, Tilley, Kornfeld, Larson, and Ream 2005; Shanks, Kornfeld, and Ream 2005) recognized the residues of three taxa with DNA analysis and four with protein analysis. Canid was the taxa identified most commonly, with several examples of deer and cat for the DNA analysis and bear, sheep, dog, and human for the protein. Most interestingly, this analysis showed a series of taxa not identified in the zooarchaeological record. Such results are intriguing and suggest that tools recovered at the Bugas-Holding site had long use lives, perhaps being used at other localities prior to the group moving to Bugas-Holding. The formally shaped tools, the flake tools, the use-wear analysis discussed below, as well as the molecular study attest to a high diversity of activities carried on during site occupation, as would be expected of a winter village.

Attempting to better understand the economic activities and group composition of this winter village, James Miller identified a total of 14 different raw materials in the chipped stone assemblage. These materials indicate that most of the raw materials at the Bugas-Holding site are available within close proximity to the site.

Figure 5.26   Bugas-Holding site bifacial tools.

However, two of the chert sources, Green River Ostracodal and Opalitic cherts, are nonlocal. These originate from formations in the Green River Basin, several hundred kilometers south of the site, but these sources are represented by only 12 pieces in the Bugas-Holding assemblage. Two other raw material types, Eocene Cretaceous Opalitic chert and Mississippian/Devonian cherts, comprise over 99% of the debitage. This pattern, in combination with the presence of debitage from the other locally available raw materials, suggests the finishing, resharpening, and maintenance of tools during the butchering and processing activities. Results of obsidian X-ray fluorescence studies by Raymond Kunselman indicate that most originate from Obsidian Cliff in Yellowstone National Park 100 km west of the site, while several pieces arrived from southern Jackson Hole (150 km southwest) or from Bear Gulch in Targhee National Forest (250 km west of the site) in Idaho. The identification of raw material in conjunction with artifact analysis also discovered that tools are represented by nonlocal or exotic raw material types, mainly the Green River Formation opalitic chert and obsidian. This suggests that these items were brought into the site and discarded with comparatively less resharpening and maintenance than the local raw materials.

Microwear analysis conducted by Doug Bamforth also indicates the diversity of activities carried on at the site. The primary microwear is from activities associated with the processing of animal foods for bone grease and the processing of hides after removal from the carcass. The analyzed tools include bifaces, end scrapers, edge-modified flakes, and a core. These show three functionally distinct classes of wear. The first, found on one of the examined bifaces known as "Shoshone knives," consists of dry hide polish on tool edges and flake ridges

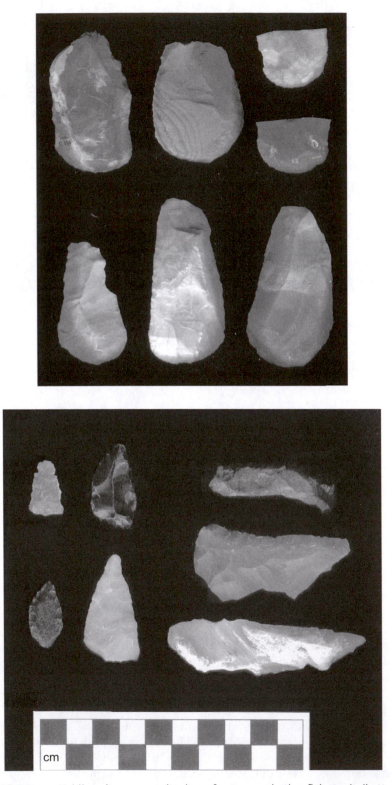

Figure 5.27   Bugas-Holding site scrapers (top), perforators, and other flake tools (bottom).

on the distal two-thirds of the surface. This suggests that transport in a leather sheath produced the wear. The second wear class of hide scraping was seen on the end scrapers in the assemblage, which were hafted judging from traces of hafting wear on the dorsal surfaces of the artifacts. Several of the end scrapers were resharpened shortly before discard, as there is a mixture of scraping wear and fresh edges along the working portion of the scrapers. The third wear type consists of tools used to skin and butcher animals. Most of these tools were discarded with very distinct use-wear traces, suggesting heavy use before discard. In short, virtually all of the worn pieces show traces of use in the processing of animal carcasses. Interestingly, the "Shoshone knife" shows use-wear traces indicating woodworking. This specimen is from a test unit 20 m to the west of the block excavation area and is the only piece examined with microwear that contains polish not normally associated with butchery or meat processing. In combination with the results from the analysis of material collected prior to the University of Wyoming's excavations at the Bugas-Holding site, the use wear on the Shoshone knife suggests that there may be unexcavated areas of the site that are functionally distinct from the excavated zone.

The high diversity of activities suggested by the chipped stone tools is also supported by the 22 bone and antler implements. Among these are an elk antler flesher/hide-working tool (Figure 5.28e), four antler weaving tools (needles; Figure 5.28a–d), six bone awls (Figure 5.28g–k), and one bipointed awl or possibly a leister or barbed gorge (Figure 5.28f). In addition there are several bone and antler ornaments, including an elk tooth pendant, bone beads, a shell bead, elk antler rasp (a musical instrument; Figure 5.29), and an incised bone. The antler

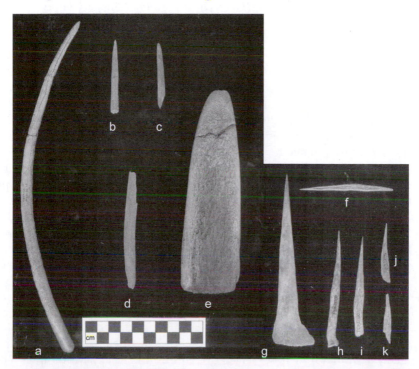

Figure 5.28 Bugas-Holding site bone and antler implements: basket-weaving needles (a–d), elk antler flesher or hide-working tool (e), bone awls (g–k), and an leister or barbed gorge (f).

Figure 5.29   Bugas-Holding site elk antler rasp. (Drawing by Allen Denoyer.)

weaving needles include one complete specimen, two tips, and one midsection. The complete specimen is 28.5 cm long, tapering from one end of the implement to the other. The thicker end is approximately 10.5 mm in diameter and well blunted, while the thinner end tapers to a fine, but not sharp point. The elk antler flesher shows evidence of the manufacturing technique. First, the antler was grooved longitudinally as well as perpendicularly to the long axis of the element before being snapped. The cancellous bone interior was scooped out to form a slightly U-shaped cross section, while the grooved sides were well rounded. The distal end was undoubtedly shaped into a relatively sharp, spatulate form that is now heavily polished from use. The bone awls were manufactured on a sheep/deer-sized scapula, a sheep/deer-sized rib, a possible canid radius, and various elements unidentified to taxa. The working ends of the awls all came to carefully manufactured, extremely sharp points. The four bone beads were likely manufactured from bones of small mammals, usually these are small carnivores. Of the four beads, one is a long breast plate bead, while the rest are short, and one of the latter is probably unfinished. The presence of tubular bone beads, grooved bone, and an elk antler pendant (Figure 5.30) are indicative of further craft activities occurring at the site.

The *Olivella* sp. bead and elk antler rasp are of particular interest. *Olivella* beads manufactured from the columella of the shell are well documented as money beads in California (King 1978) and have been found in several archaeological sites in our study area. The presence of the bead at Bugas-Holding suggests an exchange system that may have reached well into the Rocky Mountains. The elk antler rasp was manufactured by grooving and snapping the antler prior to placing a series of grooves on the outside antler surface. Bone and antler rasps are

Figure 5.30 Bugas-Holding site miscellaneous osseous objects: elk canine pendant (a), tubular bone bead (b), and grooved bone fragments (c and d).

well known in Plains archaeological assemblages (e.g., Henning 1998) and elk have a ritual significance to many Plains and Rocky Mountain groups (Densmore 1992:176). The rasp may be a part of such ritual activity.

The 129 pottery fragments from Bugas-Holding are mostly body sherds and represent several vessels. A few rim and base sherds, however, are part of the assemblage, and these show the typical basal flange of an Intermountain pottery style (see Figure 6.79). Along with the small tri-notched projectile points, Cottonwood Triangular preforms, and the radiocarbon dates (490 ± 80 BP, Beta 69729; 380 ± 100 BP, RL1871; and 200 ± 60 BP, Beta 69793; corrected dates overlap at AD 1400–1600), the pottery places the site firmly as a Late Prehistoric, Shoshonean occupation. Other sites in the region, currently under investigation, have similar assemblages, but appear to be slightly more recent, as evidenced by small quantities of European trade goods (Eakin 2005).

Although the artifact assemblage is significant for interpreting the Bugas-Holding site and the procurement and use of bighorn sheep, much of the evidence comes from the sheep remains themselves. Over 45,000 faunal remains were point provenienced, with the majority being either sheep or bison (Figure 5.31). Of the identified specimens, 780 are sheep (MNI=14) and 1108 are bison (MNI=15). A battery of tests were performed on this assemblage, in particular on the spatial distribution and positional data recovered and including the most in-depth integrated taphonomic analysis of fauna in North America (Rapson 1990).

According to the investigator, the timing of sheep mortality at the Bugas-Holding site differs from that of bison: sheep were killed in one or several episodes

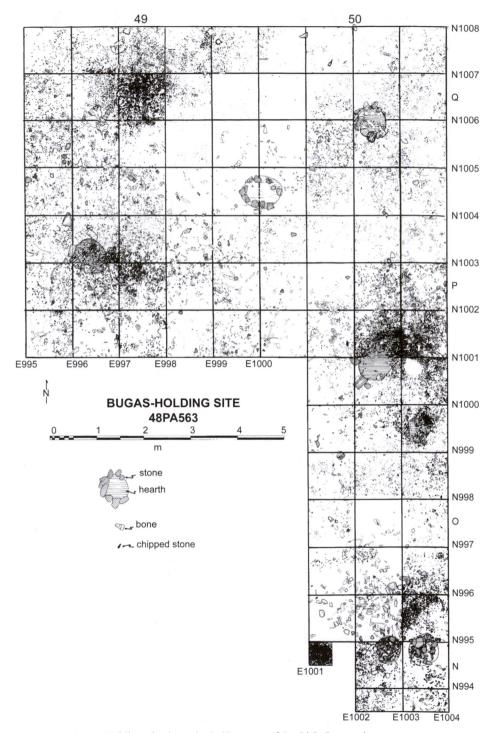

Figure 5.31   Bugas-Holding site bone bed. (Courtesy of David J. Rapson.)

in late fall or early winter, while the bison were procured over the season of site occupation. To reach this conclusion, Rapson (1990) has examined the sex of animals, cut marks, impact marks, and bone fragments, as well as their site context. While bison were apparently selected by sex (more males were procured than females and males were more heavily processed), there was no sexual selection of sheep. Sexual selection of bison is common as females are in a poorer nutritional state during pregnancy than males and are often not procured in mid to late winter (Speth and Spielman 1983). Sheep, on the other hand, were procured prior to the season where nutritional issues would be considered.

On the basis of butchering and processing of carcasses as well as bone, it can be surmised that Bugas-Holding occupants hunted sheep early in the winter and stored the products for later use. The location of the butchering marks on bone suggests that whole carcasses were stored and processed while frozen. Several nearby sheep traps were most likely the facilities used to capture the animals. Bison, on the other hand, appear not to have been brought to the camp complete. Discrepancies in the frequencies of distal limb elements suggest that some parts were left at kill locations where primary butchering occurred. Although Bugas-Holding is a mixed bison and sheep bone bed, the sheep from the site provide one of the most significant assemblages for understanding the role of these animals in Northwestern Plains and Rocky Mountain prehistoric economies.

DEER

Mule deer remains appear in archaeological sites from Folsom to the Historic period. There is no known conclusive evidence of mass trapping of either mule or whitetail deer in prehistoric times, even though the faunal evidence indicates that they were continually hunted in small numbers. The extensive McKean complex Dead Indian Creek site (Figure 2.60) in the Sunlight Basin of northwestern Wyoming (Frison and Walker 1984) yielded at least 50 deer that were taken throughout the winter (Simpson 1984) and smaller numbers of mountain sheep (no seasonality) between 4500 and 4000 BP. Occupants were living in pit houses, one of which was over 1 m in depth (Figure 2.61). Evidence argues strongly for some sort of ceremonialism connected with deer procurement.

Several large male skullcaps were given unusual treatment. One was placed in a depression in the center of a rock cairn and others were placed to one side of it (Figure 5.32). At least one set of antlers is large enough to be regarded as a trophy today. Stone artifacts of the McKean complex were directly associated with the skulls, and all of this was alongside a large campsite rich in cultural materials. There are a number of questions concerning the preservation of these skulls. They were covered with alluvium to a depth of just over 0.6 m. No evidence indicated that they had been placed in artificial pits, but a strong argument can be made for the covering of the entire feature with alluvium shortly after placement. Porcupine remains were common in the site deposits and are common there today; these animals cannot resist chewing antler but none of the antlers or bone demonstrated more than superficial rodent chewing. In addition, the antlers demonstrate no evidence of weathering, which quickly accelerates the deterioration process.

Located in the same mountain basin as the Bugas-Holding site, the Dead Indian Creek site contains mule deer and mountain sheep bones, but no bison, while the

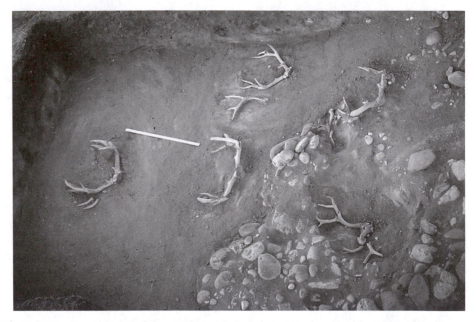

Figure 5.32   Arrangement of deer antlers and skullcaps at the Dead Indian Creek site.

Bugas-Holding site has both mountain sheep and bison skeletal remains as well as deer DNA. Mule deer, especially the mature males, often occupy about the same kind of rough, rimrock country that mountain sheep favor. Mule deer are not able to negotiate rough terrain as well as mountain sheep, but in many ways they run a close second. It is not at all unlikely that a combination mountain sheep/mule deer trap was located somewhere in the extremely rough country surrounding the Dead Indian Creek site. Further comparison of these two sites would elaborate on the procurement of medium-sized mammals at different times in prehistory.

Whitetail deer behave differently from mule deer and are smaller in size. They favor stream bottoms and brushy areas. In terms of hunting the two species, the whitetails are more difficult. They hide in brushy areas and demonstrate the frustrating trait of keeping trees, brush, and other obstacles between them and the hunter, although once the hunter becomes familiar with their behavior patterns, they are not difficult to procure. However, based on the archaeological record, the whitetail deer was a relatively insignificant prehistoric food source on the Northwestern Plains. A single whitetail deer is reported for the Lindenmeier site in northern Colorado (Wilmsen and Roberts 1978:46) and possibly one from the Cody complex Jurgens site (Wilmsen 1970:31). Whitetail deer are known from the 450-year-old Big Goose Creek site on the eastern slopes of the Bighorn Mountains in a context that produced what are believed to be Crow Indian ceramics (Frison et al. 1978). The site contained a number of whitetail deer skulls (identified from antlers), antlers, antler tool handles, and antlers discarded during tool manufacture.

Deer Bone Beds

The earliest known deer bone bed is at the Helen Lookingbill site. The site, important for several reasons, is located at the high (2621 m), wet mountain meadow in the southern Absaroka Mountains above Bear Creek. A spring in the site vicinity provides water, while limber pine, arrowleaf balsamroot, and innumerable other plants are potential food resources. The site represents 10,500 years of intermittent occupation; however, of interest here is the Early Plains Archaic deer bone midden dating to between about 6460 and 7140 BP (Figure 5.33). The midden is at least 15 cm thick and contains over 2497 bone specimens, of which 482 could be identified as deer and 11 as sheep. Other species included in the assemblage are bison, porcupine, jackrabbit, rodent, and carnivore. The dominance of deer is surprising, given the abundance of sheep traps in the vicinity of the site. The nearby sheep traps, however, are all recent and may not have been there at the time of the deposition of the Lookingbill bone midden.

The assemblage of body size 3 and deer specimens at Lookingbill can be described as lightly to moderately weathered, exhibiting some chemical deterioration of exterior surfaces as well as some root etching, showing very little carnivore modification, and extensively fragmented (Kornfeld et al. 2001). Only 17% (n=383) of the bones display burning on at least some part of their surface. Although root etching has obscured some cut marks, this applies primarily to specimens with more than 10% of their surfaces obscured, and this category represents only 6% of the total assemblage. In general, then, human beings were the primary agents responsible for the accumulation and modification of seven deer in the small excavation area of the Lookingbill Early Archaic level, and the extent of postdepositional modification of the assemblage is minimal. Finally, it appears that a significant percentage of body size 3 fauna in this assemblage are males. Tooth eruption and wear on six highly fragmentary mandibular elements indicate a midsummer to early fall death.

The overall pattern of skeletal elements (Figure 5.34) is most similar to that observed at kill/butchery locations, where essentially whole carcasses are introduced to the site from a nearby kill. The carcass is disarticulated so that high-utility

Figure 5.33   Portion of the Early Plains Archaic bone bed at the Helen Lookingbill site.

portions, such as ribs, pelvis, cervical, thoracics, and femur, can be transported. Those portions of moderate to low utility (such as the cranium, mandible, and distal limb elements) are consumed and discarded on the site. The nature of Early Archaic game procurement, processing, and use is further illustrated by comparison with other assemblages. The body size 3 bones at the Bugas-Holding site are primarily bighorn sheep taken in mass kills during the late fall, with most of the carcasses returned to the residential site and put up in stores for consumption during the course of the winter occupation. A generally positive relationship exists between the frequencies of elements with cut marks in both assemblages, as well as several potentially significant differences (Figure 5.34). The carpals, tarsals, and third phalanges, all elements of the lower limb with little economic utility, are all located along the x-axis. These elements contain virtually no cut marks or evidence of processing in the Bugas-Holding assemblage, but they are regularly marked in the Lookingbill assemblage. Whereas at Bugas-Holding, carpals, tarsals, and phalanges were imported as part of leg units, placed in stores, but never used, at Lookingbill the presence of cut marks on these elements suggests that they were discarded in the process of preparing the limbs for transport to another location. Lumbar vertebrae, astragali, and calcanei (circled in the upper left hand corner of Figure 5.34) are much more often cut at Bugas-Holding than at Lookingbill. Each of these elements represents significant meat masses that are regularly transported to residential camps. The lack of cuts on these elements at Lookingbill suggests these elements were discarded at the site without apparent butchery. The prevalence of cuts on the tibia, humerus, and pelvis at Lookingbill compared to Bugas-Holding (circled on the far right of Figure 5.34) may reflect the stripping of muscle masses from these elements in order to decrease their bulk for

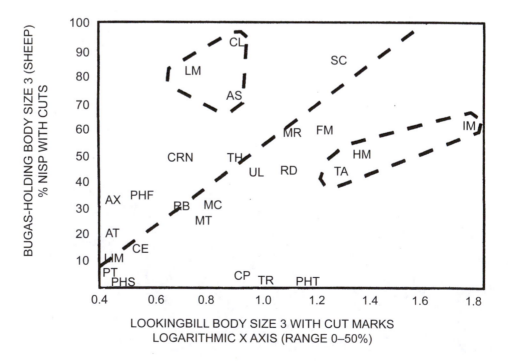

Figure 5.34 Helen Lookingbill site cut marks compared to cut marks at the Bugas-Holding site.

transport. These patterns illustrate the difference between butchering patterns at a kill/butchery (Lookingbill) site and a campsite (Bugus-Holding).

The pattern of skeletal elements at the Lookingbill site is most consistent with a relatively short-term hunting camp, occupied during the summer to fall, with small numbers of animals, predominantly males, brought essentially whole to the camp for processing. This processing was aimed primarily at the shipment of meaty portions of the axial skeleton and the upper limbs to a site of consumption located elsewhere. Because the present faunal analysis is restricted to the two square meters, it is difficult to know if the meat was moved out of the site or merely to another area of the site. It is possible that deer hunting and processing for storage elsewhere may have occurred at the end of some longer occupation not initially oriented toward deer hunting.

Many characteristics of the Lookingbill site hint at residential camping rather than solely temporary hunting camp activities. Scrapers, gravers, drills, and a wide variety of flake tools form the chipped stone tool assemblage. These are not hunting and butchering implements, but rather bespeak a variety of domestic activities. The projectile points are also equivocal. The many manufacturing stages could well be expected at a hunting camp where hunting implements are repaired (Figure 2.44). However, the reuse and recycling of these implements into nonhunting tools (Figure 5.35h and i; see also Figure 2.44) could occur at either type of occupation.

The Barton Gulch site is located in the Ruby Valley of southwest Montana. The site is significant for its data about the Alder and Hardinger complexes (9410 and 8780 BP, respectively; see Chapter 2). One of the unique features of the Barton Gulch site is its fauna. Although the investigators do not provide specimen counts, the faunal collection is extensive but includes only three species: cottontail, mink, and deer, as well as indeterminate rabbit. The MNI of the three identifiable taxa are two, one, and two, respectively. The deer, however, are heavily processed, as evidenced by cut marks on deer long bone shaft fragments and impact fractures. Numerous bones also exhibit calcinations, indicating their contact with high heat.

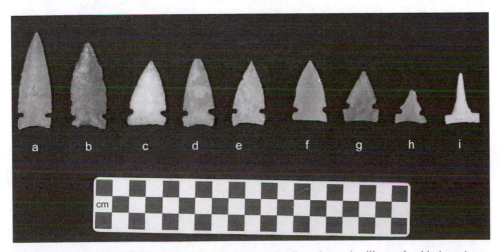

Figure 5.35 Lookingbill site Early Plains Archaic projectile point series illustrating blade resharpening and point recycling into nonhunting implements: projectile points (a–g), early-stage recycled drill (h), and late-stage recycled drill (i).

The use of deer in the absence of larger species is unusual and unexpected for mid-Paleoindian times, as is the heavy processing of the carcasses and bones. However, Barton Gulch is one of the now numerous sites that are yielding such evidence of forager behavior early in North American prehistory (Walker and Driskell 2007). Although not a deer bone bed, the faunal data are a significant addition to the Paleoindian database.

ELK

The Rocky Mountains today provide habitat for a considerable number of elk but, except for antlers, elk rarely appear in archaeological sites on the Northwestern Plains or Rocky Mountains. However, large piles of elk antlers were recorded historically as prehistoric features. A cave site (Elk Bone Cave in Bighorn County, Montana) was excavated by Nelson (1943) and elk remains (but no pile of elk antlers) are mentioned. However, Crow Indians claim there was a pile of antlers estimated to be about 6 or 7 m high (Conner 1972) in this same cave in the later decades of the nineteenth century. A mound of elk antlers located on the Missouri River above the mouth of the Yellowstone River in Montana was described by Denig (1930:398) as "covering an acre of ground and in height about 30 feet" (see also Conner 1972). These reports demonstrate intensive use of elk during Protohistoric or Historic periods. Earlier, however, elk occur only in very small numbers, with a few exceptions. The Folsom level at the Agate Basin site produced what we believe was a fluting tool made from an elk antler brow tine removed by deep groves into the main antler (Frison and Bradley 1981:13). Projectile points first thought to be bone and later identified as elk antler were recovered from the same components. The Hell Gap level at the Agate Basin site revealed two tips of two elk antler tines, one of which was thought to be the spur for an atlatl. An elk antler hammer for working chipped stone was recovered from the Frederick level at Locality I of the Hell Gap site. One pair of elk mandibles was recovered in the McKean level at the Dead Indian Creek site, although small tests in a Late Prehistoric level at the same site yielded a large number of elk bones and antler remnants that demonstrate deep grooving marks. A single elk was recorded at Pictograph Cave I (Mulloy 1958:226) at what should be a time period close to that of the Dead Indian Creek site. None was reported in Pictograph II levels, but three specimens appeared in Pictograph III and IV (Late Prehistoric and Historic) levels.

Both the camp and bison kill areas of the Big Goose Creek site provided evidence of elk, especially antlers, that were used for tools and decorative items. Remains of elk were found in the Piney Creek Buffalo Jump (Frison 1967b). Two elk antler flaking hammers are recorded from Late Prehistoric period Shoshone sites and several elk antlers were recovered in cribbed-log structures, also believed to be Shoshone, located on the eastern slopes of the Absaroka Mountains near Cody, Wyoming. A series of elk antler specimens, fleshers, tooth ornaments, hide scrapers, rasps, and other artifacts were recovered from the Shoshone-age Bugas-Holding site described above. Elk were hunted regularly by Shoshone groups in historic times (e.g., Wilson and Driggs 1919). While a large number of elk antler digging tools have been recovered from quarry sites of the Early Plains Archaic period (Figure 5.36) and the Late Plains Archaic period (Davis 1982), elk bone beds are rare and were unknown until quite recently.

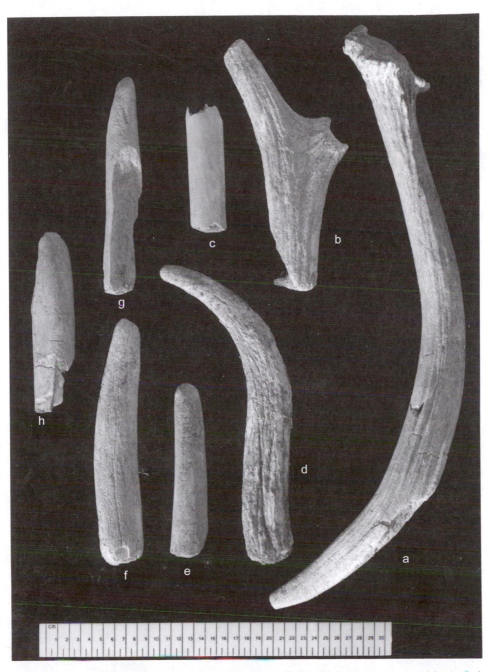

Figure 5.36 Elk antler (a, b, d–h) and large mammal rib (c) digging tools recovered in an Early Plains Archaic stone quarry.

Regardless of a rather common occurrence of elk in archaeological assemblages, the only elk bone bed currently known to us in the Central Rocky Mountains and the adjacent Plains is the Joe Miller site northwest of Laramie, Wyoming. The site is located on a ridge in the Strauss Hills that appears to be prime elk habitat and a migration corridor between the Four Mile and Cooper Creek drainages. Dan Eakin (personal communication 2008) and the site investigators (Burnett et al. 2008) report frequent sightings of elk in a depression either immediately north or south of the site. The Joe Miller site lies in a thick sand shadow deposit that covers the site with up to 120 cm of sediment. The site was discovered during a pipeline survey and has since been reinvestigated and tested during several subsequent linear survey projects. The testing included numerous scattered auger holes, test units, and one block excavation.

The Joe Miller site, about 7500 m² in size, was tested with a 59 m² block and some outlying units. The cultural material was buried between 50 and 120 cm below surface, and the eight features excavated in the block had a very restricted age between 1510 ± 40 and 1780 ± 40 BP. These data correspond well with the Late Archaic projectile point assemblage, including several Besant types. The eight hearths are very uniform in size (50–100 cm), shape (circular), and contain fire-cracked rock overlying a dark charcoal layer (Figure 5.37). Fire-cracked rock extends across the floor beyond the features, and backplots show close association of the surface marked by the features, artifacts, and bone. Excavations yielded 7795 faunal specimens of which 656 are elk, 786 are large ungulate, likely also elk, and 161 are rodent. Other taxa identified with smaller NISPs are jackrabbit, pronghorn, and bison, while many specimens not identifiable to taxa could still be categorized as diminutive ungulate, unspecified ungulate, and large carnivore.

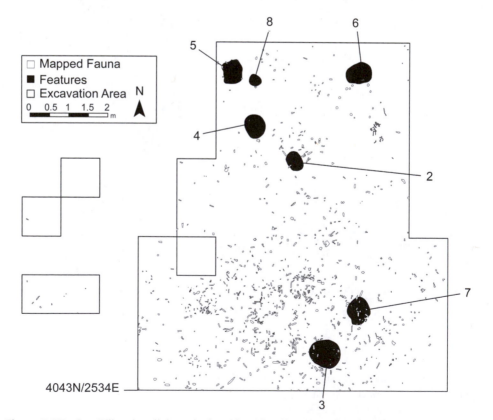

Figure 5.37   Joe Miller site elk bone bed and hearths. (Courtesy of Paul Burnett.)

The largest number of specimens (4302), mostly very small fragments, are not identifiable.

Of interest here are the remains of 11 elk. The analysis of tooth eruption and the presence of elk fetal specimens demonstrate that the time of death is May to late May/June. The elk were butchered and the bones heavily processed, as evidenced by cut marks, long bone fragmentation, and impact marks. The investigators suggest that marrow extraction and/or bone grease rendering was the purpose of this activity (Burnett et al. 2008). Coupled with the eight hearths with fire-cracked rock, such a scenario is plausible. Large quantities of fire-cracked rock are commonly a part of heavy bison bone processing assemblages, such as at Head-Smashed-In site in Alberta (Brink and Dawe 1989; Reeves 1990), and the same pattern can be expected during processing of other taxa.

The only other elk bone bed is EhPv-126. Although somewhat away from our region, in Banff National Park near the town of Banff in Alberta (Monsalve et al. 2009), its importance lies in the fact that it is one of two elk bone beds known to us. Consequently, site EhPv-126 is important for understanding procurement of this animal. A still incomplete study of the fauna has nevertheless yielded the remains of five elk and one moose from 2171 bones, of which 256 were identifiable to element. The MNI was calculated on the basis of tooth rows for elk and one incisor for moose. This would lead us to think that elk is a grossly dominant component of this assemblage. The significance of the study, however, goes further. Monsalve and colleagues analyzed DNA of a sample of the specimens not identifiable to species. The result is that one out of four of the analyzed specimens are moose, many more than would be expected on the basis of identifiable bone. This leads to a series of important questions, why is the moose bone less identifiable visually? Some and by no means all explanations for this could be 1) differential processing of moose and elk in such a way that moose is more heavily processed, thus its remains are not identifiable; or 2) moose were procured after the elk thus being above the elk in the burial process and more weathered and thus less identifiable. Whatever the reason, EhPv-126 is informative about the elk procurement system as well as its variation from other economic pursuits.

Rabbit

Each species of animal, both small and large, demands a unique method of procurement. Cottontail, snowshoe, and jackrabbits can provide a significant amount of food and, although they are relatively easy to obtain, each requires a very different procurement strategy. Whether or not communal rabbit drives prevailed in any part of the area is not known. However, the Green River Basin was apparently occupied by Shoshonean groups among whom rabbit trapping was common during Late Prehistoric and Protohistoric times and probably earlier. There is no reason to doubt that Shoshone rabbit drives on the same order as those in the Great Basin (Steward 1938) were carried out there also.

In fact, one bit of evidence supports this. One of us (Frison) visited a site that was being blown out of a sand dune in the Upper Green River Basin in the same general area and with likely cultural affiliations to the Eden-Farson site (Frison 1971b) of postulated Shoshonean origin. The site yielded only a few projectile points, tools, and flakes surrounding a small fire hearth, but associated with it were a large number (n=51) of jackrabbit tibiae. Many others had been exposed and were decomposed. Several were in the process of being made into bone beads and demonstrated evenly spaced, encircling cuts. It seems unlikely that the number of animals represented here could have been acquired during a single hunting effort by a single person. Jackrabbits are usually hidden in daylight hours and the easiest way to procure large numbers is some kind of cooperative effort using a rabbit net. The site is recent (at least Late Prehistoric) judging from the presence of small side-notched and tri-notched projectile points, but was unfortunately destroyed during pipeline construction.

Rabbits are common in archaeological assemblages of the Plains and Rockies. Even during the Paleoindian period, out of 13 taxa, rabbits rank third on the basis of maximum MNI, fourth on the basis of NISP, and fifth on the basis of presence/absence. Bighorn sheep, deer, bison, rodents, small animals, and birds rank higher in one or several of the rankings (Kornfeld and Larson 2008). Many of the sites discussed in this and previous chapters have the remains of rabbits, among them Allen, Vermillion Lakes, Hanson, Mummy Cave, Medicine Lodge Creek, Barton Gulch, Charlie Lake, and Blue Point, the last to be discussed in a bit more detail below. We name these sites not because the rabbit remains at them are necessarily abundant, but because they span the geographical, temporal, and elevational breadth of the Northwestern Plains and Rocky Mountains. Rabbits thus are not restricted in time and space, but rather appear to be used through time and throughout the region of our study and beyond.

The Blue Point site is in the Green River Basin, 9.5 km west of the Green River, 6.5 km north of the Blacks Fork River, and several hundred meters northwest of a playa lake. Blue Point Ridge is 2 km south of the site. The archaeological material was sealed in an eolian sand shadow deposit emplaced southeast of a low ridge forming the north edge of the playa.

Three cultural components were identified at Blue Point, with ages of 9540 ± 50, 8190 ± 50 to 8340 ± 420, and 7030 ± 210 to 7360 ± 90 BP, respectively, from oldest to youngest (Johnson and Pastor 2003). Component 1 yielded Cody complex Alberta and Scottsbluff projectile points; Components 2 and 3 yielded no chronologically diagnostic artifacts, but are interpreted as Late Paleoindian and Early Archaic.

According to Johnson and Pastor, the Alberta component was the richest of the three cultural assemblages, with eight projectile points, 10 stone tools, and 1628 pieces of debitage. The 363 faunal remains were dominated by jackrabbits with an NISP of 64. Deer, with an NISP of 31, rodent (NISP=13), and bison (NISP=12) are the next most common taxa. A fire hearth surrounded by a rich assemblage of tools forms an activity locus at the site, but other activity loci are also present. Component 2 also has a feature surrounded by fire-cracked rock and flakes. Although a smaller assemblage is associated with this component, a similar faunal pattern is present as in Component 1, with rabbit as the dominant and rodent as secondary taxa. However, bison is absent in Component 2 and only deer bone is present. Component 3 has the largest faunal assemblage with 681 specimens. As with Component 2, rabbit (both *Lepus* sp. and *Sylvilagus* sp.) dominates the assemblage followed by rodent-sized animals. Bison-, deer-, elk-, and pronghorn-sized bone are present in small quantities, but they were not identifiable to species.

The Blue Point site is not unique in its high relative numbers of small taxa such as rabbit and rodent. In the Green River Basin and much of the Wyoming Basin, mid to late Paleoindian sites with broad faunal and floral representation are common. Sites such as 48SW8842, Vegan, 48LN1185, 48UT3775, and Deep Hearth all date to the later portion of the Paleoindian period and all contain either evidence of use of a wide diversity of food resources or heavy processing of resources such as extraction of within-bone nutrients (Bruder and Rhodes 1992; McDonald 1993; McKern and Creasman 1991; Pool 2001; Reust et al. 2002). These sites are particularly informative of a range of Paleoindian adaptations, as such evidence is missing elsewhere. The many bison kill and processing sites we know over the Plains and Rocky Mountain areas provide very little information about economic activities other than bison procurement. The Green River Basin is one area where significant complementary economic processes have been preserved and investigated. The six sites mentioned above hold some of the most important evidence about mid to late Paleoindian lifeways. Together with Medicine Lodge Creek, numerous Bighorn Mountain rockshelters, and other sites throughout the Northwestern Plains and the Rockies, the Green River Basin sites are beginning to shape a more holistic image of Paleoindian lifeways and economic strategies, one more consistent with today's perspective on foraging peoples.

Small Mammals, Birds, Amphibians, Insects, Fish, and Shellfish

Small mammals, birds, amphibians, insects, fish, and shellfish often constitute a part of the recovered archaeological faunal assemblages, but they seldom receive detailed treatment and there has never been an intensive compilation and comparison of these data. There are perhaps two reasons for such lack of treatment. First, with few exceptions the remains of these small animals constitute a very small portion of the assemblage and are thus assumed to have contributed very little to prehistoric subsistence. Making this assumption, however, requires ignoring archaeological formation processes and taphonomic considerations. There are good reasons why even large quantities of remains of some of the animals considered here would be undetectable in the archaeological record. Second, many of these animals are considered to be intrusive or potentially intrusive into the archaeological deposit. Because rodents, insects, amphibians, as well as other taxa burrow, live, drag things, and die in their dens below ground they are viewed as the natural background to a cultural foreground. To identify intrusive rodents, a problem in many Great Basin caves, Thomas (1971) long ago proposed an analytical method. We are not aware of the application of this method to any assemblages in our region. However, to question the cultural origin of the taxa discussed here while not questioning the animals discussed in the previous part of this chapter and in Chapter 4 is inconsistent with the nature of the archaeological record. Geologic processes are nothing but giant sediment traps. Everything that gets deposited on the earth's surface, or immediately below it, is trapped in a condition of sedimentation and erosion. Cultural material is only part of the buried material—it is not any more likely that a bison bone gets trapped than a mouse skeleton. Yet the cultural association of the former is virtually never questioned, while the latter is more often than not dismissed as intrusive or otherwise noncultural. In the section below we review some of the smaller animals recovered from archaeological sites. We emphasize a few cases where cultural association is confirmed, but only as examples of numerous other cases of potential or even probable prehistoric use of such taxa.

The many species of rodents in the Plains and Rocky Mountains are perhaps the most common taxa of the smaller animals found in archaeological assemblages considered here. Rodents vary in size from voles to beavers, but here we are largely concerned with the smaller taxa, up to about one kilogram in size or about the size of prairie dogs. Rodent remains, especially porcupine, beaver, and marmot, are common in Plains Indian sites. Prairie dogs, ground squirrels, and muskrats are less frequently found. Wood rats, and to a lesser extent mice, may have been significant as food; over 600 MNI of both species, along with many others, were recovered in a Late Paleoindian food refuse midden at the Medicine Lodge Creek site in northern Wyoming discussed further below (Walker 1988, 2007). Porcupines probably require the least in the way of hunting techniques of any animal. The rewards, at least in terms of protein if not flavor, may be the greatest of any hunting pursuit with regard to expenditure of effort. The animal is clumsy, slow, and usually easy to locate. The only thing one needs to pursue and kill a porcupine is a club or a rock and the good sense to stay far enough away from the animal's tail. The beaver is quite different, requiring some sort of trap or snare and quite a bit of skill to procure. Wood rats and muskrats are easily taken provided the proper techniques are known. The Great Basin Shoshonean was quite knowledgeable about wood rat trapping, but someone unfamiliar with the ways of wood rats would have to experiment for a long time before a full belly would be the reward for efforts at wood rat trapping. Many people have lived for years in areas where wood rats are common and have never seen one because the animals tend to keep out of site and are largely nocturnal in their habits.

Simple snares could be used to take wood rats. A dry rockshelter along the Green River in southwest Wyoming in an area where wood rats abound produced a cache of over a hundred snares that were probably used for this purpose (Figure 5.38). An identical snare was recovered in a dry cave further north in the Wyoming Basin. This kind of simple snare can be used on other small animals as well as wood rats. Whether the wood rats at Medicine Lodge Creek site were procured with these kinds of traps, deadfalls, or by other means is unknown. What is clear is that over 3500 bones represent over 600 animals, many of them wood rats, but including gophers, deer mice, and voles, and that these animals were consumed 9500 years ago. A total of over 41 species are associated with this occupation and, on the basis of *Neotoma*, Walker (2007) estimates August as the time of death. This rodent midden is associated with several features, fire hearths, and stone tools.

Another case of the use of rodents comes from site 48LN787 at the southern end of the Wyoming Range at an elevation of 2160 m. A nearby ridge forms the divide between the Colorado River drainage and the Great Basin. The site is in a cold sagebrush/grassland about 4 km from the Hams Fork River, the nearest location of riparian vegetation. The site has been radiocarbon dated between 1100 and 1380 BP and has Shoshone-style tri-notched projectile points.

Seven features, five of which were excavated, were found in a relatively small excavation area of 3 x 8 m and were divided into two types. Type 1 features were deeper, contained nearly all of the bone, and most of the fire-cracked rock associated with them were within the features. Type 2 features were shallow, contained virtually no bone, and most of the fire-cracked rock was found either on top of them or surrounding them. These likely represent different kinds of processing

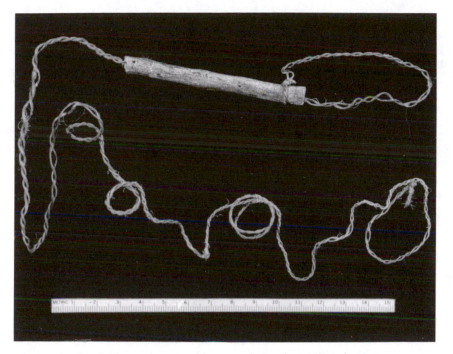

Figure 5.38   Small animal snare recovered in a cave in southwest Wyoming.

activities: Type 2 features appear to be cleanout from hearths, while Type 1 features may have been hearths or boiling pits. Sandstone slabs in the vicinity of the features may represent remnants of a lodge or lean-to.

The Type 1 facilities produced approximately 2000 bone specimens representing at least 51 individual animals, but only one with 700 specimens has been fully analyzed. Both feature types yielded evidence of nine species: deer, pronghorn, jackrabbit, weasel, sagebrush vole, least chipmunk, prairie dog, Richardson's ground squirrel, and sage grouse. A total of 31 individual animals are in the fully analyzed feature; however, four species represent 26 individuals—sagebrush vole, least chipmunk, prairie dog, and ground squirrel (Kornfeld and Chomko 1983). The ground squirrel is dominant; its remains comprise 50% of all the bone and 95% of all the identifiable bone. Twenty-one ground squirrels were processed at this site. A taphonomic analysis of the skeletal elements indicates a pattern of survival where crania and upper leg bones are the most represented; scapula, innominate, lower leg bones, and ribs are poorly represented; and axial skeleton and digits are absent. On the basis of experimental butchering of two squirrels, the investigators suggest processing as the most likely cause of this pattern, where the four legs and head were detached with most of the meat remaining on them, while the digits and the axial skeleton are discarded. These parts can then be placed in a boiling pot to produce a stew. Although this scenario is in need of further testing and comparison, the process presents an alternative to the theory of grinding small mammals on metates proposed by others.

Birds appear in archaeological sites probably in larger numbers than the recovered remains indicate because their bones have not survived as well as the bones of large animals. The sage grouse thrives best in the treeless sagebrush-covered areas where they may be found in large bunches at certain times of the year. They are easy to hunt with weaponry such as a bow and arrow. Blue grouse are also present in large numbers, but favor higher elevations and timber patches. A heavy stick to throw at birds on the ground or a noose on the end of a long pole to slip over the head of a bird roosting in a tree can usually provide a meal.

Birds are present in the Medicine Lodge Creek rodent assemblage discussed above. Fenner (2007) identified six avian species, including duck, grouse, jay, owl, and robin. On the basis of robin migration behavior, Fenner concludes that Walker's assessment of time of year of the occupation of this component is consistent with the bird data. As with the rodents from this level, the bird assemblage lacks axial elements, while leg elements are abundant and many bones are burned. This, however, is at odds with the usual element representation of overabundance of wing bones and for now its meaning remains unresolved, except to say that the Medicine Lodge Creek population apparently processed their birds differently.

Insects are rare occurrences, but Leigh Cave in the Bighorn Mountains has a rich Middle Plains Archaic deposit of Mormon crickets (Frison and Huseas 1968). Not unlike grasshoppers, Mormon crickets can provide a rich source of protein. The issue, however, is how to collect them so as not to use more energy than is returned from the harvest. The answer in the area of the Great Salt Lake has been to collect grasshoppers when they are available in mass quantities washed up on the shores of the lake (Madsen and Kirkman 1988; Madsen and Schmitt 1998). Although this may be when grasshopper collecting is most energy efficient, grasshoppers were collected in drives across the Great Basin as well (Steward 1938). The people of Leigh Cave and other Plains and Rocky Mountain localities could have collected their Mormon crickets either in drives or perhaps in a mass die-off that occurred in a setting we are not aware of. What we are sure of is that the remains of Mormon crickets survived at Leigh Cave, but they probably were used at other localities where these fragile remains did not survive the ravages of time.

We have not yet addressed fish, shellfish, and amphibians. All occur at archaeological sites on rare occasions, but how this may correspond to their significance to prehistoric diets remains to be seen (Kornfeld et al. 1995; Lippincott 2000). Although much use of mussels seems to be for decorative purposes, at least some archaeological remains suggest their recovery in subsistence contexts. It is clear that prehistoric Plains and Rocky Mountain peoples used a broad array of resources and were intimately familiar with a wide range of resources. How important such resources were in their daily lives remains to be investigated.

Conclusions

Over the past several decades perhaps one of the most significant additions to Northwestern Plains and Rocky Mountain prehistory has been some of the sites discussed in this chapter. Although several of the sites, such as Dead Indian Creek and Eden-Farson, were in the first and second editions of this book, they were unique—outliers in the sea of bison kills—and therefore difficult to use in interpreting the broad patterns of prehistory. The deer and pronghorn procurement evidence was buttressed by ethnographic accounts of Shoshone, Sheepeater, and other foragers' pronghorn drives, antelope traps, and bighorn sheep traps in North America that provide evidence that these animals were taken en mass. However, evidence of non-bison bone beds is still just too small to be meaningful.

Recently the situation has been changed by the discovery of new sites as well as reanalysis and reinvestigations of material recovered previously but not recognized as significant deposits or as having implications for understanding prehistory (Figure 5.39). Another significant addition has been the recognition

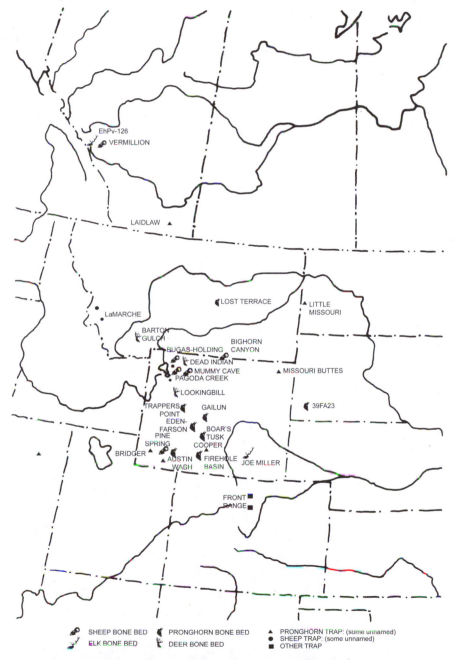

Figure 5.39   Selected sheep, deer, pronghorn, and elk bone beds and traps. All sites are cited in Figures 2.20, 2.51, 2.55, 2.63, 2.69, or in the text, except Missouri Buttes Antelope Trap (unpublished).

and emphasis placed on faunal remains at non–bone bed sites. These sites have yielded small quantities of a wide variety of fauna and have added to the overall understanding of the cultural ecology of prehistoric peoples of the Northwestern Plains and Rocky Mountains. Sites such as Blue Point in southwest Wyoming, with a faunal assemblage of jackrabbit and deer and a few rodent and bison bone and which dates to as early as the Cody period, certainly provide a broader and complementary perspective on Paleoindian subsistence strategies. Such strategies have been hinted at on the basis of data discovered at Mummy Cave, Medicine Lodge Creek, various rockshelters in the Bighorn Mountains, and the Bighorn Canyon caves among others, but now the universality of this pattern is becoming clearer and data are accumulating that provide for a more holistic image of prehistoric subsistence. The deer bone bed at Dead Indian Creek site and the 212 pronghorn at Eden-Farson are no longer unique, no longer outliers, but are rather parts of the pattern of subsistence pursuits dating to the earliest occupation of North America. Because of these recent additions to the archaeological record, we now have a more robust picture of the broad patterns of prehistory than we did 20 years ago. New discoveries, both in the field and lab, new methods, and new theories are all contributing to and providing the synergy for expanding our knowledge base of prehistoric subsistence on the Northwestern Plains and adjacent Rocky Mountains.

6

Prehistoric Lifeways and Resources on the Plains and in the Rocky Mountains

Introduction

The title of the earlier editions of this book would imply that hunting overshadowed any other means of subsistence known and practiced by the prehistoric inhabitants of the Northwestern Plains and the Rocky Mountains. However, enough data now exist to argue that this has not always been the case. Two issues arise with this switch in emphasis. One is where to make the division between hunting and gathering, since hunters did a lot of gathering and gatherers did a lot of hunting. Another issue is how to interpret a database that is biased because the evidence of hunting is relatively easy to see archaeologically, while differential preservation and other factors make the evidence of gathering more difficult to document from the same record. Since the second edition of this volume, we have come to realize that prehistoric people of the Rocky Mountains and Northwestern Plains ran the gamut from a heavy reliance on large and medium mammals when stores of meat were needed for survival through lean times or when the economic system demanded it to a heavy emphasis on gathered plants, small animals, and other creatures (similar to some of their Great Basin relatives). At many times, the seasonal differences in resource availability dictated which was emphasized the most. At other times, the choice was economic or cultural.

Many new techniques, methods, and collaborations mean that we understand much more about hunter-gatherer human existence than we did in 1991. We are more secure in the determination of seasonality from animal remains and are beginning to have the means by which to infer seasonality from plants and a host of other resources. Many of the methods discussed in previous chapters were new when the 1991 volume was published and are now employed commonly by archaeologists; other methods, such as DNA, were on the horizon but not yet realized. Higher-resolution excavation methods and changes in archaeological understanding of what the record is have released us from assuming that all archaeological sites are cultural creations, so that now we can talk confidently about the spatial patterning of human activities while ruling out those patterns brought about naturally.

This chapter presents some of our understanding of prehistoric lifeways, in particular diet, and the some of the resources that were critical for survival. Ethnographic analogy, diet breadth models, and vegetation surveys present a picture of how and which edible resources could be used by prehistoric residents. Archaeological features such as fire pits are common reminders of food processing, and much rarer, but equally important food caches form means of survival found in the archaeological record. Finally, this chapter considers stone tool resources, another significant part of human existence on the plains and in the mountains.

ETHNOGRAPHIC ANALOGY, TOOLS, AND FIRE PITS

The Gosiute and several other Basin-Plateau groups lived at a "bare subsistence level" (Steward 1938:1) where "seeds were the most important foods" (Steward 1938:52), at least from time to time. However, hunting was important also: "Game provided not only essential foods but skins for clothing and materials for certain implements" (Steward 1938:231). In setting up a gradational scale with hunters on one end and gatherers on the other, the Gosiute can be placed at one end as gatherers. However, the Gosiute were still creditable hunters; they were hunting pronghorn, deer, mountain sheep, and in some localities, even an occasional bison. Pronghorn were taken communally in traps and, although of less importance, mule deer were sometimes taken in communal efforts in the northern part of the Great Basin by constructing "V-wings between which was a hurdle with a pit beyond. The deer's propensity to jump carried him [sic] over the hurdle into the concealed pit. In a few localities a shaman charmed deer for these drives" (Steward 1938:36). Mountain sheep "though formerly fairly abundant … were taken with great difficulty" (Steward 1938:37). However, during the rut, rams could be taken by concealed hunters thumping logs to mimic the clashing of heads in dueling contests. Jackrabbit drives using nets were an important economic activity in providing food and also hides for fur blankets.

Archaeologically, the epitome of true hunting groups on the Northwestern Plains would have been the Besant bison hunters with their large bison-corral procurement sites and religious structures and, later on, the prehorse Crow with their large communal bison jumps. Both groups were utilizing these procurement complexes in order to obtain surplus meat for winter storage and potentially exchange. There is little doubt that even these sophisticated bison hunters were attracted to seasonal plant resources such as berry patches, sego lily bulbs, yucca pods, and greens after a long winter subsisting almost entirely on some form of meat. All Rocky Mountain and Northwestern Plains prehistoric groups will fit somewhere on this scale between the Gosiute hunter and gatherer and the Crow bison hunter.

The manifestations of prepared fire pits (roasting, baking, and boiling pits) consist of careful excavations of many shapes and sizes, usually in clay and/or sandy

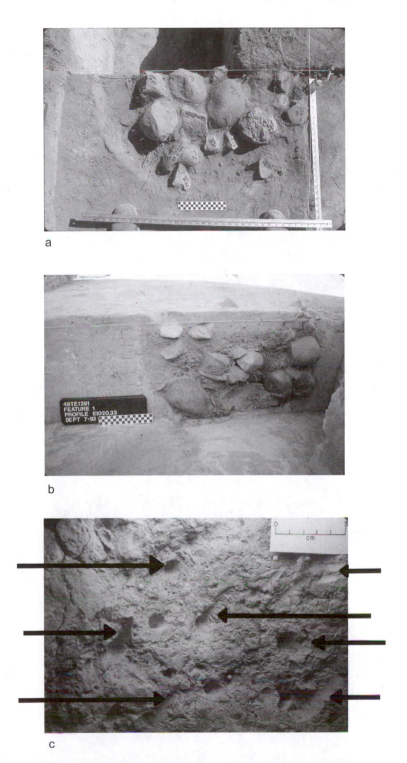

Figure 6.1 Stone-filled baking pit and evidence of digging equipment from the Henn site, Jackson Hole, Wyoming: overhead view (a), cross section (b), and close-up of interior of the pit showing impressions from digging sticks used to excavate the pit (selected impressions shown by arrows).

deposits (Figure 6.1). They contain evidence of sustained high heat, judging from thick oxidation rings around their perimeters in places where the clay contained sufficient amounts of iron particles. They are believed to have been used mainly for the preparation of plant foods. Part of this interpretation comes from the association in many sites of grinding materials (manos and metates) along with the fire pits (Figure 2.56). Occasionally, there are bones of both large and small animals associated in such a way as to suggest cooking of meat as well as plant food. One example consists of pits of different kinds associated with bison procurement sites that are probably designed for heating stone for boiling (Figure 6.2). Another kind of pit was apparently designed for cooking bison parts and has also been found in the vicinity of bison kills such as the ones at the butchering and processing area at the Wardell site in western Wyoming (Figure 6.3).

This fire pit and grinding tool complex is quite well represented on the Northwestern Plains and Rocky Mountains south of 45° north latitude or the Montana–Wyoming boundary, but north of this it begins to disappear rapidly, so that 100 km farther north it has nearly gone. This is interpreted as a loss of the Archaic lifeways to the north and a greater reliance on bison hunting. To the south it is thought to indicate a true Archaic lifeway. One major area of Archaic lifeways was the Wyoming or Green River Basin (Figure 1.1), which is adjacent to, and has good access to and from, the Great Basin. It was suggested several decades ago that this accident of geography and topography might have resulted in an influx of people to the north from the Great Basin that were the founders of the plant-gathering economy (Mulloy 1958:210). There is evidence of Great Basin contacts throughout the Archaic and Late Prehistoric times, according to investigators now working in the Wyoming Basin. Also grinding tools were

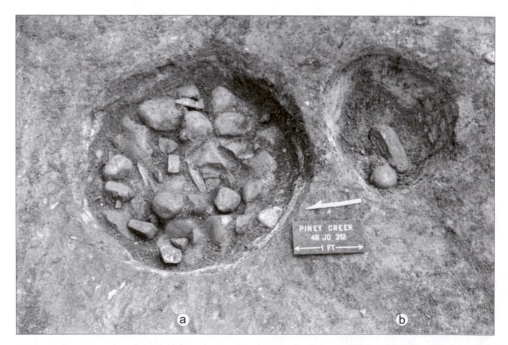

Figure 6.2 Stone-heating pit (a) and associated stone-boiling pit (b) at the Piney Creek Buffalo Jump bison processing area.

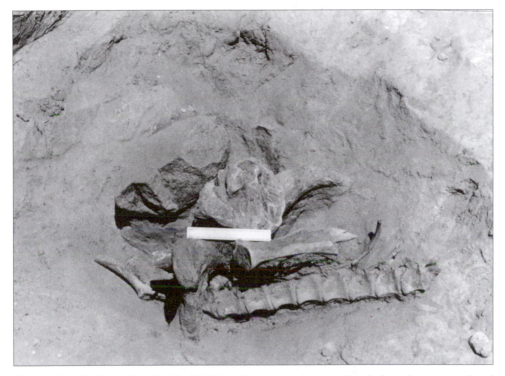

Figure 6.3 Cooking pit at the Wardell Bison Trap processing area that had not been opened and still contained the remains of bison parts.

present in the foothill/mountain areas in Late Paleoindian times, continuing on to Protohistoric times.

Simple grinding tools were recovered in late Foothill/Mountains Paleoindian Pryor Stemmed sites in Bighorn Canyon (Husted 1969) and in the same cultural complex at the Medicine Lodge Creek site (Frison 1976a). Better-developed grinding tools were recovered at an elevation of nearly 2621 m in a Late Paleoindian context in the southern Absaroka mountains at the Lookingbill site (Frison 1983b; Kornfeld et al. 2001). They were found also in the poorly understood Late Paleoindian Lusk complex at the Betty Greene site in eastern Wyoming (Greene 1967).

The presence of grinding stones at the Lookingbill site at 8600 feet (2621 m) strongly suggests plant gathering. One mano from the Early Plains Archaic levels at the site yielded cattail root starch (*Typha* spp.). Cattail roots were used as food and sometimes ground into meal. Arrowleaf balsamroot (*Balsamorhiza sagittata)* is abundant today on the Lookingbill site and was an important source of food and medicine (Moerman 1998). Another possibility would be limber pine nuts (*Pinus flexilis*) and whitebark pine nuts (*Pinus albicaulis),* which are plentiful enough in the site area so that over the past decade large numbers of producing trees (Figure 6.4) could be found within a short distance of the site, even though in this same period very few trees have produced more than a single crop. One of us (Frison) has noted a strong correlation between limber pine stands and Middle and Late Plains Archaic grinding stones. The main point to be made is that grinding tools were well in place by Late Paleoindian times in the higher altitudes.

Figure 6.4 Limber pines heavily loaded with cones in late August in the southern Absaroka Mountains, Wyoming.

The Wyoming Basin, Wind River Basin, and the Bighorn Basin all demonstrate this strong orientation toward Archaic plant gathering, but perhaps it is best demonstrated in the last of these. The Bighorn Basin lies in the rain shadow of the Absarokas to the west and, consequently, yearly precipitation in the interior basin is low. At least two weather stations report less than 18 cm/year, and this is reflected in sparse grass cover. There is little if any evidence of communal bison procurement in the basin in post-Paleoindian times and it is doubtful that the carrying capacity of the basin would have supported enough animals to make communal hunting profitable. On the other hand, there is ample evidence of Archaic occupations. Since the basin is nearly surrounded by mountain ranges, except for a corridor connecting to the true plains to the north, there is a large circling band of foothills and numerous intermittent and permanent stream valleys that extend well into the mountain slopes. These conditions, combined with certain geological formations that favor cave and rockshelter formation, resulted in an ideal situation for Archaic lifeways. Many of these rockshelters contain Archaic occupations and some are dry enough to have preserved perishable materials, which adds much to the interpretive value of the sites.

All three of these major basins have witnessed intense archaeological investigations, but we are more familiar with the Bighorn Basin. Several years of investigations associated with a major research project (The Medicine Lodge Creek Project) funded by the National Science Foundation resulted in major excavations at the deep, stratified Medicine Lodge Creek site, along with a number of peripheral sites (Frison and Walker 2007; Larson 1990, 1992). Data from long-term investigations of the rockshelters on the western slope of the Paintrock Canyon and in the Black Mountain region of the western foothills of the Bighorns and the Bighorn

Basin are providing further information (e.g., Finley 2008; Kornfeld 2007b; Larson 2007). There are data from Mummy Cave (Husted and Edgar 2002) and the investigations in Bighorn Canyon on the north end of the basin on both sides of the Montana–Wyoming border (Husted 1969). Data were also gathered from the Pryor Mountains just across the Bighorn River in Montana (Loendorf et al. 1981).

Animal Resources

Within the Bighorn Basin, the Horner site (Frison and Todd 1987) has provided the only known evidence of large-scale bison procurement during the Paleoindian period. There is at least one small bison jump in the western Bighorn Basin during Archaic and Late Prehistoric times. Otherwise bison occur only occasionally in archaeological sites, although there is an increase from Late Archaic times until they disappeared in the late nineteenth century. Bison do not appear until the Late Prehistoric period levels at Mummy Cave. This is not surprising considering the site location in a river valley far back into the Absaroka Mountains. Caves straddling the Wyoming–Montana line in Bighorn Canyon produced only token numbers of bison bone (Husted 1969). The Medicine Lodge Creek site (Frison and Wilson 1975) yielded very little evidence of bison until historic times. The Laddie Creek site in the foothills of the Bighorn Mountains (6800 feet, 2972 m) contains small numbers of bison in the Late Archaic and Late Prehistoric levels. At the higher elevations, the faunal evidence includes only an occasional bison during the entire Holocene.

Mule deer (*Odocoileus hemionus*) and mountain sheep (*Ovis canadensis*) dominate the faunal remains; pronghorn (*Antilocapra americana*) are surprisingly few until the Late Archaic and Late Prehistoric periods. Nearly every cultural level at Mummy Cave produced some mountain sheep remains, and mule deer were a distant second. Deer outnumbered mountain sheep at Medicine Lodge Creek, but at the higher elevations in sites in more open, grassy country, mountain sheep and deer are about equal in numbers until the Late Archaic, when bison become most common. The implications of this are that mule deer, as well as mountain sheep, were quite well adapted to rough country, and that the latter, although they liked to be close to rough country in order to escape predators, were strongly attached to having open, grassy country nearby for grazing. A single elk (*Cervus canadensis*) was recorded at Medicine Lodge Creek in a cultural level dating to about 8500 years ago. As already mentioned, elk are rare in sites until into the Late Prehistoric period, at which time they also become common subjects in rock art depictions. The discovery of an elk bone bed dating to the Late Archaic at the Joe Miller site suggests that such discoveries may alter our perspective on elk in prehistory.

The Sheep Mountain sheep net (Frison et al. 1986) is a strong indicator of systematic procurement of that species in Late Paleoindian times, and there is no reason to doubt a continuation of netting or some other kind of mountain sheep procurement terminating with the large traps described earlier for the Protohistoric period. For example, a significant increase of mountain sheep in cultural levels in Mummy Cave at about 4400 and 1200 years BP could indicate improved trapping methods, an increase in numbers of sheep, or both. The Laidlaw antelope (pronghorn) trap in Alberta (Brumley 1984) and the Trappers Point site in Wyoming (Miller and Sanders 2000) extend large-scale pronghorn procurement at least into the Archaic time periods. The Early Archaic deer bone bed at the Lookingbill site (Kornfeld, Larson, Rapson, and Frison 2001) also indicates there is much to learn about the procurement of medium-sized mammals within the Rocky Mountains.

Smaller mammals, especially rodents and lagomorphs, were important as food, if our evidence from Medicine Lodge Creek is an indicator. Wood rats (*Neotoma cinerea*) seem to have been of greatest significance, although cottontail rabbits (*Sylvilagus* sp.) and jackrabbits (*Lepus* sp.) may have been a close second. All three species are found from low to higher elevations. Carnivores, including bobcat (*Lynx rufus*), badger (*Taxidea taxus*), black bear (*Ursus americanus*), and coyote (*Canis latrans*), appear occasionally in archaeological sites; their osteological remains in some cases appear to have been treated in much the same manner as those of any herbivore, suggesting their use as food. The rather unusual preservation of large numbers of fish remains in two Late Paleoindian levels at Medicine Lodge Creek indicates their use as food. However, it is difficult to make any reliable assessment of their contribution to the total food supply on the basis of present evidence. Included were either lake chub or flathead chub (*Covesius plumbeus* or *Hybopsis gracilis*), sucker (*Catostomus* sp.), and either mountain whitefish or cutthroat trout (*Prosopium williamsoni* or *Salmo clarki*).

Caution is necessary in relating present behavior and distribution of animal species to the prehistoric periods. Introduction of domestic animals, control of predators, fencing, loss and change of habitats, controlled seasonal hunting, parasites and disease introduced from domestic animals, and artificial feeding, along with many other factors, have significantly altered the habits of most larger game animals. Some, such as the deer and pronghorn, have managed to adapt surprisingly well. Others, such as the elk and mountain sheep, have not fared as well.

PLANT RESOURCES

The Bighorn Basin contains six major vegetation zones (Porter 1962): (1) desert-basin, (2) grassland, (3) foothill-scrub, (4) timbered mountain slope, (5) alpine, and (6) stream bank communities. At present only one major attempt has been made to study the plant potential of the basin as a human subsistence base and this was in conjunction with the Medicine Lodge Creek Project (Galvan 2007).

The Medicine Lodge Creek site is large and complex. It spans a period of 10,000 years of continuous use by many human groups. The actual area of site use through time shifted and changed in size as the lateral movements of a permanent and an intermittent stream that came together at the site varied. These conditions resulted in a good share of the site evidence being moved out of context, but fortunately much is still in place. In addition to lateral stream movements, rockfalls at different times, some of which were quite large and covered large areas, dictated the locations of camp areas. The site is located at a transition between the desert-basin, grassland, and foothill-scrub zones and has the added advantages in terms of food resources of a stream bank plant community. Elevation increases rapidly to the east toward the western slopes of the Bighorn Mountains. The diversity of both plant and animal resources within a zone of human exploitation may have been instrumental in determining the popularity of the Medicine Lodge Creek site through time.

An east–west botanical transect of 12.8 km was made with Medicine Lodge Creek at the center (Figure 6.5). It was felt that this transect would cross the greatest number of vegetation zones within a possible radius of exploitation by plant gatherers staying at the site. The transect covered elevations from 1413 m on the west to 2073 m on the east. The investigator recognized five distinct vegetational situations in the transect range (Galvan 2007). The zones included the four already mentioned plus the disturbed area of the site itself and an area of saline soil dominated by saltbush (*Atriplex* sp.) and greasewood (*Sarcobatus* sp.). Since the site area disturbance is recent it can be regarded as insignificant. A total of 98 plant species were identified in the transect sample, and at least 37 were of some potential as sources of human food.

According to the investigator, three general groups of foods can be proposed based on both kind and seasonal availability: (1) a spring and early summer group that includes greens and a number of roots and bulbs, (2) a late summer/early fall group of ripening fruits and seeds, and (3) fruits and seeds that remain on the plants during at least part of the winter. The first group includes tender young stems and leaves of plants such as arrowleaf balsamroot (*Balsamorhiza sagittata*), bee plant (*Cleome* spp.), biscuitroot (*Lomatium)* and chenopods (*Chenopodium* spp.), roots of the bitterroot (*Lewisia rediviva*), bulbs of the sego lily (*Calochortus nuttallii*), and wild onion (*Allium* sp.) (Figure 6.6). The second group includes fruits of the chokecherry (*Prunus virginiana*), buffalo berry (*Shepherdia argentea*), and gooseberry (*Ribes inerme*), and seeds of yucca (*Yucca glauca*), Indian rice grass (*Oryzopsis hymenoides*), wild rye (*Elymus canadensis*), limber pine (*Pinus flexilis*) and whitebark pine *(Pinus albicaulis)*, to mention a few of the more important (Figure 6.7). Saltbush (*Atriplex canescens*) and amaranths (*Amaranthus* spp.) are examples of plants whose leaves can be eaten in the spring and whose edible seeds are available later on in the summer. The third group includes fruits of wild roses (*Rosa* spp.), buffalo berries, and seeds of the saltbush (*Atriplex canescens*). A complete documentation of the plant food resources would expand the list considerably (Figure 6.8).

The fruits are generally confined to stream banks, areas close to springs, and the north slopes of canyons. Grasses are most prolific in the grassland-sagebrush zone but are found also in the foothill-scrub zone. Greens grow best along stream banks and in other areas of abundant moisture, although the arrowroot demonstrates the most prolific growth on steep talus north slopes from low to middle elevations. Saltbushes favor saline soils of the desert-basin area. Root and bulb plants generally favor light, sandy soils from low to high elevations. Limber pines grow best in the rough, deeply dissected sandstone canyons from about 1900 to 2500 m elevation, while whitebark grows in the higher elevations.

Many of the plants mentioned grow at different elevations, so that at a given time a particular species may be mature at one elevation but still growing at a higher elevation. Many plants (especially tender shoots and greens) are desirable as food only for short periods of time. With the distribution of resources at various elevations, the human group merely had to move short distances to prolong the period of availability. For example, Leigh Cave (Frison and Huseas 1968), a small rockshelter site with dry deposits of the Early and Middle Plains Archaic periods at an elevation of 1700 m, produced evidence of intensive use of wild onion (*Allium* sp.). The floor of the shelter was covered with a hard-packed layer of outside coverings of wild onion bulbs up to 2 cm thick in places. Preparation methods

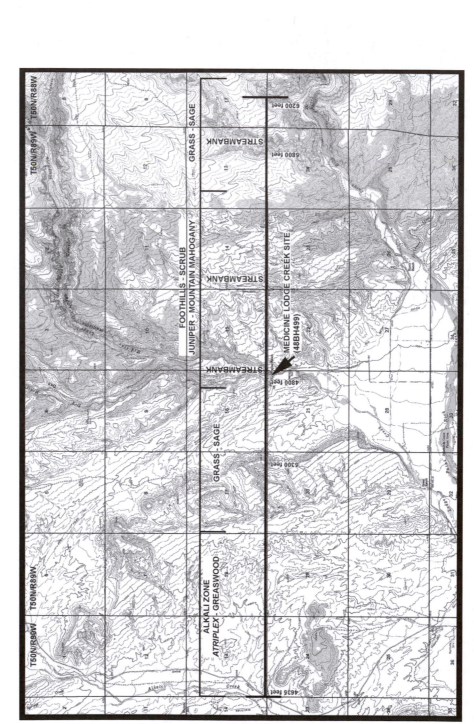

Figure 6.5 An east-west botanical transect for ethnographically and archeologically documented floral resources. The transect is centered on the Medicine Lodge Creek site. Major areas of vegetational zonation are indicated.

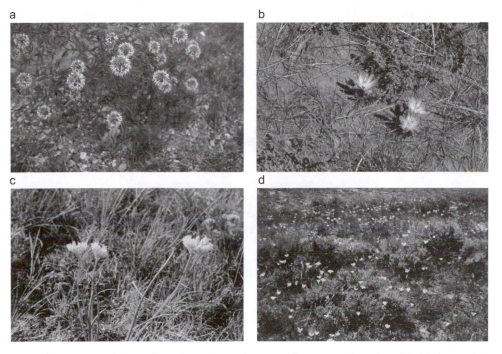

Figure 6.6   Selected plants from the spring and summer plant group: bee plant (a), bitterroot (b), wild onion (c), and sego lily (d). (From Galvan 2007.)

Figure 6.7   Selected plants from the late summer/early fall group: chokecherry (a), yucca (b), Indian rice grass (c), and wild rye (d). (From Galvan 2007.)

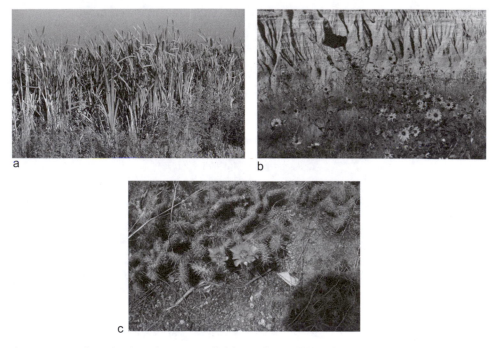

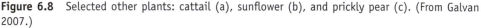

Figure 6.8   Selected other plants: cattail (a), sunflower (b), and prickly pear (c). (From Galvan 2007.)

are not known, but roasting pits were present. At least nine other plants probably utilized as food were represented, including buffalo berry, prickly pear (*Opuntia polyacantha*), chokecherry, juniper (*Juniperus* sp.), limber pine, thistle (*Cirsium* sp.), wild rose (*Rosa woodsii*), wild rye, and seeds, pods, and leaves of yucca. One of the roasting pits and its immediate area was littered with parts of several hundred roasted Mormon crickets (*Anabrus simplex*). Insects may have been of minor value but were still good sources of protein. Mormon crickets were found also in a Protohistoric Shoshonean campsite along with several other smaller insects (Frison 1971b).

The larger herbivores such as deer, mountain sheep, and bison that live in close proximity to mountain ranges are able to follow patterns of transhumance in response to plant resources. There is an added impetus to these movements, because the lower elevations may have an adequate food supply during the hot summer, but the grass is tenderer and conditions in general are more pleasant at the higher elevations. Those same species of animals that live away from the mountains are usually tied to—and well adapted to—patterns of nontranshumance. But in the Bighorn Basin a good share at least of the large herbivore population could and did move from summer to winter feeding areas. Their movements would have also affected the movements of human groups dependent to some extent on them for part of their food.

Diet Breadth on the Plains and in the Rockies

Moving out of the Bighorn Basin into what is termed the western Black Hills uplift, one of us (Kornfeld) created a diet breadth model based on several proposed plant procurement systems in the area (Figure 6.9; Kornfeld 2003). Many of the resources present in the Bighorn region are also available to populations of the Black Hills; in fact, a total of about 500 edible plants are available, but some occur in quantities not economically feasible to exploit. Of these 25 were used in modeling five plant procurement systems: seeds, roots, greens, fruits, and other.

Seeds

Seed procurement is the most complex system in terms of its organization and in terms of the number of component subsystems (e.g., Steward 1938; Yanovsky 1936). Various resources including saltbush, goosefoot, bulrush, wild rye, cattail pollen, and others require different procurement and processing techniques and are constrained by different scheduling concerns. Like large animal procurement,

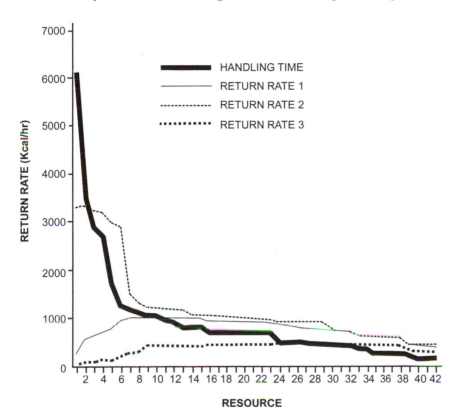

Figure 6.9   Diet breadth model for a portion of the Northwestern Plains (from Kornfeld 2003): 1. cattail pollen, 2. deer, 3. yucca, 4. pronghorn, 5. big horn sheep, 6. prairie dog, 7. saltbush (shadscale), 8. goosefoot (pigweed), 9. bulrush (tule seed), 10. marmot, 11. bison, 12. muskrat, 13. plums (and cherries), 14. wild rye (squagrass), 15. porcupine, 16. jackrabbit, 17. snowberry (wolfberry), 18. wild rose, 19. sarvice berry, 20. juniper, 21. prickly pear, 22. currant (goose-berry), 23. sumac, 24. sunflower (several varieties), 25. 13-lined ground squirrel, 26. plains pocket gopher, 27. beaver, 28. bushy-tailed wood rat, 29. cottontail, 30. junegrass, 31. wheat-grass, 32. ground squirrel, 33. ponderosa pine, 34. Indian rice grass, 35. muhli, 36. dropseed (alkali sakatoon), 37. northern pocket gopher, 38. foxtail barley, 39. cattail roots, 40. sago lily, 41. wild onion, 42. microtus (and other small mammals).

storage or immediate consumption are important considerations, but precise timing is often crucial because of competition from other consumers as well as the resource's own dispersal mechanisms. Some species can be gathered from the ground, but such gathering depends on other competing consumers and may result in altered processing techniques. The abundance of some species, like limber pine in the Rocky Mountain coniferous forest, may allow for band-level aggregations as well as fairly large-scale storage (although handling time suggests that limber pine would only be used in the broadest diets), while other species are much less clustered and are easier to exploit under conditions of extreme fission (nuclear-family level). The seed procurement system operates in the summer and fall, with late summer/early fall being the most productive time. At the least, the implements necessary for the seed procurement system include carrying equipment (baskets), ground stone (or mortar and pestle; see Figure 2.56), and heat (fire). Timing of procurement is critical; limber pine cones open rapidly and a blanket or hide spread on the ground beneath the tree is more efficient than picking up seeds after they fall to the ground.

Roots

Tubers are not predicted in any of the optimal diets modeled by Kornfeld (2003), but are known from direct evidence (e.g., Frison and Huseas 1968; Scott-Cummings 1995) and are inferred from indirect evidence (large, stone-filled earth ovens, e.g., Francis 2000; Mulloy 1954a; Smith and McNees 1999) to have been used prehistorically. Thus, wild onion, which is relatively abundant in selected portions of the landscape, and other species are expected to be a part of a tuber procurement system. The tuber procurement system should also be complex because it includes a number of species that require different gathering and processing strategies (Aaberg 1983; Ewers 1958:86). In addition, processing strategies should vary depending on the nature of consumption. For example, some tubers can be processed for flour (ground meal), roasted, or boiled (Aaberg 1983). The flour can, furthermore, be either consumed immediately or stored. Midspring to summer is the best time to procure tubers. We expect at least the following tubers and roots to have been procured: wild onion, sego lily, prairie potato, arrowleaf balsamroot, bitterroot, biscuit root, and yampa.

The tools required for tuber procurement included digging stick (see Figure 2.68), knife (flake), ground stone (if tubers are dried and made into paste; see Figure 2.56), carrying equipment (e.g., baskets), and baking ovens. Digging sticks and baskets should be used where the food is gotten, but these artifacts are unlikely to leave any traces behind. An exception might be a broken digging stick, in which case a knife (flake) would be used to repair a stick on the spot. The flake could be all that is preserved for the archaeologist. Ground stone could be located at a camp (even a short-term camp) where baking ovens would indicate food preparation.

Greens

This system includes the collection and consumption of green plant parts, namely stems and leaves (Steward 1938:19). Greens contain a variety of vitamins, minerals, and other nutrients. Most species of grasses, some leaves, and some flowers (e.g., yucca) are included in this system. Different types of preparation (e.g., no preparation, boiling, boiling with meats or other foodstuffs) can substantially alter the nutrient values of component foods (Konlande and Robson 1972; Robson 1975). Nutritional values can be either enhanced or reduced by the preparation process. Although different species are included, procurement of greens is likely not very complex, since gathering and processing strategies are similar. While not a major energy source, greens are important for a variety of essential nutrients. They are available from midspring to midfall and generally are not storable. Tools for procurement and processing include carrying equipment (baskets), boiling containers (skin pouch, pottery, stone vessels), and fire.

Fruits

Fruit procurement is a late summer to fall occupation, with minor activity continuing through the winter. The most important species are a rich variety of berries, but chokecherries, yucca pods, and rose hips are also included (e.g., Grinnell 1972:250). All tree and shrub vegetation communities contain various types of fruit. Fruits are generally consumed immediately, but when dried and stored provide an important, although poor, source of winter vitamin C (Roll and Deaver 1980:81). Some fruits are processed and stored jointly with other foods (e.g., pemmican). Yucca pods are likely a major subsystem of fruit procurement, but are different from other fruits in that they are not eaten raw. Fruits occur in great abundance, but vary in most productive location from year to year. In addition, most fruits are available only for a short time because of interspecific competition and poor self-storage capacity (i.e., they rot). Tools required for the fruit procurement system vary from none (for immediately consumed fruit), to carrying equipment (baskets), ground stone (for storing and processing as dried fruit or pemmican; see Figure 2.56), and fire (probably roasting pits or baking ovens for yucca pods).

Other

A number of resources, in addition to the ones discussed in the various procurement systems above, are relatively important from time to time and hence play an important role in sociocultural processes. Such resources include, but are not limited to, honey and insects (grubs, Mormon crickets, and possibly ants). Honey requires containers for collection, while insects must be collected and can be eaten raw or processed with ground stone, boiling equipment (pouches, pots), and fire.

PREHISTORIC FOOD PREPARATION

Most of the foods hunted and gathered by human groups required some measure of preparation to enhance palatability, improve their taste, and remove undesirable parts. For example, the hard shells of grass, other seeds, and nuts had to be cracked and the insides reduced to grits or flour, otherwise they would not be properly digested and would pass on through the human digestive system. Some form of cooking both animal and vegetable food usually improves taste, while boiling certain greens and bulbs removes their bitter taste. Certain parts of animals, large or small, must be removed when killed in order to prevent spoilage. Some of these could later be eaten while others were discarded.

Plains hunter-gatherers used a stationary grinding slab, usually a hard, fine-grained sandstone, in conjunction with a smaller hard stone or mano to crack the seeds (Figure 2.56). The grinding slab was pecked to form a small depression that would catch and hold the seeds just enough so that the mano could break them. The appearance of such grinding tools is documented in terminal Paleoindian times, and they formed an integral part of the tool assemblages until historic times.

The total range of functions for grinding tools is not entirely resolved, but it is generally assumed they indicate preparation of plant foods. It has been suggested, but not proven, that they may have also been used for reducing rodent bones to a paste (Mulloy 1954a:59). It is quite possible that a small-animal bone midden at the 9500-year-old level at the Medicine Lodge Creek site may have been destined for this kind of preparation. Rodent bone numbers in most sites do not seem commensurate with their availability, which may indicate that small animals were not used extensively, their bones disintegrate easily, or that the bones were eaten for marrow or other substances. The Foothill/Mountain Paleoindian component at Medicine Lodge Creek suggests that we ought to seriously begin to investigate the use of rodents and other small animals as food. We should also make quantitative evaluations of their food value.

Fire Pits

These features are generally considered to have been used for cooking food products, but they were also used to produce light and heat. Stones were placed on a bed of hot coals in the pits. When properly heated, the stones served as a source of heat for cooking. Whatever was to be cooked could have been put in a green hide, animal paunch, or fiber bag, placed directly on the hot stones, covered with earth or some sort of mulch, and left for a period of time, which could have been several hours or even a day. With practice, this can be done without burning or contaminating the food with the surrounding matrix.

The heat ultimately fractured the stones to the extent that they were of no further use and another pit was dug and the process repeated, or the original pit was cleaned out and fresh rock was used. This kind of earthen oven use is clearly demonstrated at the Wardell Bison Trap site (Frison 1973b), where an unopened pit contained several parts of a bison carcass or carcasses that presumably were being cooked (Figure 6.3). This feature had never been opened nor the contents utilized. Pits of this nature were also used to heat stones for boiling during the Late Archaic and Late Prehistoric periods. In this case, there was another pit or pits nearby where the stone boiling took place. The latter was usually lined with a green hide or paunch. Stones of proper size arranged in a small circle with a hide or animal paunch liner could also serve as the pit (see Figure 4.43b), as was the case at several sites near the end of the Late Prehistoric period associated with the Crow Indian occupation in the area.

In other instances, ovens were made by lining a pit with slabs of sandstone; sometimes a slab was placed at the base of the pit and the cavity was capped with another sandstone slab. Such features occur in Archaic sites in the Rocky Mountains and Northwestern Plains. Contents of these features, when present, include seeds, prickly pear pads, and burned bone (Thompson and Pastor 1995). The largest number of these features occurs during the Archaic and Late Prehistoric. In southwest Wyoming they occur most often during the Early Archaic Opal Phase.

PROTECTION OF STORED FOOD SUPPLIES: FOOD CACHING

Protection of stored food must have been a major problem. Frozen storage associated with cold-weather, communal kills of large animals has been suggested earlier as part of the subsistence strategy for the Paleoindian period on the Northwestern Plains, based on the time of year animals were killed and the configuration of faunal materials in several Paleoindian sites. Examples of frozen storage included the mammoth bone piles at the Colby site (Figures 4.3 and 4.4) and a pile of butchered bison units in an Agate Basin component at the Agate Basin site (Figure 6.10). This does not rule out the possibility that some meat was also dried for temporary storage. Dry storage would appear to have been a practical solution for both animal and plant foods, although there were limited locations for this kind of storage where protection from both the elements and rodents could be reasonably guaranteed.

Figure 6.10 Badly deteriorated pile of butchered bison carcass units from the Agate Basin bone bed at the Agate Basin site.

There were many ways that stored food could be lost. Moisture can cause spoilage of dried meat or plant food. Scavengers and carnivores can detect meat products very well and, unless stores are deeply buried or otherwise well protected, the ability of animals such as bear, wolf, coyote, or badger to dig or gain access to things cannot be taken lightly. Rodents are also a problem and do a surprising amount of burrowing. Badgers often burrow after the rodents, which can create havoc should their burrowing come into contact with anything stored underground. Rodents tend to burrow along the contact between the fill and solid walls of rockshelters and into some cultural levels, which tend to be less compacted than levels of fill. The optimum place for dry storage is well away from rockshelter walls and also well away from the drip line.

There is some evidence that strongly suggests the use of dry storage features in rockshelters. In some of the Paleoindian levels at the Medicine Lodge Creek site (see Frison 2007:61–64) there are globular-shaped pits in compact clay deposits that vary in size from about 25 cm to 50 cm in diameter. Distributed through three cultural levels dated at about 8300 years BP, there are at least 14 of these pits (Figure 6.11) in an area of two square meters. In another part of the site, but of the same age, six of these same kinds of pits formed a circle around a central pit (Figure 6.12). All were filled with what appeared to be trash from an occupation floor and, although some pieces of charcoal were contained in the fill material, they were definitely not fire pits and contained no evidence of ever having fires in them, nor was there any evidence of fire-fractured stones commonly associated with food preparation features. It is postulated that these were storage pits used from year to year, and when not used for storage, they were filled with trash to protect the sidewalls of the pits from collapsing.

Similar features were found in Paleoindian age deposits in Schiffer Cave (Figure 6.13), a small but dry rockshelter on the eastern slopes of the Bighorn

Figure 6.11   Storage pits of Late Paleoindian age at the Medicine Lodge Creek site.

Figure 6.12 Storage pits of Late Paleoindian age at the Medicine Lodge Creek site, possibly located in a pithouse.

Figure 6.13 The Schiffer Cave site on the eastern slopes of the Bighorn Mountains.

Mountains (Frison 1973a). Several genera of dried and partially charred seeds were recovered, including *Helianthus*, *Opuntia*, *Amaranthus*, *Prunus*, *Pinus*, and *Juniperus* along with several unidentified ones. The circumstances strongly suggested that larger quantities of these seeds had been stored in these features.

The Medicine Lodge Creek deposits were damp because of percolation of water through gravel and cobble levels during high-water periods. This wet condition destroyed much perishable material so that only a few charred seeds were found in the deposits filling the Medicine Lodge Creek pits and only *Juniperus* and *Prunus* have been identified. This is suggestive but not conclusive of use as food storage since these shrubs grow around the entrance of rockshelters and the seeds are often found in noncultural contexts. Fire pits were common features in the lower levels of the Bighorn Canyon cave sites (Husted 1969), and several of these were described as filled with ash and bits of charcoal. There is a strong possibility that some of these were storage features rather than fire pits since they were recovered from cultural levels of about the same age and in similar site contexts as those from Medicine Lodge Creek and Schiffer Cave.

During the summer of 1976, investigations were initiated in the foothill/mountain slope areas of the Bighorn Mountains in an attempt to gain a better understanding of the Early Plains Archaic occupations. A rockshelter (Southsider Cave) at just over 2600 m elevation provided evidence of possible food storage features. The site was a true cave and the kind not usually demonstrating evidence of human occupation in this area, since the opening was small and the living area was located deep into the hillside.

Two features in the rockshelter are believed to have been storage pits. They were cylindrical in shape and larger than the ones mentioned above (75 cm in diameter and about 60 cm deep) and were also later in time by about 1000 years. Dampness deeper in the cave deposits caused loss of perishable materials if any were present, but there was no evidence of fire or food preparation. A number of flat stones were associated but they had not been heat fractured; their positions suggested that they were used as coverings for the features. There were, however, many other features in the site that were fire and food preparation pits.

Taken as a whole, this accumulation of data now provides strongly suggestive evidence for food storage among Late Paleoindian and Early Plains Archaic cultural groups in the Bighorn Basin, and the concept of storing provisions constituted a small but vital link in the yearly round of subsistence activities.

QUARRIES, QUARRYING, AND RAW MATERIAL PROCUREMENT

The Northwestern Plains and Rocky Mountains are richly endowed with sources of raw stone flaking material, and we find that every known source has been exploited to some extent. The procurement of raw materials was more than the mere gathering of available surface materials; it involved, in addition, serious, well-planned, provisioned expeditions. In fact, the early European settlers of the Northwestern Plains, who were deeply imbued with the Protestant ethic of hard work, were so impressed with some of the obvious aboriginal stone quarrying pits such as the Spanish Diggings (Holmes 1919:210–213) that they could only attribute these to Spaniards looking for gold—hence the name given to them (Figure 6.14).

Figure 6.14   Overview of the Spanish Diggings quarries area.

Another large aboriginal stone quarry in the northern Bighorn Mountains became known as Spanish Point for the same reasons.

The number of intensive quarrying operations and the amount of quartzite and chert removed from the Spanish Diggings area is phenomenal to say the least (Saul 1969). An examination of the reject material indicates that there was an effort to obtain a high-quality product with superior flaking qualities, since large quantities of mediocre material were quarried and discarded. For several thousand years, prehistoric people on the Northwestern Plains were willing to employ the most difficult mining techniques imaginable in efforts to gain access to superior stone-flaking materials.

The Hartville uplift, a geologic feature in east-central Wyoming is nestled in a bend of the Platte River, stretching about 50 km to the north from Guernsey and 50 km east from Glendo, Wyoming. This vast area consists of Devonian, Mississippian, Pennsylvanian, Permian, Triassic, Jurassic, and Cretaceous formations, most of which are richly endowed with chert. Dakota quartzite (Cretaceous) and Hartville chert (Mississippian/Pennsylvanian) were most extensively quarried, and these formations are dotted with single or concentrations of pits, trenches, and a few tunnels (Figure 6.15). The pits can be large, up to 15 m across and 5 m deep on the surface (Reher 1991).

Twenty-five major quarry pit locations have been known for some time (Saul 1969), but more are discovered nearly every day as the area is surveyed for various development and land-exchange reasons (Reiss 1995). These show a variation in raw material acquisition methods from procurement of surface material to excavation of deep pits and tunnels. Along with material acquisition, however,

Figure 6.15   Quarry tunnel at the Spanish Creek Quarry at the Spanish Diggings with rubble mound in foreground.

the areas in the vicinity of the quarries contain thousands of domestic structures. Reher (1991) has investigated part of the area around the Barbour, Dorsey, and Spanish Creek quarries and documented 180 tipi rings, but estimates that at least 500 are present in the same area (Figure 6.16), with numerous reoccupation episodes. The camp debris associated with these occupations consists of various tools such as scrapers and other evidence of domestic activity.

There are numerous raw material acquisition localities in the same Dakota Formation sandstone from Texas to Canada (Banks 1990). At Windy Ridge in the Middle Park of Colorado, Bamforth (2006) found 182 depressions over 1.3 hectares. He suggests that these can be explained only by Indians digging down through the sandstone and into quartzite veins. To him this implies deliberate, focused procurement rather than casual embedded acquisition of raw material, as is also suggested by Reher (1991).

A less well-known example is the Spanish Point quarry in the northern Bighorn Mountains mentioned above. Several hectares are pockmarked with pits up to 3 m deep (Figure 6.17a) and trenches up to 2 m deep and 25 m in length. The material sought was an exceptionally fine chert in a wide range of colors from opaque to transparent that occurred in nodular form in sizes ranging from a fraction of a kilogram to more than 500 kg. The nodules are distributed in a relatively soft matrix and were extracted using elk antler and bison bone digging tools (Figure 6.17b).

Figure 6.16   Remains of domestic structures (tipi rings) in the area around the Spanish Diggings quarry locations.

Figure 6.17   Quarry pit of Early Plains Archaic age for chert nodules (a) and an in situ digging tool (b) in the northern Bighorn Mountains in Wyoming. Other digging tools from the pit are in Figure 5.36.

Hammerstones weighing as much as 10 kg were used to break into the larger nodules. Another large chert quarry site was discovered and excavated near Three Forks in southwest Montana (Davis 1982). The extent of mining operations, which included deep pits and tunnels, gives some indication of the value of stone flaking materials. Bone and antler tools similar to those from the Spanish Point quarry were recovered there in large quantities. On the Northwestern Plains and in the mountains there is an almost endless number of smaller surface and quarry sites attesting to the value placed on stone flaking materials. The quantity of material sought does not answer the question of why there was an expenditure of this amount of effort. There had to be other reasons, which may have included the quality of the material.

One aspect of lithic raw material that becomes obvious when looking closely at both archaeological assemblages and the behavior of raw materials in the chipped stone production process is that there is a relatively small amount of truly outstanding material. This meant that the prehistoric tool maker was forced to expend effort in direct proportion to the level of quality that was desired in the finished product. The production of superior-quality (in terms of lithic technology and not necessarily functional utility) flaked stone items required that the knapper, someone, or several persons were forced to expend great effort to provide a constant supply of high-quality material. Quarrying chert is much like archaeology itself; no one knows what the quality of the next nodule will be, and this offers the constant hope of rewards as the next nodule is opened. On the other hand, the cost of acquisition was reduced by camping at or near quarries, as at Spanish Diggings described above, or at the Barger Gulch site in the Middle Park of Colorado.

The Barger Gulch procurement location has a series of campsites near a source of raw material. One of these, Locality B, is of Folsom age. The camp at Locality B is perhaps 500 m south to southeast of the main source of Troublesome Formation chert outcrops (Locality A; Kornfeld et al. 2001), but clearly close enough to bring significant quantities of raw material to the site. The site is relatively shallowly buried, up to about 50 cm; however, erosional areas with material on the surface are present as well (Surovell et al. 2005). The site is at least 2000 m², but may be larger as its limits have not yet been defined. So far Locality B has been excavated with block excavations, exploratory units, and auger holes (Figure 6.18). Surface mapping showed areas with high artifact concentrations and these seem to be complementary to areas with low artifact densities. This has led us to think that the occupation layer is exposed on the surface in some areas and buried in others.

Barger Gulch Locality B has yielded chipped stone production debris (tens of thousands if not hundreds of thousands of specimens), broken finished and exhausted projectile points (Figure 6.19), pieces broken in several manufacturing stages (Figure 6.20) scrapers, gravers (Figure 6.21a), ultrathin bifaces (Figure 6.21b and 6.22d), several other types of flake tools, Levallois-like cores (Figure 6.22b), small quantities of distant raw materials, concentrations of burned specimens suggesting hearth locations, several types of activity areas, and dwellings (Figures 6.23).

In many ways similar to Barger Gulch Locality B is a significant recent discovery of a Folsom component in Two Moon shelter in the western Bighorn Mountain foothills of north-central Wyoming. Two Moon is a rather small, nondescript rockshelter among thousands of others in the region (Figure 6.24). The shelter is

Figure 6.18   Barger Gulch in the Middle Park of Colorado. Arrow points to site location.

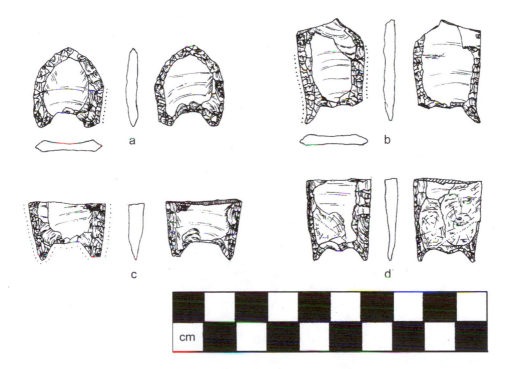

Figure 6.19   Exhausted projectile points from the Barger Gulch site: (a) Trout Creek chert, (b–d) Troublesome Formation chert.

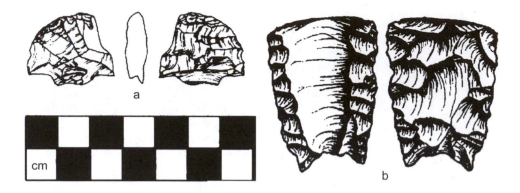

Figure 6.20   Selected preforms and manufacturing failures from the Barger Gulch site. (Figure 6.20b courtesy of Todd A. Surovell.)

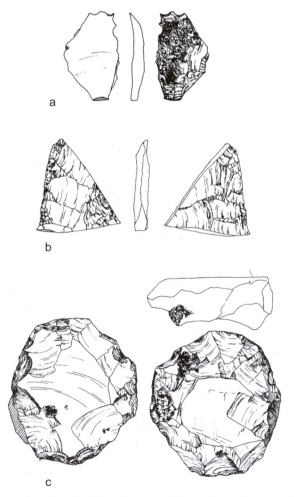

Figure 6.21   Graver (a), ultrathin biface fragment (b), and Levallois core (c) from the Barger Gulch site. Length of Figure 6.21a is 45 mm.

Figure 6.22   Selected refitted artifacts from Barger Gulch: refitted early stage preform (a), refitted late stage perform manufactured on an ultrathin biface made from Trout Creek chert (b) , and late stage preform (c). (Photo by John Laughlin.)

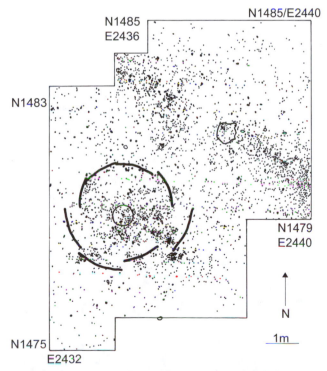

Figure 6.23   Point-provenienced artifacts (dots), and postulated structure location (dark gray arcs) at the Barger Gulch site. (Modified from electronic illustration provided by Nicole Waguespack.)

Figure 6.24   Two Moon shelter excavation.

located on the southwest flank of Black Mountain, a somewhat prominent feature of the midlevel foothills at an elevation of 2000 m. Although the shelter has seen some looting, it appears minimal and several Paleoindian strata do not seem disturbed. So far less than 5 m² of the Folsom component has been excavated. Only two projectile points are in this assemblage: a quartzite base and a tip of a Phosphoria point (Figure 6.25d, e).

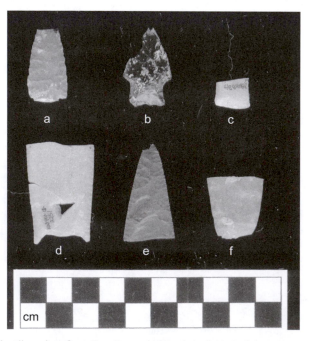

Figure 6.25   Projectile points from Two Moon shelter: Late Archaic (a), unknown Late Paleoindian (b), Pryor stemmed (c), Folsom (d, e), and Foothill/Mountain (f).

The Two Moon Folsom age assemblage consists predominantly of relatively large biface thinning flakes, most if not all with unprepared or barely prepared platforms. Nearly 100% of the raw material is red chert of the Phosphoria, Amsden, Madison, or Nowood formations. The surface of Black Mountain is littered with this material as are the drainages. The flakeability of these cherts vary from excellent to poor. Thus the Two Moon inhabitants needed only go several hundred meters and no more than 1 km to acquire the raw material. Interestingly, there are no channel flakes in an assemblage of over 10,000 pieces of debitage. This puts Two Moon at a rather extreme end of the Folsom assemblage pattern (Kornfeld 2002). However, given the use of red chert at the nearby Hanson site in the later stages of Folsom point manufacture, it may be suggested that Two Moon and Hanson are at the opposite ends of the point manufacturing trajectory. That is, early stages (without fluting) occurred in the upper foothills, at Two Moon or similar sites, while later stages (including fluting) occurred at large base camps in the lower foothills.

The workshop aspect of Two Moon must be tempered by the large number of flake tools recovered in the assemblage. These provide evidence of a variety of domestic activities, and the manufacturing of a wide variety of implements from perishable materials. In addition to this, Two Moon is one of a few fluted-point rockshelter occupations in North America. A longstanding argument in North American archaeology has been whether rockshelters were used by the first inhabitants of the continent (e.g., Collins 1991; Walthall 1998). While many early diagnostics in rockshelters are in questionable contexts and provenience, Two Moon appears to present excellent integrity of the archaeological record. Continuing research at the site will likely yield significant new data on Folsom behavior.

We might also observe the modern flint knapper and his or her emotional attitude toward an exceptionally fine piece of material. Nothing is dearer to a flint knapper than the exceptionally fine piece of flaking material, and the best way to get a piece of this kind of material is to have something of about equal value to trade. Another aspect is that when the knapper does acquire such a piece of material, it is used to produce something of excellence. It is not unreasonable to postulate that the aboriginal flint knapper placed similar value on raw materials.

The specific quarry locations discussed thus far are, however, only a part of the raw material procurement story. Undoubtedly many tons of raw material were removed from Spanish Diggings in southeast Wyoming, Windy Ridge in north-central Colorado (Bamforth 2006), South Everson Creek and Schmitt Mine in southwest Montana (Davis 1982; Davis et al. 1997), Camp Baker in west-central Montana (Roll 2003), Reeder Creek in the Middle Park of Colorado (Metcalf et al. 1991), and other quarry locations. Like the Barbaur, Schultz, and Spanish Creek quarries, some of these have large pits (for example Camp Baker, Windy Ridge, and South Everson Creek), and at some procurement was through soft sediment overburden and a layer of sandstone to reach higher-quality raw material (for example South Everson Creek and Windy Ridge). As with Spanish Point, several have bone or antler quarrying tools (for example Reeder Creek), while most have heavy quarrying and knapping tools, including a grooved maul at Camp Baker. However, the ubiquity of raw material in the region results in widespread procurement possibilities. The Wyoming State Historic Preservation Office data suggest that nearly the entire state is covered with some kind of procurement localities

(Figure 6.26). This is not to say that the distribution is uniform in space or quality. On the contrary, some areas are densely packed with procurement locations, others are not, and some surface material is of excellent quality, while other is not.

Procurement locations can be divided into primary and secondary type (Leudtke 1976). Primary locations are those where raw material is procured (usually quarries) directly from the geological formation (usually of origin). Secondary procurement locations are those containing redeposited raw material, usually gravel deposits. The specific quarries, such as Spanish Diggings discussed above, are generally the loci of primary procurement from a geologic formation. Secondary procurement is generally the collection of raw material from surface exposures of cobbles that tend to be in secondary context. Southwest Wyoming has broad exposures of tertiary river terraces that contain an abundance of raw material. Because of such ubiquity of this material and because of its relatively good quality, the terrace cobbles were frequently used as a source of raw material for tool making. As any modern knapper will tell you, cobbles are commonly the source of good-quality raw material. This is because Mother Nature has weeded out the poor-quality pieces or reduced them to unworkable small cobbles. In essence, what anyone procuring raw material at a primary quarry does is done naturally in secondary cobble deposits. Cobbles in the process of being rolled down rivers are battered against each other, similar to being purposefully broken up by a flintknapper, cracking along fault lines and inclusions and leaving a homogeneous cobble. This is the same process done by a "miner" at a quarry: cobbles are tested and those that break at fault lines or inclusions are rejected. The cobbles on the terraces are also tested prior to removal and additional poor-quality pieces are found and rejected.

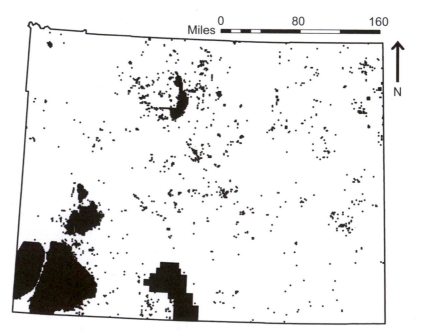

Figure 6.26 Raw material procurement sites in Wyoming. (Courtesy Wyoming State Historic Preservation Office, Ross Hilman, 2009.)

Southwest Wyoming is particularly well endowed with cobble terraces, but they are also found elsewhere, particularly in the Bighorn Basin, as well as Jackson Hole (Figure 6.26). This ubiquity in southwest Wyoming has caused the archaeologists in the area to define a new type of site, a "lithic landscape," to describe these localities. The cobble exposures can be traced for many kilometers; indeed, no boundaries can realistically be assigned to them. The quarried pieces are commonly not densely concentrated, but rather widely scattered; however, such scatters cover 10,000 km² nearly continuously. Whether this represents more or less procured material than point quarries such as Spanish Diggings is hard to estimate, but the yield has been substantial. Flakes, cobbles with one or two flakes removed, and cores are found on these lithic landscapes, occasionally interspersed with campsites. The importance of the lithic landscapes and the quarries is that the Central Rocky Mountains and the nearby Plains are clearly amply endowed with raw material sources for chipped stone tools. Although not all of the materials are high quality, prehistoric peoples in this region rarely had to travel more than several hours to reach a raw material procurement location.

One of the persistent debates about foragers, including prehistoric ones discussed here, is just how do they go about procuring ("provisioning" in Steve Kuhn's 1995 terminology) raw material. Two models have been around for some time, direct and embedded procurement (Binford 1979; Luedtke 1976), and the Central Rocky Mountains have been in the focus of this debate. Direct procurement is defined as an intentional trip to a source for the sole purpose of obtaining raw material. One may eat, sleep, or do other activities, but the purpose of the trip is to gather stone. Embedded procurement is the obtaining of raw material while in the pursuit of other activities. Thus the purpose of the trip is foraging, camping, or other activities and in the process the nearby stone is obtained.

Reher (1991) has argued that the sheer massiveness of the Spanish Diggings quarries, as well as the effort placed on individual pits, argue for direct procurement. He sees groups visiting such quarries and producing preforms, cores, other partially manufactured pieces, or finished tools and removing these to other localities for future use. According to the investigator, this is the gearing-up process to acquire sufficient tools for fall communal hunts. A slightly different view is presented by Francis (1983) and a number of other investigators, who see provisioning in the Central Rocky Mountains and vicinity as a process with both embedded and direct procurement components. Francis has argued that in the Bighorns, prehistoric stone-tool-using peoples obtained stone from secondary sources, along with other resources, on their annual seasonal movements. In the Bighorns, therefore, several simultaneous models are possible, all of which utilize different environmental zones from the riverine riparian communities in the center of the basin to the alpine areas of the mountain ranges. Most, if not all, contain raw material. Thus, the secondary source material was obtained while using the zones for various subsistence activities, while the primary sources such as Spanish Point may have been targeted for direct procurement.

Of course, Francis and Reher are talking about different regions. Spanish Diggings material may have been procured directly, while raw material in the Bighorn region and other areas may have been procured both directly and while undertaking other activities. On the other hand, both strategies may have been used in both areas depending on other issues facing prehistoric peoples. The domestic use of Spanish Diggings area, as evidenced by the tipi villages surrounding the quarry pits, certainly suggests more than direct procurement, but it does not preclude direct procurement. Although direct procurement may have been chosen by prehistoric people under certain conditions, the ubiquity of raw material in the Central Rocky Mountains and nearby Plains makes an embedded strategy an efficient possibility as well. What prehistoric people chose to do was thus likely based on factors other than economic necessity alone.

Caching Stone Tools

Caches are common components of the archaeological record on the Northwestern Plains and Rocky Mountains. The dictionary defines "cache" as "a place in which stores of food, supplies, etc., are hidden" and "anything stored or hidden." These definitions imply that hidden items will be recovered for later use and eliminate so-called mortuary or burial caches from consideration of caching behavior. Archaeological objects that are either caches or mortuary offerings are, however, difficult to separate, unless in direct association with an interment. Economic caches include food and implement stores. Implement stores may include a variety of cache types, each with specific implication for technology. Caching of both food and implements is a response to anticipating future needs in the face of spatial or temporal disparities in resources (Binford 1976). Implement caches provide tools in places where none would be available without a cache.

Implement caches are known from most of the North American Plains, although their incidence seems low. In the vicinity of the Black Hills, for example, perhaps two dozen caches have been reported. However, there are probably many more that have gone unreported. Given that only those caches that were not removed because their owner had died or forgotten the location (Tunnell 1978:1) are recoverable, the few dozen known facilities demonstrate that implement storage was one of the technological strategies employed on the Northwestern Plains and vicinity.

The context of Northwestern Plains implement caches varies a great deal. Some caches can be considered to be isolated facilities, occurring away from other cultural debris such as sites or at locations with only low density of debris, while other caches occur at large, sometimes multicomponent sites (Kornfeld et al. 1990). Such caches vary in size from a few to over 200 items, and this variation appears independent of the context described above. Most commonly, caches contain only bifaces, but they can contain bifaces and flakes, and occasionally a variety of tools. Below we discuss several caches from the Northwestern Plains and adjacent Rocky Mountains.

Clovis Caches and Burials: Anzick

The Anzick site, located on a drainage of a Yellowstone River tributary near Wilsall, Montana, was apparently a burial of the Clovis period (Figure 6.27). The site was discovered through earth-moving activity and unfortunately was badly disturbed before systematic study could be made. The site contained fragments of the skulls of two (one Clovis, one other) red-ocher-covered subadults and over 100 stone and bone offerings. The "cache" included bifaces in several stages of production

Figure 6.27   Location of the Anzick burial in southern Montana.

and several completed projectile points (e.g., Figure 2.21a). Bone items, presumably of mammoth long bone, were cylindrical shaped, one with a single-beveled, cross-hachured end and the other end vaguely conical shaped, reminiscent of a foreshaft designed to fit in the distal end of a mainshaft (Figure 2.22c). Both ends of another specimen demonstrate the single-beveled, cross-hachured treatment (Figure 2.22b). A method for their use as foreshafts has been proposed (Lahren and Bonnichsen 1974).

The Anzick site, along with the Simon Cache (Butler 1963) found at Big Camas Prairie along the Snake River Plain in Idaho, were first regarded as anomalies of the Clovis complex. However, the discovery of the Richey-Roberts Clovis Cache in Washington State (Mehringer 1988, 1989) and the presence of another Clovis Cache, the Fenn Cache, found several years ago but of uncertain provenance, suggest that these features were more likely an institutionalized part of Clovis culture. If they all prove to be burial caches, which seems likely, then the best raw materials were being removed from the system, in which case the term "cache" is not appropriate since there was no intention of recovering the materials for further use. Each assemblage contains some exotic stone flaking materials, suggesting contact across territorial boundaries with distant Clovis groups. The presence of red ocher in these collections also suggests ritual. The possibility that the caches represent interments of somehow differentiated individuals in Clovis groups cannot be dismissed.

The Fenn Clovis Cache

Found several decades ago in the southwest Wyoming, northwest Utah, or southeast Idaho area, we do not know the exact location where the cache was recovered. Stone flaking materials are from several sources, including the Green River Formation (Eocene), found mainly in southeastern Wyoming with smaller deposits extending into western Colorado and Utah; Phosphoria (Permian) and Madison (Mississippian) deposits, probably from northern Wyoming; obsidian from extreme southeast Idaho; and quartz crystal from an unknown source or sources.

Most of the cache consists of bifaces (projectile point preforms) in various stages of production. They demonstrate Clovis biface production strategy very well, with percussion flakes initiated at one margin and terminating at the opposite margin (Figure 6.28). Completed projectile points include unbroken and unreworked specimens (Figure 6.29) and reworked ones (Figure 6.30). A unique style of diagonal-parallel percussion flaking is expressed on some specimens (Figure 6.29), and two demonstrate the rounded corners on the proximal ends as seen in the specimens from the Colby Mammoth Kill site located in northern Wyoming (Figures 4.5 and 6.30).

One obsidian projectile point from the Fenn Cache demonstrates distinctive longitudinal striations on the fluted surfaces (Figure 6.31b) similar to those observed on specimens from the Great Basin (see Wormington 1957:61). The cause of these striations is unknown, although some relation to hafting has been proposed. Three of the Fenn cache specimens have, however, been investigated in

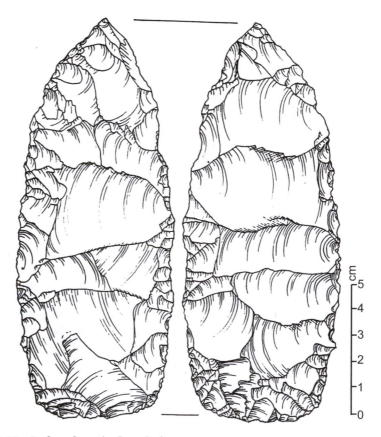

Figure 6.28 Preform from the Fenn Cache.

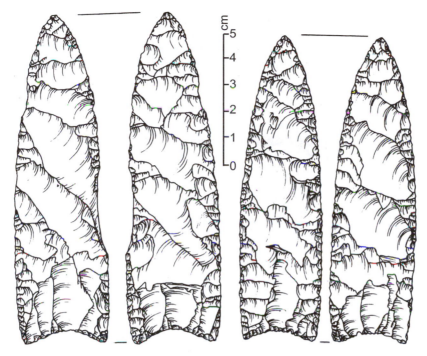

Figure 6.29 Clovis points from the Fenn Cache.

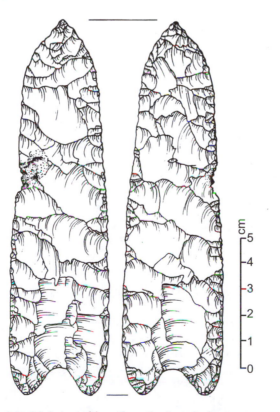

Figure 6.30 Clovis point with indented base from the Fenn Cache.

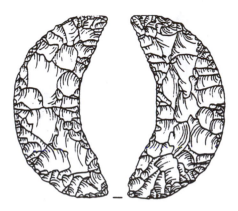

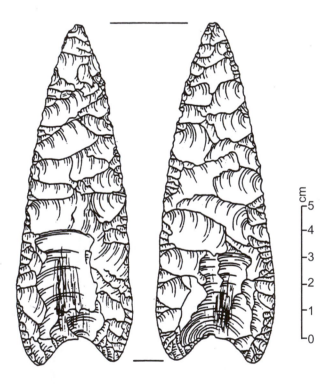

Figure 6.31 Crescent (a), and obsidian Clovis point (b) from the Fenn Cache.

more detail microscopically for "wear," and all show some aspect of specimen and thus assemblage history (Figure 6.32).

A crescent of Green River Formation chert from the Fenn Cache (Figure 6.31a) is also strongly suggestive of a western contact, since these are hitherto unknown from Clovis sites in the Plains-Rocky Mountain area. A single blade tool was in the cache. Three quartz crystal projectile points demonstrate the ability of Clovis knappers to flake this very difficult material. The quartz crystal appears similar

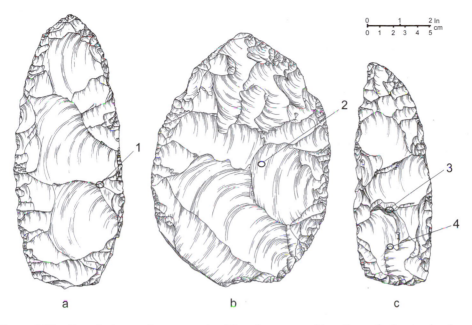

Figure 6.32 Fenn Cache specimens examined for microwear and locations of micrographs shown in Figures 6.33 and 6.34: specimen no. 109 (a), no. 100 (b), no. 126 (c). (Courtesy of Forrest Fenn.)

to that of the large crystal bifaces in the Simon Cache. A large preform in the Simon Cache is of Phosphoria (Permian) Formation chert identical to two projectile points from the Fenn Cache and possibly from the same source in the Bighorn Mountains in northern Wyoming. Each of the 56 items in the Fenn Cache was heavily coated with red ocher.

The large obsidian biface (Figure 6.32b) has heavy abrasions over its entire surface (Frison and Bradley 1999). A few of the linear ridges between flake scars show heavy abrading, while a number of abrasions are on flake scar interiors. Clearly these are from manipulation and storage of this large obsidian object by prehistoric peoples, modern curators, and burial processes, and most likely all of these, and probably other processes, combined. One photomicrograph shows the multidirectional nature of the striations on one of the interior flake scar surfaces (Figure 6.33a). These striations are of different widths, probably indicating differentiation in the morphology of the contact surface, and linear as well as curvilinear in shape. There are numerous episodes of the processes that caused striations, indicated by the directionality of the striations and overlapping of different striations of different widths. The thinner abrasions are rather reminiscent of soil abrasions on bone, and the same cause may be acting on this piece as well as other obsidian specimens from the Fenn Cache. In fact, the obsidian artifacts in the Fenn Cache appear to be most heavily affected by random abrasion, as would be expected of this rather soft and brittle material.

A ridge between two flake scars was examined on another large biface manufactured from Green River Formation chert (Figure 6.32a). This relatively tough material shows less abrasion than the obsidian specimen described above; nevertheless, it exhibits considerable selective abrasion. One high ridge scar shows bright spots (Figure 6.33b), formed when rock is rubbed on another rock under wet conditions (Levi-Sala 1986; Vaughan 1985). We can certainly imagine a variety of instances where this might have occurred with this assemblage: in the wet ground, while being transported in a nonwaterproof carrying bag while it was raining or snowing, and other possible scenarios. The difference in wear patterns between the chert and obsidian bifaces mentioned here may also be the result of material differences, while the processes remain the same. Thus, bright spots on chert and striations on obsidians may both be the result of heavy abrasion.

The last of the Fenn specimens examined was manufactured on pink to translucent Utah agate, probably of similar toughness or tougher than the Green River chert (Figure 6.32c). Like the Green River specimen, it is not as heavily abraded; however, numerous flake scar ridges and other locations show wear. As with the Green River specimen, the ridges show heavy bright spots, which under increased magnification show the intensity of abrasion by the faceting (Figure 6.34a–d). At 400x magnification, heavy striations are seen overlying bright polish (Figure 6.34d), showing the intensity of the abrasive force at this location. Such heavy abrasion suggests that not only were the artifacts rubbing against other rocks or each other, but that a considerable force was pushing them together. We can suggest perhaps that they were tightly bound for transport by prehistoric peoples to prevent breakage. Tankersley (2002) has proposed such a scenario for another Clovis cache/burial assemblage. Differences in transport intensity, in combination with other wear characteristics of the specimens, may be one avenue for differentiating caches from burials.

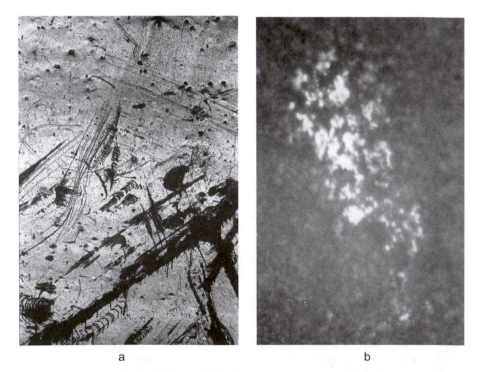

a   b

Figure 6.33 Micrograph of polishes and striations on specimens a and b in Figure 6.32. Numbers 1 and 2 on Figure 6.32 show locations of the micrographs: number 2 at 50x (a), and number 1 at 100x (b).

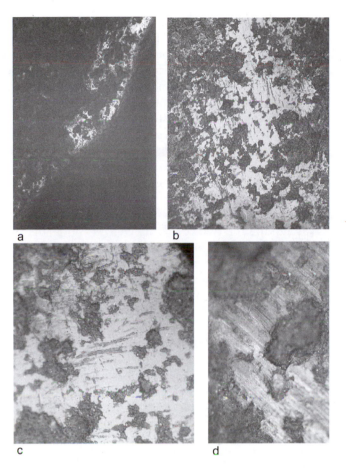

Figure 6.34 Micrograph of polishes and striation on specimen c in Figure 6.32. Numbers 3 and 4 on Figure 6.32 show locations of the micrographs: number 3 at 50x (a), number 4 at 250x (b), number 4 at 400x (c), and number 3 at 400x (d).

Crook County Fenn Cache

The Crook County Fenn Cache was apparently discovered in the early 1960s (Tankersley 2002). It was found during road construction that exposed a long red stain in the road cut (Haynes, personal communication 2008). The red stain is apparently a natural geologic feature, perhaps related to the red scoria formation in this area. The location of the cache is northwest of the Black Hills and in the Pine Breaks of northeastern Wyoming in Crook County. It was the fourth such assemblage of Clovis-age artifacts discovered (following Fenn, Simon, and Anzick), although it did not become known until two other, subsequently discovered caches were described (the Drake and Ritchey-Roberts caches). Four of the six Clovis caches are in the Central Rocky Mountains, Simon is close on the Snake River Plain of Idaho, while only Ritchey-Roberts is some distance away in central Washington. Only the latter was excavated professionally (Mehringer 1988, 1989), while the others, including the Crook County Cache, were collected by avocational archaeologists or are the result of earth-moving activity or both.

Compared to the other caches, the Crook County Fenn Cache is the smallest assemblage with only nine specimens. Of these eight are large bifaces, while one is a finished Clovis point (Figure 6.35). One of the eight bifaces has minimal facial modification, with only the base exhibiting bifacial flaking and the tip exhibiting some unifacial flaking (Tankersley 2002:114). There is also ample marginal retouch on this specimen as well as what appear to be marginal use-wear scars. Examination of the specimens suggests that they were covered with red ochre and tightly wrapped together (Tankersley 2002:116). Such transportation practices may have caused the wear patterns on the Fenn Cache described above. The cache unfortunately has yet to be examined microscopically.

The raw material from which the Crook County Cache bifaces were manufactured is from southwest Wyoming, perhaps 500 km to the southwest of the find location. Some Fenn Cache specimens were also manufactured from this chert, in some way linking the two caches as well as Clovis peoples across vast expanses of the Central Rocky Mountains. The sole projectile point in the collection was manufactured from distinct yellow chert, perhaps of Mississippian age, but possibly from some other similar source. The point is distinct from the other specimens in raw material as well as in surface characteristics and must be considered a suspect part of the assemblage given the uncontrolled circumstances of its discovery.

The Crook County Fenn Cache is an important addition to Clovis social and technological strategies. Why did Clovis folk bury their dead (children in the only documented case of a Clovis burial, the Anzick site) with what appear to

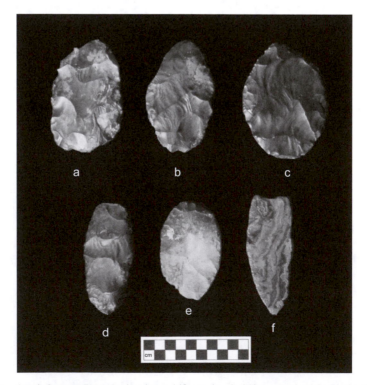

Figure 6.35   Crook County Fenn Cache: large bifaces (a–c), bifaces and preforms (d–f). (Courtesy of Forrest Fenn.)

be such elaborate objects? If some of these groups of artifacts are actually caches rather than burials, what does this say about Clovis technological systems? At least several investigators have suggested a link between the first peoples entering an empty, unknown landscape and this caching or burial behavior. The caches are proposed to act as ritual links to the landscape, a way to learn and remember the unknown (Gillespie 2007; Kornfeld, Harkin, and Durr 2001). Whether these proposals are proven correct in the future or not, clearly the Clovis people put considerable effort into these objects and valued them highly, as they valued the individuals they buried them with.

Larson Cache or Burial

A questionable case for caching is the Larson Cody complex cache (Ingbar and Frison 1987) that contained over 40 complete and broken Scottsbluff-type projectile points and several tools, including a Cody knife, graver, and end scraper (Figure 6.36). Two items (Figure 6.36p) do not appear to be related to the Cody complex. The materials were found in a deflated sand dune area and removed from their original context by sand transport. They very likely represent a human interment, but all of the bone material has been lost and there was no red ocher recorded, either by the Larsons who found the cache or by testing for its presence on the artifacts. Its identity as either a burial or utilitarian cache cannot be determined, but its contents strongly suggest a burial offering.

McKean Site Caches

Three caches were recovered from the McKean site on the western edge of the Black Hills. Two of these are tool caches that contain scrapers and a variety of other tools, while one is a biface cache. The tool scraper caches were recovered from the Middle Plains Archaic component of the site, while the biface cache was recovered from an eroded context and reported by an avocational archaeologist.

One tool cache of seven items was recovered from a shallow depression in bedrock, suggesting that it was purposefully left there for later recovery (Figure 6.37). The seven items stored include six scrapers and one flake (Figure 6.38). Six of the cached items were made from Morrison silicified siltstone (essentially a fine-grained quartzite), while the seventh was manufactured from Cloverly Formation quartzite. Morphologically, the scrapers are large end scrapers, but they exhibit other employable units and can be considered multiedged tools. In comparison to another Middle Plains Archaic period cache, the Dodge Cache (Davis 1976), the McKean site cache is smaller and the types of items limited. Direct behavioral association of the cache with other facilities and artifacts at the site cannot be demonstrated, but the site is a large base camp discussed in Chapter 2.

The employable units in this cache exhibited rounding and polish on all but one of the items, indicating significant use of the implements. Microwear analysis showed that the cached items contained edges in good, relatively fresh condition, but heavily utilized and incompletely resharpened edge sections were also present (Figure 6.39). The few items with signs of dorsal-ridge rounding suggest either contact with a container or prolonged prehension, the latter being less likely

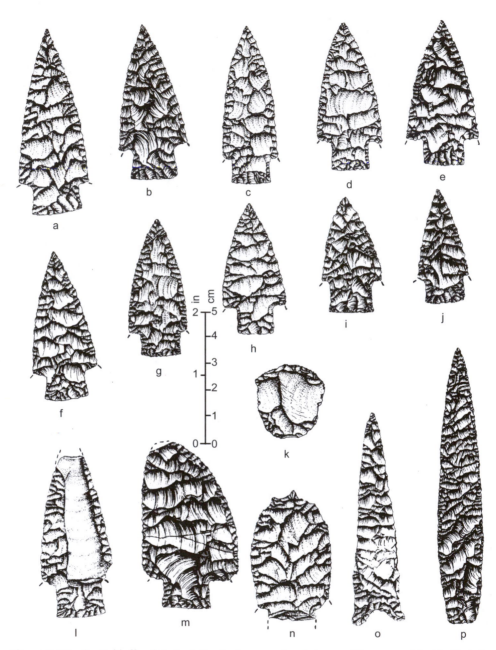

Figure 6.36 Scottsbluff points (a–j, l), single-spurred end scraper (k), asymmetrical knife (m), double graver (n), and non-Cody complex points (o, p) from the Larson Cache in southwest Wyoming.

because of large amount of handling time necessary to produce such polish. The materials worked with these items probably include at least wood and hide. The various stages of microwear traces suggest that these items had been used for a substantial period of time prior to being cached.

That the cache was transported before it was cached may be inferred from the wear on the dorsal ridges of the large tools. This inference is supported by the

Figure 6.37   McKean-age cache from the McKean site in northeastern Wyoming in situ.

type and intensity of wear. Furthermore, one unmodified flake has wear on its dorsal face, suggesting that transportation preceded the removal of the flake from a larger piece of raw material. The presence of one unmodified flake among the six tools, the use of the tools on at least two different materials, and the variation in the number of edges and degree of modification all suggest tool manufacture was carried out as needed for a particular task. Evidence of resharpening prior to storage, however, implies a desire to maintain the tools in working order. That is, if an implement is damaged during resharpening, a replacement can be brought in during the subsequent visit to the location, but once resharpened, the tool is ready for the next time it is needed. Binford (1979:266) has argued that gear carried by an individual for particular tasks and for emergencies can be called "personal gear," and caches, which are commonly recycled or used to meet the needs of the moment, can be considered as "situational gear." The McKean tool cache suggests a trajectory for the stored items from personal gear to the caching of the implements as gear stored in various parts of the landscape in case they might be needed in that location ("insurance gear"), to long-term expedient use of stored tools.

The second McKean cache was discovered during the original site investigations. Mulloy's (1954b:449) account of the materials within the cache mentions that "three were found together with a slender, retouched lamellar flake on the lower level surface as if they might have been in a bag." Although the investigator mentions a bag, the context is otherwise quite similar to the tool cache described

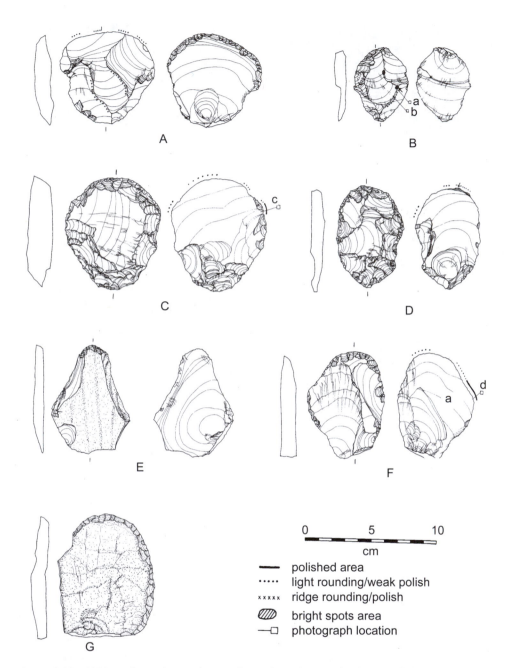

Figure 6.38   McKean site cache specimens. Illustrations show production morphology and location of polish on specimens A–G. Letters a, b, c, d refer to micrographs shown in Figure 6.39. Drawings are in Japanese technical style. (Drawing by Kaoru Akoshima.)

above. The Mulloy cache consists of four large scrapers and one elongated flake all manufactured on Morrison silicified siltstone (Figure 6.40). The one "lamellar" flake has acute, thin edges that are nibbled from use along the entire circumference. This is likely a cutting implement. The three scrapers are all thick and generally round. All of the curved edges are retouched and exhibit significant use with

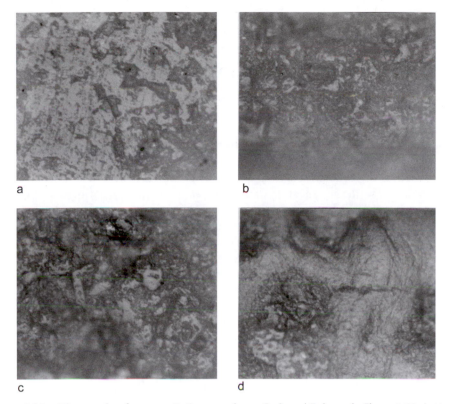

Figure 6.39   Micrographs of wear on McKean specimens B, C, and F shown in Figure 6.38. Letters a through d on Figure 6.38 indicate locations of the micrographs and correspond to figures a though d here. Polish includes rounded, ridge rounding/polish (a) and bright spot (b) (Figure 6.38, specimen B, letters a and b) ; polished area (c) (Figure 6.38, specimen C, letter c) ; and polished area (d) (Figure 6.38 , specimen F, letter d). (Photos by Kaoru Akoshima.)

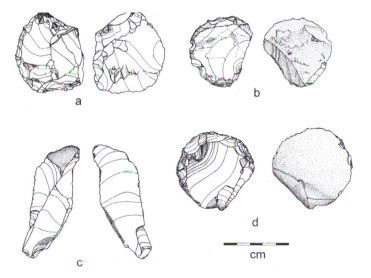

Figure 6.40   McKean-age cache from the McKean site discovered during original investigation in the 1950s (Mulloy 1954b).

at least some step fracturing and rounding on each piece. The implements have clearly been used and retouched and stored in a still usable state, hence this cache is very similar to the one discussed above.

A third cache was recovered at the McKean site by an avocational archaeologist. Although we have not studied this cache, its location leaves no doubt that it came from the McKean site, but its cultural affiliation is unknown and may never be known. The cache of some 20 or 30 bifaces, however, speaks of different structural poses of the McKean site residents. The organizational role of a biface cache is rather different than the other two caches discussed above, perhaps more congruent with preparing for future activities than with base camp activities. Like the Helen Lookingbill site discussed below, the McKean site likely played different roles in the settlement system depending on season, occupation duration, and other contingencies.

These are but a few of the caches found throughout the Northwestern Plains and Rocky Mountains, but it is not yet clear, nor has it been fully investigated, how and whether their distribution is related to quarry locations, campsites, and other components of settlement systems. Although only Paleoindian to Middle Archaic caches were discussed, a number of caches date to later periods (Lippincott 1985). What may be differences in caching strategies through time has yet to be fully investigated. The caches also vary in composition; some contain solely tools (e.g., McKean site caches), others contain predominantly bifaces, some are dominated by plain (usually large) flakes, others contain projectile point preforms as well as finished projectile points. All this indicates that caches are very diverse technological features and that caching served a number of different functions.

7

COMMUNITIES AND LANDSCAPE

INTRODUCTION

Prehistoric hunter-gatherers of the Northwestern Plains and Rockies are expected to have lived in groups best described as bands (e.g., Fried 1967; Service 1962). Bands—that is, groups composed of several related or fictive kin families—create an economic entity, although the basic economic unit remains a family. Bands are flexible in composition and generally egalitarian in social relations; they disperse into smaller extended-family groups periodically as well aggregate into macrobands. The periodicities of these several scales of dispersal and aggregation remain a matter of debate; suffice it to say that economic, social, and ideological pressures are almost certainly intertwined in such decisions.

Various structural remains that date to the earliest occupation of the region provide evidence of prehistoric communities. Pithouses (often occurring in multiples), wooden structures, and stone circles, sometimes clearly evidence of larger multiband villages (Reher 1983), are the archaeological records that provide evidence of community organization and living spaces. Living spaces, however, also include huge landscapes where rock cairns, sometimes arranged in alignments, are evidence of animal procurement activities (animal trap drive lines) or transportation routes (trails). Other constructed features on the landscape are ritual. Medicine wheels, vision quests, and shaman's structures provide a glimpse into ceremonial aspects of prehistoric life. As important as these aspects of the archaeological record are for understanding prehistoric societies, they are relatively understudied. In this chapter we present some information that bears on these aspects of prehistoric communities and their landscapes.

STRUCTURES AND VILLAGES

If one spends any time on the Northwestern Plains or in the Rocky Mountains it is difficult to imagine that the need for shelter for hunters and gatherers was not a concern throughout a good part of the year. Survival during the cold months on the plains and mountains required relatively sophisticated shelter from the elements, and harsh weather can occur at any time of the year. However, we can only now begin to discuss the evidence for shelter that we see archaeologically. Although more possibilities exist than those discussed here, given the record that we have today, four different types of structures have left clear archaeological remains. These four archaeological types include semisubterranean pit features (called interchangeably here house pits and pithouses), stone circles, rockshelters, and log structures. Within each of these types (and especially the first three) is a wide range of variation in size, shape, features, artifacts, and inferred use, and for house pits and stone circles, the number of each type of structure found at a single location varies greatly.

The past 35 years of intense energy and transportation development in the region and the large amounts of federal land with stringent requirements for archaeological investigation has brought large numbers of structure remains to the database. The number of stone circle sites in the state dwarfs the other three structure types, partially because stone circles are found during surface reconnaissance. Because not a single house pit has been found during surface survey, the numbers of house pit sites are fewer, yet evidence suggests that large numbers of these features await discovery. While rockshelters are rarely thought of as a type of "chosen" shelter, they represent the shelter type with the least amount of labor investment required to provide adequate shelter. Rockshelters have been the focus of intense research in northern Wyoming over the last 40 years. Finally, the most obvious and easy to understand type of shelter is one manufactured from wood. Yet, preservation of wooden structures is guaranteed in the best of conditions for only some 200 years, leaving only a small sample of these features to discuss.

House Pits

One of the most significant discoveries of the last three decades has been house pits. These features are defined as semisubterranean structures that are usually seen in cross section as a shallow, bowl-shaped depression (although exceptions exist). Remarkably, not a single house pit has been found through surface survey, and in some instances there have been no archaeological remains visible on the surface whatsoever. As more house pit sites come to light and are excavated in their entirety, we should be able to understand their associated settlement pattern both within sites, between sites, and through time. These features also preserve some of the best data for understanding the daily life of their inhabitants.

The earliest report of a house pit in the Northwestern Plains and Rocky Mountains came with investigations at the Shoreline site (48CR122) on the eroded beach of Seminoe Reservoir (Figure 7.1; Walker and Zeimens 1976). The next came several years later when the monitoring of an open pipeline trench revealed the remnants of a house pit in profile in a sand deposit that had been identified several

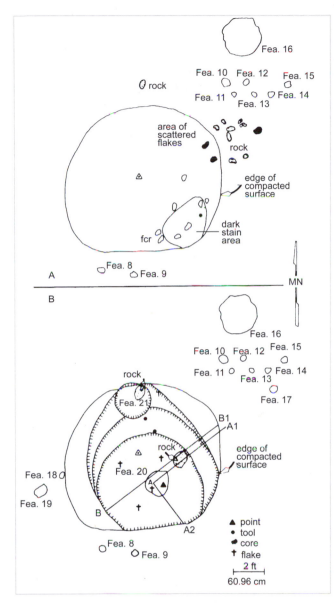

Figure 7.1 Plan view of 1976 Shoreline site pithouse: (A) after removal of beach gravel veneer, showing location of associated features relative to the pithouse, and (B) showing location of all associated features relative to the pithouse after excavation. Contours in (B) are 30.5 cm.

years before as having surface archaeology and the potential for buried remains (48SW1029; Hobbs and Garcia 1981). Additionally during those early years, several house pit features were identified in hindsight only after excavations ended. As energy development intensified and the ability of archaeologists to investigate subsurface deposits in this situation improved, more house pits were found, as did their sense of where such features might occur. By the mid-1990s, the focus on investigation of house pits and their contents resulted in the publication of several overviews of this feature type (e.g., Larson 1997; Larson and Francis 1997; Smith

2003). Since then, the number of sites with house pit features has multiplied, as has our understanding of the meaning of these features.

Stabilized sand dune areas in the interior of intermontane basins (the Wyoming, Wind River, and Bighorn basins) have produced many of the pithouses known at present (Figure 7.2), and also coincide with a number of the areas that experienced intense energy-related earth moving. Oil and gas field construction and highway work uncovered many of the early house pits, and the features were literally bladed away. The consistent use of "open-trench monitoring," where archaeologists accompany pipeline (and other) crews during construction, has resulted in the discovery of half of the know house sites. Archaeological exploration (testing and auguring) of potential locations as well as excavation of overlying levels in stratified sites have exposed the remainder of structures. The use of remote sensing to find buried features has only just been introduced as a method for identifying house pits and their associated features (Walker 2004a). The presence of buried, intact Holocene deposits in much of Wyoming, northern Colorado, and potentially southern Montana has the potential to yield much more information about these important remnants of past settlement systems.

House pit sites range in age from pre-8000 BP to the very end of the Late Prehistoric period (720 BP) and span from the Great Divide phase of the Early Archaic to the Deadman Wash phase of the Late Archaic and Late Prehistoric phases in southwest Wyoming and northwestern Colorado, as well as the Early, Middle, and Late Plains Archaic and Late Prehistoric in the Bighorn Basin and central Wyoming. Pithouses of Middle Archaic age were found in the Wyoming Basin (Harrell and McKern 1986; Newberry and Harrison 1986), which, when added to the one from the Dead Indian Creek in the Sunlight Basin of northwest Wyoming, the one from the McKean site, and those in southern Saskatchewan (Ramsay 1993), demonstrates a wide geographical spread for these features. Nearly two-thirds of the house pit sites in our study area date to the Middle Holocene (from 6500–4000 BP), with most in the 6500 to 5000 BP range. The second largest number of sites dates to the Late Archaic and Late Prehistoric periods.

In those sites where larger excavation areas have been opened up, the number of houses range from one to thirteen. Pithouses often have numerous features dug into their floors, including fire pits, cache or storage pits, and postholes. Where excavation has occurred outside of the house feature, similar features associated with activity areas have been found as well. Many of the interior features identified as fire hearths contain fire-cracked rock, charcoal, ash, charred seeds, ground stone, chipped stone, and bone. Some below-floor features within the house contain little, although in some cases their content is similar to the fire hearths, without the charcoal and dark staining of the sediment. Rose (2008) has investigated interior features found within Wyoming house pits and evaluated the potential for the former to be storage pits. Based on experimental archaeology, she concludes (Rose 2008; using DeBoer 1988) that storage pits occur in small numbers in the analyzed house pits, but more than half of the structures contained at least one storage pit, and that the majority of the storage pits in her study represent short-term use. Postholes probably indicate the presence of supports for roofs both inside and outside of the structures.

Truly representative of the Archaic way of life, the cultural remains found with house pits include ground stone (manos, metates), chipped stone, bone, shell, and rarely, bone awls, bone needles, bone, stone, or shell beads and their

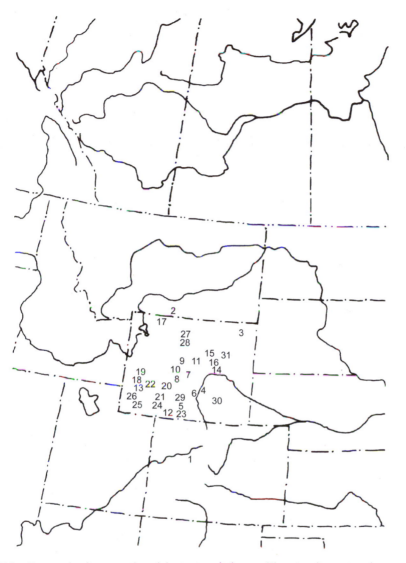

Figure 7.2 House pit sites mentioned in text and those with extensive external excavations: 1. Yarmony House (Metcalf and Black 1997); 2. Spiro (24CB13322, Walker-Kuntz et al 2006); 3. McKean (48CK7; Kornfeld et al. 1995); 4. Shoreline (48CR122, Walker and Zeimens 1976); 5. Nova (49CR4419, Creasman and Thompson 1990); 6. Sinclair (48CR4522, Smith and Reust 1992); 7. Split Rock Ranch (48FR1484, Eakin 1987); 8. Jeffrey City (48FR2339, Reiss 1990); 9. Sand Draw Village (48FR3123, Walker 2004a); 10. Lost Creek (48FR4398, WySHPO site form); 11. Moneta Divide (48FR4459, WySHPO site form); 12. 48FR4856; 13. Taliaferro (48LN1468, Smith and Creasman 1988); 14. Two Toads (48NA1079, WySHPO site form); 15. Flying A Ranch (48NA1431, WySHPO site form); 16. Natrona House (48NA2526, WySHPO site form); 17. Dead Indian Creek (48PA551, Frison and Walker 1984); 18. Birch Creek (48SU595, Thompson et al. 1989); 19. J. David Love (48SU4479; McKern and Harrell 2008); 20. Buffalo Hump (48SW5057, Harrell 1987); 21. Sweetwater Creek (48SW5170, Newberry and Harrison 1986); 22. Farson (48SW6777, Harrison and Creasman 1989); 23. 48SW8842 (Pool 2006); 24. 48SW10749 (WySHPO site form); 25. 48UT133 (WySHPO site form); 26. Hogsback (48UT2516; Eckman 2005); 27. Elk Head (48WA1181; McClelland and Martin 1999); 28. Nowater Housepit (48WA1463, Martin and Harding 1999); 29. 48SW1029 (Hobbs and Garcia 1981); 30. Medicine House (48CR2353, Miller and McGuire 1997); 31. Lembke (Lippincott 1998).

manufacturing debris. Although highly variable in quantity, chipped stone assemblages are made up of production debris (debitage, cores, bifaces), small numbers of projectile points, and occasional scrapers, drills, and other formal tools. Where faunal remains have been identified to class size or species, small mammals predominate. Heavily processed leporids (cottontail rabbit and jackrabbit) and rodents are found in a large number of the dwellings. Although many sites have yielded small numbers of deer, pronghorn, bison, mountain sheep, and elk skeletal elements, these animals do not appear to have been the focus of subsistence activities at the sites. Bird bone, amphibians (frogs, toads), lizards, and snakes are found in small numbers in some of the sites. Fresh-water mussel shells occur in the mid-Holocene sites, but have yet to be found in Late Holocene sites.

Although over three times as many house pits have been reported today than had been investigated a decade ago, only a small proportion of these sites have had any extensive excavations completed, and several of the earliest excavations were restricted to only the area within the outline of the house pit truncated by earth-moving equipment. The current strategy of house pit investigation involves extensive excavation only when destruction of the feature cannot be avoided. Unfortunately, when the damage is already done through pipeline or some other trenching, the strategy of investigators involves minimal excavation to identify the feature as a house pit, excavation of one or two 1 x 1 m test units, and collection of charcoal for a radiocarbon date if it can be found. The danger of such a method is that each subsequent undertaking monitors the site's destruction, but because the site is not excavated in its entirety it becomes extremely difficult to reconstruct the context of the site or its contents.

The Barton Gulch site is located in the Ruby Valley of southwest Montana. The site is significant for its data about the Alder and Hardinger complexes (9410 and 8780 BP, respectively; see Chapter 2). However, the site has also yielded a unique mid to late Paleoindian assemblage. The uniqueness results from recovery of domestic features and a diverse fauna. The features are perhaps the most interesting aspect of the Alder complex. The occupation surface consisted of 37 similar features distributed into four groups (Davis et al. 1989). Each group was centered around a basin that was shallow and exhibited heavy oxidation. One or two charcoal-filled features (40 cm diameter and 30 cm deep) surrounded the basin. In a 2 m diameter around this basin were a series of smaller (25 cm diameter and 10 cm deep) charcoal-filled features. Although similar pithouses are a familiar feature of the Archaic, their occurrence in the Paleoindian period had heretofore not been demonstrated. We should note, however, that a series of similar features were discovered in the 1970s and 1980s around Bairoil in Wyoming, with dates in the 8000s radiocarbon years BP. Unfortunately this discovery went largely unnoticed and remained controversial (Moore et al. 1987; John Greer, personal communication 2008). In retrospect, if any of these still remain, they deserve additional investigation in the light of Barton Gulch and the Early Archaic pithouses discussed below.

Fortunately, although excavated under the time constraints of salvage archaeology, extensive excavations at a few sites have yielded what may be considered small villages and/or longer-term camps. The Split Rock Ranch site, dating to the latter part of the Early Plains Archaic or the Opal phase of the Early Archaic, provides an example of a campsite that contained five house pits with evidence for gathering of local plant resources, use of small mammals (rodent and rabbit), and other activities commensurate with a summer occupation (Eakin 1987; Eakin et al. 1997). The Spiro site (24CB1332), a Middle Plains Archaic site located at the northern end of the Bighorn Basin, has produced nine house pits. However, because many of the hearths and houses overlap each other and because the radiocarbon date range extends beyond that of a single occupation, the site represents a reoccupation of a certain location several times over a thousand years for intensive processing of plant foods, including root/tubers such as bitterroot (*Cymopterus* sp./*Lewisia rediviva*) and prickly pear pads (Walker-Kuntz et al. 2006). The Sand Draw Village site (48FR3123) has yielded an extensive Late Prehistoric plant processing area with what is likely to be the largest number of semisubterranean pit features reported in Wyoming once final analyses are complete. All three of these sites contain other components, but the focus of discussion here is the components with pithouses.

The largest known Early Archaic house pit site that shows use of house pits as living structures over a relatively long time is the Split Rock Ranch site (48FR1484) along the Sweetwater River in central Wyoming (Figure 7.2; Eakin 1987; Eakin et al. 1997). The site was subject to broad, horizontal excavation of house pits, internal features, and external activity areas (Figure 7.3). Excavations in the Early Archaic occupation exposed five house pit features, two external activity areas, nine external features, 26 internal features, and eight internal and six external postholes.

The Split Rock house pits were generally circular and dish shaped with no evidence of prepared floors, benches, wall niches, or ventilator shafts. Three intact houses range from 2.8 to 5.5 m in diameter; the other two structures were incompletely excavated. Common to all five structures was the presence of multiple pits dug into the floor of the house (Figure 7.4). With few exceptions, these features are interpreted as storage pits, although charcoal, more indicative of fire pits, was recovered in sufficient quantities for dating from most of them (Eakin 1987). The Early Plains Archaic occupation at Split Rock Ranch dates between 6180 and 5130 BP. Calibration of the dates at the one sigma level (Stuiver and Reimer 1993 suggests overlap in the majority of the features excavated (Figure 7.4), indicating a single occupation or reuse of the house pits with some features burned at slightly later dates.

The Early Archaic occupation of Split Rock Ranch yielded thousands of chipped stone flakes and 79 tools (Table 7.1). Projectile points range from side notched to stemmed and are similar to points found in other house pits dating to this time. The remaining chipped stone assemblage consists of retouched and utilized flakes, bifaces, cores, and debitage. The raw material of the chipped stone is predominantly local in origin with a few pieces of nonlocal material from sources southwest and north of the site. Metate fragments and manos were recovered from the excavations. Other more exotic artifacts recovered include bone awls manufactured from deer/pronghorn-sized metapodials, drilled and polished dark gray green steatite bead fragments, pieces of hematite, and a fossilized fish scale, indicating some of the domestic and craft activities occurring at the site.

The faunal assemblage from the Split Rock Ranch site consisted of nearly 4000 specimens, 2800 of which were identifiable to at least size class. Small mammal, rodent, and rabbit (both cottontail and jack) comprise the bulk of the identifiable faunal remains. Deer (NISP=11) predominate in the large/medium mammal bone, with one element each of bison, pronghorn, and mountain sheep present.

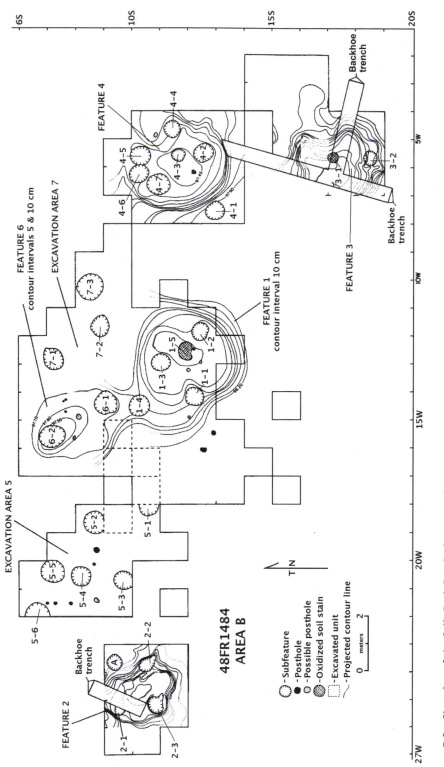

Figure 7.3 Plan view of the Split Rock Ranch site excavation area. Contour intervals are 5 cm unless otherwise noted. (Adapted from Eakin 1987; Courtesy of the Wyoming Highway Department and the Office of the Wyoming State Archeologist.)

Figure 7.4 Pithouse (Feature 4) during excavation of the Split Rock Ranch site. Interior features date to at least two Early Plains Archaic occupations. Exterior feature (upper right) is related to an even earlier Early Plains Archaic occupation. (Photo by Dan Eakin.)

Table 7.1 Comparison of the Split Rock Ranch and Spiro site assemblages. Split Rock Ranch assemblage is from the Early Archaic level only (data from Eakin et al. 1997); Spiro data is from the Middle Archaic component (Walker-Kuntz et al. 2006). Absolute frequencies are given except where noted.

Feature/Artifact class	Feature/Artifact type	Split Rock	Spiro
House pits		5	9
Features	Hearths	1	56
	Storage pits	34	0
	Postholes	14	0
Chipped stone	Projectile points	5	7
	Stone tools	79	56
	Debitage	5844	2843
Ground stone	Manos	5	2
	Metates	6	4
Bead fragments	Steatite	2	0
	Bone tube manufacturing debris	0	23
Bone	Tools	6	29
	Rabbit and rodent % of assemblage	49 %	66 %
	Artiodactyl % of assemblage	3 %	1.9 %
	Fish	0.3 %	1 %
	Unidentified % of assemblage	47 %	19 %
Fire-altered rock		7 pieces	686,027 gm

Eggshells believed to be either duck or goose and over 100 identifiable pieces of mollusk shell (*Pisidiidae* sp.) were recovered. Many small pieces of egg and mollusk shell were observed during excavations but not collected.

Large quantities of charred and uncharred plant remains in the form of seeds, fleshy fruits, and possibly greens and tubers were recovered from excavations and flotation of features. Located where it is along the Sweetwater River adjacent to both the Granite Mountains to the north and Green Mountain to the south, Split Rock Ranch was close to many different vegetation communities rich in edible plant foods. The presence of eggshells, fresh-water mussel shell, fish and snake bones, and the seasonality of some fruits and seeds suggest warm season (summer–fall) occupations of the Split Rock Ranch site.

Another site of equal significance, but with somewhat different characteristics than the Split Rock Ranch site, is the Spiro site (24CCB1332), located in the Bighorn Basin just a few miles north of the Wyoming–Montana border. Occupied at least five times during the Middle Plains Archaic (4390–3550 BP), the extensive excavation area revealed the remains of nine house pits and 49 features (Walker-Kuntz et al. 2006). House pits range from 2.3 to 6.1 m in diameter. Unlike Split Rock, the Spiro site contained large numbers of basin-shaped and straight-sided cylindrical hearths and earth ovens. The overlapping of features and house pits both vertically and horizontally indicates multiple uses of this particular location within the narrow radiocarbon range. The site contained nearly 700,000 gm of fire-altered rock distributed in the hearths, house pit fill, and across the excavated area; Split Rock Ranch, in comparison, yielded only seven pieces of fire-altered rock. Made on predominantly local raw materials, the chipped stone assemblage contains projectile points, stone tools (including cores, bifaces, and tested cobbles), and debitage. Both manos and metates are present. Leporids (cottontail and jackrabbit) and rodents make up two-thirds of the identifiable fauna. Like Split Rock Ranch, deer are the most commonly represented artiodactyl (MNI=3). Bison, elk, and mountain sheep/pronghorn make up a small number of individual elements. Unidentified small/medium/large mammals and a suite of nonmammalian creatures (fish, reptile/amphibians) constitute the remainder of the collection. Along with several larger bone tools, the Spiro site contained bone tube manufacturing debris such as grooved and snapped, and cut fragments of bird and rabbit bone (Walker-Kuntz et al. 2006). Spiro may represent one of the northernmost extensions of the Archaic house pit settlement system.

The Sand Draw Village site (48FR3123) is located southeast of Riverton, Wyoming. Its Late Prehistoric component (1430–970 BP) revealed 13 shallow house pits and 70 hearth and posthole features (Figure 7.5; Walker 2004a; Danny Walker, personal communication 2008). The houses range from just over two meters to three meters in diameter. The largest house pit appeared to have been dug, while the other structures were very shallow, suggesting they had been shaped by trampling or just ordinary activity around the central hearth or hearths (Walker 2004a). Recent excavations exposed a seven-meter-diameter work plaza. During three years of excavation over the last 15 years, the fire pit features are the most significant find at Sand Draw. Many of them are deep, cylindrical, rock-filled features containing both plant and animal remains. Plant remains include prickly pear (*Polycantha opuntia*), and roots such as wild onion (*Allium* spp.), biscuitroot (*Lomatium* sp.), and bitterroot (*Lewisia rediviva*), all of which occur on or near the site today. The hearths also contain small amounts of rabbit bone. At this point,

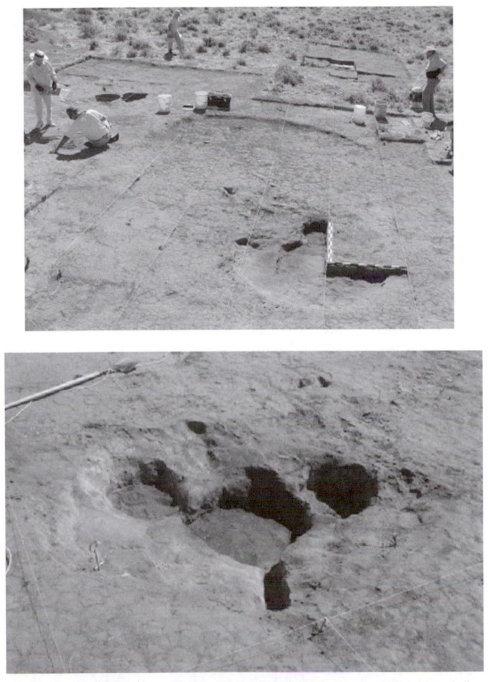

Figure 7.5 Pithouses at the Sand Draw Village site. A small house pit within a large shallow depression showing reuse of the site (top), and a small pithouse with storage facilities (bottom).

the Late Prehistoric occupation of the Sand Draw Village site appears to have been focused almost exclusively on the processing of plant food. Unlike Split Rock Ranch and the Spiro site, the Sand Draw Village has little in the way of the non-subsistence debris observed at the first two sites.

The most enigmatic evidence of a pithouse is the one at the Early Archaic Medicine House site along the North Platte River in south-central Wyoming. The pit structure measures 6 m in diameter and 1 m deep and contains well-preserved walls and internal features. A large share of the structure is still intact, and there are likely to be other similar structures in the immediate vicinity (McGuire et al. 1984; Miller and McGuire 1997). Radiocarbon dates on the site are 5300 and 5100 years BP, or close to the end of the Early Plains Archaic period. However, as the house was not completely excavated and no investigation was undertaken outside of the excavated house pit, there is still much to learn about this site.

Stone Circles

Stone circles (also called tipi rings) occur in large numbers throughout the Northwest Plains and Rocky Mountains (Figure 7.6). Unlike house pits, the vast majority of stone circles have been found on the surface with the age of the circle determined largely by the presence of diagnostic artifacts. They appear nearly everywhere that stones of proper size were available; they occur singly and in groups, where they may number well into the hundreds. Buttes and less noticeable topographic rises are common locations, and ridge tops may be lined with them. They may line terraces along live streams and dry arroyos. They occur in the arid, interior intermontane basins, on the open plains, in the foothills, and even (with less frequency) in the high mountains. Large numbers of individual rings may actually be contiguous or they may be separated by distances of several meters. Single and/or multiple outliers from large groups of rings are common. Partial rings suggest pirating of earlier rings to build later ones.

The rings themselves may be composed of a single course of stones either touching or some distance apart or they may consist of a wide band of stones, suggesting that stones were piled several deep around the base of a lodge structure and gradually became disarranged through time. Some circles contain small piles or vague circles of stones that suggest fire hearths; some of these "fire hearths"

Figure 7.6   Tipi rings in central Wyoming.

are centrally located but many are not. Some circles contain carefully prepared fire pits. Stones used may be stream boulders and cobbles or slabs of limestone, sandstone, or whatever other stone material was available.

These stone circles may represent all that remains after the removal or disintegration of various kinds of superstructures. If so, they were constructed in conjunction with some sort of circular lodge or tipi (Mulloy 1965a). Malouf (1961a) thinks that different-appearing structures may have disintegrated leaving similar-appearing stone circles. He favors a domestic or living structure origin for most of them. Malouf refers to all of these as "stone circles" but uses "tipi ring" if the circle was used to hold down the bottom of a skin-covered structure. Kehoe (1960) argues convincingly that the stone circles are tipi rings designed to hold down lodge covers, but his data are limited to observations made on the Blackfoot reservation. Other ideas on the use and distribution of stone circles have been presented by Hoffman (1953). It appears that many stone circles do represent the only nonperishable remains of living structures, but it can be strongly argued that others do not. Other less common features consist of vague stone circles made of large sandstone or limestone slabs that may be the only remains of dome-shaped, five- or six-sided, roughly circular log structures, some of which are still in existence (Figure 7.7) and are probably Shoshonean in origin. They occur mainly in the foothills and mountains of northwest Wyoming and adjoining areas of Idaho and Montana. Horizontally laid logs made up the sides of these structures and slabs of stone were laid around the outside. As the structures rotted away, only the stones were left.

The oldest documented tipi ring is found in dated context in the Frederick level at Locality I at the Hell Gap site (Irwin-Williams et al. 1973; Larson et al. 2009), although few stone circle sites are documented for the Paleoindian and Early Plains Archaic times. In the Middle Plains Archaic the density of sites with stone circles increases, but the majority of rings date to the Late Archaic, Late Prehistoric, and Protohistoric (Scheiber 1993:82). In her study of 287 stone circle sites from Wyoming with chronological indicators, Scheiber (1993) found Middle Plains Archaic stone circles to differ significantly from later rings. These stone circles are smaller and less variable in size, and have greater spacing between circles, long-axis orientations toward the northeast rather than southeast, and fewer total rocks in the ring than later time periods. As a group, Late Plains Archaic, Late Prehistoric, and Protohistoric stone circles differed little from each other (Scheiber 1993).

Stone circles believed to be a campsite associated with a buffalo jump of Crow Indian origin at the Piney Creek site in northern Wyoming (Frison 1967b) have larger stone concentrations to the windward side of the rings, suggesting a relatively long occupation (several weeks or more) with added stone for protection from strong winds that occur almost daily. Other Crow Indian tipi rings, identified on the basis of ceramics, are found close to timberline in several concentrations of a dozen or more in the northern Bighorn Mountains. These are manifest as circles of large, angular limestone blocks and are disarranged somewhat, suggesting that they had been placed on top of a lodge cover to hold it close to the ground and moved outward when the lodge was taken down. The fire hearths in many of the circles are centrally located, but in others they are outside the circle. Stone circle sites are also associated with numerous other buffalo kill locations; especially notable are those surrounding the Muddy Creek site (Figure 7.8).

Figure 7.7 Cribbed-log living structures from Logan Mountain (a), and in the Sunlight Basin of the Absaroka Mountains of northwest Wyoming (b).

Most but not all stone circle sites are noted for a lack of diagnostic cultural material. Perhaps many of these sites represent short-term occupations. Cultural materials associated with these features are usually little more than a few flakes

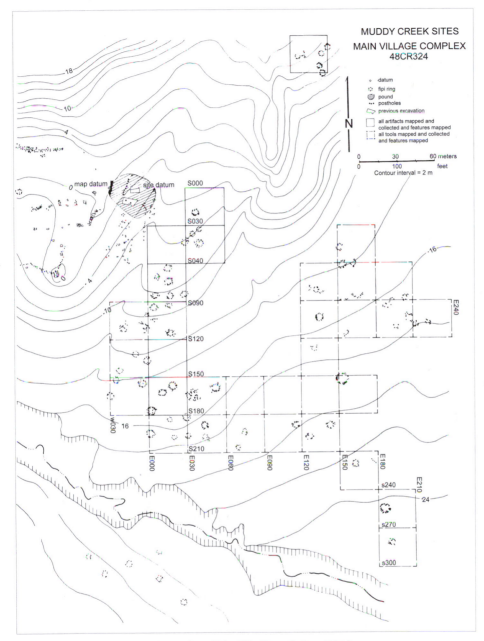

Figure 7.8   Tipi rings at Muddy Creek Buffalo Kill. (From Reher 1987.)

and an occasional broken projectile point or tool. It is possible that some circles had religious meaning; small stone circles have been observed in the vicinity of buffalo jumps and may represent locations of shamanistic activity associated with communal bison kills. On the other hand, many of the larger stone circles may also have served important religious functions. Many studies of stone circles on the plains have been made (Davis 1983; Davis et al. 1982b; Scheiber 1993) and numerous recording techniques applied (Figure 7.9), but whatever their true

Figure 7.9 Photographing tipi rings in eastern Wyoming. Overhead photographs can be used in precision mapping of the individual stones.

function, stone circles will provide Plains archaeologists with research problems for many years to come.

Wood Structures

Still in evidence are a number of deteriorated wooden structures, although these are quickly disappearing. They include the game procurement traps and associated corral structures described in Chapter 5 along with the horizontally laid log habitation structures (Figure 7.7). Also remaining are a few conical lodges (Figure 7.10) and less sophisticated habitation structures of juniper logs and trees (Figure 7.11), but these also will not survive much longer. Other living structures were built in caves and overhangs, and some are undoubtedly much older than those exposed to the elements. Some of these remain essentially intact (Figure 7.12) and consist of poles leaned against the walls with rocks and smaller branches built up around the bottom.

CAMPSITES AND SETTLEMENTS

Structures and villages such as those discussed in the previous sections are relatively rare in the archaeological record. Prehistoric peoples, however, camped every night and moved camp often. A rough estimate of between approximately one week and 4–5 months would probably cover the duration of most prehistoric group camps. These types of sites are, therefore, one of the most important segments of prehistoric lifeways and should be relatively common in the

Figure 7.10 Conical pole lodge from the East Fork of the Wind River in northwest Wyoming (a), Soapy Dale lodge from the Absaroka Mountains (b), and lodges from Painter Gulch, a tributary to the Sunlight Basin (c). The latter had begun to badly deteriorate when this photograph was taken in 1985. Lodge on the left is more complete than the collapsed lodge to the right (behind the standing tree).

Figure 7.11   Juniper log lodge from the foothills on the southern slopes of the Bighorn Mountains in central Wyoming.

Figure 7.12   Pole lodge with poles leaned against the walls of a cliff, with rocks and smaller branches built up around the bottom of the shelter, in the western foothills of the Bighorn Mountains.

archaeological record. Some campsites were already discussed earlier in this volume as they are sometimes a part of a set of interrelated localities that include kill, processing, and camp components, while other campsites were discussed as part of the development of Plains cultural chronology. However, camps also occur in other behavioral contexts, and these often have very different archaeological characteristics.

Perhaps the earliest campsites in the Central Rocky Mountains and adjacent Plains are of Folsom age. At least five of these are in the region, as is one that is located in a rockshelter. The first excavated of these camps is the Lindenmeier site on the Colorado–Wyoming border. Lindenmeier plays a significant role in the history of Paleoindian archaeology and is one of the largest if not the largest known Folsom site. Not only is it spatially extensive, but its artifact inventory is large as well. The Lindenmeier investigations are examples of interdisciplinary success. Bryan and Ray (1940) interpreted not only the reason for its discovery as due to a pirated stream deepening its drainage through the cultural deposit but, by tracing the stream terraces, were able to estimate the time of occupation (prior to the radiocarbon revolution this was the only means of estimating age) as well as model the paleoenvironments. The glaciations identified are still valid climatic events. The investigator interpreted Lindenmeier as a campsite (Roberts 1935), one of the rare examples of this type of locality at the time. Later, when ethnographic analogy was the rage and various models of hunter-gatherers (Lee and DeVore 1968) began playing a significant role in prehistoric interpretations, the site was reinterpreted as an aggregation site—a place where multiple independent groups of hunter-gatherers met for various social and ceremonial purposes (Wilmsen and Roberts 1978). A further reinterpretation questions the need for aggregations among early North American foragers living in extremely low densities across the continent (Hofman 1994). Lindenmeier thus continues to play a major role in Paleoindian interpretations.

Somewhat spatially smaller, but still a large site with a large artifact inventory, is the Hanson site in the Bighorn Basin on the western slopes of the Bighorn Range. The site is encased in the sediment of the T-2 terrace on two sides of the same arroyo. The current arroyo split the site in two and in the process eroded away a substantial portion, perhaps most of the site (see Figure 2.26). The remaining portions on both sides of the arroyo, however, hold a wealth of information regarding Folsom camping.

The Hanson site was investigated with a number of exploratory units, backhoe trenches, several small block excavations, and one large block (Figure 7.13). These revealed an approximate minimum overall extent of the site of 65 x 200 m and resulted in the recovery of tens of thousands of artifacts, mostly chipped stone, but including some bone. With the exception of a few dozen well-preserved bones, much of the bone consisted of small millimeter-sized fragments. The fragmentation is due to pre- and postdepositional destruction processes of weathering, soil chemistry, overburden weight, and so on. Whether predeposition treatment of bone—that is, heavy processing—is responsible for the fragmentation is not determinable at this time, although the fragments and breaks are largely angular, suggesting weathering (Arnold 2007). The taxa identified at the Hanson site include bison, mountain sheep, jackrabbit, and bobcat.

Three hard-packed areas are thought to represent some sort of circular structures or lodges; however, no postholes were discovered as supporting evidence

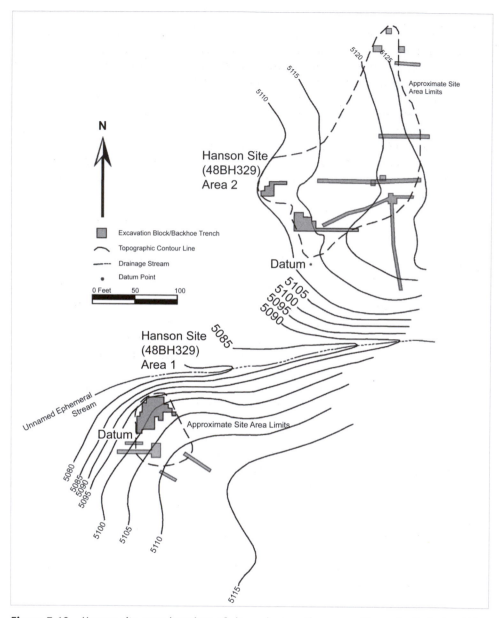

Figure 7.13   Hanson site map: locations of site and excavation areas. (Image by Craig Arnold.)

for this inference. One of these features had two superimposed hard-packed layers, suggesting multiple occupations and remodeling of the dwelling. The time
period between occupations is unknown and could have been from as little as a
few days to as long as decades. The lodge interpretation is supported by several
features, including an antler stake driven into the ground whose purpose might
have been to hold down the outside covering, presumably some sort of animal
skin, of the lodge.

Evidence of intense heat is present in many areas, including oxidized clay up
to several centimeters in thickness. Calcined bone fragments and burned chipped

stone was also abundant in these areas, but no fire hearths were obvious. The distribution of fire-altered material, however, suggests where the hearths had been (Figures 7.14 and 7.15). Paleoindian sites often lack clearly defined features, but the presence of hearths and dwellings and their location is often arrived at analytically through patterns of distribution of burned material (e.g., Jodry 1999b; Laughlin 2005; Steiger 2006; Surovell and Waguespack 2007).

A contemporary of Lindenmeier and Hanson is the Krmpotich site in the Green River Basin of southwest Wyoming. The site is on the western edge of the

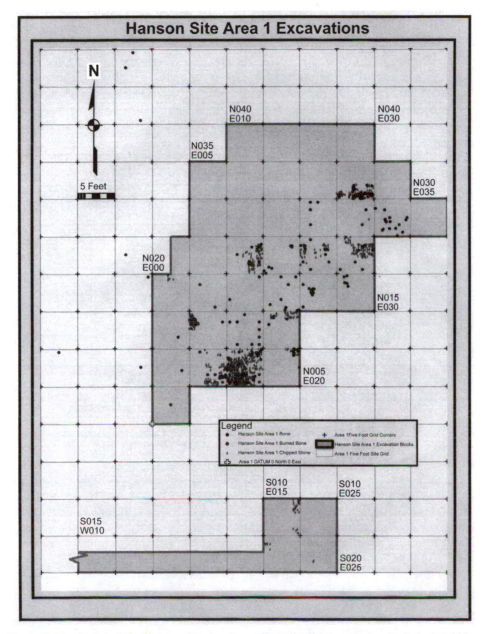

Figure 7.14 Area 1 of the Hanson site showing artifact distribution. (Image by Craig Arnold.)

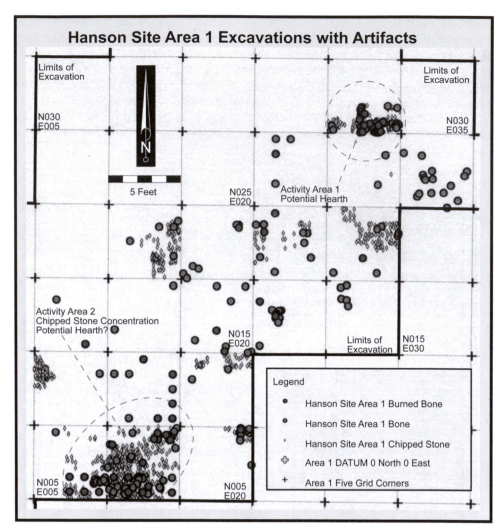

Figure 7.15   Area 1 of the Hanson site showing the location of burned material probably indicating the location of hearths. (Image by Craig Arnold.)

Killpecker dune field, a feature containing other Paleoindian localities, notably the Finley site. Krmpotich is not only a significant Folsom camp, but is an excellent example of the necessity of interdisciplinary studies and the role of avocationals in archaeology. The site was monitored for years by an avocational archaeologist, Jack Krmpotich, who brought it to our attention and finally convinced us to investigate it. Excavations began in the southern portion of the site, where surface artifact exposure was noted. The dense concentration of artifacts is now suspected to be a function of sediment deflation where smaller-sized sediment (sand) was removed by wind. A nondeflated deposit was expected to be located further to the north, buried by up to several meters of sand. A backhoe trench and adjoining units (Figure 7.16) demonstrated that Folsom-age material was buried within a paleosol extending in excess of 20 m to the north. Vertical artifact frequency showed that artifact density was the greatest at the bottom of this paleosol. Several seasons were devoted to excavating this paleosol, but generally with poor results,

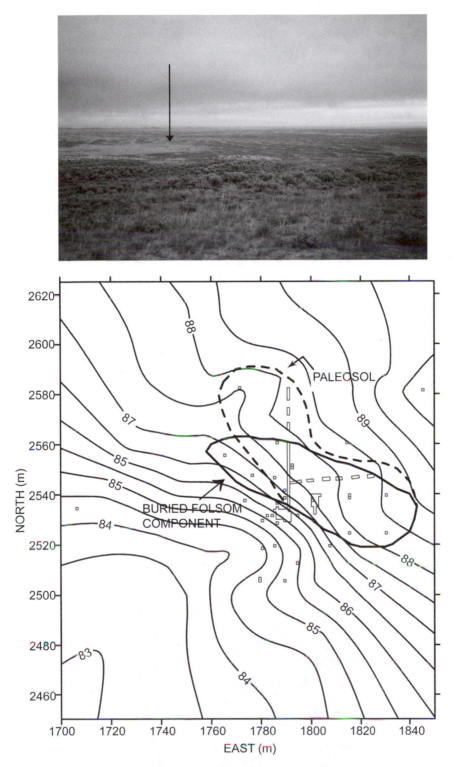

Figure 7.16 Krmpotich site (top) and excavation map (bottom). Excavation blocks, trenches, and units are indicated, as is the subsurface distribution of the Folsom component and paleosol.

the excavation yielding only a few diagnostic artifacts (channel flakes and project-ile point fragments), virtually no tools, and a large amount of very small, likely (re)sharpening flakes. A granulometric analysis of a column sample, however, showed that the greatest frequency of artifacts corresponds to the largest sedi-ment grain size, indicating that deflation is responsible for both patterns (Mayer 2002). Based on radiocarbon and optical stimulated dates bracketing the deflated surface, the age of deflation pre-dates 2000 years ago, when the recent deposition that buried the site began. All the chronologically diagnostic artifacts excavated from the deflated surface, however, are Folsom, indicating that there are no other cultural components represented. We are also still unsure whether the horizontal distribution of artifacts is a function of cultural behavior or natural processes.

Nevertheless, the recovery of only Folsom artifacts at the site suggests that the cultural assemblage recovered is Folsom and the artifacts can be informative of Folsom camping activities. To begin, many objects such as scrapers, gravers, and a variety of flake tools signal domestic tasks (Figure 7.17). Other artifacts, however, consist of broken bifaces, whole and broken preforms, exhausted projectile points, and channel flakes (Figure 7.18). These demonstrate on-site production of fairly large quantity of preforms and projectile points. On this basis, a workshop would be a better description of site function. Nevertheless, the combination of tools and production debris demonstrate the dual function of the site—a camp and a work-shop. Although several sources of raw material are located within 10–20 km of the Krmpotich site, the main material for the manufacture of Folsom projectile points and preforms is oolitic chert, and this material is the most common component of the assemblage. Within a few kilometers of the Krmpotich site oolitic chert occurs

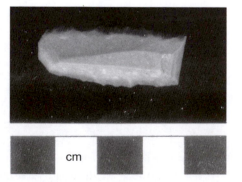

Figure 7.17   Selected tools from the Krmpotich site: channel flake graver (top), and limace (bottom).

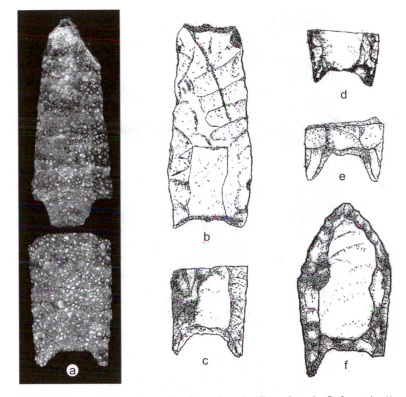

Figure 7.18   Folsom point preforms (a, b) and projectile points (c–f) from the Krmpotich site. Figure 7.18a was broken on the second fluting attempt. Not to scale. (Courtesy of Jack Krmpotich.)

as rather small flat cobbles. To manufacture Folsom projectile points, cobbles were regularized into early stage preforms, but not bifaces, before they were brought to the site. The Krmpotich tool makers took advantage of the natural "bifaces" by simply removing a series of flakes around the cobble circumference, thus making them into bifaces and in the process began setting up the platforms for fluting (Peterson 2001). Michael Peterson duplicated this Folsom point production process experimentally and found that it required the removal of about 40 flakes from an average core to complete the process.

Starting with occupations even earlier then Lindenmeier and Hanson is the stratified Hell Gap site in east-central Wyoming. The Hell Gap site is arguably the most significant Paleoindian campsite with occupations from 11,000 to 7500 BP that contain all Plains cultural complexes with the possible exception of Clovis. The site is located along the terraces of the Hell Gap Arroyo as it winds its way from the open plains into the Hartville uplift (Figure 7.19). Five separate localities were identified by the first investigations of the 1950s and 1960s (Irwin-Williams et al. 1973), however, more are now known to exist (Larson et al. 2009). Of the original five localities, four contain solely or mostly Paleoindian components, while the fifth is of much later age.

Like the sites discussed in this section, Hell Gap is unusual among large and well-reported Paleoindian sites on the Plains in that it has not a single bison kill, although some components display significant amounts of bison processing. It is located near rich sources of quartzite and chert for tool stone, a situation not

Figure 7.19   The Hell Gap site area: view east toward the open plains with the Hell Gap Valley in the foreground. (Photo by Richard Collier, Wyoming State Historic Preservation Office.)

uncommon in the Rocky Mountains, but unusual for the Plains. The site presents much more than just the bison hunting economy of Paleoindian life, one that was no doubt repeated many times up and down the Hartville uplift, but only the archaeology at Hell Gap has been preserved. Other Hell Gaps, wherever they were, have not been so fortunate.

Starting with the first clear evidence of human occupation of the Hell Gap Valley at 11,000 BP, we begin to see patterned use of the valley that continues throughout the Paleoindian occupations (Figures 2.23 and 7.20). One of the primary draws to the valley was undoubtedly the abundant Hartville uplift chert available nearby. Cloverly Formation quartzites occur not all that much further away, but seem not to have been a preferred stone at any time during the Paleoindian occupation. Hell Gap Paleoindians were involved in the production of bifaces and tools made from flake cores. Many of the bifaces were transported off the site, as were the flake tools. Flake tool production at Hell Gap in many cases rivals that of biface production and gives us a more balanced perspective on Paleoindian technological organization. The presence of tools (both bifaces and flake tools) that have no associated debitage indicates that people were replacing old tools with new. The discarded or lost flake tools of Hell Gap range from utilized and retouched flakes to scrapers and gravers (among others). Beyond serving as sources of flakes for tools, bifaces were manufactured from the preform stage into finished projectile points in many of the occupations. The relative frequency of tool types varies significantly from one component to the other at the locality that has received the most in-depth analyses, Locality I.

Some kind of heat treatment of the Hartville uplift chert may have occurred during the Paleoindian occupations, especially in the Eden/Scottsbluff and Frederick components at Locality I. Evidence for a hearth or hearths in the Frederick component in an area with a high frequency of heated flakes further supports this

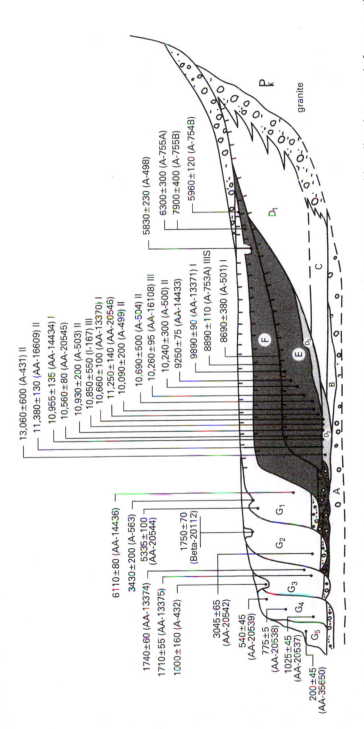

Figure 7.20 Schematic diagram and radiocarbon determination of the Hell Gap arroyo (all dates are presented in radiocarbon years before present).

suggestion. Some of the Eden/Scottsbluff and Frederick tools show evidence of heat treatment. The juxtaposition of heated and burned debitage next to the hearths in the Frederick level should be further investigated, as should the relationship between debitage, tools, and production debris (cores and bifaces) within those squares showing the highest percentage of heated and burned stone.

Not only does the Hell Gap site have hearths where stone was possibly heated, but it is the location of some of the earliest structures in North America. Beginning with the Midland component at Locality II, five Paleoindian structures were excavated, one of which was apparently rebuilt in a similar location on more than one occasion (Figure 7.21b). Four of the structures are defined on the basis of postholes that are assumed to be the support mechanism for a skin covering. Two of the structures are in the Agate Basin component at Locality II. A different structure type is located in the Frederick component of Locality I. Here a series of cobbles mark off a semicircle reminiscent of a tipi ring (Figure 7.21a). If this is in fact a tipi ring, it is one of the earliest if not the earliest such feature known from North America. These structures, as much as anything, demonstrate the campsite nature of the Hell Gap site.

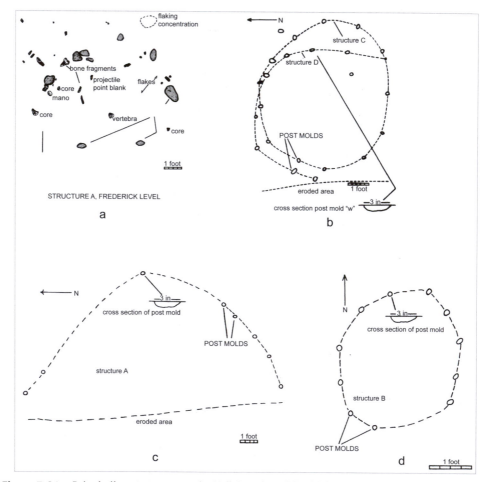

Figure 7.21   Paleoindian structures at the Hell Gap site: a) Fredrick complex stone circle; b) Agate Basin complex postholes; c) Midland complex postholes; d) Midland postholes.

Results from microwear analyses of a sample that includes material from all components (Bamforth and Becker 2009) as well as a focused study of Eden/ Scottsbluff and Alberta tools (Muñiz 2009) tell us that, in many ways, the activities occurring at Hell Gap were similar through time (Figure 7.22). Much of the

Figure 7.22   Selected use-wear polishes from the Eden/Scottsbluff components of the Hell Gap site. (Photo by Mark Muñiz.)

wear is from hide scraping, mostly of dry hides. Butchery traces, seen as meat and fresh hide polish, occurs in the Cody components (Eden/Scottsbluff and Alberta), but is rare in other complexes. The presence of wood and plant polish on two tools suggests that other materials were being processed. Many of the tools show evidence of hafting, particularly scrapers, and a number of the tools have polish, suggesting they were carried in leather sheaths of some kind.

Unfortunately, poor provenience information, missing faunal elements from the assemblage, and the inadequate and destructive use of chemical preservatives applied to the bone during 1960s excavations reduces the amount that we can say about the activities surrounding faunal exploitation at Hell Gap. However, we are able to draw some general conclusions about the faunal assemblages that broaden our understanding of Paleoindian subsistence practices. Hell Gap faunal assemblages represent a combination of bison killed in mass kills and hunted individually, but it appears that none of the animals were killed at the spot where they were recovered. Instead animals, or more likely portions of animals, were brought to Hell Gap for butchering and processing (Figure 7.23). In all instances, secondary processing to remove marrow and fat deposits was the goal of most of the subsistence-related activities at Hell Gap (Figures 7.24–7.26). The intensity of the fat recovery appears to have been greater in the earlier components, but the Locality IIIS/V Eden component sample is very small and only part of a much larger deposit. Further investigations in that deposit may answer many questions.

Figure 7.23 Locality IIIS/V of the Hell Gap Valley: exposed Eden "living floor" excavated in the French fashion by exposing all of the stratigraphic layer. Henry Irwin incorporated this field methodology into the Hell Gap investigations after spending time with Leroi-Gourhan at the site of Pincevant in France, which the latter had just started to investigate. Portions of the floor were also preserved in latex.

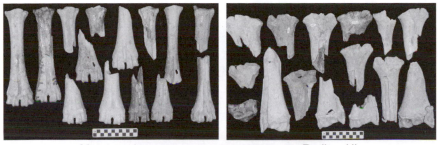

Metatarsals   Radius–Ulna

Calcaneus

Astragalus

Atlas

Figure 7.24 Butchered bison long bones (top), calcanii (middle), astragali (bottom left), and atlas vertebra (bottom right) from the Hell Gap site. (Courtesy of David J. Rapson.)

Many more campsites from all periods of prehistory are within our area. A number of these were discussed in other parts of this book as they bear on other topics of interest. Thus, the McKean site was presented in Chapter 2 and the Bugas-Holding and Helen Lookingbill sites in Chapter 5. These and other campsites are perhaps the most common archaeological localities on the Northwestern Plains and Rocky Mountains as well as in other regions with hunter-gatherer populations.

CAIRN LINES, ALIGNMENTS, FENCES, AND CORRALS

Cairn Lines

Drive lines for bison jumps have long been recognized (e.g., Frison 1967b, 1970a; Malouf 1962) and many thoughts and ideas on their use and function have been expressed. These features usually consist of relatively small piles of stones arranged in lines leading toward bison procurement features, whose location was determined usually by the natural topography. These lines, in many cases

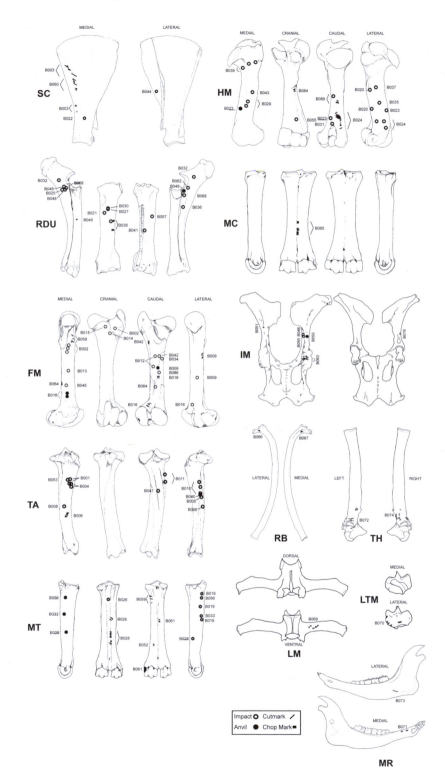

Figure 7.25 Location of butchering marks on bison bone elements. (Courtesy of David J. Rapson.)

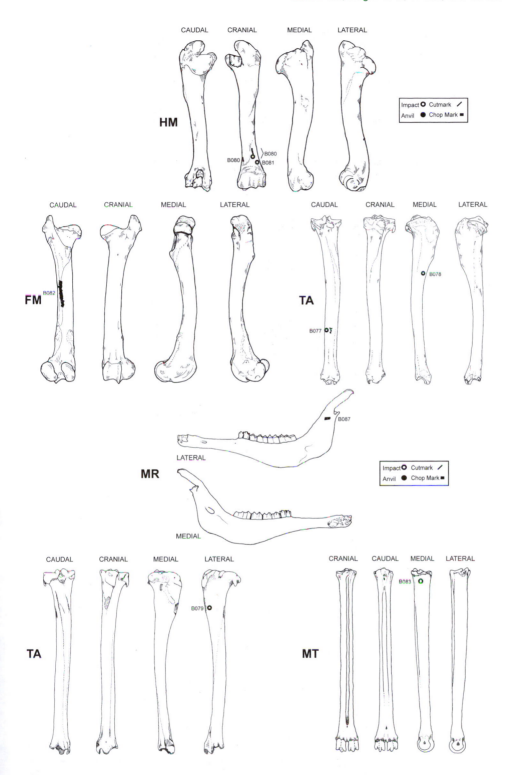

Figure 7.26 Location of butchering marks on deer- or antelope-sized bone elements. (Courtesy of David J. Rapson.)

at least, seem to have been placed in locations that suggest they were markers providing information on the control of bison herds during a drive event.
Lines of closely spaced and/or contiguous stones appear as drive-line features
in rough country and at higher elevations in communal mountain sheep procurement sites. Some of these may have had ritual significance also in animal
procurement events.

A set of drive lines in southeast Wyoming is particularly intriguing as it shows
long-term bison management strategy. This site, southwest of Lusk, Wyoming,
consists of a series of complete and partial drive lines, many leading toward a
25 m steep scarp at the edge of an unnamed drainage, while a few lines lead in
a different direction (Figure 7.27; Dewey and Janice Baars, personal communication 2008). These demonstrate a long-term redundant use of this facility and
natural physiographic features. The drive lines were built and rebuilt on many
occasions—likely the stones from older drive lines were moved into newer ones.
While one set of lines clearly ends in a scarp that must have formed a jump, other

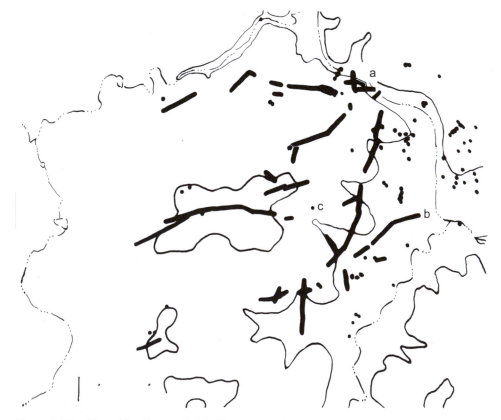

Figure 7.27 Bison drive lines and tipi villages in southeast Wyoming on the northern edge of the
Hartville uplift. Over 2000 cairns are in this complex; many lines are inferred to be drive lanes for
buffalo drives. Although the main drive system ends in a jump at the northern end of the complex
(a), some lines point in an east–west direction (b), probably indicating location of another drive
system. Individual cairns (c) may be part of older rebuilt lines, meat storage, or have served other
functions. This vast complex, covering over 9 km², is surrounded and interspersed with a number
of villages, as seen from the distribution of tipi rings (not shown). (Courtesy of Dewey and Janice
Baars.)

sets end in gentler terrain, where perhaps an artificial structure contained the animals. The entire complex consists of 1922 cairns, most constituting the drive lines. Even more intriguing are the tipi villages around this bison procurement facility. A preliminary study has partially documented the surface manifestation of this site; however, much work remains to be done if this major prehistoric site is to yield the full potential information possible. Although not unique, such sites are not common across the Northwestern Plains. A similar situation may be present in the Two Medicine area of Montana, Head-Smashed-In in Alberta, and elsewhere on the Great Plains (Brink and Dawe 1989; Zedeño et al. 2008).

Stone piles or single cairns are present in other forms, the purpose of which is sometimes unclear. With great predictability, they are present on high points. Their cultural origin is usually difficult to determine because of their context, and their age cannot be determined reliably because of a lack of diagnostic items and/or organic materials for dating. There seems to be little doubt that these cairns are not of Euroamerican origin.

Linear arrangements of various-sized cairns (Figures 7.28 and 7.29) are presently known from southern Montana and much of Wyoming. At first glance they are reminiscent of animal drive lines, but careful evaluation soon dispels this possibility because their locations do not fit in with animal behavior during procurement operations and many of the cairns are much larger than those found in animal drive lines. In many cases they do follow trails, and present-day roads have utilized the same terrain (Figure 7.30). Large areas were cleared of stones to provide enough for the cairns, but these are often in areas where it is difficult to envision a need for markers in order to follow a trail, suggesting possible ritual significance. It is obvious in most cases that these cairn lines represent considerable human effort and that they must be accorded their proper place in Plains-mountain

Figure 7.28   Piles of stones in a line in the southern Bighorn Mountains in Wyoming marking the Jensen Trail.

Figure 7.29   Cairn lines in Wyoming.

Figure 7.30   Present-day road following a line of cairns. In the background is the "Hole-in-the-Wall" country in the southern Bighorn Mountains.

prehistory. We need to know their true function or functions, the time period or periods involved, and if they were the results of casual, long-term accumulations or major, short-term efforts.

Six of these cairn lines in the southern Bighorn Mountains and foothills area have been superficially studied (Frison 1981), and others are known to exist in the Laramie Range in southeast Wyoming and in the Ferris and Green mountains in south-central Wyoming. Mulloy (1958:179–182) described cairn lines in Pryor Gap in southern Montana that extend a distance of approximately 1.6 km. Three large rock mounds are on one end, the largest of which is about 11.6 m x 10.4 m in diameter and about 1.5 m high, while the other two are smaller. Sixty-one other cairns in the line are much smaller yet and resemble closely the ones in the Bighorn Mountains. Potsherds and other Late Prehistoric items were recovered in one of the cairns (see also Nelson 1942).

A detailed study was made of another manifestation known as the Bad Pass Trail cairn line that begins in northern Wyoming and extends into southern Montana just north of the Bighorn River. It is located between the Bighorn and Pryor mountains (Loendorf and Brownell 1980) and, in its entirety, covers a distance of approximately 19 km and contains several hundred cairns of various sizes (Figure 7.31). This has been a trail in both prehistoric and historic times and about the only means of easy access between the two mountain ranges. Several cairns were completely excavated and one produced potsherds. A radiocarbon date of 1620 ± 85 years BP (Beta-1078) that the investigators feel is reliable was obtained on charcoal from another cairn, which would indicate that at least part of the cairn line could be of Late Archaic or early Late Prehistoric age.

Medicine Wheels

Few things concerning Plains-mountain archaeology has received the publicity and interest as the so-called Bighorn Medicine Wheel. Unfortunately, too many of the interpretations of this feature rely on conjecture rather than reliable data. First reported in the professional literature by Simms (1903), the number of reports that followed are numerous and only a few can be mentioned (e.g., Eddy 1974, 1977; Grey 1963a; Wilson et al. 1981). There seems little doubt that the Bighorn Medicine Wheel is authentic, although it has undergone many different disturbances since its first discovery by Euroamericans (Figure 7.32). There is a strong possibility in this case that this feature was built in more than a single stage over an unknown period of time and part or parts of it may be older than others. Cultural materials recovered within the structure itself are of Late Prehistoric and Historic age (Grey 1963a), and many of its elements have been disturbed by various individuals looking for artifacts. The Fort Smith Medicine Wheel on the Crow Indian Reservation in Montana (Brown 1963) is much smaller than the Bighorn Medicine Wheel and consists only of a central cairn with six spokes. However, it also appears to be of authentic Native American origin.

On the other hand, people other than our prehistoric inhabitants have demonstrated a compulsion to arrange stones in the same kinds of configurations. Many of these have been mistakenly identified and, after they have been in place for many decades, they can be difficult if not impossible to distinguish from the real thing. A prime example of this is a boulder structure in the Bighorn Mountains

Figure 7.31   Cairns along the Bad Pass Trail in southern Montana.

Figure 7.32   The Bighorn Medicine Wheel in 1958. (Photo by Don Grey.)

built during the 1930s by children (under adult supervision) at summer camp who were strongly influenced by a visit to the Bighorn Medicine Wheel. It was mapped with some question as to its authenticity (Grant 1981:71), but still its non–Native American origin needs to be carefully documented to prevent future misinterpretations. Although Medicine wheels and other rock alignments are better known from the far northern Plains (Brace 2005), they are common to the south as well, being documented in Colorado and New Mexico. One example is a recently described feature from Table Mountain in the Laramie Basin of southern Wyoming (Figure 7.33).

Alignments

Many high points are the locations of various stone structures (Figure 7.34) that are given a variety of names, including stone rings, vision quest structures, shaman

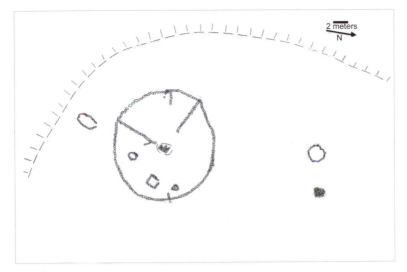

Figure 7.33   Recently documented Medicine Wheel on Table Mountain in the Laramie Basin, Wyoming, that may be of authentic Native American origin. (From field sketch by Norbert Waslik.)

Figure 7.34   Stone structure on a high point, Old Women anticline, eastern Wyoming (a), a vision quest site on top of Hunt Mountain in the Bighorn Mountains (b), and a vision quest site on a ridge below Hunt Mountain (c).

structures, eagle traps, and signal fire rings. All of these fit within the beliefs and activities of known Plains Indian groups and are described ethnographically. Careful investigation is always needed to better ensure the authenticity of these as being of prehistoric origin, since many can be documented as non-Indian in origin. Present-day people such as sheepherders with time to spare in their work have constructed numerous cairns, rock walls, and other features.

Stones arranged in the form of arrows, some quite large, occur in many locations, usually in prominent locations on ridge tops and summits. The authenticity of many and perhaps most of these as being of prehistoric origin needs to be questioned. However, at least one of some size in the western Bighorn Basin in northern Wyoming has long been accepted as authentic. Built of over 500 stream-rounded boulders, it is 17.5 m long and the shaft is about 50 cm wide (Loendorf 1978). It points to the general direction of the Bighorn Medicine Wheel, which may or may not have significance. The earliest settlers in the area claim it was there when they arrived during the latter part of the nineteenth century.

Of great interest as well are the various effigies constructed from cobbles and boulders. Although not particularly common in the Northwestern Plains and Rocky Mountains, they occur in nearby regions. Brace (2005) has documented a variety of human and animal figures as well as geometrically designed monuments in Saskatchewan, and similar features occur throughout the area. The animal figures include snakes, buffalo, salamanders, and most commonly turtles. Such figures are rather reminiscent of the intaglios of the southern California deserts.

Protohistoric Fences and Corrals

A very different type of alignment was recorded in the Powder Wash area of southwest Wyoming by Dick Murcray (1993). A juniper fence over 8 km long forms an enclosure crossing Powder Wash (Figure 7.35). There are several breaks in the fence, two notable ones being where the modern road crosses the feature and a third on the fence's northeast side. The fence encloses an area of perhaps three square kilometers. This is significantly larger than any known game traps in the region—one reason for the controversy surrounding its interpretation. Murcray first interpreted this feature as an antelope trap, but its great size and lack of topographic features conducive to known methods of animal hunting, prompted further research. Partly because of the large size, and encouraged by relatively recent dendrochronological dates, this feature was reinterpreted as of historic Euroamerican origin and related to well-documented outlaw use of the Powder Wash area (Darlington and Bodyfelt 1999). However, further intensive studies of the feature complex, which includes a multitude of rock images, wood and stone structures, as well as other features around the fence, suggest a coherent behavioral complex of historic Native American origin for this facility (Keyser and Poetschat 2008). Keyser and Poetschat suggest that the feature was used as a horse corral by the Ute people in the nineteenth century. At that time, the Utes were raiding for horses to the north among the Shoshone and the Euroamerican immigrants crossing the continent along several trails. The investigators link the rock art, many containing horses, with the use of the corral and argue that this is one of a number of such features along the northern boundary of the Ute territory (Martin et al. 2006).

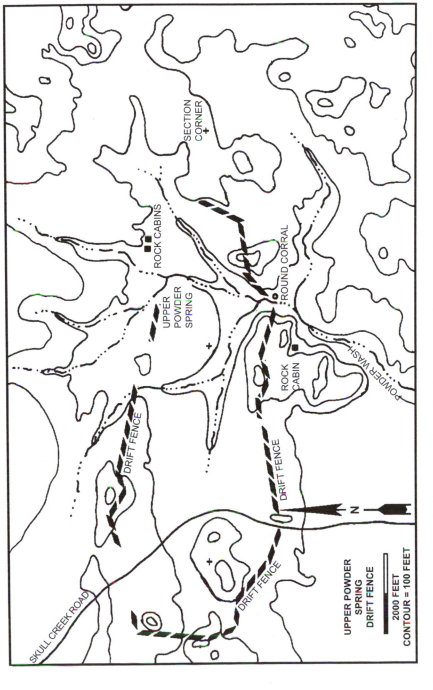

Figure 7.35 Powder Wash juniper fence. (Darlington and Bodyfelt 1999; courtesy of Dave Darlington.)

8

A Myriad of Life's Necessities

Introduction

Depictions of hunter-gatherer lifeways wax and wane between romantic—happy, affluent foragers in possession of all life's necessities and not needing very much, to the opposite—perennially starving savages who lead short and brutal lives. Perhaps both are true or perhaps neither are. Regardless, life on the Plains and nearby Rockies offered opportunities, but also significant obstacles and numerous unpredictabilities. Prehistoric people coped with life, survived, and quite clearly thrived. To do so required ingenuity expressed in material objects and behaviors other than those discussed in the previous chapters.

Here we present a myriad of rare or unusual objects that form the archeological record. It is not their scarcity or "wow" factor that make them important; rather, many are representative of specific requirements or critical behaviors for life on the Plains and Rockies. However, for various reasons (e.g., poor preservation or true scarcity), some objects occur infrequently in the archaeological record of our region. We begin with clothing and containers or the evidence for and implications of such objects. Both have survival or comfort value, but hunter-gatherers vary a great deal in how they accomplish this. Hunting equipment consists of more than just the spear or arrow tips presented throughout this book because of their diagnostic value. Atlatl weights and bows are more significant aspects of this equipment, yet both are rare in the archeological record. Red ocher, personal adornment, personal tools, and exotic items have been found in association with human remains, clearly indicating the ritual or interment. Burial offerings speak loudly of human networks, scales of social relationships, and other usually intangible but critical aspects of life. Other exotic objects clearly "imported" from great distances (from the Pacific and Gulf coasts to the Great Lakes) suggest a vastly greater awareness of the continent than we were able to show in other chapters of this book. And the completeness of prehistoric lifeways is well represented by musical instruments that undoubtedly accompanied much human activity during both working and nonworking hours of the day throughout prehistory. Thus the objects discussed in this chapter, although vastly underrepresented in the archeological record, are perhaps the most significant record of past lifeways on the Plains and Rockies.

CLOTHING

In conjunction with heat and shelter, winter survival in the Northwestern Plains and Rocky Mountains required some kind of fairly sophisticated clothing. Actual evidence for this is scarce, but some evidence is strongly suggestive. Many site assemblages contain the tools that could produce tailored and sewn clothing. In the Leigh Cave assemblage (Frison and Huseas 1968), a wide variety of two-strand twisted cordage made of milkweed (*Asclepias* sp.) and other fibers was recovered. In addition, there were fragments of hide sewed with the same fiber cordage (Figure 8.1).

In the Spring Creek Cave (Frison 1965) and Daugherty Cave (Frison 1968a) assemblages, bits of hide and twisted sinew and both plant fiber and sinew sewing elements suggest clothing manufacture. A hide moccasin of Late Plains Archaic age in the latter assemblage indicated well-made and serviceable footgear (Figure 8.2). Very few perishable assemblages of any great time depth are present in rockshelters because of the tendency for moisture to filtrate cultural levels once they are buried with roof fall.

Tailored clothing on a mummified cadaver interred about 1200 years ago in Mummy Cave (Husted and Edgar 2002) and footgear from the same site component provide further evidence of the ability of prehistoric peoples to produce adequate winter clothing. Footgear in particular must have limited food gathering activities during periods of extreme cold. Frostbitten feet require a long time to heal, and if the frostbite is severe enough, they never heal completely. Prehistoric hunters and gatherers were most certainly aware of these dangers and took the necessary precautions. Clothing manufacture is particularly evidenced by needles, several of which have been found dating to as early as Folsom times (Figure 8.3). Bone needles and awls are part of several of the assemblages from house pit structures, including Split Rock Ranch, and occur in other prehistoric campsites.

CERAMICS AND CONTAINERS

Pottery appeared on the Northwestern Plains and Rocky Mountains at the end of the Late Plains Archaic and continued through the Late Prehistoric period. Assemblages are small and frequently highly fragmented, and although present in relatively small amounts, ceramics are a valuable cultural marker. Several pottery traditions are represented. However, with one exception, the different pottery-bearing peoples were intrusive or at least peripheral to the centers of main development. The exception is the Intermountain pottery tradition (Mulloy 1958:196–200), usually regarded as having cultural affiliations with Shoshonean groups. Although it appears indigenous to the Rocky Mountains and Northwestern Plains, its original source is unknown.

Shoshonean or Intermountain tradition pottery is recognizable by a distinctive flat bottom and usually a flowerpot shape (Figure 8.4) with a flanged base, although a number of stylistic variations are now known, such as prominent shoulders and strengthened rims (Frison 1971b; Wedel 1954). The technology is generally poor in relation to other ceramics. The pottery is usually thick and poorly fired, and it contains ungraded tempering materials of widely varying sizes. Surface treatment is

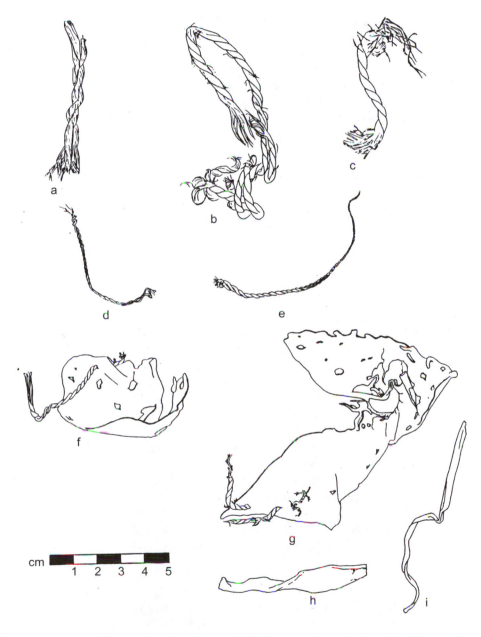

Figure 8.1 Twisted fiber cordage (a–e), tanned hide fragments sewed with twisted fiber cordage (f, g), and fragments of tanned hide (h, i) from Leigh Cave in the western foothills of the Bighorn Mountains. (From Frison and Huseas 1968.)

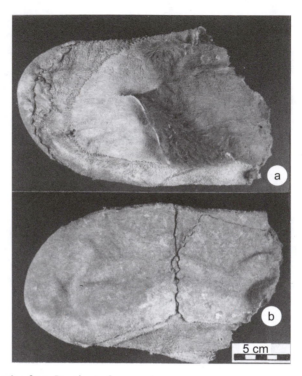

Figure 8.2 Moccasins from Daugherty Cave.

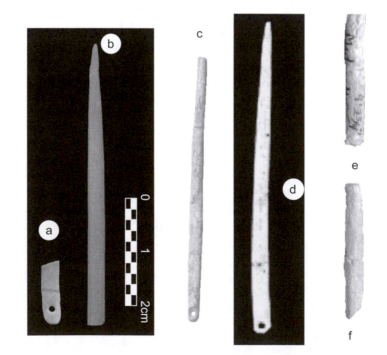

Figure 8.3 Bone needles and possible needle preforms from several sites: Medicine Lodge Creek (a, b), Hell Gap (c), Little Canyon Creek Cave (d); bone rods (probably needle preforms) from the Hell Gap site (e, f).

Figure 8.4   Intermountain tradition vessel. (Courtesy of Robert and Jo Larson.)

usually nothing more than a smoothing, although rare decorative motifs in the form of fingernail impressions appear on the shoulders of vessels. Holes drilled on both sides of a break for patching are also common, and small segments of vessels were reworked for reuse. It was common to make a smaller vessel out of a larger one by grinding a groove around the circumference at whatever distance was necessary below the rim to avoid a break. The vessel could then be broken along the groove and the lower part salvaged. Intermountain pottery has been subdivided into two traditions: Boar's Tusk Gray ware, which is characterized by globular, flowerpot-like forms with coarse grit or sand and Skull Point Gray ware, which is poorly known but thought to occur later in time than Boar's Tusk Gray (Creasman et al. 1990; Middleton et al. 2007).

Pottery from several different ceramic traditions associated with Southwestern cultures has been identified in southwestern Wyoming. Small amounts of Fremont pottery called Uinta Gray Ware have been found, and a local tradition of Fremont-like jars called Black Buttes Gray ware has been proposed for pottery found in southwest Wyoming (Middleton et al. 2007). A single site in central Wyoming, the Carter site (48NA1425), yielded ceramics similar to Uncompahgre Brown ware of northern Colorado and eastern Utah. Rather than identify the pottery as Uncompahgre and imply a Ute affiliation, Martin (2000) chose to name the pottery Waltman Brown. Pueblo pottery, both corrugated and painted sherds, has been found along the southern border of Wyoming west of the North Platte River and represent items brought into the area.

Pottery found in the camp/processing area of the Wardell Bison Trap site was originally described as coming from narrow, deep jars with pointed bottoms that appeared Woodland in shape but not surface treatment (Frison 1988a). Frison's

(1991) claim of Avonlea affiliation for the pottery has recently been confirmed by Reed (2003), who identifies the sherds from Wardell as Athabascan. Analysis of numerous sherds from the Woodard site located in central Wyoming southeast of Riverton, the Trappers Point area near Pinedale, and the Rock Springs area suggest an Athabascan affiliation as well (Frison 1988a; Reed 2003).

Because the pottery of southwestern Wyoming and northern Colorado is so frequently highly fragmented, few in number, and poorly dated, the identification of ceramic traditions for this area is still in its early stages. Future comparative work on the assemblages, petrographic and other analyses of composition, and better control of context could provide answers to questions about the Late Archaic and Late Prehistoric movement of peoples, connections to other areas, and the use of ceramics among hunter-gatherers living in the area.

Mandan tradition pottery occurs in the northeast quarter of Wyoming, a large share of southeastern Montana, and northwestern South Dakota. It is believed this pottery (Figure 2.14) was left by Crow Indians (Frison 1976b). It now appears that there were several movements of Missouri River groups to the area from AD 1400 to AD 1700 (Bowers 1965; Brooks 1995; Medicine Crow 1979). The Crow component at the Medicine Lodge Creek site contained sherds from a single vessel identified as Riggs Ware of the Extended Middle Missouri Tradition (Page 2007), and could indicate proto-Crow occupation of the area. The Big Goose Creek site at the base of the eastern slopes of the Bighorn Mountains in northern Wyoming (Frison et al. 1978) produced two radiocarbon dates between AD 1400 and AD 1500 with ceramics that could represent a derived form of Mandan tradition, based on comparison with those from the Hagen site in eastern Montana (Mulloy 1942). Most pottery attributed to the Crow has some measure of resemblance to the Hagen site ceramics. However, the identity of this pottery is usually tenuous and based on its provenience in territory traditionally known to have been occupied by the Crow. What is believed to be Crow pottery has appeared in northeast and north-central Wyoming, in places along the Yellowstone River in Montana (Mulloy 1942, 1953, 1958), and in extreme northwestern South Dakota (Over 1936).

Intermountain (Shoshonean) and Crow pottery sometimes occur together in the same campsite, which could be the result of any number of factors. The Piney Creek stone circle campsite (Frison 1967b) is considered to be a typical Crow manifestation with a small amount of Intermountain ceramics. The John Gale site is a typical Shoshonean campsite with ceramics of definite Crow shapes and styles (Brox and Miller 1974). A few reconstructed vessels of likely Crow origin have been collected and described (Frison 1976b). "Wife stealing" has been cited as an explanation for the occurrence of two pottery types in the same site. However, such a statement is likely based on perceptions of gender inequality between males and females that arose out of the economic stresses of contact period economics. Equally plausible explanations based on both ethnographic and ethnoarchaeological research among modern pottery makers include ceramic makers from one group living with another group without the stigma of human trafficking; exchange and gifting between groups; multiple occupations of a single location by different groups; or even acquisition of someone else's lost pot. Identification of the reasons for different pottery styles in some archaeological sites requires testing at numerous well-excavated prehistoric localities.

The erosional remnant known as the Pine Bluffs in extreme southeast Wyoming has attracted many prehistoric populations. It is also peripheral to the Late

Prehistoric horticultural groups that lived on the plains of western Nebraska and Kansas, so that sites with Woodland, Upper Republican, and Dismal River ceramics have been found there. A sequence of radiocarbon dates from the Pine Bluffs site and others nearby provide a good chronological record of these cultural groups.

Woodland pottery is found on the eastern edge of the area along the Wyoming–Nebraska border and in northeastern Colorado. An isolated occurrence of Woodland pottery was found in southern Montana in a campsite area associated with the Kobold Buffalo Jump site and may have been associated with a Besant component there. A nearly complete Woodland vessel was recovered at the Greyrocks site near the confluence of the Laramie and North Platte rivers in southeast Wyoming in good cultural context with a date of about 1750 BP (Figure 2.15). Farther up the North Platte River, the Butler-Rissler site produced Besant projectile points and the partial remains of a large Woodland vessel (Miller and Waitkus 1989). Wheeler (1996) found Woodland pottery at Mule Creek Rockshelter (48CK4) in northeast Wyoming. Woodland pottery was also found in extreme northeast Colorado at the Happy Hollow Rockshelter (Steege 1967).

Upper Republican tradition pottery occurs within the loop of the North Platte River in Wyoming and along the South Platte River and the plains in Nebraska and in northeast Colorado (Reher 1971). The question of whether the far western sites, such as those at Pine Bluffs, are hunting camps occupied by eastern groups or whether they represent longer-term settlement has been the subject of debate for decades. Analysis of clay sources of Upper Republican ceramics from the Seven Mile Point and Gurney Peak Butte sites in the Pine Bluffs area indicates the use of local clay sources, suggesting that these sites were not short-term hunting camps, but may represent movement of people between the Medicine Creek drainage of Kansas and the High Plains (Cobry 1999; Cobry and Roper 2002:161). Flat-bottomed pottery suggestive of Intermountain has been recorded in sites containing Upper Republican ceramics, but the contexts were not good enough to determine whether these were the results of the same or different occupations.

Middle Missouri ceramics appear in small amounts in the northeast part of the area. The Nollmeyer site in eastern Montana along the Yellowstone River is proposed as an Extended Coalescent site, and a nearly complete vessel from the Dead Horse Creek site in the Powder River Basin in Wyoming is considered to be of Middle Missouri origin. Other small finds of ceramics in the Black Hills and the buttes area of South Dakota have also been identified as Extended Coalescent (Johnson et al. 1990). The cultural affiliations of the Smiley-Evans site along the Belle Fourche River in western South Dakota appear to be well to the east along the Missouri River. The site is a fortified campsite on a narrow terrace finger overlooking the Belle Fourche River valley with a defensive ditch protecting its approach from the plains to the east. The site represents a penetration of a Plains Village group almost to the Wyoming–South Dakota border at about 1000 years BP. A small amount of unidentified ceramics was found at the site (Alex 1989). Sites with ceramics of questionable cultural affiliations are located in the butte country of northwest South Dakota and southeast Montana and need further investigation and analysis.

Along with pottery, carved steatite vessels in the same flat, flanged-based, flowerpot style (Figure 8.5) were common. Other steatite vessels demonstrate a wide variance in size and shape. Steatite sources are found in pre-Cambrian deposits in the Teton, Wind River, and Bighorn Mountains (Figure 8.6), and the

Figure 8.5   Carved steatite vessels from Wyoming; note the stone plugs used to patch holes (a, b).

Figure 8.6   Steatite quarry (a), and a natural outcrop (b) used as a source of material.

Laramie Range, and all known sources demonstrate some measure of prehistoric quarrying efforts. Steatite has excellent heat-tolerance qualities, although it is an extremely heavy material with poor structural strength. Vessel blanks obviously cached at different stages of completion are a common find at varying distances from the quarries (Frison 1982a).

We are still not sure which came first, the fired pottery or the carved steatite vessels; neither are we sure of the time depth of the two. Radiocarbon dates are known for this Intermountain ware pottery. The oldest date, of about 750 years BP, is from Myers-Hindman in southwest Montana (Lahren 1976). Other dated occurrences are from Mummy Cave (Husted and Edgar 2002), Eden-Farson (Frison 1971b), and Eagle Creek (Arthur 1966), and are much later. The characteristic flat-bottomed pottery and carved steatite vessels occur all over the area but are concentrated mainly to the north and west, especially in the Green River Basin, the Upper Snake River drainage, the Absaroka Mountains, and upper Yellowstone River drainages. A good measure of individuality was expressed in steatite vessels; although they follow a general pattern to some extent, differences such as rim form and additions such as raised rings appear occasionally on vessel bodies. On the other hand, vessel shape was limited in many cases to the size and shape of the raw material piece, which may explain much of the variance in morphology.

This issue of pottery vs. steatite vessel precedence has also been a bone of contention in the southeast United States (Sassaman 1997, 2006; Truncer 2004, 2006). At stake are vastly different explanations for the emergence of soapstone technology. However, the crux of the matter is the dating of the emergence of the two technologies. In the Northwestern Plains and adjacent Rocky Mountains this is also an issue as finds of both materials are infrequent and contexts more often leave something to be desired than not. Nevertheless, our study area may be accumulating enough data to participate in this important debate in North American archaeology (e.g., Feyhl 1997).

MISCELLANEOUS AND UNIQUE ARTIFACTS

During the past 40 years, hundreds of people have passed through our doors with objects and pictures of things they wish to have identified. These objects cover a broad range and, in addition to human artifacts, they include stones shaped by wind and stream action, fossils, natural formations, bones chewed by rodents, pictures of stone arrangements, and many others too numerous to mention. Most people come with the hope of having their objects identified; others have already decided what their treasures are and only want confirmation. This last group is always the most difficult to deal with and are never pleased when you tell them that their cobble with a groove around the center resulted from stream action and is not a grooved maul.

Pack rat middens abound in our study area, and these rodents can apply artistic and other patterns to bone with their teeth that many persons find difficult to ascribe to their real source. Many of the sedimentary geological formations contain things such as concretions that appear to be of human origin. In this case, context is important since occasional fossils and natural formations do appear in archaeological sites, suggesting that prehistoric persons expressed interest in these objects as well as those persons presently roaming the country. The role of fossils and unusual objects in American Indian life and ritual is a potentially fascinating study and has been the subject of some ethnographic research (e.g., Mayor 2005).

On the other hand, we have found it poor policy to deprecate objects persons bring in for identification. More than once, a single artifact has proven to be the key to an important site. Many persons have told us that they hesitated to bring in an object for identification because they did not want to appear unknowledgeable. Consequently, it is advantageous to build up a rapport with the public so that they will bring in their finds for identification and know that they will be received in such a way that they will not feel inferior if their objects prove to be of no archaeological value.

Another aspect of this is that many things that persons bring in for identification are the things that are difficult to place in a cultural system. They are the projectile points and/or tools that do not fit well into any standard diagnostic or functional typology. In addition, there are the items outside the tool and weaponry categories that fall into the realm of the supernatural, but there is little chance of learning in exactly what manner from the archaeological record. Other items include those moved long distances from unfamiliar cultural systems for which the cultural mechanisms responsible are conjectural. Probably the greatest problem to the professional archaeologist is the behavior of those who are continually "testing" the professional; those individuals who acquire items that are either faked or obtained from other areas and claim they were found locally.

Atlatl Weights

Atlatl weights appear to have served more than purely functional needs. One broken atlatl from Spring Creek Cave in northern Wyoming (Figure 2.66g) has notches and glue in the proper position to indicate the former presence of a weight, now missing. However, in the cultural deposits of the site that are of Late Plains Archaic age, one broken and one complete atlatl weight were recovered that were made of calcite crystal, a relatively soft material that can be shaped by grinding with relative ease. Dry deposits in Daugherty Cave (Frison 1968a) of the same Late Archaic age produced parts of identical atlatls and two atlatl weights, one of fossil belemnite (Figure 8.7c) and a part of one carved from steatite. Another weight carved from a soft unidentified stone (Figure 8.7a, b) was recovered in a site component also of Late Plains Archaic age.

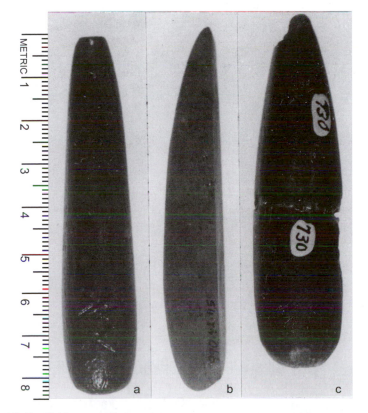

Figure 8.7 Atlatl weights.

Atlatl weights take curious shapes. One carved of steatite (Figure 8.8a, b) may represent some living object; the bottom side of this specimen is slightly concave, presumably to better fit the wooden part of the atlatl. Fossils were used to make weights, and in one case (Figure 8.8c), only one side of the object was ground flat to fit the back of the atlatl. Not always were these items made of relatively soft stone. Small river cobbles were ground flat on one side and may or may not have a shallow transverse groove centered over the top, presumably to aid in tying the object to the atlatl. Caution should be taken here, since in known but rare circumstances, small, polished river cobbles exposed on elevated river terraces may have one side smoothed by wind and sand action over long periods of time and out of context have been misidentified as atlatl weights.

Atlatl weights are occasional surface finds but not of the frequency that one would expect had they not been accorded some special status, possibly as the repositories of personal power or magic. It is debatable whether the atlatl weight

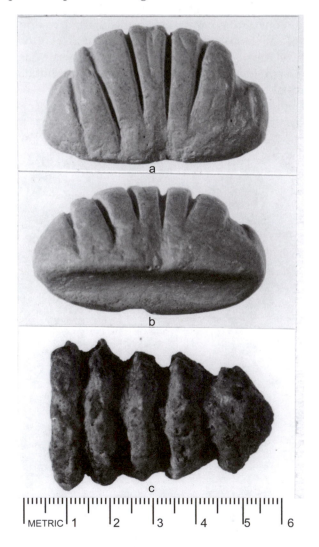

Figure 8.8 Atlatl weights; see text for discussion.

helped increase either the velocity or accuracy of the projectile, so its true function was at least partially ritualistic.

A bannerstone of green-banded slate was recovered in north-central Wyoming under circumstances that would seemingly eliminate any doubt of its authenticity or recent introduction. Both the material and the artifact are alien to the Northwestern Plains and Rocky Mountains. Although identical specimens appear regularly east of the Mississippi River, the circumstances of its appearance this far to the west are unknown (Figure 8.9; Mulloy 1954c).

Burial Offerings

In the earlier discussions of Clovis caches, the distinction was made between burial offerings which were not intended to be recovered for future use and caches of various utilitarian items that were meant to be recovered. Burial caches were removed from the system, while utilitarian caches were put aside for reentry into the system at a later date. It is an important distinction and one that is not always clear in the archaeological record, particularly in cases where the actual human osteological remains have not been preserved.

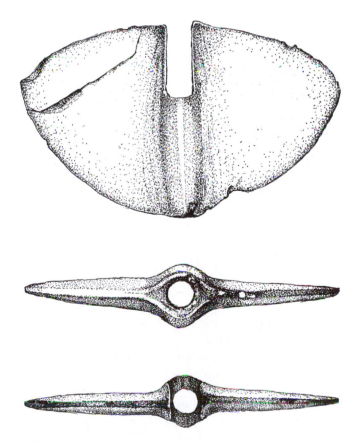

Figure 8.9   Bannerstone of exotic material found near Hyattville, Wyoming (Mulloy 1954c; courtesy of the Colorado Historical Society).

Clovis and other Paleoindian-age manifestations almost always attract more attention than those of later times, which is unfortunate but beyond control of the investigators. Consequently, the older ones receive wide publicity while those of younger age generally do not unless they contain large numbers of exotic items. The major problem in the investigation of caches is the general unpredictability of their locations. For reasons of security, they were placed so that the location was known only to the person or persons directly involved and not in obvious or predictable places. Consequently, most discoveries are accidental and, too often, not by archaeologists. Others that make such discoveries nearly always remove them so that it is seldom possible to view the materials in their original context.

The sizes of utilitarian caches vary. They may contain a few flakes, bifaces, or tools, or the number of items may be well into the hundreds. Materials may be close to or at considerable distances from sources. For example, caches recovered in southeast Montana (Clark and Fraley 1985) contained material from the Spanish Diggings and Hartville uplift nearly 300 km to the south in Wyoming. In numerous cases, caches of flakes, quarry blanks, and bifaces in early manufacturing stages have been found in the immediate vicinity of raw material sources.

In situations where human bone is lacking, red ocher, items of personal adornment, weaponry, personal tools, and exotic items are usually good indicators of burial situations. On the other hand, the nature of the items in the cache, whether they be flakes, bifaces at any of a number of manufacture stages, or complete tools or weaponry, cannot always be relied upon to separate human interments from true utilitarian caches. For example, the Rattlesnake Ridge burial cache in east-central Wyoming (Lippincott 1985) contained 41 bifaces at different stages of manufacture and a single possible formal tool. Were it not for the presence of two human bone fragments and a few pieces of red ocher, it would easily pass for a biface cache intended for later recovery and use.

At the other end of the spectrum, the Wind River burial cache in central Wyoming (Frison and Van Norman 1985), with a large quantity of artifact material, leaves little doubt of its true character. It was apparently some kind of cremation, with quantities of red ocher, tools, weaponry, and shell ornaments along with fragments of human bone and teeth. On the other hand, there were also a number of early-manufacture-stage bifaces, simple tools, and unmodified flakes that, lacking the unequivocal evidence of a human interment, would have been regarded as the contents of a utilitarian cache.

Both utilitarian caches and burial offerings continually appear, especially with the increasing number of persons, not all artifact hunters, that prowl the back country. Both manifestations were important parts of the prehistoric cultural systems and their true identity is important: burial offerings represent ritual activity and reflect status and religious beliefs while the utilitarian caches pass on information pertaining to the subsistence strategy.

Exotic items appear in burials and some come from a considerable distance. At one time, these kinds of objects were generally considered to be either fakes or else were acquired elsewhere and false claims were made as to the location of their discovery. Both of these situations have no doubt occurred, but there is evidence also that some exotic materials did get onto the Plains and Rocky Mountains and appear as burial offerings. Often the circumstances of recovery eventually provide evidence of authenticity or falsehood. A large notched biface (Figure 8.10a) was reported to have been found on the surface in southern

Figure 8.10 Corner-notched biface probably of lower Mississippi Valley origin from near the Garrett Allen (Elk Mountain) site in south-central Wyoming (a), and a side-notched biface found in a human burial at Medicine Creek Cave in northeastern Wyoming (b).

Wyoming and its authenticity was questioned. However, part of a large *Busycon* sp. shell (Figure 8.11) was found a year or so later by a different person in the same location, and it is now believed the two items were from a human burial that had eroded out nearby. Both items are diagnostic of materials from the lower Mississippi Valley that somehow found their way out onto the Plains.

There is no doubt that there is a limited amount of truly superior stone flaking materials, and when an unusually fine piece was obtained, the flintknappers tried to make something special. These items often appear as burial offerings. An example is a notched biface (Figure 8.10b) that was found in a prehistoric burial in eastern Wyoming nearly 100 years ago. It required a piece of chert of unusual quality to produce this item, but it still contained one small flaw that left a projection on one face which was removed by grinding in order to achieve more perfect symmetry of the object. Another example is a quartzite biface (Figure 8.12) that may have eroded out of a burial. It required an unusually large piece of material of high quality to produce the object. This piece has a flaw through one end that the maker tried very hard to remove with little success. This item does not correspond to any known typological tool or weaponry for this area nor are there use-wear patterns present that might identify it as a tool.

A probable burial situation that is unique for the type of artifacts that it contained was found in the southern Bighorn Basin. Over 40 years ago, four com-

Figure 8.11   Badly deteriorated *Busycon* shell recovered near the Garrett Allen (Elk Mountain) site in south-central Wyoming in the same location as the biface in Figure 8.10a.

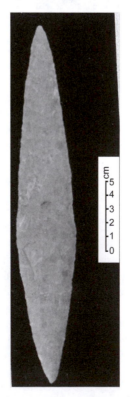

Figure 8.12   Bipointed quartzite biface from northern Wyoming.

plete and three fragments of tubular pipes or shaman's sucking tubes were found at the base of a sandstone scarp about 6 m high. Three of the complete pipes were of steatite and had apparently been deliberately broken, but all pieces were recovered and refit. The other complete specimen was of sandstone and was apparently a natural formation with a hole through the center, so that little modification was needed. Still another was a root cast in which the center had been drilled. One specimen was decorated with several incised figures (Figures 8.13b and 8.14). Recently, the site location was revisited and broken pieces were recovered that refit to pieces found earlier and still another nearly complete specimen was recovered. All together, 11 specimens and several sources of pipe stone material are represented. Red ocher was present in one of the objects and a burial, possibly of a shaman, is strongly suggested. Several large panels of petroglyphs are located on the sandstone walls above the location where the objects were recovered. The deliberate breaking of the objects suggests some form of ritual activity associated with the death of a special person such as a shaman. One human skull fragment was recovered in a nearby pack rat nest.

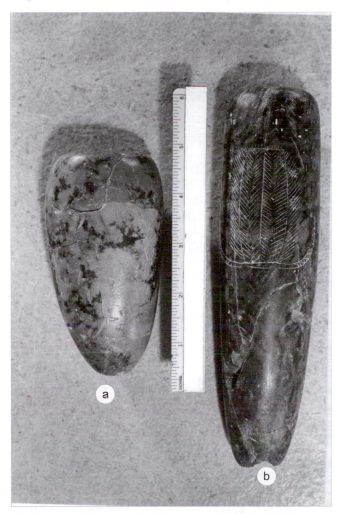

Figure 8.13   Pipes or shaman's sucking tubes from northern Wyoming.

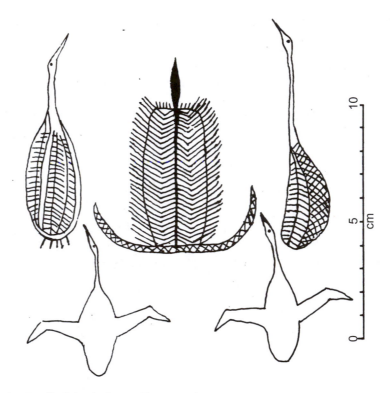

Figure 8.14   Detail of the design on Figure 8.13b.

It has been suggested that these items are not pipes but instead could be some sort of shaman's paraphernalia. One (Figure 8.13a) did have red ocher in the barrel when found. The deliberate breaking suggests "killing" the objects. The fact that the pieces were closely associated suggests they were in a special container, possibly a hide bag, when broken (Frison and Van Norman 1993).

Bows and Bow Making

Wooden and sinew-backed bows of historic age are common in Plains ethnographic collections. These were made of several different woods, including juniper (*Juniperus* sp.), chokecherry (*Prunus* sp.), and skunkbrush (*Rhus trilobata*). Provided the situation in the past was similar to the present, locating trees and shrubs that would produce the necessary quality of wood for bow manufacture required considerable effort. Juniper bow trees have been identified (Figure 8.15) and were usually relatively large trees with one side straight and free of knots. Cuts were made of desired length and the piece was split out from the standing tree (Figure 8.16).

On the other hand, the sinew-backed reflexed bow made from mountain sheep horn is a rare item. The manufacture technology involved is very different from that of a wooden bow. Its origin is unknown but could ultimately be far to the north, since they do bear a marked resemblance to composite bows made by certain Eskimo groups. The mountain sheep horn composite bow is attributed to the

Figure 8.15   Bow tree in central Wyoming. (Courtesy of Charles A. Reher.)

Figure 8.16   Section cut from a bow tree in eastern Wyoming. (Courtesy of Charles A. Reher.)

Sheepeater group of Shoshone Indians. The Sheepeaters supposedly occupied a "semiautonomous enclave" (Shimkin 1947:247) within the area claimed in historic times by the Shoshone.

A mountain sheep horn bow was found in a rockshelter in the higher elevations of the Gros Ventre Mountains in northwest Wyoming (Frison 1980); the exact time of its discovery is not known, but it was probably in the late 1950s. Its preservation was excellent, although the handgrip which held the two sections of the bow together was missing. The horn part of the bow consists of two separate parts manufactured from sections taken from two large ram horns, very likely a pair. The two parts were joined by a peg (also of horn) about 2.3 mm in maximum diameter but oval in cross section. The length of the plug is not known and can be seen only because the missing handgrip allowed the two pieces to separate and break the plug.

The bow is slightly asymmetrical (Figure 8.17a, b), being 83 cm in maximum length with one section 43 cm long and the other 40 cm long. A thick, continuous sinew backing was applied to the back of the bow, covering both sections. In the unstrung position, it was slightly reflexed (Figure 8.17c) so that when braced (Figure 8.17d) and when in use, directly opposing pressure was exerted against the joining surfaces of the two sections of horn. This is an excellent example and one of the few of this particular type known to exist. Sinew-backed bows made of

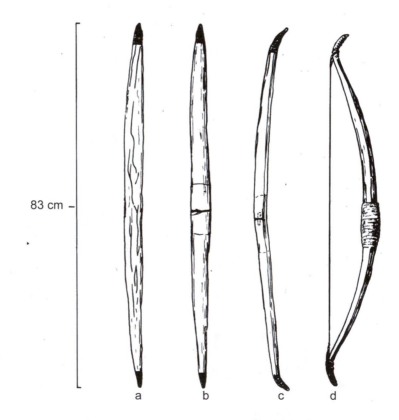

83 cm

a   b   c   d

Figure 8.17 Sinew-backed bow made from mountain sheep horn found in the Gros Ventre Mountains in northwest Wyoming.

two elk antler staves joined together are also known among the Sheepeaters but preserved specimens are rare. Single elk antler staves were also used for bows and in this case, a sinew backing was applied.

Edge-Ground and Edge-Abraded Cobbles

Stream-polished, flattened river cobbles with a ground and/or polished edge, usually of quartzite (Figure 8.18a, b) but occasionally of other stone material of similar hardness, are puzzling items. They appear regularly but with no known patterned distribution. A common function assigned to them is use in hide polishing. The nature of the wear would allow this but we know of no satisfactory evidence to confirm it. Other cobbles are edge abraded but instead of the worked edge being polished, the surface in this case is pecked (Figure 8.18c). The latter may have been caused by some form of flaking tool, as demonstrated by Crabtree and Swanson (1968). However, it is difficult to attribute the wear surfaces on Figure 8.18a and 8.18b to stone flaking.

Red Ocher

Red ocher is found in many contexts, including burials, and is widely scattered on occupation floors of a number of sites, especially those of Paleoindian age. Stone artifacts are sometimes painted with red ocher; in dry caves such as the ones in the Bighorn Mountains (see Frison 1962, 1965, 1968a), many items, especially wooden items such as foreshafts, mainshaft fragments, and atlatl fragments, were painted with red ocher. In the case of burials, its use appears to be ritualistic. In other cases it could be both ritualistic and functional, since it does serve to protect and prolong the life of wooden materials.

Red ocher occurs in many locations over the Northwestern Plains and in the Rocky Mountains. It is often found in the center of sandstone concretions and in small pockets in limestone and sandstone formations. One of the largest known sources and one that was mined extensively in prehistoric times is located in the Hartville uplift in southeast Wyoming within a few kilometers of the Hell Gap site. The area has been mined for iron ore since the late eighteenth century, but one Paleoindian-age mining area escaped total destruction. The site, known as the Powars II Site 48PL330, has only been minimally tested. It has the general appearance of most prehistoric quarrying operations but with one major difference: the tailings piles contain large numbers of simple flaked stone and large animal long bone quarrying tools but, in addition and unlike other quarrying sites, there are large numbers of broken and complete Paleoindian projectile points covering the entire range of types of the open Plains Paleoindian from Clovis to Frederick (Stafford 1990).

Use of ochre is seen at the nearby Hell Gap site from the earliest occupations. Aside from abundant small nodules occurring at many of the site's localities and layers, an ocher sphere was recovered in situ (Figure 8.19). The sphere was apparently placed on top of a shaped palette and both were placed in an area of large boulders. Both the palette and sphere may have been cached in this location and never recovered. This is one of the larger single nodules of ocher at the site,

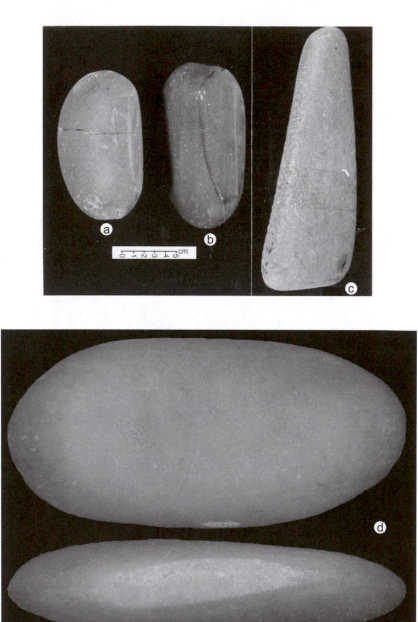

Figure 8.18   Edge-ground (a, b, d) and edge-abraded cobbles (c).

and another of similar size occurs nearby. Red ocher was also recovered from the Hanson and Sheaman sites, including concretions as well as a spherical form (Figure 8.20), while at the Medicine Lodge Creek site the ochre was found in the context of a set of objects interpreted as a flint-knapping tool kit (Figure 8.21).

Figure 8.19 Ochre sphere and palette from the Goshen component of Hell Gap site Locality I.

Figure 8.20 Ocher from Paleoindian sites: nodules from the Sheaman site (a–d), and concretion from the Hanson site (e).

Figure 8.21   Postulated Paleoindian flint knapper's tool kit from Area 2 of the Medicine Lodge Creek site: deer antler tool (a), red ocher (b), edge-grinding tool (c), and chert core (d).

Musical Instruments

Musical instruments are rare in the archaeological record; however, they have been recognized across the Plains and elsewhere in North American and the world. This infrequent occurrence is partly a function of raw material, many musical instruments being manufactured from perishable materials such as wood or hide. However, it is likely that not many musical instruments were manufactured in the first place; that is, there were probably many scrapers, points, flakes tools, baskets, and other tools made to every musical instrument. Therefore their low occurrence in the archaeological record partly reflects their low frequency in the cultural systems. Also exacerbating this rarity is their likely longevity in the cultural system. Once manufactured, such items are likely passed on to future generations, sometimes as sacred objects or as heirlooms. Regardless of their meaning, such objects are not lightly discarded and could remain with a group for dozens or even hundreds of years. Nevertheless, we are aware of several musical instruments in the region. One of these was discovered at the Shoshonean Bugas-Holding site.

The Bugas-Holding Rasp
The Bugas-Holding site rasp was manufactured on elk antler beam (Figure 5.29). The antler was grooved and split longitudinally to acquire the proper width

and perpendicular to its long axis to produce the length. The finishing on the perpendicular cut is not as uniform or as well executed as the longitudinal. The long sides are heavily rounded and nearly polished, while the ends remained somewhat jagged. The rasp is 87 mm long and 20 mm wide. The antler surface was lightly flattened from its natural circular shape and along this flattened area were incised 13 grooves. Most of the grooves and inter-ridges are perpendicular to the long axis; however, four on one end angle away to as much as 45° from perpendicular. It has been suggested that this follows a natural hand motion while scraping the rasp; the rasp would thus be played with wrist action, not by moving the entire arm (Rod Garnett, personal communication 2008).

Rasps have been described in both North American ethnography and prehistory, but have not received a great deal of attention. Driver (1953) has compiled information on ethnographic and archaeological occurrences of rasps from which it is clear that implements of perishable material are less common in the archaeological than in the ethnographic record (Garnett et al. 2006). Thus wood, hide and other materials used for rasps or rasping equipment (e.g., scrapers and resonators) were probably used prehistorically but did not survive the ravages of time, while bone and antler rasps are more durable. Although we are not aware of any elk antler rasps in the region or elsewhere on the Plains, we are familiar with a number of bone instruments. One particularly significant rasp was recovered from the Karpinsky site in Alberta (Bryan and Conaty 1975). According to the investigators, the 100-year-old site apparently functioned as a seasonal family camp. Although apparently the Karpinsky site is smaller and of shorter duration than Bugas-Holding, the two rasps nevertheless come from similar contexts. The Karpinsky rasp is of similar size and the ridges and grooves of similar spacing to the Bugas-Holding specimen. Other Plains examples tend to be on bison ribs (e.g., Henning 1998). Whether any of these rasps functioned along with a scraper or were used with a resonator is currently unknown. What we can say is that these musical instruments were present in a wide range of prehistoric Plains and Rocky Mountain societies and likely ranged in function from ritual to entertainment objects.

Exotic and Exchange Items

By exotic items we are referring to several types of unusual and unique artifacts that have been recovered in and out of context throughout the region. We are also including here items from clearly distant sources of raw material or manufacture. Although by themselves inadequate to tell the story, the accumulated occurrence of these objects is beginning to throw some light on parts of prehistory that would otherwise remain mute.

One such object is a Michigan barbed axe (Figure 8.22). Discovered in a field outside Douglas, Wyoming, this artifact was manufactured on basal porphyry. The usual range of this artifact type, as well as the raw material of its manufacture, is the Great Lakes region. Michigan barbed axes are the first of such implements to appear at the Archaic–Woodland transition, about 3000 years ago (Smith 1971:21). Trade of Yellowstone obsidian to the Hopewell area is well known, but what was received in return? It is possible that this axe is one such object.

Figure 8.22   Michigan barbed axe found near Douglas, Wyoming. (Photo by Dewey Baars.)

Another artifact found some time ago in the area of Hyattville, Wyoming was also manufactured on exotic material and represents another possible trade item (Figure 8.9; Mulloy 1954c). The bannerstone Mulloy described is also characteristic of midcontinent Archaic cultures. More recently, several discoveries of shell masks at the edge of our study area bespeak long-distance trade networks (Figure 8.23). Lippincott (1997) has assembled a series of papers on these objects. Most appear to be manufactured from marine shell from the Gulf coast, although trade with the Pacific coast is also demonstrated. The representations on the masks suggest a Mississippian age for these objects and furthermore a link to the Southern Cult. That a complex society such as the Mississippian was well connected throughout the continent is not surprising. But just what role did the Plains and Rocky Mountain nomadic peoples of our region play in these connections? Spielman (1983) has suggested trade of agricultural products and foraged products between settled and nomadic populations in the Southwest. The Pawnee and early historic hunting forays into the western Plains are well documented in the early Historic period and this pattern has been proposed during prehistory (Roper 1997; Scheiber 2001). Were such forays accompanied by trading? Did the foreigners employ the native nomadic people and are these exotic objects payment for such services? We may not soon have the answers to these questions, but clearly these exotic artifacts are part of the larger story of the prehistory of the Northwestern Plains and Rocky Mountains.

Another aspect of exchange is the more proximal exchange of goods between nearby groups. In anthropology and archaeology, this exchange among band societies has been an important topic of study. Whether objects whose sources are from distances more than 50 or 100 km were traded for or were procured during seasonal rounds in prehistory is a matter of debate. Sourcing obsidian has recently become a rather common practice, and we are seeing that this material is being distributed of hundreds to thousands of kilometers from the source (Baugh and Brosowske 2006). Others have investigated the source locations of chipped stone tools from as early as the Early Plains Archaic and found that at some sites small

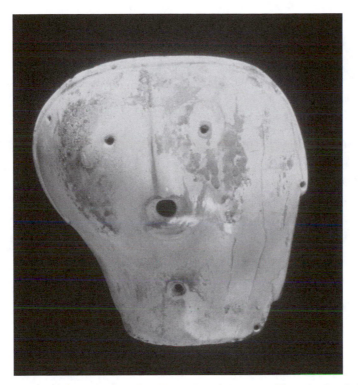

Figure 8.23   Shell mask from the Bear Paw Mountains of Montana. (Photo by Tom Roll.)

amounts of raw material are from great distances, suggesting exchange systems rather than direct procurement during seasonal rounds (Huter 2001). Great variation within and between raw material sources makes these studies difficult, but a small amount of material is distinctive enough to be traced across the landscape. The great distance some material traveled in excess of several hundred kilometers makes it highly unlikely that the Early Plains Archaic Lookingbill inhabitants traveled to procure this material (Huter 2001; James C. Miller, personal communication 2001). More likely it came to them through some kind of an exchange system.

Other Miscellaneous Objects

A full discussion or even list and descriptions of objects infrequently occurring in the archaeological record can never be complete. However, a number of unique artifacts have been discussed over the years. A few of these, in addition to the objects discussed earlier in this chapter, deserve at least to be mentioned.

One such object is the so-called Medicine Lodge Creek plaquette (Figure 8.24). Found near one of the Medicine Lodge Creek rock shelters, the object is clearly incised with a pattern. Francis (2007) argues that the pattern best fits a medicine bag. Medicine bags are powerful objects or full of powerful objects. A representation of the medicine bag on this portable item is unusual in two ways. First, representations of medicine bags are rare, and second, portable images are rare in the area of the Rocky Mountains and Northwestern Plains. Portable images and

Figure 8.24   Incised rock from the Medicine Lodge Creek site, Wyoming.

incised tablets do, however, occur in nearby areas of the Great Basin (Tuohy 1983), but are of different designs. Portable images are used by many if not all band societies and perhaps even more complex ones as well. In Australia, aborigines incise utilitarian and nonutilitarian items. The incising serves as remembrances of past events, territories, and other important facts, and to enhance oral histories. Other bands as well as more complex societies also incise tablets and frequently store them in special places.

A different decorated object was found by an avocational archaeologist in southwest Wyoming. While not incised, the small pebble has a painted design on one surface (Figure 8.25). Although somewhat damaged, the red and black pigment appears to delineated a bird. Birds do occur in rock images in the region, but not this type of bird. Both the incised Medicine Lodge Creek tablet and the painted bird portable image are hard to interpret. They are out of context; even their authenticity can be questioned. Yet not to mention such objects gives short shrift to the complexity and rich cultural heritage of prehistoric peoples of this region.

A very different object is a shaped bone from the Bugas-Holding site. Only a fragment of this artifact is preserved and was recovered; the rest is broken off (Figure 8.26). The preserved piece is less than one square centimeter (about 4 x 5 mm) in size and approximately 1 mm thick. It appears to be from a longitudinal notched or toothed object. Two and a half notches are preserved on the piece, as the object broke through one of the notches. The notches are about a millimeter deep and are separated by approximately 1.5 mm from the next notch. This is likely a utilitarian item, perhaps related to basketry or rope-production activities.

An object probably of Late Prehistoric or more likely historic age is the war club found in the early 1900s near Ten Sleep, Wyoming (Figure 8.27). This item is almost certainly a part of ritual paraphernalia, such as is often seen in historic pictures of Plains tribes and their leaders. War clubs are also common in ethnographic collections and museums. However, a few occur in archaeological collections, although most often found on the surface and of unknown age.

Figure 8.25   Painted pebble from southwest Wyoming.

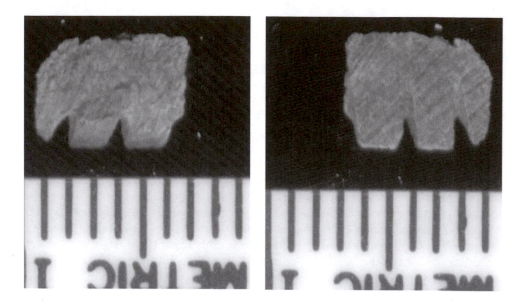

Figure 8.26   Notched bone implement from the Bugas-Holding site of Sunlight Basin in Wyoming.

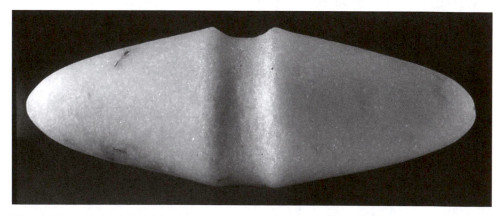

Figure 8.27   War club found in the early 1900s near Ten Sleep, Wyoming (length 143 mm).

The final objects we wish to mention are beads. Whether ornamental, ritual, currency, or exchange items, beads occur from the earliest occupations not only in the Northwestern Plains and Rocky Mountains, but in nearby areas as well. The earliest beads from the Northwestern Plains and Rockies known to us were recovered from the Folsom component of the Lindenmeier site (Wilmsen and Roberts 1978). These are followed by beads from the Agate Basin component of the Hell Gap site (Figure 8.28l and m, Plate 1c). Both of these are stone: one is calcite and the other is hematite. Also of Paleoindian age is the grooved bone bead recovered from the Frederick component (Figure 8.28k, Plate 1c). Evidence for beads continues into the Early Plains Archaic with a steatite bead fragment from the Split Rock Ranch site, and into the Middle Plains Archaic with debris from the manufacture of bird and rabbit bone tubes at the Spiro site. Bone, stone,

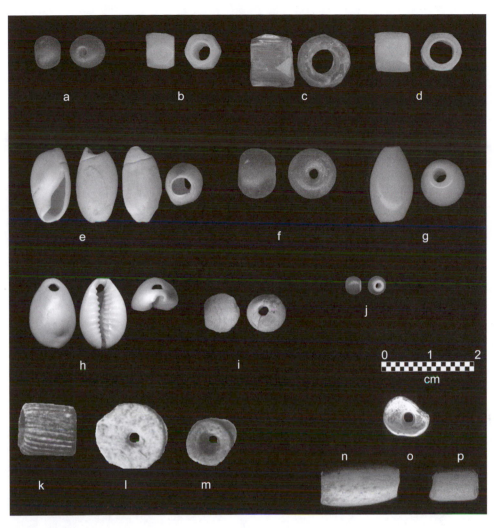

Figure 8.28 Selected beads from several Wyoming sites: Medicine Lodge Creek (a–j), Hell Gap (k–m), and Bugas-Holding (n–p).

and shell beads occur throughout later prehistory. At the Protohistoric Bugas-Holding site several tubular bone beads as well as an *Olivella* sp. shell bead were recovered (Figure 8.28o, p, Plate 1c, and Figure 5.30b). One of the tubular beads is relatively long, suggestive of a breast plate, while the others are short and indicate other uses. Several types of beads continue through the Historic period, such as *Olivella* and cowry shell; however, the new European imports tend to dominate the assemblages (Figure 8.28a–j, Plate 1c).

9

Paleoindian Flaked Stone Technology on the Plains and in the Rockies

Bruce A. Bradley
Exeter University, Exeter, UK

Introduction

The 1960s and 1970s witnessed a major change in the way researchers viewed flaked stone artifacts. No longer were "finished tools" simply classified and compared. Gone were the days of simple functional typologies. It is now generally accepted that flaked stone artifacts became part of the archaeological record as the result of manufacture, use, reuse, discard, and natural site formation processes. Artifact forms result from these complex origins. Flaked stone assemblages from the Northwestern Plains and Rocky Mountains have been increasingly analyzed within the concept of these dynamic systems. Indeed, it is the systems themselves which are being used to characterize cultural norms. The great advances in the 1960s and 1970s stemmed from general theoretical and methodological changes within archaeology as a whole, but also resulted from the growing awareness of the role of practical experiences as exemplified by the application of experimental archaeology. While these ideas were new and viewed with suspicion then, they are now part of the mainstream of archaeological method, especially in relation to artifact technologies and site formation processes.

These approaches to the study of flaked stone assemblages have been applied to artifact assemblages in the Northwestern Plains and Rocky Mountains. This has been possible because of at least four circumstances: (1) there has been continued extensive research in this region; (2) the complex nature of the area's flaked stone technologies and site contexts have been conducive to these types of studies; (3) recovery methods have improved; and (4) the circumstances of preservation of some sites have allowed archaeologists to recover and study assemblages of *associated* manufacture and use remains of stone tools. The following discussion summarizes and updates what I know about Northwestern Plains and Rocky Mountain flaked stone technology.

Earliest Materials

As yet little is known about flaked stone on the Northwestern Plains and Rocky Mountains before the advent of Clovis about 13,000 years ago. There are no known generally accepted assemblages of flaked stone, even though there are hints that at least some people may have been through the area. On the edge of the Southern Plains, however, early flaked stone artifacts are claimed to have been recovered from several strata below the well-defined Clovis levels at the Gault and Buttermilk Creek sites in central Texas (Collins and Bradley 2008). About all that can be said at this point is that the technologies include basic biface and flake manufacture. There is no evidence of blade or bladelet production, and few formal tools have been recovered. It is just a matter of time before more is known about this material, and it seems likely that more sites will be found in the not distant future. There are also hints of early people in the north on the margin of the Great Lakes, again east of the Northwestern Plains (Overstreet 2004).

Early Paleoindian

Clovis

The earliest, widely accepted, flaked stone tool assemblage in North America is known as Clovis (Wormington 1957). Although the exact distribution of this material is not well defined, it is clear that it is found throughout the Northwestern Plains and Rocky Mountains. There are fluted points and, although mostly poorly dated, they may be younger than Clovis and perhaps related to post-Clovis technologies of the Great Lakes region (Gryba 2002; Wilson and Burns 1999). Curiously, there are few Clovis points made from Knife River flint from southwestern North Dakota, even though it is considered by modern knappers to be an ideal raw material for making Clovis points. There is no indication that the material was not available and no evident reason why Clovis knappers would not have used it (Bruce Huckell, personal communication 2008). Several regional variations of Clovis projectile point types have been suggested (Frison and Todd 1986; Howard 1990:225–262) but at least one of these, Colby (Figures 9.1a and 9.6b), resulted from reworking broken segments. Nevertheless, the basic technological processes of biface and point manufacture seem to be present throughout the region. Generally speaking, Clovis flaked stone technology is characterized by bifacial tool and flake manufacture. Most Clovis tools are either bifaces or are made from flakes that resulted from the biface manufacturing process. Few, if any, individual Clovis sites have produced the entire known range of flaked stone tools, and this discussion incorporates the assemblages from a number of Clovis sites. Perhaps the greatest weakness in reconstructing Clovis technology on the Northwestern Plains and Rocky Mountains is the general lack of sites that represent primary manufacturing localities (for a possible exception see Mallouf 1989). Most Northwestern Plains and Rocky Mountain Clovis sites have been interpreted as being either kill sites (e.g., Miami; Sellards 1952) or kills with associated small campsites (Blackwater Draw; Boulldurian and Cotter 1999), and even one (Colby) has been interpreted as a meat cache (Frison and Todd 1986). Another site (Anzick) has been interpreted as a burial (Lahren and Bonnichsen 1974). Because

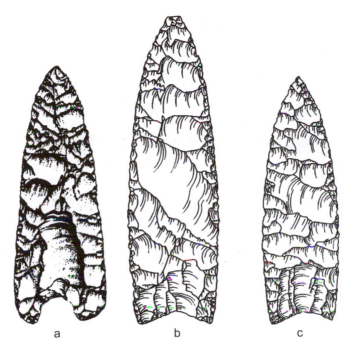

a   b   c

Figure 9.1   Clovis points from the Colby site (a) and Fenn Cache (b, c).

of this interpretation, other like sites have also been suggested to have been burial related (Butler 1963; Mehringer 1989). All are now subsumed under the category of cache, although there is no general consensus of what this means, and it is likely that all caches were not the same. However, it is these sites that may actually give us the clearest view of the sequences of flaked tool manufacture. This is because these assemblages seem to include nearly the entire range of biface manufacture. Analysis of these bifaces has revealed a reasonably consistent and unique biface production system. This technology has been observed at the Sheaman site in eastern Wyoming (Bradley 1982:203–208). In this case, the process was interpreted not from the bifaces but from the discarded debitage. Luckily, the location was preserved well enough so that several partial reduction sequences were available for study by refitting flakes to each other (Figure 9.2). This is also supported by analysis of materials from other non-Northwestern Plains or Rocky Mountain Clovis manufacturing sites (e. g., Gault) where a whole range of technologies are represented (Collins 2002).

Flakes for tools were mainly produced through two bifacial flake production approaches. The first resulted in discoidal cores (Figure 9.3). Large, flat flakes were produced from these cores, and although the cores are fairly common at source processing sites, there is little evidence that they were transported away from the material source. The second approach was the production of large, ultimately thin bifaces (Figure 9.4). These also produced large, flat flakes, but are frequently included in Northwestern Plains, Rocky Mountain, and western caches. Once they became too thin to produce further useful large flakes they were broken, sometimes intentionally, and the segments then could be used to produce projectile points. There is a clear example of this in the Anzick assemblage (Wilke 2002).

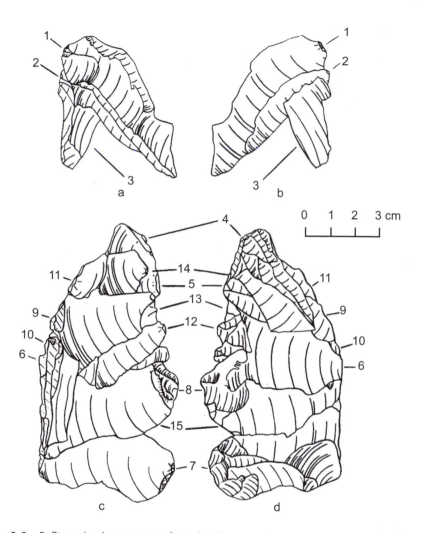

Figure 9.2   Refit production sequence from the Sheaman site.

Bifaces intended to become projectile points, whether as oversize forms for deposition in caches or for use, were usually manufactured from large pieces of high-quality raw material. In the Northwestern Plains and Rocky Mountains there is also limited evidence of the use of large flake blanks as well (Wilke 2002). This blank form may well be underrepresented because of the types of Clovis sites that have been investigated. At the East Wenatchee site in Washington there are a number of early phase bifaces that were made from flake blanks. Initial flaking produced the general form, regularity, and proportions of the object and prepared it for the removal of large thinning flakes (Figure 9.5a). The distinctive aspects of the thinning process were the platform preparation method, flake removal sequence, flake termination form, and spacing of flake removals. After initial blank regularization, the sequence continued by the removal of a large thinning flake from one margin on one face. This thinning flake often traveled across the entire face, frequently removing a portion of the opposite margin (Figure 9.5b shaded). This approach was consistently used to remove "square" edges as well

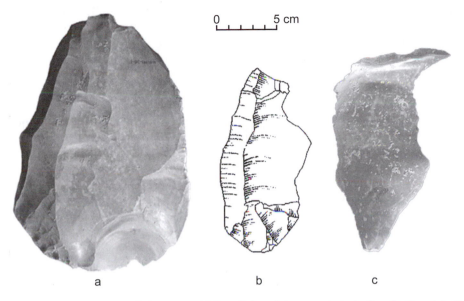

a   b   c

Figure 9.3   Clovis discoidal flake core and biface flakes: flake core photo by Sam Gardner (a), disc core flake drawing by author (b), and overshot biface flake photo by Sam Gardner (c).

Figure 9.4   Biface flake cores. (Photos by Sam Gardner.)

as other surface and edge irregularities. When feasible, the next major thinning flake was removed from the same face, but originating from the opposite margin. Then a flake was removed from the same face but from the original margin (Figure 9.5b 1–3). Primary thinning flakes were spaced so that they slightly overlapped with the previous flake scar. The result was a very flat, regular face. The process was continued, alternating margins on the same face when appropriate and possible, until the entire face was covered (Figure 9.5b). This was often accomplished by the removal of only a few large thinning flakes. The resulting large, flat thinning flakes were being selected for the majority of the other tools that make up Northwestern Plains and Rocky Mountain Clovis assemblages. When it was deemed useful, thinning flakes were removed from the base, occasionally on both faces and sometimes from the tip, throughout the production sequence (Figure 9.5a). In terms of platform preparation, these flakes were removed in the same manner as those from the sides. Although one might be tempted to call this fluting, the objective was not to produce a flake scar to be retained on the finished point. I agree with Callahan (1979), who identifies these as end thinning flake removals, distinguishing them from flutes that were done when the final base was being prepared. Thinning and shaping was repeated on the opposite face, and so on. It seems plausible that in the early phase of manufacture bifaces served primarily as cores, although there is some evidence that they may also have been used as tools themselves. When the biface became too thin and/or narrow to produce good tool blanks, the manufacturing strategy changed from the production of flakes to systematic biface shaping and thinning. In this phase, flake removal sequences tended to be selective along a single margin, and flake size and spacing was substantially reduced (Figure 9.5c). When desired, full-face and overshot flakes were still removed throughout the process (Figures 9.5b shaded and 9.6a). Although flaking tended to be perpendicular to the central axis of bifaces, there are quite a few examples of diagonal flaking as well from a number of sites (Figure 9.6). From this point on it seems that the primary objective was the production of a bifacial projectile point and/or knife. The finishing technology of projectile points varied considerably from biface to biface. Although some regional and/or temporal variants may occur, the same forms of finishing technology seem to be present throughout the region. In some cases the projectile points were

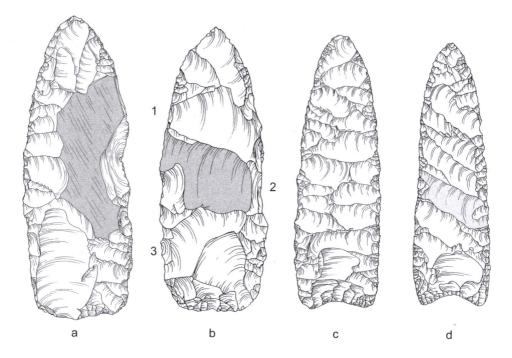

Figure 9.5   Clovis biface reduction sequence: early phase (shading indicates original exterior surface of raw material) (a), middle phase (shading indicates overshot flake scar, numbers indicate removal sequence) (b), late phase (c), and finished point (d). Images resized to fit sequence.

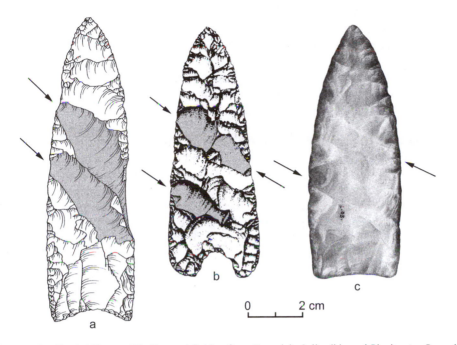

Figure 9.6 Clovis bifaces with diagonal flaking from Fenn (a), Colby (b), and Blackwater Draw (c). (Photo of cast by Sam Gardner.)

mostly percussion finished with only minimal pressure retouch (Figure 9.1b). In other cases, substantial marginal pressure retouch followed the percussion flaking (Figure 9.1a), and others underwent substantial pressure thinning and shaping (Figure 9.1c). There are also examples where pressure flaking was done over entire faces, save the flute scars, with a comedial pattern resembling the later Cody flaking style (Bouldurian and Cotter 1999: Figure 26b). Although it is not evident in every case, this style of finishing may be reworking to repair use damage. Near the end of the manufacturing sequence, the bases of most points were thinned by the removal of one or more flakes from both faces. These flakes usually ran to the point of maximum biface width and are called flutes (Figures 9.1a and 9.1c). A flute may be defined as any basal thinning flake(s) scar that terminates at or past the area of the hafting element (J. B. Sollberger, personal communication 2008). Occasionally, an earlier end thinning flake scar would be retained on one face and the point designed around it. It was also not unusual for the postfluting retouch to be done so as to shape the point around the flute scars. Postfluting flaking was done on the lateral margins of the points, but care was taken not to remove the basal flute flake scar(s).

Another trait that was part of the Clovis point manufacturing process was the intentional removal of the end of the basal thinning flake scar(s) from the lateral margins (Figure 9.6b shaded). This generally removed the step or hinge fractures present at the end of the flute flake scar(s). I consider this a diagnostic of Northwestern Plains and Rocky Mountain Clovis point manufacture technology. Curiously, some Clovis points from kill sites (Figure 9.6c) and quite a few of the Clovis points recovered from caches (Figure 9.1b, c) do not exhibit well-made flutes, if they have them at all. With a functional interpretation of fluting as a hafting enhancement, this might make sense if one contends that the cache points were never meant to be used as projectiles. On the other hand, if flute scars served a display function, one might say that fluting was not necessary as the oversize points were intended to be buried in any case.

Along with the distinctive points, Clovis biface thinning flakes also tend to exhibit diagnostic traits. These include the platform morphology, the shape of the flakes, the flake termination form, and the dorsal flake scar patterns (Figure 9.3b; see also Bouldurian and Cotter 1999: Figure 30). Early-phase biface thinning flakes have wide, straight platforms that are faceted, reduced, and ground, often heavily and frequently extending from the platform surface around to the proximal dorsal surface (Figure 9.7). The flakes tend toward a rectangular shape (parallel lateral margins), have a low count of dorsal flake scars that originate from both margins of the biface, and frequently include a section of the opposite margin on their distal edges (overshot; Figure 9.3c). Their dorsal surface flake scars also tend to produce a central ridge, indicating that platform locations were directly between previous flake removals.

The morphology of these flakes served very well for large flake tools, and various amounts of lateral unifacial retouch tended to accentuate their already elongated shape (Bouldurian and Cotter 1999: Figure 30). In some cases, this general elongation has been mistaken as an indication that Clovis flake manufacture was the result of a core blade technology. This observation has led to the conclusion that Clovis flaked stone technology was *based* upon a blade manufacturing process. Although struck blades (Green 1963) and a couple of blade cores have been attributed to Clovis assemblages in the Northwestern Plains and Rocky Mountains, this is clearly an exception to the rule in this region. Nevertheless, a well-defined blade technology was part of the Clovis repertoire in the south and east (Collins 1999). The paucity of blade technology in the north and west probably has more to do with the nature of land use than the lack of this technology. It certainly did not have to do with inadequate raw material sources. A common stone source located

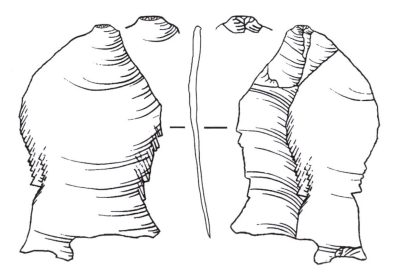

Figure 9.7 Clovis biface production flake from the Sheaman site in eastern Wyoming showing flake platform (top).

in southwestern Wyoming and used in two Clovis caches, Fenn and Crook County, occurs in large angular chunks and nodules that are ideally suited for Clovis blade manufacture, but to my knowledge no blades have been found made from it. This is also the case with other western stone sources such as Alibates dolomite in the Texas panhandle.

Raw material choice was highly selective. There are massive deposits of good flaking material in many places in the Northwestern Plains and Rocky Mountains, and most of these were used by Clovis knappers to some extent. However, it is also clear that they went out of their way to use specific sources, especially ones with high-quality and colorful raw material, and neglected others. An example of special selection is seen in the Bighorn Basin in Wyoming, where there are extensive deposits of many very good quality flaking stones, such as Morrison quartzite. This material was extensively used in post-Clovis times, but seems to have been passed over by Clovis knappers. Instead, they were trekking up into the Bighorn Mountains to get an especially excellent red chert (as seen in two of the Colby points and several points from caches). Although of excellent quality, this chert is not the easiest to obtain as it occurs at high elevation where it would have been inaccessible for much of the year and not accessible at all some years. Another example of special raw material selection is seen in the Drake cache from northern Colorado (Stanford and Jodry 1988). All of the pieces were made from Alibates dolomite, a distant source with other adequate sources in between. The Fenn (Frison and Bradley 1999), Simon (Butler and Fitzwater 1965), and Wenatchee (Mehringer 1988) caches also contain mostly exotic raw materials, including optical-quality quartz crystal.

Clovis flaked biface and blade technologies are distinctive not only in particular choices in sequencing, but they represent a bold, almost exuberant, approach to tools manufacture. They clearly exceed what was needed for simple survival. Clovis biface technology was designed for mobility and efficiency that allowed the successful exploitation of a wide range of ecological settings and subsistence practices. Clovis technology was not an adaptation to a specific circumstance, but a versatile approach that allowed people to make a living wherever they went. It was a bold technique that must have taken years to perfect and along with its evident utility, probably served nonutilitarian functions as well.

Goshen

A poorly known flaked stone assemblage is being reassessed as the result of investigations at a site in southeast Montana. The Mill Iron site (Frison 1988b) has yielded a group of projectile points and stone tools that have been identified as Goshen (Bradley and Frison 1988). Originally described from the Hell Gap site in eastern Wyoming, the assemblage was not well represented and was initially only proposed as an addition to the Paleoindian sequence (Irwin-Williams et al. 1973:46). Reexamination of the Hell Gap records in light of the new discoveries allowed George Frison to resurrect the question of the Goshen techno-facies. At the Hell Gap site the Goshen materials were found stratigraphically below Folsom artifacts (Figure 2.23), and this relative position has been borne out by dates from the Mill Iron site and stratigraphy at Jim Pitts (Sellet et al. 2009). Technologically there is a limited assemblage to describe, but it is distinct from both Clovis and Folsom.

A single incomplete biface has been recovered from the bison bone bed at the Mill Iron site. It was broken, which may have been deliberate, and two of the resulting pieces (Figure 9.8) were clearly used as tools. The biface exhibits evenly spaced percussion thinning with opposing flake scars meeting near the midline, diving into each other. It also shows bifacial marginal retouch, possibly pressure, forming sharp edges. Unfortunately, the biface is too fragmentary to determine the exact flake removal sequence. This basic process most resembles the biface manufacturing process seen at the Sheaman site in eastern Wyoming (Bradley 1982:203–208), as well as the Folsom bifaces called ultrathins (Frison and Bradley 1980; see further discussion of Folsom below). Although, based on some refit flakes from Sheaman (Bradley 1982), I originally reconstructed Clovis point manufacture as including diving flaking in the late phase, I no longer subscribe to this. Late-phase Clovis bifaces exhibit transmedial, flat flaking (occasionally including overshot flaking), not diving flaking. However, diving flaking is typical of late-phase Folsom ultrathin biface manufacture. This indicates to me continuity in biface manufacture between Goshen and Folsom, but not between Clovis and Goshen.

Knowledge of Goshen point manufacturing technology is limited because only finished and reused points have been found in good context in the Northwestern Plains and Rocky Mountains (Bradley and Frison 1988). What is apparent from points in their original form (Figure 9.9) is that the projectile points resulted from manufacturing sequences with highly controlled pressure thinning and shaping characterizing the final phase. Final pressure flaking is consistently well controlled,

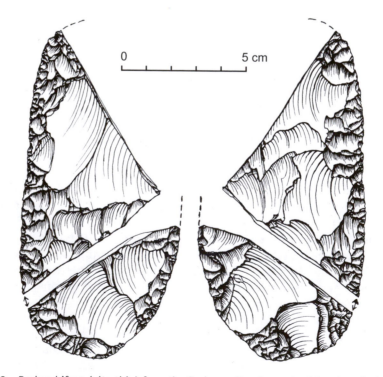

Figure 9.8   Broken biface (ultrathin) from the Goshen cultural complex bison bonebed at the Mill Iron site in southeast Montana.

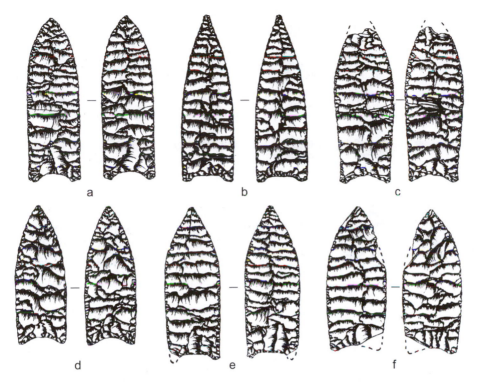

Figure 9.9 Original forms of Mill Iron site points.

with flake terminations either comedial or transmedial. Flake scar orientations are perpendicular to the point axis, except at the tip where they tend to be perpendicular to the margin. When modified and reworked points (Figure 9.10) are also considered, the range of finishing technology increases. Along with reworking, this may also be related to the form of the original raw material. The two basic results were original thin, flat points that exhibit regular transmedial and comedial flaking patterns, and reworked points that exhibit less regular flaking tending toward comedial. Based upon both the Mill Iron site artifacts and points from other sites, it looks as if the normal Goshen point exhibits a manufacturing technology very similar to that described for Plainview points in the southern High Plains (Knudson 1973). What the temporal relationships between Clovis, Goshen, Folsom, and Plainview point technologies were remains to be determined. One of the Mill Iron points exhibits final flaking and retouch typical of unfluted Folsom points, and the shape even conforms to Folsom (Figure 9.9c).

My impression is that the pressure flaking and general point technology of Goshen points more closely resembles Folsom point technology than it does Clovis. This is especially true when one notes the presence of extremely fine and well-controlled pressure retouch on most of the Mill Iron site points. Although pressure thinning is present on the bases of Goshen points, it is not comparable to the basal thinning (fluting) on either Clovis or Folsom points.

Since Goshen points seem to be older than Folsom, I suggest that Folsom derived from Goshen rather than Clovis, at least in the Northwestern Plains and Rocky Mountains. The antecedent of Goshen could well be the elusive pre-Clovis indented-base point from the Great Lakes area, or even further east.

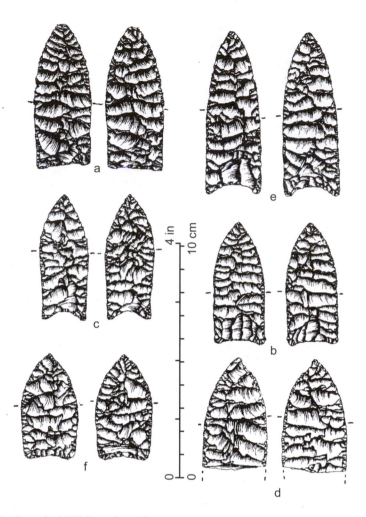

Figure 9.10   Reworked Mill Iron site points.

Midland

Midland as an independent assemblage has been the topic of a great deal of discussion (Amick 1999) and still remains unresolved. This is primarily because Midland has been used as a category into which any number of different point forms have been placed, the main criteria being that they are Folsom-like and unfluted. To further complicate the issue, Midland and Folsom points are frequently found together, but to my knowledge they have not been recovered from contexts that unequivocally indicate contemporaneity (e. g., from a single-episode kill site). Midland points, in all their various guises, have also not been found in sealed stratigraphic units without Folsom points (a possible exception is the Gault Site in central Texas). However, as it now stands, the general consensus is that "we should maintain a definition of Midland as an unfluted Folsom point" (Frison 1996:207). On technological grounds I disagree. I think it is possible to distinguish a distinct Midland point type and that unfluted Folsoms are technologically Folsoms that just are not fluted.

I recognize two different technologies within the Midland-Folsom general grouping. The two technologies do not relate to just whether or not the points are fluted, but to how the final shaping/thinning flaking and marginal retouch were accomplished. To complicate this issue, some Goshen points could easily be classified as unfluted Folsom (Figure 9.9c). It is my contention that there are indeed unfluted Folsom points (Figure 9.11d, e), but there are also unfluted points that were produced with a different, distinguishable technology, and most of these have been identified as Midland.

What I think of as Midland are those points that exhibit wide, relatively shallow flake scars that produce a very flat cross section (Figure 9.11a–c). Flaking may have included pressure, but for the most part looks like highly controlled percussion. Often the noninvasive, abrupt, continuous margin retouch narrowed the piece so that most of the negative bulbs of the thinning flake scars are nearly eliminated. This is not a technology that would be good for preparing preforms for Folsom fluting, yet many of the points look purposely made and are not just failed attempts at Folsom. It is also unlikely that they were made on thin flakes like the pseudofluted points. Until we know whether or not Midland points exist separate from Folsom, this issue will remain unresolved; however, this will not happen if we continue to identify unfluted Folsom points as Midland.

Folsom

By far the greatest amount of effort expended on the study of Paleoindian flaked stone technology, both on paper and in replication efforts, has focused on Folsom

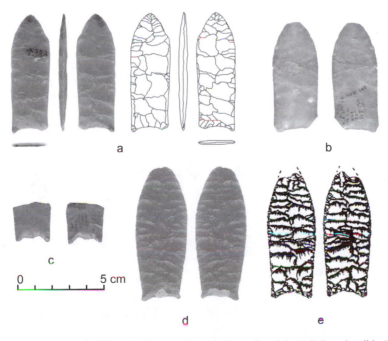

Figure 9.11 Comparison of Midland points: replica by the author (a), Hell Gap site (b), Hell Gap site (c), replica by the author (d), and Mill Iron site (e).

point manufacture (e.g., Clark and Collins 2002). The very concept that flaked stone artifacts resulted from a process may have been a product of attempting to decipher the complex production sequence of this point style. Even though the basic sequence was identified by Coffin (1937:9–10) and Roberts (1935:18–21), interest has increased as new data have become available and more investigators have attempted to interpret it (Frison and Bradley 1980). Although the minute details of the manufacturing process and the basic tools and techniques, especially fluting, are still the topic of discussion (Crabtree 1966; Flenniken 1978; Frison and Bradley 1982:209–212; Gryba 1988:53–66), there is a general acceptance of the basic manufacturing sequence of Folsom points (Figure 9.12; Flenniken 1978). Curiously, the best evidence for the tools and techniques used is generally discounted (Frison and Bradley 1982).

While much attention has been paid to point variations (Figure 9.13; Ahler and Geib 2002) and primary manufacturing, less attention has been focused on point finishing techniques, which include extensive postfluting flaking of the tip (Bouldurian and Cotter 1999: Figures 37–39), minimal margin retouch (Figure 9.13a), and distinctive fine, steep, patterned overall marginal retouch (Figure 9.13c). To my knowledge, no modern knapper has replicated the minute regular retouch with a tool that could have been used in Folsom times. It is unclear why this method of finishing was used in some cases, as it must certainly have involved a great amount of skill and effort, yet there is no apparent functional advantage to it. It is also curious that both finishing techniques co-occur throughout the Folsom range, with no evident chronological or spatial variation.

The singular focus on Folsom point manufacture, especially the fixation on the fluting technique(s), has neglected the manufacturing technology of the other

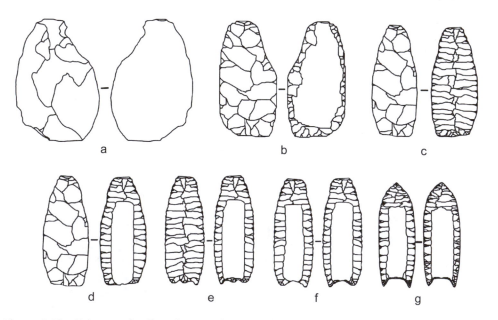

a   b   c

d   e   f   g

Figure 9.12   Folsom projectile point manufacturing phases: flake blank (a), unifacially and unilaterally modified flake blank (b), regularized preform and prepared for fluting on one face (c), preform fluted on one face (d), preform prepared for fluting on second face (e), preform fluted on both faces (f), and finished tip, base, and lateral edges (g).

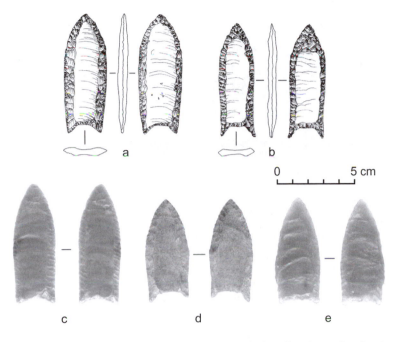

Figure 9.13 Folsom point variation: North Dakota (a, b), and replicas by author (c–e).

flaked stone artifacts in Folsom assemblages. Along with the projectile points, there is a specialized biface manufacturing process, which I used to think was an extension of Clovis biface manufacture (Bradley 1991), but now see as having a closer tie to Goshen in the Northwestern Plains and Rocky Mountains. This biface production has been described in the analysis of the Hanson site materials (Frison and Bradley 1980:31–45). In that study, it was proposed that biface manufacture functioned primarily as a flake production process (especially in the early stages) and shifted over to bifacial knife manufacture as the biface became too small and thin to produce usable flakes. Instead, bifacial cores described as discoidal are typical of the Folsom flake production process (Figure 9.14), and most unifacial tools in Folsom assemblages were made from flakes struck from bifacial cores (Frison and Bradley 1980:18) rather than biface thinning flakes as seen in Clovis assemblages.

It is also unlikely that these cores were made into Folsom points. However, Folsom biface production also included a specific process to make knives, called ultrathins (Figure 9.15; Jodry 1998). I see no clear evidence that the early phases of production of ultrathin knives were designed as flake cores, as in Clovis. Final thinning was accomplished with well-controlled diving flaking producing cross sections that at times are thinner in the middle than along the margins. These ultrathins have been interpreted as specialized filleting knives, especially used in jerking meat, and possibly a woman's tool (Jodry 1998). Technologically, Folsom ultrathin production corresponds exactly to Goshen. A composite of fragments of Goshen (Mill Iron site) and Folsom (Hanson site) gives an idea of what a complete form would have been (Figure 9.15c).

Of particular interest to me is not only the processes of Folsom point manufacture, but also the reason for its extreme complexity. It has been convincingly

Figure 9.14   Folsom discoidal flake core from the Hanson site.

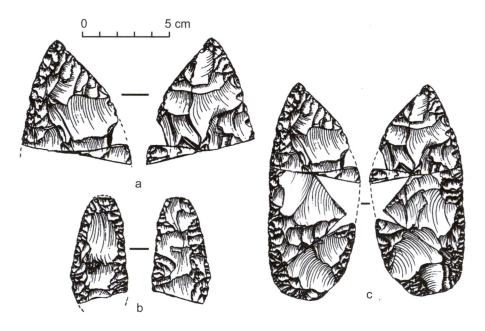

Figure 9.15   Folsom and Goshen ultrathin bifaces from the Hanson site (a, b), and composite Hanson and Mill Iron sites (c).

argued that the fluting process was functional in that it enhances the hafting process of the point (Ahler and Geib 2002). Although this may be true, my own experience has shown that producing a haft for a very thin point, using stone tools, is much more difficult than making one for a thicker point. Experimental uses of hafted Folsom point replicas have also not demonstrated a superiority over other thicker Paleoindian styles. Evidence from several sites in Wyoming, as well as reevaluation of earlier collections, has indicated to me that there may have been an additional reason for the development of the complex point manufacturing, and especially the fluting process.

Clearly, fluted Folsom points were being used on projectiles (Bement 1999; Meltzer 2006), but so were other styles at the same time (Bradley 1982:194). At the Agate Basin site in eastern Wyoming, a Folsom level was excavated which yielded a range of manufacture and use evidence (Frison 1982c:37–71). Included in this level was evidence of the killing and butchering of several bison, the manufacture and use of stone and bone tools, and the fluting of Folsom preforms. Of interest is the observation that none of the projectile points that were associated with the bison kill were fluted Folsom points. Three bone points, a small Clovis-style point, and a small point manufactured by trimming a flake were all that were recovered in association with the bison. On the other hand, there was ample evidence that the fluting of preforms was a common practice at the site. An elk antler tool (Figure 9.16) and a bison metatarsal tool (Figure 2.32) were recovered and interpreted as having been parts of fluting devices (Frison and Bradley 1982:209–212). Several associated channel flake fragments have also been fitted back onto broken and/or discarded preforms.

Well-fluted but unfinished preforms have been reported from nearly all Folsom manufacturing sites and as surface finds from Wyoming to at least Oklahoma (Bradley 1982:186–195; Frison and Bradley 1980:56; Wilmsen and Roberts 1978). Virtually all of these preforms could have been made into very serviceable points with relatively little additional effort (Figure 9.17). Why were

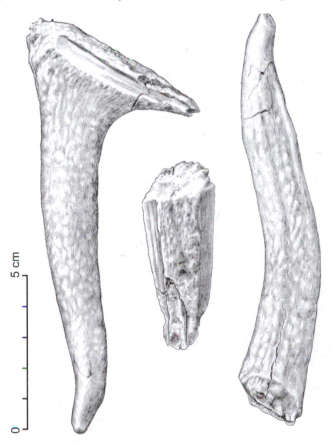

5 cm

Figure 9.16   Probable Folsom fluting tool.

Figure 9.17   Prematurely discarded Folsom point preforms from the Hanson site (a), and Agate Basin site (b).

they discarded? In one case it has been possible to document that a single pre-form was fluted successfully at least three times and then intentionally smashed (Bradley 1982:192–193), even though a very small amount of additional flaking effort would have produced one of the finest and largest Folsom points yet dis-covered (Figure 9.18). In this situation, it is reasonable to ask if it is possible that

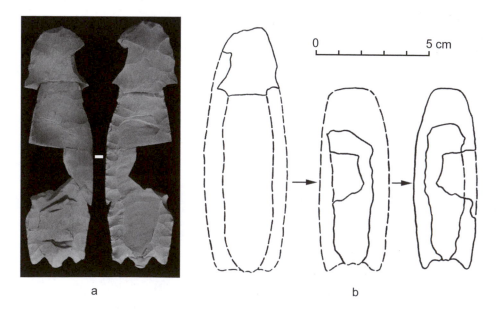

Figure 9.18   Refit broken Folsom preform: refit preform pieces (a), and reconstructed fluting intervals (b).

the projectile point may not have been the primary product of the process. What alternative is there?

It has been a decade and a half since I proposed that the complex fluting process may have originated as an expedient way to thin the base of a projectile point, but that it eventually took on other, less utilitarian, meaning (Bradley 1991:378–379). Even with new theoretical frameworks that can embrace this sort of speculation, there has not been much discussion of the nonutilitarian aspects of flaking (cf. Sinclair 1995). A common human behavior in any activity where risk of failure is involved is the invocation of the supernatural to assist in lessening the risk. This process can involve something as individual as a football player crossing himself before a field goal attempt to something that involves a large segment of a society, such as a corn dance at a Southwestern Pueblo. Frequently this ritual activity is carried out by one or more persons considered to be imbued with special powers. Since the fluting of an already thin preform was a risky business, the success or failure of the attempt may have been considered a prognostication of the success of an upcoming event such as a hunt. Is it not possible that fluting could have developed into an integral part of a prehunt ritual? I submit that it did, and that the unfinished and intentionally broken fluted preforms represent this process.

If it does turn out that Folsom technology was derived from Goshen, which lacked fluting, we need to document and explain the process by which fluting was invented/adopted with no apparent developmental stages, at least in the Northwestern Plains and Rocky Mountains. Folsom fluting may not have been a continuation and elaboration of Clovis technology. One option is that the fluting transition out of Clovis took place in the east, perhaps as expressed in such technologies as Gainey, Barnes, and Cumberland, and was then adopted by the Goshen people in the Northern Plains.

Along these same lines, I also suggest that the extreme care and artistry exhibited by many Paleoindian projectile points was symbolic of a power vested in them. Many historic and modern Native American cultures believe that stone projectile points have their own spirits and may be used to invoke supernatural power(s). Projectile points are frequently included in medicine bundles and used in various types of religious rituals. I consider it likely that this was the case since at least Folsom times. Perhaps the oversize Clovis points found in caches are an even earlier expression of this perception.

MIDDLE PALEOINDIAN

Agate Basin

Following the very complex process that went into the manufacture of Folsom points, Agate Basin points were made with a relatively simple technology. This is not to say that they were simply made; the points were made by percussion reduction of a biface and finished with pressure shaping (Figure 9.19). Remnants of percussion flaking are often still visible. Retouch was selective and invasive and covered most of both faces. Pressure flaking was seldom transmedial and on many points is comedial, but not patterned or serial. Spacing of flake scars varies widely from close (Figure 9.19a, d, h) to quite wide (Figure 9.19b, c, k). Although not patterned, this process was accomplished with care and skill, producing

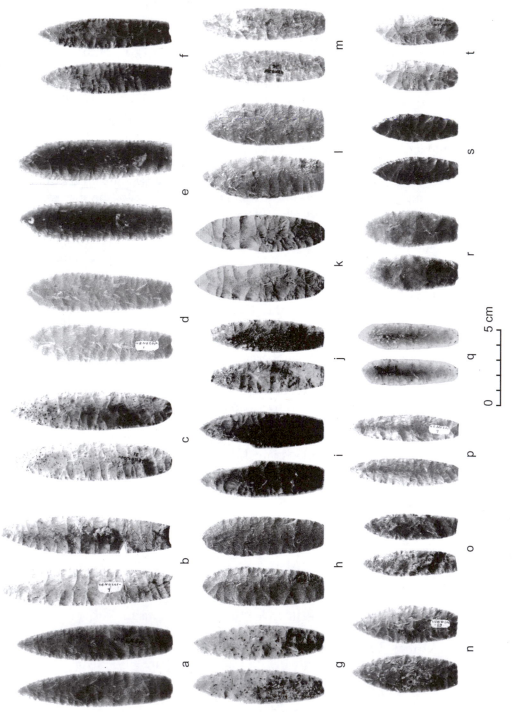

Figure 9.19 Agate Basin points from finished primary specimens (a) to reworked, heavily remanufactured pieces (t).

points that were longitudinally flat and symmetrical with very straight, even margins. As with earlier Paleoindian points in the Northwestern Plains and Rocky Mountains, Agate Basin points were finished with lower lateral and basal margin grinding/polishing.

Few instances of the early phases of Agate Basin point manufacture have been found. One example is the Hell Gap site, where a point manufacturing area was excavated (Larson et al. 2009). Analysis of the Hell Gap material shows that preforms were produced with well-controlled, widely spaced percussion thinning reduction (Figure 9.20a). The intent was to make a long, flat point. At Hell Gap there is evidence that controlled overshot flaking may have been employed (Figure 9.20b–d). This is only seen on a few pieces and only at this one locality, so it is too early to say that it was a standard part of Agate Basin biface technology, as it was in Clovis. Although some Agate Basin points were very long, they were made in all sizes, probably based on raw material size limitations.

Most Agate Basin points exhibit evidence of reworking. Some apparently unreworked points were very long (Figure 9.21a), and it seems likely to me that the style was designed in such a way that segments resulting from use breakage could be easily modified into functional points. Reworked points have been recovered that were made from tips, midsections, and bases of broken points (Figure 9.21b–d). Reworking tended to be done with pressure flaking, frequently exhibiting less attention and skill than that used to produce the original point (Figure 9.19g, m, o, s). Reworking also tended to result in relatively thickened cross sections, masking the flatness of the original form. I see Agate Basin points as a very effective way of making recyclable projectiles and possibly the most efficient design of any of the specialist bison hunters in the Northwestern Plains and Rocky Mountains.

Asymmetrically retouched bifaces have been interpreted as knives (Frison and Stanford 1982:122–123), but they were produced by the same technology as the points except that they were not as finely finished (Figure 9.22). Flake tools continued to be made mostly on large biface thinning flakes, with nonbifacial cores also present (Bradley 1982:182–183). No standardized blade-making technology has been identified in Agate Basin assemblages, but an expedient blade production was encountered at the Agate Basin site (Frison and Stanford 1982). This blade making was done on locally available chalcedony nodules (Figure 9.23), and refitting indicates that few of the products were removed from the knapping area (Frison and Stanford 1982). Although this technique may produce good blanks for end scrapers, in this case it seems more like a knapper was simply breaking a local rock in an expedient way, sort of like whittling a stick.

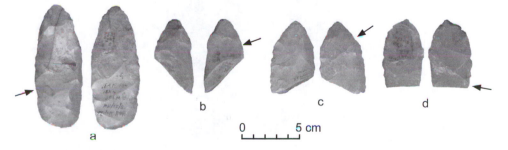

Figure 9.20   Agate Basin bifaces from the Hell Gap site.

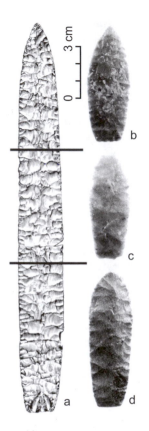

Figure 9.21   Agate Basin point reworking sequence: reconstructed Agate Basin point (a), distal three-quarters of a reworked tip (b), reworked midsection (c), and reworked base (d).

Figure 9.22   Agate Basin biface knives from the Agate Basin site.

Figure 9.23   Agate Basin "blades" and cores from the Agate Basin site.

Although Agate Basin point production technology typifies what is normally considered Paleoindian, it is substantially different from the preceding Folsom process. It is my opinion that Agate Basin technology was not derived from Folsom technology on the Northwestern Plains and Rocky Mountains. This material could represent the first expression of northeast Asian technology, coming out of the northern Great Basin.

Hell Gap

Hell Gap projectile point manufacturing technology was a continuation of the well-developed Agate Basin technology. Interestingly, the makers of Hell Gap points chose to terminate the production process at an earlier phase than the Agate Basin point makers did. The sequence was the same with percussion thinning and shaping giving way to pressure thinning/shaping. Two basic finishing techniques have been observed on Hell Gap points in the Northwestern Plains and Rocky Mountains: (1) marginal pressure flaking that invades onto the faces only in the areas of the tip and stem (Figure 9.24d, e; Bradley 1974:191–197); and (2) pressure thinning/shaping that covers, or nearly covers, the entire faces (Figure 9.24a–c, f, g; Stanford 1974:29–36). It is not clear whether these differences represent regional, chronological, or simply idiosyncratic variations. Approximately the same degree of finishing care was applied to Hell Gap points as to Agate Basin points. Margin grinding/polishing is present on the stem and basal margins. An interesting feature has been noted on several of the points from the Jones-Miller site and one from the Casper site: a shallow groove has been cut into the points, perpendicular to the point axis, at or just above the stem. I have successfully replicated this feature by using a point as a passive abrader for the grinding/polishing of the margins of another point.

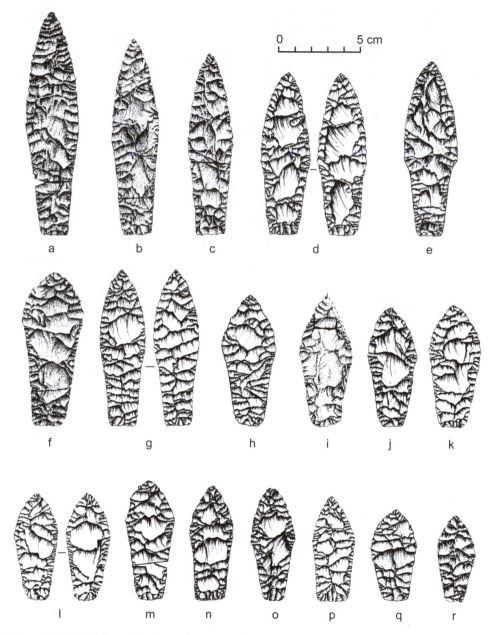

Figure 9.24   Hell Gap points from the Casper site.

This may have been occurring at the Jones-Miller and Casper sites as the result of the reuse of broken projectile points. There are few stones at the locality that could have served as abraders for margin grinding/polishing and already-hafted projectile points could have served this purpose.

A surface site exposed several kilometers up the North Platte River from the Casper site, the Seminoe Beach site, was apparently a location where Hell Gap projectile points were being manufactured (Bradley 1991:385). Several preform stages are represented that were broken during manufacture. One (Figure 9.25a) is a large

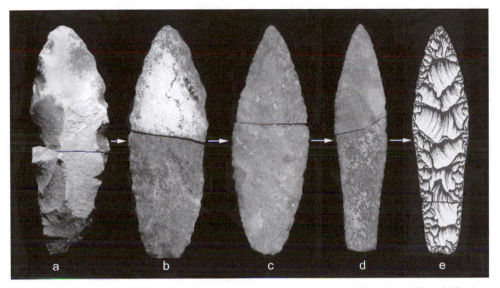

Figure 9.25 Hell Gap biface production phases: early phase (a), middle phase (b), middle-late phase (c), late phase (d), and finished point (e).

percussion flake with initial percussion shaping; two others (Figure 9.25b, c) broke in a later stage of percussion shaping; another (Figure 9.25d) was further advanced and needed only a small amount of work on the stem and point; while the last (Figure 9.25e) was essentially finished and is of the same morphology and raw material (quartzite) as several from the Casper site.

A special bifacial reduction sequence has been noted on Hell Gap points from the Casper site in central Wyoming (Bradley 1974:192–193). This involved the thinning of one face of the biface from one margin with the thinning flakes running almost to the opposite margin (Figure 9.26a). The biface was then turned over and the opposite face was thinned from the other margin. This produced a biface with a thin parallelogram cross section (Figure 9.26b). This cross section was modified by margin retouch into a lens shape. Platform preparation for the removal of the thinning flakes included specific isolation and moderate to heavy grinding. Unlike the Clovis platforms, these exhibit a smaller area and a convex shape. This type of platform is seen starting in Folsom biface production (Frison and Bradley 1980:27–30) and probably is present in Agate Basin biface production as well.

An asymmetrical bifacial tool has been reported from the Hell Gap site (Irwin-Williams et al. 1973:47–48); however, recent analysis of all of the extant artifacts did not reveal a bifacial knife from the Hell Gap component. Flake tools continued to be manufactured from a combination of flakes from bifacial and nonbifacial cores. One from the Casper site is presumably a butchering tool with heavy use wear on the working edges.

Alberta

Relatively little is known about Alberta point and biface production technologies. However, an excellent analysis of the production, use, and reuse of the points from the Hudson-Meng site has been published (Huckell 1978:153–189). In this analysis,

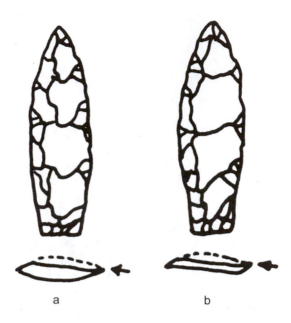

Figure 9.26 Experimental percussion thinning of a Hell Gap preform.

a special percussion process was identified on several of the points. This involved the removal of percussion flakes in a serial sequence that terminated at or near the midline of the biface, producing a comedial flaking pattern (Figure 9.27a, b). This was followed by selective, noninvasive pressure retouch along the blade edges,

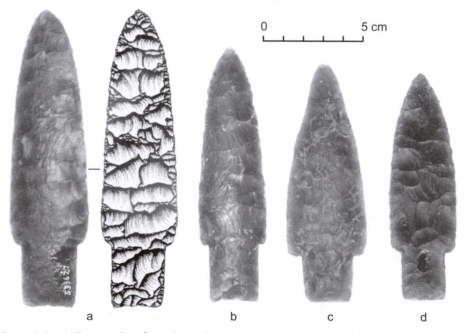

Figure 9.27 Alberta points from the Hudson-Meng site (a–c), and author's replica (d). (Figures 9.27a left, b, and c from Taylor 2006.)

pressure thinning of the stem, and margin grinding/polishing of the stem and base. This special flaking sequence has not been noted on other Alberta points from Hell Gap (Bradley 2009) nor on numerous surface finds in Wyoming. Once again, it is not clear whether this might represent regional, chronological, and/or idiosyncratic behavior. Only additional data from well-documented finds will help to answer this question.

Although platform preparation for the removal of the serial comedial percussion flakes was not discussed by Huckell, personal experience with this technique has indicated to me that isolated platforms are a must for it to be applied consistently. A small, stemmed, shouldered biface was also recovered from the Hudson-Meng site (Agenbroad 1978b). Technologically, this biface was produced with the same basic processes as many of the projectile points at the site and may even have been made from a broken projectile point. The presence of this specialized tool type and the occurrence of serial comedial flaking may be a presage to the technological system that followed.

Alberta/Cody

A projectile point production technology that may have followed Alberta has been described at the Horner site in northwestern Wyoming (Bradley and Frison 1987:199–232). The lack of a well-defined Alberta production technology has made it difficult to determine if these Alberta/Cody points actually represent a transitional stage between Alberta and Cody. Originally, these points were subsumed into the Cody complex (Frison and Todd 1987), but excavations at the Horner II site in 1977 and 1978 (Frison and Todd 1987) identified a kill area that contained only points that are now being called Alberta/Cody. This find allowed a group of artifacts to be described that chronologically precedes points that have become known as Scottsbluff and Eden (Wormington 1957:118–137).

Two styles of Alberta/Cody points are present, with the distinction based upon both form and production technology (Figure 9.28). Alberta/Cody I (Figure 9.28a–d) was produced from a percussion-shaped and thinned biface with nonpatterned pressure shaping/thinning. Percussion flake scar remnants are often visible on one (Figure 9.28b) or both faces, and pressure thinning is confined to the tip and stem. Although the points are fairly well made, they are often somewhat asymmetrical, have slightly wavy margins, and tend toward relative thickness. Selective comedial pressure flaking is occasionally present but is not well developed, and the flake scars tend to interfinger from opposite margins. There is no direct evidence of a specialized percussion sequence such as that described for some of the Hudson-Meng points. Alberta/Cody II points (Figure 9.28e–h) probably were produced in the same manner as the Alberta/Cody I points, but the production sequence was continued further. Finishing consisted of a highly specialized alternating pressure flake removal technique (Figure 9.29). This produced a point with widely spaced, comedial pressure flake scars and an extremely wavy margin (Bradley and Frison 1987:201–207). Normal pressure thinning was done on the stem, where margin grinding/polishing was also applied. Light margin retouch was applied between the pressure flake scars, reducing the degree of waviness of the margins. If additional pressure flakes, extending to the midline, were removed between the

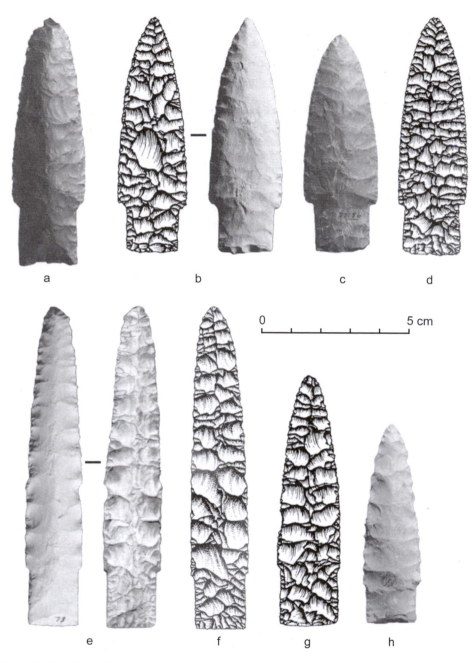

Figure 9.28 Alberta/Cody points.

flake scars, a pattern very like that found on Eden points would have been produced.

A single stemmed, asymmetrical biface was also recovered from Horner II. Although it was fractured by burning, it still retained enough features to determine that it was produced by the same techniques as those of the Alberta/Cody I points.

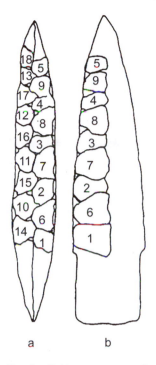

Figure 9.29 Alberta/Cody type II point flaking sequence: alternate platform selection along one margin (a), and pressure flaking sequence removal from one margin on one side (b). (From Frison and Todd 1987.)

Cody

The Cody complex includes several projectile point types (Dick and Mountain 1960:223–235; Wheat 1967:47–52; Wormington 1957:118–137). Although various types of points have been described, Scottsbluff types I and II (Figure 9.30a–f) and Eden (Figure 9.30g–j) may have been produced by the same technological sequence (Bradley and Stanford 1987:201–207). The only real differences seem to be the interval at which the sequence was terminated, the final retouch, and the way in which the hafting element was formed. Generally speaking, Cody points were produced by percussion shaping and thinning of a biface, followed by selective pressure shaping, and finished by one or more series of serial pressure-shaping flake sequences (Figure 9.31). This serial flaking became more regularized and was, for the most part, comedial. By the time three or four phases were completed, the points developed distinctive median ridges. The flaking had to be done with extreme care and control because a single step fracture would interfere with further flaking sequences. Points were finished with a variety of methods including minimal noninvasive edge regularization (Figure 9.30c, g), selective invasive retouch (Figure 9.30a, e, f), and comedial removal of ridges between flake scars (Figure 9.30h). Although it is not possible to chronologically order these various options, there seems to be a progression from the wide flaking on the Alberta/Cody II points, through the selective comedial retouch, to the final serial comedial flaking with minimal retouch. Technologically, this sequence represents flaking refinement.

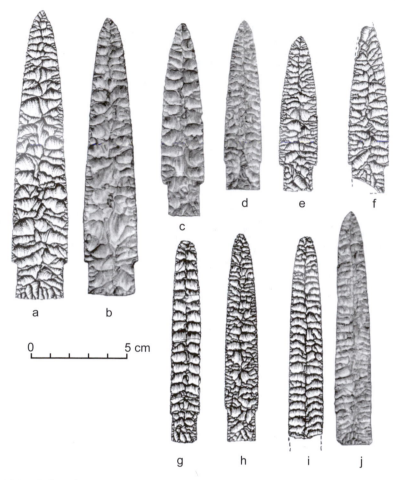

Figure 9.30   Cody points.

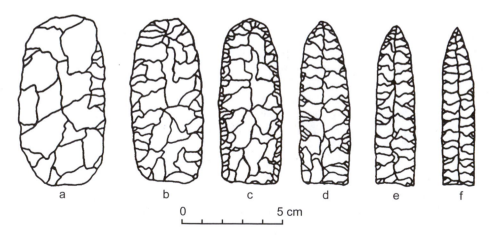

Figure 9.31   Idealized Cody projectile point production sequence by stages: stage 2 (a), stage 3 (b), stage 4 (c), stage 5 (d), stage 6 (e), and stage 7 (f).

Two point styles from eastern Colorado that also resulted from this technological process have been described but have not been included in the Cody complex (Wheat 1972, 1979). Although these points vary somewhat in minute details from Scottsbluff and Eden points, they were made by the same process. I would have no problem, on technological grounds, with including them in the Cody complex and would even go so far as to suggest that they *are* Cody points.

I have noted a variation from the normal Cody point production sequence at Locality I at the Hell Gap site (Bradley 2009). Several incomplete bifaces exhibit deep nonmarginal percussion flaking and they are relatively narrow. These bifaces were recovered in context with Eden points and could have been Eden preforms. If this was the case, there was a special Eden point technology that did not conform to other Cody approaches. Since these bifaces are smaller than usual, exhibit generally poor skill, and have only been reported from this single locality, it is not prudent to define a new technology. I therefore note it and expect that if it was more widespread it will be noted again at another site.

A third point style has also been described and called Scottsbluff III (Figure 9.32b–e). These artifacts are technologically very different from the other Cody point types and are more akin to what have been called Cody knives (Figure 9.32k–o; Ingbar and Frison 1987:461–473). The primary reduction of Scottsbluff III points and Cody knives was bifacial percussion thinning followed by pressure thinning and margin retouch. The objects are very thin (> 5:1 ratio of width to thickness), and it is clear that this was intended. Cody points were either average in relative thickness (2.5:1 width to thickness) or even intentionally relatively thick (< 2.5:1 width to thickness). Unlike Scottsbluff III "points," very few Cody knives have been recovered in their original form, but there is at least one exception (Figure 9.32k). This specimen exhibits well-controlled and closely spaced diving flaking followed by selective invasive margin retouch. This technique produced a thin, flat and sharp knife form, designed with one primary cutting edge. The opposite edge is lightly dulled by grinding. Both Cody knife forms are generally recovered in heavily used condition (Figure 9.32f–j, l–o) and have been significantly modified from their original form. Resharpening of the working edge was usually accomplished with selective, frequently abrupt bifacial pressure retouch. This is unlike later Archaic knife forms that tended to be unifacially retouched, forming a bevel.

Next to Folsom points, Cody points exhibit exceptional skill in their manufacture and consistency. The basic technological process was refined from that begun with Agate Basin points. The beginnings of the serial/comedial flaking were noted on the Hudson-Meng Alberta points, and further refinement is seen on the Alberta/Cody II points at the Horner site. This is also where we see the beginning of divergence into two distinct point forms and techniques, ultimately leading to the Scottsbluff and Eden types. Because of the continuity, it is difficult to separate one type from another, especially technologically. What is clear is that there is a continuity. As additional sites are discovered, I expect that the boundaries between types we now distinguish will begin to become less and less clear. This was certainly the case with the research at Horner II. We now have a "transition" between Alberta and Cody; I have little doubt that in time we will find "transitions" throughout the sequence from Agate Basin through Cody.

Unifacial flake tools continue to be made with selective unifacial retouch on biface thinning flakes.

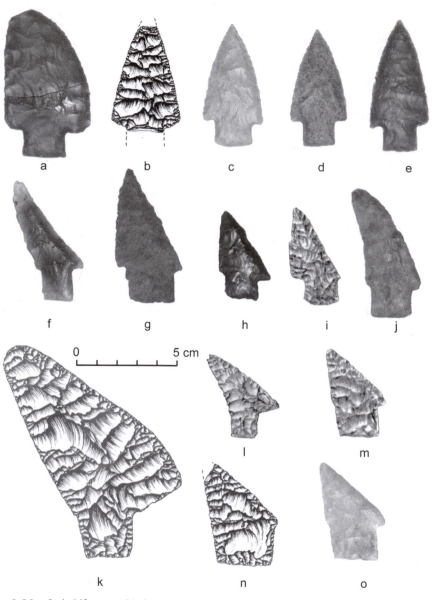

Figure 9.32 Cody bifaces and knives.

Late Paleoindian

Parallel-Oblique Point Complex

A series of projectile point styles (e.g., Pryor Stemmed and Lovell Constricted) have been found in high elevation sites in Wyoming and Montana that overlap in time with the Plains Paleoindian sequence (Frison 1978; Frison and Walker 1984; Husted 1969; Lahren 1976; Wedel et al. 1968). Although a variety of shapes are described, all share a characteristic parallel-oblique pressure flaking finishing technique and a tendency to select quartzite as a preferred raw material. There seems to be little direct technological relationship between the finishing technology of these points and contemporary points on the Plains through the Cody complex.

As a group these have been called the Frontier complex (Holder and Wike 1949) and include a variety of named types, for example, Frederick, Lusk, Allen, and Angostura (Frison 1978:34–38). Although differences in shape are present, all share a common technology. Biface/projectile point production phases are represented at the Hell Gap site in eastern Wyoming (Figure 9.33). Projectile point production phases began with percussion shaping and thinning, followed by serial, patterned pressure flaking (Figure 9.34). It is this finishing technique, however, that technologically distinguishes these points from other Paleoindian styles. Serial pressure thinning was employed, which produced parallel-oblique flake scar patterns. This technique could have developed out of the Eden flaking process in that it is usually serial, but the emphasis on oblique thinning flaking instead of comedial shaping flaking is perceptually quite different. I propose that this technology developed in the Rocky Mountains at the same time that the Alberta and Cody technologies developed on the Plains (they coexist at the Medicine Lodge Creek site; Frison and Walker 1984), and that what has come to be known as the Frontier complex originated in the Intermountain West.

The preference of quartzites and other brittle stones may be a reflection of tradition, with the ultimate origin of the flaking style being the northern Great Basin where obsidian and basalt were abundant. While fine-grained cherts and other cryptocrystaline materials tend to be elastic and support most pressure flaking techniques, obsidian, basalt and many quartzites tend to be brittle. Experience has shown me that parallel-serial and particularly diagonal flaking tend to allow pressure flakes to carry across surfaces, while other pressure flaking approaches tend to result in step fracturing on brittle materials. As knappers used to brittle materials moved into areas where there was greater choice, they probably tended to select those materials with which they were most familiar.

CONCLUSIONS

Northwestern Plains and Rocky Mountain Paleoindian flaked stone technologies were dominated by bifacial production. This frequently included the production of flakes for tools as well as the manufacture of knives and projectile points. Nonbifacial flake production did occur but tended to be expedient, both in terms of the use of locally available raw material and the limited nature of the reduction sequences employed. Complex projectile point production strategies are present in the various Paleoindian assemblages, and the expertise exhibited may have developed as an expression of perceived supernatural power. Less specialized projectile point manufacture technologies characterize the Archaic and Late Prehistoric periods, but exceptions do occur.

Flake tools included standardized forms, with most produced by simple percussion flaking techniques. Conspicuously rare or lacking are blade core and burin techniques. Flake blanks produced by bifacial core reduction dominated throughout the sequence, but unifacial core flake production is also found throughout, with a general trend toward a higher proportion through time.

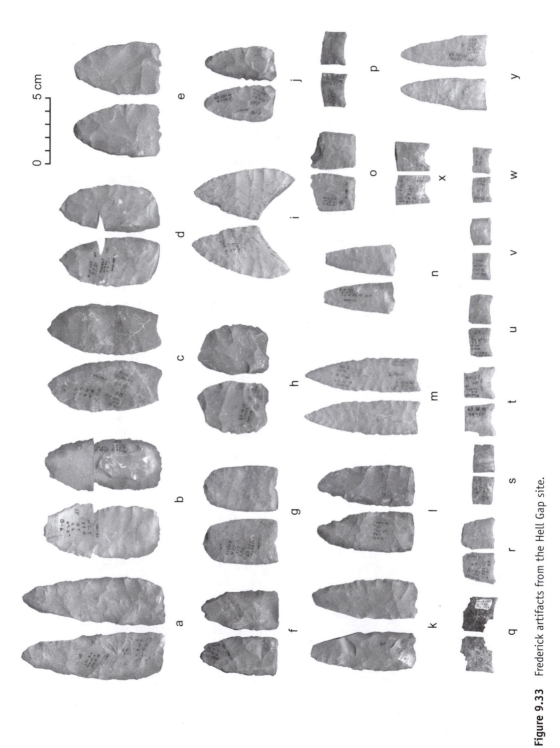

Figure 9.33   Frederick artifacts from the Hell Gap site.

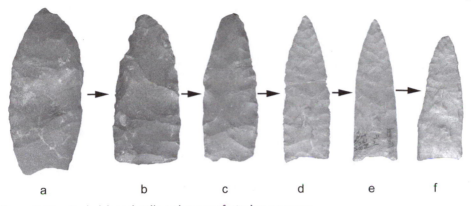

Figure 9.34   Frederick projectile point manufacturing sequence.

The earliest well-documented flaked stone assemblages of the Northwestern Plains and Rocky Mountains are Clovis, but there may be evidence of earlier assemblages in the region. Time will tell. Based on technological assessments, I see Clovis as being intrusive and possibly not resulting in any lasting occupation in the region. Evidence has also led me to suggest that Goshen overlapped with Clovis in time and that it probably developed out of an earlier technological tradition in the Upper Midwest. I also see direct technological links between Goshen and Folsom, but not between Clovis and Folsom. A different technological tradition appeared on the Northwestern Plains and Rocky Mountains after Folsom and beginning with Agate Basin. This may well have originated out of the Great Basin and ultimately northeast Asia. This general technological tradition developed and changed in the Northwestern Plains and Rocky Mountains through Cody. At that time, it was again replaced by another technological tradition that may well have also originated in the Great Basin. Whether or not this interpretation stands the test of time shall, I hope, be seen.

10

Northwestern Plains and Rocky Mountain Rock Art Research in the Twenty-First Century

Julie E. Francis
Wyoming Department of Transportation,
Cheyenne

Introduction

Rock art research around the world has been in the throes of a major revolution since the second edition of *Prehistoric Hunters of the High Plains* was published in 1991. Over the years, important advances have been made in chronometric dating techniques, interpretive models, and the technology available to document imagery. As a result, it is now possible to obtain numerical age estimates for some types of figures, to provide a much richer and deeper cultural context for understanding the meaning of many images and sites, and to record both individual images and sites in three dimensions at a far more accurate scale than ever imagined. From 1980 to 1991, *American Antiquity* and *Plains Anthropologist* published five articles in total dealing with rock art (Francis 1991:398). By way of comparison, at least eight articles in *American Antiquity* and 20 articles in *Plains Anthropologist* published since 1991 have focused on rock art or have used rock art to address other research questions of archaeological interest. The annual meeting of the Society for American Archaeology now features at least one, if not several, general sessions and sponsored symposia on rock art. In the Plains and Rocky Mountain regions, important regional syntheses (Francis and Loendorf 2002; Keyser and Poetschat 2005; Sundstrom 2004) have been published, with a broad-scale synthesis of the entire Plains region from Canada to Texas published by Keyser and Klassen (2001) and Keyser (2004). In addition, Whitley (2001) and Loendorf et al. (2005) have published important anthologies detailing breakthroughs in rock art research on the national and international fronts.

Wyoming rock art has been at the forefront of much this research. Major chronometric studies have been completed in the Bighorn and Wind River basins and in the Black Hills. As a result, numerical age estimates are now available for a variety of pecked and painted images. Many of the dating techniques, in particular for petroglyphs, must be considered

499

experimental and are not without question. Nevertheless, the body of data that has been accumulated and the general age range of many figures that has been corroborated by independent data demonstrate considerable antiquity for some images in Wyoming and documents far more complexity in chronological sequences than envisioned by most researchers.

Similar advances in the understanding and interpretation of imagery, particularly for Late Prehistoric and Protohistoric sites, have occurred since 1991. Whereas rock art was long considered of limited interpretive value and largely unknowable (Francis 1991:398), researchers in Wyoming have explored the cultural contexts in which rock art was made and have judiciously used a rich ethnographic record to aid in interpretation. It is now possible to gain a much deeper understanding of many images, in some cases to associate particular images with specific tribal groups and cultural practices, and to examine broader questions of cultural adaptation and change in the Northwestern Plains and Rocky Mountains.

Formal documentation of rock art sites in Wyoming has proceeded at a record pace. In 1991, I reported that 260 rock art sites were documented in the State Historic Preservation Office Cultural Records database (Francis 1991:397). In 2008, that number had grown to about 430 sites—an increase of nearly 70%. In addition to new discoveries, many sites known for decades have been revisited and more thoroughly mapped and recorded. Much of this work has occurred in association with specific research projects; many sites have been recorded as a result of surveys associated with energy and other types of development projects, and many more sites have been documented by dedicated avocational archaeologists and volunteers, such as Jim Stewart of Lander, Wyoming. Researchers have progressed from using 35 mm black-and-white and color slide film, tracings, and scale drawings (Francis 2005:182) to digital photography, GPS, GIS, and other techniques to document sites, panels, and individual images in three dimensions and portable machinery to chemically analyze paints in the field.

Through the considerable efforts of many researchers, Wyoming rock art now chronicles a spectacular record of cultural diversity and change among hunting and gathering peoples living in the Northwestern Plains and Rocky Mountains for thousands of years and provides new insights into native spiritual and religious practice and land use. In 1991, the state of the field permitted a general discussion of rock art site distributions, manufacturing techniques, figure types, and broad-based chronologies based upon style. Significant advances and accomplishments have occurred in every region of the state since that time. This review will proceed with a brief discussion of advances in dating and interpretive techniques, followed by more detailed discussion of rock art within specific regions of Wyoming.

CHRONOLOGICAL TECHNIQUES

Rock art dating studies were in their infancy in 1991 (Francis 1991:425), and only since the late 1980s have specialized geochemical dating techniques been used to obtain direct numerical age estimates for rock art, including both petroglyphs (pecked or engraved figures) and pictographs (painted images). Important dating research in the Bighorn and Wind River basins and in the Wyoming Black

Hills have been undertaken (Francis et al. 1993; Tratebas 1993). These two projects focused on dating petroglyphs using AMS dating of organics entombed in rock varnish or weathering rind organics and cation-ratio (CR) dating techniques. Sequences from the Bighorn and Wind River basins (Francis and Loendorf 2002:66) and the Black Hills (Tratebas 1993:164) span nearly the entire Holocene history of Wyoming and point to extremely ancient traditions of rock art manufacture.

Detailed discussions of the techniques used to date Wyoming petroglyphs and the controversies associated with some of these techniques are provided in Dorn (2001), Francis et al. (1993), and Francis and Loendorf (2002:48–67). Briefly, with the ability to date minuscule amounts of organic materials through accelerator mass spectrometry (AMS), several researchers, most prominently Ronald I. Dorn of Arizona State University, began efforts to obtain AMS ages on minute samples of organic materials encapsulated by accreting rock varnish or from organic materials contained within the weathering rinds of the host rock. These ages are presumed to provide a minimum limiting age for manufacture of the petroglyph (i.e., the petroglyph was made sometime prior to the deposition and encapsulation of organic materials and rock coatings overlying the figure).

Not all petroglyphs are suitable for AMS dating. However, well-preserved, layered rock varnish has been shown to exhibit consistent decreases in the ratios of cations (positive ions) of certain trace elements (potassium plus calcium divided by titanium, [K+Ca]/Ti) through time. AMS ages are then used to calibrate chemical changes in the layered rock varnish to generate a cation-leaching curve, from which minimum limiting age estimates for petroglyphs otherwise undatable by AMS are derived (see Francis et al. 1993 for a detailed discussion of this technique). Even when not calibrated to AMS ages, CR dates provide a relative age sequence.

AMS ages of organic material encapsulated by accreting varnish have been subject to considerably less discussion than AMS ages of weathering rind organics (WRO's), which have proven extremely controversial. Different types of organic material trapped in the weathering rinds of the host rock have been shown to yield differing ^{14}C ages. Furthermore, what had been presumed to be a closed system sealing off WRO's from contamination from either older or younger carbon sources has been shown to be more open, allowing inheritance of older carbon. Inheritance of older carbon is time transgressive: the older the petroglyph, the greater the contamination (Welsh and Dorn 1997). The effects of "older" carbon on mid to late Holocene petroglyphs (which would include most Wyoming rock art) may be relatively small. Dorn (1998) offered strong cautionary notes on the use of bulk samples of WRO's for AMS dating and noted that they must be evaluated against independent age estimates.

In addition, using geochemical techniques other than AMS dates for varnished rock surfaces, Tanzao Liu (Liu and Dorn 1996) has developed a stratigraphic sequence of rock varnishes from Pleistocene to early Holocene times for the western Great Basin. The chemical composition of the varnish microlaminations reflects climatic change and shows consistent patterning between known moist and dry climatic intervals. This technique has been used to provide age estimates for some rock art figures, and research is currently underway at the Legend Rock site in the Bighorn Basin and Whoopup Canyon in the Black Hills to determine its efficacy for Holocene-age rock varnishes.

Rowe (2001) provides a summary of AMS dating of pictographs. Figures rendered in charcoal can be directly dated; however, these ages are not without potential inaccuracies, akin to the "old wood" problem. For noncharcoal pigments, plasma-chemical extraction has been used to remove unknown organic materials, such as binders, from inorganic pigments. In Wyoming, three paintings have been dated using these techniques, all from the Bighorn/Wind River basins (Francis and Loendorf 2002:134).

INTERPRETIVE MODELS

At about the same time as the first intensive archaeological investigations and systematic rock art recording efforts began at the Legend Rock Petroglyph site in Hot Springs County (Walker and Francis 1989), South African rock art scholars David Lewis-Williams and Thomas Dowson (1988) put forth the neuro-psychological model as an interpretive framework for rock art. This article has proven seminal and radically altered rock art studies worldwide (Francis 2005:192–195). Briefly, it posits that rock art depicts the hallucinations experienced during shamanic trances. Because of the neurological structure of the brain and optic systems common to all humans, cross-culturally, people experience similar visual and physiological responses to altered states, accounting for the worldwide occurrence of numerous design elements and geometric figures.

The neuro-psychological model has been heavily criticized for being too monolithic; that is, not all rock art is the product of shamans or shamanic trance (e.g., Kehoe 2004). In many instances, particularly for Historic period rock art in the Plains, that is often the case. However, the ideas first put forth by Lewis-Williams and Dowson have led many rock art researchers to examine the broader role of trance and visionary experience in hunter-gatherer societies and the relationships of these experiences to the graphic arts, regardless of the medium (Irwin 1994). Many mundane aspects of life, for example hunting, are imbued with religious and spiritual meaning, and aspects of personal dress, decoration, and ritual are rooted in beliefs about the invocation of supernatural power that have origins in visionary experience.

All of this has led to many important changes in rock art interpretation. First, is the recognition that rock art manufacture, particularly for the prehistoric period in Wyoming and throughout the Plains, is rooted in native religious and spiritual belief. Second, rather than using Western concepts of "art" and "style" to interpret rock art, researchers have begun to explore emic concepts of supernatural power and potency, what creatures hold what types of power, and how humans (whether they are religious specialists or not) acquire this power, leading to a detailed re-examination of the ethnographic record. Third, rock art is a tangible expression of the diverse cultures, languages, and systems of religious belief among the peoples of the Plains and Intermountain West. Use of the "visionary" model has become one of the major interpretive tools for rock art in the Northwestern Plains and Rocky Mountains (e.g., Francis and Loendorf 2002; Greer and Greer 2003; Sundstrom 2004), particularly for prehistoric imagery.

The catastrophic cultural changes endured by Native Americans from Late Prehistoric to Historic times are also reflected in the rock art record of the Northwestern Plains and Rocky Mountains with the change from what Keyser

(1977) termed Ceremonial to Biographic art. Depictions of events and narratives dominate Historic period imagery. This change occurred in response to contact with Western European and American cultures, rapid technological and economic changes, warfare, forced removal from homelands, conversion to Christianity, and introduction to Western art traditions. James Keyser, recently retired from the United State Forest Service, stands at the forefront of Biographic art research.

Biographic art tends to be finely scratched or incised, and pictographs are rare (Keyser and Klassen 2001:225). Connor and Connor (1971) were among the first investigators to record Biographic art in Montana. Keyser (1977) used data from Writing-on-Stone in Alberta to define specific motifs and stylistic conventions. Through detailed analysis of hide paintings, winter counts, ledger books, and other sources, Keyser (1987, 1991, 1996) and colleagues (Keyser and Cash Cash 2002; Keyser and Mitchell 2001; Klassen et al. 2000; Sundstrom and Keyser 1998) have developed a detailed chronology and lexicon for interpretation of stylistic conventions. This has allowed for far more detailed interpretation, understanding, and identification of ethnic affiliation for Historic period rock art across the Plains and into the Columbia Plateau. Most recently, Keyser and Poetschat (2005, 2008) have used these approaches to study rock art in the Green River Basin of southwestern Wyoming.

TECHNOLOGY

In 1991, the professional digital camera, aimed at photojournalists, was released by Kodak (Bellis 2008). At that time, the standard for rock art recording was the 35 mm SLR camera, using both color and black-and-white photography. Sites were generally mapped with a hand compass and tape measure; hand sketches and measured drawings were made of panels, and for extremely detailed recording, particularly important figures were traced by hand. With advances in digital photography, computing, software, GPS, and electronic surveying equipment, rock art recording and analysis has been completely revolutionized.

Billo and Mark (1999), in conjunction with Larry Loendorf, were among the first to employ geographic information systems (GIS) to record rock art in Wyoming. At the Ring Lake Ranch sites in Torrey Valley, they used GPS to map specific panel locations and, along with digital photography and detailed panel information, to generate a database of hundreds of Dinwoody petroglyphs. By clicking on specific locations on a site map, users could access photographs and specific information that were linked in a relational database. By importing the locational data and digital images collected by Billo and Mark into a GIS using digital elevation models, Burghard (2004) was able to examine viewsheds from petroglyph panels to specific points on the landscape.

In 2006, rerecording of the Legend Rock site was initiated using high-level photogrammetric documentation techniques (Noble and Matthews 2006; Walker et al. 2007). Using these techniques, a spatially accurate photomosaic base map of the site was created. This was followed by detailed three-dimensional modeling and imaging of specific panels. With modern technology, these provide a resolution and accuracy to near 1 cm. These "virtual" models can be used to monitor and detect changes in panels and to create an accurate replica of any panel. With these tools, a user can access three-dimensional views of sites, cliff faces, and panels from almost any orientation and distance. In addition, reflection trans-formation imaging is being used to replicate lighting conditions over 24-hour periods to create far more detailed imagery of figures than observable to the human eye. The techniques being developed and refined at Legend Rock hold great promise for use in documentation and management of sites.

THE BLACK HILLS

The Black Hills of northeastern Wyoming have proven to be extremely fertile ground for rock art research over the last 17 years. This area exhibits a great diver-sity of rock art types and styles reflective of the many cultural groups of the Plains that have used the area over the course of the prehistoric and historic eras. Initial stylistic studies and chronologies were proposed by Buckles (1964), Keyser (1984), and Sundstrom (1984). These have been subsequently revised and refined with the use of numerical dating techniques (Tratebas 1993) and intensive analysis of patterns of superimposition at numerous sites throughout the region (Sundstrom 2004). Regardless of the approach, chronological sequences of rock art in the Black Hills show a complex pattern of temporally overlapping manufacturing tech-niques and styles. There is also general agreement that there is clear change in the nature of much of the rock art from the Late Prehistoric shield-bearing warriors related to the Ceremonial tradition or style defined by Keyser (1977; Keyser and Klassen 2001) to the Historic period Biographic art. This change is characteristic of much of the rock art across Wyoming.

Chronology and Numerical Dating Studies

Sundstrom (2004) has outlined the most detailed rock art chronology for the Black Hills region. An important observation made by Sundstrom (2004:23) is that engraved rock art (including both pecked and incised imagery) was made concurrently with painted rock art over the course of thousands of years. She (2004:63–67) has identified three sites at which dark red painted geometric images occur and at least two instances of superimposition of these images by pecked fig-ures, generally considered at least Archaic in age. This suggests that these painted images may be quite ancient, and she notes that at least one similar red-painted geometric figure occurs at the Medicine Lodge Creek site in the Bighorn Basin. Sundstrom does not consider these images to be closely related to painted geo-metric figures found throughout western and central Montana. To date, none of these early painted figures have been sampled for AMS radiocarbon dating.

Pecked rock art is common in the Black Hills and appears to have been manufac-tured from at least Paleoindian times and throughout the Archaic period. The ear-liest pecked rock art has been termed Pecked Realistic by Sundstrom (2004) or the Early Hunting style by Tratebas (1993). This appears to be superseded by Pecked Abstract figures in Sundstrom's terminology or the Curvilinear Abstract style in Tratebas's terminology and, in turn, by a variety of incised traditions, including the track/vulva/groove complex, Ceremonial Incised (shield-bearing warriors), and Biographical Incised imagery, spanning Late Prehistoric, Protohistoric and post-Contact times. For the painted traditions, the early geometric designs are succeeded by a variety of black- and red-painted naturalistic images, realistic images, and what has been termed vertical-series imagery (Sundstrom 2004:23).

The Pecked Realistic/Early Hunting style dominates the Whoopup Canyon site in the western Black Hills outside of Newcastle and has been the focus of intensive documentation and numerical dating studies (Tratebas 1993). The style consists of small solid-pecked humans and animals in what appear to be hunting or herd scenes (Figure 10.1). A unique characteristic of this style is the "loop line," which is thought to represent traps, corrals, or perhaps nets (see Figure 5.18). Humans are sometimes shown assisted by dogs, and occasionally, weapons protrude from the backs of animal figures (Tratebas 1993:163). Deer, elk, and mountain sheep appear to be the most common prey, and she also notes the presence of what appear to be shamans calling game in some panels.

In the early 1990s, Ronald Dorn sampled numerous petroglyphs in Whoopup Canyon resulting in 13 AMS ages using bulk samples of WRO's and 39 CR dates ranging in age from before 11,000 years ago to about 1300 years ago (Tratebas 1993:164). As discussed earlier in this chapter, later research has shown that AMS ages on WRO's may not yield accurate ^{14}C age determinations. However, the overall

Figure 10.1   Early Hunting style animal and human images from Whoopup Canyon, Weston County, Wyoming.

results of dating studies at Whoopup Canyon are consistent with relative chronologies based upon superimpositions and support the inference that Pecked Realistic/Early Hunting-style rock art is amongst the oldest rock art in the Black Hills.

These studies also confirm that Pecked Realistic/Early Hunting rock art was manufactured over the course of thousands of years, quite likely from Paleoindian times and throughout the Archaic period. Tratebas (1993) used principal components analysis of specific design elements or motifs for both human and animal figures to define figure types and associations (e.g., ball-footed versus cloven-hoofed animal figures, or body shape of human figures). She then further examined the temporal distributions of these patterns, noting some overall trends with considerable temporal overlap between the major patterns. Of note is that the loop-line complex appears to be one of the most recent patterns. She also notes considerable continuity and suggests that Early Hunting rock art reflects a cultural tradition, and emphasizes the importance of treating rock art as archaeological data in order to examine internal variability and patterning within panels (Tratebas 1993:177).

Context and Interpretation in Black Hills Rock Art

Sundstrom (2004:55–62) poses the question of what the Pecked Realistic/Early Hunting style reveals about Archaic period lifeways and notes the similarity of this rock art to imagery found throughout the Great Basin. Some panels reflect ceremonial activities, with some individuals wearing costumes and headdresses. Panels depict a variety of implements, ranging from atlatls to rabbit snares, and some panels appear to represent ideas and concepts. These include images of humans floating above some hunting scenes and depictions of mountain lions above hunting scenes. Furthermore, some human figures are therianthropic, depicting the transformation of humans into deer, which perhaps reflects the importance of trance and visionary experience among these ancient people. Sundstrom (2004:62) concludes that Pecked Realistic/Early Hunting rock art reflects a culture with a high degree of social cooperation and a well-developed religion.

Sundstrom (2004:68–77) uses the neuro-psychological model (Lewis-Williams and Dowson 1988) to interpret the Archaic-age Pecked Abstract art of the Black Hills. Panels that show only phosphene imagery likely reflect the trance state and the physiological reactions experienced by all human beings; in virtually all Native American cultures, trance and visionary experience are important elements of religious activity. Pecked Abstract imagery clearly reflects the work of people operating outside everyday experience and points to the long-term importance of visionary experience among native peoples. She notes that Pecked Abstract art generally shows less weathering and is often imposed upon the Pecked Realistic hunting scenes. She ascribes ages of about 5000 to 2000 years ago, based upon relative criteria. This is slightly older than the numerical age estimates from Whoopup Canyon (Tratebas 1993:164). Sundstrom (2004:73) also suggests a western origin for Pecked Abstract imagery.

The occurrence of deeply ground animal tracks, vulvas, and tool grooves (Figure 10.2) can be associated with the expansion of Siouan- and Algonquian-speaking peoples from the Eastern Woodlands on to the Northern Plains after about 2000 years ago (Sundstrom 2002, 2004:78–98). By about 1000 years ago,

Figure 10.2 Tool grooves (at lower left), deeply engraved animal track, and vulva design from Medicine Creek Cave, Crook County.

ancestors of the Mandan, Hidatsa, and Crow reached the Missouri River, followed by the Algonquian-speaking Cheyenne and Arapaho, and later the ancestral Dakota and Lakota people. With this influx, pecked rock art gave way to imagery produced by incising, grinding, and abrading. Two of the better-known sites containing this type of rock art include petroglyphs associated with Ludlow Cave in South Dakota and Medicine Creek Cave north of Hulett, Wyoming. Some of the carvings are actually bas-reliefs or intaglios and typically include images of bison, bison tracks, human vulvas, and tool grooves. The important spiritual relationships between bison, women, fertility, and renewal common among many Northern Plains tribes is apparent from a detailed ethnographic analysis (Sundstrom 2002). She also uncovers numerous ethnographic references describing the production of rock art by women in association with puberty ceremonies and visions through which quill designs were acquired. Sundstrom (2002) asserts that the track/vulva/groove rock art sites were made by women. Furthermore, the deep tool grooves may be the product of sharpening bone awls used for quilling. This may also have played an important role in the acquisition of imagery. Furthermore, the replacement of bone awls and porcupine quills with metal awls and glass beads in Protohistoric and post-Contact times reflects the change from quill work to beading and, along with the adoption of Christianity by many women, may explain the sudden disappearance of this type of rock art.

The shield-bearing warrior figures found throughout the Black Hills are considered to be the earliest expression of warrior art, spanning the transition between the Late Prehistoric and Historic periods (Sundstrom 2004:99–106). The large, full-body shields which mask all but the head, hands, feet, and occasionally a weapon are thought to date to prehorse times, prior to about AD 1750. She notes that these figures tend to be more concerned with warriors' prayers for supernatural aid, rather than with their actual deeds and have often been considered part of the Ceremonial tradition defined by Keyser (1977). However, some Black Hills panels do show actual scenes, including coup counts. Although quite distinct from the Historic period Biographical art. The two styles grade into one another, and she considers them a continuous expression.

Of importance to the understanding of these figures is the body of ethnographic literature which points to a visionary origin for the acquisition of shield designs. It was often the power of the design, rather than the shield itself, which was thought to protect its owner from harm. Although each design was individual and based upon the warrior's vision, it is still possible to recognize tribal styles among the corpus of Northern Plains shield designs (Sundstrom and Keyser 1998). Sundstrom and Keyser's comparison of 22 rock art shield designs from the Black Hills to 314 shields and published shield designs with known tribal affiliations shows that nine shields are likely of Cheyenne origin and three are either Cheyenne or Lakota, or Cheyenne or Crow. They also identify several motifs as specific ethnic markers and conclude that rock art shields are potential indicators of cultural affiliation.

Historic period Biographic art of the Black Hills reflects battles, coup counting, horse raids, and scalping, including two possible coup counts against women (Sundstrom 2004:107–109). The V-shouldered human motif may be associated with Algonquian-speaking tribes of the Northern Plains, specifically the Blackfeet, Cheyenne, and Arapaho (Sundstrom 2004:112). She further notes that Biographic art proper is found only along the Cheyenne River along natural passes, large prominent cliff faces, or along major trails (Sundstrom 2004:125).

Based upon ethnographic data, Sundstrom (2004) offers rich interpretations for a variety of unusual Protohistoric to post-Contact and Historic period rock art in the Black Hills. These include four sites most likely related to Mandan/ Hidatsa eagle trapping and associated spirits such as bears, snakes, coyote, bison, and eagle. Painted Realistic art is unique to Craven Canyon and includes painted bison, legless humans and animals, and tri-lobed figures. The images are possible Ponca cultural affiliations, though more research is needed to support that hypothesis (Sundstrom 2004:128). Unique "long-nosed" figures found in Medicine Creek Cave could possibly relate to Mississippian cultures. Other unusual, lightly incised, upside-down human heads found at Medicine Creek Cave and the Hulett South site (Figure 10.3) may represent the central characters, Spring Boy and Lodge Boy, of the Crow-Hidatsa origin myth or perhaps Kiowa Sun Dance effigy figures (Sundstrom 2004:143–148; Sundstrom et al. 2001). Human faces that have been either pecked or carved into rocks also occur rarely in the Black Hills, and at least some of these may be related to shell maskettes used throughout the Plains (Sundstrom 2004:160–173). Painted vertical-series art, consisting of unusual symbols arranged in vertical lines, occurs at three sites. These are most likely related to some type of visionary experience. Lastly, Sundstrom (2004:181–185) identifies several lightly incised, horned human figures as Lakota elk dreamers. Similar figures have been found near Register Cliff in Platte County, Wyoming (Figure 10.4; Reiss 2004).

Of importance in Sundstrom's analysis of Black Hills rock art is the relation of rock art sites to a variety of widely recognized sacred places in the general area. Such places include Bear Butte and Harney Peak in South Dakota, and

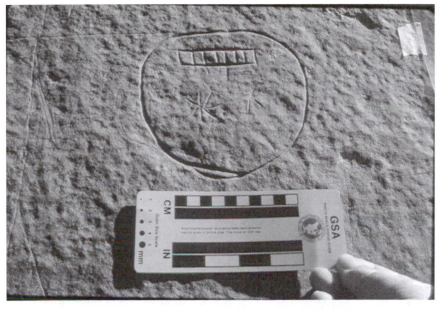

Figure 10.3   Lightly incised upside-down human head from the Hulett South site, Crook County.

Figure 10.4   At Register Cliff, two large rectangular-bodied figures hold round shields and may represent Lakota elk dreamers. Names and initials of Oregon Trail immigrants have been carved on top of Native American imagery.

Bears' Lodge Butte (better known as Devil's Tower), Inyan Kara Mountain, and Sundance Mountain in Wyoming. Many specific rock art sites are also recognized for their special, powerful nature. For example, in Mandan tradition, Ludlow Cave is said to be the sacred opening to the underworld from which bison periodically emerged to replenish the herds so that the people might live (Sundstrom 2004:81). Other localities, such as Craven Canyon and Medicine Creek Cave, stand apart as natural portals to the underworld and as places at which offerings were given for thousands of years. Less well known are several large "dance rings." Through her analysis of rock art and ethnographic data, Sundstrom conveys the cultural diversity and deeper layers of meaning and significance that these places hold for the many different peoples that have used the area over time.

THE POWDER RIVER BASIN

Documented rock art sites from the Powder River Basin were almost unknown prior to 1991. Since then, the number of known sites from the interior portion of the Powder River Basin has more than tripled, with approximately one-half of these recorded by Mavis and John Greer from Casper, Wyoming. The Eocene-age Wasatch Formation sandstones in the interior Powder River Basin tend to be softer and more erodible than the Paleozoic and Mesozoic formations of the surrounding uplifts, and outcrops are not common. Nevertheless, rock art does occur on at least some of these faces. Most of the imagery appears relatively recent, dating to the Historic period.

At least two armored horses occur at the Arminto Petroglyph site in Natrona County (Greer and Greer 2001a, 2001b, 2002a, 2002b). However, the horses are illustrated in a fairly crude boat-shaped manner, suggesting a date within the earlier portion of the time between AD 1700 and AD 1800 (Figure 10.5). Horse armor may be a logical outgrowth of personal armor common in prehorse times (Greer and Greer 2002a). However, Greer and Greer do not rule out a Spanish influence in the design and note the occurrence of a possible brand (a practice attributed to the Spaniards) or painted rump on one of the horses at Arminto. Because of the lack of associated weaponry, they conclude that the Arminto horses appear to have armor for use as protection from environmental elements rather than in expectation of hostile situations. The Arminto Petroglyph site is adjacent to an oil

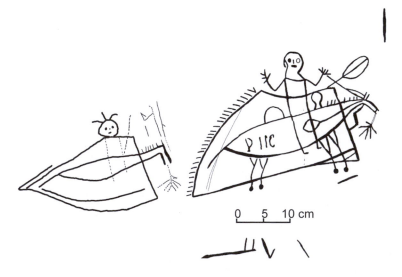

0   5   10 cm

Figure 10.5   Lightly incised armored horse figure from the Arminto site, Natrona County. (Drawing by John and Mavis Greer.)

and gas well that has been in production for at least the last 25 years, and recent visits to the site have shown considerable deterioration of the figures (Keyser et al. 2005). Documentation (T. Larson 2007) continues to determine how best to manage the site and the associated development.

Armored horses are not commonly illustrated in rock art. Mitchell (2002, 2004) has documented armored horses in the Arkansas River drainage of southeastern Colorado. Twenty armored horse figures from the Central and Northern Plains, including two from Alberta, seven in Montana, four in Wyoming, two in South Dakota, and five from the Central Plains have been reported (Greer and Greer 2007). In addition to the two Arminto horses, one other has been documented in central Wyoming and another in southwestern Wyoming. Research into armored horse figures in Plains rock art continues. Though rare, the occurrence of such images along the length of the Rocky Mountain front offers great potential for further research into the cultural dynamics of the Protohistoric and early Historic periods.

SOUTHWESTERN WYOMING

Although an image of a bow and arrow hunter from the Calpet Petroglyph site in Sublette County graced the cover of the 1991 second edition of *Prehistoric Hunters of the High Plains*, rock art in the Green River Basin has received relatively little attention until quite recently. In 1991, the majority of documented rock art sites in southwestern Wyoming were known from the uplifted and dissected area adjacent to Flaming Gorge Reservoir. In 2008, many more sites have been documented in the interior of the Green River Basin, along tributaries to the Green, in the vicinity of Fontenelle Reservoir and the Seedskadee Wildlife Refuge, and uplifted areas along the basin margins. Detailed documentation has been completed at several localities, chronologies have been constructed, and some inferences as to cultural affiliation have been put forward. Though Biographic art dominates, southwestern Wyoming rock art reflects a diversity consistent with long-term usage of the region as an important travel corridor and crossroads between the Great Basin, Great Plains, and Colorado Plateau (Keyser et al. 2004:144).

Like the Powder River Basin, many of the sandstones of southwestern Wyoming are fairly soft and erodible and not conducive to the preservation of rock art. As a result, most of the known sites are Late Prehistoric to Historic period in age. There are, nevertheless, hints of older rock art traditions. At the Black Rock site (Figure 10.6), a fortuitous overhang has protected a small area from wind damage and preserved the dark rock varnish typical of many harder sandstones. First noted by Joe Bozovich of Rock Springs, several small, fully pecked human and animals figures occur on the varnished surface. Imagery includes mountain sheep and humans, and the figures are not dissimilar to the en toto or fully pecked figures of the Bighorn and Wind River Basins. With assistance from Russell Tanner, then with the Bureau of Land Management in Rock Springs, Ronald Dorn collected several samples for AMS dating, with some surprising results. Paleoindian ages exceeding 10,000 BP were returned from a fully pecked human figure (Figure 10.7; Liu and Dorn 1996; Tanner et al. 1995). This date was obtained from a bulk sample of WRO's and may not be an accurate reflection of the true age of the petroglyph. The site nevertheless offers tantalizing hints of an older pecked rock art tradition

Figure 10.6 Overview of the Black Rock site, Sweetwater County. Pecked human and animal figures occur on the varnished overhang on the right side of the photo.

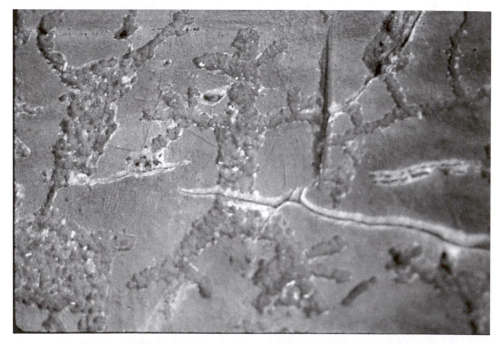

Figure 10.7 Close-up of pecked human image from the Black Rock site. A bulk sample of weathering rind organics from this figure yielded an age of 11,650 ± 50 ^{14}C years BP. Contamination from organic material from the host sandstone cannot be ruled out.

which simply has not been preserved due to the inherent characteristics of sandstones in the area.

Some rock art in the Green River Basin has been ascribed a possible Fremont affiliation (Francis et al. 1987). Incising is the most common manufacturing technique, with painted figures being exceedingly rare. In general, shield-bearing warrior figures are not common in the Green River Basin. Many human figures consist of a simple rectangular-shaped body with heads, arms, and limbs, and details of headdress and clothing are often shown. Animal depictions include horses, elk, and occasionally bears (Figure 10.8) and bison (Figure 10.9). Though Biographic art dominates the rock art of the Green River Basin, many of the animal images also reflect the continued importance of the acquisition of supernatural power from these creatures. The majority of recent research has concentrated on sites such as Cedar Canyon, White Mountain, LaBarge Bluffs, Names Hills, and other localities. Based upon these investigations, Keyser et al. (2004) and Keyser and Poetschat (2005) have defined preliminary chronologies and stylistic sequences. The predominant time frame is thought to be from about AD 1500 to AD 1875.

For Protobiographic art, three styles have been defined. The Seedskadee style is thought to be the earliest and consists of stick-figured humans (occasionally shown with shields) without headdresses and simple stick-figured or boat-shaped horses. Combat scenes are typical. They also note the presence of the slightly more elaborate Verdigris style humans at the LaBarge Bluffs site. The Green River style, identified thus far only at the LaBarge Bluffs site, is characterized by outline-pecked humans and horses with rectangular bodies. Keyser et al. (2004) and Keyser and Poetschat (2005) also identify early and late Biographical styles. These are much more elaborate, illustrate a wider range of

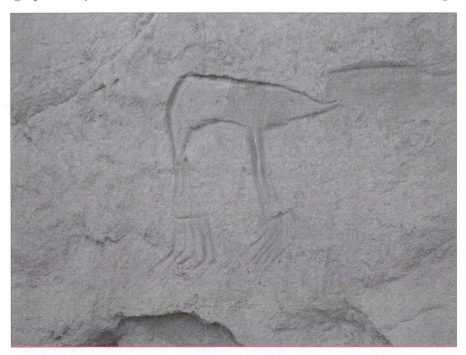

Figure 10.8 Incised bear image from the South Piney site, Sublette County. Note the elongated legs and oversized claws.

Figure 10.9   Incised bison image from the White Mountain site, Sweetwater County. Note the use of natural crevices and irregular surfaces of the cliff face to frame the head and hump, giving the impression that the animal is going into the rock.

details of posture, clothing, headdress, weaponry, and horse accoutrements. Scenes include elaborate battles and dances. Furthermore, an illustration of a train at the LaBarge Bluffs site documents the nationally important completion of the first transcontinental railroad (Figure 10.10). These authors further note

Figure 10.10   Lightly incised locomotive and train cars at the LaBarge Bluffs site, Lincoln County. A horizontal bedding plane in the sandstone conveys the impression of the railroad track.

that the elaborate scenes at the LaBarge Bluffs site are some of the most stylistically sophisticated images in Plains rock art and consider them to be one of the masterpieces of late nineteenth century Plains Indian art (Keyser et al. 2004: 147–148). Also of note is that women are illustrated at the LaBarge Bluffs site (Keyser et al. 2006). This includes elaborate depictions of what may be the capture and adoption of a woman, identifiable in several different panels (Figure 10.11). These panels are considered to have Shoshonean authorship, and reflect overall societal values about the status of women in post-Contact period Plains groups, with such depictions having great potential for gender studies (Keyser and Poetschat 2005:174; Keyser et al. 2006:67).

While still easily grouped with Biographic art, other sites, such as the Tolar site in Sweetwater County, seem to reflect a more spiritual nature. This site includes some of the most well-made horse figures in the Plains region (Figure 10.12), for which Comanche authorship has been suggested (Olson and Loendorf 2003: 40–41). However, large round-headed humans with tear-streaked eyes, horned headdresses, and a considerable amount of bear imagery also illustrate the power of the place (Figure 10.12). Tolar, located along a strategic travel corridor, may have been used to seek supernatural guidance for an impending raid (Olson and Loendorf 2003:43).

Another notable complex of Biographic art occurs in the Powder Wash area in the extreme southeastern portion of the Green River Basin (Keyser and Poetschat 2008; Murcray 1993). Generally regarded as of Ute authorship, the Powder Wash sites are predominated by numerous panels of mounted riders crayoned in charcoal. However, scenes typical of other Biographical art are uncommon, and the Powder Wash horses seem to document individual wealth and warriors' prowess

Figure 10.11   Battle scene from the LaBarge Bluffs site, Lincoln County. Mounted warriors appear to be counting coup on a female figure at the lower right of the photograph.

Figure 10.12   Distinctive mounted warrior from the Tolar site, Sweetwater County. The mounted figure wears an unusual headdress and carries a shield. A possible Comanche affiliation has been suggested for this image. Note also the mounted figure with the enlarged head, bison headdress, and tear-streaked face at the right side of the photo.

in horse raiding (Keyser and Poetschat 2008:78). Of critical importance is the association of the rock art with long, wooden drift fences, wooden wickiups, and wooden-walled rockshelters, leading Keyser and Poetschat (2008:97) to suggest that the entire complex represents a Ute redoubt for horse-raiding parties, rather than an association with game trapping or hunting.

BIGHORN AND WIND RIVER BASINS

Major research projects focusing on chronology (Francis et al. 1993), interpretation, and regional synthesis (Francis and Loendorf 2002) of the Bighorn and Wind River basins have been published since the second edition of *Prehistoric Hunters of the High Plains*. Distinctive among Bighorn and Wind River basin rock art are the pecked, interior-lined human figures considered the hallmark of the Dinwoody tradition. These figures often extend over 1 m in height and exhibit horns or headdresses, bizarre orientations of limbs often with wings or claws as appendages, complex patterns of lines in the torso, and are often associated with animal images (Figure 10.13). They stand in stark contrast to the incised and painted shield-bearing warriors and rectangular-bodied and V-shouldered human figures also common in the region (Figure 10.14). Early researchers (Gebhard 1951, 1969; Renaud 1936) believed the pecked figures to be the most ancient and constructed unilineal stylistic chronologies thought to be applicable across most of Wyoming. Relatively recent ages (i.e., Late Prehistoric, Protohistoric, and Historic periods) were generally attributed to most of the rock art in the region.

Figure 10.13   Pecked, interior-lined human figure flanked by a bird-like image from the Ring Lake Ranch site, Fremont County. Both images suggest transformation from human to animal states and exhibit many design elements which may metaphorically illustrate physiological reactions experienced during altered states of consciousness.

Subsequent investigators (Stewart 1989; Tipps and Schroedl 1985) continued to use Gebhard's stylistic chronology for documentation and investigations of rock art sites throughout the area.

Chronology and Dating

By 1991, researchers had begun to use traditional archaeological techniques to infer minimum limiting ages for some figures. These techniques included radiocarbon dating of charcoal in sediments partially burying figures or radiocarbon dating of buried features discovered below panels (Francis 1989:193–194; Loendorf 1990). These studies spurred efforts to obtain direct numerical age estimates for rock art across the study area using AMS and CR dating of petroglyphs and AMS dating of painted figures. The results of the first AMS and cation-ratio dating studies were

Figure 10.14 Simple, rectangular-bodied figure on a shield from the Red Canyon site, Fremont County. The oversized hands and V-shaped heads are also suggestive of altered states of consciousness.

published by Francis et al. (1993). This study focused primarily on the Legend Rock and other sites in Hot Springs and Fremont counties, Petroglyph Canyon and the Bear Shield site in southern Montana, and Medicine Lodge Creek on the eastern side of the Bighorn Basin. Additional AMS and CR dates were collected in 1991 and 1995 (Francis 1994; Liu and Dorn 1996). A total of 11 petroglyphs have AMS ages and 37 petroglyphs have CR ages, with paint from three pictographs dated by AMS (Francis and Loendorf 2002). Both Loendorf (2008) and Walker et al. (2007) have continued archaeological excavation at Valley of the Shields and Legend Rock to recover additional datable materials and archaeological remains associated with rock art panels.

Francis and Loendorf (2002:61–67) provide a summary of available numeri-cal age estimates for rock art in the Bighorn and Wind River basins and present an evaluation of the general reliability of these ages. Ages of petroglyphs span nearly the entire Holocene geological epoch, with at least a few figures at the Legend Rock site of likely Paleoindian age. One AMS date from the Legend Rock site was obtained from charcoal encapsulated by accreting rock varnish, considered less controversial than AMS dates on WRO's, and yielded an Early Archaic age. Francis and Loendorf also consider the time transgressive nature of AMS ages of WRO's (i.e., that the inheritance of older carbon increases with age). They conclude that since the vast majority of petroglyphs in the Bighorn and Wind River basin are comparatively young (mid to late Holocene in age), the effects of "older" carbon in bulk WRO samples may be fairly small for that particular study area. They also note the consistency of available AMS ages with independent data and the consistency of both AMS ages and CR sequences with multiple sampling, superimposition of figures on the same panel, and subject matter of known age depicted in some figures. They conclude that the AMS and CR dates provide "reasonably accurate age estimates," and that, considering temporal variation on the scale of thousands of years, the techniques provide valuable chronological data (Francis and Loendorf 2002:67).

Chronological studies of Bighorn and Wind River basin rock art yielded surprising results. In 1993, Francis et al. (1993:713–715, 731) fully expected the dating studies to reflect a unilineal chronology in which older pecked styles were supplanted by the incised and painted shield-bearing warriors and associated motifs during the latter part of the Late Prehistoric period. Instead, results showed a far greater antiquity for Dinwoody figures and a complex pattern of overlapping dates between pecked and incised figures, suggesting that all types of rock art were manufactured in the Bighorn and Wind River basins during the last 1000 years and that concurrent styles or traditions existing for a considerable period of time (Francis et al. 1993:734).

The Dinwoody Tradition

The large, pecked, other-worldly anthropomorphic figures found along the upper Wind River, Boysen Reservoir area, and lower Bighorn River were initially termed the Dinwoody (Wellmann 1979:132) or Interior-Lined style (Gebhard 1969). Though often associated with a variety of pecked animal and smaller human images, the often surreal, interior-lined anthropomorphs were considered the defining figure type for the style (Figure 10.15). Gebhard (1969:22) suggested that these figures could be attributed to the Shoshone and ranged between AD 1650 and AD 1800 in age. Results of archaeological excavation and direct numerical age estimates demonstrated that these figures range in age from the Late Archaic to the Historic period. Furthermore, AMS and CR ages suggested a complex overlapping pattern of ages for all different human and animal figure types at sites such as Legend Rock, with several different figure types manufactured over the course of thousands of years.

More in-depth study of temporal and formal variation of Dinwoody and associated figures led Francis (1994) to posit the existence of the Dinwoody rock art tradition, in contrast to the Dinwoody or Interior-Lined style. Building upon an initial typology of Dinwoody anthropomorphic and zoomorphic figures based on the Legend Rock site (Francis 1989), a rudimentary seriation showed that nearly all figure types, whether human-like or animal, exhibited some degree of chronological overlap, with some peaks in frequency of certain types through time. Anthropomorphic figures showed a general change from small, relatively simple

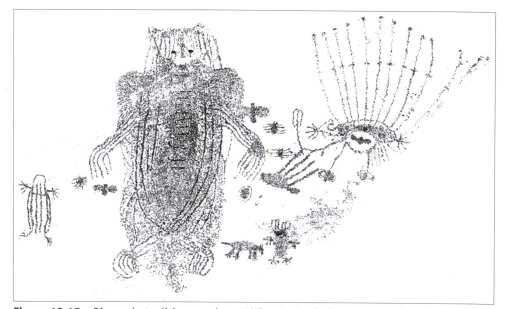

Figure 10.15 Dinwoody tradition panel at 48HO660, Hot Springs County. The dominant figure suggests transformation from human to bear and appears to emerge from a crevice in the rock surface. It is flanked by smaller human images. One canine figure is apparent, in addition to figures which appear to be flying. The large fanned image at the right side of the panel defies literal interpretation. (Tracing by Linda Olson.)

fully pecked figures during the Archaic period to the large, elaborate interior-lined images predominating during Late Prehistoric and Protohistoric times. Animal figures also showed some evidence for change through time, with large interior-lined images most common during the Archaic, and smaller, fully pecked figures, including dogs and sheep, spanning the entire sequence from Early Archaic to Late Prehistoric times.

Francis (1994:49) noted that the Dinwoody "style" consists of far more than the large interior-lined figures (Gebhard 1969; Wellmann 1979), but represents a complex of associated human and animal figures showing great time depth and continuity. In conjunction with a restricted spatial distribution in the upper Wind River Valley, Boysen Reservoir vicinity, and across the southwestern portion of the Bighorn Basin west of the Bighorn River (see also Gebhard 1969), Francis (1994:49) suggested the term "tradition" as defined by Willey and Phillips (1958:37) was applicable to Dinwoody rock art. In addition, shamanistic origins have frequently been suggested for Dinwoody rock art (Francis and Frison 1990; Hendry 1983a; Sowers 1941), and many of the figures and design elements evoke supernatural images, transformation, and out-of-body experience typical of shamanistic trances and visions. Thus, Francis (1994:49) also suggested that the Dinwoody tradition represents the material cultural expression of ideological and religious beliefs of prehistoric hunter-gatherers in that region.

This organizing principle was used by Francis and Loendorf (2002) in their analysis of formal and temporal characteristics of the Dinwoody rock art. Because of formal differences, Francis and Loendorf (2002:96) do not consider the likely Paleoindian-age figures (Figure 10.16) at the Legend Rock site to be part of the Dinwoody tradition; the earliest readily identifiable Dinwoody figures date

Figure 10.16 Unusual outline-pecked human image from the Legend Rock site, Hot Springs County. Cation-ratio dating suggests this figure may be of Paleoindian age. This image differs greatly from typical Dinwoody tradition human images. (Courtesy of Ron Dorn.)

to the Early Archaic period. They (Francis and Loendorf 2002:74–82) also suggested an extremely close relationship between the Dinwoody tradition and the en toto pecked style as originally defined by Loendorf and Porsche (1985). En toto (or fully) pecked figures exhibit a slightly greater north–south range within the Bighorn and Wind River basins, but also occur predominantly west of the Bighorn River. These figures co-occur with Dinwoody interior-lined images at many sites. As a result, Francis and Loendorf (2002) no longer consider this a distinctive style, but instead group these figures within the fully pecked human and animal figures as descriptive figure types of the Dinwoody tradition.

In their recent synthesis, *Ancient Visions*, Francis and Loendorf (2002:110–123) attribute the Dinwoody tradition rock art to Shoshonean peoples. Building upon the work of Whitley (1988, 1992, 1994a, 1994b, 1994c) that links rock art across the American West to the graphic representations of the visionary images experienced during trances, Francis and Loendorf use Shoshonean ethnography to argue that Dinwoody rock art sites were used by Shoshonean shamans as vision-questing locales to acquire knowledge and supernatural power for the purposes of curing, thereby earning elevated social position, income, and status within their communities. Direct archaeological evidence from the Coal Draw area of the Bighorn Basin, in the form of 12 steatite and sandstone sucking tubes recovered from the base of a Dinwoody panel, is also used to infer a shamanistic function for Dinwoody rock art sites (Frison and Van Norman 1993). Francis and Loendorf describe specific ritual practices, review ethnographically identified vision-quest locales, and discuss the distribution of supernatural power across the Shoshonean landscape as it relates to rock art sites. They also identify various types of supernatural beings, such as rock ghosts, water ghosts, and water babies, with several types of Dinwoody images (Figure 10.17), and they relate the spatial distribution of specific types of images to the distribution of powerful creatures and beings which inhabit the sky, earth, and underworld realms of the Shoshone.

Outline-Pecked, Incised, and Painted Imagery

Rock art on the eastern side of the Bighorn and Wind River basins presents a sharp contrast to that of the western side (Francis and Loendorf 2002:124–183). Instead of displays of closely associated human and animal images made in a

Figure 10.17   Dinwoody tradition image of Water Ghost Woman, Hot Springs County. Note the long braids, tear streak below one eye, and fringed skirt. The figure carries a bow and is flanked by a canine figure and a smaller human image. A turtle occurs on the same panel.

consistent manner over long periods of time, rock art sites east of the Bighorn and Wind Rivers often exhibit a bewildering array of figure types and manufacturing techniques. Images were made by abrasion, outline pecking, deep-line incising, fine-line incising, and several types and colors of painting; many were made using a combination of these techniques. Furthermore, nearly all different manufacturing techniques were used concurrently to depict all types of images. Common images include shield-bearing warriors and V-shouldered anthropomorphs, solid-painted rectangular-bodied anthropomorphs, and several incised and painted therianthropic figures that may be related to bear ceremonialism, common in the Northern Plains tribes. Animal images consistently associated with these figures include bear, elk, deer, bison, turtles, and birds.

Based upon the occurrence of shield-bearing warriors and V-shouldered human figures, Francis and Loendorf (2002:135) ascribe a Plains origin to most of the imagery on the east side of the Bighorn and Wind River basins. Shield-bearing warriors are one of the readily identifiable figure types common to the eastern Bighorn Basin. These figures were rendered using all the different manufacturing techniques observed throughout the area. First defined by Mulloy (1958), many investigators posited Great Basin or Shoshonean origins for the motif (Gebhard 1966; Grant 1967; Keyser 1975, 1977; Schaafsma 1971) with a spread eastward into the Great Plains. However, at Writing-on-Stone in southern Alberta, Magne and Klassen (1991) demonstrated cultural continuity between shield-bearing warriors and V-necked, hourglass, and rectangular-bodied human figures associated with Northern Plains tribes. With a widespread distribution east of the Continental Divide from Alberta to Texas, more recent research has documented the shield-bearing warrior as a common cultural symbol of nearly all Plains ethnic groups (see Keyser and Klassen 2001:211), with differences between it and the comparatively less common Great Basin shields. The diversity of shield-bearing warrior figures in the eastern Bighorn and Wind River basins certainly suggests use of the area by many different Plains peoples (Francis and Loendorf 2002:135).

Rock art on the eastern side of the Bighorn and Wind River basins does not appear to be as ancient as some of the Dinwoody sites. Most imagery appears to date to the Late Prehistoric, Protohistoric, and Historic periods. Thus far, the oldest dated figure is a black-painted turtle from Pictograph Cave outside of Billings, Montana, which yielded three overlapping ^{14}C ages of around 2100 years BP (Francis and Loendorf 2002:161). Dating studies on the eastern side of the basins have yielded somewhat disappointing results, in large part due to damage and contamination from modern chalking, charcoaling, latex molds, and casting (Francis et al. 1993:722–727).

Francis and Loendorf do not offer a specific chronology of figure types or manufacturing techniques for the eastern side of the Bighorn Basin, instead they (2002:144–147) generally ascribe Late Prehistoric period ages to outline-pecked animals, shield-bearing warriors, and deeply incised shield-bearing warriors. This inference was based on one AMS age of weathering rind organics, large shields covering nearly all the body thought to be pedestrian humans, and the lack of historic items depicted in the imagery. Fine-lined incised figures and V-shouldered anthropomorphs are generally considered to be of Protohistoric and Historic age. Late Prehistoric ages were inferred for several types of painted images.

More recent work at the Medicine Lodge Creek site (Francis 2007) may clarify some of the chronological relationships for rock art on the eastern side of the

Bighorn and Wind River basins. In conjunction with an extensive recording project completed by Charles A. Reher and the University of Wyoming Archaeological Field School, Francis provided an initial classification and chronology of figure types at Medicine Lodge Creek. This chronology was based upon previous rock art dating studies, ages of archaeological deposits at the base of panels and the lack of buried figures, and superimpositions of rock art images at the site. The occurrence of a few en toto or fully pecked human figures similar to those seen at Dinwoody sites on the western side of the basin reflects sporadic usage of the site by ancestors of modern Shoshonean groups (Francis 2007:214–216). She proposes that rock art manufacture could have begun at Medicine Lodge Creek around the terminal Late Archaic period.

Francis (2007) also elaborated on the nature of the unusual, large outlined-pecked animal figures which dominate the imagery of Medicine Lodge Creek and occur only rarely at other sites in the Bighorn Basin (Francis and Loendorf 2002:158). As defined by Francis (2007:216–218), the outline-pecked complex includes extremely large images (sometimes approaching nearly 2 m in height or length) of bears, elk, bison, and at least one ghost-line human image. A unifying characteristic of these figures is that they are pierced by large arrows that exhibit prominent fletching at the proximal end and either a projectile point or animal image at the distal end (Figure 10.18). The animal images are often surrounded by smaller outlined-pecked human figures. At Medicine Lodge Creek, one of these images may be a frontal view of a bear or a human wearing a bear costume. Smaller bear figures also can be seen around the large elk images, suggesting a

Figure 10.18   Outline-pecked elk from the Medicine Lodge Creek site, Bighorn County. This image is over 2 m long, and the creature has been pierced by several pecked arrows. A bear image appears below the elk's belly, and what may be a frontal image of a bear or human in a bear costume peers over the elk's back. One in toto pecked human can be seen above the head of the elk. Both elk and bear hold creature supernatural power in many Native American religious systems, and their power was sought by humans.

close association between the two animals. At the Greybull North site, an outline-pecked bison appears to be superimposed over an en toto pecked human. Francis (2007:218) suggests that the large outlined-pecked images may date to the beginning of the Late Prehistoric period.

Of note is that at least one of the large elk figures at Medicine Lodge Creek has been superimposed by a large pecked circle or shield, and that many of the large outline-pecked shield-bearing warriors have been placed on the same panels surrounding the elk images (Figure 10.19). This suggests a close association between the shield-bearing warriors and the extraordinary animal images. Francis (2007:225–226) posits that the positioning of the shield-bearing warrior figures around images of elk and bears may reflect the acquisition of supernatural power from these creatures, which are considered extremely powerful in many Native traditions.

Distinctive among the shield-bearing warriors of the eastern Bighorn and Wind River basins is the Castle Gardens shield style defined by Loendorf (1995). Best known from the Castle Gardens site in the eastern Wind River Basin, Castle Gardens shields exhibit a unique combination of manufacturing techniques. After abrading a sandstone surface smooth, the prehistoric artists deeply incised a shield design, often dividing it into quarters and filling each quadrant with a variety of smaller images. Then at least three colors of paint were applied to the design from a color palette that included two shades of red, two shades of orange, black, white, and green (Figure 10.20). The use of green paint stands out as a distinguishing characteristic of the style (Francis and Loendorf 2002:137). Recent XRF analysis of green paint from figures at Valley of the Shields in Montana suggests that chromium may be responsible for the green color, with possible sources in

Figure 10.19 Large, outline-pecked shield-bearing warriors surrounding the elk in Figure 10.18 at the Medicine Lodge Creek site, Bighorn County. Warriors may have sought the power of elk and bear as protection during battles.

Figure 10.20   Shield from the Castle Gardens site, Fremont County. A polychrome-painted human image adorns the shield. This figure carries oversized arrows in each hand and sports a horned headdress which terminates in zigzag lines.

southeastern Wyoming and near Ennis, Montana (Newman and Loendorf 2005). Designs on the shields include turtles, bear paws, humans, and unusual human heads.

Similar shields and shield-bearing warriors have been documented at the Valley of the Shields site in the southern Pryor Mountains and a few other sites in Weatherman Draw, with very similar examples occurring at Medicine Lodge Creek and Pictograph Cave. Wood charcoal from a buried hearth directly associated with the manufacture of these figures was radiocarbon dated to around 900 years ago (Loendorf 1990), and hearths from a site within 500 m of petroglyphs at Castle Gardens yielded radiocarbon ages around 700 BP (Walker and Todd 1984). Within the last year, Loendorf has revisited Valley of the Shields to obtain additional radiocarbon dates from the cultural level dated in 1990. Sage charcoal from the same feature yielded considerably younger ages, suggesting the "old wood" problem may have been responsible for the initial dates reported in 1990 (Loendorf 2008:189). At this time, an accurate age assessment, other than younger than 900 years, is not available for the Castle Gardens shield style. Younger ages are supported by the superimposition of a Castle Gardens–like shield figure over a large pecked arrow associated with the outline-pecked complex at the Medicine Lodge Creek site. Cultural affiliation of this style is also unknown. Both Athapaskans and the Tanoan-speaking Kiowa have been suggested as likely candidates (Loendorf 1995).

Other unusual images have been associated with specific groups living in the Bighorn Basin. One type of solid-painted anthropomorphic figure and associated plant images appear to be related to the Crow occupation of the Bighorn Mountains (Francis and Loendorf 2002:168–172). First identified from two sites in the Pryor Mountains (Loendorf and Porsche 1985), these human figures exhibit unusual flat headdresses with associated stars (Figure 10.21). These appear identical to headdresses worn by members of the Crow Sacred Tobacco Society (Francis and Loendorf 2002:172). Associated plant images strongly resemble native tobacco (*Nicotiana multivalvis, N. quadravalvis*), and tobacco pollen has been recovered from archaeological deposits in caves containing these images. Similar plant images have been found in the southern Bighorn Mountains. The various design elements can be related to many different aspects of Crow oral tradition and spiritual belief, which place the Bighorn Mountains as the origin of the Tobacco Society. Other unusual anthropomorphic figures found in the southern Wind River Basin have also been related to the Crow/Hidatsa twin heroes (Francis and Loendorf 2002:173).

Figure 10.21   Painted human image from Frozen Leg Cave in southern Montana. This image is thought to represent a member of the Crow Sacred Tobacco Society. (Larry Loendorf photo.)

Alternative Views of Prehistory

One of the remarkable aspects of rock art in the Bighorn and Wind River basins is the striking disparity in spatial distributions between the Dinwoody tradition and outline-pecked/incised/painted imagery. The restricted spatial distribution of Dinwoody petroglyphs (Figure 10.22) to the Wind River Valley, Boysen Reservoir vicinity, and the southern Bighorn Basin along streams which drain the eastern side of the Absaroka Mountains and flow into the Bighorn River from the west was first noted by Gebhard (1969). Francis and Loendorf (2002:189) view this as the core area of classic Dinwoody anthropomorphic figure types, surrounded by sites containing smaller and simpler en toto pecked figures. No classic Dinwoody anthropomorphic figures are known from the east side of the river, and the smaller en toto pecked figures occur only rarely there. By way of contrast, shield-bearing warriors and other incised and painted sites occur almost exclusively east of the river, with concentrations along the Yellowstone River and the north-flowing tributaries of the Clark's Fork of the Yellowstone (Loendorf and Porsche 1985), and at the mouths of canyons draining the west side of the Bighorn Mountains. Shield-bearing warriors are extremely uncommon west of the Bighorn River.

Francis and Loendorf (2002:190–195) relate the spatial distribution of rock art traditions in the area to other archaeological materials and patterns of site use.

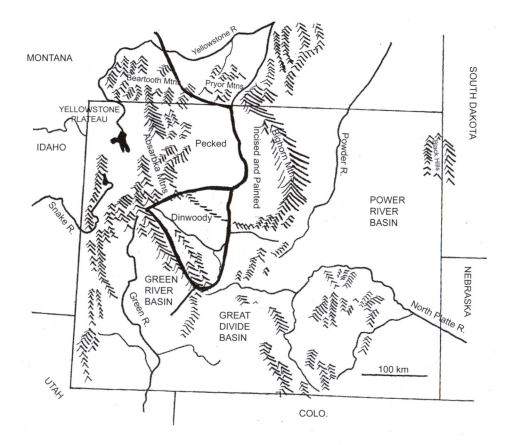

Figure 10.22   Map of rock art traditions in the Bighorn and Wind River basins, Wyoming.

They note that the distribution of Dinwoody and en toto pecked rock art generally coincides with the distribution of lithic raw materials from the west side of the Bighorn Basin, and that outline-pecked/incised/painted rock art generally corresponds with the distribution of raw materials from the western flank of the Bighorn Mountains. They further note that Dinwoody tradition rock art does not generally occur in association with major habitation or residential sites, in direct contrast to outlined-pecked/incised/painted imagery, which often occurs at major residential sites such as Medicine Lodge Creek and in several rock shelters.

Francis and Loendorf (2002) conclude that most rock art in the Bighorn and Wind River basins clearly originated in visionary experience and that the disparate spatial distribution represents a distinct ideological boundary between Great Basin and Great Plains religious systems and worldview. They note that this is most apparent in the Late Prehistoric period, but could have greater antiquity extending into the Archaic. They also argue that Dinwoody tradition rock art represents the expression of long-term occupation of the region by ancestral Shoshonean peoples. This model contradicts many traditional cultural-historical reconstructions that posit a very recent Shoshonean entry into western Wyoming (Bettinger and Baumhoff 1982, 1983). They also note that temporal changes within the Dinwoody tradition may reflect the emergence and increasing importance of the shaman in the social and political spheres of Shoshonean life (Whitley 1994c). Outline-pecked/incised/painted imagery also reflects the acquisition of sacred images through visionary experience and display in more public and non-esoteric social contexts.

Two separate religious systems coexisted among the hunting and gathering peoples of the Bighorn and Wind River basins (Francis and Loendorf 2002). The chronological overlap between two very different rock art traditions suggests that this duality has been in place since well into the Archaic period, continuing into Late Prehistoric and Historic times. Although the Late Prehistoric shield-bearing warriors exhibit the static poses typical of Keyser's (Keyser and Klassen 2001) Ceremonial tradition, Francis (2007:226) suggests that the appearance of shield-bearing warriors in the Late Prehistoric period may reflect the need to seek spiritual protection from enemies and that the Bighorn and Wind River basins may have been part of a contested landscape throughout the Late Prehistoric period.

CONCLUSIONS

Rock art research in 2008 is clearly a much different field of endeavor than it was in 1991. Instead of addressing broad distributions, stylistic sequences, and general discussion of common figure types, it is now possible to provide much more firm age estimates for many types of images, identify specific components and potentially sources of paint, address the meaning and significance of particular places on the landscape, understand individual images at a much more meaningful level, ascribe cultural affiliation to many different types of imagery, and address broad patterns of culture change. This has only been accomplished through the combination of archaeological techniques, interpretive models that are not unilaterally tied to Western thought and worldview, detailed review of ethnographic data, and use of ethnographic analogy.

Rock art data from Wyoming paints a much different, and indeed, more complex picture of the prehistory of this region than is typically gained through analysis of other archaeological artifacts and remains. Clearly, the making of rock art is an ancient tradition, dating perhaps to the earliest human occupation of this area. Analysis of the Dinwoody tradition suggests long-term occupation of the area by ancestral Great Basin peoples, likely Numic-speaking ancestors of the modern Shoshone. There are hints that this occupation could have extended well out onto the Plains and into the Black Hills for much of the prehistoric record, and that these people may have become more centered in the Bighorn and Wind River basins and west of the Continental Divide with the Late Prehistoric expansion of Siouan- and Algonquian-speaking peoples into the short-grass Plains of Wyoming, resulting in the broad culture and language areas observed during the Historic period.

Within each of the broad artistic traditions ascribed to Great Basin and Great Plains peoples, there is clear change. The Dinwoody tradition may well reflect the political and economic emergence of the Shoshonean shaman observed by ethnographers across the American West. Plains art traditions perhaps reflect conflict and competition for territory between Basin and Plains peoples over the course of the last one thousand years. And, it clearly shows the effects, changes, and disruptions of contact with European and American cultures.

The rock art data reflect an area of great long-term cultural diversity, not necessarily seen in projectile points, and it points to places of supernatural power and native views of the landscape far more so than any other type of archaeological data. In doing so, rock art research has imbued the landscape with many different layers of meaning and spiritual significance than are reflected by other archaeological sites. Indeed, rock art data can be used to interpret a great deal more of the archaeological record than just the imagery itself.

With continued technological advancements, we are far better equipped to manage these very special places. New chronological and analytical techniques will continue to be developed, and an entirely new range of research questions is waiting to be addressed. The greatest potential lies in research which continues to associate rock art with the remainder of the archaeological record to enhance and broaden our understanding of many different aspects of the past.

11

Advances in Northwestern Plains and Rocky Mountain Bioarchaeology and Skeletal Biology

George W. Gill

Department of Anthropology, University of Wyoming

Introduction

At the same time that an earlier version of this chapter (Gill 1991) appeared in the second edition of *Prehistoric Hunters of the High Plains* (Frison 1991), the very first University of Wyoming Master's thesis on the subject of Northwestern Plains and Rocky Mountain skeletal biology was just about to emerge (Zitt 1992). No comprehensive bioarchaeological paper existed at that time. Today there are six University of Wyoming Department of Anthropology Master's theses that deal with Northwestern Plains and Rocky Mountain bioarchaeology and eight that treat skeletal biology topics covering prehistoric Northwestern Plains and Rocky Mountain populations. In addition, there have been four research papers completed by McNair Scholars that cover regional questions in skeletal biology.

Scheiber's exhaustive bioarchaeological records research constituted an important part of the Central and Northern Plains Overview (CNPO) project and has added substantially to our knowledge of regional bioarchaeology (see Scheiber and Gill 1996, 1997). Furthermore, Scheiber's more recent works have expanded and updated the earlier research (Scheiber 2006, 2008). Many of the University of Wyoming Master's research projects and two of the McNair papers have been revised and updated as chapters in a recent volume, *Skeletal Biology and Bioarchaeology of the Northwestern Plains*, edited by Gill and Weathermon (2008). Included within that volume are not only several chapters by both Gill and Weathermon and several of the papers just mentioned above, but also reports pertinent to Northwestern Plains and Rocky Mountain prehistory by Douglas W. Owsley and Karin Bruwelheide of the Smithsonian Institution, Richard L. Jantz of University of Tennessee, and several others. So, these research efforts, plus a number of publications in regional and national journals since 1991, provide a considerable amount of new information to draw from in order to treat recent advances in human osteology and bioarchaeology.

It should be noted that a large amount of the data generated by the recent research just mentioned above deals with frontier whites, historic Chinese, and pioneer blacks. Since the focus of this volume is upon prehistoric hunters and gatherers from the Northwestern Plains and Rocky Mountains region, the other population groups (whites, blacks, East Asians) will not be included in this chapter.

In addition to the expanding skeletal sample within the Northwestern Plains and Rocky Mountains since 1991 (and the proliferation of reports, papers, and books dealing with them), two other events have happened that have sharpened the focus upon human bones and burials from this region of the Great Plains and Rocky Mountains. One is the passage of the Native American Graves Protection and Repatriation Act (NAGPRA) and the other is the greatly increased interest since the early 1990s in the physical characteristics and biological affinities of the earliest Americans. This interest in the biology of the Paleoindians has been spawned in part by the discoveries of some excellently preserved Paleoamerican skeletons with somewhat unusual physical characteristics (e.g., Kennewick Man and Spirit Cave Man). The broader interest in skeletal biology has been encouraged by the NAGPRA law itself and associated regulations, which require an assessment of cultural affiliation and/or biological affinity in order to properly carry out the repatriation process. Not all effects of NAGPRA, however, have been positive (e.g., Gill 2008a; Springer 2005–2006:6).

Also, with current advances in forensic applications and DNA analysis, the growing importance of the study of human skeletons cannot be disputed. Law enforcement agencies and the medico-legal community are demanding greater precision in the analysis of human remains. This "not only has helped to stimulate more skeletal biology research than ever before, but has helped sustain the sub-discipline of bioarchaeology too, through an otherwise threatening era of bureaucratic entanglements and stifling political correctness" (Gill 2008a:2). So, we are living in an admittedly schizophrenic era for skeletal biology and bioarchaeology, but clearly an era with a heightened need for these important areas of science. All of this, coupled with advances in quantitative analysis procedures and computer applications, provide a promising outlook for the future. In the quite near future some valuable collections and skeletal assemblages will undoubtedly be lost to reburial, but we will also see the development and application of new tools and methods that will allow for more scientific information than ever before to be collected from those human remains that are available for study.

The largest human skeletal series in the Northwestern Plains and Rocky Mountains is the one at the University of Wyoming. The Department of Anthropology Human Remains Repository (HRR) has over 350 skeletons physically present within the repository. These skeletons of whites, Native Americans, frontier blacks, historic Chinese, and others are largely within the human remains series (HR). Some are within the forensic case series (FC) even though most forensic cases do not remain at the repository (only some that are determined to be early historic or prehistoric in age and of little interest to law enforcement). A database series (DB) also exists as a catalog system instituted to maintain information on specimens on loan for analysis at the University of Wyoming, but that remain under the jurisdiction of another institution, individual, or agency. These records are extensive and bring the total sample to more than 600 from the Northwestern Plains and Rocky Mountains. Other collections and sets of osteological and burial records exist at the repository, but are of little interest here since they relate to populations outside of the Great Plains area (Peru, Mexico, Polynesia, etc.).

BIOARCHAEOLOGY

Prehistoric burial practices in the Northwestern Plains and Rocky Mountain region took many forms, and these forms changed noticeably through time. Situations range from accidental deaths of aged individuals (Boar's Tusk, Late Archaic male, HR044) to concealed homicides (Robber's Gulch, Late Prehistoric male, UWFC32) to well-prepared multiple graves in sacred burial mounds (Huntley, Benick Ranch, and Dicken sites of southeastern Wyoming). The most common burials throughout time, however, are lone interments of single individuals. In Plains Archaic times these tend to be primary interments, often in open areas (e.g., Dunlap-McMurry male, HR045; Falxa/Lohsic female, HR274). In Late Prehistoric times they were more often bundle burials in rock ledges and along hillsides, suggesting secondary interment from trees or scaffolds (e.g., Lund, Late Prehistoric male, HR010). Further explanation of some of these burials by time period will help elucidate the contrasts.

Earliest Burial Sites

Paleoindian burial sites from the Northwestern Plains and Rocky Mountains are exceedingly rare, but the Anzick site from Park County, Montana, which contained Clovis projectile points and subadult human remains, has been described most recently by Owsley and Hunt (2001) and dated to 11,000 BP. The Gordon Creek site on the northern Colorado border, south of Laramie, Wyoming (Breternitz et al. 1971; Swedlund and Anderson 1999), dates from a little later (9550 BP). The Gordon Creek burial contained the well-preserved remains of an adult female. At the Anzick site a thick layer of red ochre had been placed over the child's remains. This plus more than 100 finely made stone and bone artifacts (Lahren and Bonnichsen 1974) suggest that this was some kind of high-status interment. Burial goods were present with the Gordon Creek burial also (Muñiz 2004).

More skeletal remains occur somewhat later in the Early Plains Archaic, at just over 7200 BP. Fragmentary remains of adult females have been found at both the Stud Horse Butte/J. David Love site in southwestern Wyoming and the Smilden-Rostberg site in northern North Dakota. The adult female skeleton from the J. David Love site consists largely of pelvic and long bone fragments plus a number of badly worn teeth, all associated with an ancient fire pit. This very small, delicate woman had lived to a quite advanced age, and her teeth were worn well below the crowns, deep into the structure of the roots themselves (Gill 2004).

The Smilden-Rostberg remains from North Dakota are clearly at the northeastern limit (or slightly beyond) of the Northwestern Plains area, and consist of an anterior maxillary fragment (with the nasal sill and several teeth). These quite fragmentary adult female remains may not have been part of a purposeful burial at all. The fragment is of great interest, however, because it shows greater alveolar prognathism (projection of the mouth) than any other female Native American in the University of Wyoming collections, except for a single comparable example from the Late Plains Archaic of southeastern Wyoming (Huntley female, HR023). The much better-preserved Huntley site female shows the same rather extreme degree of facial projection (Gill 2008b). One other female specimen in the repository shows a comparable degree of prognathism (and reduced nasal sill), but it is a cast of a contemporary African American. Today this extreme degree of prognathism (with reduced nasal sills and spines) found among some Northwestern Plains Archaic skeletons is beginning to make sense as the skeletal record of the earliest Americans across North America expands. This facial prognathism seems to be part of a complex of craniofacial characteristics common to some Paleoamerican individuals (and probably populations) that lingers on within certain Plains Archaic populations of at least western Nebraska and southeastern Wyoming (see Gill 2005, 2008b). This whole subject of early American skeletal traits will be returned to in subsequent sections.

Other important Early Plains Archaic burials occur in this region, and clearly the one that has yielded the best-preserved skeleton is the Dunlap-McMurry burial site. This site, west of Casper, Wyoming, possessed the nearly complete skeleton of an adult male between 50 and 65 years of age and has been dated at 5300 BP. He had been buried in a shallow grave among dozens of fire pits in an ancient campsite (Zeimens et al. 1979).

It is not only of interest that the J. David Love site female and the Dunlap-McMurry male from the Early Plains Archaic are both associated with fire pits, but as Scheiber has recently pointed out, "This burial pattern of bodies buried or placed in the middle of camp deposits is also observed during the Middle Plains Archaic at the McKean site (48CK7) (Frison 1991; Haspel and Wedel 1983) and at Dead Indian Creek site (48PA551) (Gill 1984), both in northern Wyoming" (Scheiber 2008:30).

Late Plains Archaic/Plains Woodland

Many more burials are available from within the last 3000 years, beginning with the Late Plains Archaic, than from the several thousands of years before this time. This is assumed to be due to increasing human numbers. In her recent compilation of Late Plains Archaic burial sites, Scheiber (2008) lists 21 potential sites with 25 individuals represented from them. She mentions at least 19 Northwestern Plains burial sites from the temporally overlapping Plains Woodland (1000–2000 BP), with 123 individuals represented. Nearly all of the Plains Woodland sites contain multiple burials, occasionally in burial mounds, and sometimes with as many as 37 individuals at a single site, but as Scheiber mentions, the majority have less than 10. Ceramic vessels mark the introduction of the Plains Woodland culture into the Northwestern Plains, and the sites occur along the North and South Platte River drainages of southeastern Wyoming, northeastern Colorado, and western Nebraska (Scheiber 2008).

Much of the research on Northwestern Plains Woodland burial patterns has been done by Colorado archaeologists, but a few key sites have been worked by Nebraska and Wyoming professionals (see Adams 1991; Davis and Miller 2008; Gill and Lewis 1977). The best-documented Woodland site from Wyoming, the Benick Ranch site near Laramie, was initially worked by George Frison and myself, and later explored more extensively by Don Davis and Mark Miller (see

Davis 1992; Davis and Miller 2008). It shows many of the features common to other Woodland sites of the region. In these sites burial position is often flexed and these primary burials are well preserved (Figure 11.1), suggesting careful placement at a reasonable depth in the mound or pit. Shell and bone beds are often present (Davis and Miller 2008).

Probably the largest Woodland mound discovered so far in Wyoming is at the Huntley site in the extreme southeastern corner of the state. Unfortunately this large mound, containing from 19 to 30 individuals, was looted by souvenir hunters almost immediately after its discovery in September of 1963. This left very little to be salvaged by the only professional archaeologist in Wyoming at that time, Dr. William Mulloy, or by the few members of the Cheyenne chapter of the Wyoming Archaeological Society (WAS), who were also alerted. By the time these responsible parties arrived at the site, all burials had been removed and the artifacts taken (see Gill 2008b:242). A museum card entry made by Mulloy in 1963 mentions that "over 40 carloads of vandals converged on this spot immediately after discovery and completely scrambled an area of about an acre." Mulloy did manage to salvage one large male cranium, a nearly complete female skull and mandible, another adult mandible, and several long bone fragments (and other fragments). Grant Willson of the Cheyenne WAS chapter, who also searched the site in the aftermath of the vandalism, found a nearly complete skull of an adult male. These Huntley remains (HR023–HR028) and the Willson cranium (HR143; donated later to the HRR by Grant Willson) are quite valuable due to the number of so-called "Paleoamerican skeletal traits" that they exhibit. These traits will be discussed below in brief and are described in detail in Gill (2008b). The characteristics of the Huntley and Willson skulls are also compared to those of Spirit Cave Man and Kennewick Man in an earlier publication (Gill 2005).

Figure 11.1   A flexed burial of an adult male from the Woodland period Benick Ranch site.

Late Prehistoric

With the advent of the Late Prehistoric period approximately 1500 years ago, a number of dramatic cultural and biological changes occurred. Burial practices changed from the well-prepared primary interments of the Archaic and Woodland periods to crevice burials and bundle burials, indicating a less settled lifestyle. The Stone Fence burial excavated by Mark Miller and myself in the late 1970s (see Miller and Gill 1980) represents a good example of a Late Prehistoric bundle burial in a rock crevice reported and illustrated in the literature. During this time the bow and arrow replaced the atlatl and spear (Frison 1991). Not only do changes in projectile point types and pottery styles probably signify the movement of at least some new peoples into the Plains (Scheiber 2008), so do certain shifts in frequencies of physical characteristics. These physical trait changes will be discussed below and can be studied in more detail in Jantz (2008), Gill (2005), Gill and Deeds (2008), Lovvorn et al. (1999), and Stuart and Gill (2008).

Many more skeletons from the Late Prehistoric deposits show embedded projectile points and other signs of violence than do those from the earlier time periods. One of the best examples comes from the Robber's Gulch site in the southwestern badlands of the Wyoming Red Desert, northwest of Baggs, Wyoming. It dates from the early Late Prehistoric period and was excavated in 1982 by George Frison, David Eckles, Steve Martindale, and myself. It serves as a clear case of prehistoric homicide (Martindale and Gill 1983), which was followed by what appears to have been a concerted effort to conceal the body. The skeleton (Figure 11.2) gives every indication of having been thrown facedown into a deep arroyo. The young adult male in the sprawling ventral position seen in Figure 11.2 had been shot by at least 14 arrows (12 from behind and 2 from the front) by the time his body was cast into the hidden grave. Several large, flat rocks were then thrown down upon the body. These landed with enough force to shatter most of the small arrow points embedded in the dorsal skeletal elements, as if the rocks had struck rather directly against the shafts of the 12 arrows bristling from the victim's backside. Twenty-five feet of overburden subsequently slumped in over the rock-covered remains, concealing quite well the scene of the killing for several hundred years.

Protohistoric/Early Historic

With the advent of European and Euroamerican trade items lifeways continued to change, and judging from the human bones and burials, it was toward continued intensification of many of the forces set into motion during the Late Prehistoric. Longevity continued to drop (Scheiber 2008; Scheiber and Gill 1996) suggesting a continuation of armed conflict as well as the added factor of newly introduced European diseases. In addition to our own data, the historic records support these interpretations. From a bioarchaeological perspective perhaps the most dramatic change is in the alteration in richness of burial inclusions. Burial goods in the preceding Late Prehistoric are somewhat limited, while in the Protohistoric and early Historic periods most interments are quite rich with items like glass beads, metallic bracelets, buttons, and occasionally knives and firearms.

Figure 11.2   Adult male (UWFC36) from Robber's Gulch site. Position of the remains and other contextual evidence suggests a lack of intentional interment.

One such carefully prepared grave, dating to the Protohistoric period, is from the Pitchfork Rockshelter near the famous Pitchfork Ranch in northwestern Wyoming (Benedict 2003:8–11; Edgar and Turnell 1978:25–26; Gill 1976; Gill and Owsley 1985; Scheiber 1994). The two young adult males buried there were carefully wrapped in buffalo robes and placed with a rich assortment of burial goods into the recesses of a rock ledge high on the face of a cliff. They were buried in extended positions with hundreds of associated glass beads of various sizes and colors, along with *Dentallia* shells, shell hair pieces, metal earrings and bracelets, a carved wooden bowl, and a coat with brass buttons, in addition to the buffalo robes. It is not clear whether the aboriginal burial party placed the bodies there by lowering them down the cliff from above, by lines or ropes (like the rock climber who discovered them), or whether they reached the ledge from below by climbing up something like a tree or a prepared pole (rather like our archaeological recovery team, which used a 20-foot extension ladder). This unusual setting and remarkable burial sparked the interest of book author Jeff Benedict as he prepared his biography of Smithsonian's Douglas Owsley. In the prologue he states, "Carefully, Gill pulled away the rocks, and the rest of the skull gradually came into view. Doug [Owsley] was astonished at how well preserved it was. The right side of the face still held skin tissue. Two round, flat copper earrings hung from the still-intact right ear, while braided black hair ran down each side of the head" (Benedict 2003:9). The early death of these two young males coupled with an apparent state of robust health, the associated trade items, as well as the burial itself in its hidden, almost inaccessible cliffside location have caused local historians to speculate that the remains might be those of warriors possibly killed in battle. Pathological examination has failed to produce positive evidence for skeletal injury. Yet a detailed parasite study of the preserved head hair of one of the individuals does strongly suggest that the two males were for about one year away from the band or tribe (and normal grooming practices), based upon the density of the head lice and the spacing of the nits along individual hair strands (Gill and Owsley 1985). This indirect evidence for social unrest and long-term isolation prior to death at least adds to the evidence for the warrior or renegade status of these two young males.

No less impressive than the Pitchfork artifacts are the materials associated with the early Historic period Plains Indian graves from the Korell-Bordeaux site. These come from well-prepared graves near the historic Bordeaux Trading Post excavated in 1980 (Korell 1981), fully studied in 1999 (Armstrong 1999), and published in 2008 (see Furgeson and Armstrong 2008). This small cemetery was located on a bluff overlooking the famous trading post (near today's Lingle, Wyoming). The graves contained a rich assortment of both Euroamerican and Native American grave goods inside silk-lined, pine box coffins. Some had jewelry, trade blankets, knives, coins (sewn into jackets), and in the children's coffins were such things as pairs of shoes, tea sets, and bags of marbles.

The tendency for explorers and early settlers to collect items from exposed graves, especially from the numerous and lavishly equipped Protohistoric/ Historic ones (see Frison 2008), and for later pot hunters to loot burials from land not their own unfortunately did not end immediately after the western regions of the Plains were settled. A case in point is the 1983 grave desecration case brought against four men in Uinta County, Wyoming, who looted a rock crevice burial near Marbleton, Wyoming. It contained a Historic period mummy of a male, possibly a Shoshone in his late 20s. A remarkable array of burial goods was associated. The human remains and associated materials were referred by the Wyoming State Crime Laboratory to the University of Wyoming as UW Forensic Case 50. Study of the materials was made during a brief period of intensive analysis in the fall of 1983 to assist the prosecution and to establish tribal affinity in order to return the remains to the rightful tribal group. Shoshonean tribal affinities were considered most likely based upon a series of cranial and facial measurements and indices that best fit the averages for Shoshone males, plus a single design element on a well-preserved beaded moccasin. Some associated materials such as jewelry, a rifle, a saddle, and some beaded clothing were apparently sold before the looters were apprehended. These were therefore not present for subsequent analysis by archaeologists, historians, and ethnologists. Among the items that were examined, however, were beads, buttons, an elk-tooth necklace, a nickel-colored pistol (Whitney

Co. revolver 1871–1879), several .45–.70 cartridges, and the well-preserved moccasin that clearly revealed a "checker-diagonal" bead pattern. This pattern, according to Kroeber (1907:154), is "pre-eminently Shoshone and Blackfoot." The craniofacial metrics tended to rule out Blackfoot affinities, so the remains were eventually referred to the Shoshone tribe. This is perhaps one of the most lavish of the documented Historic period burials from the Rocky Mountains and Northwestern Plains.

Temporal Trends

Dramatic changes in mortality through time in the prehistoric Northwestern Plains and Rocky Mountains is perhaps the most important temporal trend identified here. The Plains Archaic average age at death calculates to 48 years (n=18), by the Late Prehistoric drops to 33 years (n=38), and by Protohistoric/Historic times falls to 25 years of age (n=42) (Scheiber 2008; Scheiber and Gill 1996). The 15-year drop in longevity from the Archaic to Late Prehistoric is even more impressive when it is realized that this is in some degree a severe underestimate. That is because of the simple fact that subadults and young adults can be aged quite accurately from the skeleton, but older adults cannot (and are therefore conservatively aged). Since so many of the skeletons from the Plains Archaic are well above 50 years of age (judging from such things as dental attrition, pubic symphysis age, vertebral changes, and cranial suture closure) and so many from the Late Prehistoric and Protohistoric are not, we therefore know that most skeletons within the latter two temporal groups are accurately aged (to within a few years) and that many within the Archaic sample are not. They are underaged. In fact, some Archaic period specimens are probably underaged by decades. It is easy to tell that a skeleton is 50 years of age or beyond, but often very difficult to tell how far beyond 50 years it might be. An excellent example of this problem comes to us from the Late Plains Archaic site of Iron Jaw Creek, Montana (Gill 1983; Gill and Clark 1983). The elderly male at this burial site had lost inches in stature from senile osteoporotic changes and had lost all teeth so many years prior to death that his mandible had atrophied to a tiny, thin remnant of 11 mm in diameter. He was awarded a conservative age at death of 70 years, which is the age entered into the mortality calculations. Yet his actual age may have been over 100 years. So, along with many other Archaic specimens, the Iron Jaw Creek burial may have helped us drastically underestimate longevity within the Plains Archaic period. In sum, longevity dropped *at least* 15 years from Archaic to Late Prehistoric times, and another eight years on into the Protohistoric/Historic period. The imbedded projectile points in some of the Late Prehistoric skeletons undoubtedly explain much of the drop in longevity. Clearly escalating violence was well underway by 1000 years ago. Some of the continued decline in longevity during Protohistoric/Historic times is probably due to new diseases. Also, equestrian activity introduced new risks of injury and death as well as the new benefits in mobility and subsistence advantages (Johanson and Owsley 2002; Owsley and Bruwelheide 2008).

These dramatic shifts in lifestyle and death rates seem to be reflected in changes in burial practices as well. During the relatively peaceful Archaic period, many of the graves were primary interments that suggest a reasonable amount of time investment in their preparation. They were often lone burials and sometimes associated with fire pits. These graves yield fewer associated artifacts, however, than those from the later time periods. Common grave goods are bone tools, projectile points, ground stone implements, tubular bone beads, *Olivella* shells, and occasional bone pendants and antler knapping tools (Truesdale 1987). Some very early burials also show associated red ocher (Frison 1978; Lahren and Bonnichsen 1974; Owsley and Hunt 2001).

By Plains Woodland times, ceramic vessels occur and actual burial mounds and cemeteries are often encountered. Primary interments continue to be the rule, but more of them are flexed than extended (Scheiber 2008).

Big changes occur by Late Prehistoric times. Burials in rock crevices and rock shelters increase in frequency. Some of these are flexed, primary interments, but show very little, if any, signs of digging (more often rock covered). Some are also secondary bundle burials. In spite of these indicators of a more mobile lifestyle and of hastier burial, a slight increase in the amount of burial goods is seen. For instance, by Late Prehistoric times the occurrence of tubular bone beads in graves increases. *Olivella* shells continue, as well as ground stone implements, projectile points, antler tools, and bone tools. No common items disappear, but some new items are added; ritual burial offerings in the Late Prehistoric that are not evidenced from the Plains Archaic include bone disk beads, shell pendants, *Dentallium* shells, juniper seed beads, steatite, and bear claws (Scheiber 2008; Truesdale 1987).

As the Protohistoric/Historic periods begin, the mortuary inclusions are much more striking. Large numbers of glass trade beads are found in at least half of all of these burials, and many contain brass, bronze, and copper items (earrings, bracelets, and buttons). Guns, knives, and coins appear too, as well as Euroamerican household items. Robes and hides are preserved for the mortuary inventory, and projectile points (some metal), *Dentallium* shells, and tubular bone beads continue. Perhaps not so surprisingly, as the glass beads and other trade items enter the Northwestern Plains and Rocky Mountains the majority of the bone, shell, and juniper beads disappear from the inventory of grave goods, as well as the bone and shell pendants.

The most common type of burial in the Northwestern Plains and Rocky Mountains, especially during the Late Prehistoric period, is the flexed primary interment placed under a rock ledge within a rock outcrop. These are usually found along a high ridge overlooking a well-watered valley below. As Frison (1978) points out, erosion normally uncovers these graves. They are generally just out of reach of the common activities of the modern population, who inhabit the valleys below, and so actions of nature are much more likely to threaten these graves.

Extended primary burial is an alternate form to the flexed primary form found in the Plains Archaic, and secondary bundle burial is an alternate form to the flexed form found in the Late Prehistoric. Flexed burials also continue on into the Protohistoric/Historic periods, but an increasing number are found in the extended, on-the-back position. Bundle burials also continue on into these later periods. This suggests that maybe the scaffold and tree burials described in early Historic times (Figure 11.3) were already in use in Late Prehistoric times, since the secondary remains of bundle burials are normally gathered up from such exposed locations.

Figure 11.3   Burial platform in a large ponderosa pine in north-central Wyoming.

SKELETAL BIOLOGY

Since the late 1930s, the Northwestern Plains has been an area of interest with regard to morphological patterns of craniofacial traits (Howells 1938). Analysis of the Torrington crania by Howells in those days did reveal a high frequency of what has come to be regarded as "archaic" features of the skull and face (mostly the midface). These traits common to Paleoindian skeletons include such features as marked alveolar prognathism, dull or absent nasal sills, modest (Caucasoid-looking) malars, cranial rugosity (males), and occasionally high cranial vaults, long skulls, and prominent chins (Gill 2005, 2008b; Jantz and Owsley 2001; Steele and Powell 1992). Few of these traits are common to the so-called Mongoloid populations generally, nor are they particularly common to Native North Americans either, over at least the last 1500 years (Gill 2005; Steele and Powell 1992). According to Spencer and Jennings (1977), J. B. Birdsell has referred to this overall pattern of Paleoindian traits as "vaguely Caucasoid" in appearance. Others have pointed out a certain "Australoid" or "Negroid" aspect as well. This Australoid/Negroid component is valid if one considers the alveolar prognathism and dull nasal sills (particularly common among females). One of the most Caucasoid-looking Archaic period skeletons ever found comes from Harlan County Lake, Nebraska (Baker 1989), just east of the Northwestern Plains region. Late Pleistocene populations of northwestern China (Upper Cave Zhoukoudian) exhibit this same vaguely Caucasoid (and Australoid) pattern as well. So do existing cranial series of eastern Polynesians and the Ainu of northern Japan. These are populations of continental Asiatic origin, but they have largely escaped the most recent waves of population movement and gene flow out of East Asia (see Gill 2001a, 2005; Powell and Rose 1999).

Population Traits

Skeletal studies in the Northwestern Plains and Rocky Mountains that attempt to examine prehistoric population characteristics suffer from one major limitation: the few remains available for study do not, in all probability, belong to a single biological population. At best, individuals from *related* populations are being pooled into samples. Fortunately, in recent years sample sizes have grown to the extent that some regional and temporal trends in morphology do seem to be emerging and to be making sense in terms of the broader picture.

Several physical characteristics of Native Americans of the Northwestern Plains and Rocky Mountains show continuity both temporally and geographically. From a current sample of 100 adult skulls, it can be seen that a medium (mesene) upper facial proportion existed throughout the region from at least as far north as northern Montana to southern Wyoming/northern Colorado and from the earliest to the most recent populations (Stuart and Gill 2008). Nose form is likewise seen to be quite medium, yet the orbits somewhat low and wide (Stuart and Gill 2008).

The crania are medium to large in size and medium (mesocranic) in proportion. There are two notable exceptions to this rule. First are the smaller people from the Wyoming Basin (Red Desert) who sometimes show wider faces and skulls. Second are the long-headed (dolichocranic) people from the Late Plains Archaic in southeastern Wyoming (Huntley and Willson sites) who seem to retain a number of Paleoamerican features (Gill 2005, 2008b).

In the earlier version of this chapter (Gill 1991), it was postulated that a population somewhat different from the large-statured High Plains hunters of northern and eastern Wyoming and Montana developed in the Red Desert. Today, with much better samples and more thorough analyses, that is seen to almost certainly be the case (Stuart and Gill 2008). Stature differences remain the most apparent difference between these two groups. In fact, almost no overlap in height exists between the two female samples. With few exceptions the shortest of the High Plains females are taller (based on femur metrics) than the tallest of the Red Desert females. The High Plains female sample (n=18) averages 159.54 cm or a little under 5 feet 3 inches, while the Red Desert/Wyoming Basin sample (n=6) averages 155.78 cm or a little over 5 feet 1 inch. Even with the small sample sizes these differences are statistically significant (Stuart and Gill 2008:170). High Plains males (n=15) average 166.93 cm or a little under 5 feet 6 inches and Wyoming Basin males (n=8) average 165.76 cm or little over 5 feet 5 inches. The half-inch difference between male samples is not statistically significant and perhaps not to be trusted as much as the female difference. This is because craniofacial comparisons also reveal a range of variation between the two female subsamples that is greater than that observed for the male subsamples. As Stuart and I explain, "Greater variation between groups of females suggests less mobility and therefore the tendency for females to remain within a smaller territory. The high degree of similarity between High Plains and Wyoming Basin males, on the other hand, suggests great mobility, which ultimately increases the possibility of researchers placing male specimens into the wrong subsample" (Stuart and Gill 2008:174–175). In other words, the more highly mobile male hunters, because of their mobility, tend to die outside of their home territories more frequently and thus are more often included within the wrong population sample. This tends to have a leveling effect on the male subsamples and suggests that the females better reflect true population variation within the Northwestern Plains and Rocky Mountain area.

Biological Affinities

Statistical tests conducted by Stuart (2000) between the two Northwestern Plains and Rocky Mountain population samples and comparative samples of Sioux, Algonquian, and Numic (based upon craniometric variables) also show more definitive patterns in the case of the female subsamples. These tests show the High Plains females to be close to the Algonquian females and the Wyoming Basin females to be very close to the Numic females (Stuart 2000; Stuart and Gill 2008). The male subsamples show similar tendencies, but not as clearly as do the females.

Interestingly, Stuart's statistical comparisons show that High Plains samples and the Wyoming Basin samples are more similar to each other than either one is to the comparative samples. Rogers (2008) has found precisely the same degree of similarity between these two populations in her thorough examination of discrete nonmetric cranial traits. These similarities could be related to the problem of sample composition mentioned above, or to actual gene flow between High Plains and Red Desert peoples, or some combination of the two factors. It does seem clear at this point, however, that the Siouan influence in the Northwestern Plains and Rocky Mountains was not particularly great, even within the High Plains samples; "Where the High Plains samples seem to differ from the Numic and the Wyoming Basin samples would appear to be more in the direction of Algonquian relationships than Siouan affinities" (Stuart and Gill 2008:175).

Microevolutionary Trends

Some microevolutionary changes of real significance are now well supported for the Northwestern Plains and Rocky Mountain Native American populations. These changes through time are (1) a reduction in cranial vault height (Jantz 2008; Stuart and Gill 2008), (2) an increase in the development of the nasal sill (Gill and Deeds 2008), and (3) a reduction in alveolar and midfacial projection (Stuart and Gill 2008). Also, some trend toward brachycephalization seems to likewise be suggested by recent data (Stuart and Gill 2008), as well as changes in jaw bone morphology (Gill and Jimenez 2004).

All three of the major microevolutionary trends were suggested in the earliest skeletal biology studies within the region. Howells (1938) discusses the prognathism and reduced nasal sills of the Torrington crania in contrast to the later populations, and Stewart (1940) and Neumann (1942) identify the lowering of cranial vault height through time in the entire western region of the United States. Skeletal samples from Montana and Wyoming were quite limited, however, at the time of these earliest studies.

The most systematically and extensively treated of these temporal trends has been the documentation of the cranial vault height changes. This metric trend within the Northwestern Plains and Rocky Mountain population data was detected during my earliest synthetic study of our regional materials (Gill 1974:101) and further strengthened by later examination of a larger sample (Gill 1981:62).

About the time of my own initial studies, Jantz (1977) and Jantz and Willey (1977) announced similar findings from a much larger sample of Plains Indians from the north-central Great Plains, and expanded this to even wider samples a little later (Jantz et al. 1981). In more recent years, Stuart added several more Northwestern Plains and Rocky Mountain specimens with good measurable cranial vaults (Stuart 2000), and even more recently I was able to add a few more to that sample (Stuart and Gill 2008).

Our most recent metric data (Stuart and Gill 2008) do seem to demonstrate that the alterations in cranial vault height from the Late Plains Archaic to more recent times are real and not a function of inadequate sample sizes. This is especially clear in the case of the High Plains males (n=24), which reveal a clear drop in mean basion-bregma height from the Archaic (134.1 mm) to the Late Prehistoric (130.1 mm) to the Protohistoric/Historic (126.4 mm). The lower-vaulted Wyoming Basin population seems to be reflecting a similar trend, but sample sizes are very small (Stuart and Gill 2008:165–166). Jantz (2008) is now able to treat this micro-evolutionary trend in much greater depth with excellent samples from the north-central Plains, and the trend is essentially the same.

The larger question as to the *cause* of this dramatic change in cranial height over such a wide area of the Northern Plains and Rocky Mountains (and the entire West), and over a relatively short period of time, is still not answered. It would seem, though, that migration and gene flow on the one hand, augmented by unknown natural selection forces on the other, probably constitute the best explanation, especially given the timing and geographic extent of this phenomenon (Stuart and Gill 2008:172).

The idea of greater alveolar and midfacial projection of earlier regional populations postulated by Howells in 1938, based upon his analysis of the Torrington remains, is now well born out. My own collection of craniometric data from Northwestern Plains Indian skeletons that relate to midface projection (i.e., basion-nasion, basion-prosthion, porion-prosthion, and other similar facial diameters) has gone on for over 35 years. Yet no compilation of these data had been undertaken until the year 2000. In that year, Stuart (2000) completed a full compilation of these data by sex group, region, and time period, and the results show significant changes by Late Prehistoric times, at least among the High Plains samples. Some of these results are also now published with brief comment (Stuart and Gill 2008). Reductions in all five of the facial projection diameters studied are seen in the High Plains male samples from the Late Plains Archaic through the Late Prehistoric and on into the Protohistoric/Historic periods. The smaller female sample seems to reflect the same trend.

The Wyoming Basin samples are simply too small regarding facial projection metrics right now to say much about the temporal trends, but the overall picture in that subregion of the Northwestern Plains seems to be one of much less projection of the face. In other words, these data show a shorter distance from the base of the cranium to the midface for the Wyoming Basin people as compared to the High Plains hunters. The finding likewise further corroborates the impression from other metrics that flatter, wider faces occurred in the Red Desert/Wyoming Basin than among the High Plains peoples (Stuart and Gill 2008:173).

At least as dramatic as any of the foregoing microevolutionary changes within the Northwestern Plains and Rocky Mountains is the alteration in the form of the nasal sill among the prehistoric and protohistoric peoples. The nasal sill is the inferior margin of the nasal aperture. The degree of development of this margin differs widely within populations of modern *Homo sapiens*, and it has therefore been a morphological feature of great interest to skeletal biologists and forensic anthropologists. Since the nearest living relatives to humans, the great apes of Africa and Asia, have no nasal sill, and neither do certain taxa of fossil hominids, paleoanthropologists also find this trait of the facial skeleton of great interest. It is normally described within one of four categories of development: absent, dull (or blurred), medium, or sharp. These categories are well defined and/or illustrated in most standard textbooks of human osteology (Bass 2005; Buikstra and Ubelaker 1994; Olivier 1969; White and Folkens 2000, 2005) and forensic anthropology (Burns 1999; Byers 2008; Gill and Rhine 1990; Krogman and Iscan 1986; Stewart 1979).

In general, people of European ancestry have very sharply defined nasal sills, African blacks have very dull ones (or none at all), and East Asian people and Native Americans have medium sills. The complete lack of nasal sill or a very dull sill is a condition common not only to blacks but to many Polynesians and Paleoamericans as well. That is why Howells (1938) was intrigued by the reduced nasal sills within the Torrington series, and why we have been looking at this trait for many years in this region of the Plains and Rocky Mountains and attempting to document changes through time in its manifestation (Gill 1974, 1981, 1991; Gill and Deeds 2008).

Exact reasons for development of a nasal sill are not known, either in terms of its evolution or in terms of individual growth and development (even though some correlation with prognathism is known to exist). One of the few things that does seem to be known about the nasal sill with certainty is its high heritability. Like some other traits of the midfacial skeleton, direct action of the environment seems to have little if any effect on this trait.

Recent attention to certain well-preserved Paleoamerican skeletal remains has not produced the degree of focus upon nasal sills that one might expect, but an exception is the thorough report by Powell and Rose (1999) on the 8400-year-old Kennewick Man skeleton from Washington state. According to Powell and Rose, the Kennewick skeleton reveals a "blurred development of the nasal sill" (1999:12). My own 2006 examination of this skeleton confirms their assessment of that particular trait. Similar reduced sill development on many Archaic specimens from Wyoming and Montana has for years encouraged our own focus upon this trait. Only recently, however, has a systematic study of results been completed (Gill and Deeds 2008).

Over the last few thousand years on the Northwestern Plains and Rocky Mountains, the nasal sill does appear to have been evolving toward a sharper margin. Our recent study (Gill and Deeds 2008) on 60 adult crania presents the percentage occurrence for each category of nasal sill for each time period (Archaic, Late Prehistoric, Protohistoric/Historic). It is seen that the majority of Archaic period skeletons show no nasal sill development at all. Things clearly change by the Late Prehistoric, and skulls with dull nasal sills are slightly more common than those with none at all. An even more dramatic change is revealed by the data from the Protohistoric/Historic period. By this time the occurrence of medium nasal sills goes from 12% to 48%. During this same time period, the first sharp nasal sills are encountered, and the "absent" condition drops from over 40% to only 4%. Such sweeping biological change in such a short time, for a trait that is so stable genetically, must certainly suggest significant migration and gene flow into this area of the Plains and Rockies. Natural selection alone would simply not be able to account for such dramatic change over such a short temporal span of just a few centuries.

Dental Health and Diet

The thorough study on dental health by Zitt (1992) alluded to at the beginning of this chapter, and recently published (Zitt 2008), reveals a very low caries rate of 2.62% carious teeth from a sample of over 700 teeth from the Northwestern Plains and Rocky Mountain region. Caries frequencies this low are typical of hunters and gatherers who subsist on a diet high in meat protein and raw, abrasive vegetable foods (roots, etc.). As Turner (1979:622) states, "Dental caries is almost wholly a disease involving carbohydrate consumption." Webster (1985) suggests that among groups practicing intensive agriculture the rate of decayed teeth is generally above 8%, those with mixed economies (hunting and some farming) show a rate of 3–7.9%, and hunters and gatherers show the lowest rates of 0–2.9%.

In her comparison with a mixed-economy group of Protohistoric/Historic populations from Nebraska, Zitt has found significant differences in caries frequencies. Among 2445 teeth of Central Plains groups (Lower Loup focus and Pawnee), the rate of caries is seen to be about twice as high (5.31%) as for the Wyoming and Montana populations. Perhaps of even more interest is the change through time within the Northwestern Plains and Rocky Mountain area. The Archaic caries rate from her study is 6.79%; this drops to 3.10% during the Late Prehistoric, 0% during the Protohistoric, and 0.69% within the Historic period. These dramatic changes through time would seem to clearly indicate a sharp increase in meat consumption and a corresponding drop in the utilization of carbohydrate foods (Zitt 2008:229).

Warfare and Injury

The beginning of the Late Prehistoric period witnesses remarkable increases in the levels of conflict, as evidenced not only by the lowering of longevity noted earlier, but also by injury levels and patterns. Three examples supporting this come from the Red Desert area of southern Wyoming. The early Late Prehistoric period homicide at Robber's Gulch (Figure 11.2, and described above) is certainly one of the most dramatic. Another, also from the Red Desert region, is the Deer Butte 2 skeleton (DB 138) from near Rock Springs, Wyoming. This skeleton of an adult male of approximately 60 years of age shows the tip of a projectile point embedded in the sternum. It was an old injury with signs of healing around the embedded fragment. The Bairoil skeleton (Figure 11.4) is another case of dramatic skeletal trauma. This skeleton of a Native American male of possible Shoshonean affinities suggests that the individual was probably in his 40s at the time of death. Excavation of the burial was by Van Gerven and Greer (see Sheridan and Van Gerven 1988; Shields et al. 1989). Full descriptions of the skeleton and context of the grave are available (Gill 1988; Sheridan and Van Gerven 1988; Shields et al. 1989). The most remarkable features of this find are the severe skeletal traumas to both the skull and face and to parts of the postcranial skeleton. Furthermore, the individual did survive the confrontation and exhibited a degree of healing from the severe traumas (without serious infection). Figure 11.4 illustrates a depressed cranial fracture, a damaged and completely severed right malar, loss of the right lateral orbit, penetration of the right maxillary sinus, an ectocranial bone spur, and atrophic changes of the ascending ramus of the mandible. Not shown in Figure 11.4 are a fractured and displaced left zygomatic arch and several postcranial injuries. Most notable among the postcranial traumas is a fractured and healed right clavicle, a fractured and deformed left second metacarpal, and a lesion (cut mark) on the right patella associated with a projectile point embedded in the proximal right tibia. Surrounding the projectile point is an osteolytic area of response to the foreign object.

According to Miller (1988), the projectile point embedded in the knee (and later removed for study) is a bow and arrow point known as a "Rose Springs Variant." It shows great similarity to the 14 projectile points embedded in the skeleton of the Robber's Gulch individual. These point types are assumed to date from 500 to 1500 years ago (Miller 1988).

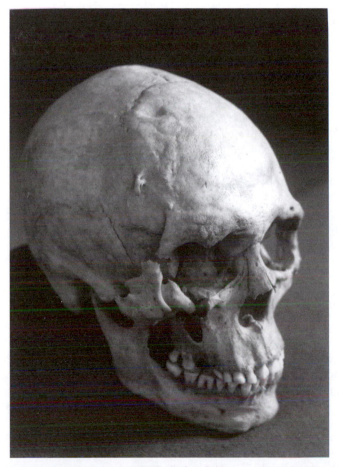

Figure 11.4 Adult male (GLM-1) from the Bairoil site. Evident here is a depressed fracture of the frontal bone, an anomalous osseous spicule, a severed and detached right malar, a missing right lateral orbital margin, and an opening into the right maxillary sinus.

Regarding this particular case of armed conflict, one is able to reconstruct some aspects of the confrontation(s) from the specific pattern of injuries: (1) while facing (probably running toward) one or more adversaries, an arrow wound was received to the right knee; (2) he was struck by a very sharp and heavy instrument; (3) in an attempt to block some blows with his left arm, he was struck at least once on the hand (fracturing the second metacarpal); (4) at least one blow was delivered to the frontal area (creating the depressed fracture) and one blow to the left zygomatic area (fracturing and displacing the arch); and (5) at least two sharp blows were delivered to the right side of the face and shoulder (which severed the malar in two places and detached the bone, removed nearly half of the eye orbit, opened the right maxillary sinus, and cut through the right clavicle). Some scene of conflict involving these basic elements must have happened in or near the Red Desert over 500 years ago.

It is of real interest that this Bairoil skeleton, which shares so much in common with Robber's Gulch in terms of biological affinities, temporal placement, and geographical proximity, also carries an embedded projectile point of the same style as the 14 points lodged in the bones of the Robber's Gulch male. As Miller (1988) points out in his lithic analysis report, "Between the Bairoil and Robber's Gulch specimens, we have convincing evidence for armed conflict during what may have been a fairly narrow window of time during the Late Prehistoric period." The Deer Butte 2 skeleton now adds one more example to this basic scenario.

Maxine Miller (1999, 2008) has advanced our knowledge considerably in the last few years with regard to prehistoric disease and injury in the Northwestern Plains and Rocky Mountains. Her study of skeletal pathology on 219 skeletal specimens from the region includes a look at sex differences, regional patterns, and temporal changes. Particularly interesting are the sex differences in patterns of healed fractures. Imbedded projectile points and severe traumas such as those just mentioned on the Bairoil skeleton are found on males, but certain facial and cranial traumas are more common on female skeletons. During the Archaic and Late Prehistoric periods the frequency of depressed cranial fractures is higher in males, but during the Protohistoric and Historic periods this pattern reverses and the rate of depressed cranial fractures is slightly higher among females (Miller 1999). Differences in patterning of depressed cranial fractures between the sexes include both position on the skull and shape of the depression. Females received injuries on both sides of the cranium while males received more blows to the left side, as if facing a right-handed assailant (Miller 1999:80). Miller concludes that females were injured while both facing and fleeing their attackers. Male crania tend to have round depressed fractures while the female skulls display a variety of oval, crescent-shaped, and kidney-shaped fractures (Miller 1999:80). Females also show more rib fractures than males.

Attempting to interpret these varying patterns (between sexes) and changing patterns (through time) is not straightforward, as Basgall (2008) has discovered in her recent study of skeletal evidence for the changing roles and status of Northwestern Plains and Rocky Mountain Indian women. She has found close parallels to our situation in data from a prehistoric site in southeastern Michigan. At this site, Wilkinson (1997) documents four times as many cranial fractures on female crania as males. Also, as Basgall (2008:33) points out, the injuries on the women's skulls are of varying sizes, as she and Miller found in the University of Wyoming HRR sample. A high mortality rate for women between 21 and 25 years old at that site, coupled with the severity, location, and the discrepancies between the sexes, suggest to Wilkinson (1997:33) intentional violence. Abduction, or attempted abduction, of women and violence toward captives by co-wives or husbands are given as the most likely explanations for the majority of injuries (Wilkinson 1997:38). Martin (1997) also suggests violence against captive women as a cause for the higher prevalence of cranial injuries among females in a prehistoric population from the Southwest.

Since fractures to the nasal bones are also more common among the females in the Northwestern Plains and Rocky Mountain populations, as well as rib fractures and more variation in types and sizes of cranial injuries, Miller (1999, 2008) has concluded that some type of domestic violence (spontaneous, unplanned strikes with whatever implement was available) is more likely than wife capture or warfare-related injury. Basgall (2008) points out that other possibilities exist, especially since Northwestern Plains and Rocky Mountain Native American societies were polygynous, which increases the likelihood of violence between women (Basgall 2008:35). Basgall also points out that female captives were more valued in the Protohistoric and Historic periods as workers for the buffalo robe trade and that this would promote a rise in the number of women captives taken or kept alive.

Even more convincing than the injury patterns in her argument for the changing roles for women in the Northwestern Plains and Rocky Mountains during the Protohistoric/Historic period is Basgall's own quite original work on femur and forearm bone morphology (Basgall 2008). Her discovery that the bowing of some forearm bones (attributed by some physician consultants and former researchers to postmortem damage) actually occurred during life is a significant finding. She has tested this with careful anatomical examination and contextual information. First, all of these bowed long bones are either ulnae or radii, and they come almost invariably from the right forearms of Protohistoric/Historic female specimens. Furthermore, the bowed specimens articulate perfectly with the matching forearm bones, rather than misaligning as they would if they had become warped from postmortem pressures. These are clearly bowed bones from muscular hyperdevelopment as Basgall states, and her argument that this resulted from the scraping of *Bison* hides during the Protohistoric/Historic period of buffalo robe trade is compelling.

Femoral neck torsion (FNT), or the twist of the femoral neck in relation to the shaft of the femur, can be easily observed and measured on a complete femur when it is placed on a flat surface (Basgall 2008:41; Gill 2001b). The FNT angle has become important in skeletal biology, forensic anthropology, and bioarchaeology studies for many reasons. For one thing there is a fairly high heritability for this trait, and the various major human populations have different average FNT angles. Whites and blacks almost always show low angles (Gill 2001b; Parsons 1914; Steindler 1955; Stewart 1962; Tamari et al. 2006) and Native Americans and some Polynesian groups have fairly high FNT angles (Gill 2001b; Schofield 1959; Stewart 1962; Young 2004). This makes the trait valuable in population comparisons and forensic identification. There is also an environmental/developmental factor involved that can be important if the environmental pressures are strong enough and occur early enough in an individual's bone development. Significant early environmental forces can not only change FNT angle but can produce asymmetry in these angles (i.e., the right femur quite different from the left on the same individual). A number of studies seem to indicate that the asymmetry in FNT is caused by mechanical influences, and in several bioarchaeological studies it is the female bone samples that show FNT asymmetry (Basgall 2008:50–51).

In the 13 sets of complete or nearly complete Northwestern Plains and Rocky Mountain female femora from the University of Wyoming HRR, Basgall has found asymmetrical FNT in 12. The one with no obvious side differences is the only Red Desert female (DB181) in the sample. All High Plains females show some degree of asymmetry, and the Protohistoric females tend to show more asymmetry than the earlier ones. The two Historic period females show even more (Basgall 2008:52). Basgall cites child development studies and controlled experiments on developing young rabbits that point to "continuous adoption of a certain sitting position" as the primary cause of these developmental changes. She goes on to say that habitually sitting with legs folded to one side (usually the right) beginning in adolescence "would cause medial rotation of the upper leg and a lateral rotation of the bottom leg, causing asymmetrical FNT like that seen in the HRR collections ... Women might sit in this position while carrying out certain tasks that required or allowed sitting on the ground, such as hide processing, pounding or grinding, quillwork, and sewing" (Basgall 2008:54). Basgall provides numerous examples from the ethnographic literature that Northwestern Plains Indian women at the time of contact did both; that is, they sat at work in a "gender-prescribed" posture and began the work activities associated with it at an early age.

Spondylolysis—a separation of the vertebral neural arch from the centrum, or body of the vertebra—is another stress-related skeletal condition that can indicate lifestyle activities. It is attributed to both genetic and mechanical influences (Brandtmiller 1984), but the mechanism actually triggering the physical separation is some mechanical force, normally to the lower back (most often affecting lumber vertebra #5, the lowest one in the spinal column). Among the Northwestern Plains and Rocky Mountain Indians the incidence of spondylolysis is about equal between the sexes, but the frequency almost doubles in the Protohistoric and Historic periods (Miller 1999, 2008). Miller attributes the higher frequency to the introduction of the horse, since equestrian activity places a strain on the lower back.

Another skeletal indicator of certain activities is the incidence of Schmorl's nodes. These are depressed lesions found in vertebral centra (bodies) that are caused, at least in younger individuals, by a fall, heavy lifting, or other physically demanding activities. Frequent horseback riding has also been suggested as a cause of Schmorl's nodes (Johanson and Owsley 2002; Reinhard et al. 1994; Wentz and DeGrummond 2008). Miller (2008) found that the rate of Schmorl's nodes among Northwestern Plains and Rocky Mountain Indian males remained fairly constant through time, but that the rate in females rose during the Protohistoric and Historic periods. In fact, there is not one incidence of Schmorl's nodes within a combined sample of all temporal levels of prehistoric females, and yet a 69% frequency is found in the Protohistoric/Historic sample. It seems that both equestrian activity and an increase in work load could account for this remarkable increase among the women. In the case of the men, it seems possible that the stress relief from the constant transport of large game meat to the base camp provided by the horse was exchanged for the new stress to the spinal column created by the acquired equestrian activities.

Conclusions

Much more knowledge comes from the Northwestern Plains and Rocky Mountain burial information and skeletal data today than was even thought possible in 1991, when the earlier version of this chapter was published (Gill 1991). The following statement appeared in the conclusions to that chapter:

> A great potential exists for gaining cultural information, from not only the burial data, but from the skeletons themselves, about religious practices, culture change, diet, disease, migration, conflict, and social interactions. Sample sizes are adequate to begin to erect mortality curves in some limited contexts, to examine differences in patterns of such things as caries and diet, or trauma and conflict between different sex groups, physiographic areas, and temporal horizons. Already some studies have begun and a few important trends in culture change and microevolution have been identified … The whole question of Archaic skeletal traits is another problem with great future potential for research. Just how Caucasoid and/or Australoid were the Paleoindians and Archaic Indians of North America generally, and of the Great Plains specifically, and with regard to what traits? (Gill 1991:447)

Today, as can be seen from the current chapter, important insights have been gained in all of the areas mentioned in that 1991 statement. Perhaps the most surprising thing in the new information is the *magnitude* of biological and social change indicated by the bones and burials from the Archaic to the Late Prehistoric and then on into the Protohistoric/Historic periods.

Ethnographic and historical records suggest a considerable amount of change and upheaval in the Protohistoric/Historic periods, with the coming of the horse, firearms, and new diseases, and this is certainly supported here, in part by the eight-year drop in longevity. Yet who would have suspected that a drop in average life expectancy of twice that magnitude had happened a thousand years earlier in the transition from the Archaic to the Late Prehistoric? And even though ethnographic accounts indicate changes in Plains Indian women's roles and status during Protohistoric/Historic times, who would have suspected the degree of impact on the skeletal system with the degree of alteration in forearm and femur morphology demonstrated in Basgall's work? It is also difficult to imagine so much change in diet toward increased meat consumption that the Protohistoric caries rate shows a drop to 0%. These biological impacts are not trivial and suggest significant social changes.

Neither of these significant periods of cultural transition (Archaic to Late Prehistoric, Late Prehistoric to Protohistoric) happened without population movement, that is, without new arrivals to the region. Of the various microevolutionary changes discussed here (e.g., cranial vault reduction, increase in nasal sill development) none seems more suggestive of new migrations into the region than the rapid alterations in nasal sill morphology. A change from nearly 90% dull or absent nasal sills in the prehistoric time periods to over half medium or sharp sills by Protohistoric/Historic times could not happen without the influx of new people. The changes were well underway before, but arrival of new populations certainly appears to have accelerated these physical changes.

A more clear separation than before is now suggested between the High Plains groups of the grasslands of northern and eastern Wyoming and Montana, on the one hand, and the Wyoming Basin peoples on the other. The High Plains people were larger in size and their skulls reflect Algonquian affinities, and the Red Desert/Wyoming Basin people were smaller in stature and demonstrate closer ties to the Numic people to the west. It should be kept in mind, however, that so far in the metric analyses the two populations resemble each other more than either one does the documented Algonquian or Numic samples.

The survival into the Late Plains Archaic in southeastern Wyoming and western Nebraska of an ancient Paleoamerican pattern of physical characteristics is also of interest. These traits are exemplified especially well by the Huntley and Willson crania. These ancient people had long, lofty heads, reduced cheek bones, and prominent chins rather like Kennewick Man and Spirit Cave Man. These traits are also shared with the East Polynesians, the Ainu of Japan, and certain very generalized European people. This pattern is clearly interesting and deserving of further study. Are those possessing these traits representative of a separate, early element in the Americas as some believe, or do they merely represent one end of the spectrum within a highly variable Paleoamerican/Archaic population, as postulated by others?

Advances in our knowledge of regional burial practices and temporal changes in these practices are likewise significant. As seen here, these data augment well the biological indicators of lifeway and lifestyle changes, and the two lines of investigation working hand in hand are clearly advancing our knowledge of regional prehistory.

12

LITHIC RESOURCES

James C. Miller
Dominguez Anthropological Research
Group, Grand Junction, Colorado

INTRODUCTION

Lithic resources are stone materials used as raw material for the production of tools and utilitarian items, or used in ceremonial contexts or as ornaments. The term "lithic resource" is broadly applied to include tool stones for chipped stone tools; clays and lithic fragments (temper) for pottery and figurines; steatite (and related rock types) for carved bowls, pipes, and banner stones or atlatl weights; minerals used in ceremony; and a variety of rock types used for grinding and boiling stones. These resources were procured in various manners ranging from deliberate quarrying through extensive excavations to simply collecting materials available on a surface.

Archaeology attempts to reconstruct and explain prehistoric behavior, including lithic procurement. Aspects of lithic procurement include the effort expended at a procurement site and in reaching the site, the technological applications to make the procured materials useful, and in a broader context, the social or trade relations involving these materials. Admittedly, lithic procurement is only one component of a way of life, but it is an important one since prehistoric technology required it. Since stone artifacts comprise the bulk of archaeological evidence, they assume critical importance.

A number of geological terms and descriptions are introduced and used in this chapter to define lithic materials. The purpose is to provide a common, accurate, and workable terminology for the definition of these resources that has advantages for the archaeologist and interested amateur alike. Accurate descriptions identify environments of formation, which in turn identify stratigraphic units that can contain a particular type of material. Success relies on a full understanding of what produces the material and leaves its mark on it.

Formation processes are a critical part of identification. Exsolution (Table 12.1) chert formed in limestone possesses a particular set of features, as does porcellanitic chert

Table 12.1   Definitions of rock types and terminology used in Chapter 12.

Agate	Banded chalcedony, such as episodic quartz crystal growth in geodes
Amorphous	Concerning opalitic chert, amorphous describes randomly oriented crystalites of quartz (SiO_2)
Aphanite	Fine crystalline igneous rock used as manos, mauls, and other artifacts, e.g., rhyolite, andesite, and basalt
Arkosic arenite	Sandstone composed primarily of quartz and feldspars with ferruginous, calcareous, or silica cement
Authigenic	Describes formation of chert through exsolution (chemical unmixing) some time after deposition of the host rock, but before lithification; normally forms nodules in definable stratigraphic zones; also called diagenetic
Carnotite	Vanadium oxysaly containing uranium oxide, i.e., "yellow cake," formed in roll fronts in sandstones; a Middle Archaic burial in the Park Range of Colorado contained "yellow cake"
Catlinite	Low-grade metamorphosed clay (Berg 1938; Morey 1984); contains a number of mineral inclusions such as sericite, hematite, and diaspore, and smaller quantities of pyrophyllite, kaolinite, and chlorite
Chalcedony	Cryptocrystalline SiO_2 rock identified under cross-polarized light by parallel laths representing individual quartz crystals; normally formed in void spaces during diagenesis
Cinnabar	Mercury sulfosalt, forms in weathered volcanic necks in the Southern Rocky Mountains; makes a brighter red pigment than hematite
Clay minerals	Kaolinite, illite smectite, and chlorite are the major clay mineral groups; all but chlorite are important in ceramics
Clinker	Altered sedimentary rock formed by low-heat alteration of sediment caused by burning coal seams; high grade is called nonvolcanic glass; medium grade is referred to as "porcellanite" on the Northern Plains; low grade is baked mudstone
Coquina	Rock composed of invertebrate hard parts, sometimes silicified; best examples are ostracode and gastropod coquinas from the Green River Formation (Eocene) in Wyoming, Colorado, and Utah
Epigenetic	Describes formation of chert during subaerial weathering where silica is stranded as a residue, such as in karst in limestone or dolomite
Exsolution	The removal or exclusion of minerals or chemicals through unmixing
Flint	SiO_2 rock composed primarily of silica sponge spicules and the silica tests (hard parts) of diatoms and radiolarians
Iron oxyhydroxides	Limonite and goethite (yellow ochre) and hematite (red ochre)
Magadi chert	Penecontemporaneous opalitic chert formed from mixing fresh and hyperalkaline water in playa or ephemeral lakes, or in pools on the marine littoral; normally associated with tephra hyperalkaline water; forms with porcellanite; named for Lake Magadi in Kenya (Surdam and Eugster 1976)
Metaquartzite	Near-pure SiO_2 rock formed in medium to high heat/pressure metamorphism from orthoquartzite or quartz arenite

Obsidian/ignimbrite	A glassy, transparent hydrid rhyolite produced by rapidly cooling extrusive flows; normally displays flow banding; ignimbrite is obsidian with lots of tephra mixed in either in discrete beds or throughout, the latter type resembles obsidian but is opaque except on thin edges
Oolite	Small mineral grain or other matter (commonly ostracodes in the West) that has an accreted rind composed of layers of calcite (later replaced with silica); formed by rolling in the surf of hyperalkaline bodies of water and is most common in Eocene lake deposits in Wyoming, Colorado, and Utah and in Paleozoic limestones; also called ooids or oolids
Opalitic chert	SiO_2 rock containing a small percentage of water that forms in limestone or volcanic tephra; chert is amorphous and does not show parallel crystal laths under cross-polarized light like chalcedony
Orthoquartzite	Silica-cemented sandstone (clasts bigger than 1/16in. or 0.0625 mm) (Krynine 1948); forms in fossil soils (Leeder 1982:308), in sandstones associated with coal or lignite beds (Goldschmidt 1958:367), or on the marine littoral through migration of fresh water of sediments saturated with hyperalkaline water that favor silica suspension (Knauth 1979) (also, see arenite)
Penecontemporaneous	Describes formation of chert at the time of deposition of the host sediment; Magadi cherts are one type
Phanerite	Coarse crystalline igneous rock used as manos, mauls, and other artifacts, e.g., granite, diorite, and gabbro
Porcellanite	Silica-cemented mudstone (clasts smaller than 1/16 in. or 0.0625 mm); forms in fossil soils, playa lakes, and sabkas through migration of fresh water through sediments saturated with hyperalkaline water that favor silica suspension (Knauth 1979); termed impure chert by Jackson (1970:406)
Quartz arenite	Sandstone composed primarily of quartz, chert, and other hard mineral grains with ferruginous, calcareous, or silica cement
Red ochre	Iron oxide, hematite
Replacement	Describes SiO_2 that fills voids left by the dissolution of other substances, such as the calcareous hard parts of invertebrates; forms as opalitic chert or chalcedony
Sepiolite	Also meershaum (sea foam), a fibrous clay mineral that forms in the evaporite facies in the Green River Formation (Eocene) (Milton 1971)
Steatite	Hydrous magnesium silicate mineral formed during low-temperature, low-pressure metamorphism of ultrabasic rocks or dolomite; normally olive or dark green, but can be light brown or red with increased nickel and iron
Wacke	A "dirty" sandstone, contains more than 10% mud (silt and clay)
Yellow ochre	Iron oxyhydroxide, limonite or goethite

formed from weathered volcanic deposits and Magadi-type chert formed in alkaline lacustrine environments. The features are visible macroscopically and microscopically with as little as 10x magnification using a hand lens or loop.

Much is currently known about source formations; however, much remains unknown. Parts of the following discussion focus on the known source areas and stratigraphic units that contain them. It is doubtful that the catalog is complete.

DEFINITION AND FORMATION OF PRIMARY SOURCES

Geological science defines rocks as sedimentary, metamorphic, and igneous according to process and environment of formation. Each of these major groups contains subclassifications. Sedimentary rocks are defined by modes of deposition and clast size; metamorphic rocks are classified by mineralogical content and the degree of heat and pressure alteration; and igneous rocks are classified as either intrusive or extrusive by mineral content and the size of the mineral crystals. The system of classification presents clear-cut boundaries for the most part, but some boundary problems are present. Chalcedony, for example, can and does form in all three environments; and volcanic tephra (ash, tuff, and lapilla) is volcanic in origin but is deposited as sediment on a landscape. Some of these boundary distinctions are relevant, others are not. The boundary-problem rock types are included in the category in which they best fit relative to their prehistoric use and not strictly according to their geological classification, and alternate occurrences are noted.

Sedimentary Rocks

The major sedimentary rock and mineral types are opalitic chert, flint, agate and chalcedony, porcellanite, orthoquartzite, sandstone, clay minerals, and various oxides formed as weathering residues (Table 12.1). Opalitic chert is a translucent, amorphous, near-pure silica rock. Amorphous refers to the random or haphazard arrangement of individual silicon dioxide globules or blebs and lack of crystal alignment in these rock types when viewed under cross-polarized light (Figure 12.1, Plate 2a). Luster is waxy or dull, and hardness is 6.0–6.5 on the Mohs scale of mineral hardness. Magadi-type penecontemporaneous chert (Table 12.1) is frequently bedded and is an important opalitic chert (Figures 12.2 and 12.3, Plate 2b, c). Some types are banded, like the so called "tiger" chert in the southern Green River Basin in southwest Wyoming. The bands are preserved varves in most cases, and typically the bands are alternate layers of opalitic chert and porcellanite. This type of chert also displays mottling with discreet boundaries (Figure 12.4, Plate 2d).

Flint is a hybrid silica rock (Table 12.1). True flints are authigenic and epigenetic (Table 12.1) rather than penecontemporaneous and form exclusively in chalk cliffs (Deer et al. 1966:351). Whole or partial remains of the varied silica hard parts or tests compose the matrix of flint, as well as any number of other remains of plant and animal life and dark organic debris.

Chalcedony and agate are cryptocrystalline rocks (Figure 12.1, Plate 2a, Table 12.1) that can be clear, even glasslike. Elemental impurities tint the stone. Luster is waxy

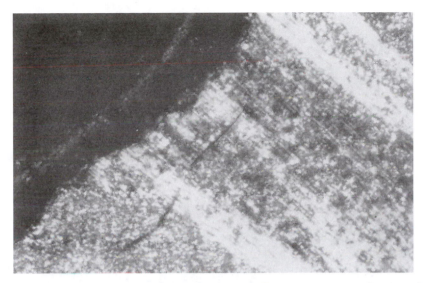

Figure 12.1   Photograph of a thin section of Knife River flint, about 400 magnification, showing randomly aligned blebs of opalitic chert (lower left) and chalcedony that replaced a palm leaf (parallel crystal alignment in upper right). (From Miller and Larson 1990.)

Figure 12.2   Magadi-type cherts: on left, top to bottom, are Browns Park Formation (Miocene) from northwest Colorado and southwest Wyoming; Troublesome Formation (Miocene), known as Kremmling chert, from Middle Park in Colorado; and Brule Formation (Oligocene), also known as Table Mountain chert from the western plains in Nebraska, Wyoming, and Colorado. On right, top, is plate "chalcedony," and on bottom, Scenic chert, both from White River Group (Oligocene) in western South Dakota.

Figure 12.3   More penecontemporaneous opalitic chert: on left, top to bottom, are Golden Valley Formation (Eocene) with cortex, known as Knife River flint or KRF, from western North Dakota; Bridger Formation (Eocene) from near Lone Tree, Wyoming; and Tipton Member of Green River Formation (Eocene) from Mexican Flats, south of Wamsutter, Wyoming. On right, top, is Burro Canyon Formation (Jurassic-Cretaceous); below is Morrison Formation (Jurassic).

Figure 12.4   Types of banding and mottling in chert from the Green River and Bridger formations (both Eocene) of southwest Wyoming. Top shows banding in a concretion from a stratified lake; bottom, left, shows banding with soft sediment deformation (light-colored band at top of specimen); and bottom, right, displays rip-up clasts or mud chips (lighter masses in dark center).

or vitreous and hardness is near 7.0. Chalcedony almost always occurs within opalitic chert in sedimentary depositional environments because plant and invertebrate fossils in chert are commonly replaced by chalcedony. In late-stage igneous and high-grade metamorphic environments, chalcedony and agate vary only in crystal size. Agate is banded chalcedony. Varved bedding (Figure 12.4, Plate 2d) in some lake chert, lithologically interlayered opalitic chert and porcellanite, indicates that many chert beds probably formed over a period of many years, with each cycle of silica precipitation and clastic deposition (eventually becoming porcellanite) representing an annual or seasonal cycle. Thin-bedded, banded chert, typically from Tertiary playa lakes or the marine littoral in Jurassic-Cretaceous times, is interpreted similarly based on algal mat growth (Figure 12.5, Plate 2e).

Orthoquartzite and porcellanite (in some cases referred to as silcrete) represent a continuum in sedimentary rocks (Figure 12.6, Plate 2f, Table 12.1). The difference in definition rests in the size of the clasts or grains that constitute the rock. Penecontemporaneous porcellanite and orthoquartzite have poorly sorted sediments on bedding planes that form impermeable boundaries, so they are most commonly platy in exposure. Orthoquartzite is granular and frequently translucent on thin edges. Mesozoic orthoquartzites are sometimes labeled "salt and pepper" because of a minority of dark chert grains mixed in a greater mass of quartz grains, or "sucrosic" because of the resemblance to granulated sugar in reflected light. Tertiary orthoquartzites are distinguishable by a wide range of minerals including substantial feldspars, especially potassium or K-feldspars,

Figure 12.5 Algal banding in chert from a hyperalkaline-hypersaline pond on the marine littoral; sample from Burro Canyon Formation (Jurassic-Cretaceous) in the Uncompahgre uplift in western Colorado.

Figure 12.6 Porcellanites and orthoquartzites. Top row, from left to right: Morrison Formation (Jurassic) and Cloverly Formation (Cretaceous) from the Hartville uplift in eastern Wyoming. Middle row, left to right: Fort Union Formation (Paleocene) from eastern Montana, known as Tongue River silicified sediment or TRSS; Aspen Mountain porcellanite from the Rock Springs uplift, part of Pettijohn's Eocene fossil soil; and Green River Formation (Eocene) platy porcellanite formed in the mud flat of Eocene Lake Goshiute, northern Green River Basin. Bottom row, two porcellanites formed from weathered igneous rocks: on the left, a sample from Table Mountain near Granby, Colorado; on the right, a sample from the Gros Ventre Mountains in the Yellowstone volcanic area in northwest Wyoming, unique for its copper content.

but some Mesozoic orthoquartzite also contains feldspar. Porcellanite is opaque with a waxy to dull luster. Dolomite and dolomitic concretions are preferentially silicified (Leeder 1982:307) and the concretions exhibit concentric banding; a similar process may form concentric banding in stratified lake deposits (Figure 12.4, Plate 2d). Diffuse mottling is sometimes apparent, but it is probably due to later (diagenetic) ionic migrations.

Authigenic or diagenetic chert (Table 12.1), porcellanite, and orthoquartzite form some time after primary deposition has occurred. Chert of this type is normally replacement chert (Table 12.1), the result of silica precipitation that crowds out the original deposits (Figure 12.7, Plate 2g) or is formed in voids vacated by other matter, chiefly organic compounds, clay, or polymorphs of calcium carbonate (mainly aragonite). Most are fossiliferous. Silica-permineralized wood (permineralized is more accurate than "petrified," although the latter is commonly used), algae, stromatolites (i.e., colonial algae), and coquinas (rocks composed of invertebrate hard parts, Table 12.1) are the common fossiliferous types. Silica-permineralized wood is easily recognized and frequently displays details such as tree rings or cellular structure. Algal chert is identified by bifurcated (Figure 12.8, Plate 2h)

Figure 12.7 Exsolution chert from Phosphoria Formation (Permian) in the Bighorn Mountains of Wyoming. The original clay laminae were crowded out and replaced by the chert mass, but clay bits have been incorporated in the mass.

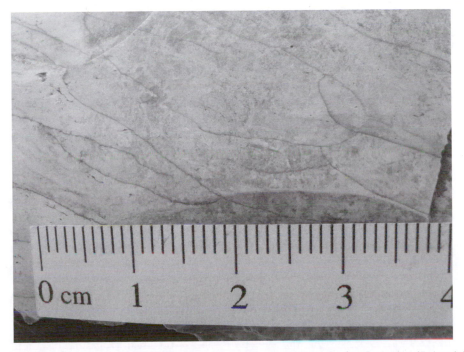

Figure 12.8 Bifurcated banding due to algal growth; sample from Fowkes Formation (Eocene) in the Fossil Basin, western Wyoming.

or parallel banding that represents algal growth and alternate fine clastic deposition. Diffuse, broad laminae in short-lived environments, such as growth on logs (Figure 12.9, Plate 3a), are also best defined as algal. Stromatolitic chert is identified by fine laminae representative of continual algal reef growth in stable environments (Figure 12.10, Plate 3b). Silicified coquina is best defined by the organisms that are identifiable in them, commonly gastropods or ostracodes (Figure 12.11, Plate 3c), and occasionally brachiopods, graptolites, and coral.

The only non-organic replacement chert that was regularly used for tool stone is oolitic chert (Figure 12.12, Plate 3d, Table 12.1). Oolitic chert is more common in Paleozoic rocks. Ostracode (clam shrimp) coquina replacement chert is more common in Tertiary rocks, but is commonly identified as oolitic chert because many ostracode chert rocks bear evidence of accreted rinds on the ostracode carapaces. Ostracodes are easy to identify by their bean or kidney shapes (among other shapes), chalcedony-replaced carapaces, muscle attachments in some specimens, and lack of concentric laminae.

Epigenetic chert, porcellanite, and orthoquartzite form through subaerial weathering of silica-bearing sediment or rock and the subsequent concentration of the silica in zones (Figure 12.13, Plate 3e, Table 12.1). Brecciated (subaerially weathered) limestone and dolomite form silica nodules through this process (Krumbein and Sloss 1963:184). Diffuse mottling, distinct globules or blebs of calcium and iron minerals or complexes, manganese dendrites, and clastic inclusions serve to identify opalitic chert formed in this environment. The chert is variegated, but can

Figure 12.9 Algal log from the Whiskey Butte Member of the Bridger Formation (Eocene). The light colored area at the bottom center of the piece is the location of a branch of an inundated tree; concentric rings surrounding it are relics of algal growth.

Figure 12.10   Replaced stromatolite from the Green River Formation (Eocene) in southwestern Wyoming.

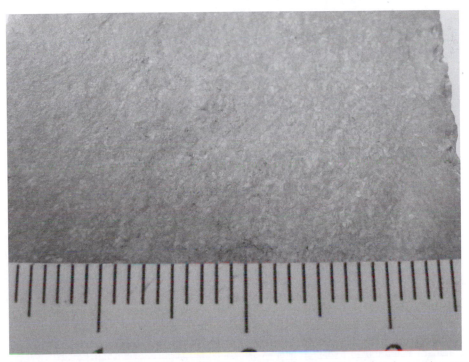

Figure 12.11   Silicified ostracode coquina from the Green River Formation in southwestern Wyoming (scale in millimeters).

Figure 12.12 Oolitic chert from the Green River Formation in eastern Utah (Eocene); many of the centers of the oolites are ostracodes.

Figure 12.13 Paleozoic cherts: far left, with white background, is a black chert nodule similar to nodules in the Jefferson Formation (Devonian) in western Montana. Second column from left shows two samples of Madison Group (Mississippian) chert: exsolution type (top) and from karst (bottom). Third column from left shows two varieties of Phosphoria Formation (Permian) chert from the Bighorn Mountains in Wyoming; bottom sample is more typical of Phosphoria chert. Far right column is exsolution chert from Nowood Formation (Permian-Pennsylvanian) limestone from the Bighorn Mountains in Wyoming, near Shell Canyon.

be clear. Much of this chert formed in Paleozoic rocks that were involved in two mountain building episodes, so chert of this type commonly displays annealed fractures filled with high refractory quartz (i.e., chalcedony) and brecciated masses (Figure 12.14, Plate 3f).

Subaerial weathering of tephra and volcanic rocks in conduits and surface flows produces a crystal-laden porcellanite that is quite distinct (Figure 12.15, Plate 3g). The process of formation is similar to the dissolution of limestone and concentration of silica, but in the case of porcellanite of volcanic origin, more easily erodible minerals are removed leaving silica as a residue, as well as some more resistant or newly formed crystals contained in the rock.

Epigenetic porcellanite and orthoquartzite (the variety known as silcrete) are commonly associated with fossil soils or, more precisely, with mineralized horizons partially related to fossil soils. They form as a result of prolonged pedogenic activity (podzolization) in warm, humid climates (Leeder 1982:308), particularly in quartz sandstones in association with superadjacent coal or lignite beds (Goldschmidt 1958:367). Some varieties exhibit trace or ichnofossil relics of bioturbation, such as root tubules and worm burrows or fucoids (Figure 12.16, Plate 3h). Orthoquartzite and porcellanite formed in sandstones (Table 12.1) subjacent to coal or lignite, however, usually lack bioturbation features.

Color in opalitic cherts is the result of metal content and oxidation states. Red, yellow, or orange are relics of iron oxyhydroxides—hematite, goethite and limonite, and ferrihydrite (Table 12.1), respectively, although more than one of the iron species is almost always present. Red ochre is hematite, yellow ochre limonite. Cinnabar (Table 12.1) makes a brighter red pigment than hematite. Dark green,

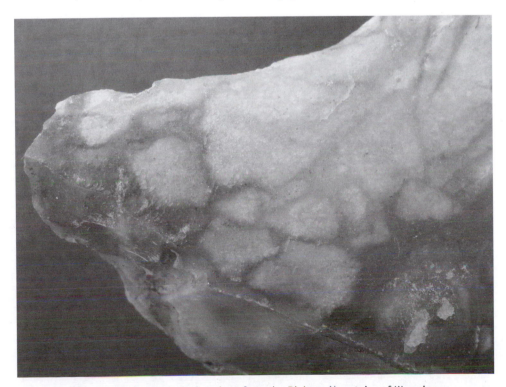

Figure 12.14 Breccia in Mississippian chert from the Bighorn Mountains of Wyoming.

Figure 12.15 Close-up of porcellanite formed from weathered volcanic material showing rock fragments and crystal laths; sample is from Miocene extrusive igneous rocks north of Grandby, Colorado.

Figure 12.16 Close-up of Morrison Formation (Jurassic) porcellanite showing root and rhizome traces and small worm burrows or fucoids in cross section.

olive, and brown are a result of reduced iron (Fe^{+2}), while gray or even black is from manganese oxide, either pyrolusite or birnessite. Heat treating advances the oxidation state of metals.

Even a small change in metal content can make a big difference in appearance. In an analysis of major elements in two parts of the same sample of Mississippian opalitic chert, one part was clear to milky, the other yellow-orange and almost opaque. Adjusted silica content in the clear sample was 98.9%, that of the yellow-orange sample, 98.5% (i.e., the content of other elements varied by only 0.4%). Most of this difference (0.3%) was accounted for by iron, and that small fraction was sufficient to completely alter the rock's appearance.

Fluorescence in UV light is another character influenced by accessory compounds in chert, chiefly calcite. While not particularly useful for identifying specific sources, the method does identify the environment of deposition. In opalitic chert, ferroan calcite fluoresces orange. Magadi-type chert (Table 12.1) has the highest calcite content and the greatest fluorescence because of it, while exsolution chert (Table 12.1) in limestones and chert formed in karst are less spectacular.

Swan River chert (actually an orthoquartzite) is thought to have originated in karst features in Devonian carbonates. Grasby et al. (2002) suggest the karst features and the orthoquartzite are a result of silica-rich solutions moving upward, hinting at a hydrothermal connection. However, the borders of the features are marked by siderite (iron carbonate) and orthoquartzite nodules, which both indicate formation via dissolution of carbonates and karst formation. The unconsolidated quartz sand in the interior of the features represents either the original clastic content of the limestone or overlapping postkarst deposition, or both. The identification of a conodont of the same age as the dolomite in the middle of the feature also indicates karst.

Distribution of Chert Types in the Sedimentary Rock Column

Vastly different environments span segments of the sedimentary rock record, and types of chert are largely restricted to certain environments. Paleozoic cherts formed in shallow epicontinental seas, with most chert bodies forming via exsolution of silica. The bodies range in size from a few centimeters to over a meter (Figure 12.17, Plate 4a). Silica bodies form along fracture zones, and at times, these sediments were emergent and weathered subaerially, forming karst. The most important early episode of karst formation was at the end of the Mississippian period, but the process continued whenever the rocks were re-exposed and continues today, as at the Schmitt Chert Quarry in Montana. Many chert nodules in immediate post-Mississippian rocks are erosional detritus.

Most chert in the Mesozoic has terrestrial origins, either on the marine littoral or in ephemeral or playa lakes, the latter usually limited to Morrison (Jurassic) and Burro Canyon (Jurassic-Cretaceous) formations. A poor chert and porcellanite is normally present in Mesozoic shale deposits, notably from replacement of dolomite concretions; these sometimes contain invertebrates, mainly gastropods.

Tertiary chert deposits are largely related to ephemeral or playa lakes, except those in the Eocene fossil lakes in southwest Wyoming, northwest Colorado, and northeast Utah. The former are high-quality, nearly pure opalitic chert, and normally exhibit lighter colors, although dark brown is common enough. Most

Figure 12.17 Exsolution chert mass in Belden Formation limestone (Pennsylvanian) on Clark Ridge on the White River Plateau, about 16 miles north of Silt, Colorado.

dark-colored chert forms in stratified lakes and contains a variety of features including the suite of features in playa lake chert, but also others indicative of deep-water formation in reducing environments, which produces dark brown and black chert that is sometimes more like porcellanite than chert.

The types of silica deposition that lead to the formation of chert, orthoquartzite, and porcellanite are related to the source of the excess silica in terrigenous rocks. Aside from epigenetic processes, which concentrate silica already present in the rock, most, if not all, opalitic chert is derived from the weathering of volcanic tephra or redeposited volcanically derived sediment. Major periods of volcanic activity in the Miocene, Oligocene, and Eocene epochs and the Jurassic period extending into the early Cretaceous produced most of the highest-quality opalitic chert.

Fossil Assemblages in Chert

In Magadi-type chert and chert formed in karst or by replacement of silica, the calcareous hard parts of the fossil are replaced by silica so that the chemical and physical attributes of rock and fossil are practically identical, although weathering frequently exposes the ghosts of organisms. While the original aragonite (a polymorph of calcite) is replaced by chalcedony or opalitic chert sometime after the original chert precipitation, the empty spaces left after the soft parts of the organism are gone are filled with opalitic chert, which absorbs a residue of calcium in some form. Weathering typically enhances the visibility of the calcareous residue which outlines the chalcedony that replaced the hard parts of the fossil (Figure 12.18, Plate 4b).

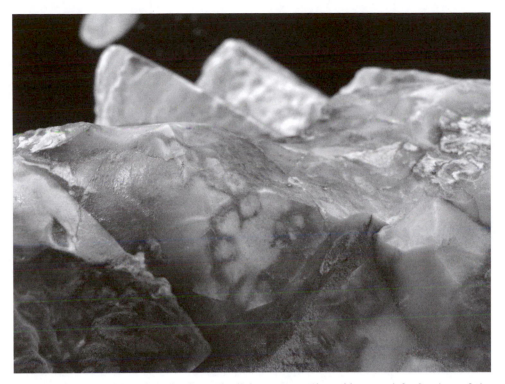

Figure 12.18   Coral in Paleozoic chert. The light areas are the void spaces left after loss of the organism's soft parts; the surrounding dark areas are chalcedony or opalitic chert that replaced the original shell material, aragonite (an organic polymorph of calcite).

The Paleozoic invertebrate fossil assemblages have more variety (Figures 12.19 through 12.21, Plate 4c). Graptolites are present in some Devonian chert and might be present in Ordovician materials. Mississippian, Pennsylvanian, and Permian cherts commonly display a number of extinct forms. Most common are crinoids and related forms (usually stem sections), various fusilinids, sponge spicules, bryozoans, fennestra or sea fans, brachiopods, scaphopods, horn corals, and a variety of Paleozoic foraminifera. Although single fossils are typical, so are mixed fossils in a "hash" that represents a litter of invertebrate hard parts settled on a former sea floor (Figure 12.22, Plate 4d). Fusilinids, which generally have small football-shaped tests or shells, show variation through time and if clearly recognized can be used to identify specific ages and rock units.

Eocene chert related to the fossil lake that once occupied the adjacent parts of Wyoming, Colorado, and Utah commonly contains gastropods and ostracodes, and both occur in coquinas. Chert from the Golden Valley Formation (Eocene) in western North Dakota, known as Knife River flint or KRF, is unique in that it formed in cutoff meanders and contains copious palm leaf or frond fragments. It is the only opalitic chert I know of that contains copious plant fossils (Figure 12.1, Plate 2a).

Oligocene and Miocene cherts, most formed in playa or ephemeral lakes, have a more restricted fossil assemblage, but almost always contain ostracodes and small pelecypods or bivalves, chiefly *Pisidium* and *Sphaerium* species. Pelecypod shells are normally seen in cross section and appear as curved lines that thicken

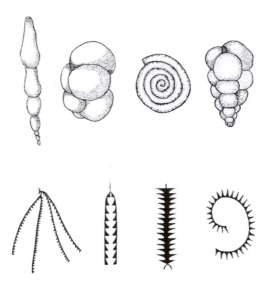

Figure 12.19 Invertebrate fossils identified in chert. Top row shows varieties of foraminifera; most are around 1 mm in size. Bottom row shows a variety of graptolites; most are one or a few centimeters in length. (Drawing by Nicole Darnell.)

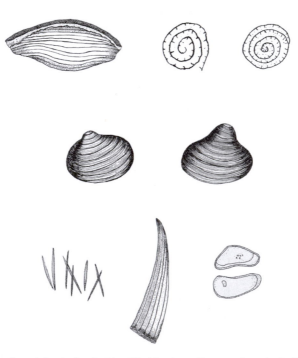

Figure 12.20 More invertebrate fossils identified in chert. Top row shows a fusilinid and two fusulinid cross sections; fusilinids are commonly about a centimeter in length or smaller, with diameters measured in millimeters. Middle row shows two bivalves usually found in Magadi-type chert; sizes range from a few millimeters to over a centimeter in the longest dimension. Bottom row shows silica sponge spicules (left), normally a centimeter or more in length; a scaphopod (center), usually a few centimeters in length; and an ostracode (right), with sizes ranging around a millimeter. (Drawing by Nicole Darnell.)

Figure 12.21   Some common, now extinct, Paleozoic fossils: two brachiopods (top row), horn coral (bottom left), and crinoid stems (bottom right).

Figure 12.22   Fossil hash from the Permian in Kansas, mostly crinoid stem segments.

toward the hinge or umbo. Ostracodes in Tertiary chert display change through time and can be used to identify specific ages and rock units.

Thermal Alteration of Chert

Heat treating some opalitic chert improves flaking or knapping quality. Between heated and unheated samples in the same rock, XRF measurements show crystallite size increases with heating. This appears to allow the fracture plane to split the crystallites, allowing for more predictable results and finer edges. Some SiO_2 blebs realign to the same orientation of those surrounding it. The change is probably apparent microscopically under reflected light, but subjectively so at this point. Unheated opalitic chert normally exhibits a textured, bumpy, or hummocky surface on a fresh break, which results when a fracture plane passes between individual crystallites or blebs rather than splitting them.

An analogy to improved flaking quality is found in the geothermal alteration of orthoquartzite and porcellanite. As individual quartz grains and silica cement are similarly realigned, fracture planes tend to split grains rather than shunt around them and overall improve the flaking quality. Heat turns most iron-bearing chert red and manganese-bearing chert grey. Calcium and sodium content produces a white or light grey.

Heat treating was intentional in many cases, for example with Swan River "chert" obtained in till (Grasby et al. 2002; Low 1996), but could also be fortuitous. In Paleozoic limestones along the Smith River in central Montana, aboriginal fires were started under chert masses in limestone to separate them from the host rock. Similarly, differential heating can be used to spall exterior parts of nodules to expose the interior of nodules; the innermost parts of nodules characteristically have better flaking qualities.

Patination of Chert

Patination occurs when a small amount of silica is removed from an artifact. As silica activity increases in hyperalkaline conditions, hydration of the surface leaves a calcium residue that is likely some form of oxide. Chert patinas appear light or dark. White patination is described as desilicification (VanNest 1985) or hydration (Miller and Larson 1990) depending on the focus of the researcher; both are correct. The usual result is a whitish patina. Opalitic chert, with its amorphous crystal habit and a higher solubility constant than cyptocrystalline quartz, is more easily affected.

Patination of this type is common on opalitic chert artifacts that are buried in or in contact with calcareous sediments. Latest Pleistocene and Early Holocene alluvium contain the largest group of calcified deposits that accelerate patination—typically braided stream deposits in ephemeral drainages—and early to middle Holocene aeolian deposits throughout the west; maximum pH values of about pH 10 are reported in several site deposits throughout the Plains and Rocky Mountains (Miller 1992). The process of desilicification is a slow one, and the total silica involved in the reactions is always small. Many hundreds or perhaps a thousand years or more are required before patination becomes visible to the naked eye.

Howard (1999, 2002) discusses another type of patination and suggests a process of dissolution and reprecipitation of silica on artifact surfaces to account for what he calls "river patina" and "gloss patination." He attributes both types of patina to an undefined chemical process that requires excess silica from somewhere (even from the artifact itself) to re-adhere to the weathering surface. Gloss patination purportedly takes place in acid soils.

Howard's idea is that the observed traits of surface smoothness and luster are due in both cases to silica adhesion rather than abrasion in the case of river patina (although abrasion remains a contributing factor), or uptake of iron from the soil in the case of gloss patina. In discounting abrasion as a major factor in formation of river patina, he only considers high-energy abrasion and ignores the effects of low-energy abrasion, which is more important; sediment in a slurry increases density of the fluid and polishes artifacts remarkably well. In the case of gloss patina, he discounts one study that indicates adhesion of iron oxide that more adequately addresses the formation of dark patina via accretion of iron oxyhydroxides (Kelly and Hurst 1956; Hurst and Kelly 1961).

Silica concentration anywhere except in hyperalkaline conditions is extremely low. Any release of silica from an artifact in environments where pH is less than 8.5 is not because of the dissolution of silica, but the weathering of other minerals in the rock (Hurst and Kelly 1961:253–254). For example, as goethite, an iron oxyhydroxide (Hurst and Kelly 1961), dehydrates it alters to hematite, an iron oxide (Deer et al. 1992). The same process forms desert varnish, "gloss" patina, and "river" patina where hematite is the major addition (Engel and Sharp 1958). The observed sheen in reflected light is due to goethite and specular hematite. Streak tests on dark patina frequently yield a faint brown or reddish-brown streak that identifies mixed-phase goethite-hematite.

Metamorphic Rocks

Metamorphic rocks used as lithic resources include steatite, catlinite and related rocks, metaquartzites, and a hybrid, technically metamorphic rock type associated with spontaneously combusted or burned-out coal seams that grade from baked shale or clinker to nonvolcanic glass (Figure 12.23, Plate 4e, Table 12.1).

Steatite, or talc, is a metamorphosed hydrous magnesium silicate commonly used in the production of bowls, platters, banner stones or atlatl weights, pipes, and other carved items. Steatite is one of several minerals in a related group of mostly dark crystalline rocks that are soft enough to be carved by stone implements.

An XRD analysis of nine steatite pipes and seven known steatite sources suggests that sourcing is a firm possibility. I identified five primary phases: steatite, minnesotaite (pure iron talc), willemseite (nickel-magnesium talc), antigorite (a serpentine, but also a hydrous magnesium silicate) and pyrophyllite; and three weathering products—chlorite, palygorskite (both fibrous clay minerals), and an unidentified phase with a bulk composition of $5MgO \cdot Al_2O_3 \cdot 3SiO_2 \cdot 4H_2O$.

None of the source areas exactly matched the artifacts in the analysis, but the diffractograms of both pipes and source materials appear relatively distinct. Samples from source areas in the Bighorn Mountains were closer to each other than other sources, and samples of sources in the Teton and Wind River mountains were closer to each other than to any others. Seven of the pipes fell into two

Figure 12.23   Metamorphic rock types: metaquartzite (top left), steatite (top right), catlinite (bottom left), and medium-grade clinker (bottom right); medium-grade clinker is called porcellanite by Fredlund (1976).

groups, but matched no sources. Another pipe was chemically unique. The last pipe, catalogued as 48HO469-4, is closely related to the sources in Sioux Creek and the Powder River Pass in the Bighorn Mountains.

Catlinite (Figure 12.23, Plate 4e, Table 12.1), with main quarry areas in Minnesota (Woolworth 1983), is a specifically identified variety of soft, red rock used for carving. A number of other sources of catlinite-like materials are described by Emerson and Hughes (2001), including Missouri flint clay and red argillites obtained from what they label a Precambrian paleosol. So far, four or more varieties are identified by Emerson and Hughes.

Metaquartzite (Table 12.1) is another metamorphic rock used in many prehistoric contexts as tool stone and more commonly as boiling stones because of its durability under thermal stress and its heat-retention qualities. A hackly fracture and surface crazing caused by differential contraction in cooling, and red or pink oxidation, marks pieces used as boiling stones (spalls are caused by differential expansion during heating). Metaquartzite differs from orthoquartzite in that the individual clastic grains are no longer distinguishable, and fracture planes in metaquartzite commonly exhibit many small-scale, subparallel, accessory fracture planes on a flaked surface (Figure 12.24, Plate 4f).

Clinker (Table 12.1) has been classified into low, intermediate, and high grades. Baked shale is a low-grade, low-heat clinker (Figure 12.25, Plate 4g), "porcellanite" (Fredlund 1976) is medium-grade clinker (Figure 12.23, Plate 4e), and nonvolcanic glass (Table 12.1) is a high-grade or high-heat clinker (Frison et al. 1968).

Igneous Rocks

Prehistorically used igneous rocks include a variety of phanerites and aphanites defined by mineral composition (Table 12.1). Phanerites were typically used as

Figure 12.24 Comparison of metaquartzite, left, with numerous accessory fractures, and orthoquartzite, right. Metaquartzite is derived from a Precambrian source; the orthoquartzite is from the Cloverly Formation (Cretaceous) in the Hartville uplift in eastern Wyoming.

Figure 12.25 Low-grade clinker.

manos, grooved mauls, and hammer, pecking, nutting, and polishing stones; aphanites, normally extrusives, were used as tool stone (e.g., obsidian and basalt) and ground stone or related artifacts, and in the case of pumice stones, abraders. Colors for all these rocks are light or dark. Lusters are overall dull, although phenocrysts (crystal inclusions) are often glassy. Obsidian, ignimbrite, and basalt are the most commonly used of these varieties for chipped stone tools, but one instance of trachyte use has been reported (Blasing and Pawlikowski 1990).

Density and durability are the characteristics of phanerites that make them useful for ground stone and other objects, and the rock chosen for these tools varies greatly. In an analysis 54 grooved mauls, the igneous/metamorphic material types, in order of dominance, include granite (17 specimens), rhyolite (14), granitic gneiss (5), metaquartzite (5), granodiorite (3), rhyolite porphyry (3), diorite (1), and dacite (1). At the Helen Lookingbill site (Shepherd 1992), raw materials of ground stone include andesite (8), and dacite, diorite, rhyodacite, and rhyolite (one each). The rock types run the gamut of useful igneous and high-grade metamorphic rock.

Igneous rock varieties commonly used as chipped stone are obsidian and ignimbrite (Figure 12.26, Plate 4h), basalt (but infrequently the other aphanites), and quartz crystals (Table 12.1). There is a hazy border between the obsidian and

Figure 12.26 Obsidian and ignimbrite: pebble obsidian from the Green River Basin, Wyoming (top left), snowflake obsidian (top right), ignimbrite (bottom left), and banded ignimbrite (bottom right) from Obsidian Cliff in Yellowstone Park.

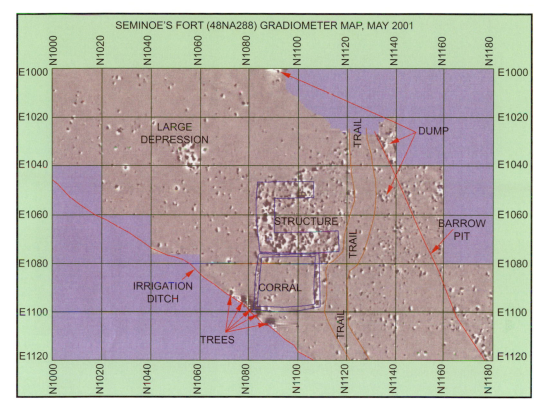

SEMINOE'S FORT (48NA288) GRADIOMETER MAP, MAY 2001

LARGE DEPRESSION

TRAIL

DUMP

STRUCTURE

TRAIL

BARROW PIT

IRRIGATION DITCH

CORRAL

TRAIL

TREES

a

b

c

Plate 1 (a) Gradiometer map of Seminoe Fort; (b) minimum analytical nodules of Madison Formation chert from the Laddie Creek site; (c) selected beads from several Wyoming sites. See text for more discussion.

Plate 2 (a) Photograph of a thin section of Knife River flint, about 400 magnification, showing randomly aligned blebs of opalitic chert (lower left) and chalcedony that replaced a palm leaf (parallel crystal alignment in upper right); (b) Magadi-type cherts; (c) more penecontemporaneous opalitic chert; (d) types of banding and mottling in chert from the Green River and Bridger formations (both Eocene) of southwest Wyoming. Top shows banding in a concretion from a stratified lake; bottom, left, shows banding with soft sediment deformation; and bottom, right, displays rip-up clasts or mud chips; (e) algal banding in chert from a hyper-alkaline-hypersaline pond on the marine littoral; (f) porcellanites and orthoquartzites; (g) exsolution chert from Phosphoria Formation (Permian) in the Bighorn Mountains of Wyoming. The original clay laminae were crowded out and replaced by the chert mass, but clay bits have been incorporated in the mass; (h) bifurcated banding due to algal growth. See Figures 12.1–12.8 for more discussion.

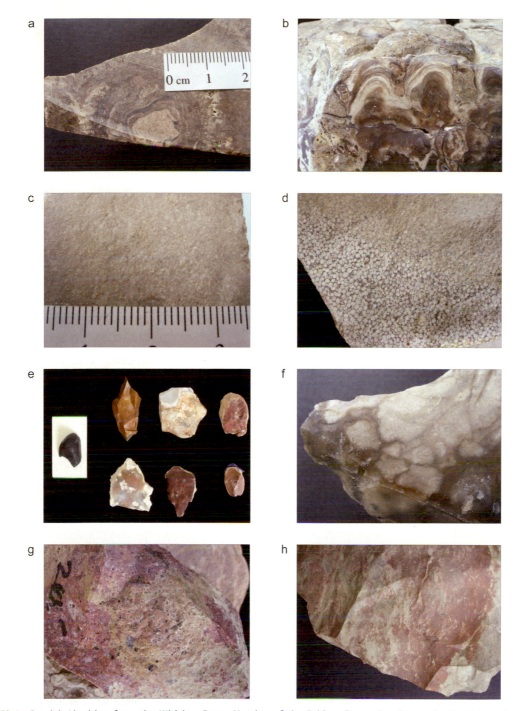

Plate 3   (a) Algal log from the Whiskey Butte Member of the Bridger Formation (Eocene). The light colored area at the bottom center of the piece is the location of a branch of an inundated tree; concentric rings surrounding it are relics of algal growth; (b) replaced stromatolite from the Green River Formation (Eocene) in southwestern Wyoming; (c) silicified ostracode coquina from the Green River Formation in southwestern Wyoming; (d) oolitic chert from the Green River Formation in eastern Utah (Eocene); many of the centers of the oolites are ostracodes; (e) Paleozoic cherts; (f) breccia in Mississippian chert from the Bighorn Mountains of Wyoming; (g) close-up of porcellanite formed from weathered volcanic material showing rock fragments and crystal laths; (h) close-up of Morrison Formation (Jurassic) porcellanite showing root and rhizome traces and small worm burrows or fucoids in cross section. See Figures 12.9–12.16 for more discussion.

Plate 4 (a) Exsolution chert mass in Belden Formation limestone (Pennsylvanian); (b) coral in Paleozoic chert. The light areas are the void spaces left after loss of the organism's soft parts; the surrounding dark areas are chalcedony or opalitic chert that replaced the original shell material, aragonite; (c) some common, now extinct, Paleozoic fossils: two brachiopods (top row), horn coral (bottom left), and crinoid stems (bottom right); (d) fossil hash from the Permian in Kansas, mostly crinoid stem segments; (e) metamorphic rock types: metaquartzite (top left), steatite (top right), catlinite (bottom left), and medium-grade clinker (bottom right); (f) comparison of metaquartzite, left, with numerous accessory fractures, and orthoquartzite, right; (g) low-grade clinker; (h) obsidian and ignimbrite: pebble obsidian (top left), snowflake obsidian (top right), ignimbrite (bottom left), and banded ignimbrite (bottom right). See Figures 12.17–12.18 and 12.21–12.26 for more discussion.

ignimbrite. Obsidian flows may incorporate tephra, and ignimbrite may flow after remelt. Obsidian and ignimbrite have a hardness of about 5.5 on the Mohs scale, and edges are unusually sharp because flaking produces a mono-molecular edge. Obsidian is usually black, but red and brown obsidian (called mahogany) are fairly common, and green obsidian has turned up in archaeological assemblages.

Basalt (Table 12.1) is easily identified by its black color and consistently dull luster. Phenocrysts usually present include olivine (a green, glassy mineral) or laths of pyroxene (an opaque, black to dark green or brown mineral). Weathered surfaces on basalt are brown or reddish brown from oxidation of iron. The knapping quality of basalt, as with some other volcanic extrusives, varies widely. The variability is likely the result of elemental and mineral composition and rate of cooling, although no firm relationships have been ascertained.

As noted, trachyte was identified in one assemblage. Trachyte is usually lighter in color, although it is possible to have dark varieties depending upon the mineral composition of the rock; it has no or very low quartz. Phenocrysts are commonly feldspathoid minerals; nepheline and leucite are the most common. Both are clear, glassy minerals with a square or rectangular shape.

Finally, crystal quartz is frequently encountered in archaeological assemblages. With a hardness of 7.0 on the Mohs scale, it is essentially glass. Impurities alter the otherwise clear, colorless crystal producing varieties such as rose quartz, smoky quartz, and citrine.

GEOLOGIC OCCURRENCE OF LITHIC RESOURCES

Stratigraphic rock units are defined by age in a hierarchical system. All of geological time is divided into eons, eons into eras, eras into periods, and periods into epochs (Palmer 1983). Depositional environments and facies are defined by lithology within that time scale. Stratigraphic names are also hierarchical. A group is composed of formations; a formation, of members; and a member, of beds. Stratigraphic names change within a region because of alternate provenance or depositional facies. A formation in one area may be termed a group in an adjacent area because of the thickness and varying composition of the rock body. Members become formations for the same reasons. An additional complexity originates in competing names for the same rock units in adjoining states, jokingly referred to as "state-line faults."

In the sections below, formation, member, and bed names will be used in conjunction with period and epoch names; figures previously presented with images of particular types mentioned are referenced. The discussion will proceed from the oldest rock stratigraphic units to the youngest. Differentiation will be made between primary sources and secondary sources in the discussions. A primary source is defined as a source where the rock of interest is still in the primary depositional context in which it formed through whatever process is applicable. A secondary source is defined as a source where the material of interest has been removed from its primary source area through erosion and redeposited in gravel in alluvium, till, or in diamictites or pediment gravel (the weathered remnants of ancient river beds).

An attempt will be made to define the range of materials in an area that includes the northern half of the Great Plains Province, the western portion of the Central

Lowlands Province (both of the Interior Plains Division), most of the Rocky Mountain System Division, and the Colorado Plateau Province physiographic areas defined by Fenneman (1946) (Figure 12.27).

Precambrian Sources

Steatite (Figure 12.23, Plate 4e) and the related mineral species are an important source material procured from Precambrian rocks. Known sources of steatite in Wyoming (Frison 1982a) are in Archean rock units exposed throughout the Rocky Mountain System. Logically, steatite and related mineral species should also occur throughout the Rocky Mountains, but not in a predictable manner. Archean rocks are among the oldest on Earth, and as a quality of their age, they have been severely altered, deformed, and faulted. Finely detailed maps will be required to discover all the potential sources, and determined field work will necessarily have to be conducted to separate the real sources from the potential ones.

Catlinite (Figure 12.23, Plate 4e) is a specifically identified variety of soft, red rock used for carving and procured from southwestern Minnesota. Catlinite comes from claystone facies interbedded with the Sioux quartzite (Early Proterozoic) (Morey 1984). It is harder than steatite and related rock types (between 2.5 and 3.0 on the Mohs scale). A secondary source of catlinite and similar rocks is in till.

Red and yellow cherts from banded iron formations, although commonly dense, brittle, and of rather poor quality, were used occasionally as a lithic resource in parts of southwest Montana. Diamictites (i.e., gravels on ancient pediment surfaces) that are composed of metamorphic lithologies commonly contain chert derived from banded iron formations, but there is no evidence that would indicate that they were procured from these secondary deposits.

Metaquartzite (Figures 12.23 and 12.24, Plate 4e, f) is variegated, durable, hard, and sometimes mottled. It was used for tool stone, boiling stones, and large utilitarian tools. The knapping quality varies with the degree of remelt in metamorphosis, impurities, and structural planes of weakness inherent in some types. Most, if not all, metaquartzites are procured from secondary sources where they are commonly abundant. One example is in the Bishop conglomerate from the Uinta Mountains of Utah and Wyoming. Commonly red, Uintah metaquartzite (Precambrian) has been widely distributed by alluvial processes in the surrounding basins.

Paleozoic Sources

Many of the lithic resources found in the western portion of the Central Lowlands physiographic province are from Paleozoic rocks (Butler and May 1984; Meyers 1970; Vehik 1985). Most of these materials are chert and orthoquartzite, some fossiliferous, but the sources are too numerous to cover in detail here. The greatest proportion of sources from the southern and eastern parts of the province are from the Mississippian, Pennsylvanian, and Permian periods; most of the important Paleozoic chert-bearing stratigraphic units in the west are also from these rock units.

Banks's (1990) thorough discussion of a number of Paleozoic sources from the south central United States, between the Ouachita Province (Interior Highlands

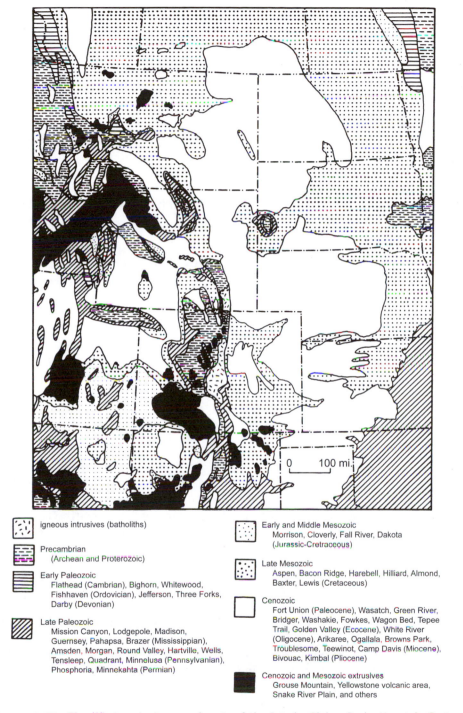

igneous intrusives (batholiths)

Precambrian
(Archean and Proterozoic)

Early Paleozoic
Flathead (Cambrian), Bighorn, Whitewood,
Fishhaven (Ordovician), Jefferson, Three Forks,
Darby (Devonian)

Late Paleozoic
Mission Canyon, Lodgepole, Madison,
Guernsey, Pahapsa, Brazer (Mississippian),
Amsden, Morgan, Round Valley, Hartville, Wells,
Tensleep, Quadrant, Minnelusa (Pennsylvanian),
Phosphoria, Minnekahta (Permian)

Early and Middle Mesozoic
Morrison, Cloverly, Fall River, Dakota
(Jurassic-Cretraceous)

Late Mesozoic
Aspen, Bacon Ridge, Harebell, Hilliard, Almond,
Baxter, Lewis (Cretaceous)

Cenozoic
Fort Union (Paleocene), Wasatch, Green River,
Bridger, Washakie, Fowkes, Wagon Bed, Tepee
Trail, Golden Valley (Ecocene), White River
(Oligocene), Arikaree, Ogallala, Browns Park,
Troublesome, Teewinot, Camp Davis (Miocene),
Bivouac, Kimbal (Pliocene)

Cenozoic and Mesozoic extrusives
Grouse Mountain, Yellowstone volcanic area,
Snake River Plain, and others

Figure 12.27   Simplified geologic map of parts of the Interior Plains, Rocky Mountain System, and Interior Plateaus physiographic divisions. Many of the formations discussed in the text are indicated. (Source: U.S. Geological Survey.)

Division) in the east and the eastern part of the Basin and Range Province (Interior Plateaus Division) in the west, includes a number of lithic resources from later time periods, both primary and secondary. In southeast Minnesota there are sources of white to gray oolitic chert in the Oneota and Prairie du Chien formations (Ordovician). The Galena Formation (Ordovician) contains a gray, tan, and white, mottled, opaque porcellanite that contains brachiopods. The Cedar Valley Formation (Devonian) contains white, gray, and red cherts and porcellanites that are mottled or banded. All of these sources are in limestones and appear to be diagenetic or epigenetic in origin.

The banded, mottled, and variegated Alibates chert and porcellanite from the Texas panhandle and eastern New Mexico is a material that is commonly identified in archaeological assemblages in Texas, Oklahoma, New Mexico, Colorado, and Kansas (Shaeffer 1958). The Alibates material has its source in Permian and possibly Triassic rocks (Green and Kelley 1960).

Flathead, Sawatch, Lodore, Tintic, and Ignacio Formations (Cambrian)
The earliest rocks in the sedimentary section of the Cambrian are a series of arkose or quartzose arenites shed from the North American craton and other high topography at the time. In many places the arenites (Table 12.1) are cemented by silica. These orthoquartzites were frequently used as groundstone. The Flathead sandstone has exposures in southwest Montana and north-central and northwest Wyoming; the Sawatch, Lodore, Tintic, and Ignacio formations, in Utah and Colorado (Berg 1960). A primary source area reported at Copper Mountain in the Owl Creek Mountains in central Wyoming (Enders and Schock 1979) is possibly in the Flathead Formation.

Gallatin Formation (Cambrian)
The Gallatin limestone contains nodular chert that is orange or black in color, and these nodules sometimes contain fossils of brachiopods and trilobites. The pebble-sized chert nodules are common on some bedding planes in the Open Door Limestone Member (the upper member of the formation) in the northwestern part of the Wind River Basin in Wyoming (Martin et al. 1980), as well as in southwest Montana, and this may represent the range of occurrence of this material in a primary context. This chert has been observed in pediment gravels, but like most Paleozoic chert, it is dense and brittle and was rarely used prehistorically.

Bighorn, Whitewood, Fishhaven, Manitou, Arbuckle, Harding, Fremont, and Viola Formations (Ordovician)
The Bighorn dolomite has widespread exposures in Wyoming. The equivalent units are the Whitewood limestone in the Black Hills, the Fishhaven limestone in northern Utah and western Wyoming, the Manitou Formation in the Colorado Rockies, and extending onto the Plains, the Arbuckle Group.

Beds of nodular replacement chert occur in the lower part of the Bighorn Formation, and a brecciated cherty dolomite is found in the upper or Leigh Member (Cygan and Koucky 1963:30). The brecciated surface has been identified in the Crawford Mountains as well, but there is little chert present (Baer et al. 1980:185). The Leigh Member of the Bighorn dolomite also has a fossil soil at its base in northern Lincoln County, Wyoming (Boeckerman and Eardley 1956:180), but the extent of this fossil soil is not known.

Material used prehistorically from the Bighorn Formation in the Bighorn Mountains in north-central Wyoming is a variegated quartzite (Craig 1983; Francis 1979, 1983). Loendorf (1973:57) reports bedded cherts in the Bighorn in the Pryor Mountains. His Big Springs quartzite may be a source in the Bighorn Formation as well (Craig 1983:34–35). The Whitewood Formation in the Black Hills is considered to be a questionable source (Craig 1983:34).

The quartzite reported is orthoquartzite and is associated with either or both fossil soils or brecciated zones in these formations. Orthoquartzites formed in the brecciated zone are the result of the clastic content of the dolomite and the concentration of the clasts and free silica precipitation during weathering.

The Manitou and Arbuckle dolomites are cherty; the Arbuckle chert is oolitic (Berg 1960:11–12). Chert pebbles are found where the Harding Formation sandstone overlies the Manitou Formation. Fremont dolomite in the South Park contains nodular black chert, and Viola dolomite in southeast Colorado is "abundantly cherty" (Berg 1960:15), although no description is offered.

Jefferson, Threeforks, Darby, and Souris River Formations (Devonian)

The Jefferson dolomite and the Threeforks Formation have exposures in western Wyoming and Montana, and minor exposures in the Bighorn Mountains. The Jefferson and Threeforks grade south and east into the Darby Formation. The Jefferson is roughly equivalent to the lower Darby; the Threeforks is roughly equivalent to the upper Darby. Mertie et al. (1951:25) and Nelson (1963:36) note nodular chert in thin, discontinuous beds parallel to the bedding planes in the Jefferson Formation in the Limestone Hills and Belt Mountains south and southeast, respectively, of Helena, Montana. These nodules are gray to black, brittle, and generally pebble sized (Figure 12.13, Plate 3e), and the chert has been noted in archaeological assemblages in the area, but not in great quantity. Some of the chert contains fossils of graptolites, a colonial organism that went extinct at the end of the Devonian, and probably trilobites. The Jefferson is brecciated on its upper contact, and this brecciated zone is present in the lower Darby in the Teton and Gros Ventre mountains in northwestern Wyoming (Andrichuk 1956:45). The Jefferson has been mapped in the Crawford Mountains in Utah and Wyoming, but there is little chert in that area (Baer et al. 1980:187).

The Souris River Formation in Manitoba, Canada, is now identified as the probable primary source of Swan River "chert" (an orthoquartzite) (Grasby et al. 2002). The description of the feature in which the material formed identifies it as karst, and the identification of a Devonian fossil inside a feature at the Mafeking Quarry supports the karst interpretation. Swan River is otherwise an important secondary source derived from till over a broad area of Manitoba, Saskatchewan, and Alberta, Canada, and in the glaciated parts of North Dakota and Montana (Low 1996).

Madison Group: Mission Canyon, Lodgepole, Madison, Guernsey, Pahapsa, Brazer, Leadville, Williams Canyon, and Gilman Formations (Mississippian)

Mississippian rocks are an important source for prehistoric tool stones over much of the mountain west. Madison Group chert and related rocks (Figures 12.13,

12.14, and 12.18, Plates 3e, f, and 4b) occur throughout Wyoming. Equivalent units are Pahapsa in the Black Hills, Guernsey in eastern Wyoming, Madison Formation in northern Wyoming, Mission Canyon and Lodgepole in southwestern Montana (Boeckerman and Eardley 1956:180; Freeman et al. 1958; Maughan 1963; Strickland 1956:53). In southeast Idaho and northern Utah, the Madison grades into a sandy limestone, the Brazer (Baer et al. 1980:187). Equivalent units in Colorado are the Leadville Formation, which has exposures from the Front Range to the west into Utah (Rothrock 1960), and Williams Canyon limestone, which has exposures in the Wet Mountains and Raton Basin west of Pueblo, Colorado (Tweto 1979).

The Mississippian rocks began to rise in the east in late Mississippian time and weathered subaerially to produce a karst terrane that extended from New Mexico to Montana (Henbest 1958:37–38). The upper cherty beds were stripped from the eastern part of the region and redeposited to the west and in karst features throughout the area (Lageson 1980:57). Authigenic chert nodules from these units are characteristically an even color of purple to red to orange or yellow, commonly contain manganese oxide in dendrites, and exhibit a suite of now extinct invertebrate life forms. The nodules vary in size, up to cobble and boulder size, and are sometimes platy. Nodules occur in the Madison, Mission Canyon, and Lodgepole formations. Thayer (1983) reports a massive bedded white chert at the base of the Madison in well cores in Montana and Wyoming.

Chert formed in karst features (epigenetic cherts) are mottled and variegated. The mottling rarely exhibits distinct borders, and if it does, the shapes are globular, wispy, and distorted, and rarely banded. The epigenetic varieties are variegated and grade from opal to porcellanite and orthoquartzite. Mineral inclusions are common, especially manganese oxides (dendrites) and blebs of iron oxyhydroxides. Many karst features contain pieces of nodular authigenic chert.

Denson and Morrisey (1952) divided the Madison in the Bighorn Mountains of Wyoming into upper Madison, upper and lower Mission Canyon, and Lodgepole. The upper karst zone is at the upper Madison–upper Mission Canyon contact, and a second "breccia" zone is at the contact between lower Mission Canyon and Lodgepole (Heiner et al. 2007). Nodular yellow and red cherts are present throughout most of the Mission Canyon and upper Madison.

Several source areas of this material are found in the Bighorns, including the Spanish Point "agate" quarry (Francis 1979, 1983). The Schmitt Chert Quarry (Davis 1982) at the Three Forks of the Missouri, near Trident, Montana, is in one of the brecciated zones. Sources from the Guernsey Formation in the Hartville uplift are called Hartville chert (Craig 1983). Although the material is said to be of poor quality (Craig 1983:34–35), Mississippian-age cherts from the Guernsey and Hartville formations located in Goshen, Niobrary, and Platte counties, Wyoming, including the Joss and Bass quarries, are examples of good-quality chert. A procurement area exists in the Pahapsa Formation in the Black Hills (Tratebas 1978), and Gardner et al. (1983) describe Mississippian chert from the Cross Mountain quarry in northwest Colorado. The Brazer Formation brecciated zones are sources of chert in the Wyoming Overthrust Belt west of La Barge, Wyoming. An inselberg of Madison limestone in the vicinity of Boulder, Wyoming, in the northern Green River Basin is another source of this material. Still another prehistorically used source is on Beaver Rim in the southern Wind River Basin, on the east flank of the Wind River Range. The massive white chert (and orthoquartzite) reported in well cores by Thayer (1983) is exposed in places in western Montana and in the Bridger Mountains between the Bighorn and Owl Creek mountains in central Wyoming.

Rothrock (1960) mentions chert in formations in the Denver Basin and southeast Colorado, but it is uncertain whether these formations actually have a surface exposure in the adjacent Front Range; none are shown on the geologic map of Colorado (Tweto 1979), but this may be because the outcrops are too small for the scale of the map. The basal Kinderhook Formation contains a variegated chert; chert in the Osage is opaque white and described as spicular, but contains other fossils, notably brachiopods, corals, and bryozoa. A fossiliferous (crinoids, coral, and foraminifera), buff to pink mottled chert is noted in the Spergen Formation, and the upper member is oolitic (Rothrock 1960:19), although it is unclear if oolitic chert is present. The St. Louis Formation contains a gray chert, and the St. Genevieve Formation, an orange and tan chert (Rothrock 1960:19–20), which are the most common colors of Mississippian chert.

The Leadville limestone has cherty zones: an opaque white chert in the bottom zone, possibly equivalent to Osage chert of the same description; variegated nodular chert throughout the main part; and light gray to white chert in the upper part, as well as karst-related chert. The Gilman sandstone in the South Park and Eagle basins, a time equivalent of the Leadville, displays a brecciated chert horizon probably related to Leadville limestone.

Amsden, Morgan, Round Valley, Hartville, Wells, Tensleep, Quadrant, and Minnelusa Formations, and Nowood Formation and Equivalent Rocks (Pennsylvanian and Pennsylvanian-Permian)

After the retreat of the Mississippian seas and the period of subaerial erosion, the seas transgressed eastward, depositing a series of related, shallow marine rocks in an epicontinental sea. The Amsden, Morgan, and Round Valley formations are subjacent to the Tensleep, Quadrant, and Wells formations. The Minnelusa is a Tensleep equivalent in the Black Hills. The Hartville Formation is the near time equivalent to all these rocks but spans a much broader interval of time, probably from the late Mississippian. It is similar sedimentologically to the Wells, Tensleep, Quadrant, and Minnelusa, consisting of limy or dolomitic sandstone and orthoquartzite that are cherty in places.

The Amsden, Morgan, and Round Valley chert are commonly nodular. The Amsden nodular chert, usually gray, blue, and sometimes tan, displays a dull luster (most of this chert is actually porcellanite). Mississippian chert lag is incorporated in the base of the Amsden, but the nodular chert stratigraphically above the base is related to limestone beds within the Amsden. Amsden chert zones have been reported in northwestern Wyoming (Bachrach 1956:54), the northern Wyoming Overthrust Belt (Boeckerman and Eardley 1956), the eastern, southern and western Bighorn Mountains (Fisher 1963:54; Francis 1983; Gorman 1963:67; Heiner et al. 2007), and near the western end of the Rattlesnake Range in the central Wind River Basin (Soister 1967:11). The Morgan and Round Valley formations in the Wyoming Overthrust Belt contain similar chert and cherty limestone or dolomite (Randall 1960:169, 174). The Cross Mountain site in northwestern Colorado (Gardner et al. 1983) is a source of Round Valley chert.

The later series of rocks in the Pennsylvanian include the Tensleep, Quadrant, Minnelusa, Wells, and part of the Hartville formations, and Nowood-equivalent rocks in the Owl Creek and middle and southern Bighorn Mountains. These rocks are predominantly thin-bedded limestone and sandstone that are variously described as dolomitic, limy, and cherty. The Quadrant contains gray, cherty dolomite locally in the Townsend Valley south of Helena, Montana (Freeman et al. 1958:449). The Tensleep is locally, albeit rarely, cherty on the east slope of the Bighorn Mountains of Wyoming (Fisher 1963:54). The upper part of the formation is orthoquartzite and a solution breccia that contains gray and black chert in pebble-size nodules (Fisher 1963:56). In the central Wind River Basin of Wyoming, the Tensleep is partly cherty dolomite (Soister 1967:11). Several cherty and dolomitic sandstones in the Tensleep Formation in northwestern Wyoming contain variegated cherts in a number of measured sections (Bachrach 1956:64).

Thin-bedded limestone and breccia stratigraphically above Tensleep and below the Opeche Member of the Phosphoria on the western monocline of the Bighorn Mountains are part of Nowood Formation rocks, a Minnelusa equivalent identified by Todd (1996); these rocks were previously mapped as either the upper part of the Tensleep or the lower part of the Phosphoria. The materials south of Shell Canyon, on Black Mountain and extending eastward to the so-called "pineapple" rock and westward on the western monocline above the Tensleep exposure there, are also part of the complex (Figure 12.13, Plate 3e; Heiner et al. 2007). Chert bodies on the western monocline are over a meter long and 50 cm thick in some exposures.

Orthoquartzite is reported in the Wells Formation in the Overthrust Belt of western Wyoming, southeastern Idaho, and northern Utah (Baer et al. 1980:187; Conner and Hatch 1980:266). The "blue chert limestone member" of the Minnelusa Formation exposed in the Black Hills is identified as a regional member (Brady 1958:45) although it appears to be discontinuous. Even where the limestone members have been stripped away in the northern Black Hills, the chert nodules are present (Brady 1958:45). Fisher (1963:54) has traced the brecciated zone in the Minnelusa east to the Bighorn Mountains in Wyoming.

A possible procurement area in the Hartville Formation near Marshall, Wyoming, contains a variegated, waxy, opaque, dendritic chert (Craig 1983:37), which may be a relic of Lageson's (1980:57) "upper red bed unit" of the Mississippian Madison Formation. Blue and grey opalitic cherts coming from the Marshall area may be the actual Hartville Formation cherts. The opalitic cherts are similar to the "Tepee Trail Agates" from the Minnelusa Formation in the Black Hills (Craig 1983:37). The orthoquartzites from the later Pennsylvanian formations were not apparently used to any great extent. Procurement of Tensleep orthoquartzite and porcellanite may have taken place in the southern Bighorn Mountains near the head of E-K Creek; the source formation of a tan porcellanite there has not been precisely determined.

The Pennsylvanian system in Colorado includes carbonate rocks bearing chert. Chert is present in exposures of Belden and Minturn limestones in the Eagle, South Park, and Sand Wash basins; chert bodies in the Belden Formation on Clark Ridge north of Silt, Colorado, range up to a meter in length and 20 cm thick (Figure 12.13, Plate 3e). The Hermosa and Rico formations in western Colorado and eastern Utah have limestone beds and some chert.

Phosphoria, Goose Egg, Minnekahta, Park City, Ingleside, and Lyons Formations (Permian)

The Phosphoria is exposed in western Wyoming, southwestern Montana, southern Idaho, Colorado, and Utah, and thickens to the south and west. There are three chert beds exposed throughout the area (Sheldon 1955, 1956). In southwest Montana, the Phosphoria Formation consists of brownish yellow and grayish yellow bedded chert 20–30 feet thick (Freeman et al. 1958); chert from the formation in the Limestone Hills west of Townsend, Montana, are characteristically brittle and tend to shatter. Phosphoria chert is exposed in the Crawford Mountains of Wyoming and Utah (Baer et al. 1980:187), the northern Overthrust Belt (Boeckerman and Eardley 1956:180), southeastern Idaho (Conner and Hatch 1980), and Jackson Hole and the Wind River Range (Sheldon 1955, 1956); in these areas, the chert is commonly gray to black and sometimes fossiliferous, containing spirifer brachiopods and fusilinids. The time equivalent in the Eagle and Sand Wash basins is the Park City Formation, which is composed of calcareous siltstone and sandstone. The best chert from these formations is commonly impure, opaque, and with a dull luster; it is technically a porcellanite. The western variety of chert has not been consistently identified in archaeological assemblages to my knowledge.

The exposures of the Phosphoria chert and porcellanite facies in the Bighorn Mountains of Wyoming (Craig 1983; Francis 1979, 1983; Frison and Bradley 1980; Peebles 1981) and the Pryor Mountains of Montana and Wyoming (Loendorf 1973) have been the result of archaeological investigations. Phosphoria chert and porcellanite (Figures 12.7 and 12.13, Plates 2g and 3e) in the Bighorn and Pryor mountains are variegated; maroon, red, purple, green, black, and white are commonly listed colors. The chert occurs as nodules or in bedded facies, especially at the base. The deposition of chert was penecontemporaneous and authigenic and took place in quiet, deep water in an isolated basin (Warner 1955). Exsolution chert occurs in the lower part of the Phosphoria Formation and is bluish-white opalitic chert that formed in nodules in shale facies. It fluoresces green in short-wave ultraviolet light.

The Minnekahta Limestone Member of the Goose Egg Formation contains chert nodules (Craig 1983:38–39). The nodules are described as dark red with green inclusions. This chert shares many traits with the Phosphoria chert. The Minnekahta (or Harriman) Formation extends into northern Colorado and has some exposures in the Front Range.

The materials discussed above are Upper Permian. Lower Permian rocks in the Colorado Rockies are arenites and conglomerates and have few carbonate beds, but both Maroon and Ingleside formations contain limestone beds. Chert in Ingleside limestone is nodular, and the upper beds of the formation are porcellanous (Maughan and Wilson 1960). Finally, the Lyons Formation is an arkosic arenite exposed along the Front Range of Colorado and has been used as groundstone.

Mesozoic Sources

Morrison, Burro Canyon, Summerville, Wanaka, Cloverly, Fall River, Lakota, and Dakota Formations (Jurassic and Cretaceous)

Some of the most distinctive rocks used prehistorically are the porcellanite and orthoquartzite in the Morrison, Cloverly, Fall River, and Dakota formations. The Morrison is thin in southwest Montana, consisting of a chert-rich salt and pepper sandstone in the Limestone Hills (Freeman et al. 1958:501) and a red orthoquartz-ite in the Bridger Mountains just east of Bozeman, Montana. The formation thick-ens to the south and has wide exposures in Wyoming (Love and Christiansen 1985) and Colorado (Tweto 1979).

There is no reliable contact between the Cloverly and Morrison in western Wyoming, but eastward the contact is formed by the Lakota Conglomerate of the Inyan Kara Group (Love 1956:76). The Rusty Beds form the upper part of the Morrison-Cloverly formations in northern Wyoming (Love 1956) and are the source of a red orthoquartzite. Hematite in the cement gives the red color.

Resource procurement areas have been noted in the Bighorn Mountains of Wyoming (Craig 1983; Francis 1979, 1983; Frison and Bradley 1980); northwest of Cody, Wyoming, in the western Bighorn Basin; in the mountains that make up the Sweetwater Arch in central Wyoming; in the Black Hills (Peebles 1981; Tratebas 1978) and Bear Lodge Mountains (Church 1996); and in the Laramie Range (Craig 1983). The typical Morrison-Cloverly porcellanite and orthoquartzite is varie-gated, but they are also commonly gray, blue, yellow, or red, and often mottled (Figures 12.3, 12.6, and 12.16, Plates 2c, f, and 3h). They contain root traces and fossil burrows (fucoids), which give them a streaked appearance.

The Spanish Diggings Quarry (Saul 1969) in the Hartville uplift in eastern Wyoming is a source of Morrison-Cloverly orthoquartzite; the material there lacks the fucoidal marks and is commonly tan, brown, purple, maroon, and gray in color (Figure 12.24, Plate 4f). The Fall River sandstone in the southern Black Hills is the source of "Black Hills quartzite," with quarries at Flint Hill, Parker Peak, and Butte Mountain (Tratebas 1978), and in the Bear Lodge Mountains, part of the Black Hills uplift (Church 1996).

The orthoquartzites and porcellanites of the Morrison, Cloverly, and Fall River formations are probably related to fossil soils, but silicification has a strong authigen-ic component; in the Morrison Formation, the source of silica was probably derived from tuff (King and Merriam 1969). The common lithic constituents of these mater-ials are quartz and chert grains far removed from provenance areas, but the mineral assemblage broadens closer to provenance areas. The quartz-chert composition is the key character that identifies most Mesozoic orthoquartzite and porcellanite.

Two other lithic resources come from these formations. The first are polished chert pebbles commonly interpreted as gastroliths (Dondanville 1963) that were occasionally used for tool stone (Francis 1979, 1983; Frison and Bradley 1980). The second is permineralized wood in the Dakota Formation in the Black Hills (Tratebas 1978). Another possible source from the Morrison-Cloverly is north of Cody, Wyoming. The material there is a banded and mottled, brown-, gray-, and cream-colored chert and porcellanite. The chert and porcellanite weather out of a limestone above the Morrison Formation but below the Cody Shale.

In the Colorado Plateau, the Summerville/Wanaka, Burro Canyon, and Dakota formations are the source of a variety of lithic materials. The Summerville contains black chert and porcellanite (Martin et al. 2002:37), but also white opalitic chert in western Colorado and eastern Utah; the Wanaka is the terrestrial time equiva-lent to the Summerville (Scott et al. 2001). Exposures of Wanaka in the Colorado National Monument contain little useful chert. Upper Burro Canyon (Figures 12.3 and 12.5, Plate 2c, e) and lower Dakota formations contain an opalitic chert formed in hyperalkaline, hypersaline ponds on the marine littoral that were created dur-ing the expansion of the Cretaceous seas at the time. The material is variegated, ranging from white to yellow to red to green, even in small specimens, and has algal banding and other fossils, including foraminifera and possibly marine ostracodes. Typically, the chert forms in discontinuous beds that leave a litter of chert rocks on a stripped surface. Burro Canyon Formation also contains a green to gray porcellanite and orthoquartzite, and conglomerates sometimes contain red chert nodules (O'Neil 1993:21). Another source of both the opalitic chert and green porcellanite is located north of Rifle Gap in western Colorado.

The Dakota Formation orthoquartzites are widespread in Colorado. In most places they consist primarily of quartz and black chert grains, and the best quality materials show various stages of silica cementation, both penecontemporaneously and authigenically. The Windy Ridge orthoquartzite in Middle Park is a well-known source, and Black Ridge in the Uncompahgre uplift is another source. In most places, the occurrence of tool stone–quality orthoquartzite is spotty.

Aspen, Bacon Ridge, Harebell, Hilliard, Almond, Baxter, and Lewis Formations, and Mesa Verde Group (Cretaceous)

The Aspen Formation is a nonmarine unit in the Overthrust Belt of Wyoming. Its upper contact is a series of porcellanite beds (Entzminger 1980:167). Love mapped three white and pink porcellanite beds in the Aspen in the Jackson Hole area and provides a possible correlation to a similar porcellanite bed in the vicinity of Frontier, Wyoming (Love 1956:78–79). Love also identified a blocky, pearl gray porcellanite in the Bacon Ridge Formation (Love 1956:80) and a light green tuffaceous porcellanite in the Harebell (Love 1956:82), both in northwestern Wyoming. Exposures of Hilliard Formation west of Kemmerer, Wyoming, have a variety of platy, opaque porcellanites that grade from tan to dark brown in color. These materials were used as tool stones. A porcellanite is exposed sporadically in the interior of the Baxter Basin, east of Rock Springs, Wyoming, and comes from the Baxter shale, the Hilliard equivalent. The Baxter material is of poor quality for applications in stone tool manufacture, but was used locally.

A purple orthoquartzite that comes from the upper contact of the Almond Formation of the Mesa Verde Group in the eastern Rock Springs uplift was locally used as a tool stone. Mesa Verde units in western Colorado also contain orthoquartzite. This orthoquartzite apparently formed through exsolution. The Lewis Formation, also on the eastern flank of the Rock Springs uplift, contains silicified dolomite concretions, and the medium brown porcellanites in the centers of the concretions were sometimes used as a tool stone in the local area. Mancos shale in the Grand Valley north of Loma, Colorado, also has dolomite concretions that are partly silicified and form a tan porcellanite; they were also used locally. The Mesa Verde Group in western Wyoming and western Colorado is the source of low-grade clinker that was sometimes used; however, the clinker could not have formed until after epeirogenic uplift in the Miocene, when the strata were elevated above sea level and ignited.

Cenozoic Sources

Fort Union Formation and Equivalents (Paleocene)

The Fort Union Formation is a series of continental rock units deposited in the wake of the retreating interior seaway. The Fort Union or its equivalents are exposed over a wide area from eastern Montana south along the western plains and in the numerous basins in the Rocky Mountain System. In the Powder River Basin of Wyoming and eastern Montana, the Fort Union has three members: the Tullock, Lebo, and Tongue River (in ascending order) (Brown 1958). In North Dakota, the Tullock and Lebo members are combined in the Ludlow Member, and the Tongue River Member is the Sentinel Butte Member. In the Wind River Basin of Wyoming, the Fort Union is composed of, in ascending order, the Lower Member, Waltman Shale Member, and the Shotgun Member (Keefer 1969).

In eastern Colorado, the equivalents of the Fort Union Formation are the Poison Canyon and Dawson formations, and in south-central Colorado, the South Park Formation; the latter has volcaniclastic conglomerate and might be a potential source of tool stone, but I am not aware of any specific sources. In northwest Colorado, Fort Union persists; the Coalmont and Middle Park formations are near equivalents, and they are arbitrarily divided by the continental divide (Tweto 1979). In southwest Colorado, the Nacimiento Formation is the equivalent. Green porcellanite pebbles and cobbles in conglomerates in Paleocene and Eocene rocks exposed on Grand Mesa in western Colorado are a secondary source probably derived from the Burro Canyon Formation (Jurassic).

The best tool stone sources in the Fort Union and equivalents appear predominantly to be related to fossil soils or silcretes—orthoquartzite and porcellanite. In the western Wyoming Basin in the area of the Rock Springs uplift, Fort Union fossil soils (Ritzma 1965) on Black Buttes, Aspen Mountain (Figure 12.6, Plate 2f), and to a lesser extent, the east flank of the Rock Springs uplift were important tool stone sources. In the Powder River Basin and the Northern Plains, Tongue River "silicified sediment," or TRSS, was an important tool stone (Figure 12.6, Plate 2f) also related to a fossil soil.

The designation of these sources as Paleocene is somewhat misleading. Silcrete formation in the Fort Union Formation started in the Paleocene and continued into early Eocene, and similar silcretes formed in the Wasatch Formation, at least in the Powder River Basin.

In the Wind River Basin, the lower member of the Fort Union Formation contains abundant chert, orthoquartzite, porcellanite, and siliceous shale (Keefer 1969:21). The quality of this material is not known, nor the extent that this material was used as tool stone, although it probably was used to some degree.

The Fort Union fossil soils (and those in the Wasatch as well) are more commonly porcellanite and characteristically gray, yellow, or red. They exhibit fine mottling and streaks resulting from root bioturbation and possibly burrows or fucoids. The stone commonly appears sucrosic, or sugary, and is opaque except on thin edges. Some varieties, notably those in the western Wyoming Basin, are orthoquartzite.

Permineralized wood and, less commonly, stromatolites are other major lithic resources from the Fort Union Formation. Permineralized wood used in the western Powder River Basin is probably from the Fort Union Formation (Reher 1979). Permineralized wood was used in the eastern Powder River Basin, northeastern Wyoming, and northwestern South Dakota, and these too are probably from the Fort Union (Craig 1983:45). In western Wyoming on the western flank of the Rock Springs uplift, the Fort Union permineralized wood was commonly procured and used, especially along the course of Killpecker Creek where the major outcrops are found. Most of the utilized permineralized wood from the Fort Union is translucent, brown to clear opaline chert. Wood grain textures are commonly preserved on the exterior and sometimes tree rings in the interior.

Another major source in the Fort Union is the variable grades (low, medium, and high) of clinker formed adjacent to spontaneously combusted coal seams. Southeast Montana and northeast Wyoming are the center for this material (Clark 1982; Fredlund 1976). Low-grade clinkers extend far to the east, into central North Dakota.

Wasatch, Green River, Bridger, Washakie, Fowkes, Wagon Bed, Tepee Trail, and Golden Valley Formations (Eocene)

The Wasatch Formation is another continental deposit, similar to the Fort Union in most respects. The Wasatch Formation exposures in the western Powder River Basin contain a porcellanite similar to the Fort Union (Tongue River "silicified sediment"). In the western Wyoming Basin and the Fossil Basin in southwest Wyoming, a series of silicified, thin-bedded ostracode coquinas (Figure 12.11, Plate 3c), commonly gray or light purple in color, was locally used as a lithic resource. Some of these are exposed along the base of White Mountain and along the west flank of Killpecker Creek north of Rock Springs. Others are exposed southeast of Sage Junction, Wyoming. Similar materials are found in the Green River Formation west of Granger, Wyoming.

The Green River Formation has extensive exposures in southwest Wyoming, northwest Colorado, and northeast Utah and consists largely of lacustrine deposits related to a series of fossil lakes that covered the region from latest Paleocene through the early late Eocene (Grande 1984:3–6). Lake Gosiute occupied most of the Green River, Great Divide, and Washakie basins in southwest Wyoming and northwest Colorado; Lake Uinta occupied the Uinta Basin in northeast Utah extending into Colorado; and Fossil Lake occupied the Fossil Basin in western Wyoming. A variety of lithic resources are available from these deposits.

The Green River Formation is the source of penecontemporaneous chert, porcellanite, and a variety of replacement or fossiliferous cherts. Penecontemporaneous chert has been reported in the Parachute Creek Member in the Piceance Creek Basin (Lundell and Surdam 1975) and the Sand Wash Basin (Kornegay and Surdam 1980); Johnson (1984) maps a number of chert-bearing horizons in the lower Green River Formation in the Piceance Creek Basin. In the Bridger Basin in southwest Wyoming, the penecontemporaneous cherts are labeled "tiger" cherts (Figure 12.4, Plate 2d) because of their distinctive banding (Love 1977); "Shavetail" is another name for the banded chert in northwest Colorado. The bulk of this chert is black, dark brown, or medium brown. The banding represents preserved lake varves and the darker, near-pure silica component is interbedded with lighter colored bands of fine clastic sediment (porcellanite). The bands are commonly subparallel and sometimes distorted by soft sediment deformation that occurred at the time of deposition (Figure 12.4, Plate 2d). Concretions with alternate dark and light banding are present (Figure 12.4, Plate 2d). The largest source of this chert is in the area of the Pine, Cedar, and Sage mountains northeast of Lone Tree, Wyoming. Similar chert and a variety of chert and porcellanite are found in the Sand Wash Basin in Colorado (Figure 12.4, Plate 2d; Stucky 1977). There is banded chert in the northern and central Green River Basin exposed between Opal Bench east of Kemmerer, Wyoming, and Wildcat Butte, west of Little America,

Wyoming. The northern extremity of the fossil lake at the time of formation was shallower, and the bands in the chert are less regular and the impurities greater. Most of the material is technically a porcellanite. Irregular banding from varve-like deposition and mottling from disturbance at the wave base at the time of formation are apparent. Dolomitic concretions are common and silicified dolomitic nodules exhibit arcuate banding that is subperpendicular to the bedding planes. Rip-up clasts, mud chips, and similar materials deposited in the beds are common and consist of fine, calcareous sediment. Opalized fossil molds of ostracods are common and appear to be small-scale, light blue inclusions in the otherwise dark brown chert. The Jack Morrow Hills, between the Killpecker Dunes and the southern end of the Wind River Range, is another source of this chert. The varves are less apparent, and the material itself is a brown opalitic chert.

In the northern Green River Basin, a thin, platy porcellanite, gray and medium brown in color, comes from the Laney Member of the Green River Formation (Figure 12.6, Plate 2f). This material is dolomitic and was formerly the mud flat or sabkha-like fringe of the fossil lake at the time of silicification. Another porcellanite, usually green or grayish green in color, containing root casts and indistinct mottling, and formed in nodules and limited beds occurs in mudstone deposits in the Bridger Formation interbeds with Green River Formation. Sources of this material have been found in the vicinity of Granger, Wyoming, in the Green River Basin, where it is often referred to as "Granger Green," and near Baggs, Wyoming, on the southern edge of the Washakie Basin. In Sand Wash Basin in northwest Colorado, a similar material forms inside fossil trees.

Useful identifying characteristics of the majority of the Green River cherts and porcellanites described above are the presence of light blue, opal-filled ostracod molds and an orange- or rust-colored fluorescence under long-wave ultraviolet light caused by ferran calcite. In addition, the porcellanites formed in shallow lake waters are dense and release a "flinty" odor when freshly broken.

The Bridger Formation is a terrigenous time equivalent for the Laney (upper) Member of the Green River Formation. The Bridger deposits contain a series of playa lake deposits (white layers) that contain chert and porcellanite in nodules and beds. The interiors of the nodules are translucent brown opalitic chert; the exteriors are white to gray porcellanite and contain planispiral gastropod fossils. "Lone Tree" opalitic chert and porcellanite is restricted in exposure to the southern Bridger Basin in Wyoming near Lone Tree (Figure 12.3, Plate 2c). No less than six chert- and porcellanite-bearing white layers are exposed on Hickey Mountain north of Lone Tree, but the number of white layers are fewer to the north and east, farther from the Bridger Basin. In Sand Wash Basin, limestones in the Bridger Formation contain Green River–like cherts described above.

There are numerous fossiliferous or replacement cherts in the Green River and Washakie formations. The knappable quality of the chert is generally better in the Washakie Basin than in the Green River Basin. Knappable-quality fossiliferous chert from the Great Divide Basin is much rarer and does not seem to extend farther east than the northwest margin of the basin. The base of the Tipton Member of the Green River Formation contains silicified gastropod coquinas; *Goniobasis tenera* is the most obvious species. The gastropod fossils in most instances give the chert an unpredictable flaking habit, and they were not used in any great extent prehistorically. In the Green River and Fossil basins, porcellanous and opaque silicified ostracode coquina are abundant (Figure 12.11,

Plate 3c). The ostracode-bearing chert and porcellanite are commonly identified as oolitic chert. Some are not, but in most the oolites are formed around ostracode carapaces (Figure 12.12, Plate 3d).

In the Washakie Basin fossiliferous or replacement cherts are commonly brown, translucent opalitic chert, although some varieties exposed on the east flank of Delaney Rim at Mexican Flats, south of Creston Junction, Wyoming, are porcellanite (Figure 12.3, Plate 2c). Algal and stromatolitic cherts are common throughout the area where the fossil lake sediments are exposed. Algal cherts are defined by the imperfect laminae common to them. In the Whiskey Basin and north to the Blue Forest east of Fontenelle, Wyoming, an important local source of tool stone known as Whiskey Buttes chert consists of silicified algal logs (Figure 12.9, Plate 3a) that occur in the Laney Member of the Green River Formation and the Whiskey Butte Bed of the Bridger Formation. A similar material occurs in Sand Wash Basin. It is opaque, porcellaneous, and ranges from black and dark brown to tan. Light blue opal inclusions are common and almost always present. Another type of algal chert comes from the western edge of the Fossil Basin from the Fowkes Formation. The Fowkes Formation algal cherts are marked by widely spaced, dark, bifurcated laminae in a tan- or cream-colored chert and porcellanite (Figure 12.8, Plate 2h). The algal varieties are restricted in exposure, but this is not true of the stromatolites. Algal reefs, (i.e., stromatolites; Figure 12.10, Plate 3b) occur in western Wyoming and northwestern Colorado. The reefs are differentially silicified, and occurrences of knappable-quality materials are not predictable throughout the range of their exposure (Bradley 1929).

Permineralized wood is available in the Laney Member of the Green River Formation and parts of the Bridger Formation. A great quantity of bluish opalized wood is present in the Blue Forest, east of Fontenelle, Wyoming. The opalized wood usually occurs on the interior of algal logs; it generally exhibits poor flaking qualities but was used to some extent prehistorically. The use of various materials is reported in the Sand Wash Basin (Stucky 1977), Colorado, and several sources in the Washakie Basin, Wyoming (Michaelsen 1983) and the Green River Basin, Wyoming (Love 1977). There are no less than 40 lithic procurement and quarry sites recorded 15 years ago and probably more now.

The Wagon Bed and the Tepee Trail formations in the Wind River Basin are less certain sources of tool stone. A siliceous limestone in the upper part of the Wagon Bed Formation contains siliceous zones 3–5 feet thick that can be traced for miles (Van Houten 1964:36). "Chalcedony" and silicified algae (stromatolites?) are reported in the Hendry Ranch Member of the Tepee Trail Formation in northern Fremont County, Wyoming (Reidel 1969:39).

The last Eocene formation of interest is the Golden Valley Formation in western North Dakota, the source of the Knife River "flint" or KRF (Figures 12.1 and 12.3, Plate 2a, c). The Knife River material is opalitic chert, commonly brown and translucent. The original chert deposition in the primary source areas occurred in the base of channel deposits (Hickey 1972:116) and also in ponds bordering the drainage systems established in the Eocene of western North Dakota (Miller and Larson 1990); the "primary" quarry areas identified by Ahler (1986) are in Quaternary lag deposits (i.e., secondary deposits). The Knife River material has a complex history, mostly penecontemporaneous, but with elements produced authigenically and epigenetically; it has been previously identified as "silicified lignite" (Clayton et al. 1970), but this is not correct for most of the material. It does contain vegetal fossils, predominantly fragments of palm leaves or fronds, and some ostracode molds that are filled with chalcedony (Miller and Larson 1990:86–87). A minimum of three beds of the material are reported at one location in the Golden Valley (Miller and Larson 1990). The Golden Valley Formation also contains two porcellanite beds (Hickey 1972). One is known as the "Hard Siliceous" or HS bed, once reported to be the probable source of the Knife River material (Clayton et al. 1970), and the other is the Taylor Chert Bed, which forms the contact between the upper and lower members of the Golden Valley Formation. The porcellanites from these beds are generally of poor quality for use as tool stone, but they were apparently used. The HS bed is probably a remnant of a fossil soil (Pettyjohn 1966) and has a much wider exposure.

White River Group or Formation (Oligocene)

The White River Group (formation in the west) has extensive exposures on the Plains of South Dakota, Wyoming, Nebraska, and Colorado and in some of the intermontane basins in the Rocky Mountain System. Singler and Picard (1979) report a chalcedony- and opal-bearing limestone at the top of the Chadron Formation or Member of the group or formation in western Nebraska and eastern Wyoming called "Flattop chalcedony" (Ahler 1977). Flattop is also applied as a designator for Kimbal Formation (Pliocene) chert and opal from northwest Colorado (Craig 1983:46). Another material from the Oligocene rocks is the "plate chalcedony" (Figure 12.2, Plate 2b), also from the Chadron (Carlson and Peacock 1975) but possibly the Brule (Ahler 1977:136), which is reportedly deposited in vertical fissures or fractures in the rock. The chert has algal banding parallel to the plates, so it is doubtful that it formed in vertical fissures. Plate chalcedony is a true chalcedony in some cases, but this is not true for most samples. The Flattop (both the Chadron and Kimbal types) and plate chalcedonies are opalitic chert and vary in color from clear or milky to opaque white and gray. Translucent varieties exhibit gray, pink, or purple shades. Some samples are mottled, containing minor globular inclusions or blebs. These are generally penecontemporaneous Magadi-type chert, but some parts may be epigenetic.

Carlson and Peacock (1975) report a "purple and white chalcedony" in the Brule Formation of the South Dakota Badlands that appears to be like the Flattop materials and is probably related. The "Scenic chalcedony" (Figure 12.2, Plate 2b; Nowak and Hannus 1985) is a brown, translucent, opalitic chert from southwest South Dakota that is a variety of Oligocene White River Group material.

The Table Mountain quarries (Koch and Miller 1996) on the Wyoming–Nebraska border west of Scottsbluff, Nebraska, are another source in the Brule Member of the White River Group. The Magadi-type chert ranges in color from almost clear to red to pink to purple (Figure 12.2, Plate 2b). The Oligocene materials from the Plains fluoresce green under short-wave ultraviolet light.

In northwest Colorado and adjacent parts of Utah, the Duchesne River Formation is the equivalent unit, but it is uncertain if the formation has any quality chert. The Florissant Lake Beds and Antero Formation in western Colorado are tuffaceous and probably contain Magadi-type opalitic chert and related porcellanite.

The Bishop Conglomerate is also Oligocene and was shed from the Uinta Mountains into Wyoming, Utah, and the northwest corner of Colorado. It is a secondary source of red Uinta Mountain metaquartzite of Precambrian age, but in a stratigraphic context. Many of the Oligocene deposits in the Rocky Mountain basins are gravel deposits and probably contain a suite of useful tool stones derived from older rock units.

Arikaree, Ogallala, Browns Park, Troublesome, North Park, Dry Union, Sante Fe, Los Pinos, Teewinot, and Camp Davis Formations (Miocene)

The Arikaree and Ogallala formations have exposures on the Plains and in some of the intermontane basins in the Rocky Mountain System. Arikaree opalitic chert commonly contains manganese dendrites and is found at Oregon Buttes south of the southern end of the Wind River Range (Zeller and Stephens 1969). Francis (1988:9) reports a white to tan, banded chert with roundish, white inclusions from the Arikaree Formation. Opalitic and white opaque chert is present in the Arikaree on the Plains in southeast Wyoming, and similar cherts in the eastern parts of Wyoming and Colorado and western Nebraska and South Dakota. "Bijou Hills silicified sandstone" (Ahler 1977; Carlson and Peacock 1975), an orthoquartzite and porcellanite, is present in the Ogallala in central South Dakota and Nebraska. The Ogallala and Arikaree materials fluoresce green under short-wave ultraviolet light.

The Browns Park Formation has exposures on the west side of the Gore Range in north-central Colorado and extends into southwest Wyoming. The Troublesome Formation is located in the Middle Park, on the east side of the Gore Range in north-central Colorado. The chert from these formations is similar (Figure 12.2, Plate 2b; Miller 1990). Milky, translucent opalitic and opaque chert that exhibits banding, most related to algal growth, occurs in thin beds. The lower parts of both formations contain penecontemporaneous cherts deposited in shallow playa lakes; the upper parts of both formations contain a greater quantity of epigenetic cherts formed during the subaerial weathering of thin-bedded, freshwater lime- stones. The epigenetic cherts contain globular inclusions and are mottled. The Browns Park and Troublesome materials fluoresce green under short-wave ultra- violet light.

The North Park Formation in northwest Colorado, Dry Union and Sante Fe Formations in south-central Colorado, and Los Pinos Formation in southwest Colorado are equivalent-aged rock units, also incorporating volcanic deposits. Los Pinos is largely of volcanic origin. Opalitic chert and porcellanite is possible, especially in the Los Pinos Formation.

The Teewinot and Camp Davis formations are exposed in northwest Wyoming. A diatomite in the Camp Davis Formation and the Teewinot is diatomaceous in parts and contains a welded rhyolite tuff (Love 1956:89–91). It is not known if and to what extent these sources may have been used prehistorically.

Bivouac, Kimbal, and Grouse Mountain Basalt Formations (Pliocene)

The Bivouac Formation is the source of another welded rhyolitic tuff (Love 1956:90–91), but again, it is not known if it was used prehistorically. The Kimbal Formation in northeastern Colorado is the source of the Kimbal "chalcedony" (Carlson and Peacock 1975), or the Kimbal-Flattop "chalcedony" (Craig 1983:46). It is a translucent, tan, brown, gray, and purple opaline chert with globular inclu- sions (blebs and ostracodes). Grouse Mountain tool stone, from Grouse Mountain in central Middle Park in north-central Colorado, is derived from weathered tuff. This material is opaque porcellanite with colors ranging from red to orange, yellow, brown and occasionally purple (Figures 12.6 and 12.15, Plates 2f and 3g). It usually contains crystal inclusions and sometimes small voids filled with mineral matter. Similar materials are found farther east in the vicinity of the Colorado River and Willow Creek confluence, and still farther north and east on a feature named Table Mountain, where it is called Table Mountain jasper.

Pliocene and Pleistocene Igneous Extrusives

Extensive extrusive volcanic deposits span the Rocky Mountain System, the Interior Plateaus, and the Pacific Mountain System physiographic divisions (Hunt 1967). Banks (1990) discusses a number of lithic resources procured from volcanic rocks in the south-central part of the United States. For the present discussion, the sources in the vicinity of Yellowstone Park and the Colorado Rockies are most important.

Obsidian, ignimbrite, basalt, crystalline quartz, and some knappable rhyolites come from the Yellowstone Plateau in northwest Wyoming, eastern Idaho, and southwest Montana; the Idaho Batholith in Idaho and Montana; and the Snake River Plain in southern Idaho. The area has been active volcanically since the early Tertiary, with a period of great activity since the beginning of the Pleistocene (Smith and Christiansen 1980). Trace element analysis of obsidian and ignimbrite (e.g., Wright and Chaya 1985) indicates there is little difficulty for the most part in assigning specific source locales for analyzed artifacts (e.g., Reher and Kunselman 1990). Basalt flows in the Colorado Rockies are present in many places.

Secondary Sources

Secondary sources are those that have been removed from their place of origin and redeposited by physical forces or processes somewhere else. The primary processes that create secondary deposits that contain a variety of lithic resources are alluvial, glaciofluvial, and glacial processes. Important secondary sources for lithic materials include till surviving the advance of the continental ice sheets and glaciofluvial runoff channels in the Northern Plains and, in unglaciated parts of the continental interior, river channels and stratigraphically defined pediments or diamictites. The context and occurrence of alluvial, glaciofluvial, and glacial deposits is fairly straightforward, as these processes occurred rather late in geological time and the provenance or source area of the lithologies they contain can be traced easily with modern maps. Alluvial and glaciofluvial deposits are still near the modern equivalents of the drainages that deposited them. Alluvial deposits are more easily traced, although complications can and do occur. One example is the case of Bitter Creek in southwestern Wyoming. Alluvial lag deposits on the high terraces that flank Bitter Creek were eroded from the Wind River Mountains and deposited at a time when the Green River flowed eastward through the Bitter Creek valley, draining to the Gulf of Mexico (Hansen 1985).

Ancient pediment gravels or diamictites present a different case for two reasons. First, they are more widely separated in geological time and contain different lithologies relative to the stratigraphic units exposed and weathering, and thus contributing to the diamictite at the time of its deposition. It is possible, with a little familiarity of geologic history, to predict what lithic resources are available in them. Second, the diamictites are largely restricted to continental deposits. In the region discussed here, the majority of the secondary sources from diamictites are Tertiary and Mesozoic in age.

Numerous Eocene diamictites derived from older rocks exist in procurement areas that were used prehistorically for tool stone. Important sources include a diamictite in the Cathedral Bluffs Tongue of the Wasatch Formation (Eocene) in the northern Great Divide Basin and diamictites in the western Green River Basin. A diamictite exposed at Moss Agate Knoll, west of Granger, Wyoming, is the source of numerous materials from the late Paleozoic through the Miocene. In the western Powder River Basin of Wyoming, favored tool stones were Phosphoria chert and porcellanite procured from diamictites as well as terrace gravels. Black chert pebbles, probably from Paleozoic rocks in the Lysite Member of the Wind River Formation, and black chert occur in the lithic assemblages in the region (Keefer 1969:25).

The "Chadron chert" (Ahler 1977:134), thought to be from Mississippian rocks in the Black Hills, is found in the basal conglomerate of the Chadron Formation (Oligocene) in the Big Badlands of South Dakota. Another Oligocene secondary source is from the Beaver Divide Conglomerate of the White River Formation. Lohman and Andrews (1968:39) state that cherty limestone slide blocks from the Wagon Bed Formation (Eocene) are incorporated in the conglomerate.

"Sweetwater agates" (Love 1961), a commonly used lithic resource, are found in the Granite Range in the southern Wind River Basin. The probable source is the Arikaree Formation (Oligocene) (Zeller and Stephens 1969:22). The Arikaree Formation may also be the original source of "moss agate" noted by Craig (1983:44–45) in the Powder River Basin, near Moorcroft, Wyoming, and on the western margin of the Plains near Lusk, Wyoming.

Pebble obsidian (Figure 12.26, Plate 4h) in the Green River Basin (Love 1977), probably deposited in the Pliocene or Pleistocene, was an important local resource. The source of these pebbles is most likely the Yellowstone volcanic area in northwest Wyoming, although trace element analysis on one specimen indicated something different. In the late 1970s, I mapped the extent of the occurrence of the obsidian pebbles along the flanks of the Green River from an area north of La Barge, Wyoming, south across the Little Colorado Desert to an area north of Green River, Wyoming. Numerous sites in the vicinity of this linear trend contain obsidian from this source.

Originally derived from the Golden Valley Formation (Miller and Larson 1990) in Dunn and Mercer counties, North Dakota, Ahler's (1986) "primary" source area of Knife River "flint" is actually a secondary source. The quarry pits excavated to procure this material are in Quaternary glaciofluvial gravels.

Rainy Buttes silicified wood (Loendorf et al. 1984) is a possible secondary source from southwestern North Dakota. Loendorf et al. (1984:335) imply that it is a secondary source, but their description is inadequate to determine the true nature of the deposit. They note that the size of the natural pieces grades up to small boulders (i.e., greater than 25 cm in diameter), but they do not mention if there are other lithologies present. If the material occurs isolated on the top of Rainy Buttes, it is doubtful that the material is lag. In isolation, it would be an erosional erratic or remnant, but still a primary source locale.

Along the Colorado River valley in western Colorado, most important materials are probably obtained from lag. Normally white from heavy patination, Miocene opalitic chert appears in almost every site in the area, but there are no exposures of Miocene rocks for a considerable distance east and north of where the chert is found. The chert survives river transport and is found in most lag deposits related to the various stages of dissection.

A number of materials are obtained from till. Swan River "chert" (again, an orthoquartzite) has a broad distribution across three Canadian provinces and the northern parts of Montana and North Dakota. Catlinite is similarly distributed in older till southward of its bedrock source. Other materials are also present.

SOURCING LITHIC MATERIALS

A variety of techniques have been applied to the problem of lithic source identification, including neutron activation (Christensen 1990; Hoard et al. 1990), X-ray fluorescence (Ingbar et al. 1990; Miller et al. 1990), and ultraviolet fluorescence (Collins 1990). The effort is to be applauded, but the results are problematical. Trace element analysis has been applied to obsidian and ignimbrite for a number of years with great success. The application to volcanic rock in general should be successful because of the evolution of magmas at a single source through time (Windley 1977:259–276). Trace element analysis of steatites seems to be successful as well (Adams and Kunselman 1990), but XRD will probably prove to be a better tool for steatite, catlinite, and other metamorphic rock types. Trace element analysis of opalitic chert derived from volcanic sources, however, met with ambiguous results (Miller and Larson 1990), but indicated that specific depositional environments of sediments (i.e., depositional facies), whether they were volcanically derived or not, are more important in determining trace element constituents than the provenance (Ingbar et al. 1990). Luedtke and Meyers (1984:297) applied trace element analysis to a localized outcrop of Burlington chert and found the variation in trace element content to be large but "structured." The variation was probably the result of unrecognized variations in the deposition in the host limestone. In view of these results, it seems that the trace element analysis of a specific source material is limited in application until all source materials have been similarly analyzed (e.g., Chistensen 1990).

If elemental analysis is to be useful in sourcing sedimentary lithic resources, a project of immense proportions will have to be undertaken to isolate the major and minor trace elements that are suitable to the application. This means nothing short of testing a variety of stratigraphically defined samples from all the known source locations of a single material for elemental composition. The elemental composition will necessarily have to be complete and include the major elements. The same testing procedure will have to be applied to all lithic resources. Closer attention to the macroscopic properties of the material seems most useful at the present time, not to mention less expensive in time, effort, and cost.

Some sources can be defined by their mineral composition. For example, the recognition of potassium feldspars in an orthoquartzite or porcellanite usually assigns it to a Tertiary source (i.e., the Fort Union). Fluorescence under long- and short-wave ultraviolet light is promising and seems to consistently identify Oligocene, Miocene, and Eocene cherts, as well as the bluish white variety of

Phosphoria (Permian) chert. Feature types (e.g., banding, mottling, and mineral inclusions) are extremely useful in defining the type of rock in which a specific lithic material formed. The fossils contained in some materials would be infinitely useful for source location, especially in detailed study (e.g., Reid 1984). All this information is immediately available, inexpensive, and accurate, but it requires study. Rarely is there a single trait, such as palm leaves in Knife River "flint," that is a surefire identifier. Identification requires a combination of evidence visible in one or a few flakes of the same material, including fossils, bedding features, mineral inclusions, and color. Every institution, contractor, and amateur has a different terminology for rock types and features, which are usually misleading but nonetheless remain useful because people understand what is meant. For example, "chalcedony" and "flint" appear frequently in the literature, but in reality, rarely in archaeological assemblages. Many times lithic analysis deals only in colors, which is largely useless. Culling information from this lithic terminology Babylon is frustrating because of the abuse and misuse of geological terms, usually by people with the best intentions in mind.

Church (1996) makes a plea for standardization of terms and the use of comparative collections, and warns that reliance solely on published descriptions will lead to invalid or misleading conclusions. Not every worker will have opportunity or funding to travel to the locations where the comparative collections are stored, and the identifications in collections I have seen are frequently inaccurate and the geologic associations often misleading. With a firm understanding of geological terms applied to lithic resources and the fossils, features, and minerals they contain, published descriptions are more than adequate. Of course, this requires learning the little bits of geology that are useful in archaeology.

Many workers are familiar with any number of lithic resources in their areas already, so it is really a matter of looking at those sources more closely with just a hand lens and learning the various features that the rocks display. The same features identify other lithic materials that share a common origin, whether in playa lakes, karst, volcanic necks, or by exsolution from carbonate rocks.

CONCLUSIONS

Defining lithic raw material procurement behavior requires understanding bedrock geology. Many procurement and quarry areas have been identified, and the geologic occurrence and area of distribution of the sought-after lithic materials can be readily defined once the geologic context is identified. Detailed analysis of the lithic materials in an assemblage can define the territory over which the inhabitants had access, in seasonal movements or through trade. Analysis of the same pattern through stratified sequences may show shifts in territorial limits, migrations through time, or a pattern in the aboriginal discovery of lithic resources. Analysis of a number of stratified sites in larger regions will show the overlap of the territories of different groups and illuminate the nature of their interactions, perhaps expressed in the presence of exotic materials. Detailed analysis of lithic assemblages will not answer all the questions but, by virtue of the durability of stone artifacts through time, it can provide significant data contributing to the resolution of some of the critical ones. This will in large part depend on accurate, technical descriptions of source materials and will be greatly aided by the use of a common terminology and a common understanding of the features useful to accurately identify a source. To reiterate, there are no easy solutions. Macroscopic identifications provide an inexpensive and proven way to accurately define source locations and formations.

13

FINAL THOUGHTS AND REMARKS

The Plains and Rocky Mountains of North America are shrouded in lore of nineteenth-century horse-mounted bison hunters, a lore that is oft repeated in books and art of the time and afterwards. The Crow, Cheyenne, Arapaho, Sioux, Kiowa, Pawnee, Blackfeet, Shoshone, Sarsi, and numerous other groups of the region, however, had many predecessors. A century ago the Plains were thought not to have been occupied until historic times, when these famous Native American bison hunters on horseback made their living on this quintessential Plains animal (Wedel 1983). Much has changed since. William Duncan Strong and his student Waldo Wedel discovered a deep history in the region dating back thousands of years, and it is now fully accepted that the Great Plains, the Northwestern Plains, and the Rocky Mountains have a human history going back nearly 14,000 calendar years before present. William Mulloy, one of us (Frison), Barney Reeves, and others developed the cultural sequences of this deep Native American history, and this volume contributes to the endeavor; this book is the third edition of a series that shows the rich and temporally deep life of Northwestern Plains and Rocky Mountain Indians.

The first glimpses of the region's prehistory less than a century ago focused on the bison hunting economy of both nomadic groups to the west and more settled village peoples to the east. Yet this was an oversimplification. While bison provided important resources for both subsistence and raw material, many other substances were important for both the nomadic and settled groups. Over a century of archaeology in the region has shown the superb adaptability of prehistoric Americans to a wide variety of resources and, sometimes adverse, climatic conditions. Their desire for variety was always there, even if we did not always see it archaeologically. This book, we hope, illustrates the rich, fruitful, and complex life of the past occupants of the Northwestern Plains and adjacent Rockies. The prehistoric Native Americans not only made a daily living, but participated in rich social and ritual networks with their neighbors, perhaps their contacts even reaching across the entire North American continent.

Data on the prehistory of this area have grown by leaps and bounds over the past several decades. Today's population growth, development, and mineral extraction in the region have all contributed to the expanding archaeological database, catalyzing both salvage and academic archaeological studies. These studies have investigated a wide array of sites from deep prehistory to recent times; from animal procurement to plant procurement to lithic raw material procurement localities; from residential, long-term camps to temporary, overnight stations; from rockshelters to open-air sites; from deep stratified sites to shallow single components to isolated artifacts on the landscape; from artifact-rich localities (with hundreds of thousands of objects) to artifact-poor sites (with 10 objects or less); from rock outcrops with carved or pecked images to those with incised images to those with painted designs; from sites with mammoth bone to those with bison bone to those with rabbit and rodent fauna.

Not only has more variability in the archaeological record been observed and recorded over the past several decades, but field, analytical, and interpretive methods have blossomed. Rarely is an archaeologist seen in the field today with a ¼″ screen and shovel. Artifact recovery with small hand tools, fine water-screening techniques, flotation devices, precise total station and GPS survey instrument recording, computerized recording techniques, and in-field preliminary analyses are becoming the norm rather than an exception. Also standard field procedures today are the various nondestructive survey techniques such as ground-penetrating radar, resistivity, and magnetometer methods designed to detect a variety of subsurface features and objects. Then there is the more frequent use of interdisciplinary studies with pollen, phytolith, soils, and geological specialists participating in field projects almost on a regular basis. Not only has this resulted in the recovery of the archaeological record undreamed of several decades ago, but it has changed our perspective on that record, what the record is, and what it can teach us.

Analytical procedures and interpretive possibilities have also developed at an unprecedented pace. Twenty years ago obsidian hydration, XRF, neutron activation, protein detection, and various other analyses were at the cutting edge of archaeological science. Many are now routinely incorporated in site reports. The new cutting edge has shifted to genetic (DNA) studies, stable isotope analyses, laser and nanotechnology, and other analytical techniques that provide new, different, and sometimes better data on paleoclimates, diets of humans or the animals they consume, stone tool and pottery use, and so on.

All the data generated by new recovery and analytical improvements has engendered rethinking of the results posed by the older data—sometimes requiring revision of our thinking about the past, sometimes supporting older explanations and theories. The new methods alone, however, are not responsible for the reinterpretation. Archaeology, for better or worse, has become a more eclectic field. Much of this eclecticism is fueled by questions not raised before or at least not seriously entertained. Where this will lead us in the future is hard to predict, but a broader range of questions is being asked the community of archaeological scientists, who are accepting a wider variety of answers from different theoretical perspectives.

Attempting to bring the mass of data included in the second edition of *Prehistoric Hunters of the High Plains* up to date and put it in some semblance of order after a lapse of nearly 20 years has provided an interesting and different perspective on the region's prehistory than that of the earlier attempt. Different attitudes usually prevail between the time an investigator first reaches the point of compiling and publishing the results of several years of research and many years later, when the old data have been continually mulled over by the original investigator and subjected to long-term scrutiny and critical analysis by other investigators. In addition, during the last two decades, massive quantities of new data have been gathered, analyzed, and applied to the same problems. This is particularly true in the case of Northwestern Plains and Rocky Mountains archaeology, where interpretations are usually based on small samples of cultural systems and, as a result, each investigator can easily arrive at a different explanation. It is a situation also where even small increments added to the database can bring about significant changes in everyone's interpretation.

Revision attempts such as this can also be somewhat humbling, which is a good thing because interpretations that appeared immutable earlier become less so as more data accumulate and the old data are reconsidered. New and improved methodologies of data gathering and analysis can be applied to existing databases, and these can modify, change completely, and sometimes negate entirely conclusions derived from earlier analyses. Continual reworking of old data, as well as collecting new data, has proven to be productive in terms of meaningful research. The old sites and the old data should be continually revisited and rethought. And the present volume has presented the positive results of many such studies.

On the other hand, much of what was presented in the second edition of this book remains relatively unchanged, which is reassuring to us and is also on the positive side for earlier investigators whose work laid the foundations that we build upon. Many new discoveries have brought about major changes in our thinking. For example, the information on pithouses of the Early Archaic period was nebulous at the time the 1st edition of *Prehistoric Hunters of the High Plains* was published, while at the time of the 2nd edition their existence was well established but not well understood, not only for the Early Archaic but for the Middle and Late Archaic as well. Since the 2nd edition, not only have the Paleoindian and Late Prehistoric periods been added to the time frame of pithouses, but the database on all pithouses has grown. More importantly, however, the data have been synthesized as well as applied to theoretical problems of human energy expenditure, acquisition, risk management, and other processes affecting foragers everywhere.

The Paleoindian Goshen complex was more or less unknown and even less well understood 20 years ago but, on the basis of new data, at least some subsistence and technological strategies are now better understood, although we still need more and better site data in order to answer questions of its relationships to Clovis and Folsom. There are still questions surrounding the radiocarbon dates that have been obtained for the Goshen complex from the Mill Iron site 24CT30 in southeast Montana. These dates allow several possibilities; according to one series of dates, the Goshen complex could be the same age as Clovis and according to another series, it could be the same age as Folsom. Only further research can resolve the problem, and ongoing reinvestigations of the Hell Gap site in southeast Wyoming would appear to be the best option at this time. Data from the Jim Pitts and Sewright sites in South Dakota will provide significant new information on dates as well as expand the Goshen database.

The Clovis occupation as represented at the Colby site suggests a strong hunting orientation, but we have no evidence of their gathering activities. However, the distribution of Clovis diagnostics from the lowest elevations to nearly timber-line and in a wide variety of ecological niches could indicate more than a strictly hunting economy. Folsom diagnostics have a distribution similar to Clovis and the Hanson Folsom site in the northern Bighorn Basin (Frison and Bradley 1980) strongly suggests foraging as opposed to a strictly hunting economy. Shortly after Folsom times, there is unquestionable evidence in the Bighorn Basin of a contin-ual succession of cultural groups with Archaic lifeways that lasted until historic times. Other mountain areas appear to have similar cultural sequences (Black 1991; Pitblado 2003; Steiger 2002).

The evidence for Archaic lifeways can be found in a number of contexts that include campsites located in response to the distribution of plant and animal resources, and many of these are in rockshelters of the Bighorns. From an overall view, the evidence suggests well-established, cyclical transhumant groups adapt-ing successfully to an environment that witnessed many short-term and long-term climatic changes. In the Bighorn Basin, the evidence for communal bison kills appears to be lacking, except during the Paleoindian period, so that subsist-ence there depended on broad-spectrum foraging. Scheduling of food procure-ment activities in response to food resources that were unpredictable from year to year was the key to survival in prehistoric times throughout the Northwestern Plains and Rockies. A stronger hunting focus may have prevailed in areas of the Northwestern Plains that provided better animal carrying capacity than the Bighorn Basin, and this is confirmed by the presence of numerous communal kills of bison in the former areas and a definite lack of them in the latter area. The Bighorn Basin contrasts with the Powder River Basin to the east (see Figure 1.1) where at certain times, Besant and Yonkee periods for example, communal bison hunting appears as a significant economic activity. However, even in this area there is a strong indication that climatic change led to discontinuities. Lifeways were more Archaic, with a broader, often changing diet and commensurate social and settlement systems. The same situation is true further to the north in the northern part of the Northwestern Plains and the Rocky Mountains, where bison bone beds suggestive of communal hunting activities are prevalent in the arch-aeological record. This communal hunting focus, however, coincides with general intensification of food production across the region. Not only are there commu-nal bison hunts, but the resource is intensely processed beginning in the Middle Plains Archaic (Fisher and Roll 1999; Reeves 1990). Bone and marrow cracking, bone fat rendering, and pemmican production are all evidence of both intensifi-cation and buffering strategies for annual or longer periods of low productivity. Such intensification is also clear in other economic activities. Grinding equipment and hearth numbers show an exponential increase from the Early Plains Archaic through the Middle Plains Archaic and into the Late Plains Archaic periods. These types of facilities and tools are designed to extract more usable resources out of the same amount of raw resource.

The dichotomy between mountains and plains subsistence strategies during part of Paleoindian times is now supported by a better database, but there is much to learn because the data necessary to understand the relationships between groups in the two areas are only now becoming known. Part of this problem is that systematic study of archaeology in the higher altitudes is just beginning to come into its own. It has been easier logistically to expend our research efforts on easily accessible sites that produce large bodies of data, but in so doing, part of the overall picture has been neglected. The confirmation of true grinding stone tools (manos and metates) at the higher altitudes at the end of Paleoindian times has forced some rethinking about the source of these tools and how they were used at the higher elevations. Thought earlier to have been imported from the Great Basin at about the beginning of Middle Plains Archaic times, grinding tool presence there by at least 8000 years ago changes the picture and forces us to change earlier concepts. Further complicating the picture is a little-known body of data on the Betty Greene site in eastern Wyoming, which is the type site of the poorly known and understood Lusk Paleoindian cultural complex that, according to the investigator (Greene 1967), produced grinding tools (metates) in unequivocal context with this terminal Paleoindian manifestation out on the open plains. Obviously, the Betty Greene site should be a prime candidate for future reinvestigation. The site is in an area of extremely fast erosion and its investigation should be an item of high priority before it is irrevocably gone.

The Foothill/Mountain complexes have, however, been somewhat clarified. Completion of one stage of investigations at Helen Lookingbill and the preliminary results from the Barton Gulch sites, as well as collections studies in the southern Rocky Mountains (Davis et al. 1988; Kornfeld and Frison 2000; Kornfeld, Larson, Rapson, and Frison 2001; Pitblado 2003), appear to have placed several Late Paleoindian complexes in clearer focus. A better understanding of the variation and time ranges of Alder, Hardinger, and possibly Lovell Constricted complexes seems to have begun the process of elaborating the Late Paleoidian Foothill/Mountain chronology.

Archaeologists have long lamented the fact that rock art could not be accurately dated, and the chance of associating stratified levels in sites to pictures on a nearby wall stood little chance of becoming a reality. This appears to no longer be the case, based on new methods of dating the residues collected on the pecked and incised surfaces (see Chapter 10, this volume). Theoretical advances in rock art research are bringing new perspectives on social and ideological aspects of Northwestern Plains and Rocky Mountain hunter-gatherers. This promises to be a major breakthrough in archaeology, particularly in many areas where geological formations were favorable for the application of pecked and painted figures.

Our knowledge of the osteology of the region was in its nascent stages two decades ago. Diligent and intensive research into these remains by students and scholars alike are bringing a completely different and much fuller understanding of human populations during the past 13,000 calendar years, and in particular of those groups that made the Rocky Mountains their home (Chapter 11, this volume).

Our reflections on the reworking of old data, collecting of new data, and changes in the potential for interpretation based on theoretical and methodological advances rapidly dispels any doubts that we know all there is to know. Paleoindian studies appeared to have reached a plateau two decades ago, but now new data appear regularly and many new sites are being sealed unless they are in danger of loss through development, looting, or natural causes. As new highways, access roads, reservoirs, mines, and other earth disturbances uncover previously hidden archaeological sites, new discoveries come to light that change our views on prehistoric life. Students today need not worry that the database is or will be exhausted in the foreseeable future.

One of the pitfalls of archaeology is that the protagonists often get too emotionally involved with their own research area and data. Too often also, their research area takes on the character of the navel of the world, with surrounding areas subordinate to and revolving around it. Admittedly, any neutral observer reading this book could easily arrive at this conclusion, although this is not intended. On the other hand, it is dangerous for any archaeologist to look over the fence into unfamiliar territory and, on a basis of poorly understood data, attempt to interpret someone else's data. Even so, a quick look at research results from areas peripheral to the Northwestern Plains and Rocky Mountains confirms that prehistoric settlement and subsistence changes rapidly over short distances. The cultural relationships between these areas have not been adequately explored or explained. Discussion of these changes constitutes what might be a fruitful area in which future researchers can become involved.

The Colorado Front Range immediately south of Wyoming contains a large land mass well above timberline. Twenty years ago, few investigators had the courage to carry out long-term research there except for Benedict (1991). The logistics of carrying out research there are difficult, but the results continually remind us that the area contains more archaeological evidence than before realized, and that this must be better understood before the final chapters on prehistory can be written. Added to this is information from the Middle Park area of Colorado close to the headwaters of the Colorado River. It was thought a short time ago that the prehistoric inhabitants moved out of such basins as winter approached. There is now evidence to the contrary: Paleoindian bison procurement occurred there in early winter (Kornfeld et al. 1999), while Early Archaic pithouses there were apparently occupied all winter (Metcalf and Black 1991, 1997). These new data will undoubtedly force us to rethink ideas of intermountain basin occupations (Pitblado 2003). In the same area there is newly discovered evidence indicating Folsom and Goshen occupations at elevations around 8000 feet. Bison kills of this age and at this elevation promise to be exciting areas for future research, since the procurement strategies appear to be different than those known on the open plains.

Farther west on the Yampa and Green rivers in northern Colorado and southern Wyoming is an ever-increasing body of evidence of the northern extent of Fremont Basketmaker occupations. Archaic evidence with roots in the Colorado Plateau and Great Basin apparently do not fit in the Northwestern Plains chronology, nor should this be expected (see Metcalf et al. 2006). Extreme southeastern Idaho, northwestern Wyoming, and northeast Utah is a rich archaeological area. Grey's Lake and Blackfoot Reservoir in Idaho, for example, have produced large collections of surface material, but few systematic investigations have been made. Some of the material looks similar to that farther east in the direction of the plains but much does not. A prime example is a tool type called the Wahmuza lanceolate point that has been found occasionally in northwest Wyoming and usually identified with great confidence and certainty as a projectile point of Late Paleoindian age (Figure 2.43). However, evidence from the Snake River Plain indicates that it is of Late Prehistoric and Early Historic age (Holmer 1986; Wood 1987). Situations such as this can be humbling and bring about much greater caution when identifying materials based on incomplete evidence.

The Bitterroot projectile point was recognized in caves and rockshelters in the mountains north of the Snake River in southern Idaho many years ago (Swanson et al. 1964) and may have relationships to the Early Plains Archaic farther east. Certainly, the time periods coincide quite well. However, the appearance of the side-notched projectile points at the end of Paleoindian times over a large area of North America remains unexplained. What adaptive change in the cultural system engendered such a change in material culture? We may be a long time in coming up with a satisfactory explanation.

Large, communal mountain sheep traps of Early Historic age abound in the mountains of northwest Wyoming and very likely also in the immediately adjacent area of Montana and Idaho (Frison et al. 1990), but similar traps are apparently lacking in the mountain sheep country along the Salmon River farther north and west in Idaho. This could reflect different procurement strategies or smaller sheep populations. This is an intriguing problem open for further investigation. We now also know that such traps are associated with extensive camps in the high altitude mountain areas (Scheiber and Finley 2009). Historic changes in social systems were apparently rapid and significant, and these high-altitude sites may yield some information on such processes.

Throughout the area, human skeletal data (Chapter 11) evidences the economically deteriorating condition of women brought about by the fur trade and other new economic processes. Historical data explicating such social processes are meager, and archaeological data are neither abundant nor are they easy to use for understanding these types of changes. Nevertheless, a fresh look at these critical times of rapid change is breathing new life into our interpretations of mountains as well as basins (e.g., Sutton 2004).

Southwest Montana has suddenly blossomed as a rich Paleoindian area (Davis et al. 1988; Hill and Davis 2005) with diagnostics that appear different than those farther east. Investigations in the same general area by Robson Bonnichsen further confirm this and have yielded excellent results (Bonnichsen et al. 1992). However, Bonnichsen's results also show the western continuation of the Cody complex. This has been further elaborated by in situ components of the Osprey Beach site on the Yellowstone Plateau and the ubiquitous stemmed point finds in the Great Basin that Dan Amick argues are Cody (Amick 2007; Johnson et al. 2004). As these investigations show, the Cody complex in western North America still leaves us with a lot of questions. Analysis of pottery from northeastern Montana (Jerde and Joyes 2009) and surveys of eastern Montana (Deaver and Deaver 1986) reveal a wealth of archaeological materials that are starting to tell us much more about the prehistory of the northeastern reaches of the Northwestern Plains.

The Knife River flint quarry areas in North Dakota have been under investigation for some time (Ahler 1977, 1986) but only during the last 10 years has there been systematic investigation of Paleoindian flint procurement. The Lake Ilo project has recovered evidence of major Folsom lithic procurement localities with ubiquitous data on production strategies from chipped stone workshops (Root 2000; Root et al. 1986). The discovery has opened the way for long-term investigations in the future. The butte country of northwest South Dakota and southeast Montana is a rich archaeological area (Keyser and Davis 1984, 1985) that deserves much more attention.

The archaeological potential of the South Dakota and Wyoming Black Hills is just beginning to be explored (Kornfeld 2003; Sundstrom 1989; Tratebas 1978, 1985; Tratebas and Vagstad 1979). The discovery of a fortified village site on the Belle Fourche River in western South Dakota demands new thinking on the migrations of Middle Missouri groups westward (Alex 1989), as does the Harrier Nest site in the Powder River Basin (Winham et al. 2000). Results of analyses of pottery from southeast Wyoming and northern Colorado (Cobry and Roper 2002; Page 2009) are beginning to shed light on our understanding of group movements into and out of the Northwestern Plains. Western Nebraska has witnessed limited archaeological exploration (Agenbroad 1978b; Barbour and Schultz 1932; Bell and Cape 1936; Strong 1935), but here too there has been significant progress (MacDonell and Wandsnider 2003) with indications that, literally, only the surface has been scratched. The Pine Bluffs of extreme southeast Wyoming is an area rich in archaeological resources that are only now witnessing a major long-term research effort that promises good results. Their extension into Colorado (the Pawnee Buttes), and the area of northeast Colorado in general, is one of the richest Paleoindian areas of North America (see Dick and Mountain 1960; Fulgham and Stanford 1982; Kornfeld et al. 2007; Stanford 1978; Wheat 1967, 1979; Wormington 1988). Between here and into the foothills of the Colorado Front Range is a wealth of archaeological resources both in the foothills and out onto the plains (see Irwin and Irwin 1959; Irwin-Williams and Irwin 1966; Metcalf 1973; Morris et al. 1985; Muniz 2009).

It is within this disciplinary context that we have revised the present volume on the Plains and Rockies prehistory. Bison procurement and processing, notably the communal procurement of these animals, still dominates the story of the region's prehistory. But noncommunal bison hunting, procurement, and processing and the consumption of a wider variety of resources from deer to roots to insects are beginning to tell their own story. Subsistence on the Plains and in the Rockies was diverse in prehistory. Diets and dietary supplements were many, and prehistoric groups had wide choices to make in their dietary preferences.

Other components of the archaeological record—hearths and various heating facilities, domestic structures, storage caches, human remains, and rock images—all add significantly to the understanding of past peoples of the Plains and Rockies. While most of these are not new discoveries in the archaeological record, most have been found in sufficient numbers (e.g., house pits) or have been studied in sufficient detail (e.g., rock images) to yield synthetic interpretations. Although field discoveries are occasionally made, the discipline has outgrown this childish enthusiasm of "finding" and replaced it with a myriad of alternative interpretations that the data and new analyses can yield. Plains and Rockies prehistory shows that past peoples of this region adapted to the changing environmental conditions, changed and intensified their diets at times, invented new technologies on a regular basis, shifted their social and exploitation territories, altered their social structures, exchanged goods with their far-flung neighbors, participated in long-distance interactions, and altered their ideological systems. All this shows a dynamic, vibrant, and evolving society over the 14,000-year history of the region.

REFERENCES

Aaberg, Stephen A.
1983 Plant gathering as a settlement determinant at the Pilgrim Stone Circle site. In *From Microcosm to Macrocosm: Advances in Tipi Ring Investigation and Interpretation*, edited by Leslie B. Davis, pp. 279–303. Plains Anthropologist Memoir 19. Lincoln, Nebraska.

Adams, Richard
1991 A Preliminary Report on the Dicken Site: A Multiple Burial in Southeastern Wyoming. Manuscript on file, Department of Anthropology, University of Wyoming, Laramie.

Adams, Richard, and R. Kunselman
1990 A Preliminary Report on Sourcing Steatite Artifacts by Means of X-ray Fluorescence. Paper presented at the 48th Plains Anthropological Conference, Oklahoma City.

Agenbroad, Larry D.
1978a Cody knives and the Cody Complex: A reassessment. *Plains Anthropologist* 23:159–161.
1978b *The Hudson-Meng Site: An Alberta Bison Kill in the Nebraska High Plains.* University Press of America, Washington, DC.
1978c Buffalo jump complexes in Owyhee County, Idaho. In *Bison Procurement and Utilization: A Symposium*, edited by L. B. Davis and M. C. Wilson, pp. 213–221. Plains Anthropologist Memoir 14. Lincoln, Nebraska.

Agogino, George A.
1972 Excavations at a Paleo-Indian site (Brewster) in Moss Agate Arroyo, eastern Wyoming. *National Geographic Research Reports* 1955–1960:1–6.

Agogino, George A., and W. O. Frankforter
1960 A Paleo-Indian bison kill in northeastern Iowa. *American Antiquity* 25:414–415.

Agogino, George A., and Eugene Galloway
1963 The skulls from Torrington, Wyoming: A re-evaluation. *American Antiquity* 29(1):106–109.
1965 The Sister's Hill site: A Hell Gap site in north-central Wyoming. *Plains Anthropologist* 10:190–195.

Ahlbrandt, T. S.
1974 Dune stratigraphy, archaeology, and the chronology of the Killpecker dune field. In *Applied Geology and Archaeology: The Holocene History of Wyoming*, edited by M. Wilson, pp. 51–57. The Geological Survey of Wyoming Report of Investigations No. 10. Laramie.

Ahler, Stanley A.
1977 Lithic resource utilization patterns in the Middle Missouri sub area. In *Trends in Middle Missouri Prehistory: A Festschrift Honoring the Contributions of Donald J. Lehmer*, edited by W. Raymond Wood, pp. 132–150. Plains Anthropologist Memoir 13. Lincoln, Nebraska.
1986 *The Knife River Flint Quarries: Excavations at Site 32DU508.* State Historical Society of North Dakota, Bismark.

Ahler, Stanley A., and P. R. Geib

2002 Why the Folsom point was fluted: Implications from a particular technological explanation. In *Folsom Technology and Lifeways*, edited by J. E. Clark and M. B. Collins. *Lithic Technology*, Special Publication No. 4:372–390. University of Tulsa, Oklahoma.

Aikens, C. Melvin

1966 *Fremont-Promontory-Plains Relationships; Including a Report of Excavations at the Injun Creek and Bear River No. 1 Sites, Northern Utah*. University of Utah Anthropological Papers No. 82.
1967 Plains relationships of the Fremont culture: A hypothesis. *American Antiquity* 32:198–209.

Albanese, John P.

1971 Geology of the Ruby site area, Wyoming, 48CA302. *American Antiquity* 36(1):91–95.
1978 Archeogeology of the Northwestern Plains. In *Prehistoric Hunters of the High Plains*, by George C. Frison, pp. 375–389. Academic Press, New York.
1985 Geology of the McKean site (48CK7). In *McKean/Middle Plains Archaic: Current Research*, edited by Marcel Kornfeld and Lawrence C. Todd, pp. 63–78. Occasional Papers on Wyoming Archaeology 4. Office of Wyoming State Archaeologist, Laramie, Wyoming.
1986 The geology and soils of the Colby site. In *The Colby Site: Taphonomy and Archaeology of a Clovis Kill in Northern Wyoming*, edited by George C. Frison and Lawrence C. Todd, pp. 143–163. University of New Mexico Press, Albuquerque.
1987 Geological investigations. In *The Horner Site: The Type Site of the Cody Cultural Complex*, edited by George C. Frison and Lawrence C. Todd, pp. 279–326. Academic Press, Orlando.

Alex, Lynn M.

1989 *Archaeological Testing and Analysis of Prehistoric Fortifications in Butte County, South Dakota*. Project 46–88–30125B018. State Historical Preservation Center, Rapid City, South Dakota.

Alley, Richard B., and Anna Maria Ágústsdóttir

2005 The 8k event and consequences of a major Holocene abrupt climate change. *Quaternary Science Reviews* 24:1123–1149.

Amick, Daniel S.

1999 New approaches to understanding Folsom lithic technology. In *Folsom Lithic Technology: Exploration in Structure and Variation*, edited by D. S. Amick, pp. 1–11. International Monographs in Prehistory, Archaeology Series 12. Ann Arbor.
2007 Way Out West: Cody Complex Occupations from the Northwestern Great Basin. Paper presented at the 65th Plains Anthropological Conference, Rapid City, South Dakota.

Ammerman, A. J., and M.W. Feldman

1978 Replicated collection of site surfaces. *American Antiquity* 43(4):734–740.

Anderson, Duane C., and Holmes A. Semken (editors)

1980 *The Cherokee Excavations: Holocene Ecology and Human Adaptations in Northwestern Iowa*. Academic Press, New York.

Anderson, Elaine

1968 Fauna of the Little Box Elder Cave, Converse County, Wyoming. The Carnivora. *University of Colorado Studies, Series in Earth Sciences* 6:1–59. Boulder.
1974 A survey of the late Pleistocene and Holocene mammal fauna of Wyoming. In *Applied Geology and Archaeology: The Holocene History of Wyoming*, edited by Michael Wilson , pp. 78–87. Geological Survey of Wyoming Report of Investigations No. 10. Laramie.

Andrichuk, J. M.

1956 Devonian stratigraphy in northern Wyoming and adjoining areas. In *Wyoming Geological Association Eleventh Annual Field Conference Guidebook*:43–50. Wyoming Geological Association, Casper.

Anonymous

1985 Summary of the archaeology of the Bozner site—artifacts. *Journal of Intermountain Archeology* 4(2). Western Prehistoric Research, Boulder, Colorado.

Antevs, Ernest

1948 Climatic changes and pre-white man. *Bulletin of the University of Utah* 38:168–191.
1955 Geologic-climatic dating in the West. *American Antiquity* 20(4):317–335.

Armitage, C. L., S. D. Creasman, and L. C. Mackey

1982 The Deadman Wash site: A multi-component (Paleo-Indian, Archaic, Late Prehistoric) site in southwestern Wyoming. *Journal of Intermountain Archaeology* 1.1–11.

Armstrong, Anne K.

1999 A Bioarchaeological Examination of the Korell-Bordeaux Site (48G054). Unpublished Master's thesis, Department of Anthropology, University of Wyoming, Laramie.

Arnold, Craig R.

2007 Assembling Intrasite Spatial Data at the 10,500 YBP Hanson Site (48BH329). Unpublished Master's thesis, Department of Anthropology, University of Wyoming, Laramie.

Arthur, George W.

1962 The Emigrant bison drives of Paradise Valley, Montana. In *Symposium on Buffalo Jumps*, edited by Carling Malouf and Stuart Connor, pp. 16–27. Montana Archaeological Society Memoir No. 1.

1966 *An Archaeological Survey of the Upper Yellowstone River Drainage, Montana*. Montana State University, Agricultural Economics Research Report No. 26.

Bach, Dan

1997 Interpreting the Cultural Significance of Charred and Uncharred Seeds Recovered from Prehistoric Hearths and Living Floors: Theory, Method and Implications. Unpublished Master's thesis, Department of Anthropology, University of Wyoming, Laramie.

Bachrach, J. L.

1956 Tensleep-Amsden sections of the Gros Ventre-Snake River area, northwestern Wyoming. *Wyoming Geological Association Eleventh Annual Field Conference Guidebook*:64–65. Wyoming Geological Association, Casper.

Baer, J. L., V. D. Ott, and R. L. Chamberlain

1980 Stratigraphy of the Crawford Mountains, Rich County, Utah, and Lincoln County, Wyoming. *Wyoming Geological Association Thirty-first Annual Field Conference Guidebook*: 185–190. Wyoming Geological Association, Casper.

Baker, Scott J.

1989 Osteological analysis. In *Archaeological and Osteological Analysis of Two Burial Sites Along Harlan County Lake, Nebraska: Chronological and Evolutionary Implications*, edited by W.L. Tibesar, pp. 69–87. Report to the U.S. Army Corps of Engineers, Kansas City District. Prepared by Larson-Tibesar Associates, Laramie.

Bamforth, Douglas B.

1988 *Ecology of Human Organization on the Great Plains*. Plenum Press, New York.

2006 The Windy Ridge quartzite quarry: Hunter-gatherer mining and hunter-gatherer land use on the North American continental divide. *World Archaeology* 38(3):511–527.

2007 *The Allen Site: A Paleoindian Campsite in Southwestern Nebraska*. University of New Mexico Press, Albuquerque. (editor)

Bamforth, Douglas B., and Mark Becker

2009 Microwear, tools, and handles: A pilot functional investigation of the chipped stone assemblage. In *Hell Gap: A Stratified Paleoindian Campsite at the Edge of the Rockies*, edited by M. L. Larson, M. Kornfeld, and G. C. Frison, pp. 285–302. University of Utah Press, Salt Lake City.

Banks, Larry D.

1990 *From Mountain Peaks to Alligator Stomachs: A Review of Lithic Resources in the Trans-Mississippi South, the Southern Plains, and Adjacent Southwest*. Oklahoma Anthropological Society Memoir No. 4. Oklahoma City.

Barbour, E. H., and C. Bertrand Schultz

1932 *The Scottsbluff Bison Quarry and Its Artifacts*. Bulletin No. 34. Nebraska State Museum, Lincoln.

Basgall, Ashly L.

2008 Northwestern Plains Indian Women: A Bioarchaeological and Ethnographic Analysis. Unpublished Master's thesis, Department of Anthropology, University of Wyoming, Laramie.

Bass, William M.

1964 The variation in physical types of the prehistoric Plains Indians. *Plains Anthropologist Memoir* 1:65–145.

1970 Excavations of a Paleo-Indian site at Agate Basin, Wyoming. *National Geographic Society Research Reports* 1961–1962:21–25.

2005 *Human Osteology: A Laboratory and Field Manual.* 5th ed. Special Publication No. 2. Missouri Archaeological Society, Columbia.

Bass, William M., and Donald C. Lacy

1963 Three human skeletons from the P. K. Burial. *Plains Anthropologist* 8(21):142–157.

Baugh, Timothy G., and Scott D. Brosowske (organizers)

2006 The Distribution of Obsidian in the Great Plains and its Relationship to Trade and Exchange. Symposium at the 64th Plains Anthropological Conference, Topeka, Kansas.

Bedord, Jean Newman

1974 Morphological variation in bison metacarpals and metatarsals. In *The Casper Site: A Hell Gap Bison Kill on the High Plains,* edited by George C. Frison, pp. 199–240. Academic Press, New York.

Behrensmeyer, Anna K.

1973 Taphonomic and ecologic information from bone weathering. *Paleobiology* 4:150–162.

Beiswenger, Jane M.

1991 Late Quaternary vegetational history of Grays Lake, Idaho. *Ecological Monographs* 61(2):165–182.

Bell, E. H., and R. E. Cape

1936 The rock shelters of western Nebraska. In *Chapters in Nebraska Archaeology,* edited by E. H. Bell, pp. 357–399. University of Nebraska, Lincoln.

Bellis, Mary

2008 History of the Digital Camera. Electronic document, http://inventors.about.com/library/inventors/bldigitalcamera.htm, accessed August 18, 2008.

Bement, Leland

1999 *Bison Hunting at Cooper Site: Where Lighting Bolts Drew Thundering Herds.* University of Oklahoma Press, Norman.

2003 2002 field work at the Jake Bluff and Certain sites. *Oklahoma Archaeological Survey Newsletter* 22(3&4):1–2.

Benedict, James B.

1975 The Murray site: A Late Prehistoric game drive system in the Colorado Rocky Mountains. *Plains Anthropologist* 20(69):161–174.

1981 *The Fourth of July Valley: Glacial Geology and Archaeology of the Timberline Ecotone.* Research Report No. 2. Center for Mountain Archaeology, Ward, Colorado.

1985 *Arapaho Pass: Glacial Geology and Archaeology of the Crest of the Colorado Front Range.* Research Report No. 3. Center for Mountain Archaeology, Ward, Colorado.

1991 People of the Shining Mountains: High-altitude cultural ecology of the Colorado Front Range, U. S. A. *Acta Archaeologica Carpathica,* Krakow, Poland.

1996 *The Game Drives of Rocky Mountain National Park.* Research Report No. 7. Center for Mountain Archeology, Ward, Colorado.

Benedict, James B., and Byron L. Olson

1973 Origins of the McKean complex: Evidence from timberline. *Plains Anthropologist* 18(62):323–327.

1978 *The Mount Albion Complex: A Study of Man and the Altithermal.* Research Report No. 1. Center for Mountain Archaeology, Ward, Colorado.

Benedict, Jeff

2003 *No Bone Unturned: The Adventures of a Top Smithsonian Forensic Scientist and the Legal Battle for America's Oldest Skeletons.* Harper Collins, New York.

Bentzen, Raymond C.

1962a The Powers-Yonkee Bison Trap. *Plains Anthropologist* 7(18):113–118.

1962b The Mavrakis-Bentzen-Roberts Bison Trap, 48SH311. *Report of the Sheridan Chapter, Wyoming Archaeological Society.*

Berg, E. L.

1938 Notes on catlinite and the Sioux quartzite. *American Mineralogist* 23:258–268.

Berg, Robert R.

1960 Cambrian and Ordovician history of Colorado. In *Guide to the Geology of Colorado,* edited by Robert J. Weimer and John D Haun, pp. 10–17. Geological Society of America, Rocky Mountain Association of Geologists, and Colorado Scientific Society joint publication. Geological Society of America, New York.

Bettinger, Robert L., and Martin A. Baumhoff

1982 The Numic spread: Great Basin cultures in competition. *American Antiquity* 47:485–503.

1983 Return rates and intensity of resource use in Numic and pre-Numic adaptive strategies. *American Antiquity* 48:830–834.

Billo, Evelyn, and Robert Mark

1999 Wind River Petroglyph GIS Project. Paper presented at the Fourth Biennial Rocky Mountain Anthropological Conference, Glenwood Springs, Colorado.

Binford, Lewis R.

1967 Smudge pits and hide smoking: The use of analogy in archaeological reasoning. *American Antiquity* 32(1):1–12.

1976 Forty-seven trips—a case study in the character of some processes of the archaeological record. In *Contributions to Anthropology: The Interior Peoples of Northern Alaska,* edited by Edwin S. Hall, pp. 299–351. Archaeological Survey of Canada Paper No. 49. National Museums of Canada, Ottawa.

1978a *Nunamiut Ethnoarchaeology.* Academic Press, New York.

1978b Dimensional analysis of behavior and site structure: Learning from an Eskimo hunting stand. *American Antiquity* 43(3):330–361.

1979 Organization and formation processes: Looking at curated technologies. *Journal of Anthropological Research* 35(3):255–273.

1980 Willow smoke and dogs' tails: Hunter-gatherer settlement systems and archaeological site formation. *American Antiquity* 45:1–17.

1981 *Bones: Ancient Men and Modern Myths.* Academic Press, New York.

2001 *Constructing Frames of Reference.* University of California Press, Berkeley.

Birkby, Walter H., and William M. Bass

1963 Possible Shoshonean skeletal material from the Turk Burial site, 48WA301. *Plains Anthropologist* 8(20):103–114.

Black, Kevin D.

1991 Archaic continuity in the Colorado Rockies: The Mountain Tradition. *Plains Anthropologist* 36(103):1–30.

Black, Stephen L., Linda W. Ellis, Darrell G. Creel, and Glenn T. Goode

1997 *Hot Rock Cooking on the Greater Edwards Plateau.* Texas Archaeological Research Laboratory, University of Texas at Austin, and Texas Department of Transportation, Austin.

Blackmar, Jeannette M.

2002 The Laird site. *Cultures: University of Kansas Museum of Anthropology Newsletter* 65:3.

Blasing, Robert K, and Maciej Pawlikowski

1990 Mineralogical Identification of Trachite in Trego County, Kansas. Paper presented at the 48th Plains Anthropological Conference, Oklahoma City.

Bliss, Wesley L.

1950 Birdshead Cave, a stratified site in the Wind River Basin, Wyoming. *American Antiquity* 15(3):187–196.

Boeckerman, R. B., and A. J. Eardley

1956 Geology of the Southwest Jackson quadrangle, Lincoln County, Wyoming. *Wyoming Geological Association Eleventh Annual Field Conference Guidebook:*179–183. Wyoming Geological Association, Casper.

Bonnichsen, Robson

1972 Millie's Camp: An experiment in archaeology. *World Archaeology* 4(1):277–291.

Bonnichsen, Robson, Marvin Beatty, Mort D. Turner, Joanne C. Turner, and Diane Douglas
1992 Paleoindian lithic procurement at the South Fork of Everson Creek, southwestern Montana: A preliminary statement. In *Ice Age People of the Rockies*, edited by D. J. Stanford and J. S. Day, pp. 285–321. University of Colorado Press, Niwot.

Booth, Robert K., Stephen T. Jackson, Steven L. Forman, John E. Kutzbach, E. A. Bettis, J. Kreig, and David K. Wright.
2005 A severe centennial-scale drought in mid-continental North America 4200 years ago and apparent global linkages. *The Holocene* 15(3): 321–328.

Borresen, Jennifer A.
2002 A Faunal Analysis of the Frazier Site, an Agate Basin-Age Bison Kill-Butchery Site in Northeastern Colorado. Unpublished Master's thesis, Department of Anthropology, University of Tennessee, Knoxville.

Bouldurian, A. T., and J. L. Cotter
1999 *Clovis Revisited: New Perspectives on Paleoindian Adaptations from Blackwater Draw, New Mexico*. University Museum Monograph No. 103. University of Pennsylvania, Philadelphia.

Bowers, Alfred W.
1965 *Hidatsa Social and Ceremonial Organization*. Bureau of American Ethnology Bulletin 194. Washington, DC.

Brace, G. Ian
2005 *Boulder Monuments of Saskatchewan*. Saskatchewan Archaeological Society, Saskatoon.

Bradley, Bruce A.
1974 Comments on the lithic technology of the Casper site materials. In *The Casper Site: A Hell Gap Bison Kill on the High Plains*, edited by George C. Frison, pp. 191–197. Academic Press, New York.
1982 Flaked stone technology and typology. In *The Agate Basin Site: A Record of the Paleoindian Occupation of the Northwestern Plains*, edited by George C. Frison and Dennis Stanford, pp. 181–212. Academic Press, New York.
1991 Flaked stone technology in the northern High Plains. In *Prehistoric Hunters of the High Plains*, by George C. Frison, pp. 369–395. Academic Press, San Diego.
2009 Bifacial technology and Paleoindian projectile points. In *Hell Gap: A Stratified Paleoindian Campsite at the Edge of the Rockies*, edited by M. L. Larson, M. Kornfeld, and G. C. Frison, pp. 259–273. University of Utah Press, Salt Lake City.

Bradley, Bruce A., and George C. Frison
1987 Projectile points and specialized bifaces from the Horner site. In *The Horner Site: The Type Site of the Cody Cultural Complex*, edited by George C. Frison and Lawrence C. Todd, pp. 199–231. Academic Press, Orlando.
1988 Typology and Technology of the Mill Iron Site Flaked Stone Tools. Paper presented at the 53rd Annual Meeting of the Society for American Archaeology, Phoenix, Arizona.
1996 Flaked-stone and worked-bone artifacts from the Mill Iron site. In *The Mill Iron Site*, edited by G. C Frison, pp. 43–69. University of New Mexico Press, Albuquerque.

Bradley, Bruce A., and Dennis Stanford
1987 The Claypool study. In *The Horner Site: The Type Site of the Cody Cultural Complex*, edited by George C. Frison and Lawrence C. Todd, pp. 405–434. Academic Press, Orlando.

Bradley, Raymond S.
1999 *Paleoclimatology*. Academic Press, New York.
2000 Past global changes and their significance for the future. *Quaternary Science Reviews* 18:391–402.

Bradley, Wilmot H.
1929 *Algal Reef and Oolites of the Green River Formation*. U. S. Geological Survey Professional Paper 154G.

Brady, F. H.
1958 Evaporite deposits in the Minnelusa Formation in the Sundance-Beulah area, Crook County, Wyoming. *Wyoming Geological Association Thirteenth Annual Field Conference Guidebook*:45–47. Wyoming Geological Association, Casper.

Brain, C. K.
1981 *The Hunters or the Hunted?* The University of Chicago Press, Chicago.

Brandtmiller, Bruce
1984 Congenital anomalies of the lower spine in two Arikara skeletal series. *Plains Anthropologist* 29(6):327–333.

Brawn, Barnum
1932 The buffalo drive. *Natural History* 32(1):75–82.

Breeden, Stanley
1988 The first Australians. *National Geographic* 173(2):266–289.

Breternitz, David A. (editor)
1971 Archaeological investigations at the Wilbur Thomas Shelter, Carr, Colorado. *Southwestern Lore* 36(4):53–99.

Breternitz, David A., Arthur A. Rohn, Jr., and Elizabeth Morris (compilers)
1974 *Prehistoric Ceramics of the Mesa Verde Region.* Museum of Northern Arizona Ceramic Series No. 5. Northern Arizona Society of Science and Art.

Breternitz, David A., Alan C. Swendlund, and Duane Anderson
1971 An early burial from Gordon Creek, Colorado. *American Antiquity* 36(2):170–182.

Brink, Jack W.
2008 *Imagining Head-Smashed-In: Aboriginal Buffalo Hunting on the Northern Plains.* AU Press, Athabaska University, Edmonton.

Brink, Jack W., and Bob Dawe
1989 *The 1985 and 1986 Field Season at Head-Smashed-In Buffalo Jump, Alberta.* Archaeological Survey of Alberta Manuscript Series No. 16. Alberta Culture and Multiculturalism, Edmonton, Alberta.

Brooks, James F.
1995 Sing away the buffalo: Faction and fission on the Northern Plains. In *Beyond Subsistence: Plains Archaeology and the Postprocessual Critique*, edited by Phillip Duke and Michael C. Wilson, pp. 143–168. University of Alabama Press, Tuscaloosa.

Brose, David S.
1975 Functional analysis of stone tools: A cautionary note on the role of animal fats. *American Antiquity* 40(1):86–94.

Brown, Barnum
1932 The buffalo drive. *Natural History* 32(1):75–82.

Brown, Lionel
1963 The Fort Smith medicine wheel, Montana. *Plains Anthropologist* 8(22):225–230.

Brown, Roland W.,
1958 Fort Union Formation in the Powder River Basin, Wyoming. *Wyoming Geological Association Thirteenth Annual Field Conference Guidebook*:111–113. Wyoming Geological Association, Casper.

Brox, George, and Mark Miller
1974 The John Gale site 48CR303: A preliminary report. *The Wyoming Archaeologist* 17:13–26.

Bruder, J. S., and L. E. Rhodes (editors)
1992 *Kern River Pipeline Cultural Resources Data Recovery Report. Wyoming Segment.* Dames and Moore, Phoenix, Arizona.

Brumley, John H.
1973 Quantitative methods in the analysis of butchered faunal remains: A suggested approach. *Archaeology in Montana* 14(1):1–40.
1975 *The Cactus Flower Site in Southeastern Alberta: 1972–1974 Excavations.* National Museum of Man, Mercury Series No. 46. National Museums of Canada, Ottawa.
1984 The Laidlaw site: An aboriginal antelope trap from southeastern Alberta. In *Archaeology in Alberta*, edited by Dave Burley, pp. 96–127. Archaeological Survey of Alberta Occasional Paper No. 23. Edmonton.

Bryan, Alan, and Gerald Conaty
1975 A prehistoric Athapaskan campsite in Northwestern Alberta. *The Western Canadian Journal of Anthropology* 5(3–4):64–87.

Bryan, Karina M.
2006 Periodic Holocene Human Resource Intensification in the Bighorn Mountains: Evidence from BA Cave. Unpublished Master's thesis, Department of Anthropology, University of Wyoming, Laramie.

Bryan, K., and L. L. Ray
1940 *Geological Antiquity of the Lindenmeier Site in Colorado*. Smithsonian Miscellaneous Collections No. 99. Washington, DC.

Bryant, Laureen M.
2007 *A Reanalysis of the Long Creek Site: 45 Years After the Excavation*. Occasional Papers of the Archaeological Society of Alberta No. 8.

Bryson, Reid A., and Robert U. Bryson
2009 Site specific high-resolution climate models of Paleoindian sites in the Plains. In *Hell Gap: A Stratified Paleoindian Campsite at the Edge of the Rockies*, edited by M. L. Larson, M. Kornfeld, and G. C. Frison, pp. 103–110. University of Utah Press, Salt Lake City.

Bryson, Reed, David A. Baerreis, and Wayne M. Wendland
1970 The character of late-glacial and post-glacial climatic changes. In *Pleistocene and Recent Environments on the Central Great Plains*, edited by Wakefield Dort, Jr., and Knox Jones, Jr., pp. 53–74, Special Publication No. 3, Department of Geology. University of Kansas Press, Lawrence.

Buckles, William G.
1964 An Analysis of Primitive Rock Art at Medicine Creek Cave, Wyoming, and Its Cultural and Chronological Relationships to the Prehistory of the Plains. Unpublished Master's thesis, University of Colorado, Boulder.

Buikstra, J. E., and D. H. Ubelaker (editors)
1994 *Standards for Data Collection from Human Skeletal Remains*. Arkansas Archaeological Survey Research Series No. 44. Arkansas Archaeological Survey, Fayetteville.

Bupp, Susan L.
1981 The Willow Springs Bison Pound: 48AB130. Unpublished Master's thesis, Department of Anthropology, University of Wyoming, Laramie.

Burghard, Elizabeth R.
2004 Rock Art and the Perception of Landscape: Dinwoody Tradition Rock Art at Site 48FR311. Unpublished Master's thesis, Department of Anthropology, University of Wyoming, Laramie.

Burnett, Paul, Charles Bollong, John Kennedy, Chris Millington, Cary M. Berg, Venesa Zietz, Ashley Fife, Karen Reed, and Maxine Seletstewa
2008 *Archaeological Data Recovery for the Rockies Express/Entrega Pipeline Project at the Joe Miller Site (48AB18), Albany County, Wyoming*. Prepared by SWCA Environmental Consultants for Kinder Morgan, Inc., Federal Energy Regulatory Commission, and Bureau of Land Management. Broomfield, Colorado.

Burns, Karen R.
1999 *Forensic Anthropology Training Manual*. Prentice Hall, Upper Saddle River, New Jersey.

Butler, B. Robert
1963 An Early Man site at Big Camas Prairie, south-central Idaho. *Tebiwa* 6(1):22–33.
1965 A report on investigations of an Early Man site near Lake Channel, southern Idaho. *Tebiwa* 8(2):1–20.
1968 An introduction to archaeological investigations in the Pioneer Basin locality of eastern Idaho. *Tebiwa* 11(1):1–14.
1971 The origin of the upper Snake country buffalo. *Tebiwa* 14(2):1–20.
1978 Bison hunting in the desert west before 1800: The paleo-ecological potential and the archaeological reality. In *Bison Procurement and Utilization: A Symposium*, edited by L. B. Davis and M. C. Wilson, pp. 106–112. Plains Anthropologist Memoir 14. Lincoln, Nebraska.

Butler, B. Robert, and R. J. Fitzwater
1965 A further note on the Clovis site at Big Camas Prairie, south-central Idaho. *Tebiwa* 8(1):38–39.

Butler, Brian M., and Ernest E. May
1984 *Prehistoric Chert Exploitation: Studies from the Midcontinent*. Occasional Paper No. 2. Southern Illinois University Center for Archaeological Investigations, Carbondale.

Byers, Steven N.
2008 *Introduction to Forensic Anthropology*. 3rd ed. Allyn and Bacon, Boston.

Byrnes, Allison M.
2009 Frederick component at Locality I. In *Hell Gap: A Stratified Paleoindian Campsite at the Edge of the Rockies*, edited by M. L. Larson, M. Kornfeld, and G. C. Frison, pp. 216–228. University of Utah Press, Salt Lake City.

Cahen, D., and L. H. Keeley
1980 Not less than two, not more than three. *World Archeology* 12(2):166–180.

Callahan, E.
1979 The basics of biface knapping in the eastern fluted point tradition: A manual for flintknappers and lithic analysts. *Archaeology of Eastern North America* 7(1):1–180.

Capaldo, S. D., and Blumenschine, R. J.
1994 A quantitative diagnosis of notches made by hammerstone percussion and carnivore gnawing on bovid long bones. *American Antiquity* 59: 724–747.

Carlson, Gayle F., and Curtis A. Peacock
1975 Lithic distribution in Nebraska. In *The Lithic Source Notebook*, edited by Ronald A. Thomas, p. R-6. Section of Archaeology, Division of Historical and Cultural Affairs, State of Delaware, Milford.

Carpenter, L. H., R. B. Gill, D. J. Freddy, and L. E. Sanders
1979 *Distribution and Movements of Mule Deer in Middle Park of Colorado*. Special Report No. 46. Colorado Division of Wildlife, Denver.

Catlin, George
1844 *North American Indian Portfolio: Hunting Scenes and Amusement of the Rocky Mountains and Prairies of America*. Catlin, London. On file at the Toppan Rare Books Library, American Heritage Center, University of Wyoming, Laramie.

Chittenden, H. R., and A. T. Richardson (editors)
1905 *Life, Letters, and Travels of Father Pierre-Jean De Smet 1801–1873*. Volume 3. Francis P. Harper, New York.

Chomko, Stephen A., and B. Miles Gilbert
1987 The Late Pleistocene/Early Holocene record in the northern Bighorn Mountains, Wyoming. In *Late Quaternary Mammalian Biogeography and Environments of the Great Plains and Prairies*, edited by Russell W. Graham, Holmes A. Semken, Jr., and Mary Ann Graham, pp. 394–408. Illinois State Museum Scientific Papers 32.

Christensen, Robert C.
1990 Neutron Activation Characterization of Knife River Flint from the Primary Source Area in West Central North Dakota. Paper presented at the 48th Plains Anthropological Conference, Oklahoma City.

Church, Tim
1996 Lithic resources of the Bearlodge Mountains, Wyoming: Description, distribution, and implications. *Plains Anthropologist* 41(156):135–164.

Clark, Gerald R.
1982 The Distribution and Procurement of Lithic Raw Materials of Coal Burn Origin in Eastern Montana. Paper presented at the joint 40th Annual Plains Anthropological Conference and the 15th Chacmool Conference, Calgary, Alberta, Canada.

Clark, Gerald R., and David Fraley
1985 Three lithic material caches from southeastern Montana: Their implications for cultural adaptation and interaction on the Northwestern Plains. *Archaeology in Montana* 26(2):5–42.

Clark, Gerald R., and Michael Wilson
1981 The Ayers-Frazier Bison Trap (24PE30): A Late Middle Period bison kill on the Lower Yellowstone River. *Archaeology in Montana* 22(1):23–77.

Clark, J. E., and M. B. Collins (editors)
2002 *Folsom Technology and Lifeways. Lithic Technology*, Special Publication No. 4. University of Tulsa, Oklahoma.

Clark, W. P.
1885 *The Indian Sign Language, with Brief Explanatory Notes of the Gestures Taught Deaf-Mutes in Our Institutions for Their Instruction, and a Description of Some of the Peculiar Laws, Customs, Myths, Superstitions, Ways of Living, Code of Peace and War Signals of Our Aborigines.* L. R. Hammersly and Company, Philadelphia.

Clayton, Lee, W. B. Bickley, Jr., and W. J. Stone
1970 Knife River flint. *Plains Anthropologist* 15:282–290.

Cobry, Anne Marie
1999 Sourcing the Middle Ceramic Period: Investigations of Upper Republican Ceramics on the Central and High Plains. Unpublished Master's thesis, Department of Anthropology, University of Wyoming, Laramie.

Cobry, Anne M., and Donna C. Roper
2002 From loess plains to High Plains: The westward movement of Upper Republican pots. In *Geochemical Evidence for Long-Distance Exchange,* edited by Michael D. Glascock, pp. 153–166. Greeenwood Publishing Group, Westport, Connecticut.

Coffin, Roy G.
1937 *Northern Colorado's First Settlers.* Colorado State University, Ft. Collins.

Collins, Gary
1970 Deception Creek Points. Manuscript on file, Colorado Historical Society, Office of Anthropology and Historic Preservation, Denver, Colorado.

Collins, Michael B.
1990 Ultraviolet Fluorescence in Chert Identification. Paper presented at the 48th Plains Anthropological Conference, Oklahoma City.
1991 Rockshelters and the early archaeological record in the Americas. In *The First Americans: Search and Research,* edited by T. D. Dillehay and D. J. Meltzer, pp. 157–182. CRC Press, Boca Raton, Florida.
1999 *Clovis Blade Technology: A Comparative Study of the Kevin Davis Cache, Texas.* University of Texas Press, Austin.
2002 The Gault Site, Texas, and Clovis research. *Peopling of the Americas,* Athena Review 3(2).
2005 Clovis – a fresh look at an ancient culture. Paper presented at Clovis in the Southeast, October 26–29, 2005. Manuscript on file, Department of Anthropology, University of Wyoming, Laramie.

Collins, Michael B., and Bruce A. Bradley
2008 Evidence for pre-Clovis occupation at the Gault Site (41BL323), Central Texas. *Current Research in the Pleistocene* 25:70–72.

Conkey, Margaret W.
1984 To find ourselves: Art and social geography of prehistoric hunter gatherers. In *Past and Present in Hunter Gatherer Societies,* edited by Carmel Schrire, pp. 253–276. Academic Press, New York.

Conner, Carl E., Nicole Darnell, and Barbara Davenport
2007 *Class III Cultural Resource Inventory for the Wagon Park Hazardous Fuels Reduction Project (Phase I) in Mesa County, Colorado.* Prepared by Grand River Institute, Grand Junction, Colorado, for USDI Bureau of Land Management, Grand Junction Field Office, Grand Junction, Colorado.

Conner, J. L., and J. F. Hatch
1980 Stratigraphy of the Sage Valley and Elk Valley quadrangles, western Wyoming and southeastern Idaho. *Wyoming Geological Association Thirty-first Annual Field Conference Guidebook:*263–277. Wyoming Geological Association, Casper.

Conner, Stuart
1962a Unusual characteristics of the Keogh Buffalo Jump. In *Symposium on Buffalo Jumps,* edited by Carling Malouf and Stuart Connor, pp. 8–11. Montana Archaeological Society Memoir No. 1.
1962b *A Preliminary Survey of Prehistoric Picture Writing on Rock Surfaces in Central and South Central Montana.* Anthropological Paper No. 2. Billings Archaeological Society, Billings, Montana.

Conner, Stuart

1972 Elk antler piles made by Indians on the Northwestern Plains. Manuscript on file, Department of Anthropology, University of Wyoming, Laramie.

1984 The petroglyphs of Ellison's Rock. *Archaeology in Montana* 25(2–3):123–145.

Conner, Stuart, and Betty Lou Conner

1971 *Rock Art of the Montana High Plains.* Exhibition for the Art Galleries, University of California, Santa Barbara.

Connor, Melissa A.

1987 *Site Testing at Jackson Lake: A Jackson Lake Archaeological Project Interim Report.* U. S. Department of the Interior, National Park Service, Midwest Archaeological Center, Lincoln.

Conway, Thor

1987 Shamanistic Rituals and the Interpretation of Ojibwa Rock Art. Paper presented at the 52nd Annual Meeting of the Society for American Archaeology, Toronto.

Crabtree, Don E.

1966 A stoneworker's approach to analyzing and replicating the Lindenmeier Folsom. *Tebiwa* 9:3–39.

Crabtree, Don E., and Earl H. Swanson

1968 Edge-ground cobbles and blade-making in the Northwest. *Tebiwa* 11(2):50–58.

Craig, Carolyn

1983 Lithic Resource Analysis and Interpretation in Northwest Wyoming and Southeastern Montana. Unpublished Master's thesis, Department of Anthropology, University of Wyoming, Laramie.

Creasman, Steven, and Kevin Thompson

1990 *Excavations at 48CR4419: The Nova site.* Report prepared for Nova Petroleum by Western Wyoming College. Report on file at the Wyoming SHPO Cultural Records Office, Laramie.

Creasman, Steven D., Kevin W. Thompson, and Beth Sennett

1990 Prehistoric Pottery of Southwest Wyoming: A Preliminary Assessment. Paper presented at the 48th Annual Plains Anthropological Conference, Oklahoma City.

Crompton, A. W., and K. Hiiemae

1969 How mammalian teeth work. *Discovery* 5:23–24.

Cygan, N. E., and F. L. Koucky

1963 The Cambrian and Ordovician rocks of the east flank of the Bighorn Mountains, Wyoming. *Wyoming Geological Association and Billings Geological Society, First Joint Field Conference,* pp . 26–37. Wyoming Geological Society, Casper.

Dahms, D. E.

2002 Glacial stratigraphy of Slough Creek Basin, Wind River Range, Wyoming. *Geomorphology* 42:59–83.

Damon, P. E., C. V. Haynes, Jr., and A. Long

1964 Arizona radiocarbon dates. *Radiocarbon* 6:91–107.

Darlington, David, and Josh Bodyfelt

1999 Outlaws and horse corrals. *The Wyoming Archaeologist* 43(2):71–84.

Davis, Don P.

1992 The Archaeology and Human Osteology of the Benick Ranch Site (48AB571). Unpublished Master's thesis, Department of Anthropology, University of Wyoming, Laramie.

Davis, Don P., and Mark E. Miller

2008 An introduction to the archaeology and human osteology of the Benick Ranch site (48AB571). In *Skeletal Biology and Bioarchaeology of the Northwestern Plains,* edited by G. W. Gill and R. L. Weathermon, pp. 48–63. University of Utah Press, Salt Lake City.

Davis, Leslie B.

1971 The Lindsay Mammoth Site (24DW501): Paleontology and Paleoecology. Paper presented at the 20th Annual Meeting of the Plains Anthropological Society.

1972 The Prehistoric Use of Obsidian in the Northwestern Plains. Unpublished Ph.D. dissertation, Department of Anthropology, University of Calgary, Alberta.

Davis, Leslie B.

1976 The Dodge site (24RB225): A McKean phase lithic "cache" in the Tongue River Valley. *Archaeology in Montana* 17(1&2):35–51.

1978 The 20th-Century commercial mining of Northern Plains bison kills. In *Bison Procurement and Utilization: A Symposium*, edited by L. B. Davis and M. C. Wilson, pp. 254–286. Plains Anthropologist Memoir 14. Lincoln, Nebraska.

1982 Archaeology and geology of the Schmitt Chert Mine, Missouri Headwaters. *Guidebook for Field Trip, 35th Annual Meeting of the Geological Society of America.* Montana State University, Bozeman.

1983 *From Microcosm to Macrocosm: Advances in Tipi Ring Investigation and Interpretation.* Plains Anthropologist Memoir 19. Lincoln, Nebraska. (editor)

1984 Late Pleistocene to Mid-Holocene adaptations at Indian Creek, west-central Montana. *Current Research in the Pleistocene* 1:9–10.

1988 *Avonlea Yesterday and Today: Archaeology and Prehistory.* Saskatchewan Archaeological Society, Saskatoon. (editor)

Davis, Leslie B., Stephen A. Aaberg, William P. Eckerle, John W. Fisher, and Sally T. Greiser

1989 Montane Paleoindian occupation of the Barton Gulch site, Ruby Valley, southwestern Montana. *Current Research in the Pleistocene* 6:7–9.

Davis, Leslie B., Stephen A. Aaberg, and Sally T. Greiser

1988 Paleoindians in transmontane southwestern Montana: The Barton Gulch occupations, Ruby River Drainage. *Current Research in the Pleistocene* 5:9–11.

Davis, Leslie B., Stephen A. Aaberg, Michael Wilson, and Robert Ottersberg

1982a Floodplain archaeology at the Holmes Terrace site (24FR52), Fergus County, Montana. *Archaeology in Montana* 23(2):1–151.

1982b *Stone Circles in the Montana Rockies: Systematic Recovery and Culture Ecological Inference.* Department of Sociology, Montana State University, Bozeman.

Davis, Leslie B., and John W. Fisher, Jr.

1988 Avonlea predation on wintering Plains pronghorns. In *Avonlea Yesterday and Today: Archaeology and Prehistory*, edited by Leslie B. Davis, pp. 101–118. Saskatchewan Archaeological Society, Saskatoon.

1990 A late prehistoric model for communal utilization of pronghorn antelope in the Northwestern Plains region, North America. In *Hunters of the Recent Past*, edited by L. B. Davis and B. O. K. Reeves, pp. 242–276. Unwin Hyman, London.

Davis, Leslie B., John W. Fisher, Jr., Michael C. Wilson, Stephen A. Chomko, and Richard E. Morlan

2000 Avonlea phase winter fare at the Lost Terrace site, Montana: The vertebrate fauna. In *Pronghorn Past and Present: Archaeology, Ethnography, and Biology*, edited by J. V. Pastor and P. M. Lubinski, pp. 53–69. Plains Anthropologist Memoir 32. Lincoln, Nebraska.

Davis, Leslie B., Thomas S. Foor, and Donald L. Smith.

1997 Cattleguard no. 3: Mitigation excavations at the South Everson Creek chert quarry/workshop site (24BE559), southwestern Montana. *Archaeology in Montana* 38(1):1–66.

Davis, Leslie B., and Sally T. Greiser

1992 Indian Creek Paleoindians: Early occupation of the Elkhorn Mountains southeast flank, west-central Montana. In *Ice Age Hunters of the Rockies*, edited by D. J. Stanford and J. S. Day, pp. 225–284, University Press of Colorado, Niwot.

Davis, Leslie B., and Emmett Stallcop

1965 *The Keaster Site (24BW559): A Stratified Bison Kill Occupation in the Missouri Breaks Area of North-Central Montana.* Montana Archaeological Society Memoir No. 2. Montana State University, Bozeman.

1966 *The Wahkpa Chu'gn Site (24HL101): Late Hunters in the Milk River Valley, Montana.* Montana Archeological Society Memoir No. 3, Billings.

Davis, Leslie B., and Michael Wilson (editors)

1978 *Bison Procurement and Utilization: A Symposium.* Plains Anthropologist Memoir 14. Lincoln, Nebraska.

Davis, Leslie B., and Charles D. Zeier
1978 Multi-phase Late Period bison procurement at the Antonson site, southwestern Montana. In *Bison Procurement and Utilization: A Symposium*, edited by L. B. Davis and Michael Wilson, pp. 222–235. Plains Anthropologist Memoir 14. Lincoln, Nebraska.

Davis, W.E.
1985 The Montgomery Folsom site. *Current Research in the Pleistocene* 2:11–12.

Dawson, Jerry, and Dennis Stanford
1975 The Linger site: A reinvestigation. *Southwestern Lore* 41(4):22–28.

Deaver, Sherri, and Ken Deaver
1986 *An Archaeological Overview of Butte District Prehistory.* Bureau of Land Management Cultural Resource Series No. 2. Bureau of Land Management, Montana State Office, Billings, Montana.

DeBoer, Warren R.
1988 Subterranean storage and the organization of surplus: The view from eastern North America. *Southeastern Archaeology* 7(1):1–20.
2004 Little Bighorn on the Scioto: The Rocky Mountain connection to Ohio Hopewell. *American Antiquity* 69(1):85–107.

Deer, W. A., R. A. Howie, and J. Zussman
1992 *An Introduction to the Rock-Forming Minerals.* Longman Group, Essex, England.

Deevey, E. S.
1947 Life tables for natural populations of animals. *Quarterly Review of Biology* 22:283–314.

Denig, Edwin T.
1930 Indian tribes of the upper Missouri. *Forty-sixth Annual Report of the Bureau of American Ethnology*:375–628. Washington, DC.

Densmore, Frances
1992 *Teton Sioux Music and Culture.* University of Nebraska Press, Lincoln.

Denson, M. E., and N. S. Morrisey
1952 The Madison Group (Mississippian) of the Bighorn and Wind River Basins, Wyoming. *Wyoming Geological Association Guidebook, Seventh Annual Field Conference, Bighorn Basin, Wyoming*, pp. 37–43. Wyoming Geological Society, Casper.

Dibble, H. L., P. G. Chase, S. P. McPherron, and A. Tuffreau
1997 Testing the reality of "living floor" with archaeological data. *American Antiquity* 62(4):629–651.

Dick, Herbert W., and Bert Mountain
1960 The Claypool site: A Cody Complex site in northeastern Colorado. *American Antiquity* 26(2):223–235.

Dillehay, Tom D.
1997 *Monte Verde: A Late Pleistocene Settlement in Chile.* Volume 2. Smithsonian Institution Press, Washington, DC.

Dippie, Brian W.
1982 *The Vanishing American.* University Press of Kansas, Lawrence.

Dobyns, Henry F.
1983 *Their Number Became Thinned: Native American Populations Dynamics in Eastern North America.* University of Tennessee Press, Knoxville.

Dondanville, R. F.
1963 The Fall River Formation, northwestern Black Hills: Lithology and geologic history. *Wyoming Geological Association and Billings Geological Society First Joint Field Conference*, pp. 87–89. Wyoming Geological Society, Casper.

Dorn, Ronald I.
1989 Cation-ratio dating of rock varnish: A geographic assessment. *Progress in Physical Geography* 13:559–596.
1998 Age determination of the Coso rock art. In *Coso Rock Art: A New Perspective*, edited by Elva Youngkin, pp. 67–96. Maturango Press, Ridgecrest, California.

Dorn, Ronald I.
2001 Chronometric techniques: Engravings. In *Handbook of Rock Art Research*, edited by David S. Whitley, pp. 167–189. Altamira Press, Walnut Creek, California.

Dorn, Ronald I., D. B. Bamforth, T. A. Cahill, J. C. Dohrenwend, B. D. Turrin, D. J. Donahue, J. T. Jull, A. Long, M. E. Macko, E. B. Weil, D. S. Whitley, and T. H. Zabel
1986 Cation-ratio and accelerator-radiocarbon dating of rock varnishes on archaeological artifacts and landforms in the Mojave Desert, eastern California. *Science* 231:830–833.

Dorn, Ronald I., William R. McGlone, and Phillip M. Leonard
1990 Age determination of petroglyphs in southeast Colorado. *Southwestern Lore* 56(2):21–36.

Dorn, Ronald J., Margaret Nobbs, and Tom A. Cahill
1988 Cation-ratio dating of rock engravings from the Olary Province of arid south Australia. *Antiquity* 62(237):681–689.

Dorn, Ronald I., and T. M. Oberlander
1982 Rock varnish. *Progress in Physical Geography* 6:317–367.

Dorn, Ronald I., and David S. Whitley
1984 Chronometric and relative age determination of petroglyphs in the western United States. *Annals of the Association of American Geographers* 74(2):308–322.

Dowson, Thomas A.
1989 Dots and dashes: Cracking the Entoptic Code in Bushman rock paintings. *South African Archaeological Society Goodwin Series* 6:84–94.

Dowson, Thomas A., and Anne L. Holliday
1989 Zigzags and eland: An interpretaion of an ideosyncratic combination. *South African Archaeological Bulletin* 44:46–48.

Drever, James I.
1997 *The Geochemistry of Natural Waters: Surface and Groundwater Environments*. Prentice Hall, Upper Saddle River, New Jersey.

Driver, Harold E.
1953 The spatial and temporal distribution of the musical rasp in the New World. *Anthropos* 48:578–592.

Duguid, James O.
1968 The Irvine site: A possible Avonlea site in eastern Wyoming. *The Wyoming Archaeologist* 11(2):24–34.

Duke, Phil, and Michael C. Wilson
1994 Cultures of the mountains and plains: From Selkirk Mountains to the Bitterroot Range. In *Plains Indians, A.D. 500–1500*, edited by K. H. Schlesier, pp. 56–70. University of Oklahoma Press, Norman.

Dunlap, Ian, John Martin, and Robert Tonkinson
1966 *The Desert People*. Film. Australian National Film Board Production, Australian Commonwealth Film Unit, Australian Institute of Aboriginal Studies, Canberra.

Dyck, I., and R. E. Morlan
1995 *The Sjovold Site: A River Crossing Campsite in the Northern Plains*. Mercury Series, Archaeological Survey of Canada Paper No. 151. National Museums of Canada, Ottawa.

Eakin, Daniel H.
1987 *Final Report of Salvage Investigations at the Split Rock Ranch Site (48FR1484)*. Highway Project SCPF-020-2(19), Fremont County, Wyoming. Prepared for the Wyoming Highway Department.
1989 Report of Archaeological Test Excavations at the Pagoda Creek Site 48PA853. Manuscript on file, Office of Wyoming State Archaeologist, University of Wyoming, Laramie, Wyoming.
2005 Evidence for Shoshonean mountain sheep trapping and early Historic occupation in the Absaroka Mountains of northwest Wyoming. *University of Wyoming, National Park Service Research Center 29th Annual Report*, edited by Henry J. Harlow and Maryanne Harlow, pp. 74–86. University of Wyoming, Laramie.

Eakin, Daniel H., Julie E. Francis, and Mary Lou Larson
1997 The Split Rock Ranch site: Early Archaic cultural practices in southcentral Wyoming. In *Changing Perspectives of the Archaic on the Northwestern Plains and Rocky Mountains*, edited by Mary Lou Larson and Julie E. Francis, pp. 395–435. University of South Dakota Press, Vermillion.

Ebert, James Ian
1986 Distributional Archeology: Nonsite Discovery, Recording and Analytical Methods for Application to the Surface Archeological Record. Unpublished Ph.D. dissertation, Department of Anthropology, University of New Mexico, Albuquerque.

Eccles, Cindy
1997 The Shoshone Knife: An Issue of Style and Function. Unpublished Master's thesis, Department of Anthropology, Brigham Young University, Provo, Utah.

Eckles, David G.
1985 Analysis of Rock Art at 48HO4: The Legend Rock Site. Manuscript on file, Office of the Wyoming State Archaeologist, Department of Anthropology, University of Wyoming, Laramie.

Eckles, David G., Jeffrey Lockwood, Rabinder Kumar, Dale Wedel, and Danny N. Walker
1994 An early Historic period horse skeleton from southwestern Wyoming. *The Wyoming Archaeologist* 38(3–4):55–68.

Eckman, Jason C.
2005 Archaeological investigations at the Hogsback site 48UT2516. In *Kern River 2003 Expansion Project, Wyoming: Cultural Resources Mitigation Report*, compiled by Alan C. Reed for Alpine Archaeological Consultants, Inc, pp. 103–216. Report on file at the WYSHPO Cultural Records Office, Laramie.

Eddy, J. A.
1974 Astronomical alignment of the Bighorn Medicine Wheel. *Science* 184:1035–1043.
1977 Mystery of the Medicine Wheels. *National Geographic* 15(1):140–146.

Edgar, Robert, and J. Turnell
1978 *Brand of a Legend*. Stockade, Cody, Wyoming.

Efremov, I.A.
1940 Taphonomy: A new branch of paleontology. *PanAmerican Geologist* 74:81–93.

Egan, Major Howard
1917 *Pioneering the West: 1846 to 1878*, edited by William M. Egan. Salt Lake City.

Eisenbarth, Dennis, and Harry Earl
1989 News from the High Plains chapter. *The Wyoming Archaeologist* 32(1–2):iv–xvii.

Elias, Scott A.
1996 Late Pleistocene and Holocene seasonal temperature reconstructed from fossil beetle assemblages in the Rocky Mountains. *Quaternary Research* 46:311–318.

Eltringham, S. K.
1982 *Elephants*. Blandford Press, Dorset, England.

Emerson, A.
1990 Archaeological Implications of Variability in the Economic Anatomy of *Bison bison*. Unpublished Ph.D. dissertation, Department of Anthropology, Washington State University, Pullman.

Emerson, Thomas E., and Randall E. Hughes
2001 De-mything the Cahokia catlinite trade. *Plains Anthropologist* 46(175):149–161.

Enders, Richard, and Sue Schock
1979 Progress Report on Archaeological Investigations at Rocky Mountain Energy's Copper Mountain Uranium Project. Manuscript on file, Archaeological Services, Western Wyoming College, Rock Springs.

Engel, Celeste G., and Robert P. Sharp
1958 Chemical data on desert varnish. *The Geological Society of America Bulletin* 69(5):457–518.

Enloe, James G.

1993 Ethnoarchaeology of marrow cracking: Implications for the recognition of prehistoric subsistence organization. In *From Bones to Behavior*, edited by J. Hudson, pp. 82–97. Southern Illinois University Press, Carbondale.

Entzminger, D. J.

1980 The Upper Cretaceous stratigraphy in the Big Hole Mountains, Idaho. *Wyoming Geological Association Thirty-first Annual Field Conference Guidebook*:163–172. Wyoming Geological Society, Casper.

Ewers, John C.

1955 *The Horse in Blackfoot Indian Culture*. Bureau of American Ethnology Bulletin No. 159. Washington, DC.

Fall, Patricia L.

1985 Holocene dynamics of the subalpine forest in central Colorado. *American Association of Stratigraphic Paleontologists Contribution Series* 16: 31–46.

Fall, Patricia L., P. Thompson Davis, and Gregory A. Zielinski

1995 Late Quaternary vegetation and climate of the Wind River Range, Wyoming. *Quaternary Research* 43:393–404.

Fawcett, William B., Jr.

1988 Communal Hunts, Human Aggregations, Social Variation, and Climatic Change: Bison Utilization by Prehistoric Inhabitants of the Great Plains. Unpublished Ph.D. dissertation, Department of Anthropology, University of Massachusetts, Amherst.

Fawcett, William B., Jr., and Thomas K. Larson

1984 A remote sensing project at South Pass City State Historic Site, Wyoming. In *South Pass City: Changing Perspectives on a Nineteenth Century Frontier Town*, edited by Marcel Kornfeld and Julie Francis, pp. 39–44. Occasional Papers on Wyoming Archaeology No. 3. Department of Anthropology, University of Wyoming, Laramie.

Fawcett, William B., Jr., and Alan C. Swedlund

1984 Thinning populations and population thinners: The historical demography of Native Americans. *Reviews in Anthropology* 11(4):264–269.

Fedje, Daryl W., James M. White, Michael C. Wilson, D. Erle Nelson, John S. Vogel, and John R. Southon

1995 Vermilion Lakes site: Adaptations and environments in the Canadian Rockies during the latest Pleistocene and early Holocene. *American Antiquity* 60(1):81–108.

Fenn, Forrest

2004 *San Lazaro Pueblo*. One Horse Land and Cattle Company, Santa Fe.

Fenneman, Nevin M.

1946 *Physical divisions of the United States*. U. S. Geological Survey, Washington, DC.

Fenner, Jack N.

2007 Prehistoric Hunting on the Range Where the Antelope Play: Archaeological Pronghorn Bonebed Formation Analysis. Unpublished Ph.D. dissertation, Department of Anthropology, University of Wyoming, Laramie.

Fenner, Jack N., and Danny N. Walker

2008 Mortality date estimation using fetal pronghorn remains. *International Journal of Osteoarchaeology* 18:45–60.

Ferris, Warren A.

1940 *Life in the Rocky Mountains*, edited by P. C. Philips. Old West Publishing Co., Denver.

Feyhl, Kenneth

1980 Tool grooves: A challenge. *Archaeology in Montana* 21(1):1–31.

1997 Steatite: Some sources and aboriginal utilization. *Archaeology in Montana* 38(2):55–83.

Figgins, Jesse D.

1927 The antiquity of man in America. *Natural History* 27(3):229–239.

1933 A further contribution to the antiquity of man in America. *Proceedings of the Colorado Museum of Natural History* 12(2):4–8.

Finley, J. B.
2008 Rockshelter Formation Processes, Late Quaternary Environmental Chance and Hunter-Gatherer Subsistence in the Bighorn Mountains, Wyoming. Unpublished Ph.D. dissertation, Department of Anthropology, Washington State University, Pullman.

Finley, J. B., M. Kornfeld, G. C. Frison, C. C. Finley, and M. T. Bies
2005 Rockshelter archaeology and geology in the Bighorn Mountains, Wyoming. *Plains Anthropologist* 50(195):227–248.

Fisher, J. H.
1963 Tensleep sandstone of the eastern Bighorn Mountains, Wyoming. *Wyoming Geological Association and Billings Geological Society First Joint Field Conference*, pp. 54–60. Wyoming Geological Society, Casper.

Fisher, John W., Jr., and George C. Frison
2000 Site structure at Boar's Tusk site, Wyoming. In *Pronghorn Past and Present: Archaeology, Ethnography, and Biology*, edited by J. V. Pastor and P. M. Lubinski, pp. 89–108. Plains Anthropologist Memoir 32. Lincoln, Nebraska.

Fisher, John W., Jr., and Tom E. Roll
1999 Prehistoric human exploitation of bison in the Great Plains of Montana (USA) during the last 3000 years. In *Le bison: gibier et moyen de subsistance des hommes du Paléolithique aux Paleoindiens des Grandes Plaines*, edited by J.-Ph. Brugal, F. David, J. G. Enloe, and J. Jaubert, pp. 417–436. Actes du Colloque International, Toulouse 1995. Editions APDCA, Antibes.

Fladmark, Knut R.
1996 The prehistory of Charlie Lake Cave. In *Early Human Occupation in British Columbia*, edited by R. L. Carlson and L. D. Bona, pp. 11–20. University of British Columbia Press, Vancouver.

Flayharty, R., and E. A. Morris
1974 T-W Diamond: A stone ring site in northern Colorado. *Plains Anthropologist* 19(65):161–172.

Flenniken, J. Jeffrey
1978 Reevaluation of the Lindenmeier Folsom: A replication experiment in lithic technology. *American Antiquity* 43(3):473–480.

Forbis, Richard G.
1962 *The Old Women's Buffalo Jump, Alberta*. National Museum of Canada Bulletin No. 180:56–123.
1968 Fletcher: A Paleo-Indian site in Alberta. *American Antiquity* 33:1–10.
1977 *Cluny, An Ancient Fortified Village in Alberta*. Occasional Papers No. 4. Department of Archaeology, University of Calgary, Alberta.

Forbis, Richard G., and J. D. Sperry
1952 An Early Man site in Montana. *American Antiquity* 18:127–133.

Forbis, Richard G., William Duncan Strong, and Maurice E. Kirkby
1965 Signal Butte and MacHaffie: Two Stratified Sites on the Northern Great Plains. Manuscript on file, Department of Anthropology, University of Wyoming, Laramie.

Forman, Steven L., Robert Ogelsby, Vera Markgraf, and Thomas Stafford
1995 Paleoclimatic significance of late Quaternary eolian deposition on the Piedmont and High Plains, central United States. *Global and Planetary Change* 11:35–55.

Forman, Steven L., Robert Oglesby, and Robert S. Webb
2001 Temporal and spatial patterns of Holocene dune activity on the Great Plains of North America: Megadroughts and climate links. *Global and Planetary Change* 29:1–29.

Fosha, Michael
2001 The Licking Bison site (39HN570): An Early Archaic bison kill in northwest South Dakota. *Newsletter of the South Dakota Archaeological Society* 31(3&4):1–5.

Fox, John W., Calvin B. Smith, and Kenneth T. Wilkins
1992 *Proboscidians and Paleoindian Interactions*. Baylor University Press, Waco, Texas.

Francis, Julie E.
1979 Chipped Stone Raw Material Sources in the Bighorn Mountains of North Central Wyoming: A Preliminary Statement. Paper presented at the 37th Plains Anthropological Conference, Kansas City, Missouri.

Francis, Julie E.

1983 Procurement and Utilization of Chipped Stone Raw Materials: A Case Study from the Bighorn Mountains and Basin of North-Central Wyoming. Unpublished Ph.D. dissertation, Department of Anthropology, Arizona State University.

1986 Fear and Loathing in Wyoming: Documentation and Evaluation of Lithic Procurement Sites. Paper presented at the 44th Plains Anthropological Conference, Denver, Colorado.

1988 Chipped Stone Raw Materials at the Mill Iron Site, Southeast Montana. Paper presented at the 53rd Annual Meeting of the Society for American Archaeology, Phoenix, Arizona.

1989 Rock art at Legend Rock. In *Legend Rock Petroglyph site 48H04, Wyoming: 1988 Archaeological Investigations*, edited by Danny N. Walker and Julie E. Francis, pp. 151–208. Manuscript on file, Office of Wyoming State Archaeologist, Department of Anthropology, University of Wyoming, Laramie.

1991 An overview of Wyoming rock art. In *Prehistoric Hunters of the High Plains*, 2nd edition, by George C. Frison, pp. 397–430. Academic Press, San Diego.

1994 Cation-ratio dating and chronological variation within Dinwoody tradition rock art in northwestern Wyoming. In *New Light on Old Art: Recent Advances in Hunter- Gatherer Rock Art Research*, edited by David S. Whitley and Lawrence L. Loendorf, pp. 37–50. Monograph No. 26. Institute of Archaeology, University of California, Los Angeles.

2000 Root procurement in the Upper Green River Basin: Archaeological investigations at 48SU1002. In *Intermountain Archaeology*, edited by D. B. Madsen and M. D. Metcalf, pp. 166–175. University of Utah Anthropological Papers No. 122, Salt Late City.

2005 Pictographs, petroglyphs, and paradigms: Rock art in North American archaeology. In *Discovering North American Rock Art*, edited by Lawrence L. Loendorf, Christopher Chippendale, and David S. Whitley, pp. 181–195. University of Arizona Press, Tucson.

2007 The imagery of Medicine Lodge. In *Medicine Lodge Creek: Holocene Archaeology of the Eastern Big Horn Basin, Wyoming*, Vol. 1, edited by George C. Frison and Danny N. Walker, pp. 209–226. Clovis Press, Avondale, Colorado.

Francis, Julie E., A. D. Darlington, William P. Eckerle, and Skylar Scott

1986 *Archaeological Investigations at Middle Fork Reservoir.* Office of Wyoming State Archaeologist, SHPO Cultural Records Office, Department of Anthropology, University of Wyoming, Laramie.

Francis, Julie E., and George C. Frison

1990 Age and Chronology of Rock Art in Northwestern Wyoming and Implications for its Changing Role in Shamanism. Paper presented at the 55th Annual Meeting of the Society for American Archaeology, Las Vegas, Nevada.

Francis, Julie E., and Lawrence L. Loendorf

2002 *Ancient Visions: Petroglyphs and Pictographs of the Wind River and Bighorn Country, Wyoming and Montana.* University of Utah Press, Salt Lake City.

Francis, Julie E., Lawrence L. Loendorf, and Ronald I. Dorn

1993 AMS radiocarbon and cation-ratio dating of rock art in the Bighorn Basin of Wyoming and Montana. *American Antiquity* 58:711–738.

Francis, Julie E., Danny N. Walker, Kyle Baber, and Karin Guernsey

1987 *Archaeological Investigations at 48SU354, Calpet Rockshelter: Fremont Occupation in the Northern Green River Basin, Wyoming.* Office of Wyoming State Archaeologist, Department of Anthropology, University of Wyoming, Laramie.

Fredlund, Dale E.

1976 Fort Union porcellanite and fused glass: Distinctive lithic materials of coal burn origin on the Northern Plains. *Plains Anthropologist* 21(73):207–212.

Fredlund, Glen G.

2009 Phytolith evidence for vegetation and climate change during the Pleistocene/Holocene transition. In *Hell Gap: A Stratified Paleoindian Campsite at the Edge of the Rockies*, edited by M. L. Larson, M. Kornfeld, and G. C. Frison, pp. 90–98. University of Utah Press, Salt Lake City.

Fredlund, Glen G., and Larry L. Tieszen

1997 Calibrating grass phytoliths assemblages in climatic terms: Application to late Pleistocene assemblages from Kansas and Nebraska. *Paleogeography, Paleoclimatology, Paleoecology* 136:199–211.

Fredlund, Lynn B.

1979 *Benson's Butte 24BH1726*. Report of Investigations No. 8. Cultural Resources Division, Montana Tech Alumni Foundation, Butte, Montana.

1981 Southeastern Montana in the Late Prehistoric Period: Human Adaptation and Projectile Point Chronology. Unpublished Ph. D. dissertation, Department of Archaeology, Simon Fraser University, Vancouver, BC.

Freeman, Andrea

2006 Radiocarbon age estimates from the SCAPE project 2000–2005. In *Changing Opportunities and Challenges: Human-Environmental Interaction in the Canadian Prairies Ecozone*, edited by B. A. Nicholson and D. Wiseman, pp. 451–486. Plains Anthropologist Memoir 28. Lincoln, Nebraska.

Freeman, V. L., E. T. Ruppel, and M. R. Klepper

1958 *Geology of Part of the Townsend Valley, Broadwater and Jefferson Counties, Montana*. U. S. Geological Survey Bulletin 1042N. United States Government Printing Office, Washington, DC.

Fremont, General J. C.

1887 *Memoirs of My Life*. Belford, Clark & Company, Chicago and New York.

Fried, Morton H.

1967 *The Evolution of Political Society*. Random House, New York.

Frison, George C.

1962 Wedding of the Waters cave: A stratified site in the Bighorn Basin of northern Wyoming. *Plains Anthropologist* 7(18):246–265.

1965 Spring Creek Cave, Wyoming. *American Antiquity* 31(1):81–94.

1967a Archaeological Evidence of the Crow Indians in Northern Wyoming: A Study of a Late Prehistoric Economy. Unpublished Ph. D. dissertation, Department of Anthropology, University of Michigan, Ann Arbor.

1967b The Piney Creek sites, Wyoming. *University of Wyoming Publications* 33(1):1–92. Laramie.

1968a Daugherty Cave, Wyoming. *Plains Anthropologist* 13(42):253–295.

1968b A functional analysis of certain chipped stone tools. *American Antiquity* 33(2):149–155.

1968c Site 48SH312: An Early Middle Period bison kill in the Powder River Basin of Wyoming. *Plains Anthropologist* 13(39):31–39.

1970a *The Glenrock Buffalo Jump, 48CO304: Late Prehistoric Buffalo Procurement and Butchering*. Plains Anthropologist Memoir 7. Lincoln, Nebraska.

1970b The Kobold Site, 24BH406: A post-Altithermal record of buffalo-jumping for the Northwestern Plains. *Plains Anthropologist* 15(47):1–35.

1971a The buffalo pound in Northwestern Plains prehistory: Site 48CA302, Wyoming. *American Antiquity* 36(1):77–91.

1971b Shoshonean antelope procurement in the upper Green River Basin, Wyoming. *Plains Anthropologist* 16(54):258–284.

1973a Early Period marginal cultural groups in northern Wyoming. *Plains Anthropologist* 18(62):300–312.

1973b *The Wardell Buffalo Trap 48SU301: Communal Procurement in the Upper Green River Basin, Wyoming*. Anthropological Papers of the Museum of Anthropology No. 48. University of Michigan. Ann Arbor.

1974 *The Casper Site: A Hell Gap Bison Kill on the High Plains*. Academic Press, New York.

1976a The chronology of Paleo-Indian and Altithermal Period groups in the Bighorn Basin, Wyoming. In *Cultural Change and Continuity: Essays in Honor of James Bennett Griffin*, edited by Charles E. Cleland, pp. 147–173. Academic Press, New York.

1976b Crow pottery in northern Wyoming. *Plains Anthropologist* 21(71):29–44.

1978 *Prehistoric Hunters of the High Plains*. Academic Press, New York.

1979 Observations on the use of tools: Dulling of working edges on some chipped stone tools in bison butchering. In *Lithic Use-Wear Analysis*, edited by Brian Hayden, pp. 259–268. Academic Press, New York.

1980 A composite, reflexed, mountain sheep horn bow from western Wyoming. *Plains Anthropologist* 25(88):173–176.

Frison, George C.

1981 Linear arrangements of cairns in Wyoming and Montana. In *Megaliths to Medicine Wheels: Boulder Structures in Archaeology: Proceedings of the Eleventh Annual Chacmool Conference*, edited by Michael Wilson, Kathie L. Road, and Kenneth J. Hardy, pp. 133–147. Archaeological Association of the University of Calgary, Alberta.

1982a Sources of steatite and methods of prehistoric procurement and use in Wyoming. *Plains Anthropologist* 27(98):273–286.

1982b Paleoindian winter subsistence strategies on the High Plains. In *Plains Indian Studies: A Collection of Essays in Honor of John C. Ewers and Waldo R. Wedel*, edited by D. H. Ubelaker and H. J. Viola, pp. 193–201. Smithsonian Contributions to Anthropology No. 30. Smithsonian Institution Press, Washington, DC.

1982c The Folsom components. In *The Agate Basin Site*, edited by G. C. Frison and D. J. Stanford, pp. 37–76. Academic Press, New York.

1983a Stone circles, stone-filled fire pits, grinding stones and High Plains archaeology. In *From Microcosm to Macrocosm: Advances in Tipi Ring Investigation and Interpretation*, edited by Leslie B. Davis, pp. 81–92. Plains Anthropologist Memoir 19. Lincoln, Nebraska.

1983b The Lookingbill Site, Wyoming 48FR308. *Tebiwa* 20:1–16.

1983c Comments on native subsistence adaptations in the Great Plains. In *Man and the Changing Environments on the Great Plains*, edited by Warren W. Caldwell, C. Bertrand Schultz, and T. Mylan Stout, pp. 111–113. Transactions of the Nebraska Academy of Science and Affiliated Sciences, Vol. XI, special issue, August 1983. Lincoln, Nebraska.

1984 The Carter/Kerr-McGee Paleoindian site: Cultural resource management and archaeological research. *American Antiquity* 49(2):288–314.

1987 Prehistoric, Plains-Mountain, large-mammal, communal hunting strategies. In *The Evolution of Human Hunting*, edited by Matthew H. Nitecki and Doris V. Nitecki, pp. 177–211. Plenum Press, New York.

1988a Avonlea and contemporaries in Wyoming. In *Avonlea Yesterday and Today: Archaeology and Prehistory*, edited by Leslie B. Davis, pp. 155–170. Saskatchewan Archaeological Society, Saskatoon.

1988b Paleoindian subsistence and settlement during post-Clovis times on the Northwestern Plains, the adjacent mountain ranges, and intermontane basins. In *Indians Before Columbus: Ice-Age Origins*, edited by Ronald C. Carlisle, pp. 83–106. Ethnology Monographs No. 12. Department of Anthropology, University of Pittsburgh, Pittsburgh.

1989 Experimental use of Clovis weaponry and tools on African elephants. *American Antiquity* 54(4):766–784.

1991 *Prehistoric Hunters of the High Plains*. 2nd edition. Academic Press, San Diego.

1996 *The Mill Iron Site*. University of New Mexico Press, Albuquerque. (editor)

2004 *Survival by Hunting*. University of California Press, Berkeley.

2008 Before bioarchaeology: Early day records of human burials on the Northwestern Plains. In *Skeletal Biology and Bioarchaeology of the Northwestern Plains*, edited by G. W. Gill and R. L. Weathermon, pp. 14–21. University of Utah Press, Salt Lake City.

Frison, George C., James M. Adovasio, and Ronald C. Carlisle

1986 Coiled basketry from northern Wyoming. *Plains Anthropologist* 31(112):163–167.

Frison, George C., R. L. Andrews, J. M. Adovasio, R. C. Carlisle, and Robert Edgar

1986 A late Paleoindian animal trapping net from northern Wyoming. *American Antiquity* 51(2):352–361.

Frison, George C., and Bruce Bradley

1980 *Folsom Tools and Technology of the Hanson Site, Wyoming*. University of New Mexico Press, Albuquerque.

1981 Fluting Folsom points: Archaeological evidence. *Lithic Technology* 10(1):13–16.

1982 Fluting of Folsom points. In *The Agate Basin Site: A Record of the Paleoindian Occupation of the Northwestern High Plains*, edited by George C. Frison and Dennis Stanford, pp. 209–212. Academic Press, New York.

1999 *The Fenn Cache, Clovis Weapons and Tools*. One Horse Land and Cattle Company, Santa Fe, New Mexico.

Frison, George C., and Carolyn Craig

1982 Bone, antler, and ivory artifacts and manufacture technology. In *The Agate Basin Site: A Record of the Paleoindian Occupation of the Northwestern High Plains*, edited by G. Frison and D. Stanford, pp. 161–173. Academic Press, New York.

Frison, George C., and Donald C. Grey

1980 Pryor Stemmed, a specialized Paleo-Indian ecological adaptation. *Plains Anthropologist* 25(87):27–46.

Frison, George C., and Marion Huseas

1968 Leigh Cave, Wyoming, Site 48WA304. *The Wyoming Archaeologist* 11(3):20–33.

Frison, George C., and Marcel Kornfeld

2008 *Mammoths in Wyoming*. Special Paper No. 1. George C. Frison Institute of Archaeology and Anthropology, University of Wyoming, Laramie.

Frison, George C., and Charles A. Reher

1970 Age determination of buffalo by teeth eruption and wear. In *The Glenrock Buffalo Jump, 48CO304*, edited by George C. Frison, pp. 46–50. Plains Anthropologist Memoir 7. Lincoln, Nebraska.

Frison, George C., Charles A. Reher, and Danny N. Walker

1990 Prehistoric mountain sheep hunting in the central Rocky Mountains of North America. In *Hunters of the Recent Past*, edited by L. B. Davis and B. O. K. Reeves, pp. 208–240. Unwin-Hyman, London.

Frison, George C., and Dennis J. Stanford (editors)

1982 *The Agate Basin Site: A Record of the Paleoindian Occupation of the Northwestern High Plains*. Academic Press, New York.

Frison, George C., and Lawrence C. Todd

1986 *The Colby Mammoth Site: Taphonomy and Archaeology of a Clovis Kill in Northern Wyoming*. University of New Mexico Press, Albuquerque.

1987 *The Horner Site: The Type Site of the Cody Cultural Complex*. Academic Press, Orlando. (editors)

Frison, George C., and Zola Van Norman

1985 The Wind River Canyon burial and cache. *Archaeology in Montana* 26(2):43–52.

1993 Carved steatite and sandstone sucking tubes: Pipes for smoking or shaman's paraphernalia? *Plains Anthropologist* 38(143):163–176.

Frison, George C., and Danny N. Walker (editors)

1984 The Dead Indian Creek site: An Archaic occupation in the Absaroka Mountains of northwest Wyoming. *The Wyoming Archaeologist* 27(1–2):11–122.

2007 *Medicine Lodge Creek Site*. Clovis Press, Avondale, Colorado.

Frison, George C., Danny N. Walker, S. David Webb, and George M. Zeimens

1978 Paleo-Indian procurement of *Camelops* on the Northwestern Plains. *Quaternary Research* 10(3):385–400.

Frison, George C., and Michael Wilson

1975 An introduction to Bighorn Basin archaeology. *Wyoming Geological Association, Twenty-seventh Annual Field Conference Guidebook*:19–35. Wyoming Geological Society, Casper.

Frison, George C., Michael Wilson, and Danny N. Walker

1978 *The Big Goose Creek Site: Bison Procurement and Faunal Analysis*. Occasional Papers on Wyoming Archaeology No. 1. Office of Wyoming State Archaeologist, Laramie.

Frison, George C., Michael Wilson, and Diane J. Wilson

1976 Fossil bison and artifacts from an Early Altithermal Period arroyo trap in Wyoming. *American Antiquity* 41(1):28–57.

Frison, George C., Gary A. Wright, James B. Griffin, and Adon A. Gordus

1968 Neutron activation analysis of obsidian: An example of its relevance to Northwestern Plains archaeology. *Plains Anthropologist* 13(41):209–217.

Frison, George C., and George M. Zeimens

1980 Bone projectile points: An addition to the Folsom Cultural Complex. *American Antiquity* 45(2):231–237.

Fry, Gary R.
1971 Preliminary report on the Foss/Thomas site. *The Wyoming Archaeologist* 14(1):15–22.

Fulgham, Tommy, and Dennis J. Stanford
1982 The Frasca site: A preliminary report. *Southwestern Lore* 48(1):1–9.

Furgeson, Thomas A., and Anne K. Armstrong
2008 The Korell-Bordeaux site: A rare Native American cemetery in frontier Wyoming. In *Skeletal Biology and Bioarchaeology of the Northwestern Plains*, edited by G. W. Gill and R. L. Weathermon, pp. 64–76. University of Utah Press, Salt Lake City.

Galloway, Eugene
1962 The Leath burial—a preliminary report. *The Wyoming Archaeologist* 5(2):2–9.
1968 The Billy Creek burials. *The Wyoming Archaeologist* 11(1):16–19.

Galloway, Eugene, and George A. Agogino
1961 The Johnson site: A Folsom campsite. *Plains Anthropologist* 6(13):205–208.

Galvan, Mary Elizabeth
2007 Vegetative ecology. In *Medicine Lodge Creek Site*, edited by G. C. Frison and D. N. Walker, pp. 155–175. Clovis Press, Avondale, Colorado.

Ganopolski, Audrey, Claudia Kubatzki, Martin Claussen, Victor Brovkin, and Vladamir Petoukov
1998 The influence of vegetation-atmosphere ocean interaction on climate during the Mid-Holocene. *Science* 280:1916–1919.

Gant, Robert, and Wesley Hurt
1965 The Sturgis archaeological project: An archaeological survey of the northern Black Hills. *South Dakota Museum News* 26(7–8):1–51.

Gardner, A. Dudley, Russel L. Tanner, and Douglas Heffington
1983 Final Recommendations for the Cross Mountain Quarry Site. Manuscript on file, Archaeological Services, Western Wyoming College, Rock Springs.

Garnett, Rodney A., Marcel Kornfeld, and Mary Lou Larson
2006 Rasping the Rockies: A Musical Instrument from the Bugas-Holding Site. Paper presented at the 61st Plains Anthropological Conference, Topeka.

Gebhard, David
1951 The petroglyphs of Wyoming: A preliminary paper. *El Palacio* 58:67–81.
1966 The shield motif of plains rock art. *American Antiquity* 31:721–732.
1969 *The Rock Art of Dinwoody, Wyoming*. The Art Galleries, University of California, Santa Barbara.

Gebhard, David, Fred Heaton, and Jonathan Laitome
1987a *The Rock Drawings of Whoopup Canyon, Wyoming*. SHPO Cultural Records Office, Department of Anthropology, University of Wyoming, Laramie.
1987b *The Rock Drawings of Cedar Canyon, Wyoming*. Stanley Associates, Lafayette, California. Submitted to the Bureau of Land Management, Wyoming State Office, Contract No. YA-512-CT9-283. Copies available, SHPO Cultural Records Office, Department of Anthropology, University of Wyoming, Laramie.

Gerhardt, Kim (compiler)
2001 Lithic Source Materials Classification Standards. Notebook evolved from the Lithics Workshop, BLM Anasazi Heritage Center, Dolores, Colorado.

Gilbert, Randi, and George W. Gill
1990 A metric technique for identifying American Indian femora. In *Skeletal Attribution of Race*, edited by George W. Gill and Stanley Rhine, pp. 97–99. Anthropology Papers No. 4. Maxwell Museum of Anthropology, Albuquerque.

Giles, Eugene, and O. Elliot
1962 Race identification from cranial measurements. *Journal of Forensic Sciences* 7:147–157.

Gill, George W.
1974 Human skeletons from Wyoming and their bearing on the concept of morphological dating. In *Applied Geology and Archaeology: The Holocene History of Wyoming*, edited by Michael Wilson, pp. 100–107. Geological Survey of Wyoming Report of Investigations No. 10. Laramie.

Gill, George W.

1976 Two mummies from the Pitchfork Rockshelter in northwestern Wyoming. *Plains Anthropologist* 21:301–310.

1981 Human skeletal populations of the Northwestern Plains: A preliminary analysis. In *Progress in Skeletal Biology of Plains Populations*, edited by Richard L. Jantz and Douglas H. Ubelaker, pp. 57–70. Plains Anthropologist Memoir 17. Lincoln, Nebraska.

1983 Additional comment and illustration relating to the Iron Jaw skeleton. *Plains Anthropologist* 28:335–336.

1984 The partial skeleton of a child from Dead Indian Creek. In *The Dead Indian Creek Site: An Archaic Occupation in the Absaroka Mountains of Northeastern Wyoming*, edited by G. C. Frison and D. N. Walker. *The Wyoming Archaeologist* 27(1–2):97.

1988 Osteological analysis of the human skeleton GLM 1 from Bairoil, Wyoming. In *A Prehistoric Human Burial from Bairoil Locality P-139 (48SW7101), Amoco LSU Reservoir 2, Sweetwater County, Wyoming*. Report WY-2535–27. John and Mavis Greer Archaeological Consultants, Casper, Wyoming.

1991 Human skeletal remains on the Northwestern Plains. In *Prehistoric Hunters of the High Plains*, 2nd edition, by George C. Frison, pp. 431–447. Academic Press, San Diego.

2001a Basic skeletal morphology of Easter Island and East Polynesia, with Paleoindian parallels and contrasts. In *Pacific 2000: Proceedings of the Fifth International Conference on Easter Island and the Pacific*, edited by C. M. Stevenson, Georgia Lee, and F. J. Morin, pp. 447–456. Easter Island Foundation, Los Osos, California.

2001b Racial variation in the proximal and distal femur: Heritability and forensic utility. *Journal of Forensic Sciences* 46(4):791–799.

2004 J. David Love/Stud Horse Butte Site: A Report on the Human Skeletal Remains. Report submitted to Current Anthropological Research, Inc., Rock Springs. Report on file, Human Osteology Laboratory, University of Wyoming, Laramie.

2005 Appearance of the "Mongoloid skeletal trait complex" in the Northwestern Great Plains: Migration, selection, or both? In *Paleoamerican Origins: Beyond Clovis*, edited by Robson Bonnichsen, B. T. Lepper, Dennis Stanford, and M. R. Waters, pp. 257–266. Texas A&M University Press, College Station.

2008a Introduction: An overview of the region. In *Skeletal Biology and Bioarchaeology of the Northwestern Plains*, edited by G. W. Gill and R. L. Weathermon, pp. 1–13. University of Utah Press, Salt Lake City.

2008b Northwestern Plains Archaic skeletons with Paleoamerican characteristics. In *Skeletal Biology and Bioarchaeology of the Northwestern Plains*, edited by G. W. Gill and R. L. Weathermon, pp. 241–262. University of Utah Press, Salt Lake City.

Gill, George W., and Gerald R. Clark

1983 A Late Plains Archaic burial from Iron Jaw Creek, southeastern Montana. *Plains Anthropologist* 28:191–198.

Gill, George W., and Cresta V. Deeds

2008 Temporal changes in nasal sill development within the Northwestern Plains Region. In *Skeletal Biology and Bioarchaeology of the Northwestern Plains*, edited by G. W. Gill and R. L. Weathermon, pp. 263–270. University of Utah Press, Salt Lake City.

Gill, George W., Susan S. Hughes, Suzanne M. Bennett, and B. Miles Gilbert

1988 Racial identification from the midfacial skeleton with special reference to American Indians and whites. *Journal of Forensic Sciences* 33(1):92–99.

Gill, George W., and Carlos J. Jimenez

2004 Paleoamerican skeletal features surviving into the Late Plains Archaic. In *New Perspectives on the First Americans*, edited by B. T. Lepper and R. Bonnichsen, pp. 137–141. Texas A & M University Press, College Station.

Gill, George W., and Rhoda Owen Lewis

1977 A Plains Woodland burial from the Badlands of western Nebraska. *Plains Anthropologist* 22:67–73.

Gill, George W., and Douglas W. Owsley

1985 Electron microscopy of parasite remains on the Pitchfork mummy and possible social implications. *Plains Anthropologist* 30:45–50.

Gill, George W., and Stanley Rhine (editors)
1990 *Skeletal Attribution of Race: Methods for Forensic Anthropology*. Maxwell Museum of Anthropology Anthropological Papers No. 4. University of New Mexico, Albuquerque.

Gill, George W., and Rick L. Weathermon (editors)
2008 *Skeletal Biology and Bioarchaeology of the Northwestern Plains*. University of Utah Press, Salt Lake City.

Gillam, Christi
1989 Human skeletal remains from the Shute Creek site, southwestern Wyoming. *The Wyoming Archaeologist* 32(3–4):54–59.

Gillespie, Jason D.
2007 Enculturating an unknown world: Caches and Clovis landscape archaeology. *Canadian Journal of Archaeology* 31:171–189.

Gilmore, M. R.
1924 Old Assiniboine buffalo-drive in North Dakota. *Indian Notes* 1:204–211.

Glenn, Elizabeth J.
1974 *Physical Affiliations of the Oneota People*. Office of State Archaeologist Report No. 7. Iowa City.

Goldschmidt, V. M.
1958 *Geochemistry*. Oxford University Press, London.

Gooding, John D.
1981 *The Archaeology of Vail Pass Camp*. Highway Salvage Report No. 35. Colorado Department of Highways, Boulder.

Gorman, D. R.
1963 Stratigraphic-sedimentational aspects of the Amsden Formation, Bighorn Mountains, Wyoming. *Wyoming Geological Association and Billings Geological Society, First Joint Field Conference*, pp. 67–70. Wyoming Geological Society, Casper.

Graham, Russell W., and Ernest L. Lundelius, Jr. (and the Faunmap Working Group)
1994 *Faunmap*. Scientific Papers Vol. 25, No. 1. Illinois State Museum, Springfield, Illinois.

Grande, Lance
1984 *Paleontology of the Green River Formation, with a Review of the Fish Fauna*. Geological Survey of Wyoming Bulletin No. 63. Wyoming Geological Survey, Laramie.

Grant, Campbell
1967 *Rock Art of the American Indian*. Promontory Press, New York.

Grant, Marcus
1981 *Aboriginal Settlement and Land Use Patterns in the Bighorn Mountains, Wyoming*, Vol. 1. Western Cultural Resource Management, Inc., Boulder, Colorado.

Grasby, Stephen E., Eugene M. Gryba, and Ruth K. Bezys
2002 A bedrock source for Swan River chert. *Plains Anthropologist* 47(182):275–281.

Gray, Stephen T., Julio L. Betancourt, Christopher L. Fastie, and Stephen L. Jackson
2003 Patterns and sources of multidecadal oscillations in drought-sensitive tree-ring records from the central and southern Rocky Mountains. *Geophysical Research Letters,* 30(6):1316.

Gray, Stephen T., Christopher H. Fastie, Stephen L. Jackson, and Julio L. Betancourt
2004 Tree-ring based reconstruction of precipitation in the Bighorn Basin, Wyoming, since 1260 A.D. *Journal of Climate* 17:3855–3865.

Gray, Stephen T., Stephen T. Jackson, and Julio Betancourt
2004 Tree-ring based reconstruction of interannual to decadal scale precipitation variability for northeastern Utah since 1226 A.D. *Journal of the American Water Resources Association* 40:947–960.

Great Plains Cooperative Ecosystem Studies Unit
2009 Little Missouri Antelope Trap. Electronic document, http://snr.unl.edu/gpcesu/Antelope_trap.htm, accessed October 10, 2009.

Green, D'Arcy C.

2005 *A Re-evaluation of the Oxbow Dam Site (DhMn-1): Middle Holocene Cultural Continuity on the Northern Plains*. Occasional Papers of the Archaeological Society of Alberta No. 5.

Green, F. E.

1963 The Clovis blades: An important addition to the Llano complex. *American Antiquity* 29: 145–165.

Green, F. E., and J. H. Kelley

1960 Comments on Alibates flint. *American Antiquity* 25:413–414.

Greene, Ann M.

1967 The Betty Greene Site: A Late Paleo-Indian Site in Eastern Wyoming. Unpublished Master's thesis, Department of Anthropology, University of Pennsylvania, Philadelphia.

1968 Age and Archaeological Association of Oblique Flaked Projectile Points at the Betty Greene Site, Eastern Wyoming. *Abstracts of Papers, 33rd Annual Meeting of the Society for American Archaeology*. Santa Fe, New Mexico.

Greer, John W.

1978 Worthan shelter: An Avonlea site in the Bighorn River canyon, Wyoming. *Archaeology in Montana* 19(3):1–104.

Greer, Mavis, and John W. Greer

2001a Armored Horses in Natrona County Rock Art. Paper presented at the Annual Meeting of the Wyoming Archaeological Society, Laramie.

2001b Armored Horses in Central Wyoming Rock Art. Paper presented at the 27th Annual Conference of the American Rock Art Research Association, Pendleton, Oregon.

2002a Cultural Properties Form, 48NA991. Manuscript on file at the Wyoming Cultural Records Office, State Historic Preservation Office, Laramie.

2002b Armored Horses in Northwestern Plains Rock Art. Paper presented at the 67th Annual Meeting of the Society for American Archaeology, Denver, Colorado.

2003 A test for shamanic trance in central Montana rock art. *Plains Anthropologist* 48(186): 105–120.

2007 Armored Horses in the Musselshell Rock Art of Central Montana. Paper presented at the 65th Annual Plains Anthropological Conference, Rapid City, South Dakota.

Greiser, Sally T.

1994 Late Prehistoric cultures on the Montana Plains. In *Plains Indians, A.D. 500–1500*, edited by K. H. Schlesier, pp. 34–55. University of Oklahoma Press, Norman.

Greiser, Sally T., T. Weber Greiser, and Susan M. Vetter

1985 Middle Prehistoric period adaptations and paleoenvironment in the Northwestern Plains: The Sun River site. *American Antiquity* 50(4):849–877.

Grey, Donald C.

1962a The Bentzen-Kaufmann Cave site 48SH301. *Plains Anthropologist* 7(18):237–245.

1962b Radiocarbon date list, Sheridan College, Sheridan, Wyoming. Manuscript on file at the Department of Anthropology, University of Wyoming, Laramie.

1963a Bighorn Medicine Wheel, 48BH302. *Plains Anthropologist* 8(19):27–41.

1963b The Turk Burial site, 48WA301, Washakie County, Wyoming, *Plains Anthropologist* 8(20):98–102.

2004 Site 48JO303. *The Wyoming Archaeologist* 48(1):18–25.

Griffin, James B.

1965 Prehistoric pottery from southeastern Alberta. In *An Introduction to the Archaeology of Alberta, Canada*, edited by H. M. Wormington and Richard Forbis, pp. 209–248. Denver Museum of Natural History Proceedings No. 11. Denver, Colorado.

Grinnell, George B.

1923 *The Cheyenne Indians, Their History and Ways of Life*, Volume 1. Yale University Press, New Haven.

1961 *Pawnee Hero Stories and Folk Tales*. Reprint of C. Scribner's Sons, New York, 1893, 1909, 1912, 1920, 1925, 1929. University of Nebraska Press, Lincoln.

Grinnell, George B.

1972 *The Cheyenne Indians,* Vol. 1. Reprint of the 1923 edition. University of Nebraska Press, Lincoln.

Grund, Brigid

2009 Understanding the Great Plains Paleoindian Projectile Point Chronology: Radiocarbon Dating and Potential Coevality of Point Types. Senior Honor's thesis, University of Colorado, Boulder. Manuscript on file, Department of Anthropology, University of Wyoming.

Gryba, Eugene M.

1975 The Stampede Site (DjOn-26): Deeply Stratified, Multi-component Site in the Cypress Hills Provincial Park, Alberta. Manuscript on file, Alberta Parks Planning Division, Parks Branch, Alberta Department of Parks, Recreation, and Wildlife, Edmonton, Alberta.

1983 *Sibbald Creek: 11,000 Years of Human Use of the Alberta Foothills.* Archaeological Survey of Alberta Occasional Paper No. 22. Alberta Culture, Edmonton, Alberta.

1988 A stone age pressure method of Folsom fluting. *Plains Anthropologist* 33(119):53–66.

2002 Evidence of the fluted point tradition in western Canada. In *Folsom Technology and Lifeways,* edited by J. E. Clark and M. B. Collins. *Lithic Technology,* Special Publication No. 4:113–134. University of Tulsa, Oklahoma.

Guilday, John L., H. W. Hamilton, and E. K. Adam

1967 Animal remains from Horned Owl Cave, Albany County, Wyoming. *University of Wyoming Contributions to Geology* 6:97–99.

Gundersen, James N.

1991 *The Mineralogical Characterization of Catlinite from its Sole Provenance, Pipestone National Monument, Minnesota.* Research/Resource Management Report MWR 17. National Park Service, Midwest Archaeological Center, Lincoln, Nebraska.

Hack, John T.

1943 Antiquity of the Finley site. *American Antiquity* 8(3):235–241.

Haines, Francis

1938 The northward spread of horses among the Plains Indians. *American Anthropologist* 40(3):429–437.

Hannus, L. Adrien

1990 Mammoth hunting in the New World. In *Hunters of the Recent Past*, edited by L. B. Davis and B. O. K. Reeves, pp. 47–67. Unwin-Hyman, London.

1994 Cultures of the heartland: Beyond the Black Hills. In *Plains Indians, A.D. 500–1500*, edited by K.H. Schlesier, pp. 176–198. University of Oklahoma Press, Norman.

Hansen, Wallace R.

1985 Drainage development of the Green River Basin in southwestern Wyoming and its bearing on fish biogeography, neotectonics, and paleoclimates. *The Mountain Geologist* 22(4):192–204.

Harrell, Lynn L.

1987 *The Buffalo Hump Site.* Cultural Resource Management Report No. 18. Archaeological Services of Western Wyoming College, Rock Springs.

Harrell, Lynn L., and Scott T. McKern

1986 *The Maxon Ranch Site: Archaic and Late Prehistoric Habitation in Southwest Wyoming.* Cultural Resource Management Report No. 18. Archaeological Services of Western Wyoming College, Rock Springs.

Harris, A. H., and P. Mundel

1974 Size reduction in bighorn sheep (*Ovis canadensis*) at the close of the Pleistocene. *Journal of Mammology* 55:678–680.

Harrison, Cheryl, and Steven D. Creasman

1989 *Archaeological Investigations of Three Sites along the Eden Valley Landfill Access Road, Sweetwater County, Wyoming.* Cultural Resource Management Report No. 46. Archaeological Services of Western Wyoming College, Rock Springs.

Haspel, Howard L., and George C. Frison
1987 The Finley site bison bone, In *The Horner Site: The Type Site of the Cody Cultural Complex*, edited by George C. Frison and Lawrence C. Todd, pp. 475–491. Academic Press, Orlando.

Haspel, Howard L., and Dale L. Wedel
1983 A Middle Plains Archaic child burial from the McKean site in northeastern Wyoming. In *McKean/Middle Plains Archaic: Current Research*, edited by Marcel Kornfeld and Lawrence C. Todd, pp. 105–108. Occasional Papers on Wyoming Archaeology No. 4. Department of Anthropology, University of Wyoming, Laramie.

Haury, Emil W., E. B. Sayles, and William W. Wasley
1959 The Lehner mammoth site, southeastern Arizona. *American Antiquity* 25(1):2–30.

Hayden, Brian (editor)
1979 *Lithic Use-Wear Analysis*. Academic Press, New York.

Haynes, C. Vance, Jr.
1967 Carbon-14 dates and early man in the New World. In *Pleistocene Extinctions: The Search for a Cause*, edited by P. E. Martin and H. E. Wright, Jr., pp. 267–286. Yale University Press, New Haven.
1968 Geochronology of late Quaternary alluvium. In *Means of Correlation of Quaternary Successions*, edited by R. B. Morrison and H. E. Wright, Jr., pp. 591–631. University of Utah Press, Salt Lake City.
1969 The earliest Americans. *Science* 166:709–715.
1970 Geochronology of man-mammoth sites and their bearing on the origin of the Llano complex. In *Pleistocene and Recent Environments of the Central Great Plains*, edited by Wakefield Dort, Jr., and J. Knox Jones, Jr., pp. 75–92. University of Kansas Special Publication No. 3. University of Kansas Press, Lawrence.
1992 Contributions of radiocarbon dating to the geochronology of the peopling of the New World. In *Radiocarbon after Four Decades*, edited by R. E. Taylor, A. Long, and R. Kra, pp. 355–374. Springer-Verlag, New York.
1993 Clovis-Folsom geochronology and climatic change. In *From Kostenki to Clovis*, edited by O. Soffer and N. D. Praslov, pp. 219–236. Plenum Press, New York.
2008 Younger Dryas "black mats" and the Rancholabrean termination in North America. *Proceedings of the National Academy of Science* 105:6520–6525.
2009 Geochronology. In *Hell Gap: A Stratified Paleoindian Campsite at the Edge of the Rockies*, edited by M. L. Larson, M. Kornfeld, and G. C. Frison, pp. 39–52. University of Utah Press, Salt Lake City.

Haynes, C. Vance, Jr., Paul E. Damon, and Donald Grey
1966 Arizona radiocarbon dates VI. *Radiocarbon* 8:1–21.

Haynes, C. Vance, Jr., Donald Grey, Paul Damon, and Richard Bennett
1967 Arizona radiocarbon dates VII. *Radiocarbon* 9:1–14.

Haynes, C. Vance, Jr., and Bruce B. Huckell (editors)
2007 *Murray Spring: A Clovis Site with Multiple Activity Areas in the San Pedro Valley, Arizona*. University of Arizona Press, Tucson.

Haynes, C. Vance, Jr., M. McFaul, R. H. Brunswig, and K. D. Hopkins
1998 Kersey-Kuner Terrace investigations at the Dent and Bernhardt sites, Colorado. *Geoarchaeology* 13(2):201–218.

Haynes, G.
1980 Evidence of carnivore gnawing on Pleistocene and recent mammalian bones. *Paleobiology* 6:341–351.

Heffington, Douglas
1985 The Altithermal side-notched knife: A Northwest Plains and eastern Great Basin horizon style. *Journal of Intermountain Archaeology* 4:35–46. Boulder, Colorado.

Heiner, Price B., Jack N. Fenner, James C. Miller, Judson B. Finley, Paul Santoro, and Marcel Kornfeld
2007 *Preliminary Report of 2006 and 2007 Field Seasons in the Bighorns: Black Mountain Archeological District and White Creek Canyon*. Technical Report No. 45. George C. Frison Institute of Archaeology and Anthropology, University of Wyoming, Laramie.

Heizer, Robert F., and M. A. Baumhoff
1958 Great Basin petroglyphs and prehistoric game trails. *Science* 129:904–905.

Henbest, L. G.
1958 Significance of karst terrane and residuum in upper Mississippian and lower Pennsylvanian rocks, Rocky Mountain region. *Wyoming Geological Association, Thirteenth Annual Field Conference Guidebook*:36–38. Wyoming Geological Society, Casper.

Hendry, Mary H.
1983a *Indian Rock Art in Wyoming*. Augstums Printing Service, Inc., Lincoln, Nebraska.
1983b *Rock Art Depictions, 48HO4*. Office of Wyoming State Archaeologist, Department of Anthropology, University of Wyoming, Laramie, Wyoming.

Henning, Dale R.
1998 The Oneota tradition. In *Archaeology on the Great Plains*, edited by W. Raymond Wood, pp. 345–414. University of Kansas Press, Lawrence.

Hibbard, C. W., and S. A. Wright
1956 A new Pleistocene bighorn sheep from Arizona. *Journal of Mammology* 37:105–107.

Hickey, Leo J.
1972 Stratigraphic summary of the Golden Valley Formation (Paleocene-Eocene) in western North Dakota. In *Depositional Environments of the Lignite Bearing Strata of Western North Dakota*, edited by F. T. C. Ting, pp. 105–122. North Dakota Geological Survey Miscellaneous Series No. 50. Bismark, North Dakota.

Hill, Christopher L., and Leslie B. Davis
2005 *The Merrell Locality*. Bureau of Land Management Cultural Resources Series No. 4. Montana State Office, Billings.

Hill, Matthew E., Jr.
2007 A movable feast: Variation in faunal resource use among central and western North American Paleoindian sites. *American Antiquity* 72(3):417–438.

Hill, Matthew G.
2005 Late Paleoindian (Allen/Frederick complex) subsistence activities at the Clary Ranch site, Ash Hollow, Garden County, Nebraska. *Plains Anthropologist* 50(195):249–263.
2008 *Paleoindian Subsistence Dynamics on the Northwestern Great Plains*. British Archaeological Reports International Series 1756. Oxford, England.

Hill, Matthew G., Marcel Kornfeld, and George C. Frison
1999 Inferring season of kill for a Cody complex bison bonebed in the Middle Park, Colorado. *Current Research in the Pleistocene* 16:30–32.

Hilman, Ross G., Keith H. Dueholm, and Rhoda O. Lewis
1987 *Results of Archaeological Investigations at Sites 48SW1961 and 48SW6333 along the Champlin 534-B and 534-C Pipeline*. Prepared for Northwest Central Pipeline Corporation by Larson-Tibesar Associates. Report on file at the Wyoming SHPO Cultural Records Office, Laramie.

Hoard, Robert J., Steven R. Holen, Michael Elam, Michael Glascock, and Hector Neff
1990 Neutron Activation Analysis of Chadron Formation Cryptocrystalline Silicates from Flattop Butte, Northeastern Colorado, Nelson Butte/West Horse Creek, Southwestern South Dakota, and the Eckles Clovis Site in North Central Kansas. Paper presented at the 48th Plains Anthropological Conference, Oklahoma City.

Hobbs, A., and M. T. Garcia
1981 *An Archaeological Report on the Monitoring of the CSG Ringer 20-inch Lateral Pipeline, Sweetwater County and Carbon Counties, Wyoming*. Report on file at the SHPO Cultural Records Office, Laramie, Wyoming.

Hoffman, J. Jacob
1953 *Comments on the Use and Distribution of Tipi Rings in Montana, North Dakota, South Dakota, and Wyoming*. Anthropology and Sociology Papers No. 14. Montana State University, Bozeman.

Hofman, Jack L.
1986 Vertical movement of artifacts in alluvial and stratified deposits. *Current Anthropology* 27:163–171.

Hofman, Jack L.

1992 Putting the pieces together: An introduction to refitting. In *Piecing Together the Past: Applications of Refitting Studies in Archaeology*, edited by Jack L. Hofman and James G. Enloe, pp. 1–20. British Archaeological Reports International Series 578. Oxford, England.

1994 Paleoindian aggregations on the Great Plains. *Journal of Anthropological Archaeology* 13:341–370.

Hofman, Jack L., and Jeannette M. Blackmar

1997 The Paleoindian Laird bison bone bed in northwestern Kansas. *The Kansas Anthropologist* 18(2):45–57.

Hofman, Jack L., Matthew E. Hill, Jr., William C. Johnson, and Dean T. Sather

1995 Norton: An Early-Holocene bison bone bed in Western Kansas. *Current Research in the Pleistocene* 12:19–21.

Holder, Preston, and Joyce Wike

1949 The Frontier Culture Complex: A preliminary report on a hunter's camp in southwestern Nebraska. *American Antiquity* 14(4):260–265.

Holen, S. R.

1995 Evidence of the first humans in Nebraska. *Museum Notes* 90. University of Nebraska State Museum, Lincoln.

2008 La Sena, Nebraska and Lovewell, Kansas Sites, 18,000 C14 years BP. Paper presented at Paleoamerican Origins Workshop, Texas Archaeological Research Laboratory, Austin, Texas.

Holen, Steven R., and David W. May

2002 The La Sena and Shaffert mammoth sites: History of investigations 1987–1998. In *Medicine Creek*, edited by Donna C. Roper, pp. 20–36. The University of Alabama Press, Tuscalusa.

Holliday, Vance (editor)

1988 *Guidebook to the Archaeological Geology of the Colorado Piedmont and High Plains of Southeastern Wyoming*. Geological Society of America. Department of Geography, University of Wisconsin, Madison.

Holliday, Vance T., Eileen Johnson, and Thomas W. Stafford

1999 AMS radiocarbon dating and the type Plainview and Firstview (Paleoindian) assemblages: The agony and the ecstasy. *American Antiquity* 64:444–454.

Holmer, Richard N.

1986 Shoshone-Bannock culture history. *Swanson/Crabtree Anthropological Research Laboratory, Reports of Investigation* (85-16:111–122). Pocatello.

Holmes, W. H.

1919 *Handbook of Aboriginal American Antiquities*. Bureau of American Ethnology Bulletin No. 60. Washington, DC.

Honess, F., and Nedward Frost

1942 *A Wyoming Bighorn Sheep Study*. Bulletin No. 1. Wyoming Game and Fish Department, Cheyenne, Wyoming.

Hoppe, Kathryn A.

2004 Late Pleistocene mammoth herd structure, migration patterns, and Clovis hunting strategies inferred from isotopic analysis of multiple death assemblages. *Paleobiology* 30:129–145.

Howard, Calvin D.

1990 The Clovis point: Characteristics and type description. *Plains Anthropologist* 35(129):255–262.

1999 River patina on flint artifacts. *Plains Anthropologist* 44(169):293–295.

2002 The gloss patination of flint artifacts. *Plains Anthropologist* 47(182):283–287.

Howard, Edgar B.

1943 The Finley site: Discovery of Yuma points *in situ* near Eden, Wyoming. *American Antiquity* 8(3):224–234.

Howard, Edgar B., Linton Satterthwaite, Jr., and Charles Bache

1941 Preliminary report on a buried Yuma site in Wyoming. *American Antiquity* 7(1):70–74.

Howells, W. W.

1938 Crania from Wyoming resembling "Minnesota Man." *American Antiquity* 3(4):318–326.

Hower, J.

1981 Shale diagenesis. In *Clays and the Resource Geologist*, edited by F. J. Longstaffe, pp. 60–80. Mineralogical Association of Canada, Toronto.

Hrdlicka, Ales

1927 Catalogue of human crania in the United States National Museum Collection. *Proceedings of the United States National Museum* 69(5):1–127.

Huckell, Bruce B.

1978 Hudson-Meng chipped stone. In *The Hudson-Meng Site: An Alberta Bison Kill in the Nebraska High Plains*, edited by Larry D. Agenbroad, pp. 153–189. University Press of America, Washington, DC.

Hudson, Jean

2007 Faunal evidence for subsistence and settlement patterns at the Allen site. In *The Allen Site*, edited by D.B. Bamforth, pp. 194–226. University of New Mexico Press, Albuquerque.

Hughes, Jack T.

1949 Investigations in western South Dakota and northeastern Wyoming. *American Antiquity* 14(4):266–277.

Hughes, Richard E. (editor)

1989 *Current Directions in California Obsidian Studies*. Contributions of the University of California Archaeological Research Facility No. 48. Berkeley, California.

Hughes, Susan S.

1981 Projectile Point Variability: A Study of Point Curation at a Besant Kill Site in Southcentral Wyoming. Unpublished Master's thesis, Department of Anthropology, University of Wyoming, Laramie.

1985 A modern analog to a bison jump. In "Papers for George C. Frison Wyoming State Archaeologist 1967–1984," edited by D. N. Walker. Special issue, *The Wyoming Archaeologist* 29(1–2):45–67.

2003 Beyond the Altithermal: The Role of Climate Change in the Prehistoric Adaptations of Northwestern Wyoming. Unpublished Ph.D. dissertation, Department of Anthropology, University of Washington, Seattle.

Hultkrantz, Ake

1958 Tribal divisions with the Eastern Shoshone of Wyoming. *Proceedings of the 32nd International Congress of the Americanists*:148–154. Munsgaard, Copenhagen.

1961 The Shoshones in the Rocky Mountain area. *Annals of Wyoming* 33(1):19–41.

Hunt, Charles B.

1967 *Natural Regions of the United States and Canada*. W. H. Freeman and Company, San Francisco.

Hurst, C. T.

1943 A Folsom site in a mountain valley of Colorado. *American Antiquity* 8(3):250–253.

Hurst, Vernon J., and A. R. Kelly

1961 Patination of cultural flints. *Science* 134:251–256.

Husted, Wilfred M.

1969 *Bighorn Canyon Archaeology*. Smithsonian Institution River Basin Surveys, Publications in Salvage Archaeology No. 12. Smithsonian Institution, Lincoln.

1978 Excavation techniques and culture layer analyses. In *The Mummy Cave Project in Northwestern Wyoming*, edited by Harold McCracken, pp. 50–145. Buffalo Bill Historical Center, Cody, Wyoming.

Husted, Wilfred M., and Robert Edgar

2002 *The Archeology of Mummy Cave, Wyoming*. United States Department of the Interior National Park Service, Midwest Archaeological Center, Lincoln, Nebraska.

Huter, Pamela

2001 Analysis of Non-local Lithic Material from the Helen Lookingbill Site. Paper presented at the Annual Meeting of the Wyoming Archaeological Society.

Huter, Pamela
2003 Assessment of Changing Diet-Breadth at Southside Shelter. Unpublished Master's thesis, Department of Anthropology, University of Wyoming, Laramie.

Hyde, George E.
1974 *Spotted Tail's Folk: A History of the Brule Sioux.* 2nd edition. University of Oklahoma Press, Norman.

Ingbar, Eric E., and George C. Frison
1987 The Larson Cache. In *The Horner Site: The Type Site of the Cody Cultural Complex*, edited by George C. Frison and Lawrence C. Todd, pp. 461–473. Academic Press, Orlando.

Ingbar, Eric E., Raymond Kunselman, and James C. Miller
1990 Chert Source Characterization Using Selected XRF Trace Element Analysis: Knife River Flints and Look Alikes. Paper presented at the 48th Plains Anthropological Conference, Oklahoma City.

Irwin, Henry T. and Cynthia C. Irwin
1957 Archaeology of the Agate Bluff area. *Plains Anthropologist* 8:15–38.
1959 *Excavations at the LoDaisKa site in the Denver, Colorado, Area.* Proceedings No. 8. Denver Museum of Natural History, Denver.
1961 Radiocarbon dates from the LoDaisKa site, Colorado. *American Antiquity* 27(1):114–115.

Irwin, Henry T., and H. M. Wormington
1970 Paleo-Indian tool types in the Great Plains. *American Antiquity* 35(1):24–34.

Irwin, Lee
1994 *The Dream Seekers: Native American Visionary Traditions of the Great Plains.* University of Oklahoma Press, Norman.

Irwin-Williams, Cynthia, and Henry T. Irwin
1966 *Excavations at Magic Mountain.* Proceedings No. 12. Denver Museum of Natural History, Denver.

Irwin-Williams, Cynthia, Henry T. Irwin, George Agogino, and C. Vance Haynes
1973 Hell Gap: Paleo-Indian occupation on the High Plains. *Plains Anthropologist* 18(59):40–53.

Isaac, Glynn L.
1967 Towards the interpretation of occupation debris: Some experiments and observations. *Kroeber Anthropological Society Papers* 37:31–57.

Jackson, Kern C.
1970 *Textbook of Lithology.* McGraw Hill, New York.

Jackson, Stephen T., Mark E. Lyford, and Julio Betancourt
2002 A 4000-year record of woodland vegetation from Wind River Canyon, central Wyoming. *Western North American Naturalist* 62(4):405–413.

Jameson, John H., Jr.
1977 Archaeological Investigations in the Area of the Proposed Middle Fork Dam and Reservoir, Johnson County, Wyoming. Unpublished Master's thesis, Department of Anthropology, University of Wyoming, Laramie.

Jantz, Richard L.
1977 Craniometric relationships of Plains populations: Historical and evolutionary relationships. In *Trends in Middle Missouri Prehistory: A Festschrift Honoring the Contributions of Donald J. Lehmer*, edited by W. Raymond Wood, pp. 162–176. Plains Anthropologist Memoir 13. Lincoln, Nebraska.
2008 Temporal and geographic variation in vault height in the Great Plains, Great Basin, and Northwestern Plains, In *Skeletal Biology and Bioarchaeology of the Northwestern Plains*, edited by G. W. Gill and R. L. Weathermon, pp. 271–280. University of Utah Press, Salt Lake City.

Jantz, Richard L., and D. W. Owsley
2001 Variation among early North American crania. *American Journal of Physical Anthropology* 114(2):146–155.

Jantz, Richard L., D. W. Owsley, and P. Willey
1981 Cramiometric variation in the Northern and Central Plains. In *Progress in Skeletal Biology of Plains Populations*, edited by Richard L. Jantz and Douglas Ubelaker, pp. 57–90. Plains Anthropologist Memoir 17. Lincoln, Nebraska.

Jantz, Richard L., and P. Willey

1977 Temporal and Geographic Patterning in Relative Head Height in the Central and Northern Plains. Paper presented at the 35th Annual Plains Anthropological Conference, Lincoln, Nebraska.

1983 Temporal and geographic patterning of relative head height in the Central Plains and Middle Missouri areas. *Plains Anthropologist* 28:59–67.

Jepsen, Glen L.

1953a Ancient buffalo hunters. *Princeton Alumni Weekly* 53(25):10–12.

1953b Ancient buffalo hunters of northwestern Wyoming. *Southwestern Lore* 19:19–25.

Jerde, Tom, and Dennis C. Joyes

2009 Pots from the hills: Prehistoric ceramics from northeastern Montana. *Archaeology in Montana* 50(1):33–68.

Jodry, Margaret A.

1987 Stewart's Cattle Guard Site: A Folsom Site in Southern Colorado; a report of the 1981 and 1983 Field Seasons. Unpublished Master's thesis, Department of Anthropology, University of Texas, Austin.

1998 The possible design of Folsom ultrathin bifaces as fillet knives for jerky production. *Current Research in the Pleistocene* 15:75–77.

1999a Paleoindian stage. In *Colorado Prehistory: A Context for the Rio Grande Basin*, by M. A. Martorano, T. Hoeffer II, M. A. Jodry, V. Spero, and M. L. Taylor, pp. 45–114. Colorado Council of Professional Archaeologists, Denver, Colorado.

1999b Folsom Technological and Socioeconomic Strategies: Views from Stewart's Cattle Guard and the Upper Rio Grande Basin, Colorado. Unpublished Ph.D. dissertation, Department of Anthropology, American University, Washington, DC.

Jodry, Margaret A., and Dennis J. Stanford

1992 Stewart's Cattle Guard site: An analysis of bison remains in a Folsom kill-butchery campsite. In *Ice Age People of the Rockies*, edited by D. J. Stanford and J. S. Day, pp. 101–168. University of Colorado Press, Niwot.

Johanson, S. Ryan, and Douglas Owsley

2002 Welfare history on the Great Plains: Mortality and skeletal health, 1650–1900. In *Backbone of History*, edited by R. H. Steckle and J. C. Rose, pp. 524–560. Cambridge University Press, Cambridge.

Johnson, Ann M.

1977 The Dune Buggy site 24RV1, and Northwestern Plains ceramics. *Plains Anthropologist* 22(75):37–49.

Johnson, Ann M., Becky Kallevig, Richard Krause, and Steven Chomko

1990 Nollmeyer. Manuscript on file, Department of Anthropology, University of Wyoming, Laramie.

Johnson, Ann M., Brian O.K. Reeves, and Mack W. Shortt

2004 *Osprey Beach, A Cody Complex Camp on Yellowstone Lake.* Prepared for Yellowstone Center for Resources, Yellowstone National Park. Lifeways of Canada Limited, Calgary, Alberta.

Johnson, Dave, and Jana V. Pastor

2003 *The Blue Point Site.* Prepared for FMC Corporation. Western Archaeological Services, Rock Springs, Wyoming.

Johnson, Eileen

2008 Hebier and Mud Lake Sites, Wisconsin, 12,500–13,500 Radiocarbon Years B.P. Paper presented at the Paleoamerican Origins Workshop, Texas Archaeological Research Laboratory, Austin, Texas.

Johnson, Ronald C.

1984 *New Names for Units in the Lower Part of the Green River Formation, Piceance Creek Basin, Colorado.* United States Geological Survey Bulletin 1529-I. Washington, DC.

Jones, William A.

1875 *Report on the Reconnaissance of Northwestern Wyoming, Including Yellowstone National Park, Made in Summer 1873.* Army Corps of Engineers, U. S. Government Printing Office, Washington, DC.

Joyce, Dan

2008 Schaefer Site, Wisconsin. Paper presented at the Paleoamerican Origins Workshop, Texas Archaeological Research Laboratory, Austin, Texas.

Karlstrom, Eric

1977 Genesis, Morphology and Stratigraphy of Soils at the Laddie Creek Archaeological Site, Bighorn Mountains, Wyoming. Unpublished Master's thesis, Department of Geography, University of Wyoming, Laramie.

Kay, Marvin

2003 New Radiocarbon Dates for Dalton at Rodgers Shelter, Missouri. Paper presented at the 61st Plains Anthropological Conference, Fayetteville, Arkansas.

Keefer, W. R.

1969 General stratigraphy and depositional history of the Fort Union, Indian Meadows, and Wind River Formations, Wind River Basin, Wyoming. *Wyoming Geological Association, Twenty-first Annual Field Conference Guidebook:*19–28. Wyoming Geological Society, Casper.

Kehoe, Alice B.

1959 Ceramic affiliation in the Northwestern Plains. *American Antiquity* 25(2):237–246.

2004 Testing for "shamanic trance" in rock art: A comment on Greer and Greer. *Plains Anthropologist* 49(189):79–80.

Kehoe, Thomas F.

1958 Tipi rings: The "Direct Ethnological" approach applied to an archaeological problem. *American Anthropologist* 60(5):861–873.

1960 *Stone Tipi Rings in North-Central Montana and the Adjacent Portion of Alberta, Canada. Their Historical, Ethnological, and Archaeological Aspects.* Bureau of American Ethnology Bulletin No. 173, Anthropological Papers No. 62. Washington, DC.

1967 *The Boarding School Bison Drive Site.* Plains Anthropologist Memoir 14. Lincoln, Nebraska.

1973 *The Gull Lake Site: A Prehistoric Bison Drive Site in Southwestern Saskatchewan.* Publications in Anthropology and History No. 1. Milwaukee Public Museum, Milwaukee.

Kehoe, Thomas F., and Bruce A. McCorquodale

1961 The Avonlea point—horizon marker for the Northwestern Plains. *Plains Anthropologist* 6(13):179–188.

Keller, Sarah A. C.

1971 The Middle Period: Wyoming and Adjacent Plains. Unpublished Ph. D. dissertation, Department of Anthropology, Harvard University.

Kelly, A. R., and Vernon J. Hurst

1956 Patination and age relationship in South Georgia flint. *American Antiquity* 22:193–194.

Kelly, Robert L.

1985 Hunter-Gatherer Mobility and Sedentism: A Great Basin Study. Unpublished Ph.D. dissertation, Department of Anthropology, University of Michigan, Ann Arbor.

Kelly, Robert L., and Lawrence C. Todd

1988 Coming into the country: Early Paleoindian hunting and mobility. *American Antiquity* 53(2):231–244.

Keyser, James D.

1974 The LaMarche game trap: An early historic game trap in southwestern Montana. *Plains Anthropologist* 19(65):173–179.

1975 A Shoshonean origin for the Plains Shield Bearing Warrior motif. *Plains Anthropologist.* 20(69):207–216.

1977 Writing-on-Stone: Rock art on the Northwestern Plains. *Canadian Journal of Archaeology* 1:15–80.

1981 Pictographs at the DesRosier Shelter. *Plains Anthropologist* 26(94, part 1):271–276.

1984 *Rock Art of Western North Dakota, the North Cave Hills.* South Dakota Archaeological Society Publication No. 9. Augustana College, Sioux Falls, South Dakota.

1987 A lexicon for historic Plains Indian rock art: Increasing interpretive potential. *Plains Anthropologist* 32(115):43–72.

Keyser, James D.

1991 A thing to tie on the halter: An addition to the Plains rock art lexicon. *Plains Anthropologist* 36(136):261–267.

1996 Painted bison robes: The missing link in the Biographic art style lexicon. *Plains Anthropologist* 41(155):29–52.

2004 *Art of the Warriors: Rock Art of the American Plains*. University of Utah Press, Salt Lake City.

Keyser, James D., and Phillip Cash Cash

2002 A carved quirt handle from the Warm Springs Reservation: Northern Plains Biographic Art in the Columbia Plateau. *Plains Anthropologist* 47(180):51–60.

Keyser, James D., and Carl M. Davis

1984 Lightening Spring: 4000 years of pine parkland prehistory. *Archaeology in Montana* 25(2):1–64.

1985 Lightening Spring and Red Fox: McKean research in the Grand River Drainage. In *McKean/ Middle Plains Archaic: Current Research*, edited by Marcel Kornfeld and Lawrence C. Todd, pp. 123–126. Occasional Papers on Wyoming Archaeology No. 4. Office of Wyoming State Archaeologist, Department of Anthropology, University of Wyoming, Laramie.

Keyser, James D., Mavis Greer, and John Greer

2005 Arminto petroglyphs: Rock art damage assessment and management. *Plains Anthropologist* 50(193):23–30.

Keyser, James D., and Michael A. Klassen

2001 *Plains Indian Rock Art*. University of Washington Press, Seattle.

2003 Every detail counts: More additions to the Plains Biographic rock art lexicon. *Plains Anthropologist* 48(184):7–20.

Keyser, James D., and George C. Knight

1976 The rock art of western Montana. *Plains Anthropologist* 21(71):1–12.

Keyser, James D., and Mark Mitchell

2001 Decorated bridles: Horse tack in Plains Biographic rock art. *Plains Anthropologist* 46(176): 195–210.

Keyser, James D., and George R. Poetschat

2005 *Warrior Art of Wyoming's Green River Basin: Biographic Petroglyphs along the Seedskadee*. Oregon Archaeological Society Publication No. 15. Portland, Oregon.

2008 *Ute Horse Raiders on the Powder Rim: Rock Art at Powder Wash, Wyoming*. Oregon Archaeological Society Publication No. 19. Portland, Oregon.

Keyser, James D., Linea Sundstrom, and George R. Poetschat

2006 Women in war: Gender in Plains Biographic rock art. *Plains Anthropologist* 51(197):51–70.

Keyser, James D., Russel L. Tanner, and David T. Vlcek

2004 Pictures by the Seedskadee: A preliminary analysis of the Biographic rock art of the Green River Basin, southwestern Wyoming. *Plains Anthropologist* 49(190):129–152.

King, Chester

1978 Protohistoric and historic archeology. In *California*, edited by Robert F. Heizer, pp. 58–68. Handbook of North American Indians, Vol. 8, William C. Sturtevant, general editor. Smithsonian Institution, Washington, DC.

King, Robert J., and Daniel F. Merriam

1969 Origin of "welded chert," Morrison Formation (Jurassic), Colorado. *Bulletin of the Geological Society of America* 80:1141–1148.

Kittel, Timothy G. F., Peter E. Thornton, J. Andy Royle, and Thomas N. Chase

2002 Climates of the Rocky Mountains: Historic and future patterns. In *Rocky Mountain Futures: An Ecological Perspective*, edited by Jill S. Baron, pp. 59–82. Island Press, Washington, DC.

Kivett, Marvin E.

1962 Logan Creek Complex: Site 25BT3. Paper presented at the 17th Plains Anthropological Conference, Lincoln.

Klassen, Michael A., James D. Keyser, and Lawrence L. Loendorf

2000 Bird Rattle's petroglyphs at Writing-on-Stone: Continuity in the Biographic rock art tradition. *Plains Anthropologist* 45(172):189–201.

Klein, Alan M.

1983 The political-economy of gender: A 19th century Plains Indian case. In *The Hidden Half: Studies of Plains Indian Women*, edited by Patricia Albers and Beatrice Medicine, pp. 143–173. University Press of America, Washington, DC.

Knauth, L. P.

1979 A model for the origin of chert in limestone. *Geology* 7:274–277.

Knell, Edward J.

2004 Course-scale chipped stone aggregates and technological organization strategies in the Hell Gap Locality V Cody complex component, Wyoming. In *Aggregate Analysis in Chipped Stone*, edited by C. T. Hall and M. L. Larson, pp. 156–183. University of Utah Press, Salt Lake City.

2009 The Organization of Late Paleoindian Cody Complex Land Use on the North American Great Plains. Unpublished Ph.D. dissertation, Department of Anthropology, Washington State University, Pullman.

Knight, Dennis H.

1994 *Mountains and Plains: The Ecology of Wyoming Landscapes*. Yale University Press, New Haven.

Knudson, Ruthann

1973 Organizational Variability in Late Paleoindian Assemblages. Unpublished Ph.D. dissertation, Department of Anthropology, Washington State University, Pullman.

1983 *Organizational Variability in Late Paleo-Indian Assemblages*. Reports of Investigations No. 60. Washington State University, Laboratory of Anthropology, Pullman, Washington.

Knudson, Ruthann, and Marcel Kornfeld

2007 A new date for the James Allen site, Laramie Basin, Wyoming. *Current Research in the Pleistocene* 24:112–114.

Koch, Amy, and James C. Miller

1996 *Geoarcheological Investigations at the Lyman Site (25SF53) and Other Cultural Resources Related to Table Mountain Quarry Near the Nebraska/Wyoming Border*. Nebraska State Historical Society, Lincoln.

Kolm, K. E.

1974 ERTS imagery applied to mapping of sand dunes in Wyoming. In *Applied Geology and Archaeology: The Holocene History of Wyoming*, edited by M. Wilson, pp. 34–39. Geological Survey of Wyoming Report of Investigations No. 10. Laramie.

Korell, Alan

1981 Comments on the Korell-Bordeau site. *The Wyoming Archaeologist* 24(1):28–34.

Konlande, J. E., and J. R. K. Robson

1972 The nutritive value of cooked camas as consumed by Flathead Indians. *Ecology of Food Nutrition* 1:193–195.

Kooyman, B., L. V. Hills, P. McNeil, and S. Tolman

2006 Late Pleistocene horse hunting at the Wally's Beach site (DhPg-8), Canada. *American Antiquity* 71(1):101–121.

Kornegay, G. L., and R. C. Surdam

1980 The Laney Member of the Green River Formation, Sand Wash Basin, Colorado, and its relationship to Wyoming. *Wyoming Geological Association, Thirty-first Annual Field Conference Guidebook*:191–204. Wyoming Geological Society, Casper.

Kornfeld, Marcel

1985 Geophysical Survey of the Bugas-Holding Site. Poster session presented at the 50th Annual Meeting of the Society of American Archaeology, Denver, Colorado.

1998 *Early Prehistory of Middle Park: The 1997 Project and Summary of Paleoindian Archaeology – Diagnostic Paleoindian Artifact Forms*. Technical Report 15b, Department of Anthropology, University of Wyoming, Laramie. (editor)

1999 Clovis in the Rockies: How High Do They Get. Poster paper presented at Clovis and Beyond, sponsored by the Center for the Study of the First Americans. Santa Fe, New Mexico.

Kornfeld, Marcel

2002 Folsom technological organization in the Middle Park of Colorado: A case for broad spectrum foraging. In *Folsom Technology and Lifeways*, edited by J. E. Clark and M. B. Collins. *Lithic Technology*, Special Publication No. 4:47–68. University of Tulsa, Oklahoma.

2003 *Pull of the Hills, Landscape Archaeology and Great Plains Foraging Economy.* British Archaeological Reports International Series 1106. Oxford, England.

2007a Are Paleoindians of the Great Plains and the Rocky Mountains subsistence specialists? In *Foragers of the Terminal Pleistocene in North America*, edited by R. B. Walker and B. N. Driskell, pp. 32–58. University of Nebraska Press, Lincoln.

2007b Rockshelters of the Rocky Mountains: 70 years of research. In *Prés du bord d'un abri: Les hitoires, théories et méthods de recherché sur les abris sus roche/On Shelter's Ledge: Histories, Theories and Methods of Rockshelter Research*, edited by M. Kornfeld, S. Vasil'ev, and L. Miotti, pp. 51–60. British Archaeological Reports 1655. Oxford, England.

2009 Modified chipped stone and implications for Paleoindian technology and adaptation. In *Hell Gap: A Stratified Paleoindian Campsite at the Edge of the Rockies*, edited by M. L. Larson, M. Kornfeld, and G. C. Frison, pp. 243–258. University of Utah Press, Salt Lake.

Kornfeld, M., K. Akoshima, and G. C. Frison

1990 Stone tool caching on the U.S. Plains: Implications from the McKean site tool kit. *Journal of Field Archeology* 17(3):301–309.

Kornfeld, Marcel, and Steven Chomko

1983 Pre-Shoshonean Rodent Utilization. Paper presented at the 48th Annual Meeting of the Society for American Archeology, Pittsburgh.

Kornfeld, Marcel, and George C. Frison

2000 Paleoindian occupation of the high country: The case of Middle Park, Colorado. *Plains Anthropologist* 45(172):129–153.

Kornfeld, Marcel, George C. Frison, and Mary Lou Larson (editors)

1995 *Keyhole Reservoir Archeology, Glimpses of the Past from Northeast Wyoming.* Occasional Papers on Wyoming Archeology No. 5. Laramie.

Kornfeld, Marcel, George C. Frison, Mary Lou Larson, James C. Miller, and Jan Saysette

1999 Paleoindian bison procurement and paleoenvironments in the Middle Park of Colorado. *Geoarchaeology* 14(7):655–674.

Kornfeld, Marcel, George C. Frison, and Patrice White

2001 Paleoindian occupation of Barger Gulch and the use of Troublesome Formation chert. *Current Research in the Pleistocene* 18:32–34.

Kornfeld, Marcel, Michael Harkin, and Jonnathan Durr

2001 Landscapes and peopling of the Americas. In *On Being First: Presenting the First Peoples in the Americas: Proceedings of the 31st Annual Chacmool Conference*, edited by J. C. Gillespie, S. Tupakka, and C. de Mille, pp. 149–162. The Archaeological Association of the University of Calgary, Alberta.

Kornfeld, Marcel, and Mary Lou Larson

2008 Bonebeds and other myths: Paleoindian to Archaic transition on North American Great Plains. In *Zooarchaeology of the Late Pleistocene/Early Holocene in the Americas and Zooarchaeological Evidence of the Ancient Maya and their Environment*, guest editors K. F. Emery, C. M. Götz, M. E. Hill, and J. Arroyo-Cabrales. *Quaternary International* 191(1):18–33.

Kornfeld, M., M. L. Larson, C. Arnold, A. Weiwel, M. Toft, and D. J. Stanford

2007 The Nelson site, a Cody occupation in northeastern Colorado. *Plains Anthropologist* 52(203):257–278.

Kornfeld, Marcel, Mary Lou Larson, David J. Rapson, and George C. Frison

2001 10,000 years in the Middle Rocky Mountains: The Lookingbill. *Journal of Field Archaeology* 28(3/4):1–18.

Kornfeld, Marcel, and Lawrence C. Todd (editors)

1985 *McKean/Middle Plains Archaic: Current Research.* Occasional Papers on Wyoming Archaeology No. 4. Office of Wyoming State Archaeologist, Laramie, Wyoming.

Kreutzer, L. A.

1992 Bison and deer bone mineral densities: Comparisons and implications for interpretation of archaeological faunas. *Journal of Archaeological Science* 19:271–294.

Kreutzer, L. A.

1996 Taphonomy of the Mill Iron site bison bonebed. In *The Mill Iron Site*, edited by G. C. Frison, pp. 101–143. University of New Mexico Press, Albuquerque.

Kroeber, A. L.

1907 *Ethnology of the Gros Ventre*. Anthropological Papers Vol. 1, Pt. 4. American Museum of Natural History, New York.

Krogman, W. M., and M. Y. Iscan

1986 *The Human Skeleton in Forensic Medicine*. 2nd ed. C. C. Thomas, Springfield, Illinois.

Krumbein, W. C., and L. L. Sloss

1963 *Stratigraphy and Sedimentation*. W. H. Freeman, San Francisco.

Krumbein, W. E., and K. Jens

1981 Biogenic rock varnishes of the Negev Desert (Israel): An ecological study of iron and manganese transformation by cyanobacteria and fungi. *Oecologia* 50:25–38.

Krynine, P. D.

1948 The megascopic study and classification of sedimentary rocks. *Journal of Geology* 56:130–165.

Kuhn, Steven L.

1995 *Mousterian Lithic Technology*. Princeton University Press, Princeton, New Jersey.

Kunselman, Raymond

1998 X-ray fluorescence signatures of Wyoming obsidian sources. *The Wyoming Archaeologist* 42(1):1–8.

Kurten, Bjorn

1953 On the variation and population dynamics of fossil and recent mammal populations. *Acta Zoologica Fennica* 76:1–122.

Kuzmin, Yaroslav V., and Susan G. Keates

2005 Dates are not just data: Paleolithic settlement patterns in Siberia derived from radiocarbon records. *American Antiquity* 70(4):773–789.

LaBelle, Jason M.

2005 Hunter-Gatherer Foraging Variability During the Early Holocene of the Central Plains of North America. Unpublished Ph.D. dissertation, Department of Anthropology, Southern Methodist University, Dallas, Texas.

Lageson, David R.

1980 Depositional environments and diagenesis of the Madison limestone, northern Medicine Bow Mountains, Wyoming. *Wyoming Geological Association, Thirty-first Annual Field Conference Guidebook*:53–65. Wyoming Geological Society, Casper.

Lahren, Larry A.

1971 Archaeological investigations in the upper Yellowstone Valley, Montana. In *Aboriginal Man and Environments on the Plateau of Northwest America*, edited by Arnoud H. Stryd and Rachel A. Smith, pp. 168–182. Archaeological Association, University of Calgary, Alberta.

1976 *The Myers-Hindman Site: An Exploratory Study of Human Occupation Patterns in the Upper Yellowstone Valley from 7000 B.C. to A.D. 1200*. Anthropologos Researches International Incorporated, Livingston, Montana.

Lahren, Larry A., and Robson Bonnichsen

1974 Bone foreshafts from a Clovis burial in southwestern Montana. *Science* 186:147–150.

Lanning, Edward P.

1963 *Archaeology of the Rose Spring site INY-372*. University of California Publications in American Archaeology and Ethnology 49(3):236–335. Berkeley.

Larson, Mary Lou

1990 Early Plains Archaic Technological Organization: The Laddie Creek Example. Unpublished PhD dissertation, Department of Anthropology, University of California, Santa Barbara.

1992 Site formation processes in the Cody and Early Plains Archaic Levels at the Laddie Creek Site, Wyoming. *Geoarchaeology* 7(2):103–120.

1994 Toward a holistic analysis of chipped stone assemblages. In *The Organization of North American Stone Tool Technology*, edited by Philip J. Carr, pp. 57–69. International Monographs in Prehistory, Archaeological Series 7. Ann Arbor.

Larson, Mary Lou

1997 Housepits and mobile hunter-gatherers: A consideration of the Wyoming evidence. *Plains Anthropologist* 42(161):353–369.

2007 GIS perspectives on rockshelter landscapes in Wyoming. In *Prés du bord du abri: Les Histories, Théories et Méthodes de recherches sur les abris sous roche/On Shelter's Ledge: Histories, Theories and Methods of Rockshelter Research*, edited by M. Kornfeld, S. Vasil'ev, and L. Miotti, pp. 163–171. British Archaeological Reports 1655. Oxford, England.

Larson, Mary Lou, and Julie E. Francis

1997 *Changing Perspectives of the Archaic on the Northwestern Plains and Rocky Mountains.* University of South Dakota Press, Vermillion.

Larson, Mary Lou, and Eric E. Ingbar

1992 Perspectives on refitting: Critique and a complementary approach. In *Piecing Together the Past: Application of Refitting Studies in Archaeology*, edited by Jack L. Hofman and James Enloe, pp. 1–15. British Archaeological Reports International Series No. 578. Oxford, England.

Larson, Mary Lou, and Marcel Kornfeld

1997 Chipped stone nodules: Theory, method, and several Northwest Plains examples. *Lithic Technology* 22(1):4–18.

Larson, Mary Lou, M. Kornfeld, and G. C. Frison (editors)

2009 *Hell Gap: A Stratified Paleoindian Campsite at the Edge of the Rockies.* University of Utah Press, Salt Lake City.

Larson, Mary Lou, Marcel Kornfeld, and J. P. Matheson

1992 Archeological research at the Hutton-Pinkham site, eastern Colorado, *Southwestern Lore* 58(2):1–15.

Larson, T. A.

1978 *History of Wyoming.* 2nd edition. University of Nebraska Press, Lincoln.

Larson, Thomas K.

2007 Wyoming Cultural Properties Form Update, 48NA991. Manuscript on file at the Wyoming Cultural Records Office, Wyoming State Historic Preservation Office, Laramie.

Laughlin, John P.

2005 149 Refits: Assessing Site Integrity and Hearth-Centered Activities at Barger Gulch Locality B. Unpublished Master's thesis, Department of Anthropology, University of Wyoming, Laramie.

Laws, Richard M., I. S. C. Parker, and R. C. B. Johnstone

1975 *Elephants and Their Habitats: The Ecology of Elephants in North Bunyoro, Uganda.* Clarendon Press, Oxford.

Lee, Richard B., and Irven DeVore

1968 *Man the Hunter.* Aldine, Chicago.

Leeder, M. R.

1982 *Sedimentology: Process and Product.* Allen and Unwin, London.

Leopold, Luna B., and John P. Miller

1954 A postglacial chronology for some alluvial valleys in Wyoming. *U. S. Geological Survey Water Supply Paper* No. 1261.

Levi-Sala, I.

1986 Use wear and post-depositional surface modification: A word of caution. *Journal of Archaeological Science* 13:229–244.

Lewis, H.P.

1947 *Buffalo Kills in Montana.* Report on file at the National Park Service, Midwest Archaeological Center, Lincoln, Nebraska.

Lewis-Williams, J. David

1984 Ideological continuities in prehistoric southern Africa: The evidence of rock art. In *Past and Present in Hunter Gatherer Studies*, edited by Carmel Schrire, pp. 225–252. Academic Press, New York.

Lewis-Williams, J. David, and Thomas A. Dowson
1988 The signs of the times: Entoptic phenomena in Upper Paleolithic art. *Current Anthropology* 29(2):201–217.

Libby, W. F.
1952 *Radiocarbon Dating*. University of Chicago Press, Chicago.

Lippincott, Kerry
1985 Introduction to the symposium. *Archaeology in Montana* 26(2):1–2.
1985 The Rattlesnake Ridge burial/biface cache site, 48WE487, in east central Wyoming. *Archaeology in Montana* 26(2):53–61.
1996 *A Late Prehistoric Period Pronghorn Hunting Camp*. Special Publication of the South Dakota Archaeological Society No. 11. Sioux Falls, South Dakota.
1997 *Marine Shell Ornaments from the Plains*. Central Plains Archeology Vol. 5, No. 1. Nebraska State Historical Society. (compiler)
1998 The Lembke House at site 48CO1712. *The Wyoming Archaeologist* 42(2):33–48.
2000 *Freshwater Mussels in the Great Plains*. Central Plains Archeology Vol. 8, No. 1. Nebraska State Historical Society. (editor)
2005 Freshwater mussel identification and analysis from the River Bend site, 48NA202. *The Wyoming Archaeologist* 49(1):39–48.

Lischka, Joseph J., Mark E. Miller, R. Branson Reynolds, Dennis Dahms, Kathy Joyner-McGuire, and David McGuire
1983 *An Archaeological Inventory in North Park, Jackson County, Colorado*. Bureau of Land Management, Cultural Resources Series No. 14. Denver, Colorado.

Liu, Tanzhuo, and Ronald I. Dorn
1996 Understanding the spatial variability of environmental change in drylands with rock varnish microlaminations. *Annals of the Association of American Geographers* 86(2): 187–212.

Lobdell, John E.
1973 The Scoggin Site: An Early Middle Period Bison Kill. Unpublished Master's thesis, Department of Anthropology, University of Wyoming, Laramie, Wyoming.

Loendorf, Lawrence L.
1973 Prehistoric Settlement Patterns in the Pryor Mountains, Montana. Unpublished Ph.D. dissertation, Department of Anthropology, University of Missouri, Columbia.
1978 The Great Arrow, 48PA66. Manuscript on file at the Wyoming Historic Preservation Office, Laramie, Wyoming.
1984 *Documentation of Rock Art, Petroglyph Canyon, Montana, 24CB601*. Contribution No. 207. Department of Anthropology, University of North Dakota, Grand Forks, North Dakota.
1989 *Nine Rock Art Sites in the Pinon Canyon Maneuver Site, Southeastern Colorado*. Contribution No. 248. Department of Anthropology, University of North Dakota, Grand Forks, North Dakota.
1990 A dated rock art panel of shield bearing warriors in south central Montana. *Plains Anthropologist* 35(127):45–54.
1995 *The Great Turtle Shield, Castle Garden Site, Wyoming*. Loendorf and Associates, Las Cruces, New Mexico. Submitted to the Bureau of Land Management, Wyoming State Office, Cheyenne.
2008 *Thunder and Herds: Rock Art of the High Plains*. Left Coast Press, Inc., Walnut Creek, California.

Loendorf, Lawrence L., and Joan L. Brownell
1980 The Bad Pass Trail. *Archaeology in Montana* 21(3):11–102.

Loendorf, Lawrence L., Christopher Chippendale, and David S. Whitley (editors)
2005 *Discovering North American Rock Art*. University of Arizona Press, Tucson.

Loendorf, Lawrence L., James C. Dahlberg, and Lori O. Western
1981 *The Pretty Creek Archaeological Site, 24CB4 and 5*. Prepared for the Department of the Interior, National Park Service, Midwest Archaeological Center. University of North Dakota, Grand Forks.

Loendorf, Lawrence L., Ronald I. Dorn, Julie E. Francis, and George C. Frison
1989 A Proposal to Establish a Chronology of Cation-Ratio Dating for Rock Art Sites on Public and State of Wyoming Lands in the Southern Pryor Mountains and the Bighorn Basin, Wyoming and Montana. Manuscript on file, Office of Wyoming State Archaeologist, Department of Anthropology, University of Wyoming, Laramie, Wyoming.

Loendorf, Lawrence L., and Julie E. Francis
1987 Three rock art sites on the Middle Fork of the Powder River, Wyoming. *Archaeology in Montana* 28(2):18–24.

Loendorf, Lawrence L., Kerry Hackett, John D. Benko, Dori M. Penny, Judy K. Michaelsen, and Thomas K. Larson
1990 *The Cottonwood Creek Rock Art Survey.* Larson-Tibesar Associates. USDI Bureau of Land Management, Montana State Office, Billings, Montana.

Loendorf, Lawrence L., David D. Kuehn, and Nels F. Forsman
1984 Rainy Buttes silicified wood: A source of lithic raw material in western North Dakota. *Plains Anthropologist* 29(106):335–338.

Loendorf, Lawrence L., and Audrey Porsche
1985 *The Rock Art Sites in Carbon County, Montana.* Contribution No. 224. Department of Anthropology, University of North Dakota, Grand Forks, North Dakota.

Lohman, K. E., and G. W. Andrews
1968 *Late Eocene Non-marine Diatoms from the Beaver Divide Area, Fremont County, Wyoming.* U. S. Geological Survey Professional Paper 593E. Washington, DC.

Lorrain, Dessamae
1968 Analysis of the bison bones from Bonfire Shelter. In *Bonfire Shelter: A Stratified Bison Kill Site, Val Verde County, Texas,* by David S. Dibble. Texas Memorial Museum, Miscellaneous Papers No. 1:77–132.

Love, Charles M.
1977 Geological influences on prehistoric populations of western Wyoming. *Wyoming Geological Association, Twenty-ninth Annual Field Conference Guidebook*:15–29. Wyoming Geological Society, Casper.

Love, J. D.
1956 Cretaceous and Tertiary stratigraphy of the Jackson Hole area, northwestern Wyoming. *Wyoming Geological Association, Eleventh Annual Field Conference Guidebook*:76–94. Wyoming Geological Society, Casper.
1961 *Split Rock Formation (Miocene) and Moonstone Formation (Pliocene) in Central Wyoming.* U. S. Geological Survey Bulletin 1121l. Washington, DC.

Love, J. D., and Ann C. Christiansen
1985 *Geologic Map of Wyoming.* U. S. Geological Survey, Reston,Virginia.

Lovvorn, Marjorie B., George W. Gill, F. G. Carlson, J. R. Bozell, and T.L. Steinacher
1999 Microevolution and the skeletal traits of a Middle Archaic burial: Metric and multivariate comparison to Paleoindians and modern Americans. *American Antiquity* 64(3):527–545.

Low, Bruce
1996 Swan River chert. *Plains Anthropologist* 41(156):165–174.

Loy, T. H.
1983 Prehistoric blood residues: Detection on tool surfaces and identification of species origin. *Science* 220:1269–1271.

Lubinski, Patrick M.
1997 Pronghorn Intensification in the Wyoming Basin: A Study of Mortality Patterns and Prehistoric Hunting Strategies. Unpublished Ph.D. dissertation, Department of Anthropology, University of Wisconsin, Madison.
2000 Prehistoric pronghorn hunting in southwest Wyoming. In *Pronghorn Past and Present: Archaeology, Ethnography, and Biology,* edited by Jana V. Pastor and Patrick M. Lubinski, pp. 109–118. Plains Anthropologist Memoir 32. Lincoln, Nebraska.

Luedtke, Barbara E.

1976 Lithic Material Distributions and Interaction Patterns during the Late Woodland Period in Michigan. Unpublished Ph.D. dissertation, Department of Anthropology, University of Michigan, Ann Arbor.

Luedtke, Barbara E., and J. Thomas Meyers

1984 Trace element study in Burlington chert: A case study. In *Prehistoric Chert Exploitation: Studies from the Midcontinent*, edited by Brian M. Butler and Ernest E. May, pp. 287–298. Center for Archaeological Investigations Occasional Paper No. 2. Southern Illinois University, Carbondale.

Lundell, Leslie L., and Ronald C. Surdam

1975 Playa lake deposition: Green River Formation, Piceance Creek Basin, Colorado. *Geology* 3:493–497.

Lyford, Mark E., Julio L. Betancourt, and Stephen T. Jackson

2002 Holocene vegetation and climate history of the northern Bighorn Basin, southern Montana. *Quaternary Research* 58:171–181.

Lyford, Mark E., Stephen T. Jackson, Julio L. Betancourt, and Stephen T. Gray

2003 Influence of landscape structure and climate variability on a late Holocene plant migration. *Ecological Monographs* 73(4):567–583.

Lyman, R. L.

1989 Taphonomy of cervids killed by the 18 May 1980 volcanic eruption of Mount St. Helens, Washington. In *Bone Modification*, edited by R. Bonnichsen and M. Sorg, pp. 149–167. Center for the Study of the First Americans, University of Maine, Orono.

1994 *Vertebrate Taphonomy*. Cambridge University Press, New York.

Lynch, Elizabeth A.

1998 Origin of a park-forest vegetation mosaic. *Ecology* 79(4):1320–1338.

MacDonell, George H., and LuAnn Wandsnider

2003 The western Niobrara River: An inter-island passage on the Plains. In *Islands on the Plains*, edited by M. Kornfeld and A. J. Osborn, pp. 89–107. University of Utah Press, Salt Lake City.

Madsen, David B., D. R. Currey, and J. H. Madsen

1976 *Man, Mammoth, and Lake Fluctuations in Utah*. Utah Division of State History, Antiquities Section Selected Paper No. 5.

Madsen, David B., and James E. Kirkman

1988 Hunting hoppers. *American Antiquity* 53(3):593–604.

Madsen, David B., and Dave N. Schmitt

1998 Mass collecting and the diet breadth model: A Great Basin example. *Journal of Archaeological Sciences* 25:445–455.

Magne, Martin P. R., and Michael A. Klassen

1991 A multivariate study of rock art anthropomorphs at Writing-on-Stone, southern Alberta. *American Antiquity* 56:389–418.

Malde, Harold E.

1988 Geology of the Frazier site, Kersey, Colorado. In *Guidebook to the Archaeological Geology of the Colorado Piedmont and High Plains of Southeastern Wyoming*, edited by V. T. Holliday, pp. 85–90. Department of Geography, University of Wisconsin, Madison.

Mallery, Garrick

1886 Pictographs of the North American Indians: A preliminary paper. *Fourth Annual Report of the Bureau of American Ethnology*:3–256. Washington, DC.

1893 Picture-writing of the American Indians. *Tenth Annual Report of the Bureau of American Ethnology*:1–822. Washington, DC.

Mallouf, Robert J.

1989 A Clovis quarry workshop in the Callahan Divide: The Yellow Hawk site, Taylor County. *Plains Anthropologist* 34(124):81–103.

Malouf, Carling

1961a Tipi rings of the high plains. *American Antiquity* 26(3):381–390.

Malouf, Carling

1961b Pictographs and petroglyphs. *Archaeology in Montana* 3(1):1–13.

1962 Notes on the Logan Buffalo Jump. In *Symposium on Buffalo Jumps*, edited by Carling Malouf and Stuart Connor. Montana Archaeological Society Memoir No. 1.

Mandel, Rolf D., and Jack L. Hofman

2002 Geoarchaeology of the Winger site (14ST401): A Late Paleoindian bison bonebed in southwestern Kansas. *Current Research in the Pleistocene* 19:61–64.

Mandelbaum, David G.

1940 *The Plains Cree.* Anthropological Papers Vol. 37, Pt. 2. American Museum of Natural History, New York.

Mann, C. John

1968 Geology of Archaeological site 48SH312, Wyoming. *Plains Anthropologist* 13(39):40–45.

Markgraff, V., and L. Scott

1981 Lower timberline in central Colorado during the past 15,000 yr. *Geology* 9:231–234.

Martin, Curtis, Carl E. Conner, Barbara J. Davenport, Jim Conner, and Richard Ott

2002 *Report of the Class III Cultural Resources Inventory of the Proposed Burn Canyon Vegetation Treatment Area [Burn Canyon Phase I Treatment Project] in San Miguel County, Colorado.* Prepared by Grand River Institute, Grand Junction, Colorado, for USDI, BLM, Uncompahgre Field Office, Montrose, Colorado.

Martin, Curtis, Richard Ott, and Nicole Darnell

2006 *The Colorado Wickiup Project Volume III: Recordation and Re-evaluation of Twelve Aboriginal Wooden Structure Sites in Eagle, Garfield, Mesa, and Rio Blanco Counties, Colorado.* Dominquez Archaeological Research Group, Inc., Grand Junction, Colorado.

Martin, Debra L.

1997 Violence against women in the La Plata River Valley (A.D. 100–1300). In *Troubled Times: Violence and Warfare in the Past*, edited by D. L. Martin and D. W. Frayer, pp. 45–75. Gordon and Breach Publishers, Australia.

Martin, James E., Robert A. Alex, and Rachel C. Benton

1988 Holocene chronology of the Beaver Creek Shelter, Wind Cave National Park, South Dakota. *Proceedings of the South Dakota Academy of Science* 67:69–72.

Martin, Paul S.

1967 Pleistocene overkill. *Natural History* 76(10):32–38.

Martin, W. D., H. J. Fischer, R. J. Keogh, and K. Moore

1980 The petrography of the limestones in the upper Gros Ventre and Gallatin limestone Formations (Middle and Upper Cambrian), northwestern Wind River Basin, Wyoming. *Wyoming Geological Association, Thirty-first Annual Field Conference Guidebook*:37–51. Wyoming Geological Society, Casper.

Martin, William

2000 The Carter site in Northwestern Plains prehistory. *Plains Anthropologist* 45(173):305–322.

Martin, William, and William M. Harding

1999 Section 6: The Nowater housepit site (48WA1463). In *Archaeological Investigations along the Wyoming Segment of the Express Pipeline. Volume 3: Big Horn Basin and Bridger Mountains*, edited by William Martin and Craig S. Smith, pp. 6:1–6:99. Prepared for Express Pipeline by TRC-Mariah Associates. Report on file at the Wyoming SHPO Cultural Records Office, Laramie.

Martindale, Steven W., and George W. Gill

1983 A Late Prehistoric Killing in Robber's Gulch, Southern Wyoming. Paper presented at the 41st Plains Anthropological Conference, Rapid City, South Dakota.

Maughan, E. K.

1963 Mississippian age rocks in the Laramie Range, Wyoming, and adjacent areas. *U. S. Geological Survey Professional Paper* 475C:c23–c27. Washington, DC.

Maughan, E. K., and R. F. Wilson

1960 Pennsylvanian and Permian strata in southern Wyoming and northern Colorado. In *Guide to the Geology of Colorado*, edited by Robert J. Weimer and John D. Haun, pp. 34–42. Geological

Society of America, Rocky Mountain Association of Geologists, and Colorado Scientific Society joint publication, Denver.

Mayer, Frank H., and Charles B. Roth
1958 *The Buffalo Harvest*. Sage Books, Denver.

Mayer, James H.
2002 Evaluating natural site formation processes in eolian dune sands: A case study from the Krmpotich Folsom site, Killpecker Dunes, Wyoming. *Journal of Archaeological Sciences* 29:1199–1211.
2003 Paleoindian geoarchaeology and paleoenvironments of the western Killpecker Dunes, Wyoming, USA. *Geoarchaeology* 18:35–69.

Mayer, James H., and Shannon A. Mahan
2004 Late Quaternary stratigraphy and geochronology of the western Killpecker Dunes, Wyoming, USA. *Quaternary Research* 61:72–84.

Mayewski, Paul A., Eelco E. Rohling, J. Curt Stager, Wibjörn Karlén, Kirk A. Maash, L. David Meeker, Eric A. Meyerson, Fransoise Gasse, Shirley van Kreveld, Karin Holmgren, Julia Lee-Thorp, Guhild Rosqvist, Frank Raak, Michael Staubwasser, Ralph R. Schneider, and Eric J. Steig
2004 Holocene climatic variability. *Quaternary Research* 62:243–255.

Mayor, Adrienne
2005 *Fossil Legends of the First Americans*. Princeton University Press, Princeton, New Jersey.

McClelland, Bruce R., and William Martin
1999 Section 3: The Elk Head Site (48WA1181). In *Archaeological Investigations along the Wyoming Segment of the Express Pipeline. Volume 3: Big Horn Basin and Bridger Mountains*, edited by William Martin and Craig S. Smith, 3:1–3:108. Prepared for Express Pipeline by TRC-Mariah Associates. Report on file at the Wyoming SHPO Cultural Records Office, Laramie.

McDonald, Jerry N.
1981 *North American Bison*. University of California Press, Berkeley.

McDonald, K. (editor)
1993 *Archaeological Excavations at 48LN1185*. Report prepared for Archaeological Energy Consulting, Inc., Casper, Wyoming, by Metcalf Archaeology Consultants, Eagle, Colorado. Submitted to Wyoming Bureau of Land Management, Rock Springs District.

McGovern, T. H.
1994 Management for extinction in Norse Greenland. In *Historical Ecology: Cultural Knowledge and Changing Landscapes*, edited by C. Crumley, pp. 127–154. School of American Research Advanced Seminar Series. School of American Research Press, Santa Fe.

McGrew, Paul O.
1961 The Rawlins mammoth. *Wyoming Geological Association, Sixteenth Annual Field Conference Guidebook*:315–317. Wyoming Geological Society, Casper.

McGuire, David A., Kathryn Joyner, Ronald Kainer, and Mark Miller
1984 *Final Report of Archaeological Investigations of the Medicine Bow Mine Archaeological District in the Hanna Basin, Southcentral Wyoming*. Prepared by Mariah Associates, Inc., for the Arch Mineral Corporation. Report on file at the Wyoming SHPO Cultural Records Office, Laramie.

McHugh, Tom
1972 *The Time of the Buffalo*. Knopf, New York.

McKee, Dave F.
1988 A Faunal Analysis of the River Bend Site (48NA202): Evidence of Protohistoric Subsistence on the Northwest Plains. Unpublished Master's thesis, Department of Anthropology, University of Wyoming, Laramie.

McKern, Scott T., and Steve Creasman
1991 *Salvage Excavations at the Vegan Site (48LN1880) in the Green River Basin, Wyoming*. Cultural Resource Management Report No. 58. Archaeological Services of Western Wyoming College, Rock Springs.

McKern, Scott T., and Lynn L. Harrell

2008 Archaic way stations: a prelude of things to come. Electronic document, http://www.blm.gov/wy/st/en/field_offices/Pinedale/arch/way_stations.html, accessed August 31, 2008.

McKibbin, Anne, Kevin D. Black, Ronald J. Rood, Margaret A. Van Ness, and Michael D. Metcalf

1988 *Archaeological Excavations at 48CA1391, Campbell County, Wyoming.* Prepared by Metcalf Archaeological Consultants, Inc., for Cordero Mining Company and John Albanese. Report on file at the Wyoming SHPO Cultural Records Office, Laramie.

McPherron, Shannon J. P., Harold L. Dibble, and Paul Goldberg

2005 Z. *Geoarchaeology* 20(3):243–262.

Medicine Crow, Joseph

1962 The Crow Indian buffalo jump legends. In *Symposium on Buffalo Jumps*, edited by Carling Malouf and Stuart Connor, pp. 35–39. Montana Archaeological Society Memoir No. 1.

1979 The Crow migration story. In *Symposium on Crow–Hidatsa Separation*, edited by L. B. Davis, pp. 63–72. Archaeology in Montana 20(8).

Mehringer, Peter J., Jr.

1988 Clovis cache found: Weapons of ancient Americans. *National Geographic* 174:500–503.

1989 Of apples and archaeology. *Universe* 1(2):2–8.

Meltzer, David J.

2006 *Folsom: New Archaeological Investigations of a Classic Paleoindian Bison Kill.* University of California Press, Berkeley.

Mertie, J. B., Jr., R. P. Fischer, and S. W. Hobbs

1951 *Geology of the Canyon Ferry Quadrangle, Montana.* U. S. Geological Survey Bulletin 972. Washington, DC.

Metcalf, Michael D.

1973 Archaeology at Dipper Gap: An Archaic Campsite, Logan County, Colorado. Unpublished Master's thesis, Colorado State University, Fort Collins, Colorado.

1987 Contributions to the prehistoric chronology of the Wyoming Basin. In *Perspectives on Archaeological Resources Management in the "Great Plains,"* edited by Alan J. Osborn and Robert C. Hassler, pp. 233–261. I & O Publishing Company, Omaha.

Metcalf, Michael D., and Kevin D. Black

1991 *Archaeological Excavations at the Yarmony Pit House Site, Eagle County, Colorado.* Cultural Resources Series No. 31. Bureau of Land Management, Denver, Colorado.

1997 Archaic period logistical organization in the Colorado Rockies. In *Changing Perspectives of the Archaic on the Northwest Plains and Rocky Mountains*, edited by M. L. Larson and J. E. Francis, pp. 168–209. University of South Dakota Press, Vermillion.

Metcalf, Michael D., and Michael McFaul

2006 Lessons from the dirt. In *Wyoming Interstate Company Piceance Basin Expansion Project: Final Report of Cultural Resource Inventory and Evaluation, Rio Blanco and Moffat Counties, Colorado and Sweetwater Country, Wyoming.* Metcalf Archaeological Consultants, Inc. Submitted to Wyoming Interstate Company, Colorado Springs. Report on file at the WYSHPO Cultural Records Office, Laramie.

Metcalf, Michael D., Ronald J. Rood, Patrick K. O'Brien, and Bret R. Overturf

1991 *Kremmling Chert Procurement in the Middle Park Area, Colorado: 5GA1144 and 5GA1172.* Report prepared by Metcalf Archeological Consultants, Inc., Eagle, Colorado for J. F. Sato and Associates, Golden, Colorado.

Metcalf, Michael D., Stephanie Slaughter, and Kelly J. Pool

2006 Appendix E. In *Wyoming Interstate Company Piceance Basin Expansion Project: Final Report of Cultural Resource Inventory and Evaluation, Rio Blanco and Moffat Counties, Colorado, and Sweetwater County, Wyoming.* Metcalf Archaeological Consultants, Inc. Submitted to Wyoming Interstate Company, Colorado Springs.

Meyer, Crystal, Mary M. Prasciunas, Derek T. Anderson, Norbert Wasilik, Marcel Kornfeld, C. Vance Haynes, Jr., and George C. Frison
2005 *Preliminary Results of the 2004 Field Season at the Agate Basin Site*. Technical Report No. 36. George C. Frison Institute of Archaeology and Anthropology, University of Wyoming, Laramie.

Meyers, J. Thomas
1970 *Chert Resources in the Lower Illinois Valley*. Report of Investigations No. 18. Illinois State Museum, Springfield.

Miao, Xiaodong, Joseph A. Mason, William C. Johnson, and Hong Wang
2007 High-resolution proxy record of Holocene climate from a loess section in southwestern Nebraska. *Paleogeography, Paleoclimatology, Paleoecology* 245:368–381.

Michaelsen, Judy K.
1983 A Study of Lithic Procurement Behavior in the Red Desert Region of Wyoming. Unpublished Master's thesis, Department of Anthropology, University of Wyoming, Laramie.

Middleton, Jessica L., Patrick M. Lubinski, and Michael D. Metcalf
2007 Ceramics from the Firehole Basin site and Firehole phase in the Wyoming Basin. *Plains Anthropologist* 52(201):29–41.

Millar, J. F. V., H. Epp, T. W. Foster, J. S. Wilson, and G. Adams
1972 The Southwest Saskatchewan Archaeological Project. *Napao* 3(2):1–39.

Miller, James C.
1990 Lithic resources in the Troublesome Formation. Manuscript on file, Archaeological Service, Western Wyoming College, Rock Springs.
1992 Geology in Archaeology: Geology, Paleoclimates, and Archaeology in the Western Wyoming Basin. Unpublished Master's thesis, Department of Anthropology, University of Wyoming, Laramie.

Miller, James C., and Thomas K. Larson
1990 Knife River flint studies: Part I, geological and physical characterization. In *The Highway 22 Project: Archaeological Excavations at 32DU178 and 32DU179, Dunn County, North Dakota*, edited by Thomas K. Larson and Dori M. Penny, pp. 83–95. Report on file, Larson-Tibesar Associates, Laramie.

Miller, Karen G.
1988 A Comparative Analysis of Cultural Materials from Two Bighorn Mountains Archaeological Sites: A Record of 10,000 Years of Occupation. Unpublished Master's thesis, Department of Anthropology, University of Wyoming, Laramie.

Miller, Mark E.
1976 Communal Bison Procurement during the Middle Plains Archaic: A Comparative Study. Unpublished Master's thesis, Department of Anthropology, University of Wyoming, Laramie.
1986 Preliminary investigations at the Seminoe Beach site, Carbon County, Wyoming. *The Wyoming Archaeologist* 29(1–2):83–96.
1988 Projectile point analysis. Appendix to *A Prehistoric Human Burial from Bairoil Locality P-139 (48SW7101) at Amoco LSU Reservoir 2, Sweetwater County, Wyoming*. Report WY-2535–27 by William Lane Shields, John Greer, and Mavis Greer. John and Mavis Greer Archaeological Consultants, Casper, Wyoming.

Miller, Mark E., and Galen R. Burgett
2000 The Cache Hill site (48CA61): A bison kill-butchery site in the Powder River Basin, Wyoming. *The Wyoming Archaeologist* 44(1):27–43.

Miller, Mark E., and George W. Gill
1980 A Late Prehistoric bundle burial from southern Wyoming. *Plains Anthropolologist* 25:235–245.

Miller, Mark E., and David J. McGuire
1997 Early Plains Archaic adaptations: A view from the Medicine House site in the Hanna Basin, south-central Wyoming. In *Changing Perspectives of the Archaic on the Northwestern Plains and Rocky Mountains*, edited by Mary Lou Larson and Julie E. Francis, pp. 368–393. University of South Dakota Press, Vermillion.

Miller, Mark E., and Paul H. Sanders

2000 The Trappers Point site (48SU1006): Early Archaic adaptations and pronghorn procurement in the Upper Green River Basin, Wyoming. In *Pronghorn Past and Present: Archaeology, Ethnography, and Biology*, edited by J. V. Pastor and P. M. Lubinski, pp. 39–52. Plains Anthropologist Memoir 32. Lincoln, Nebraska.

Miller, Mark E., and Brian R. Waitkus

1989 The Butler-Rissler site: Plains Woodland occupation along the North Platte River, Wyoming. *The Wyoming Archaeologist* 32(1–2):1–37.

Miller, Mark E., Bryan R. Waitkus, and David G. Eckles

1987 A Woodland-Besant occurrence in Central Wyoming. *Plains Anthropologist* 32:420–423.

Miller, Maxine J.

1999 The Paleopathology of Northwestern Plains Indians. Unpublished Master's thesis, Department of Anthropology, University of Wyoming, Laramie.

2008 Disease and injury among Northwestern Plains Indians. In *Skeletal Biology and Bioarchaeology of the Northwestern Plains*, edited by G. W. Gill and R. L. Weathermon, pp. 200–211. University of Utah Press, Salt Lake City.

Miller, Sharon A., Barry L. Weaver, and Susan C. Vehik

1990 Trace Element Analysis of Northern Oklahoma Cherts by X-ray Fluorescence. Paper presented at the 48th Plains Anthropological Conference, Oklahoma City.

Miller, Susan J.

1978 Early man at Owl Cave: Current investigations at the Wasden site, eastern Snake River Plain, Idaho. In *Early Man in America from a Circum-Pacific Perspective*, edited by A. L. Bryan, pp. 129–139. Occasional Papers No. 1. Department of Anthropology, University of Alberta, Edmonton.

Milton, C.

1971 Authigenic minerals of the Green River Formation. *University of Wyoming Contributions to Geology* 10(1):57–64.

Mitchell, Mark

2002 Protohistoric Rock Art in the Arkansas River Basin: Integrating Archaeology, Rock Art and Ethnohistory. Paper presented at the 67th Annual Meeting of the Society for American Archaeology, Denver.

2004 Tracing Comanche history: Eighteenth-century rock art depictions of leather- armoured horses from the Arkansas River Basin, south-eastern Colorado, USA. *Antiquity* 78(299):115–126.

Moerman, Daniel E.

1998 *Native American Ethnobotany*. Timber Press, Portland.

Mollyneaux, Brian L., Nancy J. Hodgson, and Rachel M. Hinton

2001 *The Archaeological Survey and National Register Evaluation of Devil's Tower National Monument, Crook County, Wyoming, 1997–1998*. National Park Service, Denver.

Monsalve, Maria Victoria, Dongya Y. Yang, and E. Gwin Langemann

2009 Molecular analysis of ancient cervid remains from two archaeological sites: Banff National Park and Rocky Mountain House National Historic Site, Alberta. In *Methods, Techniques, and Innovative Approaches in Archaeology*, edited by Jayne Wilkins and Kirsten Anderson, pp. 167–181. University of Calgary Press, Calgary.

Moore, Gary L., Brad Noisat, and Jeff Campbell

1987 *Archaeological and Historical Investigations on the Amoco Bairoil CO2 Project*. Overland Associates, Inc., Boulder, Colorado. Prepared for Amoco Production Company, Bairoil, Wyoming. Report on file at the Wyoming SHPO Cultural Records Office, Laramie.

Morey, G. B.

1984 Sedimentology of the Sioux quartzite in the Fulda Basin, Pipestone County, southwestern Minnesota. In *Shorter Contributions to the Geology of the Sioux Quartzite (Early Proterozoic), Southwestern Minnesota*, edited by D. L. Southwick, pp. 59–73. Minnesota Geological Survey, Report of Investigations No. 32. St. Paul.

Morlan, Richard E.

1994 Oxbow bison procurement as seen from the Harder site, Saskatchewan. *Journal of Archaeological Sciences* 21:757–777.

Morris, Elizabeth A., Richard C. Blakeslee, and Kevin Thompson

1985 Preliminary description of McKean sites in northeastern Colorado. In *McKean/Middle Plains Archaic: Current Research*, edited by Marcel Kornfeld and Lawrence C. Todd, pp. 11–20. Occasional Papers on Wyoming Archaeology No. 4. Wyoming Recreation Commission, Cheyenne, Wyoming.

Moss, John H., Kirk Bryan, G. William Holmes, Linton Satterthwaite, Jr., Henry P. Hansen, C. Bertrand Schultz, and W. D. Frankforter

1951 *Early Man in the Eden Valley*. University Museum Monographs No. 6. University of Pennsylvania Museum of Archaeology and Anthropology, Philadelphia.

Mulloy, William T.

1942 *The Hagen Site, a Prehistoric Village in the Lower Yellowstone*. Publications in the Social Sciences No. 1. University of Montana, Missoula.

1953 The Ash Coulee site. *American Antiquity* 19(1):73–75.

1954a Archaeological investigations in the Shoshone Basin of Wyoming. *University of Wyoming Publications* 18(1):1–70. Laramie.

1954b The McKean site in northeastern Wyoming. *Southwestern Journal of Anthropology* 10(4):432–460.

1954c A bannerstone from Wyoming. *Southwestern Lore* 20(1):7–8.

1958 A preliminary historical outline for the Northwestern Plains. *University of Wyoming Publications* 22(1). Laramie.

1959 The James Allen site near Laramie, Wyoming. *American Antiquity* 25(1):112–116.

1965a Archaeological investigations along the North Platte River in eastern Wyoming. *University of Wyoming Publications* 31(2). Laramie.

1965b The Indian village at Thirty-Mile Mesa, Montana. *University of Wyoming Publications* 31(1):1–21. Laramie.

Mulloy, William T., and Louis C. Steege

1967 Continued archaeological investigations along the North Platte River in eastern Wyoming. *University of Wyoming Publications* 33(3). Laramie.

Muñiz, Mark Peter

2004 Exploring technological organization and burial practices at the Paleoindian Gordon Creek site (5LR99), Colorado. *Plains Anthropologist* 49(191):253–279.

2005 The Cody Complex Revisited: Landscape Use and Technological Organization on the Northwestern Plains. Unpublished Ph.D. dissertation, Department of Anthropology, University of Colorado, Boulder.

2009 Microwear, typology, and the Cody component. In *Hell Gap: A Stratified Paleoindian Campsite at the Edge of the Rockies*, edited by M. L. Larson, M. Kornfeld, and G. C. Frison , pp. 195–215. University of Utah Press, Salt Lake City.

Munroe, J. S.

2003 Holocene timberline and palaeoclimate of the northern Uinta Mountains, northeastern Utah. *The Holocene* 13:175–185.

Murcray, Dirk

1993 An assessment of the newly discovered Upper Powder Spring sites: A hunting complex in southwest Wyoming. *The Wyoming Archaeologist* 37(1–2):13–26.

Myers, Thomas P., George Corner, and Lloyd G. Tanner

1981 Preliminary report on the 1979 excavations at the Clary Ranch site. *Transactions of the Nebraska Academy of Sciences* 9:1–7. Lincoln.

Nabokov, Peter, and Lawrence L. Loendorf

2000 *American Indians and Yellowstone National Park*. Loendorf and Associates, Red Lodge, Montana. Report prepared for the Department of the Interior, National Park Service, Rocky Mountain Region.

Nelson, Nels C.

1942 Camping on ancient trails. *Natural History* 49:262–267.

1943 Contribution to Montana archaeology. *American Antiquity* 9(2):162–169.

Nelson, W. H.

1963 *Geology of the Duck Creek Pass Quadrangle, Montana.* U. S. Geological Survey Bulletin 1121J. Washington, DC.

Nero, Robert W., and Bruce A. McCorquodale

1958 Report on an excavation at the Oxbow Dam site. *The Blue Jay* 16(2):82–92.

Neumann, George

1942 American Indian crania with low vaults. *Human Biology* 14:178–191.

1952 Archaeology and race in the American Indian. In *Archaeology of the Eastern United States,* edited by James B. Griffin, pp. 13–34. University of Chicago Press, Chicago.

1969 The Siouan peoples of the East and the Plains. *Plains Anthropologist* 14(46):315–316.

Newberry, Janice C., and Cheryl Harrison

1986 *The Sweetwater Creek Site.* Cultural Resource Management Report No. 19. Archaeological Services of Western Wyoming College, Rock Springs.

Newman, Bonita, and Lawrence Loendorf

2005 Portable X-ray fluorescence analysis of rock art pigments. *Plains Anthropologist* 50(195):277–283.

Nimmo, Barry W.

1971 Population dynamics of a Wyoming pronghorn cohort from Eden-Farson site, 48SW304. *Plains Anthropologist* 16(54):285–288.

Niven, Laura B.

1997 Seasonal Variability of Prehistoric Bison Procurement and Utilization on the Northwestern Plains. Unpublished Master's thesis, Department of Anthropology, University of Wyoming, Laramie.

Niven, Laura B., and Matthew G. Hill

1998 Season of bison mortality at three Plains Archaic kill sites in Wyoming. *Plains Anthropologist* 43(163):1–26.

Noble, Tom, and Neffra Matthews

2006 *Proposal for Photogrammetric Documentation of Legend Rock.* Submitted to the Wyoming Department of State Parks and Cultural Resources. Bureau of Land Management National Science and Technology Center, Denver, Colorado.

Nowak, Timothy R., and L. Adrien Hannus

1985 Lithic raw materials from the West Horse Creek site (39SH37). *South Dakota Archaeology* 8–9:98–114.

Olivier, Georges

1969 *Practical Anthropology.* C. C. Thomas, Springfield, Illinois.

Olson, Linda, and Lawrence L. Loendorf

2003 *Tolar Petroglyph Site.* Report prepared for the Wyoming Department of Transportation. Loendorf and Associates, Albuquerque, New Mexico.

O'Neil, Brian

1993 *The Archaeology of the Grand Junction Resource Area: Crossroads to the Colorado Plateau and the Southern Rocky Mountains, a Class I Overview.* Prepared for the USDI, BLM Grand Junction Resource Area Office, Grand Junction, Colorado. Manuscript on file, BLM, Grand Junction.

Ono, Akira

2001 *Flake Bone Tools.* University of Tokyo Press, Tokyo.

Outram, A.K.

2001 A new approach to identifying bone marrow and grease exploitation: Why the "indeterminate" fragments should not be ignored. *Journal of Archaeological Sciences* 28(4):401–410.

Over, William H.

1936 The archaeology of Ludlow Cave and its significance. *American Antiquity* 2:126–129.

Overstreet, D. E.
2004 Pre-Clovis occupation in southeastern Wisconsin. In *New Perspective on the First Americans*, edited by B. Lepper and R. Bonnichsen, pp. 41–48. Texas A & M Press, College Station.

Owsley, Douglas W., and Karin S. Bruwelheide
2008 Cranial trauma in Historic period Central and Northern Plains Indians. In *Skeletal Biology and Bioarchaeology of the Northwestern Plains*, edited by G. W. Gill and R. L. Weathermon, pp. 212–225. University of Utah Press, Salt Lake City.

Owsley, D.W., and David R. Hunt
2001 Clovis and Early Archaic crania from the Anzick site (24PA506) Park County, Montana. *Plains Anthropologist* 46(176):115–124.

Page, Michael K.
2007 Appendix B: Pottery from the Crow component. In *Medicine Lodge Creek: Holocene Archaeology of the Eastern Bighorn Basin, Wyoming*, edited by George C. Frison and Danny N. Walker, pp. 245–250. Clovis Press, Avondale, Colorado..
2009 The High Plains Upper Republican Reconsidered: Stylistic and Petrographic Analysis of Central Plains Tradition Ceramics from the High Plains. Unpublished Master's Thesis, Department of Anthropology, University of Wyoming, Laramie.

Palmer, Allison R.
1983 The decade of North American geology: 1983 geologic time scale. *Geology* 11:503–504.

Palmer, F. E., J. T. Staley, R. G. E. Murray, T. Counsell, and J. B. Adams
1985 Identification of manganese-oxidizing bacteria from desert varnish. *Geomicrobiology Journal* 4:343–360.

Parsons, F. G.
1914 The characteristics of the English thigh bone. *Journal of Anatomy and Physiology* 48:238–267.

Pastor, Jana V., and Patrick M. Lubinski (editors)
2000 *Pronghorn Past and Present: Archaeology, Ethnography, and Biology*. Plains Anthropologist, Memoir No. 32. Lincoln, Nebraska.

Peebles, Thomas C.
1981 *A Class II Cultural Resource Inventory of the Eastern Powder River Basin*. Metcalf-Zier Archaeologists, Eagle, Colorado. Submitted to the Casper District, Wyoming Bureau of Land Management.

Petraglia, Michal D., and David T. Nash
1987 The impact of fluvial processes on experimental sites. In *Natural Formation Processes and the Archaeological Record*, edited by D. T. Nash and M. D. Petraglia, pp. 108–130. British Archaeological Reports International Series 352. Oxford, England.

Peterson, Michael
2001 Folsom Mobility and Technological Organization at the Krmpotich Folsom Site. Unpublished Master's thesis, Department of Anthropology, University of Wyoming, Laramie.

Pettyjohn, Wayne A.
1966 *Eocene Paleosol in the Northern Great Plains*. U. S. Geological Survey Professional Paper 550C. Washington, DC.

Pitblado, Bonnie L.
2003 *Late Paleoindian Occupation of the Southern Rocky Mountains*. University of Colorado Press, Boulder.

Pitblado, Bonnie L., and Robert H. Brunswig
2007 That was then, this is now: Seventy years of Paleoindian research in Colorado. In *Frontiers in Colorado Paleoindian Archaeology*, edited by R. H. Brunswig and B.L. Pitblado, pp. 39–84. University of Colorado Press, Boulder.

Pool, Kelly
2001 Eating Roots and Rabbits for 7600 Years in Southwest Wyoming: Results of Data Recovery at 48SW8842. Paper presented at the Colorado Council of Professional Archaeologists Annual Meeting, La Junta, Colorado.

Pool, Kelly
2006 *Colorado Interstate Gas Company Uinta Basin Lateral: Final Report of Excavations, Moffat and Rio Blanco Counties, Colorado and Sweetwater Country, Wyoming. Volume 29: 48SW8842*. Metcalf Archaeological Consultants, Inc. Submitted to Colorado Interstate Company, Colorado Spring. Report on file at the WYSHPO Cultural Records Office, Laramie.

Porter, C. L.
1962 Vegetation zones of Wyoming. *University of Wyoming Publications* 27(2):6–12. Laramie.

Powell, Joseph F., and Jerome C. Rose
1999 Report on the osteological assessment of the "Kennewick Man" skeleton (CENWW97. Kennewick). In *Report on the Non-Destructive Examination, Description, and Analysis of the Human Remains from Columbia Park, Kennewick, Washington*, by the National Park Service. Electronic document, http://www.nps.gov/archaeology/kennewick/powell_rose.htm, accessed May 5, 2006.

Prasciunas, Mary M., George C. Frison, Marcel Kornfeld, Mark E. Miller, and Steven J. Sutter
2008 Clovis in Wyoming. *Current Research in the Pleistocene* 25:135–137.

Putnam, J. D.
1876 Hieroglyphics observed in Summit Canyon, Utah, on Little Popo Agie River in Wyoming. *Proceedings of the Davenport Academy of Natural Sciences* 1867–1876, Vol. 1.

Quigg, J. Michael, Mary E. Malainey, Roman Przybylski, and Mark Mitchel
2001 No bones about it: Using lipid analysis of burned rock and groundstone residues to examine Late Archaic subsistence practices in south Texas. *Plains Anthropologist* 46(177):283–303.

Ramsay, Charles L.
1993 The Redtail Site: A McKean Habitation in South Central Saskatchewan. Unpublished Master's thesis, Department of Anthropology and Archaeology, University of Saskatchewan, Saskatoon.

Randall, A. G.
1960 Catalog of formation names for the Overthrust Belt and vicinity, western Wyoming. *Wyoming Geological Association, Fifteenth Annual Field Conference Guidebook*:169–177.

Rapson, David J.
1990 Pattern and Process in Intra-Site Spatial Analysis: Site Structural and Faunal Research at the Bugas-Holding Site. Unpublished Ph.D. dissertation, Department of Anthropology, University of New Mexico, Albuquerque.

Rapson, David, and Laura Niven
2009 Faunal assemblage: 1960–1966. In *Hell Gap: A Stratified Paleoindian Campsite at the Edge of the Rockies*, edited by M. L. Larson, M. Kornfeld, and G. C. Frison, pp. 111–134. University of Utah Press, Salt Lake City.

Ray, Jack H., Neal H. Lopinot, Edwin R. Hajic, and Rolfe D. Mandel
1998 The Big Eddy site: A multicomponent Paleoindian site on the Ozark Border, southwest Missouri. *Plains Anthropologist* 43:73–81.

Reed, Alan D., and Michael D. Metcalf
1999 *Colorado Prehistory: A Context for the Northern Colorado River Basin*. Colorado Council of Professional Archaeologists, Denver.

Reed, Lori Stephens
2003 *Athabascan Research Project Ceramic Analysis*. Report prepared for Athabaskan Research, Green Valley, Arizona. On file at the University of Wyoming Archaeological Repository, University of Wyoming, Laramie.

Reeve, Stuart A., Gary A. Wright, and Priscilla Mecham
1979 Archeological Investigations of the Lawrence Site (48TE509): Grand Teton National Park, Wyoming. Manuscript on file, Midwest Archeological Center, Lincoln, Nebraska.

Reeves, Brian O. K.
1973 The concept of an Altithermal cultural hiatus in Northern Plains prehistory. *American Anthropologist* 75(5):1221–1253.

Reeves, Brian O. K.

1978 Head-Smashed-In: 5500 years of bison jumping in the Alberta Plains. In *Bison Procurement and Utilization: A Symposium*, edited by Leslie B. Davis and Michael Wilson, pp. 151–174. Plains Anthropologist Memoir 14. Lincoln, Nebraska.

1983a General remarks on native subsistence adaptations in the Great Plains. In *Man and Changing Environments in the Great Plains, Transactions of the Nebraska Academy of Science* 11:115–118. Special issue edited by Warren W. Caldwell, C. Bertrand Schultz, and T. Mylan Stout. Lincoln.

1983b *Culture Change in the Northern Plains: 1000 B.C.–A.D. 1000.* Occasional Paper No. 20. Archaeological Survey of Alberta, Edmonton.

1990 Communal bison hunter of the Northern Plains. In *Hunters of the Recent Past*, edited by L. B. Davis and B. O. K. Reeves, pp. 168–194. Unwin Hyman, London.

Reeves, B. O. K., and J. F. Dormaar

1972 A partial Holocene pedological and archaeological record from the southern Alberta Rocky Mountains. *Arctic and Alpine Research* 4(4):325–336.

Regan, A. B.

1934 Some notes on the history of the Uintah Basin in northeastern Utah to 1850. *Proceedings of the Utah Academy of Science, Arts, and Letters* 11:55–64.

Reher, Charles A.

1970 Population dynamics of the Glenrock *Bison bison* population. In *The Glenrock Buffalo Jump, 48CO304*, edited by George C. Frison. Appendix II. Plains Anthropologist Memoir 7. Lincoln, Nebraska.

1971 A Survey of Ceramic Sites in Southeastern Wyoming. Unpublished Master's thesis, Department of Anthropology, University of Wyoming, Laramie.

1973 The Wardell *Bison bison:* Population dynamics and archaeological interpretation. In *The Wardell Buffalo Trap 48SU301: Communal Procurement in the Upper Green River Basin, Wyoming*, edited by George C. Frison, pp. 89–105. Appendix II. Anthropological Papers No. 48. University of Michigan Museum of Anthropology, Ann Arbor.

1974 Population study of the Casper site bison. In *The Casper Site: A Hell Gap Bison Kill on the High Plains*, edited by George C. Frison, pp. 113–124. Academic Press, New York.

1978 Bison population and other deterministic factors in a model of adaptive process on the shortgrass plains. In *Bison Procurement and Utilization: A Symposium*, edited by L. B. Davis and Michael Wilson, pp. 23–39. Plains Anthropologist Memoir 14. Lincoln, Nebraska.

1979 *Western Powder River Survey.* Report for the Bureau of Land Management. Report on file at the Office of Wyoming State Archaeologist, University of Wyoming, Laramie.

1983 Analysis of spatial structure in stone circle sites. In *From Microcosm to Macrocosm: Advances in Tipi Ring Investigation and Interpretation*, edited by Leslie B. Davis, pp. 193–222. Plains Anthropologist Memoir 19. Lincoln, Nebraska.

1987 *Documentation and Evaluation of The Muddy Creek Archaeological Site Complex.* Report prepared by Department of Anthropology, University of Wyoming. Submitted to Wyoming Bureau of Land Management. Report on file at Wyoming Historic Preservation Office, Laramie.

1991 Large scale lithic quarries and regional transport systems on the High Plains of eastern Wyoming. In *Raw Material Economies Among Prehistoric Hunter-Gatherers*, edited by A. Montet-White and S. Holen, pp. 251–284. University of Kansas Publications in Anthropology No. 19. Lawrence.

2006 The Distribution of Obsidian in the Great Plains and its Relationship to Trade and Exchange. Paper presented at the 61st Plains Anthropological Conference, Topeka.

Reher, Charles A., and George C. Frison

1980 *The Vore Site, 48CK302, a Stratified Buffalo Jump in the Wyoming Black Hills.* Plains Anthropologist Memoir 16. Lincoln, Nebraska.

Reher, Charles A., and Raymond Kunselman

1990 Obsidian Source Use in the High Plains of Southeast Wyoming. Paper presented at the 48th Plains Anthropological Conference, Oklahoma City.

Reher, Charles A., George M. Zeimens, and George C. Frison

1985 The Cordero site 48CA75: A Middle Plains Archaic bison processing station in the central Powder River Basin. In *McKean/Middle Plains Archaic: Current Research*, edited by Marcel Kornfeld and Lawrence C. Todd, pp. 109–121. Occasional Papers on Wyoming Archaeology No. 4. Wyoming Recreation Commission, Cheyenne, Wyoming.

Reid, Kenneth C.

1984 Fusulinacean sourcing of late Paleozoic cherts in the western Midwest. In *Prehistoric Chert Exploitation: Studies from the Midcontinent*, edited by Brian M. Butler and Ernest E. May, pp. 253–270. Occasional Paper No. 2. Southern Illinois University Center for Archaeological Investigations, Carbondale.

Reidel, D. W.

1969 Geology of the Tepee Trail Formation, Badwater area, Fremont and Natrona counties, Wyoming. *Wyoming Geological Association, Twenty-first Annual Field Guidebook:*39–42. Wyoming Geological Society, Casper.

Reider, Richard G.

1985 Soil formation at the McKean archaeological site, northeastern Wyoming. In *McKean/Middle Plains Archaic: Current Research*, edited by Marcel Kornfeld and Lawrence C. Todd, pp. 51–61. Occasional Papers on Wyoming Archaeology No. 4. Wyoming Recreation Commission, Cheyenne, Wyoming.

1990 Late Pleistocene and Holocene pedogenic and environmental trends at archaeological sites in plains and mountain areas of Colorado and Wyoming. In *Archaeological Geology of North America*, edited by P. Lasca and J. Donahue, pp. 335–360. Geological Society of America, Centennial Special Volume 4. Boulder, Colorado.

2009 Soil development. In *Hell Gap: A Stratified Paleoindian Campsite at the Edge of the Rockies*, edited by M. L. Larson, M. Kornfeld, and G. C. Frison, pp. 53–71. University of Utah Press, Salt Lake City.

Reinhard, Karl J., Larry Tieszen, Karin L. Sandness, Lynae M. Beiningen, Elizabeth Miller, A. Mohammad Ghazi, Christina E. Miewald, and Sandra V. Barnum

1994 Trade, contact and female health in northeast Nebraska. In *In The Wake of Contact: Biological Responses to Conquest*, edited by C. S. Larsen and G. R. Milner, pp. 63–74. Wiley-Liss, New York.

Reiss, David

1990 *Archaeological Investigations at Site 48FR2330, Wyoming. Muddy Gap-Lander, Fremont County, Wyoming.* Prepared for WYDOT. Report on file at the Wyoming SHPO Cultural Records Office, Laramie.

1995 *A Class III Cultural Resource Inventory of WYARNG North Training Area, Platte County, Wyoming.* Report prepared by the Office of the Wyoming State Archaeologist for the Wyoming Army National Guard. On file at the Wyoming State Historic Preservation Office, Laramie.

2004 Elk Dreamers in Wyoming. Paper presented at the 62nd Plains Anthropological Conference, Billings, Montana.

Renaud, E. B.

1936 *Pictographs and Petroglyphs of the High Western Plains.* Archaeological Survey of the High Western Plains, Eighth Report. Department of Anthropology, University of Denver. Manuscript on file, Department of Anthropology, University of Wyoming, Laramie.

Renfrew, Collin

1973 *Before Civilisation: The Radiocarbon Revolution and Prehistoric Europe.* Jonathan Cape, London.

Renfrew, Colin, and Paul Bahn

2008 *Archaeology Theories, Methods and Practice.* 5th edition. Thames and Hudson, New York.

Rennie, P. J., and T. S. Hughes

1998 Archaeological investigations at the Quinn Creek site. *Archaeology in Montana* 39(2):1–65.

Reust, T., R. Russell, W. E. Eckerle, S. Taddie, C. S. Smith, and D. Newton

2002 *Data Recovery Excavations at Site 48UT375, Uinta County, Wyoming.* Report prepared by TRC Mariah Associates, Laramie, Wyoming, for Pioneer Pipeline Company.

Richings-Germain, Samantha
2002 The Jerry Craig Site: A Paleoindian Bison Bonebed in the Colorado Rocky Mountains. Unpublished Master's thesis, Department of Anthropology, University of Wyoming, Laramie.

Rick, John W.
1987 Dates as data: An examination of the Peruvian Preceramic radiocarbon record. *American Antiquity* 52:55–73.

Ritzma, H. R.
1965 Fossil soil at the base of Paleocene rocks, southern Rock Springs Uplift, Wyoming. *Wyoming Geological Association, Nineteenth Annual Field Conference Guidebook:*136–139. Wyoming Geological Society, Casper.

Roberts, Frank H. H.
1935 A Folsom Complex: A preliminary report on investigations at the Lindenmeier site in northern Colorado. *Smithsonian Miscellaneous Collections* 94:1–35.
1936 Additional information on the Folsom Complex. *Smithsonian Miscellaneous Collections* 95:1–38.
1943 A new site. *American Antiquity* 8:100.
1951 The early Americans. *Scientific American* 184(2):15–19.
1961 The Agate Basin complex. In *Homenaje a Pablo Martinez del Rio,* pp. 125–132. Instituto Nacional de Antropología y Historia, Mexico City.

Robson, John R. K.
1975 Problems in assessing nutritional status in the field. *Yearbook of Physical Anthropology* 19:158–165.

Rogers, Martha
2008 An analysis of discrete cranial traits of Northwestern Plains Indians. In *Skeletal Biology and Bioarchaeology of the Northwestern Plains,* edited by G. W. Gill and R. L. Weathermon, pp. 177–199. University of Utah Press, Salt Lake City.

Roll, Tom E.
2003 *The Camp Baker Quarry (24ME467): 2001.* Report prepared by the Department of Sociology and Anthropology, Montana State University, for the Bureau of Land Management, Montana.

Roll, Tom E., and Ken Deaver
1980 *The Bootlegger Trail Site, A Late Prehistoric Spring Bison Kill.* U.S. Department of the Interior, Heritage Conservation and Recreation Service, Interagency Archaeological Services.

Roll, Tom E., William P. Eckerle, and Ken Deaver
1992 Trapped by an Arroyo: The Powers-Yonkee Bison Kill. Unpublished manuscript on file, Department of Sociology, Montana State University, Bozeman, Montana.

Roper, Donna
1997 On Coalescent and Lower Loup hunting camp sites in Nebraska. *South Dakota Archaeology* 21:33–41.

Rood, Ronald J.
1993 Deception Creek projectile points: A Late Paleoindian type for the Foothill-Mountain regions. *Southwestern Lore* 59:26–33.

Root, Matthew J. (editor)
2000 *The Archaeology of the Bobtail Wolf Site: Folsom Occupation of the Knife River Flint Quarry Area.* Washington State University, Pulman.

Root, Matthew J., Stanley A. Ahler, Carl R. Falk, John E. Foss, Herbert Haas, and Joe A. Artz
1986 *Archaeological Investigations in the Knife River Flint Primary Source Area, Dunn County, North Dakota: 1982–1986 Program.* Contribution No. 234. Department of Anthropology, University of North Dakota, Grand Forks.

Root, M. J., J. D. William, M. Kay and L. K. Shifrin
1999 Folsom ultrathin biface and radial break tools in the Knife River Flint quarry area. In *Folsom Lithic Technology: Explorations in Structure and Variation,* edited by D. S. Amick, pp. 144–168. International Monographs in Prehistory, Ann Arbor, Michigan.

Rose, Victoria
2008 The Interior Features of the Wyoming Housepit. Unpublished Master's thesis, Department of Anthropology, University of Wyoming, Laramie.

Rothrock, David P.
1960 Devonian and Mississippian systems in Colorado. In *Guide to the Geology of Colorado*, edited by Robert J. Weimer and John D. Haun, pp. 17–22. Geological Society of America, Rocky Mountain Association of Geologists, and Colorado Scientific Society joint publication. Geological Society of America, New York.

Rothwell, Sarah J.
1996 Intermountain Ceramics at the Eden-Farson Site (48SW304): An Evaluation. Unpublished Master's thesis, Department of Anthropology, University of Wyoming, Laramie.

Rowe, Marvin W.
2001 Dating by AMS radiocarbon analysis. In *Handbook of Rock Art Research*, edited by David S. Whitley, pp. 139–166. Altamira Press, Walnut Creek, California.

Russell, Osborne
1921 *Journal of a Trapper.* Syms-York, Boise, Idaho.

Rux, Marjorie, George C. Frison, and Larry Tiezen
2000 Paleoclimate and Amerindians: Evidence from stable isotopes and atmospheric circulation. *PNAS* 98(5):2485–2490.

Sanderson, Ivan D.
1984 Recognition and significance of inherited quartz overgrowths in quartz arenites. *Journal of Sedimentary Petrology* 54(2):473–486.

Sassaman, Kenneth E.
1997 Refining soapstone vessel chronology in the southeast. *Early Georgia* 25(1):1–20.
2006 Dating and explaining soapstone vessels: A comment on Truncer. *American Antiquity* 71(1):141–156.

Saul, John M.
1969 Study of the Spanish Diggings, aboriginal flint quarries of southeastern Wyoming. *National Geographic Society Research Reports, 1964 Projects*, pp. 183–199. Washington, DC.

Saunders, Jeffrey J.
1977 *Late Pleistocene Vertebrates of the Western Ozark Highlands.* Reports of Investigations No. 33. Illinois State Museum, Springfield.

Schaafsma, Polly
1971 *Rock Art of Utah.* Papers of the Peabody Museum of Archaeology and Ethnology Vol. 65. Harvard University, Cambridge.
1986 Rock art. In *Great Basin,* edited by Warren L. D'Azevedo, pp. 215–227. Handbook of North American Indians, Vol. 11, William C. Sturtevant, general editor. Smithsonian Institution, Washington, DC.

Scheiber, Laura Lee
1993 Prehistoric Domestic Architecture on the Northwestern High Plains: A Temporal Analysis of Stone Circles in Wyoming. Unpublished Master's thesis, Department of Anthropology, University of Wyoming.
1994 A probable early nineteenth century Crow burial: The Pitchfork Rockshelter reexamined. *Plains Anthropologist* 39(147):37–51.
2001 Late Prehistoric Daily Practice and Culture Contact on the North American High Plains. Unpublished Ph.D. dissertation, Department of Anthropology, University of California, Berkeley.
2006 Skeletal biology: Plains. In *Environment, Origins, and Population*, edited by Douglas Ubelaker, pp. 595–609. Handbook of North American Indians, Vol. 3, William C. Sturtevant, general editor. Smithsonian Institution, Washington, DC.
2008 Life and death on the Northwestern Plains: Mortuary practices and cultural transformations. In *Skeletal Biology and Bioarcheology of the Northwestern Plains,* edited by G. W. Gill and R. L. Weathermon, pp. 22–41. University of Utah Press, Salt Lake City.

Scheiber, Laura L., and Judson Byrd Finley
2009 Mountain Shoshone technological transition across the Great Divide. In *Across the Great Divide: Continuity and Change in Native North American Societies 1400–1900*, edited by L. L. Scheiber and M. D. Mitchell, University of Arizona Press.

Scheiber, Laura L., and George W. Gill
1996 Bioarcheology of the Northwestern Plains. In *Archaeological and Bioarcheological Resources of the Northern Plains*, edited by George C. Frison and Robert C. Mainfort, pp. 91–119. Arkansas Archaeological Survey Research Series No. 47. Fayetteville.
1997 Bioarcheology of the Northwestern Plains. In *Bioarcheology of the North Central United States*, edited by D. W. Owsley and J. C. Rose, pp. 88–114. Arkansas Archeological Survey Research Series No. 49. Fayetteville.

Schick, Kathy D.
1986 *Stone Age Sites in the Making*. British Archaeological Reports International Series 319. Oxford, England.

Schlesier, Karl H. (editor)
1994 *Plains Indians, A.D. 500–1500*. University of Oklahoma Press, Norman.

Schofield, Graeme
1959 Metric and morphological features of the femur of the New Zealand Maori. *The Journal of the Royal Anthropological Institute of Great Britain and Ireland* 89(1):89–105.

Schultz, C. Bertrand
1943 Some artifact sites of early man in the Great Plains and adjacent areas. *American Antiquity* 8(3):242–249.

Schuster, Helen H.
1987 Tribal identification of Wyoming rock art: Some problematic considerations. *Archaeology in Montana* 28(2):25–43.

Scoggin, William E.
1978 The Sand Creek burial from central Wyoming. *The Wyoming Archaeologist* 21(3):10–29.

Scott-Cummings, Linda
1995 Pollen analysis final report. In *High Altitude Hunter-Gatherer Adaptations in the Middle Rocky Mountains 1988–1994 Investigations*, by M. L. Larson, M. Kornfeld, and D. J. Rapson. Technical Report No. 4. Department of Anthropology, University of Wyoming, Laramie.

Scott, Robert B., Anne E. Harding, William C. Hood, Rex D. Cole, Richard F. Livaccari, James B. Johnson, Ralph E. Shroba, and Robert P. Dickerson
2001 *Geologic Map of the Colorado National Monument and Adjacent Areas, Mesa County, Colorado*. Geologic Investigations Series I-2740. U.S. Geological Survey, Denver.

Secoy, Frank R.
1953 *Changing Military Patterns on the Great Plains*. Monographs of the American Ethnological Society No. 21.

Sellards, E. H.
1952 *Early Man in America: A Study in Prehistory*. University of Texas Press, Austin.
1955 Fossil bison and associated artifacts from Milnesand, New Mexico. *American Antiquity* 20(4):336–344.

Sellet, Frederic
1999 A Dynamic View of Paleoindian Assemblages at the Hell Gap Site, Wyoming. Unpublished Ph.D. dissertation, Department of Anthropology, Southern Methodist University, Dallas.

Sellet, Frederic, James Donohue, and Matthew G. Hill
2009 The Jim Pitts site: A stratified Paleoindian site in the Black Hills of South Dakota. *American Antiquity* 74(4):735–758.

Service, Elman R.
1962 *Primitive Social Organization: An Evolutionary Perspective*. Random House, New York.

Shaeffer, J. B.
1958 The Alibates flint quarry, Texas. *American Antiquity* 24(2):188–191.

Shanks, Orin C.

1997 Immunological Identification of Ancient Proteins. Unpublished Master's thesis, Department of Anthropology, University of Wyoming, Laramie.

2003 DNA Recovery and Identification from Stone Tool Microcracks. Unpublished Ph.D. dissertation, Department of Microbiology, Oregon State University, Corvallis.

Shanks, Orin C., Robson Bonnichsen, A.T. Vella, and Walt Ream

2001 Recovery of protein and DNA trapped in stone tool microcracks. *Journal of Archaeological Sciences* 28(9):965–972.

Shanks, Orin C., L. Hodges, L. Tilley, M. Kornfeld, M.L. Larson, and W. Ream

2005 DNA from ancient stone tools and bones excavated at Bugas-Holding, Wyoming. *Journal of Archaeological Science* 32:27–38.

Shanks, Orin C., M. Kornfeld, and D. Hawk

1999 Protein analysis of Bugas-Holding tools: New trends in immunological studies. *Journal of Archaeological Science* 26:1183–1191.

Shanks, Orin C., M. Kornfeld, and W. Ream

2005 DNA and protein recovery from washed experimental stone tools. *Archeometry* 46(4):663–672.

Shapiro, Beth, Alexei J. Drummond, Andrew Rambauyt, Michael C. Wilson, Paul E. Matheus, Andrei V. Sher, Oliver G. Pybus, M. Thomas P. Gilbert, Ian Barnes, Jonas Binladen, Eske Willerslev, Anders J. Hansen, Gennady F. Baryshnikov, James A. Burns, Sergei Davydov, Jonathan C. Driver, Duane G. Froese, C. Richard Harington, Grant Keddie, Pavel Kosintsev, Michael L. Kunz, Larry D. Martin, Robert O. Stephenson, John Storer, Richard Tedford, Sergei Zimov, and Alan Cooper

2004 Rise and fall of the Beringian Steppe bison. *Science* 306:1561–1565.

Sharrock, Floyd W.

1966 *Prehistoric Occupation Patterns in Southwest Wyoming and Cultural Relationships with the Great Basin and Plains Culture Areas.* University of Utah Anthropological Papers No. 77. Salt Lake City.

Shaw, Leslie

1980 Early Plains Archaic Procurement Systems During the Altithermal: The Wyoming Evidence. Unpublished Master's thesis, Department of Anthropology, University of Wyoming, Laramie.

Shay, C. Thomas

1971 *The Itasca Bison Kill Site: An Ecological Analysis.* Minnesota Historical Society, Prehistoric Archaeology Series. St. Paul.

Sheldon, R. P.

1955 Stratigraphy of the Phosphoria Formation in the Wyoming and Windriver ranges, Wyoming. *Wyoming Geological Association, Tenth Annual Field Conference Guidebook:*64. Wyoming Geological Society, Casper.

1956 Stratigraphy of the Phosphoria Formation in the Jackson Hole region, Wyoming. *Wyoming Geological Association, Eleventh Annual Field Conference Guidebook:*66–69. Wyoming Geological Society, Casper.

Shepard, Anna O.

1968 *Ceramics for the Archaeologist.* Carnagie Institution of Washington Publication No. 609, Washington, DC.

Shepherd, Ruth

1992 A Cultural Model for Ground Stone Use in the Middle Rocky Mountains: The Helen Lookingbill Site. Unpublished Master's thesis, Department of Anthropology, University of Wyoming, Laramie.

Sheridan, Susan G., and Dennis P. Van Gerven

1988 Report on the human remains GLM-1, Bairoil, Wyoming. Appendix to *A Prehistoric Human Burial from Bairoil Locality P-139 (48SW7101) Amoco LSU Reservoir 2, Sweetwater County, Wyoming.* Report WY-2535-27 by William Lane Shields, John Greer, and Mavis Greer. John and Mavis Greer, Archaeological Consultants, Casper, Wyoming.

Shields, William Lane, John Greer, and Mavis Greer
1989 *A Prehistoric Human Burial from Bairoil Locality P-139 (48SW7101) at Amoco LSU Reservoir 2, Sweetwater County, Wyoming*. Report WY-2535–27. John Greer and Mavis Greer, Archaeological Consultants, Casper, Wyoming.

Shimkin, D. B.
1947 Wind River Shoshone ethnogeography. *Anthropological Records* 5(4). University of California Press, Berkeley.

Shipman, Pat
1980 Applications of scanning electron microscopy to taphonomic problems. In *The Research Potential of Anthropological Museum Collections*, edited by Anne-Marie Cantwell, J. B. Griffin, and N. A. Rothschild, pp. 357–386. Annals of the New York Academy of Sciences Vol. 376. New York.

Shipman, Pat, Giraud Foster, and Margaret Schoeninger
1984 Burnt bones and teeth: An experimental study of color, morphology, crystal structure and shrinkage. *Journal of Archaeological Science* 11:307–325.

Shippee, J. M.
1971 Wickiups of Yellowstone Park. *Plains Anthropologist* 16(51):74–75.

Simms, S. C.
1903 A wheel-shaped stone monument in Wyoming. *American Anthropologist* n. s. 5(1):1107–1110.

Simpson, J. H.
1876 *Report of Explorations across the Great Basin of the Territory of Utah*. U. S. Government Printing Office, Washington, DC.

Simpson, Tana
1984 Population dynamics of mule deer. In *The Dead Indian Creek Site: An Archaic Occupation in the Absaroka Mountains of Northwestern Wyoming*, edited by George C. Frison and Danny N. Walker. *The Wyoming Archaeologist* 27(1–2):83–96.

Sinclair, Anthony
1995. The technique as a symbol in Late Glacial Europe. *World Archaeology* 27(1):50–62.

Singler, C. R., and M. D. Picard
1979 Petrography of White River Group (Oligocene) in northwest Nebraska and adjacent Wyoming. *University of Wyoming Contributions to Geology* 18(1):51–67. Laramie.

Sjostrom, Derek J., Michael T. Hren, and C. Page Chamberlin
2004 Oxygen isotope records of geothite from ferricete deposits indicate regionally varying Holocene climate change in the Rocky Mountain region, U.S.A. *Quaternary Research* 61:64–71.

Skinner, Morris F., and Ove Kaisen
1947 The Fossil bison of Alaska and a preliminary revision of the genus. *Bulletin of the American Museum of Natural History* 89:123–256. New York.

Slessman, Scott
2004 The Frazier Site: An Agate Basin Occupation and Lithic Assemblage on the Kersey Terrace, Northeastern Colorado. Unpublished Master's thesis, Department of Anthropology, Colorado State University, Fort Collins.

Smallwood, Ashley
2008 Paleoamerican origins workshop. *Mammoth Trumpet* 23(3):1–3, 16–17.

Smiley, Francis E.
1979 Analysis of Cursorial Aspects of Biomechanics of the Forelimb in Wyoming's Holocene Bison. Unpublished Master's thesis, Department of Anthropology, University of Wyoming, Laramie.

Smith, Craig S.
2003 Hunter-gather mobility, storage, and houses in a marginal environment: An example from the mid-Holocene of Wyoming. *Journal of Anthropological Archaeology* 22:162–189.

Smith, Craig S., and Steven D. Creasman
1988 *The Taliaferro Site: 5000 Years of Prehistory in Southwest Wyoming*. Cultural Resources Report Series No. 6. Bureau of Land Management, Cheyenne, Wyoming.

Smith, Craig S., and Lance M. McNees

1999 Facilities and hunter-gatherer long-term land use patterns: An example from southwest Wyoming. *American Antiquity* 64(1):117–136.

2000 Pronghorn and bison procurement during the Uinta phase in southwest Wyoming: A case study. In *Pronghorn Past and Present: Archaeology, Ethnography, and Biology*, edited by Jana V. Pastor and Patrick M. Lubinski, pp. 71–87. Plains Anthropologist Memoir 32. Lincoln, Nebraska.

Smith, Craig S., and Thomas Reust

1992 Sinclair site: Use of space at an Early Archaic housepit site, southcentral Wyoming. *North American Archaeologist* 13:42–66.

Smith, Robert B., and Robert L. Christiansen

1980 Yellowstone Park as a window on the Earth's interior. *Scientific American* 242(2):104–117.

Smith, William A.

1971 A grooved axe typology. *Wisconsin Archaeologist* 52(1):20–41.

Soister, P. E.

1967 *Geology of the Puddle Springs Quadrangle, Fremont County, Wyoming*. U. S. Geological Survey Bulletin 1242c. Washington, DC.

Sowers, Ted C.

1941 *The Wyoming Archaeological Survey: A Report*. Federal Works Progress Administration, Archaeological Project Report, Casper, Wyoming. Original on file at the Coe Library, University of Wyoming, Laramie.

Spencer, Robert F., and Jesse D. Jennings (editors)

1977 *The Native Americans*. 2nd ed. Harper & Rowe, New York.

Speth, John D., and Katherine A. Spielman

1983 Energy source, protein metabolism, and hunter-gatherer subsistence strategies. *Journal of Anthropological Archaeology* 2:1–31.

Spielman, Katherine

1983 Late Prehistoric exchange between the southwest and southern Plains. *Plains Anthropologist* 28:257–272.

Spiess, Arthur E.

1979 *Reindeer and Caribou Hunters*. Academic Press, New York.

Springer, James W.

2005–2006 Scholarship vs. Repatriationism. *Academic Questions* 19(1):6–36.

Stafford, Michael D.

1990 The Powars II Site 48PL330: A Paleoindian Red Ochre Mine in Eastern Wyoming. Unpublished Master's thesis, Department of Anthropology, University of Wyoming, Laramie.

Stafford, Thomas W., Jr., P. E. Hare, Lloyd Currie, A. J. T. Jull, and Douglas J. Donahue

1991 Accelerator radiocarbon dating at the molecular level. *Journal of Archaeological Science* 18:35–72.

Stanford, Dennis J.

1974 Preliminary report of the excavation of the Jones-Miller Hell Gap site, Yuma County, Colorado. *Southwestern Lore* 40(3–4):29–36.

1978 The Jones-Miller site: An example of Hell Gap bison procurement strategy. In *Bison Procurement and Utilization: A Symposium*, edited by L. B. Davis and M. Wilson, pp. 90–97. Plains Anthropologist Memoir 14. Lincoln, Nebraska.

1979a The Selby and Dutton sites: Evidence for a pre-Llano occupation of the High Plains. In *Pre-Llano Cultures of the Americas: Paradoxes and Possibilities*, edited by Robert L. Humphrey and Dennis Stanford, pp. 101–123. The Anthropological Society of Washington, Washington, DC.

1979b Bison kill by ice age hunters. *National Geographic* 155(1):114–121.

1999 Paleoindian archaeology and Late Pleistocene environments in the Plains and southwestern United States. In *Ice Age Peoples of North America*, edited by Robson Bonnichsen and Karen L. Turnmire, pp. 281–339. Oregon State University Press, Corvallis.

Stanford, Dennis J., and Margaret A. Jodry
1988 The Drake Clovis cache. *Current Research in the Pleistocene* 5:21–22.

Steege, Louis C.
1960 A probable Middle Period burial in Wyoming. *Plains Anthropologist* 5(10):82–84.
1967 Happy Hollow Rockshelter. *The Wyoming Archaeologist* 10(3):11–23.

Steele, D. Gentry, and Joseph F. Powell
1992 The peopling of the Americas: The paleobiological evidence. *Human Biology* 64(3):303–366.

Steidtmann, J. R.
1973 Ice and snow in eolian sand dunes of southwestern Wyoming. *Science* 179:796–799.

Steiger, Mark
2002 *Hunter-Gatherer Archaeology of the Colorado High Country*. University of Colorado Press, Niwot.
2006 A Folsom structure in the Colorado Mountains. *American Antiquity* 71(2):321–351.

Steindler, Arthur
1955 *Kinesiology of the Human Body*. Charles C. Thomas, Springfield, Illinois.

Steward, Julian H.
1938 *Basin-Plateau Aboriginal Sociopolitical Groups*. Bureau of American Ethnology Bulletin No. 120. Washington, DC.

Stewart, James J.
1989 Distribution analysis of a petroglyph motif from Legend Rock petroglyph site (48HO4), Hot Springs County, Wyoming. In *Legend Rock Petroglyph Site (L48HO4), Wyoming: 1988 Archaeological Investigations*, edited by Danny N. Walker and Julie E. Francis. Office of the Wyoming State Archaeologist, Laramie. Submitted to the Wyoming Recreation Commission, Cheyenne.

Stewart, T. Dale
1940 Some historical implications of physical anthropology in North America. *Smithsonian Miscellaneous Collections* 100:15–50.
1954 The lower level human skull. Appendix in *The McKean site in northeastern Wyoming*, William T. Mulloy. *Southwestern Journal of Anthropology* 10(4):457–459.
1962 Anterior femoral curvature: Its utility for race identification. *Human Biology* 34:49–62.
1979 *Essentials of Forensic Anthropology*. Charles C. Thomas, Springfield, Illinois.

Stokes, S., and D. R. Gaylord
1993 Optical dating of Holocene dune sands in the Ferris dune field, Wyoming. *Quaternary Research* 39:274–281.

Strickland, J. W.
1956 Mississippian stratigraphy, western Wyoming. *Wyoming Geological Association, Eleventh Annual Field Conference Guidebook*:51–57. Wyoming Geological Society, Casper.

Strong, William D.
1935 *An Introduction to Nebraska Archaeology*. Smithsonian Institution Miscellaneous Collections 39(10). Washington, DC.

Stuart, L. Jaimeson
2000 Metric Analysis of Northwestern Plains Amerindian Skeletal Remains. Unpublished Master's thesis, Department of Anthropology, University of Wyoming, Laramie.

Stuart, L. Jaimeson, and George W. Gill
2008 Northwestern Plains Indian skeletal remains: Metric analysis. In *Skeletal Biology and Bioarcheology of the Northwestern Plains*, edited by G. W. Gill and R. L. Weathermon, pp. 160–176. University of Utah Press, Salt Lake City.

Stuart, Robert
1935 *The Discovery of the Oregon Trail*, edited by Philip Ashton Rollins. Charles Scribner's Sons, New York.

Stucky, R. K.
1977 Archaeological Survey of Sand Wash Basin, Northwestern Colorado. Unpublished Master's thesis, Department of Anthropology, University of Colorado, Boulder.

Stuiver, Minze, and Paula J. Reimer

1993 Extended 14C database and revised CALIB radiocarbon calibration program. *Radiocarbon* 35:215–230.

Stuiver, M., P. J. Reimer, E. Bard, J. W. Beck, G. S. Burr, K. A. Hughen, B. Kromer, F. G. McCormac, J. V. D. Plicht, and M. Spurk

1998 INTCAL98 radiocarbon age calibration 24,000-0 cal BP. *Radiocarbon* 40:1041–1083.

Sundstrom, Linea

1984 *Rock Art of Western South Dakota and the Southern Black Hills.* South Dakota Archaeological Society, Special Publication No. 9. Archaeology Laboratory, Augustana College, Sioux Falls, South Dakota.

1989 *Culture History of the Black Hills with Reference to Adjacent Areas of the Northern Great Plains.* Reprints in Anthropology Vol. 40. J & L Reprint Company, Lincoln, Nebraska.

2002 Steel awls for Stone Age plainswomen: Rock art, religion, and the hide trade on the Northern Plains. *Plains Anthropologist* 47(181):99–119.

2004 *Storied Stone: Indian Rock Art of the Black Hills Country.* University of Oklahoma Press, Norman.

Sundstrom, Linea, and James D. Keyser

1998 Tribal affiliation of shield petroglyphs from the Black Hills and Cave Hills. *Plains Anthropologist* 43(165):225–238.

Sundstrom, Linea, Linda Olson, and Lawrence L. Loendorf

2001 *Hulett South Site, 48CK1544.* Report prepared for the Wyoming Department of Transportation. Loendorf and Associates, Albuquerque, New Mexico.

Surdam, Ronald C., and H. P. Eugster

1976 Mineral reactions in the sedimentary deposits of the Magadi region, Kenya. *Geological Society of America Bulletin* 87:1739–1752.

Surovell, Todd A., and Nicole M. Waguespack

2007 Barger Gulch Locality B. In *Frontiers in Colorado Paleoindian Archaeology*, edited by R. H. Brunswig and B. L. Pitblado, pp. 219–259. University of Colorado Press, Boulder.

Surovell, Todd A., N. M. Waguespack, J. H. Mayer, M. Kornfeld, and G. C. Frison

2005 Shallow site archaeology: Artifact dispersal, stratigraphy, and radiocarbon dating at Barger Gulch, Locality B. *Geoarchaeology* 20(6):627–650.

Sutton, Wendy Ann Swanson

2004 Economic and Social Change during a Critical Transition: The Protohistoric in the Powder River Basin and Big Horn Mountains. Unpublished Ph.D. dissertation, Department of Anthropology, Columbia University, New York.

Swaim, Charles R.

1975 A Survey of the Trail Lake Petroglyphs. Unpublished Master's thesis, Department of Anthropology, University of Wyoming, Laramie, Wyoming.

Swanson, Earl H., Jr., B. Robert Butler, and Robson Bonnichsen

1964 *Birch Creek Papers No. 2: Natural and Cultural Stratigraphy in the Birch Creek Valley of Eastern Idaho.* Occasional Papers of the Idaho State University Museum No. 14.

Swanson, Earl H., Jr., and Paul G. Sneed

1966 *Birch Creek Papers No. 3: The Archaeology of the Shoup Rockshelters in East Central Idaho.* Occasional Papers of the Idaho State University Museum No. 17.

Swedlund, Alan, and Duane Anderson

1999 Gordon Creek Woman meets Kennewick Man: New interpretations and protocols regarding the peopling of the Americas. *American Antiquity* 64(4):569–576.

Syms, L.

1969 The McKean Complex as a Horizon Marker in Manitoba and on the Northern Great Plains. Unpublished Master's thesis, Department of Anthropology, University of Manitoba, Winnipeg.

Tamari, Kotaro, Paul Tinley, Kathy Briffa, and Kiyoshi Aoyagi

2006 Ethnic-, gender-, and age-related differences in femorotibial angle, femoral antetorsion, and tibiofibular torsion: Cross-sectional study among healthy Japanese and Australian Caucasians. *Clinical Anatomy* 19:59–67.

Tankersley, Kenneth B.
2002 *In Search of Ice Age Americans*. Gribbs Smith Publisher, Salt Lake City.

Tanner, Russel L., Joseph Bozovich, Julie E. Francis, and Ronald I. Dorn
1995 The Black Rock Petroglyphs: A Possible Clovis-Age Rock Art Site. Poster paper presented at the 53rd Annual Plains Anthropological Conference, Laramie, Wyoming.

Taylor, Jeb
2006 *Projectile Points of the High Plains*. Jeb Taylor Artifacts, Inc., Buffalo, Wyoming.

Thayer, P. A.
1983 *Relationship of Porosity and Permeability to Petrology of the Madison Limestone in Rock Cores from Three Test Wells in Montana and Wyoming*. U. S. Geological Survey Professional Paper 1273c. Washington, DC.

Thomas, David H.
1971 On distinguishing natural from cultural bone in archaeological sites. *American Antiquity* 36:366–371.

Thompson, Kevin W., and Jana V. Pastor
1995 *People of the Sage: 10,000 Years of Occupation in Southwestern Wyoming*. Cultural Resource Management Report No. 67. Archaeological Services of Western Wyoming College, Rock Springs.

Thompson, K. W., Jana V. Pastor, Linda W. Thompson, and William Current
1989 *The Birch Creek Site: Fifth Millennium B. P. Habitation in Southwest Wyoming*. Cultural Resource Management Report No. 62. Archaeological Services of Western Wyoming College, Rock Springs.

Thorne, T., G. Butler, T. Varcalli, K. Becker, and S. Hayden-Wing
1979 *The Status, Mortality, and Response to Management of the Bighorn Sheep of Whiskey Mountain, Wyoming*. Wildlife Technology Report No. 7. Wyoming Game and Fish Department, Cheyenne.

Tipps, Betsy L., and Alan R. Schroedl
1985 *The Riverton Rock Art Study, Fremont County, Wyoming*. P-III Associates, Inc. USDI Bureau of Reclamation, Billings, Montana. Cultural Records Office, Department of Anthropology, University of Wyoming, Laramie, Wyoming.

Todd, Lawrence C.
1987a Taphonomy of the Horner II bone bed. In *The Horner Site: The Type Site of the Cody Cultural Complex*, edited by George C. Frison and Lawrence C. Todd, pp. 107–198. Academic Press, Orlando.
1987b Analysis of kill-butchery bonebeds and interpretations of Paleoindian hunting. In *The Evolution of Human Hunting*, edited by M. H. Nitecki, and D. V. Nitecki, pp. 225–266. Plenum Press, New York.

Todd, Lawrence C., and Jack L. Hofman
1987 Bison mandibles from the Horner and Finley sites. In *The Horner Site: The Type Site of the Cody Cultural Complex*, edited by George C. Frison and Lawrence C. Todd, pp. 493–539. Academic Press, Orlando.

Todd, Lawrence C., J. L. Hofman, and C. Bertrand Schultz
1990 Seasonality of the Scottsbluff and Lipscomb bison bonebeds: Implications for modeling Paleoindian subsistence. *American Antiquity* 55(4):813–827.

Todd, Lawrence C., David C. Jones, Robert S. Walker, Paul Burnett, and Jeffrey Eighmy
2001 Late Archaic bison hunters in Northern Colorado: 1997–1999 excavations at the Kaplan-Hoover bonebed (5LR3953). *Plains Anthropologist* 46(176):125–147.

Todd, Lawrence C., and David J. Rapson
1988 Long bone fragmentation and interpretation of faunal assemblages: Approaches to comparative analysis. *Journal of Archaeological Sciences* 15:307–325.
1997 Formational analysis of bison bonebeds and interpretation of Paleoindian subsistence. In *Le bison: gibier et moyen de subsistance des hommes du Paléolithique aux Paleoindiens des Grandes Plaines*, edited by J.-Ph. Brugal, F. David, J.G. Enloe, and J. Jaubert, pp. 479–499. Actes du Colloque International, Toulouse 1995. Editions APDCA, Antibes.

Todd, Lawrence C., David J. Rapson, and Jack L. Hofman

1996 Dentition studies of the Mill Iron and other early Paleoindian bison bonebed sites. In *The Mill Iron Site*, edited by G. C. Frison, pp. 145–175. University of New Mexico Press, Albuquerque.

Todd, L. M.

1996 Stratigraphy at the boundary of the Tensleep Sandstone and Park City/Goose Egg formations in the southern Bighorn Mountains and eastern Owl Creek Mountains, Wyoming. *Wyoming Geological Association, Forty-Seventh Annual Field Conference Guidebook*:159–178. Wyoming Geological Society, Casper.

Tratebas, Alice M.

1978 Archaeological Surveys in the Black Hills National Forest, South Dakota, 1975–1977. Manuscript on file, South Dakota Archaeological Research Center. Rapid City.

1985 McKean settlement patterns in the Black Hills: Suggestions for future research. In *McKean/ Middle Plains Archaic: Current Research*, edited by Marcel Kornfeld and Lawrence C. Todd, pp. 137–145. Occasional Papers on Wyoming Archaeology No. 4. Wyoming Recreation Commission, Cheyenne, Wyoming.

1993 Stylistic chronology versus absolute dates for early hunting style rock art on the North American Plains. In *Rock Art Studies, the Post Stylistic Era. Where Do We Go From Here?*, edited by Michel Lorblanchet and Paul G. Bahn, pp. 163–178. Oxbow Monograph No. 35. Oxford, England.

1998 Re-examining the Plains Archaic McKean culture. In *Explorations in American Archaeology: Essays in Honor of Wesley R. Hurt*, edited by M. G. Plew, pp. 259–309. University Press of America, Lanham.

Tratebas, Alice M., and Marcel Kornfeld

2004 Missouri Buttes Antelope Trap. Paper presented at the Annual Meeting of the Society for American Archaeology. Montreal, Canada.

Tratebas, Alice M., and Kristi Vagstad

1979 *Archaeological Test Excavations of Four Sites in the Black Hills National Forest, South Dakota.* South Dakota Archaeological Research Center, Contract Investigations Series No. 6. Fort Meade, South Dakota.

Trigger, Bruce G.

2006 *A History of Archaeological Thought.* 2nd edition. Cambridge University Press, Cambridge.

Truesdale, James A.

1987 A Review of Wyoming Burials and Their Attributes. Paper presented at the 45th Annual Plains Anthropological Conference, Columbia, Missouri.

Truesdale, James A., and George W. Gill

1987 The Bridger Gap burial from southwestern Wyoming. *Plains Anthropologist* 32(115): 17–28.

Truncer, James

2004 Steatite vessel age and occurrence in temperate eastern North America. *American Antiquity* 69(3):487–513.

2006 Taking variation seriously: The case of steatite vessel manufacture. *American Antiquity* 71(1):157–163.

Tunnell, Curtis

1978 *The Gibson Lithic Cache from West Texas.* Texas Historical Commission, Office of State Archaeologist, Report No. 30. Austin.

Tuohy, Donald R.

1986 Portable art objects. In *Great Basin*, edited by Warren L. D'Azevedo, pp. 227–237. Handbook of North American Indians, Vol. 11, William C. Sturtevant, general editor. Smithsonian Institution, Washington, DC.

Turner, C. G.

1979 Dental anthropological implications of agriculture among the Jomon people of central Japan. *American Journal of Physical Anthropology* 51:619–636.

Turpin, Solveig A.

1986 Toward a definition of pictograph style: The lower Pecos bold line geometric. *Plains Anthropologist* 31(112):153–161.

Tweto, Ogden

1979 *Geologic Map of Colorado.* U. S. Geologic Survey, Reston, Virginia.

United States Geological Survey

1913 *Grass Creek Basin 15' Topographic Quadrangle Map, Hot Springs County, Wyoming.* U. S. Government Printing Office, Washington, DC.

Van Houten, F. B.

1964 *Tertiary Geology of the Beaver Rim Area, Fremont and Natrona Counties, Wyoming.* U. S. Geological Survey Bulletin 1164. Washington, DC.

VanNest, Julieann

1985 Patination of Knife River flint artifacts. *Plains Anthropologist* 30:325–339.

Vaughan, P.

1985 *Use-wear Analysis of Flaked Stone Tools.* University of Arizona Press, Tucson.

Vehik, Susan C.

1985 *Lithic Resource Procurement: Proceedings from the Second Conference on Prehistoric Chert Exploitation.* Center for Archaeological Investigations Occasional Paper No. 4. Southern Illinois University, Carbondale.

Verbicky-Todd, Eleanor

1984 *Communal Buffalo Hunting Among the Plains Indians.* Occasional Paper No. 24, Archaeological Survey of Alberta, Edmonton.

Villa, Paola

1983 *Terra Amata and the Middle Pleistocene Archaeological Record of Southern France.* University of California Press, Berkeley.

Voorhies, Michael R.

1969 *Taphonomy and Population Dynamics of an Early Pliocene Vertebrate Fauna, Knox County, Nebraska.* Contributions to Geology Special Paper No. 1. University of Wyoming, Laramie.

Walker, Danny N.

1982 Early Holocene vertebrate fauna. In *The Agate Basin Site: A Record of the Paleoindian Occupation of the Northwestern Plains*, edited by George C. Frison and Dennis Stanford, pp. 274–308. Academic Press, New York.

1987 Horner site local fauna: Vertebrates. In *The Horner Site: The Type Site of the Cody Cultural Complex*, edited by G. C. Frison and L. C. Todd, pp. 327–345. Academic Press, Orlando.

1988 Archaeological evidence for the use of small mammals by prehistoric inhabitants of the Northwestern High Plains. In *The Prairie: Roots of Our Culture; Foundations of Our Economy*, edited by Arnold Davis and Geoffrey Stanford, pp. 6.08.1–6.08.6. Proceedings of the Tenth North American Prairie Conference of Texas Woman's University, Denton, Texas. The Native Prairies Association of Texas, Dallas, Texas.

1989 Archaeological testing results. In *Legend Rock Petroglyph Site (48HO4), Wyoming. 1988 Archaeological Investigations*, edited by Danny N. Walker and Julie E. Francis, pp. 28–117. Manuscript on file, Office of Wyoming State Archaeologist, Department of Anthropology, University of Wyoming, Laramie.

2004a *Year 2000 Archaeological Investigations at the Sand Draw Dump Site, 48FR312, Fremont County, Wyoming.* Occasional Papers in Wyoming Archaeology No. 7. Wyoming State Archaeologists Office, Laramie. (editor)

2004b *Searching for Fort William: An 1834 Trading Post at Fort Laramie National Historic Site, Wyoming.* Wyoming State Archaeologist Office. Prepared for Long Distance Trails Office, National Park Service, Salt Lake City, Utah.

2007 Vertebrate fauna. In *Medicine Lodge Creek Site*, edited by G. C. Frison and D. N. Walker, pp. 177–208. Clovis Press, Avondale, Colorado.

Walker, Danny N., and Julie E. Francis

1989 *Legend Rock Petroglyph Site (48HO4), Wyoming: 1988 Archaeological Investigations*. Manuscript on file, Office of Wyoming State Archaeologist, Department of Anthropology, University of Wyoming, Laramie.

Walker, Danny N., and George C. Frison

1980 The late Pleistocene mammalian fauna from the Colby mammoth kill site. *University of Wyoming Contributions to Geology* 19(1):69–79.

Walker, Danny N., Molly Karnopp, Marit Bovee, Neffra Mattews, Tom Noble, and Mike Bies

2007 Archaeological Investigations and Rock Art Recording at Legend Rock State Archaeological Site, Wyoming. Paper presented at the 8th Biennial Rocky Mountain Anthropological Conference, Jackson.

Walker, Danny N., Marcel Kornfeld, and Eric E. Ingbar

1997 The Shoreline site and its implications for Archaic adaptations in southcentral Wyoming. In *Changing Perspectives of the Archaic of the Northwestern Plains*, edited by Mary Lou Larson and Julie E. Francis, pp. 446–463. University of South Dakota Press, Vermillion.

Walker, Danny N., and Lawrence C. Todd (editors)

1984 *Archaeological Salvage at 48FR1398: The Castle Gardens Access Road Site.* Occasional Papers on Wyoming Archaeology No. 2. Wyoming Recreation Commission, Cheyenne.

Walker, Danny N., and George M. Zeimens

1976 *Results of an Archaeological Survey of the Arch Mineral Corporation Seminoe Number One Mine, Hanna, Wyoming.* Department of Anthropology, University of Wyoming. Report submitted to the U. S. Bureau of Reclamation, Upper Missouri Region, Billings.

Walker, Ernest G.

1984 The Graham site: A McKean cremation from southern Saskatchewan. *Plains Anthropologist* 29(104):139–150.

1992 *The Gowen Sites.* Archaeological Survey of Canada, Mercury Series Paper 145. National Museum of Canada, Ottawa.

Walker, Renee B., and Boyce N. Driskell

2007 *Foragers of the Terminal Pleistocene in North America.* University of Nebraska Press, Lincoln.

Walker-Kuntz, Sunday A., Edwin R. Hajic, and Lynelle A. Peterson

2006 The Spiro site: A Middle Plains Archaic house pit site. *Archaeology in Montana* 47(2):1–55.

Walthall, John A.

1998 Rockshelters and hunter-gatherer adaptation to the Pleistocene/Holocene transition. *American Antiquity* 63(2):223–238.

Warner, Maurice A.

1955 The origin of Rex Chert. Unpublished Ph.D. dissertation, Department of Geology, University of Wisconsin, Madison.

Wasilik, Norbert

2006 Spatial Distribution of the Early Paleoindian Debitage from the Helen Lookingbill Site: Implication for Site Structure and Integrity. Unpublished Master's thesis, Department of Anthropology, University of Wyoming, Laramie.

Weathermon, Rick L., and Mark E. Miller

2008 History and development of the human remains repository at the University of Wyoming. In *Skeletal Biology and Bioarcheology of the Northwestern Plains*, edited by G. W. Gill and R. L. Weathermon, pp. 42–47. University of Utah Press, Salt Lake City.

Webster, Sean Michael

1999 Interpreting Northern Plains Subsistence Practices: An Analysis of the Faunal and Floral Assemblages from the Thudercloud Site (FbNp-25). Unpublished Master's thesis, Department of Archaeology, University of Saskatchewan, Saskatoon.

2004 A Re-evaluation of the McKean Series on the Northern Plains. Unpublished Ph.D. dissertation, Department of Archaeology, University of Saskatchewan, Saskatoon.

Webster, T. C.

1985 An Analysis of Dental Pathology from the Engelbert site. Unpublished Master's thesis, Department of Anthropology, State University of New York, Binghamton.

Wedel, Waldo R.

1954 Earthenware and steatite vessels from northwestern Wyoming. *American Antiquity* 19(4):403–409.

1961 *Prehistoric Man on the Great Plains.* University of Oklahoma Press, Norman.

1963 The High Plains and their utilization by the Indians. *American Antiquity* 29(1):1–16.

1983 Changing perspectives in Plains archaeology. *Plains Anthropologist* 28(100):89–97.

1986 *Central Plains Prehistory: Holocene Environments and Culture Change in the Republican River Basin.* University of Nebraska Press, Lincoln.

Wedel, Waldo R., Wilfred M. Husted, and John Moss

1968 Mummy Cave: Prehistoric record from the Rocky Mountains of Wyoming. *Science* 160:184–186.

Weisel, George F.

1951 The ram's horn tree and other medicine trees of the Flathead Indians. *Montana Magazine of History* 1(3):5–14.

Wellmann, Klaus F.

1979 *A Survey of North American Indian Rock Art.* Akademische Druck-u. Verlagsanstalt, Graz, Austria.

1980 Trends in North American rock art research. *American Antiquity* 45(3):531–539.

Welsh, Peter H., and Ronald I. Dorn

1997 Critical analysis of petroglyph ^{14}C ages from Côa, Portugal, and Deer Valley, Arizona. *American Indian Rock Art* 21:11–24.

Wentz, R. K., and N. T. DeGrummond

2008 Life on horseback: Paleoanthropology of two Scythian skeletons from Alexandropol, Ukraine. *International Journal of Osteoarchaeology* 19(1):107–115.

Western Regional Data Center

2008 Comparative Data for the Western States. Electronic document, http://wrcc.dri.edu/COMPARATIVE.html, accessed July 14, 2008.

Wettlaufer, Boyd

1955 *The Mortlach Site in the Besant Valley of Central Saskatchewan.* Saskatchewan Department of Natural Resources, Anthropological Series No. 1. Regina.

Wettlaufer, Boyd, and William J. Mayer-Oakes

1960 *The Long Creek Site.* Saskatchewan Department of Natural Resources, Anthropological Series No. 2. Regina.

Wheat, Joe Ben

1967 A Paleoindian bison kill. *Scientific American* 216:44–52.

1972 *The Olsen-Chubbuck Site: A Paleo-Indian Bison Kill.* Memoir No. 26. Society for American Archaeology, Washington, DC.

1979 *The Jurgens Site.* Plains Anthropologist Memoir 15. Lincoln, Nebraska.

Wheeler, Charles W., and Gary Martin

1982 The Granby site: Early-Middle Archaic wattle and daub structures. *Southwestern Lore* 48(3):16–25.

Wheeler, Richard P.

1952 A note on the "McKean lanceolate point." *Plains Anthropological Conference Newsletter* 4(4):39–44.

1954a Two new projectile point types: Duncan and Hanna points. *Plains Anthropologist* 1:7–14.

1954b Selected projectile point types of the United States: 2. *Bulletin of the Oklahoma Anthropological Society* 2:1–5.

Wheeler, Richard P.

1985 The Middle Prehistoric period in the Central and Northern Plains. In *McKean/Middle Plains Archaic: Current research*, edited by Marcel Kornfeld and Lawrence C. Todd, pp. 5–10. Occasional Papers on Wyoming Archaeology No. 4. Wyoming Recreation Commission, Cheyenne.

1995 *Archaeological Investigations in Three Reservoir Areas in South Dakota and Wyoming, Part I, Angostura Reservoir*. Reprints in Anthropology Vol. 46. J & L Reprints, Lincoln, Nebraska.

1996 *Archaeological Investigations in Three Reservoir Areas in South Dakota and Wyoming, Part II, Keyhole Reservoir*. J & L Reprints in Anthropology Vol. 47, Lincoln, Nebraska.

White, Ted E.

1952 Observations on the butchering technique of some aboriginal peoples: No. 1. *American Antiquity* 17(4):337–338.

1953 Observations on the butchering technique of some aboriginal peoples: No. 2. *American Antiquity* 19(2):160–164.

1954 Observations on the butchering technique of some aboriginal peoples: Nos. 3, 4, 5, and 6. *American Antiquity* 19(3):254–264.

1955 Observations on the butchering technique of some aboriginal peoples: Nos. 7, 8, and 9. *American Antiquity* 21(2):171–178.

White, Timothy D., and P. A. Folkens

2000 *Human Osteology*. 2nd edition. Academic Press, San Diego.

2005 *The Human Bone Manual*. Elsevier Academic Press, Boston.

Whitley, David S.

1988 Reply to commentary on Lewis-Williams and Dowson. *Current Anthropology* 29(2):238.

1992 Shamanism and rock art in far western North America. *Cambridge Archaeological Journal* 1:89–113.

1994a Ethnography and rock art in the Far West: Some archaeological implications. In *New Light on Old Art: Recent Advances in Hunter-Gatherer Rock Art Research*, edited by David S. Whitley and Lawrence L. Loendorf, pp. 81–94. Monograph No. 36. Institute of Archaeology, University of California, Los Angeles.

1994b Shamanism, natural modeling, and rock art of far western North American hunter-gatherers. In *Shamanism and Rock Art in North America*, edited by Solveig A. Turpin, pp. 1–44. Special Publication No. 2. Rock Art Foundation, San Antonio, Texas.

1994c By the hunter, for the gatherer: Art, social relations, and subsistence change in the Prehistoric Great Basin. *World Archaeology* 25(3):356–373.

2001 *Handbook of Rock Art Research*. Altamira Press, Walnut Creek, California. (editor)

Whitlock, Cathy, and Patrick J. Bartlein

1993 Spatial variations of Holocene climatic change in the Yellowstone region. *Quaternary Research* 39:231–238.

Whitlock, Cathy, Patrick J. Bartlein, and Kelli Van Norman

1995 Stability of Holocene climate regimes in the Yellowstone region. *Quaternary Research* 43:433–436.

Whitlock, Cathy, Mel A. Reasoner, and Carl H. Key

2002 Paleoenvironmental history of the Rocky Mountain region during the past 20,000 years. In *Rocky Mountain Futures: An Ecological Perspective*, edited by Jill S. Baron, pp. 41–57. Island Press, Washington, DC.

Whitlock, Cathy, Sarah L. Shafer, and Jennifer Marlon

2003 The role of climate and vegetation change in shaping past and future regimes in the north-western US and the implications for ecosystem management. *Forest Ecology and Management* 178:5–21.

Widga, Chris

2006 Niche variability in late Holocene bison: A perspective from Big Bone Lick, KY. *Journal of Archaeological Science* 33:1237–1255.

Wiesend, Christiana M., and George C. Frison

1998 Analysis of parallel-oblique flaked projectile points from Middle Park, Colorado. *Southwestern Lore* 64:8–21.

Wilke, P. J.

2002 Bifacial flake-core reduction strategies and related aspects of Early Paleoindian lithic technology. In *Folsom Technology and Lifeways,* edited by J. E. Clark and M. B. Collins. *Lithic Technology,* Special Publication No. 4:345–370. University of Tulsa, Oklahoma.

Wilkinson, Richard G.

1997 Violence against women: Raiding and abduction in Prehistoric Michigan. In *Troubled Times: Violence and Warfare in the Past,* edited by Debra L. Martin and David W. Frayer, pp. 21–43. Gordon and Breach Publishers, Australia.

Willey, Gordon R., and Philip Phillips

1958 *Method and Theory in American Archaeology.* University of Chicago Press, Chicago.

Willey, Gordon R., and Jeremy A. Sabloff

1993 *A History of American Archaeology.* 3rd edition. W.H. Freeman and Company, New York.

Wilmsen, E. N.

1970 *Lithic Analysis and Cultural Inference: A Paleo-Indian Case.* Anthropological Papers of the University of Arizona No. 16. Tucson.

Wilmsen, E. N., and F. H. H. Roberts

1978 *Lindenmeier, 1934–1974.* Smithsonian Contributions to Anthropology No. 24. Washington, DC.

Wilson, E. N., and H. F. Driggs

1919 *The White Indian Boy.* World Book Company, Yonkers-on-Hudson, New York.

Wilson, Michael C.

1974a The Casper site local fauna and its fossil bison. In *The Casper Site: A Hell Gap Bison Kill on the High Plains,* edited by George C. Frison, pp. 125–171. Academic Press, New York.

1974b History of the bison in Wyoming with particular reference to Holocene forms. In *Applied Geology and Archaeology: The Holocene History of Wyoming,* edited by Michael Wilson. Geological Survey of Wyoming Report of Investigations No. 10. Laramie.

1975 Holocene Fossil Bison from Wyoming and Adjacent Areas. Unpublished Master's thesis, Department of Anthropology, University of Wyoming, Laramie.

1978 Archaeological kill site populations and the Holocene evolution of the genus *Bison.* In *Bison Procurement and Utilization: A Symposium,* edited by Leslie B. Davis and Michael Wilson, pp. 9–22. Plains Anthropologist Memoir 14. Lincoln, Nebraska.

1996 Late Quaternary vertebrates and the opening of the ice-free corridor, with special reference to the genus *Bison. Quaternary International* 32:97–105.

Wilson, Michael C., and James A. Burns

1999 Searching for the earliest Canadians: Wide corridors, narrow doorways, small windows. In *Ice Age Peoples of North America,* edited by R. Bonnichsen and K. L. Turnmire, pp. 213–248. Oregon State University Press, Corvallis.

Wilson, Michael C., Kathie L. Road, and Kenneth J. Hardy (editors)

1981 *Megaliths to Medicine Wheels: Boulder Structures in Archaeology: Proceedings of the Eleventh Annual Chacmool Conference.* The Archaeological Association of the University of Calgary, Alberta.

Windley, Brian F.

1977 *The Evolving Continents.* John Wiley and Sons, New York.

Winfrey, James

1990 An event tree analysis of Folsom point failure. *Plains Anthropologist* 35:263–272.

Wissler, Clark

1914 Material cultures of the North American Indians. *American Anthropologist* 16(3):447–505.

Winham, R. Peter, John Albanese, Timothy V. Gillen, John Goss, L. Adrien Hannus, Kerry Lippincott, Edward J. Lueck, Linda Palmer, and Katherine Winham

2000 *Excavations at the Harrier Nest Site (48CA1366), along the Belle Fourche River, in Campbell County, Wyoming.* Archaeological Contract Series No. 157. Archaeology Lab, Augustana College, Sioux Falls, South Dakota.

Witkind, Max
1971 An Archaeological Interpretation of the Roberts Buffalo Jump Site, Larimer County, Colorado. Unpublished Master's thesis, Department of Anthropology, Colorado State University.

Wood, James C.
1987 Manufacturing and Use Damage on Pressure-Flaked Stone Tools. Unpublished Master's thesis, Department of Sociology, Anthropology, and Social Work, Idaho State University, Pocatello.

Wood, Raymond R. (editor)
1998 *Archaeology of the Great Plains*. University of Kansas Press, Lawrence.

Woolworth, Alan (compiler)
1983 The Red Pipestone Quarry of Minnesota: Archaeological and historical reports. *Minnesota Archaeologist* 42.

Wormington, H. M.
1957 *Ancient Man in North America*. Denver Museum of Natural History Popular Series No. 4. Denver.
1988 The Frazier site, Colorado. In *Guidebook to the Archaeological Geology of the Colorado Piedmont and High Plains of Southeastern Wyoming*, edited by V. T. Holliday, pp. 85–90. Department of Geography, University of Wisconsin, Madison.

Wright, G. A., and H. J. Chaya
1985 Obsidian source analysis in northwestern Wyoming: Problems and prospects. *Plains Anthropologist* 30(109):237–242.

Wycoff, Don G.
1984 The foragers: Eastern Oklahoma. In *Prehistory of Oklahoma*, edited by R. E. Bell, pp. 119–160. Academic Press, New York.

Wycoff, Don G., and W. W. Dalquest
1997 From whence they came: The paleontology of southern Plains bison. In *Southern Plains Bison Procurement and Utilization from Paleoindian to Historic*, edited by Leland C. Bement and Kent J. Buehler, pp. 5–32. Plains Anthropologist Memoir 29. Lincoln, Nebraska.

Wyoming State Historic Preservation Office
2006 Electronic document, http://wyoshpo.state.wy.us/SHPOweb2002/2002webpages/research.htm, accessed October 15, 2006.

Yanovsky, Elias
1936 *Food Plants of the North American Indians*. United States Department of Agriculture Miscellaneous Publications No. 237. Washington, DC.

Yellen, John E.
1977 *Archaeological Approaches to the Present*. Academic Press, New York.

Yellen, John, and Henry Harpending
1972 Hunter-gatherer populations and archaeological inference. In *World Archaeology*, Vol. 4, edited by Derek Rowe, pp. 244–253. Routledge and Kegan Paul, London.

Yerkes, Richard W.
1989 Lithic analysis and activity patterns at Labras Lake. In *Alternative Approaches to Lithic Analysis*, edited by Donald O. Henry and George Odell. Archaeological Papers of the American Anthropological Association No. 1. Washington, DC.

Young, Janet
2004 Bilateral differences in femoral torsion: Identifying reason for its high incidence amongst the St. Lawrence Iroquoians of the Roebuck site. In *A Passion for the Past: Papers in Honour of James F. Pendergast*, edited by James V. Wright and Jean-Luc Pilon, pp. 167–177. Mercury Series, Archaeology Paper No. 164. Canadian Museum of Civilization, Gatineau, Quebec.

Zedeño, Maria Nieves, Jesse Ballenger, William Reitze, Nicholas Laluk, and Robert Jones
2008 *Kutoyis Archaeological Project (KAP): The Kutoyis Bison Hunting Locality on the Two Medicine River, Blackfeet Indian Reservation, Glacier County, Montana*. Preliminary report prepared

for Tribal Historic Preservation Office, Blackfeet Tribe, and National Park Service Tribal Preservation Program. Prepared by the Bureau of Applied Research in Anthropology, University of Tucson.

Zeimens, George M.

1975 48AB301: A Late Prehistoric Site in the Shirley Basin of Wyoming. Unpublished Master's thesis, Department of Anthropology, University of Wyoming, Laramie.

Zeimens, George M., and Gary Alkire

2005 *Field Archaeology Practice and Procedures.* Western Plains Historic Preservation Association, Lingle, Wyoming.

Zeimens, George M., and Danny N. Walker

1974 Bell Cave, Wyoming: Preliminary archaeological and paleontological investigations. In *Applied Geology and Archaeology: The Holocene History of Wyoming,* edited by Michael Wilson, pp. 88–90. Geological Survey of Wyoming Report of Investigations No. 10. Laramie.

Zeimens, George N., Danny N. Walker, Thomas K. Larson, John Albanese, and George W. Gill

1979 The Dunlap-McMurry burial 48NA67, Natrona County, Wyoming. *The Wyoming Archaeologist* 22(1):15–25.

Zeimens, George M., and Sandy Zeimens

1974 Volumes of bison astragali. In *The Casper Site: A Hell Gap Bison Kill on the High Plains,* edited by George C. Frison, pp. 245–246. Academic Press, New York.

Zeller, H. D., and E. V. Stephens

1969 *Geology of the Oregon Buttes Area, Sweetwater, Sublette, and Fremont Counties, Southwest Wyoming.* U. S. Geological Survey Bulletin 1256. Washington, DC.

Zier, Christian J., Denise P. Fallon, and Michael D. Metcalf

1983 *Riley Ridge Natural Gas Project.* Cultural Resources Technical Report. Metcalf-Zier Archaeologists, Inc., Eagle, Colorado.

Zitt, Jennifer O.

1992 Prehistoric and Early Historic Subsistence: Patterns and Dental Pathology on the Northern Plains. Unpublished Master's thesis, Department of Anthropology, University of Wyoming, Laramie.

2008 Prehistoric and early historic subsistence patterns and dental pathology of the Northern Great Plains. In *Skeletal Biology and Bioarcheology of the Northwestern Plains,* edited by G. W. Gill and R. L. Weathermon, pp. 226–232. University of Utah Press, Salt Lake City.

SITE INDEX

SUBJECT INDEX

ABOUT THE AUTHORS AND CONTRIBUTORS

ABOUT THE AUTHORS

Marcel Kornfeld is Professor of Anthropology and director of the George C. Frison Institute of Archaeology and Anthropology at the University of Wyoming. He is past president of the Plains Anthropological Society and currently serves on the board of the Rocky Mountain Anthropological Association. He is author or editor of eight books and numerous articles on Paleoindian prehistory, hunter-gatherer subsistence and settlement, zooarchaeology, chipped stone technology, gender, closed-sites, and taphonomy.

George C. Frison is Professor Emeritus of Anthropology at the University of Wyoming and past president of the Society for American Archaeology. He served as first state archaeologist for the state of Wyoming. Unquestionably the best-known researcher on the prehistory of the High Plains, he has been responsible for major research projects in Wyoming and surrounding states. Frison is the only member of the University of Wyoming faculty elected to the National Academy of Sciences.

Mary Lou Larson is Professor of Anthropology at the University of Wyoming. She has coedited *Aggregate Analysis in Chipped Stone* and *Changing Perspectives on the Archaic in the Rocky Mountains and Northwestern Plains* and has published extensively on the analysis of chipped stone. Her interests include chipped stone production technology, pithouses, Paleoindian and Archaic prehistory, and geographic information systems.

ABOUT THE CONTRIBUTORS

Bruce A. Bradley is Senior Lecturer in Archaeology and director of the Experimental Archaeology Masters Programme at Exeter University, Exeter, UK. He has published extensively on prehistoric hunter-gatherer technology, with a special emphasis on the Paleoindian period.

Julie E. Francis is archaeologist for the Wyoming Department of Transportation. An expert on Wyoming rock art, she has most recently coauthored *Ancient Visions* on the rock art of the region.

George W. Gill is Professor Emeritus of Anthropology at the University of Wyoming. He has published extensively on the skeletal biology and bioarchaeology of the Northwestern Plains and Rocky Mountains.

James C. Miller is a Ph.D. candidate in geology at the University of Wyoming and is employed by the Dominguez Anthropological Research Group in Colorado. He has completed many geoarchaeological studies of archaeological sites throughout the Rocky Mountains and Plains.